COLUMBIANA COUNTY

OHIO

NEWSPAPER ABSTRACTS

Volume 2

Compiled by

Carol Willsey Bell, C.G.

HERITAGE BOOKS
2010

HERITAGE BOOKS
AN IMPRINT OF HERITAGE BOOKS, INC.

Books, CDs, and more—Worldwide

For our listing of thousands of titles see our website
at
www.HeritageBooks.com

Published 2010 by
HERITAGE BOOKS, INC.
Publishing Division
100 Railroad Ave. #104
Westminster, Maryland 21157

International Standard Book Numbers
Paperbound: 978-1-55613-079-3
Clothbound: 978-0-7884-8339-4

INTRODUCTION

The first newspaper published in Columbiana County was titled *Der Patriot am Ohio*, in 1808, by William D. Lepper. Mr. Lepper remarked: "...that on the 1st of December 1808, I commenced publication of a German paper, entitled *Der Patriot am Ohio*; not meeting with sufficient support, I discontinued it, and on the 7th of November 1809, the first number of the *Ohio Patriot* was issued from this office." [*Ohio Patriot* 17 June 1826]. Horace Mack's *History of Columbiana County, Ohio* (1879) notes that "In April 1867, James K. Frew began the publication of the *New Lisbon Journal*, and has since successfully conducted it as a local paper."

During the Nineteenth Century, Columbiana County published what was probably the largest number of titles in the State of Ohio. The various editors commented on the birth and death of each new title with surprising regularity. A few of these were rather unusual: the *Anti-Slavery Bugle*, published in Salem, was devoted to a special cause. Others were very political in nature, to the exclusion of local news. Some colorful titles are the *National Greenback* and the *Interregnum Pacificator*. Very few marriages and deaths appeared in the earliest issues. All such items were copied.

Columbiana County is blessed with a large collection of newspapers covering a wide span of dates. This volume is the second of several voiumes in preparation.

There is an almost complete run of the *New Lisbon Journal* during the years 1867-1876, which is one reason why this title was chosen for abstracting. A complete inventory of extant issues is included in this voiume. The abstracts from the years 1867-1872 were prepared by Carol Willsey Bell, and those from 1873-1876 were prepared by Gladys I. Mix, of Salem, a member of the Columbiana County Chapter of OGS. All of these issues are available on microfilm from the collections of the Western Reserve Historical Society in Cleveland. The microfiim is aiso available at the Salem Public Library, in the collections of the Columbiana County Chapter of the Ohio Genealogical Society.

No attempt has been made to include every item from every issue. Only those items of genealogical importance or historical interest have been copied. Interestingly, many marriage notices appeared in the newspapers which were never recorded in the county records. This fact can be blamed upon the ministers or justices who failed to return them to the courthouse. Other items may lead the user to court cases, especially to those involving the partition of land.

Carol Willsey Bell, C.G.

1867

Jan	Feb	Mar
Apr 19,26	May 3,10,17,24,31	Jun 7,14,21,28
Jly 5,12,19,26	Aug 2,9,16,23,30	Sep 6,13,20,27
Oct 4,11,18,25	Nov 1,8,15,22,29	Dec 6,13,20,27

1868

Jan 3,10,17,24,31	Feb 7,14,21,28	Mar 6,13,20,27
Apr 3,10,17,24	May 1,8,15,22,29	Jun 5,12,19,26
Jly 3,10,17,24,31	Aug 7,14,21,28	Sep 4,11,18,25
Oct 2,9,16,23,30	Nov 6,13,20,27	Dec 4,11,18,25

1869

Jan 1,8,15,22,29	Feb 5,12,19,26	Mar 5,12,19,26
Apr 2,9,12,19,26	May 3,10,17,24,31	Jne 7,14,21,28
Jly 5,12,19,26	Aug 2,9,16,23,30	Sep 6,13,20,27
Oct 4,11,18,25	Nov 1,8,15,22,29	Dec 6,13,20,27

1870

Jan 3,10,17,24,31	Feb 7,14,21,28	Mar 7,14,21,28
Apr 4,11,18,25	May 2,9,16,23,30	Jun 6,13,20,27
Jly 4,11,18,25	Aug 1,8,15,22,29	Sep 5,12,19,26
Oct 3,10,17,24,31	Nov 7,14,21,28	Dec 5,12,19,26

1871

Jan 2,9,16,23,30	Feb 6,13,20,27	Mar 6,13,20,27
Apr 3,10,17,24	May 1,8,15,22,29	Jun 5,12,19,26
Jly 3,10,17,24,31	Aug 7,14,21,28	Sep 4,11,18,25
Oct 2,9,16,23,30	Nov 6,13,20,27	Dec 4,11,18,25

1872

Jan 1,8,15,22,29	Feb 5,12,19,26	Mar 4,11,18,25
Apr 1,8,15,22,29	May 6,13,20,27	Jun 3,10,17,24
Jly 1,8,15,22,29	Aug 5,12,19,26	Sep 2,9,16,23,30
Oct 7,14,21,28	Nov 4,11,18,25	Dec 2,9,16,23,30

1873

Jan 6,13,20,27	Feb 3,10,17,24	Mar 3,10,17,24,31
Apr 7,14,21,28	May 5,12,19,26	Jne 2,9,16,23,30
Jly 7,14,21,28	Aug 4,11,18,25	Sep 1,8,15,22,29
Oct 6,13,20,28	Nov 3,10,17,24	Dec 1,8,15,22,29.

1874

Jan 5,12,19,26	Feb 2,9,16,23	Mar 2,9,16,23,30
Apr 5,13,20,27	May 4,11,18,25	Jne 1,8,15,22,29
Jly 6,13,20,27	Aug 3,10,17,24,31	Sep 7,14,21,28
Oct 5,12,19,26	Nov 2,9,16,23,30	Dec 7,14,21,28.

1875

Jan 4,11,18,25	Feb 1,8,15,22	Mar 1,8,15,22,29
Apr 5,12,19,26	May 3,10,17,24,31	Jne 7,14,21,28
Jly 5,12,19,26	Aug 2,9,16,23,30	Sep 6,13,20,27
Oct 4,11,18,25	Nov 1,8,15,22,29	Dec 6,13,20,27.

1876

Jan 3,10,17,24,31	Feb 6,14,21,28	Mar 6,13,20,27
Apr 3,10,17,24	May 1,8,15,22,29	Jne 5,12,19,26
Jly 3,10,17,24,31	Aug 7,14,21,28	Sep 4,11,18,25
Oct 2,9,16,23,30	Nov 6,13,20,27	Dec 4,11,18,25.

ABBREVIATIONS

admr	administrator of an estate
ae	aged
atty	attorney at law
CCO	Columbiana Co., Ohio
cem	cemetery
Col Co	Columbiana Co., Ohio
d/o	daughter of
deft	defendant
Eld	Elder
ELiv	East Liverpool, Columbiana Co., OH
Esq	Esquire, usually Justice of the Peace
exr	executor of an estate; indicates a will was filed
Hon	Honorable, a Judge or government official
inf	infant
inst	instant, or a date in the present month
JP	Justice of the Peace
Jeff Co	Jefferson Co., OH
Mah Co	Mahoning Co., OH
ME Church	Methodist Episcopal Church
MP Church	Methodist Protestant Church
OPen	Ohio Penitentiary, Columbus OH
OVI	Ohio Volunteer Infantry
pltf	plaintiff
Presby	Presbyterian Church
res	residence, resident of
s/o	son of
tp, twp	township
ult	ultimo, or a date in the previous month
vs	versus; plaintiff versus defendant
w/o	wife of

The first issue of THE JOURNAL was published as Vol.I, No.1, on Friday, 19 Apr 1867, by JAMES K. FREW. The masthead carries the title of JOURNAL while the corner title in each issue says NEW LISBON JOURNAL.

Fri 19 Apr 1867 Vol.1 no 1

D: 13th inst at res. in this place, JESSE HUSTON ae 53y.

D: at res of his parents near New Lisbon on 15th inst, MORRIS STRAUGHN. He was a young man.

JAS.K.FREW, Tobacco & Cigars (ad)

Fri 26 Apr 1867

M: 3d inst by SAMUEL HARDMAN ESQ., BENJAMIN HUNT of Alliance & MRS. ELIZABETH CARLISLE of Salem.

M: 6th inst by REV G.D.KINNEAR, FIRMAN S. ALBRIGHT & LIZZIE WILLIAMS, both of county.

D: 3d inst in North Georgetown, CORA ELLA BESTER, only dau of E.L. & MARY.

Fri 3 May 1867

D: at County Infirmary 28 Apr, JOHN HESTON, ae 99y.

Fri 10 May 1867

M: 11th ult by ROBT. DILWORTH, WILLIAM DILWORTH of New Waterford & MAGGIE J. NEWELL, of Enon Valley PA

M: 11th ult in New Garden by E.GARSIDE, JP, SOLOMON BLYTHE & JANE NELSON all of CCO.

M: 20th ult by REV G.D.KINNEAR, A.R. MARTIN & SALLIE E. CROOK, d/o THOMAS CROOK both of Elkton.

M: 25th ult by REV. A.B.MAXWELL, CHARLES A. RUSSELL & MARY STRATTON, both of CCO.

M: 1st inst at Salem by REV. A.B.MAXWELL, GERHARD H.A.BALKER & ANNA J. SHERMAN.

M: 30th ult by SAMUEL HARDMAN ESQ., JOSEPH HEACOCK & TACY L. JOHNSON of Salem.

D: 25th ult in Salem of consumption, EDIE G. ROGERS ae 20y

D: 17th ult in Wellsville, ROBERT W. RAMSEY ae 19y 8m 20d

D: 14th ult WILLIAM McSPADDEN of Wayne Tp ae 69y

D: 16th ult MRS. GEORGE TURNER of Elkrun Tp ae 35y

D: 23d ult at res in Salem Tp., WILLIAM BETZ ae 78y

Death of MRS. WINES: MRS. WINES, w/o HEDGEMAN WINES of this place, died Sat. last. Funeral from Presbyterian Church.

MR. HEDGEMAN WINES who has been confined to his home for several weeks, with an affection of one of his hands, is now able to be about again.

Fri 17 May 1867

SUICIDE: We learn from St.Louis papers that MR. LUKE, of the firm of BRUCE & LUKE, grocers at St.Louis, committed suicide last Fri. by arsenic; was 35y, left wife & one child; cause, pecuniary embarrassment. He was the husband of JENNIE BRUCE, formerly of this place, whom he married over a year ago.- [note: WILLIAMSON LUKE & JENNIE H. BRUCE m 5 Sep 1865 by O.M.TODD v.5 p100]

Sad accident: We learn from the SALEM REPUBLICAN that a child of BARTON ENTRIKEN of south of Salem was drowned one day last week by falling into a water trough near the spring.

M: 9th inst by REV.W.K.BROWN, SAMUEL P. LUDWICK of McKees- port, PA & MRS. ELIZABETH MILLER of New Lisbon.

M: 2nd inst by ELDER W.T.MARTIN at his res near Salem, JOHN BUSHONG & CLARISSA WILLIAMSON, both of CCO. [note: marr- iage record says LAVINA WILLIAMSON]

M: 4th inst by ELDER M. HARROD, JACOB GLECKLER & AMANDA V. RIGHT, all of CCO.

M: 4th inst at Parsonage of Mineral Charge, by I.J.DELO, ALPHEUS FARMER & LYDIA RINEHART.

M: 4th inst by I.J.DELO, SOLOMON MILLER & HARRIET LODGE, all of co.

D: 2d inst in Salem, JOHN LEMON ae 69y

D: in Salem Tp on 4th inst, JESSE IRA ROLLER s/o SAMUEL & CAROLINE H. ae 10m 8d

D: at res in New Albany, Ind.,25th ult, ZIMRI FOX in 51st yr

Fri 24 May 1867

M: 14th inst by REV.W.K.BROWN, JOHN EDGAR HUSTON & MAGGIE McCORD, both of New Lisbon.

M: 16th inst at res of J.H.HILLERMAN near Pittsburgh by REV SYLVESTER BURT, GEORGE L. MILLER & ANNIE M. GASKILL both of New Lisbon.

M: 9th inst by REV.J.R.ROLLER, WILLIAM BENNETT of CCO & PHENIAH BEATTY of Carroll Co.

M: 9th inst by REV ROBT. DICKSON, JOHN Q. ABRAHAM & MARY L. McLAUGHLIN, both of CCO.

M: 15th inst by REV. WM.BAXTER, EDWARD B. CRAWFORD & SARAH HAMILTON of Wellsville.

M: 14th inst in Wellsville by REV.J.HENDERSON, JOHN L. CARA- HAN & SUSAN E. HAMILTON.

M: 12th inst in Salem by REV I.N.BAIRD, THOMAS B. WILSON & MARY A. PAINTER.

D: MATTHEW SCHAFFER, of the boot & shoe business in Wells- ville, found dead on floor of shop by his son, of heart disease.

Fri 31 May 1867

D: 15th inst RICHARD WEBB of Salem ae 75y.

D: 16th inst ANN PAINTER late of Salem ae 83y.

D: 20th inst SUSAN WOODARD, widow of WILLIAM, of Hanover Tp ae 73y.

M: 16th inst by REV.S.W.CRITTENDEN, JAMES M. BROWN of Salem & SARAH ISABEL JOHNSTON of Philadelphia, Pa.

M: 14th inst in Atwater, Portage Co Oh by REV. DALES, D.F.- YENGLING of Salem & MARY HICK of Portage.

M: (no date) at res of bride's father by REV.JOHN WILLIAMS, WILLIAM STALCUP of Alliance & ALICE A. SHELTON of Salem Tp.

M: 14th inst by REV.J.B.MILLER, NOAH W. CRAWFORD of Clarkson & MOLLIE A. CONKLE of Mt.Union.

M: 15th inst by REV.J.B.MILLER, JOHN A. McCAMON & ELLA CRAWFORD of New Waterford.

M: 20th inst at St.Aloysius Church, East Liverpool, by Rev.P.J.McGUIRE, THOMAS M. GAREY & ANNIE M. SHEARMAN both of Wellsville.

M: 23d inst by REV.W.K.BROWN, PHILIP HAMILTON & NANCY HILL, both of co.

Fri 7 June 1867

Divorce: HANNAH M. FINDLEY vs JOHN, whose residence is unknown, petition for divorce filed 31 May 1867 for wilful absence. J.L.SMITH her atty.

D: 21st ult, EDDIE MATHEWS s/o PHILIP & MARY ANN of Salem Tp, ae 7y 1m.

D: 9th ult in Wellsville, MRS. MARY LAWSON in 87th yr.

M: 28th ult in East Fairfield, C.B.DICKEY, County Recorder, & NORA BEAN.

M: 28th ult by JOHN McVICKER, ESQ., JAMES TANNER of New Lisbon & EMMA E. ENDLY of Mansfield, Oh.

M: 16th inst by ISAAC WEAVER ESQ., DAVID BELAT & FRANCES BECK, all of co.

M: 21st inst by WM.ANDERSON ESQ., in Knox Tp, ISAAC WEAVER & KATE KELLINGER.

M: 23d ult by REV A.B.MAXWELL, REV. G.R.KERR of Allegheny Pa & JENNIE M. STEWART of Locust Grove, Ohio.

M: 23d ult by DAVID McLAIN ESQ., JOHN M. CRAWFORD & REBECCA YOUNG, all of CCO.

M: 21st ult by REV T.A.McCURDY, WILSON S. BURNET & CHARITY A. CARR, both of Wellsville.

Death of MRS. B.W.PRITCHARD: died of consumption at res of her husband in New Lisbon Sat last; she was the daughter of F. ZEPPERNICK, banker of this place. [note: B.W.PRITCHARD & SUSAN ZEPPERNICK m 6 Oct 1857. v4 p319]

The remains of ROBERT FOLGER, the murderer of DINSMORE, were buried by his father & mother in Georgetown, Beaver Co Pa.

Fri 14 June 1867

DAVID CORNWELL, with WILLARD & CHILD, wholesale grocers, Chicago, Ill., is in town visiting relatives & friends.

D: 26th ult at res in West Tp of dropsy, DAVID KING ae 73y

D: 5th inst of consumption HANNAH M. FAWCETT w/o AMOS ae 66y

D: 29 May in Ludlow KY, EMMA BELMINA HELMAN youngest d/o CHARLES M. & MARY G., of Cincinnati.

D: 6th inst in Salem MARY CORDELIA BISSELL d/o J.G. & MARY T. ae 16y

D: 7th inst in New Lisbon at res of her son in law E.WHITACRE, MRS. MARY WELCH, ae 80y.

M: 5th inst at res of bride's father in New Lisbon by REV ROBT.DICKSON, HENRY E. FROST & MARY E. CROWL all of New Lisbon.

M: 30th ult by REV.S.WAGNER, JAMES K.PIERSOL of Allegheny Co Pa & MARY E. COPE of CCO.

M: 4th inst by REV W.K.BROWN, CLEMENT L. CROSS & RACHEL TRUNICK both of CCO.

M: 30th ult by REV J.M.BRAY, DAVID SILVER of Waynesburg & ELLA J. COX of CCO.

M: 4th inst by REV.A.B.MAXWELL, C.N.SCHMICK of Canfield & JENNIE WELKER of Salem.

Fri 21 June 1867

Attempted suicide: we learn from ALLIANCE MONITOR that MRS. BARNEY NEASE of that place attempted suicide by hanging last week. She sent her children out to play; was saved by neighbors. Cause was domestic difficulties.

CAPT. IRISH, native of New Lisbon, was seriously injured in Pittsburgh at the Tournament of the Colored People last Tues. Was run down by a horse in jousting games.

Fri 28 June 1867 (Vol 1 no 11): on WRHS microfilm

Suspension of REV. O.M.TODD: The Presbytery held its session in Madison Tp last week. REV. O.M.TODD, formerly pastor of the Presbyterian Church in this place, but now of Lima, Ohio, was suspended from the ministry.

New Church: we are pleased to learn that an Episcopal church is to be erected in this place, on the lot of the "Old Bank Bldg." The building will be put under contract this summer.- It is the intention of the congregation to procure the services of a clergyman of eminent learning and piety to officiate.

M: 20th inst by REV.E.A.BRINDLEY, W.H.MELVIN of New Lisbon & MISS MELISSA E. QUEST, of Wellsburgh WVA.

M: Sun 16th inst by REV.C.H.ELLIS, JAMES LYMAN KENDALL of Des Moines, Iowa & MISS ANNA NORRIS of Salem.

D: 14th inst at res of her son, HENRY MORLAN ESQ., MRS. CATHARINE MORLAN aged 93y 5d.

Fri 5 July 1867

Church Directory:
  United Presbyterian   REV.S.T.HERRON
  Methodist Episcopal   REV. W.K.BROWN
  1st Presbyterian   REV. R. DICKSON
  Disciple   REV. WM.H.BAXTER

M: 18th inst in Fairfield by REV.S.WAGNER, SOLOMON SURTZER & SUSAN ROGERS both of co.

M: 18th inst at res of bride's father by REV.L.B.PERKINS, ENOS SEACHRIST & REBECCA E. MARLNEE, all of CCO.

M: 24th inst by REV.WM.BAXTER, WILLIAM J. GEORGE & ELIZA A. JOHNSON, both of CCO.

M: 25th inst by REV.CHARLES THORN, J.LYTTLETON CLARK of Cleveland,Oh & HATTIE A.HERRICK of New Salisbury.

D: 22d inst MRS FRANK SHARPNACK w/o DANIEL of Salem

D: 10 May suddenly at res near New Garden, BENJAMIN KEPNER ae 71y.

D: 4th inst at res of father ALFRED MITE, JAMES C. MITE ae 18y

D: 24th inst at res of her mother MISS VIOLET DONALDSON in 51st yr.

D: 18th ult JOHN STEWART of Salem Tp ae 63y.

D: 28th ult ROBERT BRINKER s/o DR.D.BRINKER of Centre Tp ae 18y

(Birth): A young woman, very young indeed, no teeth-bald headed--bare footed--can't speak--is said to look wise enough--weeps occasionally--apparently in good health-- rather small in stature--a keen appetite--a perfect stranger- --lately arrived at the residence of the Proprietor of the Journal. [Jas.K.Frew]

Fri 12 July 1867

D: 2nd inst SOPHIA STARR d/o JAMES of this place ae 36y 9m 12d

D: 30th ult near Clarkson, Middleton Tp, HENRY PYLE ae 52y

D: 30th ult in Salem, WILLIAM MAERKT ae 15y

D: 5th inst in New Lisbon CONRAD FAULKER ae 77y

M: 29th ult in Elkrun Tp by A.McCARTER JP, WILLIAM W. WEDEN & JULIA MORLAN all of co.

M: 27th ult in Salem by REV.A.B.MAXWELL, JOHN F. HANNAY & MARY E. PATTERSON.

M: 20th inst by REV.J.N.SWAN, WILLIAM M. SMITH & JOSEPHINE ARBUCKLE all of co.

M: 4th inst at res of J.B.SKILLMAN, Salem, by A.A.THOMAS Esq., ALBAN W. FORNEY & HARRIET E. SHEETS all of co.

M: 4th inst at American House, Salem by REV.A.B.MAXWELL, THOMAS J. SHAFFER & JENNIE McKERE.

M: 27th ult by REV.I.N.BAIRD, ISAAC JUDD & HENRIETTA M. TOMPKINS all of Salem.

Rat hunt in Lancaster, Ohio, resulted in slaughter of 16,598 rats.

JOHN D. KING ESQ. formerly of Columbiana, removed to Kenton Oh where he is in law practice.

LT. GEORGE A. GARRETSON just graduated from West Point with high honors, is visiting relatives & friends in New Lisbon.

JOHN LEEK, a lad aged 9y, s/o RICHARD of Guilford, drowned near there last Mon while swimming.

It is rumored that MR.RILEY, formerly Civil Engineer on New Lisbon Railway, but recently employed on Union Pacific RR, was lately killed by Indians in the far west.

Fri 19 July 1867

M: 4th inst by REV.J.McCARTY, ROBERT P. JUSTICE & MILLIE H. MURPHY, all of Salem.

M: at Oak Grove 4th inst by REV.D.V.HYDE, WILLIAM BAKER & MARY ANN DILDINE all of co.

D: 8th inst HARVEY FROST s/o EZRA & CATHARINE of this place ae 9m.

D: 11th inst HATTIE L. WADSWORTH d/o MRS. ADELINE WADSWORTH of this place, ae 3y.

D: 10th inst ELIZABETH BEAN w/o PIUS of this place ae 42y.

D: 12th inst ELIZABETH WORMAN of Salem Tp ae 81y 11m 28d.

D: 14th inst STEPHEN HENDRICKS of Centre Tp at advanced age.

D: 19th ult after lingering illness, ELI COBB, ae ----y.

JOHN MOFF of No.Georgetown, refused to pay income tax, Deputy US Marshall fined him $100.

Fri 26 July 1867

M: 10th inst by ISAAC WEAVER ESQ, CHARLES A. GRICE of No.-Georgetown & MARY J. BESTER of Salem.

M: 16th inst by REV.WM.BAXTER, F.PHILLIPS & MATTIE J. CRAW-FORD, both of co.

M: 19th inst by REV.W.K.BROWN, GEORGE M. ROBERTS & ELIZA JANE QUAIL, both of Salineville.

CAPT. WILLIAM H. ECKLEY s/o HON.E.R.ECKLEY died of typhoid fever in New Mexico on 20th ult. He was a Captain in the Regular Army.

Fri 2 Aug 1867

D: 15th ult MRS. MARIA PATTERSON w/o THOMAS of Madison Tp ae 36y

D: 21st ult ALMIRA JANE BELL w/o SAMUEL of Wayne Tp ae 21y

D: 18th ult in Salem Tp, ELIZABETH HART ae 83y.

Fri 9 Aug 1867

M: 25th ult by REV.I.N.BAIRD, J.C.ZIMMERMAN of Van Wert OH & MARY M. OVINGTON of Mahoning Co.

M: 31st ult by REV.A.B.MAXWELL, at res of bride's father, CHARLES W. GARDENER & REBECCA T. MENDENHALL.

M: 28th ult by REV.G.D.KINNEAR, WILLIAM C.STOKESBERRY & MARGARET ALLBRIGHT both of Elkrun Tp.

M: 1st inst by JOSHUA WHITACRE JP, SAMUEL D. COPE & MRS. MARY M. KREIDLER all of CCO.

M: 21st ult by REV.C.A.J.CRAMER, JULIUS T. SIGLE of Leetonia & HULDA OBENAUF of Mahoning Co.

D: 29th ult ANNORA HAWKINS d/o ROBERT & CATHARINE ae 19y 3m 12d. Sermon by REV.HYDE.

D: 29th ult at res of ERASTUS EELLS, MISS MARY BRANNEN, formerly of Franklin Tp, ae 65y.

D: 29th ult MRS. ELIZA RICHEY w/o WILLIAM of Hanover Tp ae 56y

D: 3d inst at res of THOMAS STARR of this place THOMAS STEPHENSON s/o SAMUEL of Wellsville ae 14y.

Accident: on Sun last a little son of THOMAS HOLLOWAY on the Clutter Road was kicked by a horse & so badly injured his life is despaired of.

HON.C.L.VALLANDIGHAM is in town visiting relatives & friends. He addresses the Democracy of Mah.& Col.Cos. at New Middleton, Springfield Tp, on Aug. 9th.

Fri 16 Aug 1867

M: 7th inst at res of bride's father by REV.R.DICKSON, CHARLES H. GILMAN & KATE R. ROBERTSON, all of New Lisbon.

M: 8th inst at the Reformed parsonage by REV.G.M.ALBRIGHT, JAMES G. FLUGAN & SOPHIA WAGELY both of New Lisbon.

M: 1st inst by REV.SWAN, GEORGE W. BARBER of Middlebury, Summit Co & LIZZIE McDONALD d/o JAMES of Col.Co.

M: 2nd inst by REV I.N.BAIRD, WILLIAM HENRY of Indiana & ELIZABETH HENDERSON of this co.

D: 6th inst HANNAH A. REED w/o FISHER REED of Salem ae 23y

D: 2nd inst near Salem, G.W.YERGER ae 31y

D: 27th ult MARK BARNETT ae about 60y.

D: 8th inst near New Lisbon, JOSEPH STRAUGHN ae 66y.

Fri 23 Aug 1867

M: 15th inst by REV.WM.BAXTER, WILSON VOGAN & AMELIA SPRIN-GER, both of co.

M: 15th inst RUSSELL WILLIARD & SAMANTHA WHITACRE both of New Lisbon.

D: 7th inst JOSEPH PERRY GREENLEE s/o JOSEPH & HARRIET ae 13y 6m.

Fri 30 Aug 1867

D: 16th inst DANIEL GARWOOD ae 89y.

D: 19th inst DORATHA MOFF ae 60y.

D: 4th inst of cholera infantum, MARY V. HAMMOND infant d/o J.W. & SALLIE ae 8m 8d.

M: 15th inst at Salineville by REV.J.M.BRAY, JAMES B. JOHNSON of Washingtonville & EMMA IRWIN of Salineville.

M: 10th inst by SAMUEL H.BENNETT ESQ., JOSEPH B. RAY & MARY E. JOHNSON all of co.

M: Aug 14 by REV.THOMAS Y.ORR, SAMUEL WILSON of Salem (late of Butler PA) & JESSIE N.TATEM of Pittsburgh PA

M: 21st inst in the Episcopal Church, Salem, by REV.T. McMURPHY, WILLIAM ICKES of Hanover & ELCEY M. MEEKS of Salem.

M: 19th inst by REV.D.W.TOWNSEND, E.A.WRIGHT & ANNIE E.SHURTZ all of Alliance.

Fri 6 Sep 1867

Death of ALCINUS RICHARDSON, who was killed at Platford, near Omaha, Nebr. on 20th ult by the explosion of a steam boiler in a saw mill where he was working.

D: 20th ult JOS.STEWART of Salem Tp ae 78y.

D: 24th ult MRS.KATE D.IRWIN of Wayne Tp ae 48y.

M: 28th ult at res of bride's father by REV.S.T.HERRON, SAMUEL P.MORRISON of Salem & ELLA E.STARR of New Lisbon.

M: 29th ult at res of A.A.EWING, New Lisbon, by REV. ROBT.DICKSON, ADAM KIBLER of Green Hill & ANNIE M.HOFFE of New Alexander.

Fri 13 Sep 1867

D: in New Lisbon 3d ult FREEMAN D. MORRISON s/o FREEMAN & MARY ae 1m.

D: in Metropolis City, Ill. 16th ult MARTIN BEESON formerly of Salem ae 47y.

D: 1st inst MRS.CATHARINE SHELTON of Salem Tp ae 82y.

M: 31st ult by REV.ROBT.DICKSON, GEORGE W.RUSSELL of New Lisbon & SUSAN BROWN of Franklin Tp.

M: 29 July by REV.I.N.BAIRD, FRANK M.BADLEY & ELIZA ENGLISH all of co.

M: 29th ult by REV.A.B.MAXWELL, S.MORRIS & ELIZA HUNT all from Salem.

M: 18th ult by REV.D.W.TOWNSEND, JACKSON BENNER of Col.Co. & MARY A. FOX of Stark Co.

M: 14th inst by REV.OWEN HIGGINS, JAMES STITT of Salem & MRS. ELIZABETH DICKSON of New Castle, Pa.

M: 4th inst by REV.W.K.BROWN, BAKER RICE & SARAH A. HILL both of co.

Escape: on Tues last at res of C.D.GRISELL on Lisbon St., his little grandson PAUL FAUTS, whose parents now reside in Wheeling Va, about 2y old, fell into a well over 30 feet deep & was brought up by J.A.KERR, alive & well. The little fellow was overjoyed when clasped in the strong arms of his uncle whose presence of mind soon brought him out of his perilous position.

Death of ALCINUS RICHARDSON, Plattford Neb. Yesterday (Aug 19) the steam mill belonging to HUCKLEBOUS & ROBINSON blew up & instantly killed 2 men, R.P.PUGH & ALCINUS RICHARDSON. PUGH was a Virginian, & the other from New Lisbon, Ohio.

We are indebted to JOHN N.SHENKLE of Syracuse, Morgan Co Missouri for a list of subscribers to the JOURNAL from the far west. The many friends of Mr.S. in New Lisbon will be pleased to hear he has embarked in business in Syracuse & is doing well.

Fri 20 Sep 1867

D: 14th inst ETTA L. LODGE w/o WILLIAM & d/o G.F.ADAM of this place, ae 26y.

Fri 27 Sep 1867

D: at Fremont Wisc. NEWTON McLAUGHLIN s/o JOSEPH died on 8th inst of typhoid fever. Was a young man of much promise.

SUICIDE near Columbiana: we learn from SALEM REPUBLICAN that on Fri. last, MRS. JOSEPH CONDLES, [sic: CANDLES] living about 2 mi E of Columbiana, committed suicide by hanging herself from a rafter with a skein of yarn. For several weeks she had been unwell & a fit of temporary insanity caused the deed.

Still alive & kicking: I.B.REILLY, the Civil Engineer who was reported scalped by Indians on the Pacific Railroad, is home & denies the soft impeachment.

M: 5th inst by WM.MOORE ESQ., EDWARD FINLEY & ISABELLE J. THOMPSON of CCO.

M: 8th inst by JSOEPH COULSON ESQ., MILTON BETTIS of Carroll Co & REBECCA J. TAYLOR of West Tp.

M: 5th inst by REV.HOUSTON, WILLIS B. READ & SADE J. NEVIN of New Waterford.

M: 10th inst by REV.J.N.SWAN, at parsonage of Yellow Creek Church, JOHN A. NOBLE & MAGGIE C.FRASER all of co.

M: 19th inst by A.A.THOMAS ESQ, JOSEPH CREW of Butler Tp & PHEBE TRESCOTT of Salem.

D: of flux on 11th ABEL SILVER of Salem ae 39y.

D: 13th inst LYDIA COOK w/o JAMES ae ——y.

D: 16th inst MARY BURNS w/o HUGH ae 35y.

D: 14th inst COBURN BATTIN w/o ROBERT of Salem ae 70y.

D: 10th inst in Wellsville, CHARLES BARR s/o J.W. & MATILDA ae 17y.(see next issue)

D: 18th inst in Salem, SAMUEL WYANT ae 54y.

Fri 4 Oct 1867

RICHARD BARR a lad about 15y, died in Wellsville on account of a cold contracted while playing baseball, by sitting upon the ground when very warm. (see previous issue)

D: 5th inst MRS.MARGARET SWEARINGEN of Hanover ae 39y 7m 5d

D: 16th inst in Salem MARY BURNS w/o HUGH ae 35y.

D: 20th inst in Salem infant son of DANIEL WHARTON ae 2 wks

D: 21st inst in Salem WILLIAM TAYLOR s/o CALEB M. ae 13y.

M: 23d inst by J.W.MORRISON ESQ, DANIEL McLANE & CYNTHIA M.MARTIN all of co.

M: 5th inst by REV.G.McELHENNY, THOMAS B.COPE & MARY THOMPSON both of Salineville.

M: 5th inst by same, THOMAS M.JONES of Pittsburgh PA & LIZZIE THOMPSON of Salineville.

M: 12th inst by ELDER S.S.McKOWN, EDWARD LAWSON & PHILENA A.BURSON, all of Hanover Tp.

M: 18th inst by same, GEORGE W. NICHOLSON of Jefferson Co. & LUCY KEMP of CCO.

M: 19th inst by REV.A.T.McMURPHY, SAMUEL LEWIS & MARIA PROBERT, both of Salem.

M: in Illinois Sep.12 by REV.RICE, H.H.HOPKINS of Fort Madison, Iowa & SADA PIM, formerly of East Rochester Ohio.

M: 22nd inst in Salem by REV.A.MAXWELL, AARON HAIFLY & MARTHA WHARTON.

Fri 11 Oct 1867

D: 3d inst in Salem, CHARLES F.LEASE s/o EDWIN & MARY B. of brain fever, ae 3y 3m.

M: 3d inst by REV.ROBT.HAYS, GEORGE METCHUM & ALICE CRABAUGH, all of co.

M: 3d inst by REV.ROBT.HAYS, DANIEL WRIGHT & SARAH A.BURBECK, all of co.

M: 3d inst by REV.I.N.WHITE, AARON DOBSON & FRANCES ADAMS.

M: 1st inst in Wellsville by ELDER D.J.WHITE, WILLIAM M.CARO- THERS & M.E.SPRINGER both of Wellsville.

M: 26th ult by REV.A.B.MAXWELL, at house of bride's father near Salem, JAMES D.TOLERTON & HANNAH L.CONKLE.

M: 28th ult by REV.A.B.MAXWELL, JAMES VICKERS & ALICE B. STILSON.

On Mon last week, THOMAS TAYLOR, ae 72y, fell & was killed by the breaking down of the scaffold of the new Presbyterian church at Columbiana. Four of his ribs were broken. JOEL MORELAND was badly hurt. The cause was the giving away of a joice.

"Applications for divorce are greatly on the increase. It is somewhat remarkable that some people are in such a hurry to surrender the bonds they were in just as great a hurry to take upon themselves a few months ago. The old story, however, kiss & twitter for a few weeks, then cold coffee and general neglect."

Fri 18 Oct 1867

Crime in Canton: Divorced wife slaughtered by her husband. CAROLINE YOST killed by FERDINAND HOFFMAN as she sang in the choir of the German Reformed Church. Brutally stabbed with a butcher knife. (see also 25 Oct & 1 Nov)

M: 1st inst by REV.S.S.McKOWN, GEORGE SULTNER & ELIZABETH TRANSUE all of Hanover Tp.

M: 9th inst by same, NATHAN A. KING & SARAH C. BURSON all of CCO.

M: 10th inst by JOHN McVICKER ESQ., FREDERICK G. BAKER & CATHARINE FIFE all of co.

D: in St.Louis on 2nd inst of cholera, GEORGE C.SHULL ae 26y 2m, formerly of Wellsville.

D: in New Orleans, LA Sept 18 of yellow fever, DR. THOMAS M. BENTLEY, formerly of Salem.

D: 5th inst in Butler Tp MARY INGRAM d/o JOSEPH & PHEBE.

Murder of a Wellsville citizen in Montana Territory: JOHN D. DAVIDSON, a former citizen of Wellsville, was brutally murdered at Middle Creek Montana Territory Sept 13. Some person knocked on door of cabin occupied by him & partner, 4 men entered & asked for coffee. Partner stepped out to get chips for fire, heard cry of distress. Mr.D's body found, head cut to pieces with blows from a hatchet. Robbery was motive.
His aged mother & brothers reside in Wellsville.

Fri 25 Oct 1867

Incorporated: The New Lisbon Woolen Mfg.Co., corporators are JOHN OGDEN, BENJAMIN JAGGAR & JOHN ROBINSON. Shares of stock are $50 each.

D: in New Orleans Oct 4 of yellow fever, SHERMAN P. CRAIG, ae 23y 10m. He was a printer by profession & a brother to ROBERT E. CRAIG, at one time publisher of the PATRIOT in this place.

D: at res in Madison Tp on 18th ult, DANIEL S. McLEAN ae about 55y.

D: 17th inst 2 mi N of town, SARAH BRINKER w/o ANDREW in 67th yr.

M: 16th inst by ELDER WM.BAXTER, JOHN SWITZER & E.F.BURNETT both of co.

M: 9th inst by REV.W.H.JAMISON, assisted by REV.JOHN GAILEY, DUNCAN McDONALD & ALICE BOWER, both of co.

M: 3d inst by REV.R.HAYS, HENRY J.CLARK & AGNES R.GILSON.

M: 8th inst by REV.R.HAYS, ADAM WILLIARD & MARGARET ANN CUNAR.

M: 10th inst by same, J.A.LINDSAY, M.D. of Salineville & MARIA E. CONNELL of Summitville, this co.

M: 10th inst by MAYOR L.B.LOCKARD, SAMUEL GAMBLE & MRS. MARY J. BRADWAY, all of Salem.

M: 17th inst by REV.D.X.JUNKIN, WILLIAM McCLYMONDS of Massillon & ANNA LOY of New Castle PA.

M: 15th inst by REV.A.T.McMURPHY, H.NELSON ADAMS & AMERICA CORNWELL both of Salem.

M: 13th inst in Beaver PA by REV.I.N.BAIRD, REV.WARNER LONG of the Pittsburgh Conference M.E.Church & KATE IKERT of Salem.

M: 15th inst in Newark by REV.HARVEY, H.G.KINGSBURY of Salem & HATTIE BALL of Newark.

M: Oct 1 in Mt.Pleasant,Ohio, by Rev.MITCHELL, J.H.LEWIS of Salem & EMMA SCHOOLEY of Mt.Pleasant.

Crime at Canton: FERDINAND HOFFMAN is sorry he didn't kill his ex-wife immediately; she is still lying in a precaious condition, her recovery is doubtful. (see also 18 Oct & 1 Nov)

An 11 year old son of JOHN GRIMMESEY supposed lost; he ran off, but later returned.

BASTARDY: ANNA ALBERT came before JUSTICE MORRISON last week & made her moan. A certain THOMAS SHAFFER had beguiled her innocence. He is being held on bond.

MR.DOUGHTON had added another story to his residence & tastefully ressuscitated the entire mansion.

Fri 1 Nov 1867

M: 24th inst at res of bride's parents by REV.W.K.BROWN, PETER B. YOUNG & EMMA E. HOOVER, all of New Lisbon. "Matrimonial event of the week, the wedding of EMMA E. HOOVER, daughter of our townsman WILLIAM A. HOOVER, & PETER B.YOUNG, of the firm of S.SMALL & SONS. REV.W.K.BROWN of the ME Church offic."

M: 23 Oct, D.W.CORNWELL of Chicago & EMMA F. PAINTER of Bloomington Ill. "Our friend DAVID W. CORNWELL embarked on the sea of matrimony."

M: at home of bride in Fairfield Tp, by REV.S.B.TEAGARDEN, R.L.DICKEY & SADIE E. PITZER.

M: 3d ult by REV.D.V.HYDE, HARDING BUCKMAN & SELINA COBBS.

M: 8th inst by J.W.MORRISON ESQ., JAMES JACKMAN & ELIZABETH SHECKLER both of Salineville.

M: 3d inst by REUBEN WATT ESQ., AMOS C. BILLINGSLEY & MARY C. McKANE all of Middleton Tp.

M: 18th inst by REV.W.K.BROWN, THOMAS WATSON of Alliance & NANCY WILAMAN of Salem.

M: 10th inst by ISAAC WEAVER ESQ., DANIEL WOLF & NANCY HAWKINS, all of co.

M: 10th inst by REV.SWAN, ANDREW SMITH of Celina Ohio & NANCY McGILVERY of Wellsville.

M: 22nd ult by REV.McCARTY, G.T.SWEARINGEN & MISS SARAH SWEARINGEN all of co.

M: 3d inst by REV.McCARTY, PHINEAS COOPER & MRS. SARAH C. JOBS, all of co.

M: 24th inst by REV.I.N.BAIRD, JACOB HOLE & AMELIA E.MORLAN, all of Salem.

M: 24th inst in Salem by A.A.THOMAS ESQ., J.H.FLAUGHER & LAURA PLATT.

M: 24th inst by Friends ceremony in Salem, LINDLEY BRACKEN of Belmont Co & ANN FRENCH of Salem.

D: 18th inst PHEBE NETTIE HOKE d/o JONAS of Salem Tp ae 1y 1m 23d.

D: Oct 4 at res of her mother in Wellsville, MISS ELLEN F. SHEARMAN in 24th year.

D: Oct 17 in Cleveland, MRS. VIRGINIA CREIGHTON, formerly a resident of Wellsville.

D: 25th inst JOHN HISCOCK of Centre Tp ae about 60y.

J.E.VOGLESONG ESQ. formerly of Columbiana & a son of JOHN VOGLESONG of that place died at Vicksburgh on 5 Oct.

End of the Canton Tragedy: Death of MISS YOST from wounds inflicted by HOFFMAN. After a week's suffering, MISS YOST died Sat last about 4 o'clock pm. The funeral was Monday, with between 2000 & 3000 people in attendance. Not more than half could get into the German Reformed Church. MISS YOST was aged about 26y. She was married to HOFFMAN in 1864, lived with him in all, 5 months, and never spent a pleasant hour with him due to jealousy. A few months after the marriage HOFFMAN was put in jail for stealing & rather than stand trial, he enlisted in the army. Shortly after he got out of the army he was arrested & sent to the Penitentiary. The murderer and his victim were both buried the same day & only about an hour apart. It is proper to say that MISS YOST was a woman of excellent qualities & never gave him cause for his conduct. She was much affected by the death of her little girl, about 2y old, who died a few months ago. FERDINAND HOFFMAN, the murderer of his divorced wife, put an end to his worthless life in our jail on Sunday night last. He hung himself with a bed sheet. His age was about 28. He was a man of violent passion, exceedingly jealous of his wife & when they lived together abused her.

Fri 8 Nov 1867

M: 29th ult by REV.JAMES HENDERSON, G.SHIPMAN & MARY A. CRAW-FORD, of Madison Tp.

M: 29th ult by REV.I.J.DELO, GEORGE SPRINGER & CELESTA C. RINEHART all of co.

D: 23d ult in Butler Tp, AMELIA GOODBRAKE d/o JACOB & HATTIE ae 18m 12d.

D: 22nd ult in Fairfield Tp near Columbiana, SIMEON HARDMAN ae 45y.

Sudden death in Salem: on Sun morn last MRS MARY WEAVER, relict of the late EMMOR T. WEAVER, found dead in bed.

REV.HIGGINS, Pastor of Mt.Union ME Church, died at his residence in Mt.Union last Sunday.

The new German Lutheran Church recently erected in East Liverpool was dedicated on 27th ult.

EDWIN LENHART, the young incendiary, who has been applying the torch to stables at Salem, has been sent to the Reform School til age 21.

JOHN ARTER announces the New Lisbon Tannery in business.

Fri 15 Nov 1867

D: 5th inst REUBEN F. RANDOLPH, of Achor, aged ——. (note: he was aged 28y in 1850 census.)

Fri 22 Nov 1867

M: near Summitville Oct 31 by REV.I.N.WHITE, CHRISTOPHER H. JOHNSON & NANCY HULL.

M: 7th inst by REV.W.K.BROWN, WILLIAM HEISTAND & SUSANNAH HARTMAN both of Knox Tp.

M: 7th inst by REV.EDWARD PETTIT JP, WILLIAM D. MONTGOM-ERY & MARY BURWELL, all of co.

M: 3d inst by REV.I.N.BAIRD, GEORGE L. BROOKS & MRS. HETTIE BOUTWELL all of Salem.

M: 31st ult by same, WALDEMAR U.O.THIEME & LYDIA LEORA MENTZER.

M: 12th inst by REV.J.W.TORRENCE, ROBERT RALEY of Carrollton & MARGARETTA M. SLOAN d/o GEORGE of Hanoverton.

M: 14th inst by REV.W.K.BROWN, JOHN F. PIERCE & MARTHA SHOEMAKER.

D: 6th inst in Salem, JOHN FLITCRAFT in 81st yr.

D: 2nd inst at res of her daughter in Beaver Co PA, SUSAN GOODERL w/o GEORGE ae 54y 6m 9d.

TRAGEDY AT LEETONIA: ANTHONY QUAILY, the keeper of a low doggery in that place, became insensed against MIKE DULAN for giving testimony to Grand Jury that led to indicting & fining QUAILY for violating the liquor law. QUAILY threatened DULAN & attacked him in QUAILY's saloon. DULAN died 30 hours later.
QUAILY attacked his victim with ferocity & malignity of a demon. He fled & has not yet been caught.

ABEL LODGE, the old veteran, is adding some shingles to the rear roof of "the old stone house" near the ME Church. Some other slight improvements would not injure its appearance.

PETER YOUNG & Lady returned home Sat last looking none the worse after their matrimonial tour.

On Wed last week, MATHIAS SCHOTT was found buried in a sand hole near the depot at Massillon, had been missing nearly 3 weeks. Inquest held.

JOHN MULHOLLEN was convicted of grand larceny at late term of court & sentenced to Ohio Penitentiary for 1 year.

Court adjourned suddenly Tues morn: JUDGE FRIES received a telegram announcing the death of his mother in law MRS. BEL-DEN, the wife of JUDGE BELDEN of Canton.

Fri 29 Nov 1867

M: in Vicksburg Miss, Sep 11 by REV.H.LEARY, KING DORWART, CO.D, 34th Infantry USA & ANNA L. HALL of that city.

M: 7th inst by E.P.VANSYOC ESQ., WILLIAM STRAWN & ELIZABETH HEILNER.

M: 12th inst by REV.J.W.MARTIN, ANDREW O.AZDELL & MAGGIE J. WILLIAMS all of co.

M: 14th inst by same, JACOB BARNES & ELLIE A.AZDELL all of co.

M: 20th by Friends ceremony, DANIEL KOLL & MARY J. FAW-CETT both of Salem.

M: 21st inst by REV.G.A.LOWMAN, WILLIAM McGREGGOR of New York & ANNA F. LOWMAN of Wellsville.

M: 24th inst by REV.BAXTER, G.FRANK ROGERS & MINERVA J. COWAN all of New Lisbon.

D: Oct 20 near Montgomery Texas of yellow jaundice, DAVID WOODRUFF, formerly of Salem, ae 53y.

D: 14th inst near Hanover, MRS. ABIGAL PHILLIPS widow of DAVID, ae 57y 10m.

D: 29th ult W.J.BILLINGSLEY of East Palestine ae 56y.

D: in Franklin Tp of hemorrhage, MRS.NANCY FITZPATRICK w/o HUGH, aged 55y.

D: 21st inst in Salem MRS. WILLIAMS w/o JOHN R. of heart disease.

REV.O.M.TODD, formerly of this place, now pastor of the Presbyterian Church at Lima Ohio, has received a call to the Presb.Church at Muncie, Ind. The people of Muncie must be hard up for a minister.

An old pioneer gone: Died 20th inst at his residence in Wooster, Wayne Co Oh, JOSEPH H. LARWELL, ae about 84y. He was at an early period a citizen of Col.Co. & resided we believe at Liverpool or Fawcettstown as it was then called & helped in laying out or marking the first Government surveys in CCO.

Death at a religious revival: A widow lady living in Knox Tp, having been ill for some time, asked to go to a revival. Her soul calmly resigned itself & she died. (no name)

FRANK WINES narrowly escaped drowning last Sat. Was skating at ROLLER's Dam east of town, when the ice gave way.

JOHN MORRISON is again at home. For past 18 mo has lived at Chillicothe, Livingston Co., Missouri.

Fri 6 Dec 1867

ALIMONY NOTICE: JOHN H. NEWBERRY, residence unknown, is informed that AGNES NEWBERRY filed on 30 Nov 1867 petition in CCO for wilful absence, asks alimony.

D: at New Orleans 7th ult of yellow fever, JAMES McMULLEN of Franklin Tp, ae 30y.

M: 20th ult near East Liverpool by REV.GEO.W.RIGGLE, WILLIAM R. COREY of Kansas & LAURA M. FISHER.

M: at Orange, Ill on 6th ult by REV.NEEDHAM, JOSEPH ENGLAND of Mt.Union Oh & ELLA J. JOHN of Salem.

M: 14th ult by REV.S.B.TEAGARDEN, ANDREW FLICK & E.L.LIPSEY

M: 17th ult by ISAAC WEAVER JR.,JP, JOHN RUFF & BARBARY A. BEHNER all of co.

M: 27th ult at house of JOHN MASON by REV.I.J.DELO, HARVEY LEE & LINNIE MASON, all of co.

M: 20th ult by SAML.HARDMAN ESQ., T.B.BROWN & MARY E. SHAW all of co.

Fri 13 Dec 1867

M: 28th ult by WM.ANDERSON ESQ.of Knox Tp, THOMAS POWELL & LUCINDA CAMERON.

M: 28th ult by REV.J.E.CARSON, JESSE HEPHNER & ANN M. GRAHAM, both of New Garden.

M: 21st ult by JOHN W.MORRISON ESQ., LEWIS REED of Mahoning Co & ORETTA S. BAKER of CCO.

M: 12th ult in Salem by ELDER J.D.WHITE, BARTLEY B. RITTENHOUSE & AMANDA J. STRAGER.

D: 21st ult at his res near Wellsville DAVID ROSE in 57th yr

D: in Salem 4th inst of heart disease EZEKIEL BARD ae 76y

D: in Salem 30th ult ELIZABETH FAIRFAX w/o ALLEN of lung disease ae 39y.

D: in Salem 1st inst of brain fever, REBECCA F. GARDNER w/o CHARLES W., ae 17y, & d/o ISAAC & ELIZA A. MENDENHALL.

WILLIAM ORR, of Caldwell Co Missouri, has been visiting relatives & friends here for some weeks past & left Monday.

Ran away with another man's wife: some nights since, a daguerrean artist named COLTON ran off with the wife of a MR. MOORE residing in Hanover Tp. The parties went north on the Cleveland train.

The number of births in Col.Co. for the first quarter under the new registry law was 292: 146 males & 146 females. Deaths reported: 91.

Fri 20 Dec 1867 (page 1/2 damaged)

Death of the mother of REV.S.T.HERRON, residing near Noblestown, Allegheny Co Pa. He left to attend her funeral. There will be no preaching in the UP Church this Sabbath.

Fri 27 Dec 1867

M: 18th inst M.E.TAGGART ESQ., of Leetonia & FLORA J. KIDD of Greenville PA.

M: 18th inst by REV.T.A.McCURDY, R.SPENCER BROWNSON of Waterbury CT & EMMA C. GEISSE of Wellsville.

M: 12th inst by REV.W.S.GRAY, SAMUEL S. HAGER of Pittsburgh Pa & MAGGIE J. COOKE of Salem.

M: 5th inst at Jennersville PA by Friends ceremony, DANIEL BONSALL of Salem & ELIZABETH PAXSON of former place.

M: 12th inst by REV.T.P.CHILDS, ANDREW WEAVER & EMMA B.FRIESE all of Salem.

M: 7th inst at the Weddell House, Cleveland, by GEORGE HESTER, ESQ., JOHN L. BAXTER & MISS E.A.BAXTER.

RICHARD ARTER of Shelby Ohio is in town visiting friends.

1868

Fri 10 Jan 1868

OLD MUSTER ROLL: Below we give the muster roll of Captain McLAUGHLIN's Company, 1st Regiment, 2d Brigade, 4th Division, Ohio Militia, 6 Sept 1806.

ARTHER, JOHN
ARMSTRONG, ANDREW
BAKER, JEPTHA
BEEN, JAMES
BRADY, STEPHEN
BLACKLEDGE, LEVI
BROWN, NATHAN
BAKER, GIDEON
BRADY, JAMES
BRYON, JOHN
BEEN, MOSES
BRICKER, HENRY
BAUGHMAN, HENRY
BRANDEBERRY, PHILIP
BRANDEBERRY, B.
GRIM, ABRAHAM
GOLDING, JAMES
GARRISON, THOMAS
GUTHRIE, RICHARD
GRIM, PETER
GRIM, DANIEL
GUTHRIE, WILLIAM
GREEN, HOLLAND
HOOVER, JOHN
HOLLOWAY, EPHRAIM
HOLLAND, SAMUEL
HAMILTON, HENRY
HARRISON, WM.
HARBAUGH, DANIEL
KING, THOMAS

BLACKLEDGE, R.
BOWMAN, JACOB
BURTON, ROBERT
BURSON, JOSEPH
BRANDEBERRY, JACOB
BROWN, MATHEW
CROSS, FRANCES
CALDER, DANIEL
CAMP, DAVID
CRESSINGER, PETER
CAMPBELL, JOHN
DORLAND, JAMES
DUCK, GEORGE
DILFORD, J.L.
EHRHART, DAVID
EDWARDS, JOHN
EATON, JOHN
FIFE, JOHN
FIFE, WM.
FOX, PHILIP
FOUTZ, MICHAEL
FIFE, JAMES
FIFE, DAVID
FISHER, BRICE
GREEN, THOMAS
WILLETS, GEO.
KINNEY, PETER
KING, JOHN
KING, HUGH
KOONTZ, JOHN
MOTTINGER, GEORGE
McCALLISTER, ROBERT
McLAUGHLIN, JEREMIAH
McLAUGHLIN, JOHN
MOORE, M.
MASON, MARTIN
McKAIG, PETER
MORGAN, WILLIAM
McCONNEL, JOSEPH
POE, ANDREW
PRICE, JAMES
PEARCE, AARON
POTTER, ELDRIKEN
RICHARDSON, JOSEPH
RITCHEY, ISAIAH
RANDOLPH, ISAAC
SMALLEY, ISAAC
TEEGARDEN, WILLIAM
VOTAW, JOHN
WATSON, JOSEPH
WELLS, PETER
WILSON, DAVID

M: 31st ult by ELDER WM BAXTER, WILLIAM F. FIGLEY & BIANCA E. TRIMBLE; also, GEORGE B. FIGLEY & MATTIE M. UNDERWOOD, all of New Lisbon.

M: 26th ult by WM.FULTZ ESQ., WILLIAM STRATTON & OLIVE DAVIS, all of co.

M: 17th ult at Harlem Springs by SQUIRE DANNALS, K.K. KEMBLE of Alliance & HATTIE A. HILLERMAN of Hanover.

M: 26th ult by REV.T.WAGNER, EDWARD H.KRIDLER & MARIA SWITZER all of co.

M: 1st inst by REV.I.N.BAIRD, CHARLES C.MULFORD & LAURA R. WEBB, both of Salem.

M: 31st ult by SAML.HARDMAN JP, MADISON H. ANGLEMIER & SARAH J. SHONS, all of Salem.

M: in Salem 1st inst by ELDER J.W.LANPHEAR, PERRY FIRESTONE & ANNIE C. STEEN, all of co.

CAPT. LEWIS McCOY, for many years a resident of West Tp., died of internal hemorrhage after a severe illness at his res near Alliance on 16th ult.

Fri 17 Jan 1868

OFFICERS OF THE 1ST REGIMENT, 2ND BRIGADE, 4TH DIVISION, OHIO MILITIA, SEPT. 1806:

LT. COLONEL	REASIN BEALL
MAJORS	LEWIS KINNEY, JOHN TAGGART
CAPTAINS	ALEX. SNODGRASS, ISRAEL WARNER,
	JOHN HINDMAN, GEORGE FREDERICK
	JOHN CANNON, THOMAS KEATCH
	BENJAMIN BRADFIELD, 3 VACANCIES

THE FOLLOWING IS THE LIST OF CAPTAIN KEATCH'S COMPANY:

LT. JACOB STOFFER   ENSIGN JACOB ROLLER
                    PRIVATES:

ATTERHOLT, HENRY
BRIGGS, JOHN
BROWN, HARMON
BALL, THOS.
BEESON, JOHN
BOWMAN, CHRISTIAN
COLLINS, MATHEW
CROZIER, JOHN
COPE, CALEB
DIXON, SIMON
FITZPATRICK, CHARLES
GASKILL, ISRAEL
HOLLOWAY, JOEL
HIVELY, C.
HANES, EBENEZER
ICENHOUR, JOHN
ANTRIM, JOHN
BATTERSHELL, WILLIAM
BAIR, JOHN
BOWMAN, JOSHUA
BALL, NATHAN
CALLIHAN, JAMES
COOK, JACOB
COPE, JESSE
DAVIS, HENRY
EVANS, JONATHAN
FIRESTONE, JOHN
GRANT, JOHN
HOLLOWAY, AARON
HOFFMAN, JOHN
HIVELY, JOHN
KELLEY, PATRICK

KROUCE, JACOB	MILLER, PETER
MELINGER, JACOB	MEACE, PHILIP
McCONNELL, JOHN	MELINGER, J.
OGLE, WM.	PIGEON, WILLIAM
ROBINSON, JOHN	ROLLER, HENRY
ROLLER, JACOB	SHINN, THOMAS
STEPHENSON, PETER	SCATTERGOOD, BENJAMIN
SNIDER, JOHN	STUART, HUGH
STAUFFER, HENRY	SCHOLFIELD, DAVID
TEETERS, JOHN	TEST, ISAAC
TEST, ZACHEUS	WEBB, THOMAS
WICKART, JOHN	WILSON, JAMES
WRIGHT, JOSEPH	WILLIARD, GASPER
ZIMMERMAN, HENRY	ZIMMERMAN, CONRAD
ZIMMERMAN, JOSEPH	

M: New Year's Eve, WILLIAM BAXLEY of Raymond Oh & KATE UNDERWOOD of New Lisbon.

M: 1st inst by A.A.THOMAS ESQ, DALLAS W. RENS & ARBANA RITCHEY all of Perry Tp.

M: 2nd inst by E.P.VANSYOC ESQ., JOSIAH WALTON of Damascus & ELIZA J. BENEDICT of Knox Tp.

M: 25th ult by REV.ROBT.HAYS, NATHAN HENDRICKS of Hanover Tp & MARGARET E. GARSIDE of Washington Tp.

M: 2nd inst by same, SAMUEL AIKEN of St.Clair Tp & ISABEL TODD of Centre Tp.

M: same day by same, WILLIAM MEREDITH & NANCY EDWARDS both of Salineville.

M: 31st ult in Columbiana by THOMAS CALLEN ESQ., WILLIAM KINDIG & CATHARINE GORMAN.

M: New Year's Day by REV.BANKS, JACOB SHENKLE of East Liverpool & ANNIE E. COWAN of Brownstown PA.

M: 6th inst at the National Hotel, Beaver PA by REV.POWELL, JACOB SHAUB & BETTIE LAUGHLIN, both of Franklin Tp.

M: 31st ult CHARLES F.HALL of Salem & CARRIE HULL of Warren Oh

GRAND & PETIT JURORS: The following are the names drawn for Grand & Petit Jurors for the January term of Columbiana Common Pleas:

GRAND JURORS

SALTERWAIT, HUTCHEON	BUTLER TP
HILLERMAN, J.F.	HANOVER TP
SMITH, JOHN	LIVERPOOL TP
VOTAW, MOSES	HANOVER TP
HAYES, CHARLES J.	PERRY TP
MARTIN, JOHN H.	YELLOW CREEK TP
ESTEP, JOSEPH	KNOX TP
SWITZER, SAMUEL	CENTRE TP
CABLE, PHILIP	ST.CLAIR TP
STEWART, JACOB	YELLOW CREEK TP
ALDRIDGE, HENRY	SALEM TP
WILLIAMS, DAVID	BUTLER TP
ADAMS, H.P.	PERRY TP
COPE, JOSEPH	ELKRUN TP
BATTIN, DAVID	WEST TP

PETIT JURORS

KECK, JACOB	SALEM TP
HARTLEY, JOSEPH S.	KNOX TP
RICH, DANIEL	UNITY TP
RAUCH, JONATHAN	UNITY TP
McCANN, HENRY	HANOVER TP
WICKERSHAM, WILLIAM	WEST TP
FALCONER, JOHN JR.	MADISON TP
GEORGE, WM.S.	LIVERPOOL TP
MACKALL, SAMUEL	ST.CLAIR TP
BAKER, HIRAM	HANOVER TP
WHITACRE, URIAH	FAIRFIELD TP
BOOTH, JEREMIAH	MIDDLETON TP

Fri 24 Jan 1868

D: 16th inst JOHN ZIMMERMAN of this place ae 61y

D: 17th inst MRS. ELIZABETH WILLIAMS of Wayne Tp ae 84y

Guardian Petition: LAVOY W. FITZPATRICK, ALVERDA FITZPATRICK, SUSANNA FITZPATRICK, ALWILDA FITZPATRICK & SAMUEL S. FITZPATRICK, are notified that 18 Jan 1868 JACOB FITZPATRICK, as their guardian, petitioned to sell land in Cass Twp., Hancock Co Ohio, being the undivided 1/5 part of SE 1/4 of Sec.28, Twp.2N R11E of 160 acres.

D: 11th inst at her res in Salem MRS. HATTIE COOK w/o O.R.

D: 12th inst in Butler Tp, TAMSON H. BROWN d/o ENOCH & MARY, ae 16y 2m.

M: Dec 19 by REV.J.R.DUNDAS, REUBEN MILLER of Alliance & ELIZA HUNTER of Winchester.

M: Dec 25 by same, WILLIAM H. RANDOLPH & MAGGIE A. GILSON, all of Winchester.

M: 1st inst by same, WILLIAM W. KING of Alliance & KATE KING of Winchester.

M: 2nd inst by REV.ROLLER, JACOB KEELER of Columbiana & CATHARINE ELSER of Mahoning Co

M: 2nd inst by REV.A.Y.HOUSTON, SETH MEEK & SUE E. SHEETS, all of East Palestine.

M: 8th inst by ELDER D.J.WHITE, H.C.PARMALEE & MARTHA A. URIE both of Wellsville.

M: 13th inst by Rev G.W.BURNS, BENJAMIN SMITH & LAVINIA MILLWOOD.

ERASTUS EELLS, undertaker, was not called on to make a coffin in the months of November & December. That hasn't happened in the past 38 years.

A.G.McCASKEY & family have moved to Steubenville where is is to work as Tickey Agent of the Panhandle Railroad there.

JOHN ZIMMERMAN died at his res Thurs last; left widow & family, aged 61y.

Fri 31 Jan 1868

M: 14th inst at Pittsburgh PA by REV.J.S.REED, HENRY GREAVES & MRS. S.R.WILLITS both of New Lisbon.

M: 12th ult by ISAAC WEAVER ESQ., SAMUEL STANLEY & ELIZA J. ILER, all of co.

D: 17th inst at res in Salem, JOHN SHEETS in 88th yr.

D: at res in Madison Tp 5th inst, JAMES McLAUGHLIN in 86th yr

D: 19th inst JULIA ANN CUFFEL of Centre Tp ae 70y

D: 19th inst JOSHUA PATTERSON of Wayne Tp ae 73y

D: 22nd inst at res of SOLOMON SIDLER of Salem Tp, MRS. LOUISA KIPP ae 24y 1m 27d

345 marriage licenses issued in CCO in 1867.

Fri 7 Feb 1868

M: 21st ult by REV.G.D.KINNEAR, JAMES W. KINNEAR & MALINDA COPE; also, at the same time & place, ROBERT GREY & LOUISA COPE, both daughters of NATHAN COPE of Unity Tp.

M: 31st ult by J.McVICKER ESQ., JAMES JACKSON of New Brighton PA & MARY F. SHEROW of Lisbon.

M: 21st ult by DANL.McLANE ESQ., THOMAS CHAMBERLIN & REBECCA GUY all of Madison Tp

M: 23d ult by REV.J.N.SWAN, JOHN M. AZDELL of Mexico Missouri & LYDE CABLE of St.Clair Tp.

M: same day by same, JAMES WILDWOOD of East Liverpool & MARTHA M. MILLINAUX.

M: 23d ult by SAML.HARDMAN ESQ., L.M.HENDERSON & MATTIE TATUM, all of Salem.

MRS. LYDIA IRISH, formerly of this place but now of New Castle PA, the aged & honored wife of the late WILLIAM IRISH, a few days ago donated $50 to the destitute in the South.

Farmer convicted & sent to PEN: JOHN O. ICKES, whose barn in Berlin Tp., Mahoning Co, was burned last Sept., has just been convicted at the Mah.Co.court, of arson for burning the barn of SIMON HARTZELL, his brother in law, whose barn was burned at the same time as his own. His own barn was insured for more than its value & it is supposed he burned it to get insurance, and burned HARTZELL's to prevent suspicion. He was sentenced to 3 years.

Fri 14 Feb 1868

M: 20th ult by REV.J.ESTILE, E. MARSHAL & MARY ZIMMERMAN, both of co.

M: 4th inst by REV.JOSEPH ANDREWS, EDMUND JOHN WHITTON of East Liverpool & MARY JANE SNOWDEN of Wellsville.

D: in Wellsville 29th ult MRS. MELISSA JENKINS in 27th yr.

D: at res in Salineville 6th inst SAMUEL McCOY in 92nd yr.

Information wanted: on 13 Dec 1867, PHILIP BARCH, a soldier of Co B, 12th Ohio Cavalry, called with JOHN SOUDER who keeps a public house in Clarkson, Middleton Tp. He stayed with SOUDER from 13 to 16 Dec, saying he was going to visit MARTIN THOMAS, a messmate who lives east of Clarkson 4 miles. Since leaving Clarkson said BARCH has not been seen or heard of by any person of his acquaintance.

JOSHUA TODD, Supt. of Union Schools in Hanover resigned due to ill health

JOHN TWADDLE, whose arrest for stealing a horse & sleigh at Chestnut Ridge Church, Carroll Co, the property of LAUGHLIN McKENZIE, was sentenced to 3 yrs in Ohio Pen.

Fri 21 Feb 1868

M: 30th ult at res of MRS. E.A.SMITH in Salem, JOHN MURRY of New Garden & MISS DUNN, of Glasgow, Scotland.

D: 1st inst at res of her son in law WILLIAM CRAWFORD of St.Clair Tp, MRS. HELEN HENRY ae 87y

D: at res of his son in law RICHARD ADAMS in New Lisbon on 10th inst from a stroke of paralysis, JOHN SCOTT ae 80y

JOSEPH S. LODGE, formerly a resident of this place, son of ABEL LODGE, now is Recorder in Johnson Co Iowa.

HON. JAMES BOONE of Salem died from congestion of the lungs in that place on Fri. last.

Fri 28 Feb 1868

M: 16th inst by ISAAC WEAVER ESQ., LEWIS I. STOFFER & AMANDA DIEL, all of Knox Tp.

M: 13th inst at res of bride's father by E.P.VANSYOC ESQ., BENJAMIN BARBER & HULDAH J. CREW, all of co.

D: in New Lisbon 18th inst at res of parents SARAH ANN SHERROW ae about 16y

D: 31st ult, JAMES GALBREATH ae 88y.

D: 6th inst infant son of GEORGE McDONALD.

D: at the Infirmary 17th inst, MICHAEL SHOEMAKER ae 73y.

Child burned to death in Columbiana: We learn from the SALEM REPUBLICAN that on 11th inst, MRS. B. COPELAND, of Columbiana, after lighting a candle & placing it upon a table & during her absence her youngest child, aged about 18 mo, got upon the table where the candle was & its clothes caught fire. Mrs.C., hearing cries, ran to the house & found her child completely enveloped in flames. It was so badly burned that it died in a few hours.

Fri 6 Mar 1868

M: 26th ult at the res of bride's parents by REV.R.DICKSON, WATSON C. WHITNEY & MATTIE J. ROGERS, all of New Lisbon.

M: in Hiram, Portage Co on 20th ult by RICHARD M. HANK, ESQ., CURT THOMPSON of Salem & ISA C. YOUNG of the former.

M: 23d ult in Washingtonville by REV.CUNNINGHAM, C.F.KESSELMIRE & MISS M.T.WILLIARD, both of Salem.

D: 20th ult near Salem, CORA M. ENGLAND, d/o JAMES R. & LIZZIE A., ae 2m 18d.

D: 21st ult at Logansport Ind, ISAAC GARWOOD, ae 33y, formerly of Salem.

D: 29th ult in Wayne Tp., MRS. _____ROSEBERG, ae about 90y

D: 26th ult in Wayne Tp., MRS. FRANCES FORBES ae 74y

J.M.MOWREY runs Cottage Hill Nursery, 1 mile north of New Lisbon; concord grapes, peaches, etc.

Postmaster JOHN ROBERTSON of this place arrested by U.S.-Marshall & taken to Cleveland for embezzlement of $300.-(story explains his innocence.)

Fri 13 Mar 1868

M: 27th ult by REV.JOHN ARTHUR, W.G.McINTOSH & KATE CAMERON, both of co.

M: 27th ult by THOMAS C.ALLEN, ESQ., JOSEPH O. WOODS & LAURETTA J. EDMUNDSON, all of co.

M: 27th ult by WM.ANDERSON ESQ., ALONZO WERTZ of Stark Co & MAGGIE ALTMAN of CCO.

D: 26th ult in New Garden of consumption, DAVID SCATTERGOOD, ae 72y

D: 2nd ult MARY ANN BAKER w/o WILLIAM & d/o MRS. UNGER & granddaughter of WILLIAM CALDWELL, ae 21y 4m 1d.

JOHN ROBERTSON, Postmaster, honorably acquitted.

CHARLES POWERS s/o R.J.POWERS ESQ., has been home several days from Meadville Pa where he is attending college.

Death of JOSEPH B. MORGAN: died at res in East Fairfield Thurs. night, served 2 terms as Recorder; aged about 34y; Mason, burial from M.E.Church. (see also March 20)

THOMAS BROOKS, who lived here a number of years ago, died at his res near Fort Desmoines Iowa last week, ae about 60y.

Attempted suicide: Sun last week, GEORGE SKELLEY, a res of Unity Tp, attempted to hang himself in his barn. he was discovered & cut down. Cause: temporary insanity.

Fri 20 Mar 1868

M: 8th inst in Hanover by WM.JOHNSON ESQ., S.B.MAUNTY & M.McCAN, all of co.

M: 16th ult by WM.FULTZ ESQ., MARION SAINTCLAIR & SALLIE MOORE, all of co.

Resolutions of Respect from New Lisbon Lodge No.65, F & AM for JOSIAH B. MORGAN who died 8 Mar 1868. W.M.HOSTETTER, W.M., & W.A.NICHOLS, Secy.

Fri 27 Mar 1868

M: 28 Feb at res of MR.ROBINS BLACK by REV.J.E.CARSON, HENRY MICHNER & SARAH M. SOMERS.

M: 12th inst at res of bride's parents by same, STEPHEN KEITH & A.A.WINDER.

M: 12th inst by same at res of bride's parents, JOHN W.-BLYTHE & HANNAH A. MURRY, all of co.

M: 12th inst at res of bride's parents by ISAAC WEAVER JR., GEORGE STOFFER & CATHARINE BEAR both of co.

M: 15th inst at res of bride's father in Kent by REV.ANDREW WILSON, HIRAM HOLCOMB of Salem & SYLVIA S. BUSHNELL of Kent.

M: 27th ult by W.ANDERSON ESQ., ALONZO WERTZ of Stark Co & MAGGIE ALTMAN of CCO.

M: 11th inst by Friends ceremony in Philadelphia, JONATHAN BONSALL of CCO & REBECCA W. ZELLEY of Medford, Berlington Co NJ.

M: 12th inst in Wellsville by ELDER D.J.WHITE, JOHN BILES of Steubenville & MRS. SARAH TEIL of Wellsville.

M: 17th inst by REV.T.P.CHILDS, HENRY V.CONN & ELIZABETH ANN WHITE, all of co.

D: 16th inst at res in Salem, JONATHAN SHAW ae 71y.

D: 11th inst at her res in Salem, MRS. HARRIET WOODRUFF w/o JAMES ae 59y.

D: 11th inst at res in Salem, ROBERT HENCHILLWOOD ae 70y.

D: 9th inst SAMUEL H. CONN of Butler Tp ae 73y.

D: 5th inst at res near Hanover, D.L.McQUILKEN ae about 27y.

D: 20th inst at res of his parents JOHN HENDERSON s/o DANIEL & RACHEL ae 9y.

Birth & Death reports: number of doctors reporting: 54; births: 284, males 148, females 136; legitimate births, 273; illegitimate 11; number of deaths, 85.

Accident: ISAAC SEACHRIST of Columbiana, at the Enterprise Works, had 2 of his fingers taken off with a circular saw. JACOB BRINKER residing about 3 miles north of town, had one hand badly mutilated last week while attending a circular saw.

Fri 3 Apr 1868

M: 19th inst at res of OBADIAH FRENCH near Damascoville, by REV.DR.BAIRD, JOSHUA WOODWARD of Pa & JUDITH FRENCH of CCO.

M: 17th ult at Beaver PA by REV.A.S.LOWRY, W.G.ANDERSON of Wellsville & KEZIAH MAPLE of Jefferson Co.

M: 19th ult by ELDER D.J.WHITE, CHARLES M.MELLOR & ETHELINDA LEWIS both of Wellsville.

D: 20th inst in Salem, FREDERICK VOETTER, infant son of JULIUS & MARGARET ae 1y.

D: 21st inst in Salem, ISAAC BENNETT ae ___y.

D: 22nd inst in Butler Tp, ZIMRI WHINERY ae 54y.

D: at res in Madison Tp Feb 14, DAVID R. GILSON in 39th yr

D: 14th ult EDWARD B. DAVIS, ae 18y.

Accident: we regret to learn that STEPHEN DOUGHTON, of this place, while on his way from Hubbard to New Lisbon on 26th inst, was thrown from his buggy, breaking one of his ribs & being otherwise injured.

J.E.MASKREY, Marble Works, will move to south side of diamond

Fri 10 Apr 1868

M: 20th ult at the Parsonage of Yellow Creek Congregation, Madison Tp by REV.J.N.SWAN, ELI R. WESTFALL of New Lisbon & NANNIE C. CAMERON d/o JNO.ESQ., of Wellsville.

M: 17th ult at Beaver PA by REV.A.J.LOWMAN, FRANK H. MENOUGH & MARY A. BENWOOD, both of Wellsville.

M: 31st ult at the Kennard House, Cleveland, by REV.C.H. ELLIS, JOEL BONSALL & MILLIE VAUGHN, both of Salem.

M: 19th ult at res of bride's parents by REV.P.W.WEDDLE, DANIEL BAKER of CCO & HATTIE HAMILTON of Wooster, Ohio.

D: at the Infirmary 31st ult, JOHN BARTON in 96th yr.

D: 31st ult at res of JAMES FARMER, Salem Tp, his mother, MRS. JERUSHA FARMER ae 84y 7m 1d.

D: 3d inst at res of THOMAS McCLELLAND, Centre Tp, REBECCA McCLELLAND, ae 75y.

A short time ago, CHARLES O'BRIEN, who lives in Hanover Tp, was assaulted by his son, a lunatic, who cut & knocked the old man down & held him there. The old gent raised the cry of murder & attracted the attention of neighbors who came to his rescue. The father, after his release, seized his refle & rushed upon the lunatic, declaring that he would shoot or kill him, & it was by superhuman efforts that the old man was restrained. In the melee he fired the contents of his rifle at his son, or perhaps at random, which did no injury. It is thought that the father is also partially deranged.

W.C.SHERBINE will run a milkwagon during the coming season.

Fri 17 Apr 1868 (Vol 2 no 1) on WRHS microfilm

Church Directory:
UNITED PRESBYTERIAN   REV.S.T.HERRON, PASTOR
METHODIST EPISCOPAL   REV. J.F.JONES, PASTOR
FIRST PRESBYTERIAN   REV.R.DICKSON, PASTOR
DISCIPLE   REV. WILLIAM H. BAXTER, PASTOR
FIRST REFORMED CHURCH REV. G.M.ALBRIGHT, PASTOR
TRINITY, PROT.-EPISC. corner Walnut & Beaver St.

Warren, Ohio: Apr 6: JAMES FEARNS, a young man aged 22, who for 4y has been employed by PARKS & WENTZ as clerk, committed suicide yesterday at 10 o'clock by hanging himself with a roll of crash toweling fastened over the frame of a door. No cause is assigned for the commission of the act. The deceased leaves a widowed mother & sister who reside in Longmore, Ireland.

M: 1st inst at res of bride's father by THOS.C.ALLEN ESQ., AARON C. ARMSTRONG & MISS SALOME MARTIN all of co.

M: 7th inst by REV.J.F.JONES, PIUS BEAN & MRS. P.CARTNEY both of New Lisbon.

M: 26th ult by CLARKSON BARNABY JP, WILLIAM BROOKS of CCO & MISS LYDIA REESE of Stark Co.

M: by F.M.GREEN at his res in Canfield on 2nd inst, E.J.-ARNOLD & MISS LIZZIE A. DIXON of Salem.

M: 8th inst by REV.WM.BAXTER, JONAH METZ & MISS SAMANTHA B. FARR, all of co.

M: in Crawford Co.,Ill 19th ult by REV.LEVI C.ENGLISH, at res of bride's father, ALLEN CALVIN of Mahoning Co & MISS JULIA E. REESE formerly of Espy, Columbiana Co Ohio.

D: at Granville Oh 25th ult from the effects of a wound rec'd at battle of Shiloh, ABRAHAM IKIRT in 49th yr.

D: 1st inst at Infirmary, MARGARET EMICH in 73d yr.

D: 6th inst MRS.SARAH JOHNSON w/o C.S., in 23d yr.

Fri 24 Apr 1868 (Vol.2 no 2) on WRHS microfilm

M: 4th inst at res of bride's mother by REV.T.P.CHILDS, ABRAHAM F. ROYER of Salem & MISS ALVINA CRAFT of Mah.Co.

M: 6th inst by REV.R.DICKSON, LEANDER SHRIVER & MISS MARGARET McGAFFICK both of Butler Tp

M: at the Leetonia House on 16th inst by REV.S.T.HERRON, REUBEN L. INGLEDEU & MISS ALICE R. CHAIN d/o H.CHAIN ESQ., of Leetonia.

D: 11th inst at Broadway Hotel in Salem after an illness of 1y which she bore with a Christian's hope, MRS. M.A.COLE ae 36y.

D: 11th inst at New Garden, MRS.D.JOHNSON ae 90y.

D: 13th inst infant child of J.McGAFFREY ae 1y.

Fri 1 May 1868

M: 11th ult at res of DANIEL MERCER in Butler Tp by E.GARSIDE ESQ., ALBION M. WARD & CELESTIA C. PETTIT all of co.

M: 19th ult by REV.M.HYDE at res of bride's brother in law JOHN JOINT, formerly of Connock, Ireland & MRS. HENRIETTA TUTTLE, formerly of Penna. Salem & Pittsburgh papers copy.

D: 11th ult NETTIE E. ABRAMS w/o WILLIAM in 19th yr.

W.P.LANPHEAR, artist, New Lisbon; ad with cupids & camera.

THOMAS HANNA, late a resident of this place, now of Marshall-town Iowa, is in town visiting friends.

The remains of WILLIAM B. IRISH were removed from the cemetery in New Lisbon on Mon Apr 20 & taken to New Castle PA for burial. Mr. IRISH died in 1850 near New Lisbon.

WILLIAM THOMAS, an Irishman of Leetonia, the village bully, assaulted a number of people there & was arrested by FRED MAUS to go before SQUIRE McVICKER. He made an escape.

Registry of births & deaths: the Legislature did not repeal the law.

8 May 1868

M: 25th ult at res of CAPT.J.J.SCROGGS by REV J.N.SWAN, assisted by REV S.T.HERRON, DR.H.B.HART of Akron & MISS I.C.YOUNG of West Point.

M: 16th ult by E.P.VANSYOC ESQ, JOHN C. STANLEY of Mahoning Co & EDITH C. NEILL of Middleton Tp.

D: 15th ult ELIZABETH ATKINSON W/O GEORGE in 68th yr.

D: 25th ult at his res in East Liverpool, JAMES FOSTER of the firm of FOSTER & RIGBY, proprietors of the Broadway Pottery, aged about 60y.

D: 18th ult at res near Wellsville, JANE KOUNTZ ae 87y 5m 13d

COURT: RUTH ADAMS vs JOHN Q.ADAMS, stricken off at defd.costs

ANTHONY CLUNK has taken the contract of lighting the street lamps for the next year at $215.04.

Death of JOHN McLERAN: we regret to announce the death of JOHN McLERAN, SHERIFF OF COL.CO. who died of consumption at his residence in this place Fri last in 39th yr; was elected last fall & began in January. He removed to this place from Salem & was buried in Salem last Sun with Masonic honors.- JOHN P. MORGAN, Coroner, takes the office made vacant by his death.

We learn that the wife of ANDREW BUNTING, pilot, residing at Wellsville, took arsenic last Thurs. night & in a short time was a corpse. Cause not known. Deceased leaves 2 small children.

15 May 1868

M: 30th ult by REV G M ALBRIGHT, asstd by REV R HAYES at the res of bride's parents, DAVID H. PATTERSON & ROSA WILLIARD all of co.

M: 28th ult at res of JOHN A. BLACKBURN of Victor, Iowa by REV F L ARNOLD, WILLIAM M. EDDY, M.D., of Marengo, Iowa & REBECCA A. BLACKBURN, formerly of Salem.

D: 5th inst, MRS. _____THOMPSON of East Liverpool ae 83y.

D: at Monteray, Alegan Co Mich on 12th ult, MARY ZIMMERMAN W/O JOHN, formerly of Salem in 30th yr.

Suicide of MRS. BUNTING of Wellsville, particulars: she asked him to buy new furniture & carpets & he refused; she drank arsenic. Was aged 35y; he is proprieitor of a boat that plies the Ohio River

We learn that MRS. MARGARET LYNCH committed suicide Thurs last by throwing herself into the Ohio River just below East Liverpool. She was somewhat intoxicated at the time. Deceased, with 2 small children & her husband, OWEN LYNCH, were on their way from Allegheny to Wheeling.

22 May 1868

M: 17th inst at the family res on Lisbon St. by REV I N BAIRD, asstd by REV JOHN J MOFFIT, DR. J.I.MARCHAND of Irwin Station, PA & ETTIE T. SNIDER of Salem.

M: 30th ult at res of bride's mother in Damascoville, by REV JOHN McCARTY, SURVANTUS P. KERR of Portage Co & HANNAH M. BALDWIN of this co.

M: in UP Church, Wellsville on 7th inst by REV JOSEPH ANDREWS, JOSEPH WARRICK of Franklin & MARTHA J. McLANE of West Point, both of co.

M: 29th ult by REV.ROBT HAYS, JAS.F.GLENN & ANNIE LEONARD.

M: 5th inst by same, GEORGE ARMSTRONG & ELLEN HUNTER.

M: same day by same, JOHN McELROY & ANN RAPPLES, all of Salineville.

M: 12th inst at Valley Mills by E P VANSYOC ESQ, THOMAS HARMER of Morgan Co Oh & M.E.LAMBORN of this co.

D: 25th ult at Smiths Ferry, LAVINA ORMES w/o WILLIAM JR., in 35th yr.

D: 18th Mar. in Franklin Tp of consumption, HUGH DOBSON s/o ROBERT & RACHEL ae 24y 4m.

D: 23d ult CHARLES MASON of Centre Tp ae 88y.

Partition: LEVI SUMMERS, MARY SUMMERS, ANNA SUMMERS, SARAH MITCHENOR & HENRY MITCHENOR, of Col.Co. & AMOS SUMMERS, JESSE MILLER & MARIA MILLER of Mahoning Co, petition filed by HENRY D. SUMMERS, minor, by WASHINGTON MESSIMORE his guardian re land in Knox Tp.

29 May 1868

M: 20th inst at res of bride's parents by REV J F JONES, LOUIS BURTON NELSON & SARAH DAVIDSON both of New Lisbon.

M: 4th inst by REV J N SWAN at res of bride, HOMER HUSTON & EUPHEMIA WILLIAMS.

M: 6th inst at res of bride's father by REV R V DODGE, REV SANFORD G. FISHER of East Liverpool & MISS LOUIE J. DRURY of Washington PA.

M: 14th inst by REV J J MOFFIT at res of bride's father, JOHN O. BESSON (sic: BEESON) of Waterford & R.V.HEACOCK of Salem.

M: 7th inst at the American House, Salem, by REV A MAXWELL, MILTON TRAVIS & ANNA W. WALTERS both of Wash'ville.
D: near Kingston, MO., Thurs 14th inst HELEN WOODBRIDGE ORR, only dau of JAMES S. & LIZZIE H. ORR ae 13m 13d.

D: 21st inst at res of her son JOHN FIGLEY of Hanover Tp, MRS. JEMIMA FIGLEY ae 68y.

D: 24th inst at her res in Salem Tp, MRS. REBECCA HALVER-STADT ae 57y.

D: in New Lisbon 16th inst SOLOMON GLOSS ae 58y.

D: 17th inst,consumption, in Salem, HOWELL S. BISHOP ae 49y

D: 15th inst in Salem, MARY MULHURN ae 78y.

D: 16th inst,Butler Tp, ABIGAIL MARTIN relic of JOHN ae 61y

On Fri last week, AUZY WHITE was thrown from a buggy at Salem; he had not recovered from the injuries rec'd some 2y ago at Island Run, which deprived him for a long time of the use of one of his legs.

JOHN FROST of the Massillon Independent & JAMES L. ROBERTSON, Prosecuting Attorney of Henry Co., are in town visiting relatives & friends.

5 June 1868

M: 22nd ult at res of bride's parents by REV W K BROWN, LAWRENCE THOMSON of Leetonia & SAMANTHA CLAPSADDLE of Alliance

M: 21st ult at res of bride's parents by REV.MR.MILLS, SYLVESTER S. GARWOOD of Salem, manager of Pacific & Atlantic Telegraph Co. at Harrisburg, Pa. & FANNY G. BRETZ, youngest dau of MAJOR JACOB BRETZ of Carlisle PA.

D: at res in Canton on 21st ult,consumption, L.S.DILLEY late editor of the Ohio Repository; he leaves a wife & one little one (Stark Co Democrat)

D: 28th ult AMY MURPHY w/o E.W. of Salem ae 48y.

D: 27th ult at the Infirmary, JOHN STEVENS in 50th yr.

Estate of JAMES BELL: SALOME H. BELL, admrx
Estate of ALEX. McGILLVARY: PERCILLA J. McGILLVARY admrx

Decoration of soldiers' graves: Memorial Day, in our cemetery:

CAPT. FREEMAN MORRISON	76TH OHIO
CHARLES E. LOUNSBURY	65TH OHIO
HENRY J. KING	6TH OHIO CAV
MAJOR ANSON L. BREWER,	PAYMASTER
CAPTAIN CHARLES BREWER	19TH OHIO
CLINTON STARR	78TH OHIO
CAPT. EZRA COPPOCK	104TH OHIO
CAPT. JOSIAH MORGAN	104TH OHIO
CORNELIUS Y. STRAIT	3RD OHIO
MARSHALL MILLER	126TH OHIO
GEN. JOHN ARMSTRONG	
COL. JOHN WATT	
GEORGE ATTERHOLT	104TH OHIO
LEWIS FLUGAN	87TH OHIO
JOHN ROBINSON	—— PA
JONATHAN PHILMAN	6TH OHIO CAV

A banner inscribed "To the Memory of our Absent Fallen Comrades" bore the following names:

CAPT. U. BEAN	19TH OHIO
ISRAEL BRINKER	104TH OHIO
LEVI BRANDEBERRY	3D OHIO BATTERY
ROBERT BREWER	87TH
WM. BURBECK	
WM. BROUGHTON	2ND VIRGINIA
WM. CHARTERS	78TH
MARTIN CULBERTSON	176TH
ELIAS CULBERTSON	19TH
ELI CHANDLER	19TH
JACOB CLUNK	76TH
GEORGE DOWNARD	176TH
BYRON ENTRIKEN	104TH
JASON ESTILL	5TH
ROBERT EWING	24TH
GEORGE FREEMAN	6TH OHIO CAVALRY
MILETUS GASKILL	104TH
LEONARD GASKILL	—— ILLINOIS
JAMES GROOMS JR.	76TH
CAPT. URIAH IRVIN	19TH
THOMAS JOHNSON	176TH
DAVID JOHNSON	104TH
THOMAS JESSOP	104TH
HIRAM LOUDEN	
WM. LAUGHLIN	1ST
JOSEPH LEIGHTENSTINE	76TH
HIRAM P. MYERS	32ND
JOHN McDONALD	104TH
DAVID L. McQUILKEN	38TH
JOHN MILLER	104TH
JOHN L. MITCHELL	176TH
JACOB MITCHELL	176TH
PIERCE McCARTNEY	19TH
BENJAMIN F. ORR	76TH
JOSEPH F. ORR	76TH
WM. PARSONS	104TH
FREDERICK PINEER	19TH
LIEUT. ALCINUS RICHARDSON	7TH
LEONARD SPRINGER	12TH OHIO CAV
ROBERT SCOTT	78TH
DAVID SPRINGER	13TH KENTUCKY
LIEUT. CALVIN STARR	3RD KENTUCKY
SIMON SMITH	6TH OHIO CAV
JAMES SPRINGER	1ST
JOHN THOMAS	6TH OHIO CAV
DANIEL WATT	78TH
JOHN WHITACRE JR.	76TH
HENRY OGLE	76TH
FRANK PROUSE	1ST

12 June 1868

M: 28th ult by REV J N SWAN, JOHN SMITH & KATE McKENZIE all of co

M: 31st ult at res of R G HEATON in Salem by REV J J MOFFIT, SAMUEL BARTH & MARY L. BROWN both of Salem.

Death of Kit CARSON, famous pioneer & Indian fighter; died at Fort Lynn, Colo on 23d ult; he was born in Madison Co KY Dec 24, 1809 & with his parents emigrated to Howard Co MO. (long)

Skeleton found: Wed last week a skeleton was found on the Ore banks west of town. The story was related by one of our oldest citizens: about 1806, JAMES NAUGHTON, who emigrated from Penna with a wife, 2 sons & 1 daughter, resided up the creek. On a cold day in Jan. he came to town to buy provisions & disappeared. He was under the influence of drink. He was never found & his family left here years ago.

19 June 1868

M: 17th ult by WM. ANDERSON ESQ., A.B.KNULL of Stark Co & KATE CURRY of Knox Tp, CCO.

M: 31st ult by THOS C ALLEN ESQ, JOHN A. ESTILL & MELISSA E. MARCH all of co

M: June 4 at res of bride's father, J.B.NIXON at Ark Hill Place near Alliance OH by REV D W TOWNSEND, JERRY BOYER of Pittsburgh PA & LIBBIE NIXON.

D: 5th inst at Infirmary, MARGARET DEMON in 33d yr.

D: 8th inst MALANCTHON BOWMAN s/o SAMUEL of Centre Tp ae 23y 11m

D: 6th inst at res of parents, H.WARREN CHESSMAN of Salem ae 33y

D: 4th inst near Bryan, Williams Co OH of lung fever, HENRY DUNLAP brother of M.V.DUNLAP of Salem ae 23y.

Estate of CHARLES BELAT: DAVID BELAT admr

DAVID GOLDEN was accidentally drowned Tues night last, opposite East Liverpool. He was attempting to board the steamer Lioness while under full headway with a tow; his skiff ran under the guard of the boat & swept him off. Body not yet recovered, tho a full search was instituted at once by CAPT. RENO of the Lioness. He did not hail the boat. Deceased leaves a wife & 1 child.

26 June 1868

M: 16th inst at the St.Charles Hotel, Pittsburgh PA by REV G W BURNS, MAJOR M.H.FOUTTS of East Liverpool & LIDE R. GARDNER of Hancock Co VA.

M: 9th inst at res of bride's father in Col'ana by THOMAS C.ALLEN ESQ., JOEL OBERHOLTZER & SUSAN SNYDER.

M: 6th ult at Oak Grove by REV D V HYDE, MATHIAS NOLF & LYDIA DAHOFF both of co.

D: 15th inst at res of his daughter MRS. KING in Wellsville, JOHN CREIGHTON in 80th yr.

D: 8th inst at res of his son in law WILLIAM DIEHL near Winchester OH of cancer, AQUILLA BURCHFIELD ae 72y 5m 15d.

REV. F.RICHARDS, formerly of New Lisbon but now of Chicago, spent a few days last week in town among relatives & friends.

3 July 1868

M: 18th ult at ME Ch in East Liverpool by REV GEO CROOK, JOHN W. TAYLER & BELLE C. KNOWKES (sic: KNOWLES) both of that place.

M: 17th ult at res of bride's parents by REV J H CONKLE of Elizabeth PA, J.P.TODD of New Lisbon & MAGGIE J. McGHIE of New Somerset OH

M: 25th ult in Salem by REV T P CHILDS, E.L.VICKERS & LIZZIE WATERS both of Salem

D: 23 May LILLIE HILL inf.dau.of J.G.& SOPHIA of Shelby Oh

REV.ROBERT McCASKEY, formerly publisher of the NEW LISBON BUCKEYE STATE, but now a Methodist minister stationed at Monroeville, Huron Co, spent last Sabbath in this place & preached at the M.E.Church.

NEW LISBON JOURNAL, 1867-1876

10 July 1868

M: 3d ult by HIRAM GAVER JP, SAMUEL RICHER of Washingtonville & SUSAN BELATT of Butler Tp.

M: 26th ult by same, J.E.CRUBAUGH of Hanover & EMMA SINCLAIR of Franklin Tp.

D: at her res in Pt.Harmar, Wash.Co.Oh. 3d inst, MRS. ELEANOR PECK formerly of New Lisbon, ae 63y 16d.

D: 25th ult at father's res in Wellsville MISS CATHARINE COYLE in 21st yr.

D: at Col'ana on 5th inst, MRS. SHUTS ae about 25y (see Aug 7)

Ordination of REV. JOSEPH LEPER at West Beaver Presb.Church.

Human skeleton found at West Point by workmen excavating the new road; was a middle aged white man, buried with a skeleton of a dog. Foul play is believed, but at this late date, cannot be proven.

NAPOLEAN YOUNG, the Elkrun chamption, will try to walk 100 miles in 24 hours at Pittsburgh.

17 July 1868

M: 4th inst by ED PETTIT JP, HAMILTON S. DICKEY & SUSANNA TURNER all of co.

M: 6th inst by REV A T McMURPHEY, REUBEN PROBERT & SOPHIA LARGE, both of Salem.

D: 8th inst at res in Salem Tp, SAMUEL STEWART in 48th yr

D: 9th inst at res in Wayne Tp, JOHN LOUDEN in 65th yr

Unknown man drowned, coroner's inquest; supposed to be a German about 50y old. Was buried at ME Church yard at Franklin Square.

24 July 1868

D: 6th inst, consumption, MISS SUSAN LONG of Salem 24th yr

GOV.HAYES reprieved MRS. VICTOR, condemned to be hanged Aug 20, until Nov 20 & ordered her to be removed to the Northern Lunatic Asylum at Newburgh.

Last Fri was Capt. FERDINAND BECK'S 69th birthday. For the past 30 years he has been the bellringer at the courthouse.

A young man 18y old named WALTER STEELE, s/o JOHN, recently from England, was drowned Sun July 12 opposite East Liverpool while bathing. Funeral Mon from First Methodist Church.

Col. BUCKLEY, once Major of the 19th Ohio, died in Akron some days since.

31 July 1868 (on WRHS microfilm)

M: 4 July in Salem by REV I N BAIRD, J.FRANCIS LONG & MISS ISABELLA McDONALD.

M: 23d inst by REV WM BAXTER, THOMAS GRAFTON & MISS BELLE FREDERICK both of this co.

D: Mon Jly 20 of cholera infantum, ANNIE W. FISHER, d/o CHRISTIE A. & SAMUEL L. FISHER ae 5m.

D: Wed 23d inst in New Lisbon, MRS. MARY P. ARMSTRONG in 75th yr

Arrest of DANIEL SHUTT: charged with poisoning his wife; is about 35-40 yrs of age, of German descent; is a watchmaker & jeweler by trade; he was married to MARY L. McSTEPHENSON, his 2nd wife (whom he is charged with poisoning) in Jan 1865.- Resided about 1y in Sewickley PA, 1y in Lawrenceville near Pittsburgh & the past 18mo in Col.Co.Oh. Prior to 4 July he insured wife for $5000; she died July 5, it was thought from a quantity of ice cream; burial at Sewickley. Her mother Mrs. MARY STEPHENSON made information before JUSTICE MILLS of New Lisbon alleging he had murdered her. Testimony of SHUTT was that she was a very wicked woman, she had attempted

suicide on 1 or 2 occasions by hanging & threatened to poison herself. Remanded to jail, unable to give bail of $10,000.

A Scotchman named THOMAS CARR committed suicide in Youngstown Thurs. night by butting his brains out while in the lockup.- He had the delirium tremens.

7 Aug 1868

M: 22nd ult by REV LANPHEAR, GEORGE W. PYLE of Salem & LOU STRAWN of Mahoning Co.

M: 1st inst by J B MILLS ESQ, JOSHUA WEBB & ELIZABETH WEAVER both of Salem Tp.

M: 25th ult by same, A.J.REEDER & ANNA B. RODGERS all of West Tp. (see also Aug 14)

Wife poisoning case, continued from last issue: DANIEL SHUTT discharged; had been arrested & tried before JUSTICE MILLS & JUDGE FIRESTONE; all witnesses except the sister of the deceased were present. MR. SHUTT proposes having the body taken up & the stomach examined. (see July 10)

14 Aug 1868

M: 25th ult by J B MILLS ESQ, A.J.REEDER & ANNA B. BYERS all of West Tp. (see also Aug 7)

D: 26 July infant son of CHARLES F. & S.B.LEASE of Salem ae 3m 2 wks 1d.

D: in Martin Co Ind, 8 July of remittant fever, JOSEPHINE TODD w/o JOHN A., formerly of Wayne Tp, CCO.

SAMUEL COBURN. Among the hardy pioneers who settled CCO were the SHEEHANS, McLAUGHLINS & THE COBURNS. SAMUEL COBURN, the subject of the sketch is the eldest son of the latter family, of Irish descent; was born in PA near the Susquehanna River on 5 Aug 1780; in Spring 1796 this family moved from PA to the Northwest Territory & on 9 June 1796 settled in what is now St.Clair Tp on a farm after owned by CAPT. WILLIAM FOULKS, proprietor of Foulks Town, now Calcutta. He voted in Fall 1801 & has been a voter in St.Clair for 67y & only failed to vote once, in Spring 1813, when he was in the Army. (signed) URIAH THOMAS.

MR. H. TRITT of Alliance, for many years a resident of New Lisbon, was poisoned last Fri in some unknown manner & supposed dying. He had purchased a drug store a few days before & it is thought he took poison by mistake.

NAPOLEAN YOUNG's walk in Pittsburgh (long story)

21 Aug 1868

M: in New Lisbon at Cowan House 9th inst by REV JONES, JAMES DEEVERS & SALLIE CROXALL both of East Liverpool.

M: 3d inst by HENRY C ROBINS JP, G.W.WIREBAUGH & DELILAH TOLSON both of co.

M: 9th isnt by THOS C ALLEN ESQ, PETER BARE & SARAH C. WORMLEY of Mahoning Co.

D: 1st inst in Salem MISS SOUDERS ae abt 16y.

D: 3d inst near Salem infant child of JOSEPH LANNIE.

D: 9th inst in Salem, JAMES BOONE infant son of MRS.JAMES BOONE.

D: 11th inst at Infirmary, MAHALA REEDER ae 78y.

Death of HENRY TRITT at Alliance; died last Sat from chewing something other than gensing root; buried in Minerva by Odd Fellows

MRS. ABBY KELLEY FOSTER of Worcester had an ovariotomy on 30th ult (Worcester Spy)

NAPOLEAN YOUNG accomplished walking 100 miles in a little over 22 hours. He is a yankee by birth, being born in Providence, RI; is aged about 35y; lives in Elkrun Tp.

13

Terrible accident: last Tues eve horses on Wellsville hack ran away with load of passengers: MR.DAILY, the driver; passengers, JAMES BURBECK, JUDGE S.S.CLARK of this place, his son WILLIAM CLARK of Steubenville & GEORGE MILLER also of New Lisbon. The first 3 escaped while the latter was so seriously injured that he died Wed. They ran into the buggy in front of them with JAMES SEATON & JESSE HARRIS both of Salem. MR. MILLER was an old & respected citizen. Family has sympathy.

28 Aug 1868

M: 13th inst at res of bride's father in Washingtonville by REV J J JACKSON, J.J.BUSHONG of Salem & MOLLIE E.WOODS.

M: 20th inst at Cowan House by MAYOR FROST, CHARLES SWANK & SUSAN TAYLOR of Salem.

M: 19th inst in Salem at res of MARY WEBB by DR. I.N. BAIRD, HARRY HAINES of Canton & KATE BILGER of Salem.

M: 19th in Salem by REV A B MAXWELL, ELI STRATTON of Atwater & MARY A. HILLIARD of Green Tp., Mahoning Co.

D: of cholera infantum Aug 15 at house of JAMES DAVIS of Salem, JAMES D. BUCK s/o JOHN F. & ADALINE of Franklin Co MO. ae 10m 4d.

Failure of a strike: 1500 miners of the Mahoning Valley Ohio had been on strike nearly 4 months & will resume work. A failure, as they didn't receive the additional .20 per ton.

Suicide: 17th inst the wife of ED.WELCH of Franklin Tp committed suicide by cutting her throat from ear to ear. She was laboring under a fit of temporary insanity at the time of the rash act.

The Hon. JUDGE G.W. BELDEN of Canton died 15th inst, funeral by Masons.

Obit: GEORGE MILLER ESQ. died at res in New Lisbon Aug 12; was a native of CCO & 30y citizen of New Lisbon. His business kept him away from home a lot. He was injured in hack accident.
(see Aug 21)

4 Sept 1868

D: 28th ult in Cleveland, MISS SOPHRONIA POTTER in 37th yr of typhoid fever.

M: in Salt Lake City on 16th ult in the presence of the Saints, BRIGHAM YOUNG to MRS. J.R.MARTIN, MISS EMILY P. MARTIN, MISS L.M.PENDERGRAST, MRS. R.M.JENICKSON, MISS SUSIE P. CLEVELAND, all of the county of Berks, England. No cards.

D: at res in New Lisbon 25 Aug, BENJAMIN PRITCHARD in 74th yr; over 50 yrs a resident.

D: 14th ult near Kansas City MO, ADA HUDSON d/o MAJOR J.K. & MARY W., ae 2y 2m.

4 Sept 1868

D: 24th ult at his res in Franklin Tp, ANDREW YOUNG, a soldier of 1812, in his 86th yr.

D: 27th ult at res of mother in Salem, EMMA FLORENCE RUKENBROD in 23d yr

D: 16th ult in Wellsville, MRS. ELIZA HOUSE, consort of JOHN in 57th yr.

D: 16th ult in New Lisbon, J.N.MORRISON, infant son of FREEMAN & MARY.

D: 17th ult at Salem, MARIA PRISBY (colored) ae 51y.

D: 23d ult in Salem, BYRON S. ESTILL infant s/o JAMES & ETTIE.

D: 24th ult in Salem, infant child of H.PRINCE, ae 9m.

M: 20th ult at the parsonage near Enon Valley PA by REV JOHN B MILLER, HARRISON OWENS of East Palestine & LYDIA M. BOURNAM, Elkton.

M: 25th ult at res of ERASTUS EELLS in New Lisbon by JOHN McVICKER, Esq., WILLIAM SILVER & MRS. SUSAN H. KEESEY, both of Salem.

M: 13th ult by REV J F JONES, JOHN L. WILCOXEN of Carroll Co & ALETHA B. SWEARINGEN of co.

M: 29th ult at res of JOHN DEEMER in Col'ana by THOS.C. ALLEN Esq., LEWIS J. DEEMER & CAROLINE SCHILLING.

M: 18th ult at res of CHARLES DONELLY ESQ., by Rev D V HYDE, WILLIAM MENTZER & ANNA STACKHOUSE both of Salem.

M: 13th ult at Youngstown by REV J S LYTLE, I.N.BEESON of Salem & MARY KEPLINGER of Alliance.

M: 27th ult by ELD WM. BAXTER, EDWARD P. BARNETT & MARTHA M. ROOK, both of Salem.

11 Sep 1868

M: 19th ult at New Castle PA by REV DICKEY, DAVID SHAFFER of New Castle & EMMA HOLLOWAY of New Lisbon.

M: 24th ult at res of bride's parents by REV N H WEAVER, J.H.STAMP of Mt.Union Oh & MATTIE A. BOSSERT of Washingtonville.

M: 25th ult at the Cowan House, New Lisbon, by REV ROBT DICKSON, GEORGE A. VOGLESONG & ANNA E. METZGAR both of Col'ana.

D: 21st ult near Fontnelle, Nebraska, MARY L. HISCOX d/o JAMES & ELIZABETH, formerly of this place.

D: 2nd inst at res of mother near New Lisbon, JAMES H. WILSON, late publisher of the BUCKEYE STATE, in 26th yr.

D: 4th inst EDITH ELMIRA McLAIN d/o LEONARD & HANNAH of Franklin Tp ae 2y 6m 14d.

D: 30th ult JOHN DOYLE of Franklin Tp ae 58y.

KILLED BY THE INDIANS: we regret to announce the death of ISAAC BURBECK, formerly of New Lisbon, who was killed by the Indians in Kansas a few weeks since. The following particulars we learn from a private letter received by WILLIAM STARR of this place. He left Junction City, KS on 25 July with an ox train bound for Fort Wallace for the purpose of chopping cord wood, & on 19 Aug, he, with 2 other men belonging to the same train, was killed by the Indians. He was temporarily buried where he was killed, but was subsequently removed to the cemetery at Fort Wallace.

18 Sep 1868

M: 27th ult by WM. FULTS ESQ, FRANCIS M. GRAFF & PHEBE GORE, all of co.

D: 7th inst HOMER STEWART s/o JOSIAH & SARAH of Salem Tp ae 4y 10m 9d.

D: 6th inst infant child of GEORGE & ELIZABETH DICKSON of New Lisbon.

D: 9th inst in Salem MARTHA TALCOTT ae 32y.

D: at his res in E.Liverpool on 7th inst AARON BRAWDY in 74th yr.

ROMANCE OF A YOUNG MAN: a former citizen of Columbiana, probably well known to many of our readers, is a romantic cuss. About 5 yrs ago was the proprietor of a daguerrian wagon visiting many places in Green Co PA; he after had a hotel in Ludwig, where his first wife died. He sold out & left that co. He was married to his 2nd wife in Jan. 1865. They resided about 2y in Pa, then removed to Columbiana Co. where they resided til his 2nd wife's death, which occurred 5 July 1868. His name is DANIEL R. SHUTT. Shortly after his 2nd wife's death, his mother-in-law, MRS. M. STEPHENSON, made an information against him, alleging that he had poisoned his wife to draw the money on her life insurance. Our readers will remember his arrest last July in Allegheny City PA on a requisition from Justice MILLS. He was brought here for a hearing on July 25 & put in jail; on July 30 he came before the Probate Judge, they discharged him. About a week or 10 days previous to his arrest, an ad appeared in the Pittsburgh Commercial, wanting lady correspondents, worth from one to three thousand dollars, signed, "A.B., Allegheny City, Pa." A young man of Poland, seeing the ad, thought he saw a chance for fun & answered it, stating that he was a lawyer's only daughter & the father was worth 25 to 30 thousand dollars & signed it "LULA H. MOORE." The bait took & he received his reply, saying he is 25 yrs old, of respectable parents. That his father & mother both lived north of Greensburgh & farmed for 30 yrs; his father died about 3y ago, he had 3 brothers & 4 sisters "I am the lone one..." He made an appearance in Poland, looking for "Miss MOORE." [complete letters are given] Later, DANIEL SHUTT appeared before the Mayor & made information charging his mother in law MRS. MARY STEVENSON with assault & battery. After the death of SHUTTS' wife, his children were taken charge of by Mrs. S. He visited her house when a difficulty arose regarding the little ones; she ordered him out of the house; she shied a stool at his head. Case was dismissed. We await to hear of more letters.

ELIGIBLE BACHELORS

NEW LISBON BACHELORS: The following list of celibates has been handed us for publication by a happy young Benedict of our village, who is alive to the importance of showing up our friends of the bachelor persuasion, with a view of leading them to follow his own happy example. In the record will be found the names of several of the noble youth of our village, which are now, for the first time, presented to the public gaze. (18 Sep 1868) BACHELORS OF NEW LISBON: Below will be found the continuation of an article published a few weeks ago, under the above title. We are preparing a list of the marriageable ladies of New Lisbon, and as soon as we can ascertain their ages, shall take pleasure in placing it before our readers.(16 Oct 1868)

[Ed.note: these two lists have been combined & placed in alphabetical order. The date of issue follows the item]

ADAM, FRED : A good looking bach of 31, familiarly known as the Village Blacksmith; a great favorite with the ladies; drives a good team; takes his oysters stewed; habits good; would make a good husband, but too hard to suit. (16 Oct)

ADAM, GEORGE M. : A bachelor of 28; wagon-maker by trade; was a Lieutenant in the late war; good looking & is rather fond of his pipe; sports a heavy moustache & goatee, & would marry if some young lady would propose; income moderate. (18 Sep)

ADAMS, M.W. : Another bashful bachelor; carpenter by trade; lives in the suburbs & comes to town semi-annually; was a good soldier in the late war; admires a lady on Market street; would marry if somebody would take advantage of 1868; habits good; would never be out late at night; a good catch. (16 Oct)

ATEN, LOUIS : Better known as "Bus"; a noble youth of 21; gentleman about town, takes his bitters straight & is very fond of his pipe; has an eye for a neat foot & a pretty ankle; drives his own team & pays considerable attention to the ladies; would like to marry; expectations good.(18 Sep)

CAMPBELL, JOHN : A bach of 20; swings more style than any man in town; clerk in the dry goods store of BOWER & ASHFORD; a great ladies man; likes to imagine the dear creatures can't live without him; wears good clothes & is fond of his pipe; would be inclined to marry any respectable female possessing a quantity of stamps; income unknown.(18 Sep)

HARBAUGH, DAN : a quiet old bachelor; rather above medium size; good looking; well off in this world's goods; spends his evenings on Chestnut street; good habits. If he don't soon marry, will be placed on the "retired list". (16 Oct)

HARBAUGH, DENNIS : A fine old bachelor; good looking, jovial, fond of fun; liked by everybody; a successful farmer, don't play billiards nor believe in planchette; keeps good hours & don't want to marry. (16 Oct)

HESSIN, JOE : a noble youth of 21 winters; five feet nine inches high & weighs 200 pounds avoirdupois; resides with his parents; an admirer of Blackstone & intends studying the law. Has a find figure & a large head, greatly resembling Daniel Webster's. In no hurry to marry, but would take some fair creature with plenty of ready money.

HOSTETTER, DAVY : lives on Market Street; engaged in grocery business; several summers have passed over his head; in days gone by was fond of the ladies; is the earliest riser in town; perfectly happy and don't want to marry. (16 Oct)

JOHNSON, ED. A young bachelor of 23 summers; junior partner of the firm of MILLER & JOHNSON, dealers in Hats & Caps; good looking, wears good clothes & is considerable of a sport; belongs to the Olympic Base Ball Club & is fond of his cigar; good moral character & would make a capital husband.(18 Sep)

McLEAN, DAVID B. : Dentist; a noble looking youth of 24; six feet high, straight as an arrow, curling auburn locks & beautiful Burnside whiskers; is considerable of a musician, & very fond of the society of the ladies. Good moral character & a splendid catch. Income good.(18 Sep)

McVICKERS, JOHN : A bach of uncertain age, a limb of the law, who now holds the office of Justice of the Peace; would be quite a favorite with the ladies, if he would venture more into their society; wants to marry & is only waiting for some fair creature to propose; would make a splendid husband; stamps enough for two.(18 Sep)

MOORE, FRANK : A nice young man, aged 20; parts his hair in the middle & the ladies call him "a darling"; is good looking, has no bad habits, is learning to smoke & plays an excellent game of croquet; prospects good & would make an excellent husband.(18 Sep)

MORGAN, JOHN : A handsome bachelor of 23; proprietor of the "Hotel de-Morgan"' and High Sheriff of Columbiana County; a generous landlord; keeps his boarders free of charge; requires them to be in early at night; spends his spare moments on "Sheep Hill"; a jolly fellow & wants to marry.- (16 Oct)

MORRISON, JOHN W. : A handsome old bach of 43; a lawyer by profession; can't drink anything but Mishler's Herb Bitters, therefore never practiced much before a bar; wears a large vest; would make a good alderman; admired by all the ladies; his profession and checkers occupies all his time, & has no chance to get married; all O.K. financially; a good catch.- (16 Oct)

PRITCHARD, CYRUS B. : A model young man of 22; very fond of his cigar; clerk in the hardware store of R.B.PRITCHARD; good looking, drives his own team & spends most of his spare time at the residence of a young lady on Walnut street.- Prospects good.(18 Sep)

RANDOLPH, KERSEY : A prepossessing bach, over whose head has passed several summers; late county auditor; good looking & has no bad habits; would marry if some young lady would take advantage of leap year & pop the question; income all right; no lack of seven-thirties.(18 Sep)

ROBINSON, JOHN: A gay young bach of 25; one of the city "paps"; partner in the firm of J.OGDEN & CO., woolen goods manufacturers; a great favorite with the ladies, but shows no disposition to settle down; income good.(18 Sep)

SHULTZ, LYMAN H. : A promising youth of 19; clerk in the dry goods establishment of SHULTZ & BRO.; fond of lager beer, good looking & has a splendid prospect, financially; a good catch; would make an affectionate husband.(18 Sep)

SMALL, FRANK : A youth of 24; clerk in the dry goods establishment of SMALL & SONS; rather fond of attending base ball matches; good moral habits; not over fond of the ladies, but does not let them pass unnoticed; prospects good.(18 Sep)

SMALL, PHIL. : A prepossessing youth of 21; partner in the firm of SMALL & SONS, dry goods; slings on considerable style, & is quite a favorite with the ladies; goes East pretty often but is a young man of good moral habits. Prospects good.(18 Sep)

SMITH, BILLY : A jolly little miller, small in stature, but good looking; a fine musician, sings Tenor; fond of his cigars & plays billiards; would like to marry some nice young lady with funds, so he would never be caught in the "shorts" when old age comes creeping on. (16 Oct)

SPRINGER, M.O. : Is what is termed a fast young man; a strong temperance advocate; takes his "tea" straight; puts on considerable style; has charge of the N.L.R.R., owns a book store, sports a heavy mustache, & is mortgaged to a young lady on Washington street.(18 Sep)

STARR, JAMES : A bashful bachelor of 30; rather good looking, dresses with great care; a good mechanic; a great admirer of the fair sex, but never loved; very reticent; can't be caught napping; good moral character & habits good. (16 Oct)

STARR, JOHN : A noble looking bach of about 35; proprietor of a butter-store; ought to have been caught long ago; would marry if he found the right lady; has enough stamps for two. (18 Sep)

STEEN, D.G. : Rather spare looking bachelor; a printer by trade & sticks type on the "Buckeye"; quiet, witty & "I don't care to take a weak solution;" fond of music but can't sing; takes the world easy & is in no hurry to marry. (16 Oct)

THOMPSON, SAMMY : A merry old bachelor, with frank open countenance; a great flatterer; admires the ladies all; anxious to marry; known as the good samaritan; good hanits; sings well; nimble as a cricket & whistles like a mocking bird; prospects good. (16 Oct)

THOMPSON, TOMMY : The gayest "boy" in town, aged 27; confidential clerk in the banking house of THOS. McCOY; considerable of a musician, in the vocal line; has a smile for everyone & is quite a favorite with the ladies; generally spends his evenings on Walnut street; is ready for a proposal.(18 Sep)

WHITE, THOMAS H. : One of the pioneers of the village; the fear of the draft never disturbed his tranquil mind; engaged in butter business; never traveled very much; is passionately fond of ladies society; would make a good husband & an affectionate father; Captain of the Eagle; a great temperance advocate; dame rumor says he is to be married during the holidays. (16 Oct)

WOODS, T.S. : A fine looking personage; owns "Ohio Patriot"; a lawyer, can make a good speech; commanding figure, dignified bearing; plenty of bonds; has traveled; knows a thing or tow; would make a good husband; hard to catch & will die game. (16 Oct)

25 Sep 1868

A MRS. SMITH, residing of a farm of WILLIAM HILL, some 2 1/2 miles from East Liverpool, on the Calcutta Rd., who was so severely burned last fall by the explosion of a lamp, died last Thurs eve from the effects of her injureis. Leaves husband & a large family of children.

Liverpool RECORD says that last Mon, JAMES LARKINS, grandson of WILLIAM DEVERS, Esq., was thrown & injured while riding a horse.

M: 10th ult, RAGAN ROGERS & ABBIE MOORE, both of New Lisbon.

M: 9th inst at res of bride's father in Cumminsville, Hamilton Co Oh, Brevet Major General HENRY C. BANNING of Mt.Vernon, late Col of the 87th OVI, & JULIA KIRBY, youngest daughter of TIMOTHY KIRBY Esq & sister of MRS. DONN PIATT.

M: at Broadway Hotel in Salem on 17th ult by REV A B MAXWELL, ALSINUS SWANEY & ELIZABETH McQUILKIN of Millport.

M: 9th inst in Buffalo, Washington Co PA by REV J EAGLESON, ALBERT BONSALL of Salem & MARY E. ODENBAUGH of West Middleton, Wash.Co.Pa.

M: 26 July by REV W S KENDIG at his res in Georgetown PA, JAMES P. CONN & AMANDA M. RODGERS, of Wellsville.

M: at Weddell House, Cleveland on 10th inst by REV D C OSBORNE, A.B.WRIGHT & HETTY SHARPNACK, both of Salem.

M: in New Castle on 22nd ult by JAS. DICKSON ESQ., THOS.- COOPER & ALLA TRESCOTT both of Salem.

M: 25th ult by JOHN McVICKER at New Lisbon, WM. SILVER & MISS SUSAN W. KEESEY both of Salem. (see 4 Sept)

M: 10th inst by SAML HARDMAN ESQ., THOMAS BESLEY & ANNA E. BRIGHT, all of co.

M: 15th inst at house of bride's father in Col'ana by REV ROBT DICKSON of New Lisbon, WILLIAM HARRISON STEWART, M.D., & LAURA TRAINER both of Columbiana.

M: by same on 17th inst at Cowan House, New Lisbon, JOHN NORRIS & MARGARET J. DOBSON both of Salineville.

M: Sept 17 at res of bride's father in Salineville by REV JOHN HUSTON, JOSEPH KINNEY of Hancock Co WVA & ROSE McGLENEN.

D: MRS. SARAH VENABLE, widow of late GEORGE VENABLE in Goshen Mahoning Co on June 23d in 64th yr.

D: 28th ult, JOHN CROCKERTON, infant s/o ROBERT & BARSHE- BA, ae 1y 5d; also on 31st ult, ANNIE, d/o same, ae 4y 4d.

D: 15th inst, PETER O'DONNEL, JR., of Franklin Tp. ae 26y.

D: 18th inst, HARRY SHERMAN KEITH s/o ELI & MARY ae 5m 15d.

D: 9th inst JOHN McCASLIN of Carroll Co. ae 67y.

D: 16th inst of cholera infantum, CHARLES FRANK HASSIN, infant s/o JONATHAN & ELIZABETH of Madison Tp ae 16m 2d.

D: 10th inst at res in New Lisbon, MRS. CHRISTIANA NACE, consort of the late MATTHIAS NACE SR., ae 84y.

D: 20th inst at res of son in law DR. PATTERSON in Dungannon, WILLIAM GREEN SR., of Elkrun Tp., at an advanced age.

D: 3d inst in Salem, HANNAH V. McCLURG, infant d/o F & GA, ae 11m 3d.

D: 14th inst at res of REV.JOSEPH PAXON in Elkrun Tp., MARY CROW ae 51y.

D: 16th inst at mother's res in Salem of fever, WARREN SHEETS ae 17y.

D: 16th inst HUGH LYNN of Franklin Tp., ae 92y.

SUICIDE: HENRY RAMSEY of Damascus committed suicide Thurs. Sept 10 by cutting the artery on his left arm with a razor. The deceased was 50y old. The cause was poverty & affliction.
He was buried by the Township Trustees.

Salem was last week shocked by another double murder case. A young woman named MARTHA SOLCOTT died Wed. morning after 5 days of intense suffering at the res of CAPT. GIBBS where she resided 5 or 6 yrs. Oath taken on her dying bed, she came to her death from the effects of a violent criminal abortion, produced by some physicians in Cleveland or Canandaigua, NY, but refused to testify who the perpetrator was. But she further stated the father of her child was a married man with a very respectable family & a daughter grown up to womanhood.
These victims of unbridled lust should have the protection of law & the physician who would lend himself to such a murderous purpose ought to be sent to the Pentitentiary for life. Let there be a thorough ferreting out of the guilty parties (News)

2 Oct 1868

M: on 24th ult at the res of the officiating minister by REV A B MAXWELL, CHARLES H. WEEKS of Erie PA & MISS EMMA BOONE of Salem.

M: on 9th ult at St.Louis MO by REV J H BROOKS, JAS.A. HARRIS, of Salem & MISS MATTIE C. McDONALD of St.Louis.

M: on 17th ult in Beaver PA by REV JAMES HOLLINGSHEAD, RUEL WRIGHT of Salem & MISS SARAH DAVIDSON of Beaver Co PA.

M: at the American House in Salem on 22nd ult by REV A B MAXWELL, T.C.SIMPSON & MISS M.S.ROLLER both of Washingtonville.

M: 22nd ult at res of bride's parents by R H GARRIGUES ESQ, ADDISON CARR & MISS PHOEBE HARRIS both of Salem.

16

M: 22nd ult at Salem by SAMUEL HARDMAN ESQ. ZADOCK CALLAHAN of Canfield & MISS ANN A. GEORGE.

M: 22nd ult at house of bride's mother by REV DICKSON, A.W.LEWIS & MISS MARY J. SHEARS both of Leetonia, CCO.

M: at the same place & evening by the same, E.O.WARNER of Unionville, Lake Co., & MRS. M.B.SHEARS, of Leetonia.

D: 22nd ult GRACE CLARK, infant d/o WILLIAM & ELIZA of Hanover Tp ae 19d.

D: 15th ult MRS. ALMIRA H. EATON w/o SAMUEL ae 32y 3m 9d.

D: 23d ult ANNA DAVIS of Salem Tp ae 35y.

D: 13th inst at her late res in Cleveland Oh, MRS. HATTIE A. CLARK w/o J.LYTTLETON CLARK in 27th yr.

D: 22nd ult EMMA CORA BURSON d/o GEORGE & REBECCA of Hanover Tp ae 6y 14d.

D: 22nd ult of typhoid fever ANNA CATHARINE RAY d/o HENRY W. & MARY T. of Carroll Co ae 21y.

D: 21st ult of cholera infantum, ANNA HOSTETTER d/o JAMES S. & LYDNIA A. of Hanover Tp ae 3m 5d.

D: 26th ult SARAH STEWART w/o JOSIAH of Salem Tp ae 39y 10m 24d.

FATAL ACCIDENT: As LEVI MILLER was going from town last Sat., his horses scared at the cars near the New Garden crossing & threw him out of the wagon. He fell on his head, rupturing a blood vessel in his brain, from the effects of which he died the next morning. MR. MILLER resided at centre of Butler, was a carriage maker & aged about 60y. (Salem Journal)

JOHN DALGLEISH, a traveling agent for a tobacco house in Pittsburgh, committed suicide at Alliance, Sabbath night, 20th ult. He retired to his room at the hotel some time during the previous day. When the clerk went to call him the following morning the door was found locked. On breaking it in, he was found dead, shot through the heart, a revolver lying by his side. No one knows when he did it, or the cause.

BACHELORS OF POLAND

A gentleman who resides in Poland has furnished us the following descriptive list of the bachelors of that beautiful city. It will no doubt prove interesting to quite a number of our readers, who are acquainted with many of the gentlemen whose names appear below:

BLACKMAN, IVAN : This bach is something similar to the above named gentleman (H.S.Duncan); is quite a vocalist & cana render Irish melodies in fine style; cultivates carefully a moustache & has met with good success. He is the idol of the "Ku Klux"; not easy taken in by muslin or calicos on Brady's patent tilters. He plays the Bazoo on the "KKK" orchestra.

BROWNLEE, WM. R. : A young man of good appearance & is engaged in the study of law. Pecuniary prospects good. No use in the girls winking at him, for he is tied & fastened & bound in the net of love's perplexities already.

CALHOUN, W.J. : Another young bach, a fine looking, smart & gentlemanly young fellow. He is said to be devoted to base ball, especially that part where a person lays under a tree & watches an interesting game; his morals are very good; he is employed in the secret service of the government; he will make a splendid catch for some young lady worth about $50,000; he is a lady's man & a faithful worshipper at the shrine of beauty, although he is called fickle & a a "flirt;" he is "Grand Scribe and Chief of the Grand Council of Ten" in the "Conjuncti Fratri."

CASE, CHAS. CARROL : A handsome young fellow; is confidential clerk in J.G.LESLIES dry goods store; plays base ball & belongs to the "Ku Klux" & is "Senior Warden" in the "Conjuncti Fratri"; he likes all the girls & they all like him; is a great whistler; he can shut up a mocking bird & make a canary hang its head; good steady habits & good morals.

CASE, WM. R. : A handsome young fellow, of gentlemanly address; splendid intellectual talents & oritorical powers; is a great "base ballist," and takes "flys" remarkably well; is of a social disposition & will some day be an ornament to the domestic circle, of which he will be the head. He is a great favorite with the ladies; belongs to the "Ku Kuz Klan" and "Conjuncti Fratri" and the "Resolute B.B.C.; likes New Lisbon for some mysterious reason.

DUFF, JOHN : A young student of medicine; he drives a span & rides in a handsome carriage; is very anxious to marry & will make a quiet & obedient husband. Come, ladies, one & all.

DUNCAN, EV. : A young bachelor merchant of Poland; stands high in society; possesses social & genial talents; he worships at the shrine of only one divinity in town; will make a good husband.

DUNCAN, HENRY S. : This young gentleman is mostly in Pittsburgh, but Poland claims him as one of her loved sons; he is of a theatrical turn of mind & is a very good performer; the "Ku Kluxs" presented him with a tin medal for his singing & break downs; he is heavy on "Beautiful B-I-L-E on my Knee," "Beet Be by Boon-light" & is some persimmons on several other beautiful songs; is the center of attraction at all parties on account of his comic proclivities; we guess he is not engaged. Strictly temperate & good morals.

HINE, CECIL D. : Another handsome young bach; he possesses fine scholarly attainments & has entered the Sophomore class in the Western Reserve University, Hudson, O.; he will likely make as good a "score" in college as he does in base ball, at which he is a complete success. He don't believe in scattering his affections promiscuously, but concentrates them on one object of divinity. Is "Noble Grand" of the "Conjuncti Fratri."

HUBBARD, HENRY JR. : A young gentleman of good prospects, being a junior partner in the firm of HUBBARD, BURKE & CO., manufacturers of tin war etc. No 705 Main Street. Henry is of a fast disposition & quite a sporting character; attends all base ball matches & bets heavily on the "Resolutes;" is a great admirer of the fair sex & would not hesitate to leave the state of single blessedness for one of double blessedness.

KIRTLAND, ALFRED POTTER : A young bach of about 22; is at present a student in the Civil Engineer Institute, Troy, NY; he is President of his class in college & has won some distinction in drawing & surveying; plays base ball & gallants the girls around very often; of a good disposition & steady habits. We don't hesitate to recommend him to the attention of the young ladies.

LEE, ANDREW : A bachelor of about 26 yrs of age; sole proprietor of a wagon shop & something of a gardener & horticulturist; has a high appreciation of the gentle sex.

McKINLEY, ABNER O. : Comes under the same class of fine scholarly young bachelors; don't think he is in love & his heart is open to sealed proposals from young ladies; will make a good husband for some specimen of perfection; don't drink or swear, but smokes like fury; is "Junior Warden" of the "Conjuncti Fratri."

MANSFIELD, FRANK : Bachelor of good standing; makes money in running a coal bank; he was a captain in the late war; he don't appear to be very susceptible to any tender emotions in regard to the other sex; plays base ball, but is very quiet & don't say much; will make a good protector for some gentle, confiding creature.

MATHEWS, JOHN " A handsome bachelor, a very desirable catch in the eyes of many maneuvering mamas, but as yet, John has proved himself to be not susceptible to the tender endearments of the aspiring dear creatures.

MORSE, HENRY G. : A young fellow who is the chum of the above named gentleman (Kirtland) in college in Troy; exceedingly sweet on the young ladies; takes moonlight rambles frequently & is often found going home at late hours. Good habits & morals.

POWERS, JAMES H., M.D. : A late graduate of Cleveland Medical College & not long since a partner in a drug store; he has a splendid form & wears good fitting clothes, which set it off to an advantage; moustache & Burnsides; a dark poetical eye, sparkling with love & admiration for beauty everywhere; something of a musician & plays on the violin & piano; sings basso profundo very well & is a ladies' man; belongs to the "Conjuncti" and "Ku Klux."

REYNOLDS, JAMES : A young bach of about 24; good looking & of steady habits; don't drink but smokes; has lately fell heir to an estate in Mississippi; would make a steady husband.

SCANNEL, ROBERT O. : A bachelor of uncertain age, but still young & handsome; he is a manufacturer of boots & shoes; income very good; he is noted for the invariable neatness of his attire. Did you ever see Robert without good clothes?- Did you ever see him dress unfashionably? Did you ever see him with his boots not blacked? Did you ever see him with his silk hat not brushed? Did you ever see him look anything but a gentleman (which he is) ? Did you--did you--did you--did you ever--did you--did you?

SLAVEN, ANDREW : A bachelor of about 30 summers; is a great politician & is the principal leader of the SEYMOUR & BLAIR faction in this city; he distinguished himself in the late war, especially at Carnifax Ferry, West Va; he possesses fine conversational powers & is of prepossessing manners; enquire for or address him at the "Bridge Hotel" room 20, lower floor.

STODDARD, HENRY : A fast young man with plenty of money; he is proprietor of "Stoddard's Museum," now traveling in the west; supposed to have a notion of marrying sometime.

STOUGH, CLARK : He would make a fine subject for a hero of a novel; of a noble & commanding form, an intellectual bearing, a raven moustache, a dark sparkling eye, beaming with intelligence; and a voice soft & gentle as a cooing dove; he has a high appreciation of the beautiful, consequently is a great admirer of the fair sex; he has great fascinating powers & when he exercises them among the gentle ones, they always yield--they wilt. He presides over a fashionable dry goods emporium & "goes East" very often to replenish his stock & to enjoy the "sea breezes of the Delaware." Ladies, throw out your hooks!

STOUGH, SAMUEL : A very young bach, brother to the beautiful Clark, & associated with him in the store; of sociable & gentlemanly manners; he is sweet on the fair sex & may be seen buzzing (or bussing) around them like a honey bee around a bung-hole of a molasses barrel. "Samuel, beware of widders!"

9 Oct 1868

JENNINGS ESTATE: SIMEON JENNINGS, the famous land speculator, for a time lived separate from his wife & gave deeds for land sold without her signature & release of dower.- Since his death the widow is prosecuting the holders of these lands, lying in Ottawa, Lucas, Williams, Fulton & perhaps other counties in northwestern Ohio. The JENNINGS estate was reckoned a million, & the widow, apart from personality, was assigned 5,000 acres in her right for her dower interest in the remainder.

M: 29th ult in Allegheny City PA by REV DR W.D. HOWARD, GEORGE E. BURNS & LIZZIE J. KING, both of New Lisbon.

M: 24th ult by REV ROBT DICKSON at Presbyterian Manse, New Lisbon, JOHN M. DAVIS & MARTHA A. CONKLE, both of Clarkson.

M: 10th ult by REV D W COLLINS, T.G.ARTER,M.D., of Chicago Ill., & MATTIE McCUNE d/o SAMUEL ESQ., of Blairsville.

M: 12th ult by REV A E WARD at the Parsonage in Hanover, PATRICK McCORMICK & AGNES FALOON, both of Hanover.

M: 27th ult by same at bride's res, JAMES WILSON of Hammondsville OH & MARY A. WILLIAMS of Gilford, CCO.

M: 24th ult by I S McKOWN, WM.P.BURSON & MRS. RUTH B. JAMES, all of Hanover.

M: 24th ult by REV J J ESTILL at res of JAMES COVERT in Franklin Square, SAMUEL DUNNAM & LEVARRA COVERT all of Lawrence Co PA.

M: 20th ult at res of DR. GARRETSON, in accordance with the order of the Society of Friends, HARDING BAILEY of Mahoning Co & LUCRETIA M. GARRETSON of Salem.

M: 24th ult at res of bride's father by REV E B CAKE, JAMES P. BREIGHTON of Newark, OH & CARRIE ELDRIDGE of Salem.

M: in Salem 24th ult by SAMUEL HARDMAN ESQ, PHILIP L. SMYERS & CLARA M. MULLEN.

M: 1st inst by REV A B MAXWELL at res of bride's mother, W.H.McCLOSKEY of Forrest & ANNA TRAVIS of Salem.

M: 24th ult by REV T P CHILDS at res of bride's mother, WM. MILLER of Alliance & SARAH ROYER of Salem.

M: 28th ult by DR.THOS WICKES, JAMES WILSON of East Liverpool & ABBIE F. EDGERTON of Marietta.

16 Oct 1868

M: 7th inst by REV A B MAXWELL at house of ELI FAWCETT, ALBERT B. TEST of Butler Tp & LYDIA A. FAWCETT of Perry.

M: 3d inst at Cowan House by REV ROBT DICKSON, JOHN H. MARCH & SADIE ADAMS both of co.

M: 23d ult by REV J S GIBSON, DAVID L. RUBLE of Winona & MISS FRANK M. HARTSOCK of Millsboro, Pa.

M: 1st inst by REV J J ESTILL, JOSEPH CHAIN & JENNIE GROVE all of co.

M: 8th July by REV ROBT HAYS, WILLIAM RHODES & ANNA SHARP both of Salineville.

M: 1st inst by THOS.C.ALLEN ESQ., JAMES B. BOSTON & NANCY J. BLAKE, all of co.

D: 3d inst BENJAMIN STANLEY of Damascus, ae 78y.

D: at her res in Salem, MRS. MAHALA BRADY in 71st yr.

Fri Oct 23, 1868 (Vol 2 no 28) WRHS MICROFILM

M: on 13th inst by Rev I N WHITE, ROBERT S. CROSS & MISS MARY J. GRIER

M: on 8th inst by Elder DJ WHITE, SAMUEL FARMER of Martinsville & Miss MARY A. VANFOSSAN of Madison

M: on 18th inst by JB MILLS, ESQ., at the res of the bride's father, MARTIN FINERAN of Leetonia & Miss REBECCA CLUNK of New Lisbon

M: on 13th inst at house of bride's father by Rev AB MAXWELL, A.H.HARRIS & MISS M.L. CHESSMAN all of Salem

D: on 2nd inst at the res of his son at Milltown, Crawford Co IND, JACOB HOSTETTER, ESQ., of Paris Twp.. Stark Co Oh, aged 83y; the subject moved from Hanover York Co Pa in spring of 1820 to New Lisbon & kept the hotel in that place known now as the Union House. In 1824 he moved to Stark Co in vicinity of Canton where he served as a Judge of CP Ct for sec'l years; was rep. one term in state senate after which he removed to his farm near Minerva where he resided til a few weeks prior to his death, when he accompanied his son to Milltown; but a few days after arriving there he was attacked by disease which soon resulted in death. He was known as man of strict integrity; by his death his family are deprived of an aged father whose loss they deeply feel.

D: on 11th inst at the res of her husband in Wellsville, MRS. MARY YEALY aged 25y 6m 6d

D: on 11th inst at Achor, CCO MRS. MARY M. BROWN widow of the late WILLIAM BROWN

D: on 16th inst VIRGINIA BELL McLAIN, d/o LEONARD & HANNAH McLAIN of Elkrun Tp aged 8y 3m

D: on 5th inst in Goshen Tp, SAMUEL JOLLEY aged 40y

D: on 9th inst in Salem Tp, THOMAS McCAN, aged 77y 6m

Fri Oct 30, 1868 (Vol 2 no 29) WRHS MICROFILM

M: on 1st inst at the res of Jonas HAKE in Salem Tp, by Rev A B KIRTLAND, ISAAC HALVERSTADT & MISS MINERVA SHELLENB- ARGER all of co

M: on 6th inst in Iowa city by Hon JUDGE CAVANAH at the res of Mrs. L B Harris, ALEX. R. FULLER ESQ., of Clayton Co Iowa & Miss TINE SHARPNACK, formerly of Salem OH

D: on 7th inst CATHARINE ELIZABETH STEWART, D/O JOSEPH & MARTHA E. STEWART aged 18y 3m 27d

D: on 22nd ult JAMES PHILLIPS S;O WM. & FRANCIS PHILLIPS of Franklin Tp aged 37y 4m 3d

D: on 20th inst AARON CHAMBERLIN of Elkrun Tp aged 43y

D: on 23d inst at Washingtonville, MRS. CATHARINE KINDIG dau of MRS. MARY HELMAN of New Lisbon O

D: on 23d inst at the res of his parents in NEw Lisbon, DANIEL T. McKEE in 22nd yr of his age

D: on 14th inst, DR. JAMES ROBERTSON of Hanover in the 68th yr of his age

Fri Nov 6, 1868 (Vol 2 no 30) WRHS MICROFILM

M: on 21st ult by the REV P J McGUIRE at St.John's Church, Summitville, JOHN E. McKENNA & MISS MARY J. CAVENAUGH all of Franklin Tp

M on 27th ult at the Union Hotel New Lisbon by JOHN McVIC- KER, JOHN BROWN ESQ. & MISS MARGARET YATES all of Saline- ville Oh

M on 22nd ult by Rev Robert Hayes, HON. S.C.KERR, Repre of Jeff Co, & Miss MARY CLARK, dau of STEPHEN CLARK of COL CO

M: on 24th ult at his res at East Rochester by Joseph Coulson Esq., B.T.COUSOR & MISS M. HEITSMAN all of West Tp CCO

D: at wellsville on Sat 17th ult CORA MAUD STEVENS infant dau of JOHN W. & MAGGIE STEVENS, aged 1y 7m

D: on Sun eve 25th ult in Salem Tp MRS MARY HEATON in 86th yr of her age

D: at the Infirmary 21st ult, ANDREW RISH in 66th yr

Fri Nov 13, 1868 (Vol 2 no 31) WRHS MICROFILM

A man named FRANK AMOS of Carroll Co committed suicide on 21st ult by cutting his throat; cause not known

M: on 29th ult by Rev ROBT HAYES, JOHN A. McCORMICK of Madison Tp & miss SARAH McCORD, dau of THOMAS McCORD of Wayne Tp

M: on same day by same MINUS A. WILLIAMS & MISS SARAH J. CUNAN dau of MICHAEL CUNAN dec'd both of Wayne Tp

M: on 26th ult at the ME Church in Hanover by Rev A.E.WARD, WM.S.MOFFETT & MISS SARAH T. HAMILTON all of Hanover

D: on 4th inst SUSAN BURCAW, W;O GEORGE BURXAW of Elkrun Tp aged 32y

D: on 5th inst HUGH MORROW JR. of Center Tp aged 30y

D: on 30th ult in Salem, ROBERT TAYLOR aged 29y

D: on 1st inst in Salem RACHEL MALONY, w/o JAMES MALONY AGED 65y

D: on 28th ult in Butler Tp MILLSTANT HARRIS d/o ROBT HARRIS

Fri Nov 20, 1868 (Vol 2 no 32) WRHS MICROFILM

M: on Wed 11th inst at res of bride's father by Rev R.DICK- SON, GEORGE KINNEY of Albion Mich & Miss MARY LOUNSBERY of New Lisbon

M: on 12th inst at the res of CHARLES RICHARDS near Alliance by Rev WK BROWN, EDGAR TRUNIC & MISS KATE STEMLEY both of Col Co

M: on 10th inst by the REV D A RANDALL at his res in Columbus OH, JOHN P. MORGAN, Sheriff of Col.Co. & Miss FLORENCE M. PITCAIRN both of New Lisbon OH

M: on 4th inst by J.MILLS, ESQ., JOHN W. HUM & MISS JOSEP- HINE SNYDER all of New Lisbon

M: on 15th inst by EDWARD PETTIT, J.P., JOHN KEMBLE & MISS SUSANNA STAPLETON all of co

D: on 15th inst at the Infirmary, GEORGE HOWE aged 89y

Fri Nov 27, 1868 (Vol 2 no 33) WRHS MICROFILM

M: on 12th inst by Rev I N BAIRD, JOSEPH H. GARTSIDE of Pittsburgh & Miss CATHARINE J. COLFLESH of CCO

M: on 27th ult by RH Garrigues,JP at the house of SAMUEL HARDMAN ESQ., MR. A.J.DICK & MISS E.J. MARSHALL all of Salem

M: on 12th inst BY W.FULTZ ESQ., LEMUEL T. LAMBORN & MISS NANCY CREW all of this co

M: at Salineville on 28th ult by REV JOHN HUSTON, ALBERT MONTGOMERY & MISS HENRIETTA LACOCK

M: on 12th inst by Rev GW RIGGLE, RICHARDSON FISHER & MISS ELLEN THOMPSON all of this co

M: on 5th inst by EP VANSYOC, ESQ., JESSE CREW OF IOW & MISS REBECCA WHINERY of this co

M: on 5th inst by REV GW RIGGLE, JOHN HAMBELL & MISS MATILDA SMITH, both of E.Liv O

D: on 11th inst in Salem, MRS. MARY ANN PICKETT age 78y

D: on 18th inst JESSIE ANDERSON NICHOLS dau of WM.A. & HARRIET NICHOLS, aged 10m 15d

D: ON 19TH inst DAVID WARD of Elkrun Tp aged 59y

D: on 19th inst IVANNA REEDER, dau of LYDIA REEDER of Carroll Co in 30th yr

D: on 19th inst in New Lisbon, DANIEL HARBAUGH aged 87y

DEATH OF HON. DANIEL HARBAUGH: We have today to announce the death of this old & esteemed citizen whichoccurred on the 19th inst at his res in this place. Mr. Harbaugh has been in feeble health & almost helpless for the last 5y. He was born in Uniontown PA on 21 June 1781 and at the time of his death was 87 yr of age. The judge was one of the earliest pioneers of Eastern Ohio having settled in New Lisbon in 1803. For several years he held the office of Co Commissioner, was a captain of .cavalry in the war of 1812, represented his district in both branches of the state legislature 7 for several years filled the position of one of the assoc.- judges of court of com pl in this co. His funeral on Sabbath last was largely attended.

COURT: ALFRED H. GEISSE vs REBECCA GEISSE: DIVORCE GRANTED WM.GREEN vs ELIZABETH GREEN: DIVORCE GRANTED

Fri Dec 4, 1868 (Vol 2 no 34) WRHS MICROFILM

M: on 21st ult by REV J L VALLANDIGHAM, IRVING S. VALL- ANDIGHAM, M.D., of St.George Delaware & miss KATE WHITELY, dau of ALEXANDER LOWBER MD, of Newark Delaware

M: on 3d ult by Rev ROBT HAYS, JOSEPH FALOON of Frank.Tp & Miss MAGGIE QUAIL of Salineville

M: on 22nd ult by WM.JOHNSON, JP, ISAAC DAVIS & MISS SUSANNA MORRISON both of CCO

M: on 22nd ult by Rev J J MOFFIT, WM.A.KELLEY of Iowa & Miss SARAH POST of Salem O

D: at the residence of his son in law near New Garden, WEST NEGUS aged 80(?) y (maybe 83 or 89)

D: on 25th ult SARAH FARMER w/o HENRY W. FARMER of Salem Tp aged 40y

D: on 26th ult at the res of ALBERT CHANDLER of Centre Tp, NATHAN HENDRICKS aged 80y

D: on 23d ult in Salem GEO.REED, aged 63y

D: on 23d ult in Salem URIAH BUEL aged 53y

Fri 11 Dec 1868 (Vol 2 no 35) (from WRHS microfilm)

M: on 26th ult by REV ROBT DICKSON, THOS.F.McKARNS of Franklin Tp & miss MARTHA J. MARCH of Madison Tp CCO

M on 3d inst by Elder WM.BAXTER, JAMES H. GREEN & MISS MARY E. BARCUS both of Salineville

M: on 27th ult at Oak Grove by REV DV HYDE, WM.C.HAINES & MISS ELIZABETH A. ENTRIKEN both of CCO

D: on 28th ult JOHN SHERMAN MORGAN, son of JASON & CATHARINE MORGAN of Wayne Tp age 4y

D: on Fri 4th inst at the res of ANDREW ROACH in New Lisbon, MRS ELIZABETH CONNEL aged 86y

D: on Sat 5th inst MRS POLLY WILES of this place aged 75y

D: on 6th inst at the res of his mother, HARRY W. MILLER aged 13y. The funeral of Harry W. Miller, dec'd, will take place at 2 o'clock PM Tues the 8th inst from the res of his mother

Supplement, Fri 11 Dec 1868

Fri 18 Dec 1868 (Vol 2 no 36) (from WRHS microfilm)

M: on 25th ult by Rev WHITE, ROBERT TURNER of Alliance & miss MARY J. BREENE of Summitville

M: on 9th inst by Rev JH LEIPER at the res of the bride's mother in East Liverpool, ROBERT STERLING & MISS MARIA AZDELL all of Col Co

D: on 1st inst WILLIE ROLLER, infant son of JOSHUA & LYDIA ROLLER, aged 2m 1 week 5d

D: on Nov 27 CHARLES MATHEWS of Salem aged ---years

D: on 9th inst ANNIE ARMBRUST wife of ADAM ARMBRUST of Fairfield Twp aged 60-8-6

D: on 13th inst WILLIAM MORGAN of Wayne Tp aged 74y

Fri 25 Dec 1868 (Vol 2 no 37) (from WRHS microfilm)

D: on 12th inst in Wellsville, MARY ALLISON W/O JOHN ALLISON aged about 75y

LEGAL: JACOB GOCHENAUR, of Goodhue Co Minn; SUSAN SHAWBER & PHILIP her husband, ELIZABETH GOCHENAUR, relict of ELCANY GOCHENAUR DEC'D, MARY J. KRIDLER & GEORGE her husband, ADAM ARMBRUST, relict of ANNA ARMBRUST dec'd OF COL CO OH; LYDIA A. SCHOOLY & WILLIAM her husband OF WARREN CO IOWA, & THE UNKNOWN HEIRS, IF ANY, OF DELILAH NORRIS, DEC'D FORMER WIFE OF JAMES NORRIS, WHO WERE RES OF HENRY CO IND WHEN LAST HEARD FROM...take notice that petition was filed on 16 dec 1868 in Col Co by DAVID GOCHENAUR is now pending; pet sets forth that DELILAH NORRIS died without leaving any legal reps., & that the share of said DELILAH should be divided among the other heirs at law of DAVID GOCHENAUR SR. DEC'D & for parti-tion of: NW 1/4 sec 30 twp 12 range 2, of 20 acres.... excepting out of the above 1/8 of an acre in SW corner of premises, USED AS A FAMILY BURYING GROUND.... full descrip-ion: beginning at the sw corner of 1/4 sec, thence along the south boundary of said 1/4 sec 60 perches to a post, thence north 41 degrees east, 52 3/10 perches to a post on the road leading from New Lisbon to Columbiana; thence west 95 perches to a post, thence south 41 2/10 perches to place of beginning.

20

1869

Fri 1 Jan 1869

D: 10th ult at the Infirmary, MINERVA YATES ae 54y.

D: 21st ult SUSANNA SHOEMAKER w/o JOSEPH SHOEMAKER of Centre Tp ae 57y.

D: 25th ult WILLIE CHAMBERLIN s/o AARON & CATHARINE CHAMBER-LIN of Elkrun Tp ae 7m.

D: 25th ult at the Infirmary, ANGELINE WOLF in 38th yr.

A number of colored citizens of Salem have organized a Cornet Band in that place & been presented with a fine set of silver instruments by the ORMES BROTHERS, of Island Run notoriety.

REV.A.O.PATTERSON, D.D., for many years pastor of the Presbyterian Church of this place, died at Oxford, Butler Co Ohio on Monday last week.

Patents: THOMAS STARR of Lisbon, patent for "animal power", a labor saving machine; also, THOMAS LODGE, a patent for a shifting buggy top.

Fri 8 Jan 1869 (Vol 2 no 39) (from WRHS microfilm)

M: on 22nd ult at the res of the bride's father, by Rev J.N.SWAN, EVAN McINTOSH & MISS TENIE McDONALD all of co

D: on 21st ult Mrs. LYDIA R. MYERS, wife of P.F.GEISSE of Wellsville in 51st yr of age

D: on 2nd inst, JOHNIE REDDICK, infant son of 15 months of CUMMONS C. & SARAH E. REDDICK who lived near this place & have one child remaining, a boy of 3 summers

Fri 15 Jan 1869 (Vol 2 no 40) (from WRHS microfilm)

M: on 25th ult in Nashville Tenn by Dr. JOHN GAILY, CHAS. R. ELLIOTT of Wellsville OH & Miss MAGGIE RITCHIE of Weyauwega Wisc.

M: on 26th ult at St.Alloysius' Church by Father McGUIRE, PETER AINSLEY & MISS MAY GRAFTON both of E.Liv

M: by same at same place on 29th ult, JOHN GRAFTON & MISS MAGGIE McNICHOL, BOTH OF E.Liv

M: on 24th ult at res of COL.J.A.DANKS, in Aetna, Allegh Co Pa by Rev WESLEY SMITH, WM.H.COCHRAN & MISS HATTIE HULME both of E.Liv

M: on 12th ult by J.LINDERSMITH ESQ., at Norristown, Carroll Co Oh, THOMAS CARTER Of Salineville & Miss SARAH E. WARE of Norristown

D: on 23d ult, ELIZABETH SMITH, W/O JACOB SMITH of Hanover Tp age 65y 6m

D: on 2nd inst MARY ANN WISMAN D/O LEVI & MARTHA WISMAN of Franklin Tp ae 24y

Fri 22 Jan 1869 (Vol 2 no 41) (from WRHS microfilm)

M: at the res of bride's parents in Butler Tp on 31st ult by WM.FULTS, ESQ., JOHN H. FURGERSON of Pittsburgh PA & Miss SARAH GARDENER of CCO

M: on 5th inst at the Methodist church, Sloan's Station by Rev W G BURNS, REV. SAMUEL WORCHESTER of E.Liv & MRS CHAR-LOTTE B. ROBINSON of East Corinth Maine

M: on 31st ult by REV J J MOFFIT, JAS.H.BARD & MISS AMY THOMSON all of Salem

M: on New Year's night at the residence of A.C.BLIZZARDS, BY REV B.R.MATHERS, NEWTON AYRES of Cedar Co Iowa & Miss LUCRETIA Z. COLE of New Lisbon

D: on 11th inst ELIZA A. w/o ADMIRAM HOLDERMAN of Hanover ae 44y

D on 12th inst Mrs MARY LOGAN at the residence of her son PATRICK LOGAN of Summitville Franklin Tp aged 67y

D: in Salem Tp on 7th Jan, MRS. MALL aged 85y

DIED on 16th inst SARAH W. GALBREATH W/O DAVID GALBREATH of Fair TP aged 67y 7m 19d

Fri 29 Jan 1869 (Vol 2 no 42)

MARRIED on 14th inst by Rev Wm Baxter, GEO.W.McCAN & MISS AGNES M. HILL all of this co

M: on 14th inst at Rochester PA by REV L PAINE, STEPHEN MULROY & MISS MARGARET McKEE both of Hammondsville OH

M: in Cleveland on 4th inst at the res of J.G.HUSSEY by REV DR W H GOODRICH, WILLIAM B. PETTIT & MISS KATE E. POTTER, all of Cleveland

M: on 9th inst at res of bride's father in West Tp by JOS COULSON ESQ., CHARLES C. CONNER & MISS CELESTIA F. DAVIS all of co

M: on 14th inst at res of bride's mother near Bolivar Tusc Co Oh by Rev A R Smith, DR. S.F.BOYCE formerly of Wellsville & Miss LUCINDA KAINE of Bolivar

M: on 17th inst at res of bride by Rev G.W.Riggle, WM.H.AUGH-INBAUGH of Wellsville & Mrs ELLEN DAWSON of E.Liv

M: on 12th inst at Smiths Ferry PA by Rev DAWSON, ALBERT SHENKLE & MISS SUSAN SPIRES of E.Liv

M: on 14th inst at Smithers Ferry PA by Squire McKEAG, B.F.WILSON of Phila.Pa & miss ISADORE MINER of Wellsville

M: on 19th inst at res of bride by Rev J J MOFFIT, ALEXANDER McCLEARY of Cambridge OH & Miss FANNIE M. TOLERTON of Salem

D: on 12th inst at this res in E.Liv., ISAAC FOUTS aged about 34y

D: on 17th inst LEATHY SWITZER at the res of her son in law JOSEPH WORMAN of Salem Tp aged 80y

D: in No Georgetown MRS. MAGDALINE GURMANS aged 80y

D: on 14th inst in Goshen Tp, ROBERT MARLOW aged 56y

D: on 19th inst in Butler Tp, ELIZABETH W/O ALBERT BECK

Fri 5 Feb 1869 (Vol 2 No 43)

M: on 28th ult by Rev WM.BAXTER, PETER DAVIS & MISS REBECCA J. HICKMAN both of co

M: on 14th ult at res of bride's father by Rev CHARLES BAHRENS, J.H.FIFE & MISS ELIZABETH A. WEBER, all of Jackson Co Oh

M: on 14th ult at parsonage near Enon Valley PA by REV JOHN B MILLER, FERDINAND HEACOCK of Salem & Miss MIDE FERRALL of East Fairfield, Col Co

M: on 24th ult at the Baptist parsonage by REV TP CHILDS, WM.H.UMSTEAD & MISS SAMANTHA STRAWN all of Salem

M: on 16th ult by SAMUEL HARDMAN ESQ., LEVI HOGE & MISS MARGARET INGLEDUE all of co

M: on 23th ult by SAMUEL HARDMAN ESQ., W.A.TULLIS & MISS HANNAH REED all of co

D: on 21st ult in Salem, ANNA LEORA KEEN D/O T.J.KEEN ae 6y

D: on 22nd ult in Franklin Square, THOMAS McELWEE aged 22y

Fri Feb 12, 1869 (Vol 2 no 44)

D: on 27th ult near Georgetown, DAVID ALLEN aged years & 6 mo (no years are given)

D: on 15th ult KATE BURT, D/O DAVID & ELIZABETH BURT of Hanover Tp aged 27y

D: 22nd ult CHARLES PACKSTON of Hano Tp aged 52y

D: on 22nd ult ALEXANDER KING of Hano Tp age 40y

D: 29th ult RICHARD O'HERIN of Franklin Tp age 23y

D: at infirmary Jan 28, ANNA HAGUE in her 79th yr

Mr ISAAC WEBB, an old & respected citizen of Salem was brought before the Probate Court last week on complaint of JACOB AMBLER. He is laboring under some mental derangement or delusion & we are informed will be taken to Newburgh

Fri Feb 19, 1869 (Vol 2 no 45)

Married on 9th inst by H McCORD ESQ., EDWARD THOMAS of Winchester & miss LOUISA McMULLEN of Summitville CCO

M: in Mansfield on 10th inst by ..., REV FRANK RICHARDS of Chicago & Miss CAL SUPER of Mansfield

DED on 29th ult in Wayne Co Iowa of consumption ELIZABETH R. EWING W/O JOHN D. EWING, formerly of Winchester CCO

D: on 1st inst DAVID MONCRIEF, of Carroll Co aged 67y

D: on 9th inst MARY STERLING W/O JAS of Centre Tp aged 69y

DANIEL HALLEN, residing near North Georgetown ruptured a blood vessel of his lungs while coughing which resulted in his death in a short time

COURT: J.E.BRADFIELD vs MARY BRADFIELD, DIVORCE GRANTED

Fri 5 Mar 1869 (Vol 2 no 47)

M: on 16th ult by REV W B HIGBY, CHARLES E. BOSTWICK & MISS MARY PERDUE all of Minerva OH

M: on 11th ult by Rev O N HARTZHORN, WM.W.GILTON of Winchester OH & Miss MARY McLEARN of Mt.Union

M: on 25th ult by REV IN WHITE, WM.G.FROST & MISS E.A.MC-INTIRE

D: on 31 jan MARY C. CRAIG, W/O ROBERT E.

D: on 21st ult near New Lisbon with dropsy of the heart, MRS. SUSAN W. WILSON W/O JESSE WILSON JR., aged 20y

D: on 20th ult near Col'ana GEORGE MILLER aged 87y

D: on 21st ult in Col'a, MRS HATTIE DETWILER aged 24y

D: on 22nd ult MARGARETANN H. SHOEMAKER W/O WILLIAM of Wash Tp aged 44y

D: on 19th ult CATHARINE STEWART of Salem Tp aged 63y

Fri 12 Mar 1869 (Vol 2 no 48)

M: on 27th ult by RH GARRIGUES JP, JAMES HUDSON & MISS ELIZA MADSON both of Salem

D: on 28th ult near Winchester, JOHN HUSTON formerly of New Lisbon in 63rd year

Fri 19 Mar 1869 (Vol 2 no 49)

M: on 10th inst at house of bride by Rev ROBT DICKSON, T.S.WOODS, ESQ. & MRS K.G.POTTER both of New Lisbon; will tour to eastern cities

M: on 25th ult at house of JOHN CLAPSADDLE of Franklin Square by S.BOTTLEFIELD TEEGARDEN, ELMER TAYLOR & MISS ELIZABETH CLAPSADDLE all of Alliance OH

D: on 6th inst MARY HAZEN in Salem aged 12y

D: on 8th inst of anemia, SARAH WALLACE W/O WILLIAM of Elkrun Tp age 60y 5m 11d

D: on 10th inst at res in Green Tp, Mah Co, ISAAC BONSALL in 61st yr

D: 12th inst BENNY LODGE S/O ABNER & ESTHER of Salem Tp aged 7y

D: 7th inst in Salem, infant child of E & E LUPTON

D: on 6th inst in Salem, LAURA KEEN D/O T.J.KEEN ae about 6y

D: on 1st inst at Infirmary GEORGE FOSTER in 25th yr

Fri 26 Mar 1869 (Vol 2 no 50)

M: at the res of Levi Gardner in Hanover Tp by Wm Fultz Esq., EDWIN GARSIDE & MISS SUSANNA C. GARDNER all of CCO.— "Another old bachelor friend made happy...has taken unto himself another & we trust a better half. In this case, however, our friend was not a bad speciamn of the Genus Homo, if we may judge from the trick her served us. May the happy couple enjoy a long & prosperous journey through life."

M: on 7th inst by JOSEPH COULSON, ESQ., at his residence in East Rochester, CHARLES TAYLOR & MISS LAURA MILLER, all of West Tp CCO

M: 11th inst by Rev J.ARTHUR, MATTHEW LOVE of Saline twp, Jeff Co to MISS MAGGIE SMITH of Yellow Creek Tp, CCO

M: 1st inst by JOHN ROBINSON ESQ., WM.S.VAUGHN & MISS LYDIA A. WILLIAMS, both of Wayne Tp

M: 13th inst at New Lisbon O by REV JONES, JOSEPH E. TORRENCE & MISS LYDIA A. MYERS both of Wellsville

M: on same at New Lisbon by same, WM.G.URIE & MISS ISABELLA F. MARSHALL both of Wellsville

M: 6th inst in Salem by Elder E.B.CAKE, E. WOODWORTH & MISS ANNA MONTGOMERY.

D: on 18th inst at the residence of her son in law in New Lisbon, MRS. ELIZABETH FOX, aged 66y

D: in Alliance on 21st ult of songestion of the heart, MARY A. JONES consort of CATLET JONES formerly of this county

D: on 17th inst in Salem JOSHUA REVES aged about 63y

D: 18th inst SARAH ANN LOVE W/O WM. of Leetonia formerly of Salem, aged 33y

D: 11th inst in Salem, WARREN H. WILKENS, S/O JOSEPH aged 7y 7d

D: 12th inst in Washingtonville, ANNA MARIA BERTOLETT w/o DR.BERTOLETT, aged 62y 6m

D: 11th inst MARIA LAUGHLIN W/O ROBERT of Franklin Tp ae 74y

D: 19th inst infant child of ROB'T PILLMAN of Hanoverton

D: 17th inst FANNIE GILMAN D/O C.H. & REBECCA aged 9m

D: 14th inst infant child of MR. MYERS of Dungannon

D: 14th inst CHARLES WILLINGTON S/O JASON of Dungannon ae 1y

MRS SUSAN MOORE of Wellsville was badly burned on Wed from her clothes accidentally taking fire. She is not expected to recover

Fri 2 Apr 1869 (Vol 2 no 51)

D: on 4th inst at residence of his son in law BERT ROBERTSON in Belleville, Ill of typhoid puenmonia, GEORGE WEST formerly of this county, aged 57y 19d

D: 7th ult near State Centre Iowa of lung fever, infant daughter of LEWIS & ELIZA ANN HAMBLETON

D: 19th ult infant child of ROBERT PILLMAN of Hanoverton

D: 2nd ult in Port Washington, ANNA FRANK PORTER, D/O FRANCES E. & HENRY H. PORTER aged 8m 14d

D: 21st ult near Elkton, ELIZABETH ALBRIGHT w/o DANIEL G. ALBRIGHT & D/O the late JOHN SHEETS of Salem in 50th yr

D: 21st ult in Salem MISS LYDIA HUDSON aged 29y

D: 7th ult MAUD LUPTON, & on the 22nd ult, MARY LUPTON, twin children of DANIEL & EMILY J. LUPTON, of Salem, aged near 7 mo

D: 22nd ult EDWARD JONES S/O DAVID & MARY ANN of Centre Tp aged 6 mo

D: 24th ult A.J.BLOCKSOM of this place aged 34y
(obit) The funeral of AJ BLOCKSOM took place on last Sabbath & was largely attended. The services were conducted by REV DICKSON in the Presbyterian church, after which the body was conveyed to the burying ground where services were conducted by the Masons, he being a member. MR BLOCKSON was a native of this place, much respected, leaves relatives & friends.

D: 26th ult T.S.WOODS ESQ., of this place aged 41y
(obit) Death of T.S.WOODS. The dec'd was a prominent member of the New Lisbon Bar & editor of the Ohio Patriot. He died suddenly at his residence in New Lisbon last Fri eve of apoplexy. He had but lately returned from his wedding tour & enjoyed good health & was in the best of spirits up to the time of his death. His funeral will take place at Salem, tomorrow, the 30th inst.

The first child born in the White Pine silver district, son of CURRY & SUSAN FERGUSON, has been presented with several thousand dollars in silver bars & bricks by the miners.— MRS. FERGUSON is the eldest daughter of JUDGE S.S.CLARK of New Lisbon.

Fri 9 Apr 1869 (Vol 2 no 52)

M: on 25th ult by REV J B DUNDAS, J.C.CHAIN & MISS SARAH CURREN all of Franklin Tp CCO

M: 25th ult by REV.VOGLESONG, WM.GREEN & MISS ELIZABETH McGARVEY all of this county

M: 25th ult at the residence of the bride's father in Berlin Centre by REV.CALEB BROWN, JAMES W. DERR & MISS HARRIET E. KING

M: 24th ult by SAMUEL HARDMAN, JP, JOHN BARCUS & MRS MARY ANN SIPLE both of Salem

D: at his residence in Salem on 30th ult of consumption, HENRY J. STAUFFER aged 41y

D: 31st ult LIZZIE CRAWFORD, D/O JAMES & MAGARY of Hanover aged 15y

D: 31st ult SAMUEL C. MERCER S/O DANIEL & LIZA ANN of Butler Tp aged 18y

D: 1st inst infant child of ELIZABETH RASH of Hanover Tp aged 6mo

D: 3d inst MRS MARIAH BROWN of Hanover Tp aged 72y

D: 3d inst H.W.DONALDSON of Wayne Tp aged 63y

D: 3d inst PETER McKENNA of Wayne Tp aged 22y

D: 30th ult MARGARET CROOK W/O SAMUEL of Fairfield Tp ae 71y

12 Apr 1869

M: 1st inst at res of JAMES DOBSON, Mahoning Co, by REV.W.J.SHARPE, W.J.ADAMS of New Lisbon & JENNIE E. DOBSON of Mah Co.

Also, at same time & place, JAMES K. DOBSON & MISS M.A.OYSTER; also, by the same, AMOS OYSTER & ANNIE M. DOBSON.

D: 6th inst ABIE A. RODGERS w/o Z.R.RODGERS of New Lisbon ae 28y.

D: 9th inst in New Lisbon of paralysis, MRS. MARGARET A. GLOSS formerly of Poland, Mah.Co., ae 75y.

D: 6th inst RACHEL ANN TAYLOR w/o PLUMER TAYLOR of Hanover Tp, ae 38y. (see also 26 Apr)

D: 7th inst MARY PHILIPS of Carroll Co ae 79y.

D: 8th inst JOSHUA WELDMAN of Hanover Tp ae 68y.

Wooden wedding: Tues Apr 7th was the 5th anniversary of REV. JONES, Pastor of the ME Church in this place, & his wife; party held.

ISAAC SIDWELL, formerly of the firm of STOWELL & WHITNEY of New Lisbon, died at Sharon, Mass, Mon. last week.

19 Apr 1869

M: at res of A.BALL, Salem, on 13th inst, JOSEPH WEBB & KATE BALL by Elder E.B.CAKE.

M: 16th inst by J.B.MILLS, ESQ, at res of bride's father near New Lisbon, MOSES S. WHITE of Canton & KATIE HELT.

M: 15th inst by REV.I.BAIRD, JOSHUA G. WOOD & ALICE A. BAIRD, all of Salem.

D: 6th inst at the Infirmary, JOHN CRATON, ae 59y.

D: 13th inst SAMUEL CHILEY of Wayne Tp, ae 90y.

D: 12th inst near New Garden, MARY ANN CARTNEY, ae 72y.

D: 13th inst at res of THOMAS KEEN, SARAH WEBSTER ae 70y.

D: 14th inst in Salem, ELI HAINS in 89th yr.

D: 14th inst in Salem, infant child of MR.HAZLET ae 1y.

D: at his res near Damascus of apoplexy on 14th inst, JAMES NAYLOR JR., ae about 25y.

D: 10th inst in Butler Tp, PHOEBE BROOMLEY ae 72y.

26 Apr 1869

M: 21st ult by REV.WM.DALZELL, JAMES K. GREEN & LAVINA E. WOOLAM all of West Point.

M: 14th inst at Merchant's Hotel, Pittsburgh PA by REV.M.B.-SLOAN, JAMES B. RONEY & REBECCA KENNAMAN, both of Salem.

M: 22nd inst by REV.R.DICKSON at the Union House, FREDERICK BLANCHARD & ANNIE ALBERT, all of New Lisbon.

M: 8th inst by REV.RIGGLE, THOMAS G. EDGE & ELANOR L. DOVER, all of East Liverpool.

D: of consumption at her res near Green Hill, CCO, RACHEL ANN TAYLOR, w/o PLUMMER E. TAYLOR, ae 38y 8m (see 12 Apr)

D: 18th inst MRS. ISABEL SHAW w/o JOHN SHAW of Centre Tp, ae 89y (see 3 May)

D: 21st inst WASHINGTON LOUDON of Wayne Tp ae 28y.

D: 22nd inst at res of JOSEPH HAMILTON of Elkrun Tp, REBECCA LAIRD, ae 49y.

D: 17th inst at res of her mother in Hanover Tp, MISS LUCRETIA IRA, ae 22y.

3 May 1869

M; 18th ult by REV.N.H.WEAVER, MILTON CARNS & ANNA BILGER, both of co.

D: 22nd ult at the Infirmary, MARY JANE MOFFIT, ae 30y.

D: 18th ult, MRS. ISABEL SHAW w/o JOHN SHAW of Centre Tp, ae 81y (see 26 Apr)

D: 23d ult JAMES HARRY SHAW s/o JAMES & CATHARINE ANN SHAW of Carroll Co, ae 1y 6m.

D: 25th ult ELLA J. STRATTON d/o SIMON & DELINA F. STRATTON, of Salem Tp, ae 1y.

D: 27th ult ELIZABETH WILLIARD w/o JOHN WILLIARD of Franklin Tp, ae 64y. The wife of JOHN WILLIARD of Franklin Tp died suddenly last Mon night; she had been suffering with some disease supposed to be neuralgia or rheumatism. Heart disease thought to have caused death.

10 May 1869

MOORE photographic gallery in New Lisbon (ad)

D.C.DELANO, Photograph rooms, New Lisbon; taken over the rooms from Messrs. LANPHEAR. (ad)

HOMICIDE: Steubenville has another murder: JOHN McCAFFREY was stabbed last Sat night by JAMES COULSON & died the next day, Sunday.

FATAL ACCIDENT: Last Fri afternoon, JACOB WARNER of this place, had both of his legs crushed by the passing of 5 freight cars over them; he had been drinking for a day or two, was walking down the Cleveland & Pittsburgh RR tracks towards his home in the north part of town when struck. Was taken home in a wagon where he died in about 1 1/2 hours from the accident. —Alliance Democrat.

Marriages & Divorces in Ohio: the year ending Jan. 1869, there were 28,221 marriages, about 1000 less than last year; the divorces number 847, a decrease of 128 from the previous year.

17 May 1869

M: 12th inst at res of bride's mother by REV.ROBT. DICKSON, M.O.SPRINGER & MATTIE P. SNODGRASS, all of New Lisbon.

M: 20th ult by REV.ROBT. HAYS, H. FALOON of Hanover Tp & LIZZIE CUPPOLD, youngest daughter of SAMUEL of Centre Tp

M: 3d inst at the parsonage near Enon Valley PA by REV.JOHN M. MILLER, JOHN W. HOUTZ of Canfield & JENNIE LAUGHLIN of Salem, CCO.

M: 20th ult by WM.FULTZ ESQ, MARSHALL B. HOOPES & ANNA BARBER, all of Columbiana.

D: 5th inst ABRAM BRANDY of Hanover Tp, ae 40y.

D: 13th inst MARY NEWHOUSE w/o THOMAS of Elkrun Tp ae 20y

D: —th inst ELLEN McGARY w/o JOHN of Winchester, Hanover Tp, ae 33y.

D: 1st inst at res in East Liverpool, E.T.NEVILL ae 49y.

D: in Georgetown on 3d inst, JOHN H. SHIVELY ae 23y.

D: 4th ult L.E.ELLSWORTH KALE, son of ISAAC & MARY ANN LOW of East Fairfield, ae 1y 6m 27d. [KALE or LOW??]

DR. JOHN S. ROBERTSON has located at Germantown, Montgomery Co Ohio, for the purpose of practicing his profession.

24 May 1869

M: at Oak Grove on 13th inst by REV.D.V.HYDE, LOUIS TELLIS & LYDIA ENGLES, both of co.

M: 4th inst in Centre Square PA by REV.CHAS.FISHER, W.J. DE-WILTER [DETWILER ?] of Washingtonville, OH & SOPHIA FRANTZ of Centre Square.

M: 18th ult in Salineville by H.C.ROBBINS, JP, JOHN CLECKNER & SARAH STEVENS both of New Lisbon.

D: in Pittsburgh PA on 12th inst, JOHN LANGSTAFF SR., formerly of Salem, in 68th yr.

D: 21st inst at Infirmary, ZELPHA BENNETT in 59th yr.

D: 13th inst FRANKIE HUMPHREY, s/o WILLIAM of Hanover Tp, ae 5y

D: 16th inst SUSAN REGAL of Patmos, Mahoning Co, ae 69y.

D: 17th inst, MARY ANN CALLAHAN, w/o THOMAS of Goshen Tp, Mahoning Co.

Body of unknown man found hanging in the barn on the PUMPHREY farm, 2 1/2 miles south of Salineville; taken to S'ville for inquest; seems to be a man from Steubenville, a blacksmith.

Convention of the soldiers of the War of 1812 to be held in New Philadelphia on June 20th.

31 May 1869

M: by REV.J.N.SWAN, at res of bride on 29th ult, GEORGE CAVIT of Indianola, Iowa & MAGGIE ROSS of Yellow Creek Tp CCO.

M: by same at parsonage of Yellow Creek Church May 11, JONATHAN WHITACRE & HANNAH RAMSEY, all of co.

M: 12th inst by REV.S.CROWTHER at res of bride's parents, WM.H.ELVERSON & CHARLOTTE HARKER, all of New Brighton PA.

M: 20th inst by REV.GEO.VOGLESONG at res of bride's mother, WM.A.DAVIS of Salem & SUSAN M. VOGLESONG of Hanover.

D: in Columbia, SC, on 25th inst, MISS AMY A. BOYCE d/o JOHN of Wellsville.

D: at her father's res in DeWitt, Carroll Co, Missouri, MARTHA JANE McCORMICK, w/o THOMAS, ae 36y.

D: at her res in Beaver Falls PA on 1st inst, MRS. MARY C. CILWORTH ae 39y. [corrected to MARY C. DILWORTH in issue of July 5th]

D: 23d inst NANCY ANN PAXON of Centre Tp ae 66y.

D: in Butler Tp 21st inst, RACHEL CHANDLER.

D: in Salem 22nd inst DELLA WILSON d/o M.A.WILSON ae 1y 6m

7 June 1869

M: 29th ult at res of bride's father by REV.A.B.KIRTLAND, D.W.HALVERSTADT of East Palestine & LOUISA LATTA of Unity Tp

M: 20th ult at res of bride's father by REV.J.J.JACKSON, DAVIS SHELTON & LIZZIE C. ALTERHOLT both of Salem Tp.

D: 25th ult near Salineville, HATTIE A. CARTER, w/o J.WILLIS CARTER & d/o JAMES & MARY C. CLARK, ae 19y 8m 3d.

D: 30th ult in Green Tp, Mahoning Co, infant child of MARK GODWARD, ae 5 weeks.

D: 1st inst near Salem, ELIZABETH KIRTLAND, w/o THOMAS ae 70y

D: 1st inst near New Garden, JAMES O. JOHNSON ae 24y.

D: 26th ult in Salem, S.K.LANPHEAR, ae 25y.

WILSON A. ROOSE, residing at 164 Garden St., Cleveland, left his home on Mon. May 24 about noon & was seen on Bank St. in the afternoon. Since that time, nothing has been known of his whereabouts. He is about 27y old, 6 feet high, dark hair, dark brown eyes, rather dark complexion & dark moustache. He was dressed in a black broadcloth coat, black pants, black velvet vest, high black hat & heavy new boots. Since his disappearance, it has been ascertained that he was financially embarassed. Any info regarding him or his whereabouts addressed to MRS. ELLA C. ROOSE, Wellsville, CCO, will be thankfully received. Other papers please copy. MRS. ELLA C. ROOSE, Cleveland, May 31, 1869.

REV.S.T.HERRON, lately of this place, has been assigned by the church as a missionary to Mt.Pleasant Iowa for the present year.

14 June 1869

M: 25th ult at the National Hotel, Beaver PA by REV.J.HOLLINGSHEAD, DANIEL PAULY & ZILLA A. BARNES, both of East Liverpool.

M: at res of bride's mother by Rev.KINGDON on 20th ult, J.B.FERRALL & MILLIE E. PROUTY, all of Oskaloosa, Iowa.

M: 5th inst in Salem by SAML HARDMAN ESQ, WILLIAM F. McKEE & JANE DOYLE, all of Salem.

M: 5th inst in Salem by REV.DR.COX, FRANKLIN LANDON & ISABEL BASTEL, both of Massillon.

D: 2nd inst, infant child of JAMES & MARY CROSSER of Elkton.

D: 22nd ult IDELIA WILSON d/o MRS. MARY ANN WILSON ae 1y 6m 14d.

D: 8th inst in Salem, PRESLEY ROBINSON (colored) ae about 65y

D: 6th inst MRS. MARY HUEY, w/o JOHN, late of Washington Tp, ae 79y.

FATAL ACCIDENT: last Sunday, a child of MR. & MRS. WHANG of North Georgetown, aged about 2y, while playing around the room, accidentally fell into a buckey of boiling water, scalding it so severely that it died in about 19 hours. —— Salem Journal.

The law concerning registration of births & deaths has been repealed. Instead of doctors, sextons, midwives & others making reports, it is now the duty of Ward & Township assessors to report in their districts, annually.

Petition to sell real estate: ERASTUR EELLS, admr of ALFRED PAXON, dec'd, notice to HARRIET AMELIA ENDLEY & DAVID her husband, of Kansas; ELIZABETH PAXON of Indiana & MARY ANN PAXON, residence unknown, heirs at law of ALFRED PAXON dec'd, to sell real estate in R3 T14 S18.

DR.H.C.McCOOK, of St.Louis, MO, is here visiting relatives & friends.

21 June 1869

REV.MR.ANDREWS, late pastor of Wellsville UP Church, died Wed last at his residence in Wellsville.

M: 6th inst by REV.J.REINHART at his res in Columbiana, WILLIAM H. DeRHODES & PHEBE R. BELL, both of Col'ana.

M: 10th inst at Presbyterian parsonage, New Lisbon, by REV.ROBT DICKSON, DAVID CRUBAUGH & ELIZABETH J. DOBSON, both of co.

M: 17th inst by THOS.C.ALLEN ESQ, at his res in Columbiana, AARON H. ENGLE & LORENA J. BAKER, both of co.

M: 17th inst by ELDER WM.BAXTER, RICHARD FARMER & SARAH RICE, both of co.

D: in Pittsburgh 29th ult of typhoid fever, MARTHA UMBSTAETTER McCOOK, d/o DR. GEORGE L. McCOOK ae 13y 1m 9d.

D: 13th inst of consumption, LOUISA STEWART d/o EDWARD & ROSENA, of Salem Tp, ae 28y.

D: 14th inst DANIEL THOMAN of East Lewistown, Maho.Co.

28 June 1869

M: at Cowan House, New Lisbon on 24th inst by REV.ROBT.DICKSON, FRANK P. FERRAND & LYDIA FERRALL, both of co.

M: 10th inst at res of URIAH WILSON by Rev.I.N.BAIRD, assisted by REV.WM.COX, D.D., WM.WEAVER HEATON of New York & SADIE A. WILSON of Salem.

M: at res of JACOB SANOR by REV.D.V.HYDE, LYMAN SOMERS & MARY ELLEN STURGEON both of co.

M: 16th inst by SAML POLLOCK ESQ, WILLIAM BELL of Huntersville OH & MELISSA E.M.WRIGHT, late of New Salisbury, OH

M: at Smiths Ferry PA on 2nd inst, JOHN MARTIN of Wellsville & MARY TAYLOR of Salineville.

M: 18th Mar by SAML POLLOCK, WILLIAM HUNTER of Wellsville & MARY BORING of Salineville.

M: 16th inst in Salem by SAML HARDMAN, JP, J.W.GREEN & CELESTIA RAY, both of co.

M: 16th inst in Salem by same, GEORGE RITCHLY & TILLIE HUDSON, of Salem.

D: 12th inst, JOHN B. WILSON of Elkrun Tp, in 66th yr.

D: 20th inst at res of her son JESSE FROST of Hanover Tp, MRS. MARY FROST ae 84y.

D: 21st ult LYDIA ROUDEBUSH d/o DR. BATTON of Hanover Tp, ae 24y.

D: —th inst, FRANK EMMIT WELCH s/o ROBERT & KATE of Hanover Tp, ae 18 mo.

D: 12th inst in Butler Tp, AMELIA WHITE w/o JOHN H. ae 24y

D: 26th inst CATHARINE JOHNSON w/o CHARLES of Centre Tp ae about 60y.

Little BILLY DEAN was taken before MAYOR CURRY of Salem a few weeks ago, for stealing $7 in money. He was sentenced to Reform School.

The remains of DR.HORACE POTTER & his 3 daughters, who were buried in the Presbyterian cemetery, were taken up last Wed & conveyed to Cleveland for re-interment in the family plot there.

A boy about 8 yrs old named THORNTON was drowned in the Ohio River opposite the RR shops, Wellsville, last Mon while swimming.

In a drunken spree at Youngstown on 18th inst, a Welshman named DAVID WILLIAMS was stabbed in the breast by his brother and died the next morning.

HENRY HEASLEY, residing near Poland, OH, died Tues morn last of heart disease. He had just left his residence to superintend some laborers, when death stopped him. He was a director of the First National Bank of Youngstown, aged about 65y.

5 July 1869

M: 21st ult at res of bride's parents by REV.DR.COX, A.J.-GRISILWOLD of Twinsburgh & MISS M.F.FARQUHAR of Salem.

M: 21st ult at res of bride's parents by REV.JOHN B.MILLER, HUGH KEELER of Goshen, Mah.Co. & ANNA BOIES of E.Palestine.

M: 14th ult by REV.J.HENDERSON, DANIEL W. GEISSINGER & ANNA M. HUNTER, both of Wellsville.

M: 24th ult by same, WM.H.HARDMAN & ANNA G. MILLIGAN, both of Wellsville.

D: in Beaver Falls PA on 1st ult of typhoid fever, MRS. MARY C. DILWORTH w/o S.C. in 36th yr. (see 31 May)

D: 30th ult LYCURGUS DAVIS s/o AMOS & JANE DAVIS of Wayne Tp, of billious remitting fever, in 16th yr.

D: 26th ult in Georgetown, ROSE A. WEAVER w/o JOHN ae about 70y

D: 29th ult JAENETTE KING D/O JEHU C. & HARRIET F. of Knox Tp, ae 6y.

D: 26th ult, MRS. MARY MUMFORD of Wellsville, from a cancer on the cheek.

D: 21st ult in East Liverpool, LOT G. ARMSTRONG s/o DANIEL & LEVINA ae 14y.

D: 25th ult HANNAH WHITE w/o ISAAC WHITE ae 65y.

D: 4th inst LOMEY KEYSER d/o JESSE & JULIA of Fairfield Tp, ae 3y 4m.

D: 3d inst infant child of CHARLES & LYDIA BECK of this place

MISS MARY ANN WILLETS, who a short time ago was taken to Newburgh [insane asylum], returned last week, not much improved in mind.

12 July 1869

M: 1st inst at the parsonage near Enon Valley PA, by REV.-JOHN B. MILLER, JOHN P. ALTAFFER of Alliance & ANNA SNIDER of Salem.

M: 6th inst at Cambridge, at res of bride's father by REV.BARON STOW, JOHN S. WHITACRE of New Lisbon & CELESTIA I. TRAIN, youngest dau of EDMUND TRAIN, ESQ. (long article about the wedding on page 2)

M: 8th inst by EDWARD PETTIT JP, MILES UNDERWOOD & REBECCA McLEAN all of co.

M: 1st inst by REV.ROBT HAYS, at res of bride's father, THOMAS EARL & MARY QUAIL both of Salineville

M: 26th ult by REV.N.H.WEAVER, assisted by REV.J.W.SLOAN, J.M.SITLER of Leetonia & ELLA WALTERS of Washingtonville.

M: at Dayton OH May 15th at First Baptist Church by REV.H.S.-COLBY, WEBSTER STREET of Salem & MAIMIE E. GILMORE, of Yellow Springs, OH

M: by REV J. HENDERSON July 1st, JOHN BROOKS & ELVINA DOUGLASS, both of Wellsville.

D: at res of her father in DeWitt, Carroll Co Missouri, MRS. MARTHA JANE McCORMICK, w/o THOMAS, ae 36y.

D: Sat 10th inst, ANNA WORMAN w/o JOSEPH of Salem Tp ae 61y 5m

D: 9th inst ISAAC SHAW of Hanoverton, ae 58y.

D: in Canfield on 4th inst MRS. SIMMONS SACKETT ae about 70y

D: 26th ult LAWRENCE LING of Hanoverton, ae 58y.

D: 2nd inst ZADOK DOWNER of Hammondsville, ae 60y.

Body of an unknown man found in Ohio River, about 30 yrs old, had been dead some time; buried at Spring Hill Cemetery.

19 July 1869

M: 13th inst by REV. WM.BAXTER, THOMAS C. CALDWELL & MRS. ELIZABETH HUSTON, both of co.

M: 15th inst at res of bride's father on High St by REV. WM. COX, ED.F.RUKENBROD & LIZZIE WILSON, all of Salem.

D: 13th inst in New Garden, ANN HESTON, ae 52y.

D: 12th inst at her res near Mt.Union, Maho.Co., after a brief illness, MARTHA HOILES w/o EMANUEL ae 19y 6m 9d.

D: in Salem on 13th inst CALLIE BAKER d/o THOMAS ae 20y.

D: 14th inst JAMES BALDWIN of Centre Tp ae 70y.

D: at res of her mother in Centre Tp on 14th inst, SOPHIA G. HILL w/o JACOB G. HILL, of Shelby OH.

Little EDDIE VERNER, aged about 9y, son of GIBSON VERNER, was drowned at East Liverpool last Sat. night; the body was just found by some boys who were bathing in the river, near Brooklyn opposite the mouth of Yellow Creek.

HELEN R. VANCE & ELLA POTTER, of this place, graduated at the 13th annual exam of the Music Vale Seminary, Conn.

Laying of cornerstone: The A.M.E.ZION CHURCH cornerstone will be laid by members of Boyd Lodge No.5 of colored Masons at Salem Wed. Aug 4th. A grand festival will be given by the ladies for the benefit of the church. In the evening there will be speaking by some of the best orators of the day:- FREDERICK DOUGLASS & J.W.LOGAN have been invited.

26 July 1869

D: 14th inst at res of her mother, MRS. SOPHIE C. HILL in 27th yr; leaves mother, sister, husband & brothers.

D: 20th inst at his res near North Benton of dropsy of the chest & consumption, BENJAMIN HAMILTON, ae 83y 8m.

D: 21st inst in Hanover Tp, ANN WILLIAMS ae 73y

D: 21st inst ELIMELECH SWEARENGER of Hanoverton ae 78y.

CAPT. FERDINAND BECK celebrated his 69th birthday on the 17th inst; he has been ringing the courthouse bell for 33 years.

AMOS SKEETER was instantly killed by a blow from an unknown man to whom he had presented his bill. SKEETER had been living in the suburbs of the borough for some time; he was of small stature & delicately formed, while his adversary was a man of great strength.

WILLIAM MONTGOMERY, aged about 65y, residing near Elkton, was seriously injured last Wed while leading a colt attached to a mowing machine.

2 Aug 1869

M: 29th ult at the Cowan House, New Lisbon, by JOHN McVICKER ESQ., GEO.W.HAWKINS & M.J.HINER all of co.

M: 23d ult by WM. FULTZ, ESQ., JACOB D. PETERSON & CAROLINA McGAFFICK, all of co.

M: 15th ult by WM.C.WILLIAMS ESQ, CHARLES BURLINGAME & ELIZABETH VANKIRK, both of co.

M: 17th ult by M.N.RUSSELL ESQ, JOHN WALLACE & MARGARET DEVORE, all of Jefferson Co Oh.

D: 24th ult in New Lisbon of lung fever, MARY E. DAILY, d/o THOMAS B. & MARTHA, ae 4y.

D: 20th ult in East Liverpool, WILLIE C. MURPHY, s/o J.F. & SALLIE E. ae 5m.

D: 20th inst at New Brighton PA, WILLIAM TODD, formerly of Hanoverton, ae 27y.

D: 27th ult WILLIAM CRUMLEY of Wayne Tp, ae 89y.

A mulatto boy recently stole $50 from his employer, a Mohawk Indian barber in Warren PA & ran off with a white girl, got married, & came to Youngstown, OH. The girl's father found them there & took his daughter home. The Indian also came & arranged with the husband to go back & work out the amount taken.

A Columbiana correspondent of the Salem Journal says a disgraceful affair has lately been revealed at that place.- A.A.BUSHONG, a "young man of spectacles", thinking money was not coming fast enough, thought to commit forgery to help him on in seeking worldly pleasures. He used his father's name in connection with that of DR.DEEMER, renewing the amount several times, and thereby extracting from the banking house of ZEPERNICK & LODGE, New Lisbon, over $980. His father, already too indulgent, has given security for the amount, which relieves him of a five year's penitentiary life, unless some kind friend of his will push the matter, whereby he may learn a trade which will relieve him of the necessity of committing forgery. [Ed.Note: A.A.BUSHONG is ALPHEUS A., the son of DAVID & BARBARA (STRICKLER) BUSHONG, all of whom are buried in Columbiana Cemetery. ALPHEUS served in the Civil War, and in one city directory, was listed as a Painter.- ALPHEUS' grandfather, ANDREW BUSHONG, was a brother of this compiler's ancestor, JACOB BUSHONG, 1754-1830.]

9 Aug 1869

M: 14th ult by SAML HARDMAN JP, AARON WILSON & EMMA G. WALKER, all of Salem.

D: 30th ult at res in Wellsville, DANIEL FRAZER in 48th yr

D: at res of DR.GEORGE McCOOK in Pittsburgh PA on 5th inst, of apoplexy, MISS POLLY McCOOK ae 70y; funeral in New Lisbon on Sat.

D: 9th inst in New Lisbon, JOHN V. VOGAN, ae 30y.

D: 24th ult at his res in Washingtonville, JAMES ROLLER in 66th yr.

FOUND DEAD: an old man named CASSEY was found dead in his house at New Alexandria, this co, on July 31. He lived entirely alone & was either very childish or deranged in mind & seemed to have no relatives to care for him. Mr C. had not been well for a week and the last seen of him was on Thurs.- It is supposed from appearance, he died that night. He bought his house to have a place to die.

WILLIAM LANTERMAN of Austintown, Mah.Co., committed suicide by cutting his throat a few days ago whilst sick & in bed. He was over 70 years of age.

On Sat last, while STEPHEN STONE, with his wife & child & a man named BURNS were passing up the River in a skiff, they attempted to pass around the bow of the steamer "Hunter", lying at Vanport, about 2 miles below Beaver, when the skiff was upset, precipitating the whole party into the River. MR. STONE & BURNS were rescued but the wife & child were drowned before help could reach them. —Wellsville Union.

16 Aug 1869

M: 8th inst at the Reformed parsonage by REV.G.M.ALBRIGHT, DAVID SHIVE & LUCINDA BRICKER all of co.

M: 5th inst in Salem by REV.DR.COX, DAVID B. REEDER of Hanover & ELLEN BOSWELL of New Brighton PA.

M: 27th ult by J.R.HAMILTON ESQ, JAMES M. BECK & CLARA V. PITZER both of Co.

D: 4th inst in East Liverpool, NANCY FOUTTS w/o JOHN

D: 7th inst in East Liverpool, ANDREW MILLER, ae 33y.

D: 20th inst in East Liverpool, WILLIE C. MURPHY s/o J.F. & SALLIE E., ae 5m.

D: 29th ult in Canton IN, HOWARD PINKHAM, s/o WM. & EMMA C., ae 20m 13d.

D: at East Liverpool on 9th inst, infant child of JOHN N. & BELLE C. TAYLOR.

D: 8th inst in Knox Tp, infant son of SIMON & CLARISSA WHITELEATHER, ae 4m.

D: 10th inst, infant child of WILLIAM & ELIZABETH JEFFREY of Elkton, ae 4m.

A.A.BUSHONG has left for parts unknown. (see 2 Aug)

P.W.SMITH, better known as BILLY SMITH, the "Merry Miller", formerly of this place, is now flourishing at Portland, Mich. He subscribes to the Journal.

Vital statistics: for the 9 months ending July 31, 1869, the following occurred in Columbiana Co: 323 deaths, 178 males, 145 females; males born, 469; females born, 431; marriage licenses, 247.

FATAL ACCIDENT: ANDREW MILLER, until lately Wharfmaster at East Liverpool, was instantly killed on Sat afternoon by falling back on the railroad track as the mail train bound down left the depot.

Sudden death: on 9th inst, as JACOB FOX of Knox Tp was walking around the house, he made the remark that he believed he would lie down, and died in a few moments. MR.FOX was 71 years of age, an old & respected citizen of the township.- Leaves a large circle of friends.

23 Aug 1869

M: 12th inst by REV.HENDERSON, Assisted by REV.WYCKOFF, DANIEL McKAY & MRS. MARY ANN BERRY.

D: 12th inst at his res in Wellsville of cramp cholic, THOMAS W. RIGGS, in 66th yr.

D: 13th inst at res of her son, PHILIP WICKERSHAM, Green Hill, CCO, AMY WICKERSHAM, in 91st yr. (see Sept 6)

D: 17th inst in Salem, infant child of CHARLES STRAWN ae about 1y.

D: 12th inst at res of her son in law, JOHN WILLIARD of Franklin Tp, MRS. LINDERSMITH, ae 83y.

D: 18th inst JOHN STUART of Franklin Tp, ae 81y.

D: 19th inst SOPHIA KECK d/o JACOB of Salem Tp, ae 18y.

JOHN HINER, for 17 years past Postmaster of Columbiana, died recently at that place, ae 68y.

MILO VANFOSSAN, of Wellsville, who has been running on the Pan Handle Railroad as a brakeman for about a year, was killed at Taylor's Station about 8 miles east of Columbus on Wed. 14th inst.

Sad accident: at res of MRS. BLYTHE on 19th inst near New Garden; on Wed. the house had been attempted by burlars, but the family heard & raised the alarm & the burglars left. The young man loaded a double barrel shot gun & placed it in his room. On Thurs., Miss BLYTHE had been to a picnic & returned late with neighbors. The family had retired & while she sat there, a little brother who was sleeping upstairs, looked out the window & saw her, informed his brother who seized the gun & fired, shooting her in the hip; she ran into the house for help, and the brother fired again, hitting her in the face & breast. DR.FIRESTONE was called & extracted 50 grains of shot & more than cannot be removed. She is critical, but hopes to recover.

Legal notice: T.W.BOISE, SAMUEL BOISE & SARAH A. McCONNELL, wife of ----McCONNELL, children of ELIZABETH BOISE dec'd, and JOHN BOISE of Washington Co Iowa; MATTHEW BOISE, SARAH BOISE & ----BOISE, children of NOBLE BOISE (who is supposed to be dead) who when last heard from resided in Missouri, and the unknown heirs of POLLY SCOTT dec'd, who when last heard from resided in Bureau Co Ill., non-residents, are defendants & sued by JAMES MARTIN, surviving executor of the will of WARREN BOISE dec'd, of Columbiana Co., & who filed a petition against them & others; under the 4th item of the will it is difficult to tell who are legatees and a construction of the will is necessary; mentions that heirs of POLLY SCOTT dec'd are not entitled to any part of the residue.

Legal notice: the unknown heirs of MARY ANN WISE & JOHN WISE, their father, of the state of Illinois, will take notice that SAMUEL BURGER of CCO, as guardian of GEORGE HIVELY, filed a petition against MICHAEL ROOSE & SAMUEL COFFMAN, setting forth that ROOSE & COFFMAN gave a mortgage to GEORGE HIVELY on 50 acres in West Tp, and petition is pending versus the unknown heirs of MARY ANN WISE dec'd & JOHN WISE their father & others, children & grandchildren of the said GEORGE HIVELY & those who have next estate; GEORGE HIVELY & wife on 4 May 1868 made a deed, but he was found to be insane by the Probate Court, and the deed is void.

30 Aug 1869

JOHN HARDESTY, an old soldier of the war of 1812 & said to have been the first white child born in Belmont Co., died at his home near St.Clairsville on the 10th inst, ae 80y.

D: 19th inst JOHN MONAGAN, ae about 6 mo, son of WILLIAM.

D: 21st inst at res in Salineville, ENGLEBRECHT ZELLARS, ae 56y

D: 16th inst in East Liverpool, HARRY HILL, ae 36y 2m 9d.

D: 7th inst in Salem, NINA LEVINA LEWIS, ae 7y.

D: in Salem 22nd inst SARAH J. GARRETSON, w/o DR.E.GARRETSON, ae 46y

Killed by lightning: a son of MR. WELKER of Salem, aged about 16y, was instantly killed by lightning while passing around the house for a buckey of water last Sat. eve. (see 6 Sep)

Accident: on Fri 20th inst a daughter of MR.McINTOSH of Leetonia, aged about 13y, whilst building a fire by the aid of carbon oil, her clothes caught fire & she was so severely burned that she died the same evening.

MR.SMITH, who lived at the Stone Spring House, near Wellsville, & whom we noticed last week as having been struck with paralysis, died on Friday a week ago.

I.N.WRIGHT, formerly of Salem, intends to go into the printing business in Oskaloosa, Iowa.

Attempted outrage: MRS. MARGARET INGLEDUE of Salem Tp, preferred charges before SQUIRE HARDMAN last Wed. against GEORGE FARMER for violation of the "17th section of the Crimes Act" while she was picking berries. Mr.F. plead not guilty & was bound over for $500 for appearance at the next court. —Salem Jrl.

M: 24th inst at the res of J.W.BRITTON by REV. WM. BAXTER, ROBERT JOHNSON, A.M., of Pittsburgh PA & ANNIE S. McQUILKIN of New Lisbon.

M: 25th inst at Marshaltown, Iowa, M.B.ADAMS & NETTIE HANNA, second daughter of THOMAS HANNA, formerly of New Lisbon. On Fri last, MR. & MRS. ADAMS arrived here where they will remain shortly & proceed on an eastern tour.

M: at White Cloud, Kansas on 5th inst by REV.E.W.MAUCK, DAVID YODER, formerly of Mahoning Co Oh, & DOMICILLA LEOCLOSH, the Indian Chief's daughter of the Iowa tribe in Doniphan Co.,Kan

M: 26th inst by REV.DALZELL at his res in West Point, JOHN SOWDER & LIZZIE DAVIS, all of co.

M: 15th inst by REV.J.J.JACKSON, JOHN YOUNG of Leetonia & ANNIE KEEN of Franklin Square.

M: 2nd inst by Elder E.CAKE, CHASE COALE & MATTIE VOTAW, both of Salem.

M: 25th inst in Pittsburgh PA by REV.JOHN GRAY, F.R.BIRCH of Pittsburgh & MRS. R.G.DOLE of Salem.

M: 21st inst by SAML POLLOCK ESQ, BELLE J. WICKLINE & JASPER N. NORRIS, all of co.

6 Sep 1869

M: 30th ult by SAML HARDMAN JP, ANGUS McDONALD & ELIZABETH McCAWLEY.

M: 17th ult by REV.J.R.ROLLER, ROBERT McGONAGLE of Salineville & MARTHA BEATTY of Carrollton.

D: 28th ult near Patmos, Goshen Tp, MARGARET SHINN, ae 71y

D: 29th ult in Salem, MARY SMITH, ae 32y 9m.

D: 28th ult CHARLES E. WELKER s/o JACOB & RACHEL of Salem, ae 13y 6m. (see 30 Aug)

D: 27th ult in Wellsville, CLARA J. FISHER d/o SAMUEL L. & CHRISTIE A.

D: 1st inst ELIZABETH NEWHOUSE w/o ISAIAH ae 57y

D: 13th ult at res of her son PHILIP WICKERSHAM near Lynchburgh, CCO, AMY WICKERSHAM, ae 61y. (see 23 Aug)

DR.LATIMORE A. McCOOK, son of MAJOR DANIEL McCOOK, died at Pekin, Ill. on 23d ult ae 49y. His remains were buried in the family lot in Spring Grove Cemetery, Cincinnati, Ohio. He was well known to our citizens, having studied medicine here with his uncle, DR. GEORGE McCOOK.

13 Sep 1869

M: 8th inst at the Reformed parsonage by REV.G.M.ALBRIGHT, FREDERICK BAKER & MARY K. SPRINGER, both of New Lisbon.

M: 4th inst in Salem by DR.I.N.BAIRD, W.ALLAN TUCKER & HANNAH C. BOONE, all of Salem.

M: 9th inst at res of bride's father in New Philadelphia, OH, by REV.I.G.HALL, of Leetonia OH, J.B.BERTOLETE, M.D., & MAGGIE HARDMAN.

M: 1st inst by ELDER S.S.McKOWN, CHARLES W. GARDNER & MAGGIE J. McGAVERN, all of Hanover Tp.

M: 2nd ult by same, DAVID M. HARRIS & ABIGAIL HOOPS all of Butler Tp.

M: 2nd inst at res of bride's father in West Point, CCO, by REV.DALZELL, ROBERT McBETH & SALLIE GILMORE.

D: 1 Sep of cholera infantum, CHARLES EDWARD THACKERY, s/o THOMAS & ANN, ae 5m.

D: at the Infirmary on 8th inst, MARGARET HILLIARD ae 68y.

JOSEPH S. LODGE of Iowa City, Iowa, is visiting here. He subscribes to the Journal.

Sudden death: a colored man living in Salem, WILLIAM SUTTON, who has been blind for 3 or 4 years, fell from his chair while eating dinner last Fri. He had violent spasms which lasted about 2 hours, when he died. Leaves wife & 2 children in destitute circumstances.

20 Sep 1869

M: 2nd inst at Oak Grove by REV.D.V.HYDE, THOS.LODGE & LUELLA ADAMS, all of CCO.

M: 16th inst at parsonage by REV.WM.COX, C.B.VOGAN & ELIZABETH HARRISON, all of Salem.

M: 9th inst at res of bride's parents, ERR KANNAL & LORETTA HAWKINS all of co.

M: 9th inst at res of bride's parents by REV.T.P.CHILDS, J.H.GAMBLE & ANN MEREDITH, All of co.

M: 16th inst by REV.D.V.HYDE, ALLEN LODGE & JANE REED, all of co

M: 19th inst by J.B.MILLS, ESQ., JAMES CLUNK & HATTIE CARLILE all of co.

D: 14th inst CHARLEY ELSWORTH COPE, s/o L.D. & RUTH COPE, of Hanover Tp, ae 2y 3m.

D: 15th inst, LEWIS GREEN s/o L.H. & A.E.GREEN, ae 9y.

D: 17th inst JOHN WALL s/o PETER & ELIZABETH of Salem Tp ae 2m 9d

D: 17th inst EVERETHA LONG d/o H.H. & SUSAN of Elkton ae 10m 4d

D: 14th inst JOHN HENRY BRINKER s/o JACOB & CATHARINE of Centre Tp, ae 18m.

D: 5th inst infant child of ELIAS LACEY ae 2y.

D: 14th inst ALLEN BROWN READ s/o THOMAS & MARY B. of Salem.

D: 7th inst in Salem Tp, JOHN McGAFFY, ae about 62y

The oldest prisoner in the Ohio Pen is JOHN GULL, has been there about 33 years; he was sentenced in Stark Co., Oct 14, 1869 (? should be about 1836), convicted of 2nd degree murder; the old man's mind is somewhat impaired & he enjoys many privileges of the institution.

ABIE WHINERY arrived safely in Paris. Her luggage went down with the steamer "Germania." She is studying music in the French Academy.

27 Sep 1869

M: 21st inst by REV. WM. BAXTER, JACOB EARHART & ELIZA PARKER, both of New Lisbon.

M: 5th inst by REV.ALEX SCOTT, OWEN C. BALL & ANNA MELLOR, all of East Liverpool.

M: 14th inst near Summitville, by REV.I.N.WHITE, GEORGE F. YOUNG & JANE WISMAN.

M: 16th inst at res of bride's father by REV.D.V.HYDE, JOSEPH B. WHINERY & ANNA Y. BENNETT, both of co.

M: 23d inst by REV.WM.BAXTER, JAMES HOWELL & CATHARINE WHITACRE, both of New Lisbon.

D: 25th inst ELI HARVEY BARNES, s/o ALFRED & LOUISA of Elkrun Tp, ae 4m.

4 Oct 1869

M: 29th ult by REV.DANKS, WILLIAM JOLLY & BEULAH ANN TRUNICK all of co.

M: 30th ult at res of DAVID HUM of New Lisbon, by REV.JOHN BAKER, CHARLES R. JOHNSTON & MAGGIE SILVERTHORN, all of co.

M: at Millersburgh, Ill., on 17th ult, CHAS. McDEVITT & LIZZIE A. GALLAHER, both of this county.

D: at res of JAMES McMASTER in Pittsburgh PA on 23d ult, MATILDA MARKHAM, formerly of this place, in 50th yr.

D: 26th ult in Salem Tp, MARGARET ZIMMERMAN ae 59y.

D: 29th ult in Salem, infant child of GEO.BLACK.

D; 29th ult near Salem, CATHARINE CURRY, ae 76y 3m 10d.

D: 1st inst, HENRY ATTERHOLT of Centre Tp, ae 57y

D: 1st inst CALEB COPE of Hanover Tp, ae 65y.

MISS MARY L. BOWDEN d/o JOSEPH of Minerva, aged about 20y, was found dead in bed on the 25th ult.

SUICIDE: JESSE ANDRE, residing in Hanover Tp near Dungannon, was found dead in his orchard last Fri eve with his throat cut. Not appearing at the usual suppertime, a search was made resulting in the above. When found, a pocket knife with which the act was committed was in his hand. MR.ANDRE was about 36 years of age & leaves a wife & a family or 2 or 3 children.

On 21st ult, a little daughter of ROBERT WATSON, of Leetonia, while at a neighbor's house, accidentally overturned a pot of boiling water, spilling the contents down her back. For some reason, the people at whose house the accident occurred did not render her any assistance and she started for home alone & died the next morning.

11 Oct 1869

M: 7th inst at res of bride's parents in Salem by REV.T.P.-CHILDS, ALBERT S. KIRTLAN of Knoxville Tenn & ELLA GRIMMESEY of Salem.

D: 4th inst in Elmore, OH, "LITTLE MAUD" LUCKEY, infant dau of DR. JOHN B. & KITTIE H. LUCKEY, ae 3y 4m 19d.

D: 5th inst SARAH HERRON EELLS d/o ERASTUS & CATHARINE of this place, ae 21y 10m.

D: 10th inst MARGARET DILWORTH at res of her brother BENJAMIN of Elkrun Tp, ae 50y.

D: 6th inst. SUSANNA SIMON w/o ADAM ae 66y 9m.

D: 30th ult in Salem, MARY ELLEN DORWART, w/o C. DORWART ae 28y.

18 Oct 1869

The sign at the corner of the Cowan House reading "Cross Keys 1806" was taken down & stored in the attic.

GEORGE W. HECKERT of this place received a patent for a machine for bending buggy circles.

REV.T.P.CHILDS has resigned as pastor of the Baptist church of Salem.

M: 14th inst at res of bride's parents by REV.I.N.BAIRD, WM.H.RUDESIL & HANNAH I. PIKE, all of co.

M: 12th inst by REV.WM.BAXTER, ANDREW MILLER & LOUISA BURNETT, both of co.

M: 14th inst in Salem by DR.COX, JOHN GIBBS & SALLIE HEACOCK, all of co.

M: 7th inst by WM.JOHNSON ESQ, THOMAS R. FIFE & EMMA MORRI-SON, both of co.

D: 8th inst in Salem, infant child of FREDERICK SMITH.

D: 10th inst in Salem, infant child of JAMES SHEEN ae 1y 2m.

D: 6th inst in North Georgetown, SOLOMON SHIVELY, ae 61y.

D: 7th inst in Leetonia, MAUDA LEWELLA ROLLER, infant of JONES W. & SAMANTHA A. ROLLER, ae 2 weeks & 6 days.

25 Oct 1869

M: 14th inst at house of SAMUEL ORR ESQ, by REV ROBT DICKSON, ARNER DICKSON of Canal Dover & KITTIE ORR, of New Lisbon.

M: same day by same at the LYONS & MISS HANNAH J. LEWIS, all of co. [obviously, something omitted in this item]

M: 12th inst at res of DAVID BOYCE by REV ALEX SCOTT, CASSIUS C. THOMPSON & ARA MARTIN, both of East Liverpool.

M: 30th ult by GEO HALLUM ESQ, JOHN BAUM & CEDELIA DICKEY, both of East Liverpool.

M: 12th inst at res of MRS. CONGDON, Cleveland, OH by REV.D.C.OSBORNE, CHARLES F. SMITH of Erie PA & ANNIE A.-CLECKNER of Wellsville.

M: 19th inst at res of bride's parents by REV.I.N.BAIRD, CHARLES SHARPNACK & LOUIS STEELE both of Salem.

M: 16th inst by REV.D.V.HYDE, ALLEN LODGE & JANE REED, all of co

M: 19th inst by J.B.MILLS, ESQ., JAMES CLUNK & HATTIE CARLILE all of co.

D: 14th inst CHARLEY ELSWORTH COPE, s/o L.D. & RUTH COPE, of Hanover Tp, ae 2y 3m.

D: 15th inst, LEWIS GREEN s/o L.H. & A.E.GREEN, ae 9y.

D: 17th inst JOHN WALL s/o PETER & ELIZABETH of Salem Tp ae 2m 9d

D: 17th inst EVERETHA LONG d/o H.H. & SUSAN of Elkton ae 10m 4d

D: 14th inst JOHN HENRY BRINKER s/o JACOB & CATHARINE of Centre Tp, ae 18m.

D: 5th inst infant child of ELIAS LACEY ae 2y.

D: 14th inst ALLEN BROWN READ s/o THOMAS & MARY B. of Salem.

D: 7th inst in Salem Tp, JOHN McGAFFY, ae about 62y

The oldest prisoner in the Ohio Pen is JOHN GULL, has been there about 33 years; he was sentenced in Stark Co., Oct 14, 1869 (? should be about 1836), convicted of 2nd degree murder; the old man's mind is somewhat impaired & he enjoys many privileges of the institution.

ABIE WHINERY arrived safely in Paris, Her luggage went down with the steamer "Germania." She is studying music in the French Academy.

27 Sep 1869

M: 21st inst by REV. WM. BAXTER, JACOB EARHART & ELIZA PARKER, both of New Lisbon.

M: 5th inst by REV.ALEX SCOTT, OWEN C. BALL & ANNA MELLOR, all of East Liverpool.

M: 14th inst near Summitville, by REV.I.N.WHITE, GEORGE F. YOUNG & JANE WISMAN.

M: 16th inst at res of bride's father by REV.D.V.HYDE, JOSEPH B. WHINERY & ANNA Y. BENNETT, both of co.

M: 23d inst by REV.WM.BAXTER, JAMES HOWELL & CATHARINE WHITACRE, both of New Lisbon.

M: 14th inst by REV.J.B.MILLER, assisted by REV.DAVID M.KINNEY, D.D., W.W.MILLER of Leetonia & CARRIE D. WELLMAN of Hayesville, PA.

M: 16th inst by REV.D.V.HYDE, ALLEN LODGE & JANE REED, all of co

M: 19th inst by J.B.MILLS, ESQ., JAMES CLUNK & HATTIE CARLILE all of co.

D: 14th inst CHARLEY ELSWORTH COPE, s/o L.D. & RUTH COPE, of Hanover Tp, ae 2y 3m.

D: 15th inst, LEWIS GREEN s/o L.H. & A.E.GREEN, ae 9y.

D: 17th inst JOHN WALL s/o PETER & ELIZABETH of Salem Tp ae 2m 9d

D: 17th inst EVERETHA LONG d/o H.H. & SUSAN of Elkton ae 10m 4d

D: 14th inst JOHN HENRY BRINKER s/o JACOB & CATHARINE of Centre Tp, ae 18m.

D: 5th inst infant child of ELIAS LACEY ae 2y.

D: 14th inst ALLEN BROWN READ s/o THOMAS & MARY B. of Salem.

D: 7th inst in Salem Tp, JOHN McGAFFY, ae about 62y

ABIE WHINERY arrived safely in Paris, Her luggage went down with the steamer "Germania." She is studying music in the French Academy.

The oldest prisoner in the Ohio Pen is JOHN GULL, has been there about 33 years; he was sentenced in Stark Co., Oct 14, 1869 (? should be about 1836), convicted of 2nd degree murder; the old man's mind is somewhat impaired & he enjoys many privileges of the institution.

27 Sep 1869

M: 21st inst by REV. WM. BAXTER, JACOB EARHART & ELIZA PARKER, both of New Lisbon.

M: 5th inst by REV.ALEX SCOTT, OWEN C. BALL & ANNA MELLOR, all of East Liverpool.

M: 14th inst near Summitville, by REV.I.N.WHITE, GEORGE F. YOUNG & JANE WISMAN.

M: 16th inst at res of bride's father by REV.D.V.HYDE, JOSEPH B. WHINERY & ANNA Y. BENNETT, both of co.

M: 23d inst by REV.WM.BAXTER, JAMES HOWELL & CATHARINE WHITACRE, both of New Lisbon.

M: 21st inst at res of bride's mother in Salem Tp, by ELDER E.B.CAKE, M.L.YOUNG & BARBARA FLICK, all of co.

M: 21st inst at Reformed Parsonage by REV.G.M.ALBRIGHT, ENOS BRICKER & PHEBE A. KELLEY all of Salem Tp.

Died at her res in New Lisbon on 19th inst, MRS. MAGDALENE CROWL, aged 85y. (obit) Died at res in New Lisbon on 19th Oct., MRS. MAGDALENE CROWL, widow of the late GEORGE CROWL who died 1851; her maiden name was BURGER; she was born 6 Nov 1784 & was nearly 85 years old. Oldest settler, her father came from York Co Pa to Ohio in 1807 & settled where SAMUEL BURGER now lives on Franklin Square Road. She was a member of the German Reformed Presbyterian Church. She married in 1808 to Mr. CROWL.

D: Mon last, MR.M.THOMPSON was coming to town with his team & passing HARKER'S POTTERY, when the horses ran & he was thrown from the wagon, with the horse kicking him in the temple. He died yesterday morning. Was husband & father. — East Liverpool Democrat.

D: 14th inst MRS. DALESA JONES w/o STEPHEN W. of Salem, late of Stockbridge, Mass.

1 Nov 1869

M: 20th ult at res of JOSHUA BROWN in Goshen by REV.A.B.MAXWELL, J.W.ARNOLD & S. BROWN.

M: 17th ult by LEVI KING ESQ, JNO.H.SANOR & MARTHA J.-VAMMETER, all of co.

M: 31st ult in Salem by SAML HARDMAN JP, EMMOR R. WILSON & ESTHER A. DAVENPORT, all of co.

M: same day by same, JAMES GROVES & SUSAN JAMES, all of co.

D: 25th ult at res of her daughter, MRS. JOHN ZIMMERMAN, of this palce, MRS. MARY MYERS, ae 84y.

D: 19th ult MRS. MARIAH JANE BREWSTER, w/o J.T.BREWSTER of Centre Tp, ae 52y.

D: 27th ult at West Hickory PA, JOSEPH WATSON of this place, ae 60y. (obit) JOSEPH WATSON, an old citizen of this place, died at the res of LEVI HANNA at West Hickory PA; remains brought to this place, funeral conducted by Odd Fellows, of which he was a member.

D: 21st ult at res of ALLEN BOYLE in Salem, MARGARET CAMPBELL ae 75y.

D: 21st ult at res of her son, CHARLES I. HAYES, LYDIA HAYES, ae 70y.

D: 25th ult in Butler Tp, JOHN H. MARTIN, ae 44y. (obit) SUICIDE: on 22nd ult, JOHN H. MARTIN of Butler Tp committed suicide by hanging in his barn. Was found by his son & cut down by his wife; he thought he was not getting his share of his father's estate.

D: 17th ult, SAMUEL McCLELLAN of Hanover Tp, ae 85y.

D: 18th ult, CHARLES CONNER of Carroll Co., ae 25y.

D: 21st ult, WILLIAM McFATE of Centre Tp ae 54y

Patents: to NATHAN COPE of New Waterford for a fruit house; also, to JACOB TAYLOR, of Beloit, Mahoning Co., for a carriage body brace.

A.M.E.ZION Church will have FRED DOUGLASS speak on Fri the 5th inst.

Tin wedding: MR. & MRS. L.B.LOCKARD of Salem, celebrated their 10th anniversary last Monday.

ED F.RUKENBROD, late of the Salem Republican, now with the Miami Valley News, Piqua, Miami Co., Ohio.

8 Nov 1869

M: 21st ult by REV.ROBT. HAYES, HIRAM McCORD & MARY C. EARS-MAN, all of co.

M: 4th inst at Cowan House, New Lisbon by JOHN B. MILLS, JP, ADRIAN MARIETTA & MELISSA ROSH.

D: 25th ult at res of her daughter, MRS. JOHN ZIMMERMAN of this place, MRS. MARY MYERS ae 79y. (see 1 Nov)

D: 1st inst in Salem, HANNAH C. ALLISON, ae 32y.

D: 30th ult at Clarkson, Middleton Tp, THOS. HOLE, ae 57y.

D: 28th ult at res of her brother in law near Calcutta, MRS. M.J.CRAWFORD, consort of J.Y.CRAWFORD of East Liverpool.

Accident: SYLVANUS PEPPLE & JACOB S. HALVERSTADT of Salem Tp were thrown from a buggy; SYLVANUS was badly hurt, will be a cripple for life.

Last Tues, WM. LOWELL, an employee of Iron & Coal Co. of Leetonia, was injured by the falling of an earth bank; it is feared his injuries will prove fatal.

From the Alliance Democrat: on Sat last, MR. GRANT, father of PRES. GRANT, took dinner at the SOURBECK HOUSE. He stopped off here, being on his way to Deerfield, Portage Co., where he once resided and owned a farm.

Court: Ohio vs: WM. McKEE: defendant married the prosecuting witness & case was dismissed. [bastardy?]

15 Nov 1869

Court: THOMAS T. LOVE on complaint of MAYOR BOONE, case in bastardy, continued.

M: 23d ult by REV.GEO.VOGLESONG, LORENZO D. HARDESTY & MARIAH E. SHAW, all of Hanoverton.

M: 9th inst at res of bride's parents, by REV.THOS.A.SCOTT, assisted by REV.A.B.KIRTLAND, WM.R.SMILEY & SOPHIA H. BOWMAN, all of co.

M: 4th inst by REV.DR.COX, GEORGE B. GREENWOOD of Stark Co & MATTIE C. STANLEY of CCO.

D: 16th ult in Washingtonville at res of his brother in law GEORGE W. FREED, ISAAC ESTRY ae 34y 10m 3d.

D: 28th ult JACOB F. REEDER of West Tp ae 40y.

D: 5th ult DANIEL LUPTON of Salem ae 42y 8m 23d.

MRS. WILHELMENA of Springfield, advertsies she will not be responsible for her runaway husband's debts. Sensible woman.

REV.A.B.LEONARD, who has been laboring in Leavenworth, Kan. for several years, returned to Alliance in a bad state of health.

Patents: ZADOK STREET of Salem for a patent cattle car, and AMOS RANK of Salem for a patent harvester & harvester rake.

JOHN HAINES, a former resident of this place, but laterly of Madison Wis. has opened up a photographic gallery in SPIKER'S BLDG. on Market St.

22 Nov 1869

M: 10th inst by REV.I.N.WHITE, SAMUEL C. THOMPSON, of Jacksonville FLA & V.A.LINDSAY of Salineville.

M: 18th inst by REV.T.A.SCOTT, SAMUEL J. ADAMS & MARTHA E. BRITTON, all of New Lisbon.

M: 13th inst by SAML.HARDMAN JP, WM. ISEMAN & FRANCES DUBBS, all of Salem.

M: 28th ult in Marshalltown, Iowa, by REV.R.B.BULL, ROBERT BINFORD, formerly of Salem & CADDIE C. DUNCAN.

M: 18th inst by J.B.MILLS, ESQ, ROBERT N. ESTELL & LAVINA KIBLER, all of this place.

M: 20th ult in Allegheny by REV.SWIFT, WM.V.GREEN & AMY BRIGHT, of Wellsville.

M: 4th inst in Carollton by REV.WM.EATON, JAMES W. WELTON of Wellsville & JULIA A. TAYLOR, of Carroll Co.

M: 11th inst at res of bride's mother in Mahoning Co., AQUILLA PIDGEON of Salem & LIZZIE CARLISLE.

SETH BRADFIELD, residing near East Fairfield, accidentally shot on of his thumbs off while hunting.

WILLIAM ENGLISH, on 10th inst, while walking home, was run over by horses; little hope for his recovery.

29 Nov 1869

Court: MAY J. BOVARD vs CHARLES W. BOVARD, divorce granted; she is restored to her maiden name.

DIVORCE: ELIZABETH SHRODER vs PHILIP SHRODER, divorce granted

Terrible accident: from the Journal we learn that MRS. WILDLY WARD, a colored lady of Salem, was burned to death by her clothes catching fire while sitting near a stove Thurs.-last. She threw water on them, but the fire wasn't out.

D: at res in East Liverpool on 16th inst, JOHN WEBSTER ae 87y

D: 20th inst in East Liverpool, MAY BELLA FARMER d/o L.R. & MARIA FARMER, ae 3y 9m 25d.

D: 11th inst in East Liverpool, DAVID C. MOORE ae 48y.

D: 13th inst in Salem, MRS. McCALLA, ae 91y.

D: Sept 29, ELIZABETH ELLEN MOORE, ae 10y 9m 28d.

D: Oct 5, ALMIRA MOORE, ae 9y 7d.

D: Oct 19, MAGGIE MOORE, ae 4y 6m 21d.

D: Oct 23, EMMA MOORE, ae 6y 9m 2d.

D: Oct 30, JAMES N. MOORE, ae 2y 2m 20d. All these deaths occurred from diptheria in the family of WM.S.MOORE of St.Clair Twp.

6 Dec 1869

M: 1st inst by REV.R.DICKSON, JOHN McVICKER ESQ & S.A.G.FIL-SON, all of New Lisbon; he is a member of the law firm CLARKE & McVICKER.

M: 30th ult by ANDREW ARMSTRONG ESQ, JAMES BUSH & LOUISA W. GRATE, all of co.

M: 18th ult by REV.N.H.WEAVER, assisted by the bride's father, HENRY S. PEPPEL & CORNELIA F. WEAVER d/o REV.S.WEA-VER, all of Washingtonville.

M: 25th ult in Salem by SAML HARDMAN JP, JAMES A. GILBERT & SARAH ANN LATTA, all of co.

M: 23d ult ED.M.MAHAN, conductor of the Niles & New Lisbon Railroad, & HETTIE OWREY, of Wheeling, W.Va.

D: 1st inst in this place, JOHN ROBERTSON, ae 59y. (obit) JOHN ROBERTSON, an old & respected citizen, died on 1st, funeral by REV.DICKSON, of the Presbyterian church.

NEW LISBON JOURNAL, 1867-1876

Court: SARAH DAVIDSON vs JOHN DAVIDSON, petition for alimony. Petition granted for 75 years, commencing Jan 1,1870.

DIVORCE: ELENOR FISHER vs HERMAN FISHER, divorce granted, $2,000 alimony.

13 Dec 1869

M: 18th ult by REV.J.ARTHUR, JOHN W. JENKINS & EMMA RUNYAN, all of co.

D: 2nd inst, NANCY LACY, w/o JOHN LACY (colored), of Knox Tp, ae about 55y.

20 Dec 1869

M: 9th inst by REV.J.HENDERSON at res of bride's parents, ALEX. FRAZIER of Martinsville, OH & AMANDA J. HUNTER of Wellsville.

M: 16th inst in Wooster, OH, by REV.MILLER, IRWIN STONEBRAKER of Wooster & MARY S. HAMILTON, d/o DAVID, formerly of this place.

M: 2nd inst at res of bride's parents in New Waterford by REV.JOHN N.WILSON, WILLIAM S. SILLIMAN of Blairstown, Iowa, & ARMINDA V. LITTLE.

M: 2nd inst by REV.G.W.RIGGLE, JACKSON E. MACKALL & VIRLINDA CREIGHTON both of co.

D: 18th inst STEPHEN KELLEY of Knox Tp, formerly of Salem Tp, in 51st yr.

D: 17th inst JAMES CARR of Centre Tp ae 81y.

DAVID STOFFER, of North Georgetown, while on a visit to relatives in Wisconsin, drove a span of horses 12 miles, starting while in a profuse perspiration. In a few days afterward he became a raving maniac & died shortly afterward of congestion of the bowels. His remains were brought home on the 9th & buried in the presence of a large number of friends and acquaintances.

PROBERT, the proprietor of the Iron City Saloon, was arraigned last week before Salem authorities for a violation of the new village ordinance which forbids the keeping of a drinking saloon or disorderly house. He plead guilty, fined $40, spent 20 days in the lockup.

27 Dec 1869

M: 11th inst at res of JOHN WORMAN, Salem Tp, by REV.A.B.-KIRTLAND, SOLOMON KOCH & PHEBE HALVERSTADT.

M: 22nd inst in Salem by REV.A.B.MAXWELL, LEWIS GEPHART of Niles & HETTIE OSBORN of Salem.

SAINT GEORGE is the name of the town laid out on the farm of GEORGE McKINNON near East Liverpool.

1870

Jan 3,10,17,24,31	Feb 7,14,21,28	Mar 7,14,21,28
Apr 4,11,18,25	May 2,9,16,23,30	Jun 6,13,20,27
Jly 4,11,18,25	Aug 1,8,15,22,29	Sep 5,12,19,26
Oct 3,10,17,24,31	Nov 7,14,21,28	Dec 5,12,19,26

3 Jan 1870

Fatal accident, last Mon eve as express train was heading toward Leetonia, it struck SAMUEL BOYER, residing near Columbiana, killing him instantly; his son claimed the body & conveyed it home. He was 65 or 70 years old, a farmer.

M: 30th ult by REV.WM.BAXTER, MATHEW ORR & MARY E. SMITH, eldest dau of J.L.SMITH ESQ, both of this place.

M: 19th ult in East Liverpool by REV.A.SCOTT, A.B.TAYLOR & EMMA C. ROW.

M: 23d ult by REV.S.M.HICKMAN, MART B. SIMMS of East Liverpool & ELIZA DAWSON of Glasgow, PA.

M: 14th ult at New Philadelphia by REV.BURT, JAMES GRAFTON & ICAPHENIA VANFOSSEN, both of co.

M: 25th ult by REV.I.N.WHITE, THOMAS M. CONNEL & MARTHA J. McCAUSLAND.

M: 30th ult by same, JOHN ROSEBURGH & NANCY C. BENNER, both of Wayne.

D: 22nd ult at res of JAMES MORGAN, NANCY MORGAN in 82nd yr.

D: 27th ult in this place, JOHN SAVACOOL, ae 85y.

D: 21st ult near Salem, MARIAN BLACK w/o ANDREW ae 35y.

D: 24th ult CHARLES GAILEY s/o ANDREW & ANN ae 16m.

D: 30th ult MARSHAL HOOPS aged near 30 years.

D: 30th ult, child of DAVID MESSER.

Accident last Monday, JOHN F. COYLE, Proprietor of Salem Flax Mill, working near a scutching machine, slipped & fell, one of the knives revolving at a rate of 250 times a minute, struck the top of his head, cutting off the skin to the skull. His escape from death was miraculous. He will be confined, but will recover. Salem Journal.

Attempted suicide: MRS. ISADORE MONTGOMERY, of this place, attempted suicide last Thurs., by taking laudanum; got a bottle from a neighbor, & Fri. morning was discovered in an insensible condition at the house of CAPT. MYERS, where she had been staying for a few days. The empty bottle was on the floor beside the bed. Domestic troubles is the cause; she is improving.

MATHIAS NACE SR. met with an accident last Fri, dislocating his left arm at the shoulder; was working on the roof of the Engine House, slipped & fell between two rafters.

10 Jan 1870

M: 24th ult by REV.J.C.TAGGART, WM. THOMAS & SUSAN KINSEY, all of East Liverpool.

M: 23d ult by REV.G.W.HODGEKINSON, JOSEPH BAILEY of Cincinnati & ELLEN HARRISON of East Liverpool.

M: 25th ult by REV.G.W.RIGGLE, WALTER BETTERIDGE & SARAH GREEN, all of East Liverpool.

M: 2nd inst by REV.FINK of Johnstown, PA, D.R.BAIRD of Salem & ANNIE T. HAMILTON, of Johnstown.

M: 31st ult by REV.D.V.HYDE, DANIEL HEATON & SAMANTHA CARNS, both of co.

M: 29th ult at Oak Grove by same, JOHN BADGER & MARY E. WEAVER, all of co.

M: 23d ult by G.W.RIGGLE, LEWIS THOMPSON, of Jefferson Co. & MARY A. DAVIS of CCO.

M: 25th ult by same, at res of bride's mother, JNO. H. BURGES & CAROLINE PEPIN, both of East Liverpool.

M: 7th inst at house of bride's mother by REV.ROBT.DICKSON, JAMES G. VANFOSSEN of Yellow Creek & MATTIE J. ATTERHOLT of Centre Tp.

M: 31st ult at res of GEO.HALVERSTADT in Salem Tp, by REV.A.B.KIRTLAND, JOSEPH B. KENTY & LYDIA HALVERSTADT.

M: 5th inst in Columbiana by REV.S.BAECHLER, JOSEPH DEHOFF & NANCY J. KNOWELS both of Columbiana.

M: 3d inst by SAML HARDMAN JP, JOHN H. BRONSON & ELLEN E. WILEY, all of Salem.

M: 16th ult by WM.M.CRAWFORD, ESQ., HOWARD TAYLOR & MARTHA L. PEARSON, all of co.

17 Jan 1870

M: 6th inst by REV.J.B.MILLER, S.M.EATON & MARY PALMER, both of co.

M: 11th inst by REV.I.N.WHITE, ALVIN LAUGHLIN of Franklin Tp & MAGGIE HELTZER of Gavers, CCO.

D: 2nd inst MRS. MARIAH CROXALL ae 52y 6m.

D: 10th inst in Butler Tp, HUGH MARTIN, ae 84y.

D: 10th inst at res of JOHN BLAIR, Salem, VIRGINIA THOMAS of Philadelphia, ae 30y.

D: 6th inst in St.Clair Tp, JAMES GEORGE ESQ., ae 60y.

D: 11th inst in Salem, GEO.W.KIDD, ae about 20y.

D: Dec 1, 1869, at Geneseo, Ill., ELIZABETH McCRACKEN, relict of the late NATHANIEL McCRACKEN, of Salem Tp, CCO, ae 82y.

297 marriage licenses issued in county in 1869.

24 Jan 1870

M: Dec 27, 1869, at Sherman House, Bridgeport, Belmont Co, by REV.CHALFANT, JOHN FAWCETT, of Salem, & LYDIA McMASTERS, of Concord, Belmont Co.

M: 13th inst at res of bride's father near Franklin Square by REV.A.B.KIRTLAND, G.HALVERSTADT & AMELIA M. SWITZER.

D: in Winfield, Henry Co., Iowa, at res of her son in law, EDWIN RUMMELL, on Dec.11,1869, MRS. CLARA BATCHELOR, for over 20 years a res of New Lisbon, & for the last 6 1/2 years, a res of Iowa.

D: 20th inst at this place, JAMES McNANNY, native of Ireland, ae 40y.

D: 20th inst MARGARET McGEEHEN of Wayne Tp, ae 45y.

D: 10th inst ANNA ESTERLY, w/o LEVI of Columbiana, ae 23y.

D: 13th inst WM.McLANE, near West Point, ae 41y.

PETER KNEPPER of Calcutta, charged with assault & battery, bound over to court.

31 Jan 1870

M: 12th inst by REV.D.V.HYDE at res of bride's father, JESSE TAYLOR of Chester Co Pa & SUE DAVIS.

M: 20th inst by REV.DR.COX, JAMES D. DERR of Iowa & LYDIA A. CAMERON of CCO.

M: 25th inst at Hicksville, OH by REV.I.LOWER, at res of bride's father, WM.H.CALENDER & ELLEN J. SWITZER.

D: 24 Dec 1869 at her res in Brookville, PA, MRS. HANNAH DOUTHETT, w/o REV. WILLIAM DOUTHETT, of Brookville, ae 62y. The deceased was the daughter of MATTHEW ADAMS of New Lisbon.

D: 21st inst in East Liverpool, EMMA BRATT, d/o SARAH A. & ANGUS, ae 1y 6m 7d.

D: 22nd inst MISS JESSIE McBANE, ae about 19y.

Salem had excitement: THOMAS WAY was charged with desertion from the Regular Army. He was on duty at the arsenal at Pittsburgh, PA, obtained leave to visit his parents, & overstayed the time; he served all through the late war & was a prisoner at Andersonville. He is not a skulker or a coward.

LUTHER CALVIN of East Liverpool has been arrested by U.S.Marshall for contempt in refusing to obey a subpoena.

7 Feb 1870

M: 11 Dec 1869 by G.W.BORING, ESQ., THOMAS J.W.STITT & ELIZA McPHERSON, all of Salineville.

M: 15th ult by same, JOHN P. HUSTON of Monroeville, Jefferson Co & MARY ANN POTTS of CCO.

M: 3d inst by REV.ROBT.DICKSON at res of bride's father, WILLIAM BURCAW & MAGGIE PATTERSON, both of Hanover Tp.

Haunted house: an old dwelling house situated on the road leading from Wellsville to Calcutta has for several years had the reputation of being haunted. Several braves from Wellsville were going to examine it, but they didn't have the key!

14 Feb 1870

M: 8th ult in Salem by REV. A.B.MAXWELL, JOSEPH BINSLEY & ELIZA A. McMILLEN, both of Co.

M: 10th inst at house of JAMES PATTERSON, father of the bride, JAMES McCLELLAN & NANCY PATTERSON, both of co.

M: 5th inst in Pittsburgh, PA by REV.F.A.NOBLE, DAVID T. BURCHARD & ESTHER POE, of Wellsville.

M: Dec 31 by REV.W.BAXTER, EDWARD RICHARDS & JANE CLECKNER, all of New Lisbon.

M: 2nd inst by JOSEPH FAWCETT ESQ., in Salem, KEARSEY BAILEY of East Fairfield & ASENITH JOHNS of Salem.

M: in Friends meeting, Damascus, 29 Dec 1869, SYLVESTER G. PAIK of Mahoning Co. & ELIZABETH STANLEY of Butler Tp CCO

D: 6th inst SARAH FISHER w/o DAVID of Elkrun Tp ae 76y.

D: 4th inst at res of her parents in Wellsville, EMMA FURNISS, ae 12y 7m.

D: 23d inst at res of DANIEL HIBBETS near Wellsville, ISABEL WEST, ae 56y.

D: 2nd inst near Newgarden, MARY NEGUS, relict of WEST NEGUS, ae 74y.

D: 5th inst in Salem, MARY E. THOMPSON, d/o JOSEPH W. & HANNAH A., ae 9y.

D: 6th inst near Salem, REBECCA HILLIARD, relic of JOHN, ae 75y

D: 7th inst in Butler Tp, JOHN MARTIN, ae 30y 7m.

D: 8th inst, infant child of WILLIAM BONSALL, ae 5m.

D: 8th inst, NATHAN FAWCETT, ae ---y.

D: on ---inst at Newgarden, JEFFIE GRAHAM, s/o FRANK & MARY E. GRAHAM, ae 1y.

21 Feb 1870

M: 4th inst by REV.J.DUNDAS, T.C.LINDERSMITH & CATHARINE McQUILKIN, both of Millport, OH.

M: 30 Dec 1869 by same, A.D.GRAFF & LISSA SWEARINGEN both of Hanover.

M: 9th inst at res of bride's father by REV.A.B.KIRTLAND, assisted by REV.S.S.McCOWEN, EDWIN M. CROWELL & JENNIE PIKE, all of co.

D: 9th inst MARY FIFE, of Franklin Tp ae 25y 9m.

D: 10th inst in Salem, ALLEN G. REED.

D: 11th inst in Berlin Tp, JOSEPH WILSON ae 62y.

D: 19th ult, SARAH PARK of Goshen Tp, ae 80y.

Court: Infirmary Directors of Gallia Co., versus SAREPTA DUSTON. CONRAD HUNE, ESQ., appointed guardian; order to appraise & sell real estate.

JOHN MOFF, convicted of forgery, taken to Ohio Pen for 3 years at hard labor.

WM. LODEKER & WIFE of St.Clair Tp, were arrested & brought to town Tues. on charge of threatening to burn property. A compromise effected, they were discharged.

28 Feb 1870

D: 23d inst in Salem, MRS. MARY FETTERS, ae 77y.

D: 23d inst infant child of JAMES & MARY JACKSON of this place.

D: 24th inst, infant child of EDWARD & JANE RICHARDS of this place.

D: 22nd inst, BROOKS CALDWELL of Elkrun Tp ae 54y.

Court: MARGARET BUEHECKER vs SOLOMON KIBLER, BASTARDY. He pleads guilty, order to pay $225.

7 Mar 1870

Court: MICHAEL HOOK vs MARIA HOOK, divorce granted. [this is undoubtedly the MICHAEL vs MARIA HUG case which was dismissed previously]

M: 23d ult at res of bride by REV.A.W.HOWBETT, assisted by REV.J.CROUSE, GEO.WELLS JR., of Wellsville, & MYRA MUSGRAVE of Sulphur Springs, Crawford Co.,OH.

M: 24th ult at Reformed Parsonage by REV.G.M.ALBRIGHT, SAMUEL ENTRIKEN & FRANCIS E. FILSON, both of Salem Tp.

M: 17th ult by REV.CRIST, ESQ., ALEXANDER FREED of Stark Co & LAVINA FULTZ of West Tp.

M: 17th ult by REV.J.H.CONKLE, DR.B.H.VANKIRK of West Newton, PA, & MINNIE FARRAND, of Elkton.

M: 27th ult in Concord Church, CCO, by S.B.TEAGARDEN, MARTIN BENNER & EVALYN V. FUHR.

M: 2nd ult in Salem by SAML.HARDMAN, JP, JOB W. ELTON & LOYIA A. HUDLEMYRE.

M: 16th ult by GEO.HALLUM ESQ., HOWARD SHAFER & ALLIE ORNER, both of East Liverpool.

D: 10th inst FRANK W. CARLISLE s/o DANIEL & MARY JANE ae 1m 7d

D: 24th ult in East Liverpool by an accident of C & P RR, HARRY HUNTER, of Bellair, OH, ae 25y.

D: 4th inst MARY ELIZABETH GREENAWALT, d/o JOSEPH & CAROLINA of Centre Tp, ae 7y.

D: 5th inst DAN VALLANDIGHAM GREENAWALT, son of the same parents, ae 6y.

D: 3d inst in Salem, M.M.REEP, ae 70y.

D: 19th ult in Wilkinsburgh, PA, LIZZIE LUDWICK, /o S.P., ae 29y 5m.

D: 12th ult in East Liverpool, FREDERICK CRUBAUGH, ae 70y.

D: 12th ult ADA FLORENCE MAYER, d/o WM. & HANNAH, ae 5 weeks 4d

14 Mar 1870

M: 1st inst at the Parsonage, Yellow Creek, by REV.J.N.SWAN, LAUGHLIN NOBLE & MAGGIE LOUDEN, all of co.

M: 10th inst by REV.WM.BAXTER, HENRY B. LINDERSMITH & ANNA M. REESE, both of co.

M: 3d inst by REV.ROBT.HAYS, JAMES P. PATTERSON & NANCY McINTOSH, d/o ALEX., of this co.

D: 6th inst at res of her son in law, JOS.HOLLOWAY, REBECCA SCHOFIELD, ae 86y.

D: 8th inst, OTTIE PICKET s/o J.P. & ALLIE of Salem ae 2y.

D: 4th inst near New Garden, THOMAS WHINERY, ae 58y.

D: 8th inst at res of her son, JOEL McMILLAN, near Salem, ELIZABETH McMILLAN, in 70th yr.

D: 5th inst NANCY McGUINTY of Norristown, Carroll Co, ae 80y

D: 5th inst JOHN O'CONNEL, of Dungannon, ae 30y.

D: 7th inst ROSA GREENAWALT, d/o JOSEPH & CAROLINA of Salem Tp, ae 1y.

D: 12th, EMMA GREENAWALT, dau of same, ae 3y.

21 Mar 1870

M: 10th inst by REV.A.B.MAXWELL, D.G.PORTER & MISS A.L.SCATTERGOOD, both of Salem.

M: 15th inst at res of E.M.BATCHELOR, by REV.WYCKOFF, WM.H.BATCHELOR & SUE S. BEAUMONT, all of Wellsville.

D: 23d ult of scarlet fever, LIZZIE MAE APPLE, d/o WM. & MARY JANE of St.Clair Tp, ae 3y 5m; on the 27th ult of same, JAMES ELMER APPLE, son of same, ae 7y 20d.

D: 16th inst LEWIS W. GREENAWALT, s/o JOSEPH & CAROLINA of Salem Tp, ae 3y. This makes the 5th death in the family in the last few weeks.

D: 15th inst NANCY MORGAN w/o WILLIAM deceased, at the res of her son, SAMUEL EWING of Wayne Tp, ae 86y.

28 Mar 1870

M: 13th inst by REV.W.L.NELSON, ALLEN WICKERSHAM of CCO & MISS MOORE of Carroll Co.

M: 17th inst at the Huron House, New Brighton, PA, by REV.B.C.CRITCHLOW, D.H.HILLMAN of Leetonia & CLARA T. HYDE, eldest dau of REV.D.V.HYDE of New Lisbon.

M: 10th inst by REV.S.WAGNER, DR.J.A.HISER & MISS M.L.-HINKLE, both of Co.

M: 10th inst in Hanover by WM.JOHNSON ESQ, GEO.STACKHOUSE & MATILDA MARSHALL, all of co.

D: in Salineville on 20th ult, LIZZIE FLORENCE THOMPSON, d/o KATE R. & RALPH JR., ae 4y 20d.

D: in Salineville on 8th inst GRACE MAUD DEVENEY, d/o WM. & GRACE, ae 7m 1d.

ADULTERY: Mr. M.M.RUSSELL, with a woman he passed as his wife, stopped at the St.Cloud Hotel some weeks ago & he proceeded to canvass the neighborhood for the sale of books. Last Fri., a warrant was issued, as he had left his wife & infant child boarding with strangers in Hanover, CCO; he gave the wife a few hundred dollars, & a horse & buggy, and promised not to oppose a divorce. The wife returned to her friends in Licking Co. --Stark Co. Demo.

CAPT. E.F.LEPPER, many years a resident of New Lisbon, but latterly of Parkersburg WVa, made a short visit to his old friends here.

A little child of WM. BLEAKLY of Wellsville was badly scalded last week when the boiling contents of a teapot were spilled upon it.

4 Apr 1870

M: 12th ult at the res of bride's mother in Orland, IN, by REV.FRANK PIERCE, A.J.LONG of CCO & SADE SMITH of former.

M: 22nd ult at parsonage of Yellow Creek Church by REV.J.N. SWAN, WM. TREFFINGER & MARTHA E. VANFOSSEN, all of co.

Dissolution of partnership between WM.MATHERS, A.J.COWAN & WM.C.GLENN; the books of the Mill are in the hands of A.J.COWAN, who will settle all accounts.

DR.J.J.IKERT has removed from West Point to his farm, where he will continue his practice.

D: 1st inst at his res in Hanover, JOHN RANDLES of heart disease, ae 75y 8m 22d. The deceased came from York Co Pa. in 1816. He leaves a wife, children & grandchildren.

D: 25th ult in East Liverpool, MRS. SARAH LARKINS w/o JOSEPH.

D: 24th ult MARY LOGAN d/o PATRICK & MARY of Summitville ae 4y.

D: 29th ult, EDDIE LOGAN, s/o same, ae 6y.

D: Mar 28th, SAMUEL McCREA, of Dungannon, ae 34y.

D: 22nd inst, BROOKS CALDWELL of Elkrun Tp ae 54y.

Court: MARGARET BUEHECKER vs SOLOMON KIBLER, BASTARDY. He pleads guilty, order to pay $225.

D: 2nd inst, infant child of JOSEPH & LEVINA ALBERTS of Centre Tp.

C.L.VALLANDIGHAM has sold his interest in the Dayton Ledger.

This issue closes the third volume of the Journal. The price will be raised to $1.00 per year, and the next paper will increase in size.

Mon 11 Apr 1870 (Vol 4 no 1) (from WRHS microfilm)

M: 5th inst by Rev TA SCOTT, A.L.AUGUSTINE of _____,Iowa, & MISS M.E.BREWSTER of New Lisbon Ohio

M: 30th ult at the Lutheran Parsonage, Salem Tp, by REV.A.B.-KIRTLAND, GEORGE W. McENTEE of South Ridge, Ashtabula Co & MISS SOPHIA STEWART of (near) New Lisbon

M: 24th ult in Salem by SAML HARDMAN JP, JOHN J. WHITE & MISS ELLEN S. WISNER all of this co

M: 22nd ult by JOSHUA ROHRBURGH ESQ., HENRY B WEAVER & MISS LUCENA HOLLOWAY both of this co

M: 24th ult at res of the bride's father at Union Grove Mills by REV HYDE, ALFRED ALDRIDGE & MISS LAVINA HENDRICKS

M: 17th ult at the residence of Esq HAWLEY in Salem Tp by ELDER E.B.CAKE, THORNTON McCRACKEN & MISS EMERINE HAWLEY

D: 8th inst BRIDGET MALEY at the res of her mother in Wayne Tp, aged 32y

D: 19th inst HETTIE ARTER W/O LEONARD of Hanoverton aged 24y

PATRICK McANEENY in attempting to jump from a freight train at Leetonia lately, fell under the cars & had his legs crushed below the knees. After lingering in great agony, death released him from his sufferings the same afternoon at 2 o'clock.

The Salem Republican of last week very cautiously copies our article on the death of MR.PANCAKE. Don't be so feerd, Mr Republican. If we know ourselves, the Journal is reliable.- Why didn't you credit us with the article immediately above, instead of the paper that stole it from the Journal?

A young man named FUNKHOUSER was found dead near the Railroad bridge in New Brighton on Wed morn last. The verdict of the coroner's jury was death by suffocation from falling with his face in the mud.

ISAAC GALLIGER of Winchester, COL CO while eating cake last week, partially swallowed a steel pin. A physicain tried to discover it; fianlly Dr R P JOHNSON of Alliance removed it with a magnet.

Mon 18 Apr 1870 (Vol 4 no 2) (from WRHS microfilm)

Accident near Salineville, on 10th inst, JOHN MILLER & GEORGE GESS were both thrown from buggy; MILLER was thrown & had his skull badly fractured, is still living but fears are entertained of his recovery.

M: 24th ult at residence of bride's father at Pleasant Valley Mills by REV D V HYDE, ALFRED HENRY ALDRIDGE & MISS LOVINA HENDRICKS

M: 14th inst in Hanover at the residence of DR.G.W.SANOR, by E.GARSIDE,ESQ., HENRY CLARKE & MISS NANCY NELSON all of co

Mon 25 Apr 1870 (Vol 4 no 3) (from WRHS microfilm)

D: on 20th inst, in New Lisbon, WM. MOORE, aged 92 years.

M: 10th inst by REV.J.M.DUNDAS, CHARLES W. SHERMAN of Stark Co & MISS HANNAH M. ANDERSON of Knox Tp CCO

M: 6th inst by WM.FULTZ ESQ., GEORGE M. SMITH & MISS ALCINDA HARRIS, all of co

D: 5th inst in Unity Tp, PHILLIP FETZER aged 59y 11m 2d

34

DEATH OF WILLIAM MOORE: "FATHER BILLY MOORE" as he was familiarly called, died on last Thurs afternoon. He was born near Dungannon, County Tyrone, Ireland, May 18th, 1778 and came to America shortly after becoming of age. He was pressed into the British Navy while a young man & saw hard services under English officers. He also was in the Irish rebellion & fled to America to save his life. He came to this country when few white people lived in ColCo he was a man of strong constitution until of late years, & even up to within a few hours of his death, he showed great strength for one so old & under such circumstances. About 4y ago his right leg was partially paralyzed & about 2 weeks ago, his left side was paralyzed and also his tongue.He had been boarding at Mrs HEPHNER's in Matamoras for some months & rec'd the best of attention from the family who did all in their power to relieve the old mans sufferings. He was buried at Wellsville by the Masonic fraternity to which he belonged. He was taken to Wellsville by the New Lisbon members & buried by the Wellsville Lodge. Mr Moore had belonged to the fraternity 71 years. He was the "oldest Mason" in the US at the time of his death. 71 years is a great while to live, yet he had attained his majority ere he joined the Masons. He rememberd events & dates with surprising accuracy. Events that transpired 80 yr ago he remembered well. What changes have taken place in history since his birth. For nearly a centrry he had watched the wonderful strides of science. Since his birth America has grown to be one of the great nations of the world. In 1778 the US were few in number & weak compared with today. How few of the generation of today will attain the age of 92.

D: 6th inst in Columbiana JOHN HOKE aged 69y

D: 13th inst in East Liverpool MRS. C.CROCKER in 81st yr

D: 19th inst in Salem THOMAS KEEN in 78th yr

D: 17th inst NANCY ALLISON D/O JOHN & ALICE A. of Elkrun Tp ae 2y

D: 17th inst infant child of JOHN & ELIZABETH CROWL of Centre Tp ae 2 weeks

D: 15th inst in East Liverpool, ENOCH BULLOCK ae 58y

D: 15th inst JACOB EARLY ae 50y 7m

D: 18th inst of scarlet fever LELAND TODD S/O MAGGIE J. & J.P. of Salineville ae 1y 16d

Mon 2 May 1870 (Vol 4 no 4) (from WRHS microfilm)

M: 21st ult in Leetonia by D.W.ABBOTS ESQ., OLIVER PHILLIPS & MISS CORNELIA BECK all of Fairfield Tp

M: 28th inst at res of bride's father by REV A B KIRTLAND, JOHN C.FILSON & MISS SARAH S.LINDESMITH all of Centre Tp

D: 25th ult in Butler Tp, DAVID McDONALD formerly of Hammondsville, Jeff Co, ae 75y

D: 22nd ult in Salem, GEORGE ENGLAND ae about 43y

D: 27th inst MARY WHITE W/O REV.I.N.WHITE of Wayne Tp ae 30y

D: 29th inst ALEXANDER GLENN of Madison Tp ae 71y

D: 26th ult infant child of THOMAS McCLELLAN ae 7mo

Mon 9 May 1870 (Vol 4 no 5) (from WRHS microfilm)
front page torn in half

ISABELLA DIXSON who was taken to Newburgh from Franklin Square in 1866 as insane, has been returned to the County Infirmary as incurable

KILLED BY LIGHTNING: On Fri as MISS ELIZABETH SMITH of St.Clair Twp was returning from the grave of her mother, whither she had gone to make some repairs, she was struck by lightning and instantly killed.

Session of District Court:
ISAAC SHAW vs EDWARD L. STROHN. Death of the plaintiff suggested. EDWIN GARSIDE admr made a party & case contd

M: 28th ult at REV McGOWN'S residence in Guilford, JAS.-YATES & MISS EMMA ELLIOTT both of co

M: 28th ult at New Garden by Friends ceremony, CYRUS BRANT-INGHAM & MISS SARAH KIRK, all of co

M: 21st ult at Enon Pa by REV J B MILLER, HUGH LAUGHLIN & MISS ELIZABETH PALMER both of co

M: 1st inst by REV.J.REINHART at his residence, ADOLPH ZIMMER & MISS ELIZABETH ESTERLY

M: 3d inst in Massillon by REV W LYNCH of Salem, PETER GRIBBLE & MISS LAURA L. BUCKIUS D/O S. BUCKIUS

M: in Allegheny City by J.H.McGHAR, JAMES FOLLANSBEE of Mt.Vernon NH, & miss LOU A. WILEY of Summitville Oh

M: on ...ult at res of bride in Hanover by WM.JOHNSON, J.P, THOS.J.SHIVELY & MARY C. NILES

D: 1st inst in New Waterford, ANNIE TAYLOR infant child of COLBERTSON & AMANDA aged about 1y 3m

D: 8th inst, MRS. MARY M. SHULTZ, mother of M.H. & D.C. SHULTZ of this place aged 86y 14d. (also) The funeral of MRS.SHULTZ will take place from the residence of her son D.C. SHULTZ tomorrow at 2 o'clock

D: 2nd inst in Cleveland ALONZO GRAFTON S/O THOMAS of Wellsville

D: 29th ult in Dayton OH, ARTEMUS ESTARBROOK formerly of Salem aged 78y

D: 23d ult at Middleton, JAMES McBRIDE aged 85y

Mon 16 May 1870   (Vol 4 no 6) (from WRHS microfilm)

The Rev BROWNLEE was installed as pastor of the Wellsville United Presbyterian Church last Tues

M: 2nd inst in Salem by REV E B CAKE, MR. W. PERCY GOODWIN & MISS MAGGIE WEST all of Salem

M: 4th inst in Pittsburgh by Rev JOHN A. GREY, SAM D WILSON & MISS EMMA JENNINGS both of Salem

M: 12th inst by REV J F JONES, at res of bride's parents in Hanover Tp, JOHN TRAVIS & MISS MARY J. HASTINGS

M: 3d inst at res of bride's father by REV J N SWAN, JAS. McKENZIE & MISS FRANCES WILLIAMS, all of Madison Tp

D: 8th inst in New Franklin Stark Co of consumption, J.H.HUS-TON the last son of THOMAS G HUSTON in 27th yr

D: 9th inst JERUSHA FARMER W/O GEORGE FARMER JR of Salem Tp ae 29y

D: 13th inst ELLA FRANCES RAMSEY D/O JOHN & KEZIAH of Centre Tp ae 17y

D: 7th inst near Hanover HEZIKIAH BYE ae 77y

D: 9th inst near Salineville JOHN MOORE ae 30y

D: 15th inst in Elkton MRS. REBECCA LOWREY ae 91y

D: 28th ult at her res near Col'ana MRS EVE FREESE ae 62y 1m 29d

Mon 23 May 1870   (Vol 4 no 7) (from WRHS microfilm)

M: 17th inst by JOSIAH ROHRBAUGH ESQ., THOMAS B. BLAKE & MISS E. ANN FLOWERS both of CCO

M: at North Lima Mah Co on 14th ult by REV J Q A WELLER, JOSIAH STUNMAN & MISS MARY HECKENLIVELY, the former of Col'ana & the latter of Mah Co

M: 5th inst at res of DANIEL LONGANECKER of Salem Tp by REV B F BOWEN, S.S.NEWHOUSE of Stark Co & MISS MARY A MARSH of CCO

M: 5th inst by REV ROBT HAYS, RICHARD H. HOGE & MISS NANCY N. McBANE, both of this co

D: 16th inst in New Lisbon, HENRY T. ATEN ae 29y

D: 14th inst MARY ANN COLLINS of Col'a ae 72y

D: 14th inst in Salem infant child of SAMUEL BUELL ae 7mo

D: 17th inst MATTIE STEWART D/O EMANUEL & ROSANNA of Centre Tp ae 25y

REV ROBERT DICKSON pastor of Presby ch of this place left for Phila Wed last to attend General Assembly of the church. it is his intention after the meeting to make a trip across the ocean & visit Ireland, his native land, accompanied by his wife. Congregation gave him a purse, well filled

REV. T.A.SCOTT pastor of the UP Chruch of this place will attend meeting of General Assembly at Pittsburgh Wed, & from there he will make a visit to his old home near LONDON, C.W. (Canada West)

Partition: VIRGINIA LAWSON & WILLIAM her husband, LORANZO D. COPE, THOMAS H. COPE, JOHN A .COPE, MARGARET A. COPE, MATILDA COPE & MARY A. COPE, of full age & VIRLINDA COPE, CHARLES F COPE, EMMA COPE, JAMES S. COPE & JESSE E. COPE, minors, of CCO, petition filed 7 May in CP ct by SOPHIE COPE demanding partition of NE 1/4 4-15-16 in Hanover Tp of 154 acres.

Mon 30 May 1870   (Vol 4 no 8) (from WRHS microfilm)

M: 24th inst by REV J H LEIPER, JOHN H TROTTER of Salem Tp & LIZZIE M MOORE of St.Clair Tp

M: 5th inst at Oquawka by Rev HENDERSON, JOHN WILSON of Henderson Co Ill & MRS MARY BAXTER of Middleton Tp CCO

M: 18th inst by REV A J ENDSLEY, W.W.PUMPHREY of Salineville & LIBBIE HOLM of Canton O

M: 26th inst at Salem by REV LYNCH, DAVID GRONER & LIZZIE T. McCRACKEN of Salem Tp

M: same time & place by same, HERBERT McCRACKEN & MELIZZA SILVERS, of the same township

D: 23rd inst in Wellsville, DANIEL McCLOUD ae 84y

D: 24th inst SABELLA ANN DONNELLY W/O JAMES R. of Leetonia ae 38y 6m 12d

D: 25th inst JACOB RISH S/O ANTHONY & MARY of Hanover Tp ae 8mo

D: 25th inst JOHN PAUL of Hanover Tp ae 36y

D: 26th inst SUSAN FREAT w/o PETER FREAT of Hanover Tp ae 26y

YOUNG MAN BADLY SCALDED: His stepmother bound over: recently difficulty occurred in family of ENOCH McCONNER of Franklin Square...due to her passion. She refused to be seated at table with her stepson & ordered him away; he refused, she poured pot of boiling ocffee over him, scalding his face & shoulders so that medical aid was needed. Next day, husband & wife came to New Lisbon, having concluded to settle all matters by being divorced in an amicable way. They stopped at Cowan House, took dinner, & in afternoon drove home together, with a new carpet & other household necessities without securing the object of their visit. On their return home, MRS McCONNER was arrested for assault & battery & taken before JUSTICE LONG who held her to bail for $200. [Apparently, ENOCH MCCONNER was thrice M: (1) to AMY COPE 28 May 1843; (2) to MARGARET BARNES 29 June 1862; and (3) to SUSANNA TAYLOR 23 Dec 1868, who is probably the "stepmother" referred to in this article]

JAMES BARCLAY, a highly respectable citizen of Columbiana , died at his residence on Fri eve the 20th inst at the advanced age of 73y.

REV W.C.SMITH was installed pastor of the Columbiana, Pleasant Valley & Palestine Presbyterian Churches on the 25th inst.

Mon 30 May 1870   (Vol 4 no 8) (from WRHS microfilm)

DROWNED: Stark Co Democrat says that VALENTINE EARLY, a young man about 21y, went in bathing in the Union mill dam last Thurs eve & was drowned. The body was recovered after a search of 3 hours.

MEMORIAL DAY: The German burying ground was first visited by the procession & a wreath & flowers deposited upon the grave of LOUIS F. FLUGAN. The procession then proceeded to the SPRINGER GRAVE YARD, with wreaths placed on graves of the following soldiers:
  BEAN, CAPT. U, 19TH OHIO
  BRINKER, ISRAEL, 104TH OHIO
  BRANDEBERRY, 3D OHIO BATTERY
  BREWER, ROBERT, 87TH OHIO
  BROUGHTON, WM, 2ND VIRGINIA
  BURBECK, WM., ----
  BURBECK, ISAAC, 78TH OHIO
  CARTNEY, PIERCE, 19TH OHIO
  CHARTERS, WM., 78THOHIO
  CULBERTSON, MARTIN, 176TH OHIO
  CULBERTSON, ELIAS, 19TH OHIO
  CHANDLER, ELI, 19TH OHIO
  CLUNK, JACOB, 19TH OHIO
  CLUNK, JOSEPH, 76TH OHIO
  DOWNARD, GEORGE, 176TH OHIO
  ENTRIKEN, BYRON, 104TH OHIO
  ESTILL, JASON, 5TH OHIO
  EWING, ROBERT, 24TH OHIO
  FREEMAN, GEORGE, 6TH OHIO CAV
  GASKILL, MILETUS, 104TH OHIO
  GASKILL, LEONARD, ----ILL.
  GROOMS, JAMES JR., 76TH OHIO
  JOHNSON, THOS, 176TH OHIO
  JOHNSON, DAVID, 104TH OHIO
  JESSOP, THOMAS, 104TH OHIO
  LAUGHLIN, WILIAM, 1ST OHIO
  LEIGHTENSTINE, JOSEPH JR., 76TH OHIO
  LOUDEN, HIRAM, ----
  McDONALD, JOHN, 104TH OHIO
  MORROW, HUGH, 76TH OHIO
  MYERS, HIRAM P., 32ND OHIO
  MILLER, JOHN, 104TH OHIO
  MITCHELL, JOHN L, 176TH OHIO
  MITCHELL, JACOB, 176TH OHIO
  OGLE, HENRY, 76TH OHIO
  ORR, BENJ F 76TH OHIO
  ORR, JOS F, 76TH OHIO
  PARSONS, WM, 104TH OHIO
  PINEER, FRED, 19TH OHIO
  RICHARDSON, LIEUT A., 76TH OHIO
  SCOTT, ROBERT, 78TH OHIO
  SMITH, SIMON, 6TH OHIO CAV
  SPRINGER, LEONARD, 12TH OHIO CAV
  SPRINGER, DAVID, 13TH KENTUCKY
  SPRINGER, JAS, 1ST OHIO
  THOMAS, JOHN, 6TH OHIO CAV
  WATT, DANIEL, 78TH OHIO
  WHEELER, OGDEN, 1ST OHIO
  WHITACRE, JOHN JR., 76TH OHIO
  VOGAN, JOHN V., ----OHIO

[A few of the above names are found in the Lisbon Cemetery, but not as many as are on the list; Lewis Flugan, recorded as buried at the German cemetery, has a stone at Lisbon Cem.]

Mon 6 June 1870 (Vol 4 no 9) (from WRHS microfilm)

M: 26th ult by JOSIAH ROHRBAUGH ESQ, JOSEPH SAMPSELL & MRS CATHARINE CROUSE

M: 24th ult by REV J S EASTON DD, assisted by REV W A-McCONNELL, JAMES McKENZIE STEWART of Wellsville, & SARAH MARIA CALDWELL of Hickory, Washington Co PA

M: 2nd inst by ELDER WM BAXTER, CURTIS R. PHILIPS & ANNIE McARTER both of county

M: 26th ult at res of bride's uncle, F.KEFFER, P SHRIVER of Pittsburgh PA & ALSEA HAMBRIGHT of East Liverpool

D: 29th ult at res of CHARLES E. DAVIS, SALEM, MICHAEL CRUMRINE aged 79y

D: 4th inst, J. DALLAS GRAHAM S/O JAMES of New Garden ae 23y 11m 5d; funeral yesterday by Masonic fraternity to which he was member; largest funeral ever witnessed in this county, over one mile in length, headed by Minerva Cornet Band; rain storm prevented many attending.

D: 31st ult, NATHAN GRAHAM of Hanover Tp, aged 33y

Old Pioneer Gone: JOHN YANT, probably the oldest man in Stark Co, died near Minerva Tues last at advanced age of 101 yrs

Ground was broken for the new Court House this morning.

M: Thurs morn June 2, 1870 at the residence of the bride's mother by the REV J B CLARK of Allegheny, REV T A SCOTT of New Lisbon OH, formerly of London, C.W., and Miss SADIE MARIA CALDWELL of Pittsburgh PA; trip to London via Cleveland & Niagara Falls; Mr Scott is pastor of United Presbyterian church of this place

Mon 13 June 1870 (Vol 4 No 10) (from WRHS microfilm)

M: 11th inst at Cowan House by REV BAXTER, ISAAC KOFFEL & MISS GILENA MILLER

D: 7th inst, GEORGE LEE of Centre Tp, aged 77y

D: 7th inst, CLEMENT FIGLEY of this place ae 54y
(Obit) Fatal accident: painful accident last Wed morn; CLEMENT FIGLEY of this place, in company with 2 of his sons, WILLIAM & GEORGE, has been engaged in taking out iron ore at the Jones bank about 2 1/2 mi NW of town; gravel bank gave way throwing him against the ore box; died in about 30 minutes. Sudden death cast a gloom over the community.

D: at the Infirmary on 25th ult, JOHN GOERING of Fairf Tp

June term of Common Pleas Court:
ELIZA KNOWLS vs JOHN W. KNOWLS: DECREE FOR ALIMONY

A woman named MARGARET HOWELLS was found dead in her bed at Hubbard OH Sun 15th ult & no marks being found on her person to indicate violence, jury returned a verdict of natural death

Mon 20 June 1870 (Vol 4 no 11) (from WRHS microfilm)
page 1-2 damaged

M: 9th inst by REV J N SWAN at parsonage of Yellow Creek Church, JAS N. HASSAN & MISS LUCINDA N. LOWRIE all of co

D: 27th Apr in Unity Tp after a lingering illness of the dropsy, WILLIAM HALL aged 86y 2m 12d

D: 20th inst LEONARD ARTER of Hanoverton aged about 24y

Mon 27 June 1870 (Vol 4 no 12) (from WRHS microfilm)

M: Wed 22nd inst by REV WM BAXTER, CYRUS B. PRITCHARD & MISS MARY MOORE, all of New Lisbon, at res of bride's father, DR. WM. MOORE

M: 12th inst by REV ALEXANDER SCOTT, OLIVER ASHBAUGH & MISS KATE JACKSON all of East Liverpool

M: 23d inst by REV WM LYNCH, O.SCOTT WOODS & MISS ANGELINE WEBB, all of Salem

D: 12th inst near Franklin, Stark Co, ANN JANE VANDEGRIFFT,-(formerly of Salem) aged 44y

D: 16th inst in Butler Tp, J.C.WALKER ae 23y 10m 14d

Court proceedings:
ELIZABETH BEECH vs WM. BEECH: DIVORCE GRANTED

Mon 4 July 1870 (Vol 4 no 13) (from WRHS microfilm)

M: Sabbath June 19th at Smith's Ferry, FRANK SMELTZ & MISS SARAH DENNIS of Wellsville

M: 21st ult by SAMUEL HARDMAN JP, THOMAS L. REEDER & MISS JULIAN N. SPENCER all of Salem

D: 22nd ult near Salem, MRS. C. HINCHELIFF aged 57y

Court proceedings:
ANNIE RUSSELL vs MYRON RUSSELL; divorce granted & custody of child to pltf
MARY A. SHIVES vs TIMOTHY SHIVES; divorce, wilful absence
SARAH A. GEORGE vs THOMAS GEORGE: divorce granted

CLARA A. LINGENFELTER vs BENJAMIN F. COALE: BASTARDY. pleads not guilty. Trial to jury. Verdict guilty. Defdt ordered to pay $400. Refused to pay; committed to jail.

Mon 11 July 1870 (Vol 4 no 14) (from WRHS microfilm)

DEATH OF JAMES A. BELL: last week we omitted to notice the death of JAMES A. BELL, which occurred 18th June at Milledgeville, Mercer Co PA; he was for some time foreman in the Buckeye office in this place & was well known to may of our citizens. During the war he served with credit in 7th Ohio Regt & was several times wounded; left a wife & 3 children

Last Wed, PETER WELSH of Wellsville was arrested for living in adultery with MRS ELIZABETH NOBLE on complaint of her husband ALEXANDER NOBLE. WELSH was brought before JOHN MCVICKER ESQ & committed to jail; brought before Probate Judge, plead guilty, fined $200 & 20 days in jail; the criminal intimacy has existed between these parties for several years; 20 witnesses testified.

M: at the Catholic Church in Leetonia 27th ult by FATHER E. LINDERSMITH, JOHN L. GRUBER & MISS MARIA McGLYNN all of co

M: 7th inst at ME parsonage in New Lisbon by REV J F JONES, F.T.HUSONG of Akron & MISS H. BREIDENSTINE of New Lisbon

M: 3d inst at res of bride's father, Salem by REV E B CAKE, MADISON COY & MISS MARY E. CLINE

D: 6th inst, CLEMENT H. VALLANDIGHAM at the residence of his father, DR. GEO.S.VALLANDIGHAM of this place, aged 29y

D: 4th inst at her res in Col'a, MAGDALENA KEISTER aged 66y 2m 5d

D: 6th inst CATHERINE KECK of Salem Tp ae 78y

Mon 18 Jly 1870 (Vol 4 no ??) (from WRHS microfilm)
p1-2 damaged

M: 7th inst at res of W.BEARDMORE by REV J HODGKINSON, JOHN STEWART of New York City & MARY BEARDMORE of E.Liverpool

M: 4th inst in Sharpsburg PA by REV E M WOOD, WM. HORNE & JOSEPHINE ARNOLD both of Salem

M: 28?th ult at res of bride's sister in Allegheny PA, THOMAS TURNER & MARY MOMFORD, both of Wellsville

M: 5th inst by REV J D BROWNLEE, THOS.M.WALL of Iowa & MRS. HELEN V. HUKILL of Wellsville

M: 7th inst by Rev JD BROWNLEE, ___AS LINDSAY & LUCINDA HALES both of Wellsville

D: 115th inst at res of her son in law, DR. J.M.KUHN of Salem, MRS. DR. ROBINSON, widow of the late Dr. Robinson of Hanover in 64th yr

D: 8th inst CATHARINE McGAW ? W/O HUGH of Carroll Co ae 65y

D: 9th inst in Butler Tp, GEO. HEACOCK aged about 28y

Romantic wedding: WILLIAM SEACRIST & MISS ANNA C. HAINES by REV W K BROWN, in a carriage near Mt Union; picnic lunch followed. (Alliance Monitor)

Mon 25 July 1870 (Vol 4 no 16) (from WRHS microfilm)

D: on 23d inst at res of her mother in this place, MARY A.C. MILLER in 20th yr of her age. In this sad event, the grave has claimed for its victim a most amiable young lady. "None knew her but to love her," and those who knew her best loved her most. Her sun of life has gone down before its noon on earth, but we trust it has risen again in a land of unclouded beauty.

Killed on the railroad. On Wed a young man named FRANK FEISER, brakeman on Ranger's construction train at Bernard's crossing near Beaver Falls Station on the P. Ft.W & C RR fell down between the cars & was instantly killed.

JONATHAN CREW, ESQ., of Butler Tp who was so seriously injured by falling from his porch, has since died.

JOHN GEORGE, a brakeman on the C & P RR while attempting to get on a moving train with a bucket of water, at Moultrie, fell beneath the train & was injured so severely that he died in a short time.

Wellsville items from the Union: On 15th inst, JOHN BURNETT of Wellsville was sunstruck while working on the steeple of the Presbyterian Church. (does not say he died)

Mon 1 Aug 1870 (Vol 4 no 17) (from WRHS microfilm)

M: on 25th ult by Rev B F Bowen, JAS. ROBBIN & MISS ELIZABETH A. HOWELL both of Salem

M: on 28th ult by REV W LYNCH, RICHARD H. GARDNER & MISS MARY A. CAMPBELL of Salem

D: on 25th ult JOHN S. SMITH of Wayne Tp aged 41y

D: on 17th ult GEO. CHAMBERLIN of Elkrun Tp aged 85y

D: 27th ult WILFRED C. PERINE s/o GEO. W. & LYDIE D. ae 3m 15d

D: 24th ult at the Infirmary, JOHN A. WHITE ae 70y

D: 19th ult at his residence in Franklin Sauare, THOS. McELWEE ae 64y

D: 27th ult at res of her son in law SIMON WISDEN ESQ, in this place, ELIZABETH BROUSE aged 71y

D: 27th ult HARRY MILLER s/o ABBADENIA MILLER of Centre Tp aged 14mo

BELLE DICKSON, an inmate of the Columbiana Co Infirmary, ran away from that place on Mon 18th ult. She is about 24y of age, tall & slender, black hair cut short, dark, small and sunken eyes.

Country Infirmary report: nearly 100 paupers there, over 60% are insane & idiotic.

ISAAC BENSON, a brakeman on the P.,Ft.W & C RR was killed at Carbon Hill coal works near East Palestine on Mon 25th ult. He was engaged at the time in assisting to switch a portion of a train when he accidentally fell between two cars. His head was cut entirely off. His remains were taken to Alliance for burial, where he leaves a wife and one child.

EDWIN DUTTON, of Alliance, brakeman on this road, was killed one day last week at Canton, being crushed beneath two cars.

Mon 8 Aug 1870 (Vol 4 no 18) (from WRHS microfilm)

M: on 15th ult by Rev BF BOWEN, JAMES ROBBINS & MISS ELIZABETH A. HOWELL both of Salem

M: 28th ult by Rev W LYNCH, RICHARD H. GARDNER & MISS MARY A. CAMPBELL, all of Salem

M: 5th ult by ELDER JOSEPH M. THOMAS at Massillon, ZADOK H. STREET of Salem & MISS NANCY A. BATES of Canton

M: July 14th in Salem by Rev. GRIMES, E.O. VAILE of Columbus O & miss EMMA BRAINARD of Salem

M: 2nd Aug in Salem by SAMUEL HARDMAN JP, JOHN BOWMAN & MISS LOUISA SPROWL

D: 27th ult WILLFORD C. PERINE s/o GEORGE W & LYDIA D. of Salem aged 3m 15d

D: 2nd inst MRS EMMA GIBBS w/o GEORGE W. of Salem ae 41y

D: 2nd inst after a brief illness, S.A.AVERY of Salem ae 73y

D: Tues July 19th after a lingering illness, MRS. MARY PATRICK W/O WM. A., formerly of Salem

D: Mon Aug 1, ETTA A.M. WARD, only child of E.D. & S.J. WARD of Smiths Ferry, Beaver Co PA ae 1y 2m 9d

On Mon 1st inst the Presbyterian church of Salem, at the earnest request of the Pastor, REV A B MAXWELL, agreed to unite with him in a request to the Presbytery to release him from his engagement as Pastor. Mr Maxwell expects to fill the pulpit for 3 sabbaths, after which he goes to Burlingame Kansas to take charge of the Pres.Ch in that place

Mysterious disappearance: LYMAN H. VAUGHN went away from home in Wellsville OH leaving behind a wife & 4 children. He did not make known any reason for so doing, but has always proved to be a kind husband & an affectionate parent & his distressed family are greatly concerned on his account. He is about 6 feet high, light complexion, brown hair, blue eyes and is about 27 yrs of age; had on when he left a dark vest, brown pantaloons and waterproof coat. Any person who can give any particulars as to his whereabouts will confer a fabor by addressing Mrs. JANE VAUGHN, Wellsville. Exchanges please copy.

C.L.VALLANDIGHAM & family arrived at this place on last Friday. We understand they intend remaining here for some time.

Attacked on the highway: JAMES M. JOHNSTON of firm of JM JOHNSTON & SON on way to Franklin Square, was attacked by WM. ESTEP...particulars given.

Teachers in New Lisbon schools for coming year: PROF. I.P.-HOLE, SUPT; MR. D. ANDERSON, MALE GRAMMAR SCHOOL; MISS CARRIE HOSTETTER, FEMALE GRAMMAR SCHOOL; ROOM 4, MISS LIZZIE NELSON; NO.3, MISS REBECCA DORSEY; NO 2, MISS MARY J. SCOTT; NO 1, MISS LIZZIE ROBERTSON; at exam for teachers on 30th ult, certificates were granted to: MISS CARRIE HOSTETTER, BELLE FRAZER, MAGGIE McBAINE, LIZZIE NELSON & SUE LIVINGSTON; MR CYRUS DIXON recd certif as Asst. in Supts room

Mon 15 Aug 1870 (Vol 4 no 19) (from WRHS microfilm)

Killed: a young man named JAMES RAMSEY was killed instantly Thurs last in Greenville Pa by falling out of the window of a billiard room in the second story, striking his head on the stone pavement below.

M: July 14th by REV J M BRAY, GEORGE M. BASHAW & MISS CATHARINE HOLE both of Maho Co Oh

D: Aug 4, EDWARD F. CAMPBELL, S/O JOHN & LUCY ae 3y 2m 8d

D: Aug 8, child of OSCAR THEANA aged 18 mo

M: on the 15th inst by JOHN McVICKER ESQ., ROBERT THOMAS & MISS MARY FRANCIS both of Salem

Mon 22 Aug 1870 (Vol 4 no 20) (from WRHS microfilm)

JEFFERSON THOMAS, a young man about 18y of age, was found dead in his bed on Sat last. He had been afflicted for a long time with some disease in the head, but latterly complained of a soreness in the stomach. He was able to go about & do some light work & nothing unusual appeared to ail him on Friday. (also) Died 20th inst, JEFFERSON A. THOMAS s/o HENRY THOMAS Of this place, aged 18y

DANIEL SAYLER, ESQ., Mayor of Canton, died Sat 13th inst ae 52y

M: 11th inst by REV J D BROWNLEE, EUGENE J. WARD & MISS ANNA DUNCAN, both of Portage Co Oh

M: 9th inst at Reformed Parsonage by REV G M ALBRIGHT, JONAS BRITINSTINE & MISS SARAH ZIMMERMAN both of New Lisbon

D: 7th inst in Columbiana, A.SHIVELY, aged 4y 7m 15d

D: 14th inst ANNA KELLAR, aged 64y 6m 8d

D: 19th inst at residence of her uncle, MATTHEW BLACK, JOSEPHINE BROOKS of Elkrun Tp, ae 21y

The Methodist Congregation of Salineville have commenced the erection of a fine church edifice.

A Fine Family Monument: we learn from the Salem Republican that the brothers, A. & R.G.WOODS have erected in the cemetery a very fine elegant family monument. It is composed of fine Italian marble with a grantie base, 4 feet square.- The shaft measures 19 feet. The whole weighs 13,000 pounds & cost $1600 The names of MR & MRS WOODS & THOMAS S. WOODS are inscribed on the tablet. The monument was made in NY City & is well finished & an elegantly designed piece of sculpture.

Mon 29 Aug 1870 (Vol 4 no 21) (from WRHS microfilm)

M: on 25th inst at the Union House, New Lisbon, by REV T A SCOTT, REV THOMAS HANNAY of Allegheny City & MISS CATHARINE McGILVRAY of Col Co...he is a minister in the Reformed Presbyterian Church

M: Thurs 18th inst by REV J F JONES at the Parsonage in New Lisbon, HENRY A. RICE & MISS DELLA LEVAN all of CCO

M: eve of 24th inst at res of bride's parents by REV WM.-LYNCH, P. LONSFORD GROVE & MISS MARY CORNELL all of Salem

D: 17th inst in Salem township, BENJAMIN WINDELL aged 81y

D: 21st inst in Salem HARRIET D. FAIRFAX aged 17y

D: 27th inst JESSE MOWREY S/O JACOB M & SALINDA of Leetonia aged 13m

D: 24th inst, JANE ANN MYERS W/O HIRAM of Centeer Tp ae 64y 8m 10d

D: 21st inst ENOCH GRAY of Carroll Co aged 85y

D: 25th inst at the Lutheran Parsonage in Salem Tp, MORRIS OFFICER KIRTLAND, S/O A.B. & C.B KIRTLAND, ae 3y 4m 25d

The laying of the cornerstone of the new Lutheran Church at Leetonia on Sunday last was attended by a large concourse of people. REV. BACKLER of Columbiana, REV FAST of Wooster, Stark Co & MR SIMON of this county were present. The entire arrangment was a success

Mon 5 Sept 1870 (Vol 4 no 22) (from WRHS microfilm)

JOHN McLAIN of Alliance was found dead on the railroad track 2 miles south of that place on Sat morning the 27th ult

BARNEY GRAHAM was run over by a locomotive & killed at Leavittsburg on Sat.

M: Thurs Aug 25 MISS EMMA GARLICK & JOHN C. MILLER, both of Wellsville

M: 1st Sep by REV WM BAXTER, JAMES RANDOLPH & MISS SEMANTHA J. DEEMER both of this co

D: 28th ult EVALONA BLYTHE d/o JOHN W. & HANNA B. of Hanover Tp ae 2mo

D: 31st ult MISS ELIZABETH TRUNICK D/O JOSEPH & MARIA of Center Twp ae 19y

REV JOHN B. GRAHAM of Holliday's Cove West Va spent a short time lately in New Lisbon, his old place of residence

REV. A.H.THOMAS, of the ME Church & elder of this district, died at his residence in Canton on Wed last after a brief but painful illness

Fatal accident: on Tues last week, MAHLON WHINERY, living near Winona, Butler Tp, whilst feeding a threshing machine, was struck on the head & breast & shoulder by pieces of the cylinder, breaking or bursting, causing his death in 3 hours. He never spoke after the accident. Mr. W was a man of about 50 years of age and highly esteemed by his neighbors and acquaintances

Mon 12 Sept 1870 (Vol 4 no 23) (from WRHS microfilm)

M: 3d Sept by SAMUEL HARDMAN JP at Salem, HENRY TYLER & MRS LAVINIA CARY

M: Aug 31 by RH GARRIGUES ESQ, JAMES I. LAMPSON & MRS SARAH KEEP

M: 21st ult in New Lisbon by JOHN McMICKER ESQ, MILTON DAVIS & MISS CHARLOTTE NEY both of Salem

M: Tues 6th inst , E.W.SILVER & ANNA BISHOP both of Salem

M: Mon Aug 29th by REV J JACKSON, AARON OVERHOLT & MISS EMMA McGREGOR, all of Col'ana

D: near Salineville, Aug 24, JAMES DYSART in 76th yr of age

D: morning of 7th inst LYDIA FARMER W/O ALPHEUS of Salem Tp ae 26y

A son of JAMES BROWN of Salineville was killed on the 2nd inst in a coal bank near that place, by the falling of a large quantity of slate.

M: at the residence of the bride near Leetonia, on Mon eve Spt 5 by his Honor Esq. ABBOTT, GEORGE BARTHOLOMEW to his former wife MRS. EMMA C. BARTHOLOMEW, having been separated about one year ago by a Chicago divorce.

Mon 19 Sept 1870 (Vol 4 no 24) (from WRHS microfilm)

M: 15th inst at Mount Zion Church in Centre Tp by REV A B KIRTLAND, DENNIS SMELTZ & CATHARINE WELLINGTON all of co

M: 12th inst by ESQ. HALLUM, MR. WATSON & MISS SARAH PINK-HURST all of East Liverpool

M: 14th inst in Salem by REV W LYNCH, JOS. A. SHINN of Youngstown & MISS MARY E. WOODRUFF

M: on 15th inst by same, SAMUEL R. BISHOP & MISS RACHEL BILLINGSLEY

D: 15th inst JOHN GRACE of Salem Tp ae 51y

D: 5th inst MILLER MONROE SPITLER of Hanoverton O ae 2y

D: 9th inst PHILLIP J. HOFFEY of Hanoverton ae 22y

D: 11th inst REBECCA E. DONAHUE W/O CHARLES ae 28y 10m 23d

D: 13th inst i Salem, MARTHA SERVIS BREADEN D/O WILLIAM J & JANE R., ae 14mo

MRS. JOLLY, of East Liverpool, was last Thurs attacked by palsy & died a few hours after

CAPT. JAMES WORMINGTON of Wayne Twp., this co, will be 100 years old on the 21st inst. He spent 28 years of his life on the ocean, 18 of which he commanded a merchant vessel. He is still strong and vigorous.

JOHN WILSON the Columbiana cheep Beef man, was sentenced last week by Judge Conant to 1 yr in the penitentiary; GEO SMITH the McCoy farm man, was also sentenced to the same institution for 3 yrs.

Court proceedings:
MARGARET MOFF vs JOHN MOFF: DIVORCE GRANTED

Mon 26 Sept 1870 (Vol 4 No 25) (from WRHS microfilm)
ISSUE DAMAGED, part cut out included marriages & deaths

At a late meeting of the Presbytery of Steubenville, REV J.L.R. WYCOFF was released from the pastoral charge of Wellsville

Terrible accident: the Salem Journal says on Thurs afternoon as JUDSON CALLAHAN, a workman in the Salem Planing Mills of this place, was endeavoring to shift a belt, a sharp pointed board, which he was using, caught in the belt wheel and struck him in the breast, piercing his heart and killing him instantly. He leaves a young wife and hosts of friends to mourn his sudden and terrible death.

Mon 3 Oct 1870 (Vol 4 no 26) (from WRHS microfilm)

M: 22nd ult by Rev W LYNCH, DENNIS WEISS & MISS LETTIE REGAL all of Salem

M: Sept 22 by REV J N SWAN at the parsonage of Yellow Creek Church, AUSTIN McDEVIT & MISS NANCY J. McPHERSON all of CCO

M: Sept 27th at the ME Parsonage in New Lisbon by Rev J F JONES, LEANDER GRAY & MISS MARGARET WARD

D: Sun Sept 18, MARGARET DONGES, W/O HENRY of Col'ana ae 50y 11m 9d

D: 1st inst, MATTHEW LOUDON of Wayne Tp ae 68y

The Union Church of Elkton has been completed & will be dedicated on next Sabbath at 11 o'clock

On Monday last a little son of MR. HUDSON, a merchant of New Galilee was killed. He was on his way home from school & meeting an older brother leading a pair of horses to water, jumped on the back of one. The horse was tender mouthed and when the boy took up the reins, commenced backing, and finally fell over, crushing his rider.

Mon 10 Oct 1870 (Vol 4 no ??) (from WRHS microfilm)
front page damaged

M: Thurs Oct 6, by REV J F JONES, D.B. McLAIN & MISS HATTIE S. MILLER all of New Lisbon "The Dr. & his fair partner have our best wishes"

M: 11th inst by REV T A SCOTT at res of bride's father WILLIAM H. JOHNSTON of Beaver PA & MISS HANNAH EELLS of New Lisbon

M: Thurs Sep 8 by REV I G HALL, J.S.HALVERSTADT & MISS A.C.DILWORTH all of CCO

M: 2nd inst at Reformed parsonage by REV G M ALBRIGHT, JONAS BETZ Of CCO & MISS LYDIA ROHER of Mah Co

M: 21st inst by J.B.MILLS, ESQ, W.J.ADAMS & ARABELLA PHILPOT both of New Lisbon

D: 4th inst FREDDIE H.CARLILE S/O DANIEL & MARY JANE ae 9m1d

D: Thurs morn Sept 29, MRS KATE FISHER McCOOK, wife of DR. GEORGE L. McCOOK of Pittsburgh PA

The new Methodist Episcopal Church of Elkton will be dedicated on nezt Sabbath the 16th inst; Rev I C PERSHING of Pittsburgh & other eminent ministers are expected to be present

WELLSVILLE GIRLS ELOPES WITH A M: MAN: from the Union we gather the particulars of an elopement case which occurred at Wellsville last Mon. Several months ago a man named ROBINSON having a wife & 3 children living in Wellsburgh, came to Wellsville, obtained employment & secured boarding of a worthy widow lady named LLOYD representing himself to be a single man. For a while things went on without anything worthy of note, when one day ROBINSON left town & for a time was nearly forgotten by all of the family except one, a daughter named ELLA with whom, it appears the villain had ingratiated himself & made overtures of affection & finally proposed marriage & was accepted; but the guilty pair knew full well that the mother would never countenance their union, so on Monday morning of last week, everything being duly arranged beforehand, Ella asked her mother's permission to go to the morning train to meet some friends who were expected. Here the villain met her & the twain left on the cars for parts unknown & have not been heard of.

TOO MUCH MARRIED: one VANPELT, who lives in Fox Tp, Carroll Co during the past year, is the most married man we know of. A week or two ago a second wife made her appearance in Salineville, accompanied by her brother, searching for the brother in law. It appears that VANPELT married before the war & during the war met & married wife no 2. After the war he returned to his first love. No 2 came upon the stage with an arrest warrant. The papers not being prepared in this state let the man have a chance to get away, which he improved. No 2 & No 1, together with the brother in law, stayed at the residence of Vanpelt, lately departed & talked over the situation with what result we are not informed. Of one thing we are certain: Vanpelt should represent Fox Tp in the large stone building on the banks of the Sciota (Penitentiary) (The Salineville Era)

Mon 17 Oct 1870 (Vol 4 no 28) (from WRHS microfilm)

M: on 11th inst by Rev WM.BAXTER, PETER V. SPRINGER & MISS ELIZA BARKER all of New Lisbon

M: at Winona by Friends ceremony on 4th day, 28th of 9th mon, JOHN BUTLER SR. of Maho Co & ELIZABETH JENKINS of CCO

M: 5th inst by Friends ceremony, CHARLES L. HAYES & DEBORAH FAWCETT all of Salem

M: 11th inst by REV W LYNCH, JAMES M. WOODRUFF & MISS LIZZIE BAYNE, both of Salem

M: 11th inst by RH GARRIGUES,ESQ., at res of bride's parents, in Salem, WALTER G. BENTLEY & MISS MARCIA CLEMMER

M: 6th inst by REV ROLLER, JOHN MILLER of Petersburgh & MISS MARY ZENGER of Leetonia

D: 1st inst in Salem, CATHARINE RUSLER, aged ----years

D: 2nd inst in Salem, JERRY SMITH ae 24y

D: at Damascus on 29th ult MARTHA KING aged 81y

D: in Butler Tp on 5th inst, MILLIE MOORE, aged ----yrs

D: on 8th inst in Salem, MRS. LOUA HILLIS, W/O S.D. HILLIS, aged ----yrs

D: 8th inst FREDERICK WOLF of Butler Tp aged 35y

D: 15th inst ALICE L. RHINEHART D/O SOLOMON & ELIZABETH of Centre Tp ae 22y 6m

D: 15th inst RICHARD RANDOLPH of Fairfield Tp ae 84y

The Union Church of Elkton was dedicated last sabbath, sermon by REV WILLIAM BAXTER of New Lisbon; church was filled to its utmost capacity & many were compelled to remain outside, not being able to procure seats

The wife of JOHN WILSON, the cheap beef man, lately sentenced to the Penitentiary, is asking for a divorce.

The widow of REV. JAMES RINEHART of Columbiana this co received 2004.95 in full of an insurance policy on the life of her husband lately deceased.

Mon 24 Oct 1870 (Vol 4 no 29) (from WRHS microfilm)

M: 20th inst by REV WM. DALZELL, MARQUIS H. BOUGH & MISS SARAH A. MARCH all of co

M: 20th inst at res of A.RANK by REV WM LYNCH, MARCUS LAFAY-ETTE OSBORN & MISS ELIZA FISHBURN all of this place

M: 6th inst by F.M.GREEN, ANSON B. HART & MRS MARY BAXTER of Alliance

D: in Butler Tp, infant child of JOSHUA FOUTS aged 7 mo

D: 20th inst at Salem, LEWIS DUNLAP ae 45y

Fatal accident: a boiler explosion occurred on 29th ult near Mt.Erie, Ill, in which a former resident of this county, JACOB H. GALBRAITH, was instantly killed. His back & both arms were broken & his head crushed.

Shocks of an earthquake were distinctly felt throughout the entire country last Thurs about 11 am.

Mon 31 Oct 1870 (Vol 4 no ??) (from WRHS microfilm)
front page damaged, including page of deaths & marriages

KILLED: Mr OLIVER COPE, a citizen of Salineville, was killed by a train of cars at that place Sat eve last. Mr COPE had been to the county to procure a girl to do housework & returning at the time two trains meet at Salineville was standing on the switch, watching the train coming towards him on the main track, when one coming from the other direction ran over him ahd killed him. His body was not discovered for nearly half an hour after the accident

Mon 7 Nov 1870 (Vol 4 no 31) (from WRHS microfilm)

M: Sun 23d ult at Leetonia by REV HALL, JOHN D. COMPTON & MARY A. WARD.

M: 2 Nov by EB CAKE, SAMUEL A. FOGG of Damascus Station & MISS LAVINA E. ROLLER of CCO

M: 30th ult in Pittsburgh by REV JJ JONES, HENRY BAXTER & MISS ELLA JENNINGS both of Salem

M: 23 Oct WILLIAM CROXALL of this place to MISS RUTH GARDNER of W Va

M: Tues Oct 25 by REV G W RIGGLE, N. PITTINGER ESQ & MISS ELIZABETH HARKER, of East Liverpool

M: 13 th inst at res of JOSEPH TOLSON, by G.W.BORING, ESQ., J.S.McMILLEN & MISS MAGGIE BROWN all of Salineville

M: 21st ult at Pittsburgh Pa by REV F A NOBLE, DR. T.-WOODBRIDGE of Youngstown & MRS. SARAH A. BREWER of New Lisbon

M: 27th ult at the Catholic Church in Dungannon by FATHER E. VATTMAN, CONRAD HUNE, Atty at Law, New Lisbon & MISS ALVINA M. GRUBER of Hanover Tp CCO

M: on same day at the same place by same, FRANK GRUBER & MISS BRIDGET MELLON both of this co

M: 27th ult by REV WM. LYNCH, SIMON GONGUARE of Iowa & MISS SARAH A. SCHNARENBERGER of this co

M: 26th ult in Salem Tp by REV JJ JACKSON, WILLIAM R. ZIM-MERMAN & & MISS MARY E. SHELTON all of this co

M: 27th ult by Rev WM.DALZELL, GEORGE LEWIS & MISS MATTIE WILLIAMS

M: 3d inst by same, SAMUEL M. SHAFFER & MISS TAMER WILLIAMS all of this co

M: 29th ult by REV ROBT HAYS, MR. SINGERS CRAWFORD & MISS SARAH J. LOUDEN both of Wayne Tp this co

M: at res of bride's parents in Leetonia on 25th ult by REV HALL, JOHN B. CHAPMAN of Iowa & MISS MARY E. McKEE

M: 28th ult at Dungannon by FATHER E. VATTMAN, JACOB MANTI & MISS MARY STROBLE both of New Lisbon

D: Sun Morn Oct 30, MRS. ELISA J. MOORE ae 36y

D: Tues night Oct 15th, MRS. N. LARKINS W/O HENRY

D: Oct 20 at Salineville DR. JNO. JOHNS in 67th hear of his age

D: at residence of her parents in Wellsville on Oct 23, ROSALI J. PAISLEY W/O ELIHU in 20th yr

D: in East Liverpool on 19th ult, ROSA BELL MOORE, D/O EZEKIEL J. MOORE, aged 1y 10m

D: in Butler Tp 18th ult, JEREMIAH H. WHINERY ae 43y

D: 23d ult in Salem, ANNIE E. KOPP D/O J.D. & RACHEL ae 4y

D: 4th inst, SARAH CHARITY RICE D/O ANTHONY & MARGARET A. of Wayne Tp ae 5y

D: 8th inst ADDISON HALDEMAN of Hanoverton ae 48y

The Wellsville Union says on Sat last CLAYTON AUGHENBAUGH had the forefinger of his right hand cut off while working with some machinery in the Furniture manufactory of AUGHEN-BAUGH, ANDREWS & CO

Runaway, Man Killed: At Hanoverton on last Thurs a team of horses attached to a wagon ran away, which resulted in the death of ADDISON HALDEMAN of that place. The facts as we can gather them are about as follows: Some time ago Mr H traded for a horse with MONTGOMERY. After the trade was concluded MONTGOMERY cautioned HALDEMAN against using the horse in harness as it was in the habit of running away & could not be driven at all. This advice Mr H, it would appear, did not heed but htiched the horse to a buggy. The consequence was that the horse ran away, smashing the buggy to pieces. Mr.-H. this time escaped injury. On the afteroon of the sameday, he again harnessed the horse & placed it with another in a 2 horse wagon. He attempted to drive the team but it soon became unmanageable & the result was another runaway, smashing the wagon & throwing Mr H to the ground with such force as to cause his death in about an hour & a half. Mr H's injuries were internal, several his ribs on both sides were broken, but the particulars as to the manner of his death is not known. The supposition is that he was thrown out at the front end of the wagon & crushed by the wheels passing over his body.

GEORGE SHAW of Madison Tp was arrested last Thurs for abusing his family; preliminary trial, bail $500, not being raised, he was brought her to jail.

A Colored man named WM. CLOY, lately came to Columbiana and hired to work. On the next day he was taken with fits & for a couple of days before he died was entirely out of his mind & had to be tied to prevent injury to himself & those attending him. He was buried on Sat. the 29th ult by the TWP Trustees.

Mon 14 Nov 1870 (Vol 4 no 32) (from WRHS microfilm)

D: Mon eve, 7th inst, in Salem, JAMES C. CHAMPION ae 43y

M: 10th inst at the Lutheran Parsonage in Salem Tp by REV A.B. KIRTLAND, SILVANUS PEPPLE & MISS C.A.HALVENSTADT

COURT PROCEEDINGS:
LOUSIA M. AWTHUR vs DAVID AWTHUR: PETITION FOR DIVORCE ON GROUND FOR CURELTY. DISMISSED AT PLTF COST

ELIZA WHIMPEY vs ISAAC WHIMPEY, petition for divorce on ground of extreme cruelty. Cross petiton charging that plaintiff at time of marriage with defendant had a husband living. Dismissed without prejudice

Fatal accident: WILLIAM DURKEE living at New Waterford this co and engineer on the Ft Wayne road, was run over by a locomotive in Allegheny last Sat. night and recieved injuries from which he died on the following day.

MORE NEWSPAPERS: two more newspapers are soon to be established in this co. A new one, the Wellsville LOCAL by DAVID B MARTIN formerly of the Union office, to be independent in Politics. The Liverpool RECORD is to be resuscitated by a stock company. Columbiana co has more newspapers than any other county in the State in proportion to the populations: these two new additions making eleven

Mon 21 Nov 1870 (Vol 4 no 33) (from WRHS microfilm)

M: Thur eve Nov 10 by REV JM BRAY, PROF. ALLEN J.R.TOMLINSON, principal of the Friends Academy of Damascoville, CCO to MISS ANNA FAWCETT D/O SIMEON.

M: 9th inst at home of bride in Washingtonville by EB CAKE, JACOB F. CAMPF & MISS ROSILLIA COOK

M: eve of 10th inst at res of ALBERT COOK BY EB CAKE, CHARLES E. ELLIOTT & MISS ALESTA COOK

D: at Leetonia Fri Oct 28 GERTIE WILSON D/O J.R. & M.J. ae 3y 9m

D: at Leetonia Fri Nov 11 ADA BOYER D/O DAVID & CAROLINE ae 6mo 18d

D: at Franklin Square Mon Nov 14, HARRY WARD S/O LEVI & ENGELINE ae 1y 2m

D: Nov 16 at Massillon at the res. of Hon SAMUEL BOWMAN, WILLIE F. HUDSON, S/O JOHN & REBECCA HUDSON in 17th yr

D: at res of her father MICHAEL BOWERS at Wellsville on Sun Nov 14 of scarlet fever, EVADELL BOWERS ae 7y

D: at res of his son in law NATHAN COPE on 9 Nov 1870, NATHAN HOLE, father of DR., JOHN HOLE in 78thyr of age; he was one of the early settlers of Col Co having rssided in it some 60 yrs

D: 13th inst CHARLEY WILLIS KING s/o JOHN W. & MARTHA of Hanover Tp ae 1y 2m

D: 15th inst DANIEL WOLLOM of Wayne Tp ae 57y 2m

D: 18th inst ACLIMISIA McDEVIT, D/O DAVID & MATILDA of Wayne Tp ae 5y 3m

D: at his res in Wellsville Fri Nov 11, JACOB GIBBINS at an advanced age. Mr Gibbons was one of the early inhabitants of this place, helped to raise it to what it is, and having been familiarly known to all its citizens will be missed from their society, as well as lamented by his friends. Wellsville Union

COURT PROCEEDINGS:
Ohio vs THOMAS MELLON, grand larceny, pleaded guilty, sent to State Prison 3y
OHIO vs GEORGE SHAFFER, ADULTERY; recognized in $200 for appearance at next term

41

Mon 28 Nov 1870 (Vol 4 no 34) (from WRHS microfilm)

M: 16th Nov at res of N.A.HALDEMAN, near Hanover O by the REV A. BAKER, G.W.CONNEL & MISS LOU M. CHANDLER both of this co

M: same day by same, at res of bride's parents EPHRAIM DICE & MISS LEOTA TAYLOR, both of Homeworth this co

M: Nov 15th by REV J.N.SWAN, J.G.KOUNTZ & MISS MARY E. FRASER all of this co

M: Nov 24 by REV WM. DALZELL, ABEL S. GILMORE of Pittsburgh PA & MISS HENRIETTA TOEFFINGER of West Point Ohio

M: 24th inst at the Union House by REV ROBERT DICKSON DD, assisted by REV J.F.JONES, JOHN McINTOSH & MISS ELIZA G. JOHNSON both of Wayne Tp CCO

D: in Phila.Pa at 10 o'clock am Sun Nov 20, EDWIN BARTHOLO-MEW infant son of AARON & JANE ae about 10 mo

D: 21st inst JONATHAN HARBAUGH of Centre Tp ae 60y

D: 22nd inst NOAH GLESNER of Centre Tp ae 56y [At ST.-MARTIN'S REFORMED CHURCH, WEST FORK, on the day of the funeral of NOAH GLESSNER, some wicked person stole the Bible & hymn book from the pulpit. The pastor hopes the reading of the stolen property may lead the thief to repentance. 19 Dec 1870]

D: 27th inst MARGART RICE W/o ANTHONY of Wayne Tp ae abt 33y

Col Co has sent 6 convicts to the Penitentiary during the yr

JONATHAN HARBAUGH an old & respected citizen of this place died at his residence on last Mon morn after a long & severe illness. Mr. HARBAUGH was 65y of age at the time of his death. He was a native of this place & has always lived here.

Mon 5 Dec 1870 (Vol 4 no 35) (from WRHS microfilm)

M: Tues 29th inst by REV J C TAGGART, MR. HAMP HUSTON & MISS JANIE AZDELL all of E.Liverpool

M: Nov 24 by REV WM. DALZELL, ABEL S. GILMORE of Pittsburgh PA & Miss HENRIETTA TREFFINGER of West Point

M: in Birmingham on Tues Nov 8 by REV MR BUTTS, J.M.LECLERE of Brownsville PA & MISS MARY B. HUTCHISON of Mechanicstown OH

D: Sabbath Dec 4, ABAGAIL BROWN W/o JOHN of Elkrun Tp ae 54y

D: in Mechanicstown 12 Nov MAGGIE J. HUTCHISON D/O ROBERT & ELENOR ae 16y

R.H.DIBBLE of Santa Clara Calif., formerly of this place, called at our office this morning; he looks as though the country agreed with him.

DR. THOMAS L. BANE, a resident of Ashtabula Co OH & well known to the older inhabitants of New Lisbon, died suddenly one day last week of disease of the heart. If we are correctly informed, Dr BANE, with his brother HENRY, a number of years ago was engae in the mercantile businss here & occupied a frame bldg that then stood on the corner where the Cowan House now stands.

NEWSPAPERS: the following list comprises the names & location of the newspapers published in this county:

	WEEKLY:	
JOURNAL		NEW LISBON
PATRIOT		NEW LISBON
BUCKEYE STATE		NEW LISBON
REPUBLICAN		SALEM
JOURNAL		SALEM
REGISTER		COLUMBIANA
UNION		WELLSVILLE
LOCAL		WELLSVILLE
DEMOCRAT		LIVERPOOL
	MONTHLY:	
MORTAR ; PLAIN DEALER ; BENEFACTOR		SALEM
RAINBOW		WELLSVILLE
ERA		SALINEVILLE

The East Liverpool RECORD will soon be added to the list, making 15. Col.Co.is certainly the banner newspaper county.

NEW LISBON JOURNAL, 1867-1876

Court Proceedings:
BARBARA OTT vs JOHN MARTIN OTT, divorce granted & custody of children given to plaintiff

ISADORE WILSON vs BYRON F. WILSON: DIVORCE GRANTED

CATHARINE WILSON vs JOHN WILSON: DIVORCE GRANTED

Mon 12 Dec 1870 (Vol 4 no 36) (from WRHS microfilm)

M: on 6th inst at Ashland Oh by REV S E PEARIES, STEPHEN DOUGHTON of New Lisbon & MISS AGNES S. PARMLEY of the former place

M: at the same time & place by the same, DR. JOSEPH SAMPSEL of Ashland & MRS CELIA D. PRITCHARD of New Lisbon

M: 24th ult at Mineral Ridge OH by REV B F SHARP, O.W.KYLE of New Lisbon & MRS CHARLOTTE M. TIBBETTS of the former place

M: 1st inst GALEN C. JONES of Indiana & MISS ELLA A. FAWCETT of Damascoville

M: 1st inst by REV J. HUSTON, CAPT. D.J.COOK of Denver Colo & MISS NANCY DESELLUM of Salineville

M: 13th ult by GEO.W.BORING, ESQ., GEORGE TOLSON & MISS LIZZIE RAFFLE, all of Salineville

M: 1st inst by REV J HUSTON, WILLIAM EARL & MISS SARAH MADISON all of Salineville

M: 6th inst by REV CUNNINGHAM, DAVID KEISTER & MISS MARIA POTTS all of Col'ana

D: 30th ult in Salem, MRS. SARAH A. BAIRD, W/o REV. DR. I.N. BAIRD

D: 7th inst JACOB WORMAN of Salem Tp ae 91y 8m 1d

D: 6th inst MATILDA DAVIDSON of Mt Union ae 20y

D: 7th inst in Salem, NATHAN BAUGHER ae 34y

D: in Columbiana 2nd inst LIDIE S. PEEPLES D/O WILLIAM A. & JOSIE ae 4y

D: 29th ult in West Tp of paralysis JOHN HINE ae 76y 1m 5d

D: 21st ult RACHEL McCLOSKEY D/O E & J.A. ae 15y

D: 4th inst in Col'ana, CONRAD SPONSELLER ae 65y

D: 11th inst in New Lisbon of consumption, HATTIE R. GRIFFITH ae about 16y

D: 6th inst a small child of JOHN LOUDEN of Wayne Tp ae 6mo

Court proceedings:
CHARLOTTE A. GREY vs FLETCHER W. GREY: DIVORCE GRANTED & custody of children given to plaintiff

MRS. TAMAR GLENN disposed of her household goods on Sat & starts today for Oregon with her son, G.G.GLENN with whose family she intends to reside. They will go via Union Pacific RR to San Francisco & from thence by ocean steamer to their destination....at the last State Fair in Oregon, MRS. G.G.-GLENN of Marion Co, that state, & a former resident of COL CO was awarded the highest prize for the best butter 6 months old, viz: a $75 saddle Y the Society's prize of $20. Old Columbiana always ahead. (issue of 30 Jan 1871 says that MRS. GLENN accompanied by her daughter & son, GEORGE G GLENN has arrived safely at the residence of the latter, near Salem, Oregon.)

Mon 19 Dec 1870 (Vol 4 no 37) (from WRHS microfilm)

MR. GAILY, a merchant doing business in East Liverpool, fell dead in his store room on Tues last

MR. KELLY, an old resident of Hanover Tp, died very suddenly on Mon of last week [another item says: AMOS KELLEY who lives a short distance above East Liverpool, was very seriously though it is believed not fatally, injured at Island Run last Wed. He fell a distance of 16 feet, striking a beam. This may NOT be the same man...]
42

There are 2 persons from CCO in the State Asylum for the Deaf & Dumb

The dedication of the Evangelical Lutheran St. Johns Church in Leetonia will take place on New Year's day

It is contemplated by many of the older citizens of our county to organize a PIONEER ASSOCIATION at an early day

REV A B MAXWELL has received & accepted a call from the Leetonia Presbyterian congregation & will enter upon the discharge of his duties about Jan 1

M: in Newport KY on 8th inst by REV GRANVILLE MOODY, H.J.SHIDLER of Osage Mission Kans to MISS LIBBIE P. SHORTEN, youngest dau of JAMES SHORTEN ESQ., formerly of Cincinnati

M: 12th inst in New Lisbon by REV ROBT DICKSON DD, MILTON C.D.ROBINSON of Lawrence Co PA & MISS THAMAR E. GLENN of New Lisbon

M: 3d inst by REV SIMPSON, CHRISTOPHER JOHNSON of Carroll Co & MISS ELIZABETH McCREA of CCO

M: 8th inst by REV McCURDY, JEFFERSON FISHER & MISS JOSEPHINE BUNTING both of Wellsville

M: 8th inst by REV HOWE, SAMUEL D. HAWLEY & MISS ANNA M. ROBB, all of Phila.,Pa

M: 15th inst by REV GM ALBRIGHT, ELI BRICKER & MISS ADALINE HENDRICK both of Salem

M: 8th inst by ELDER E B CAKE, at Salem, J.F.BLOCKSOM & MISS JULIANA BURSON both of Maho Co

M: 13th inst by same, FRIEDMAN RUSSI & MISS ANNA TESCHER all of Salem

D: 13th inst near Leetonia, FREDERICK BETZ ae about 75y

D: 15th inst CORNELIUS WHITACRE of Fairfield Tp ae 81y

D: 13th inst infant child of FRANCIS & ELIZABETH McINTOSH of Elkrun Tp

J.S.FREW, Recorder of Johnson Co Iowa, renewed his subscription

PIUS BEAN & EDWARD KING start for Kansas tomorrow to find a new home. (on 9 Jan 1871, the paper announces that PIUS BEAN & ED KING have located at Manhatten Kans, purchased a lot & are erecting a building to carry on the butchering business)

At ST.MARTIN'S REFORMED CHURCH, WEST FORK, on the day of the funeral of NOAH GLESSNER, some wicked person stole the Bible & hymn book from the pulpit. The pastor hopes the reading of the stolen property may lead the thief to repentance.

Mon 26 Dec 1870 (Vol 4 no 38) (from WRHS microfilm)

D: 16th inst in Butler Tp BENJAMIN HARRIS ae 65y

D: 22nd inst WILLIE BURWELL S/O LOUIS & ELIZABETH of Elkrun Tp ae 10y

M: on 15th inst by REV WM DALZELL, WM.H.CRAWFORD & MISS ELIZABETH GASTON all of this co

M: 12th inst in New Lisbon by REV ROBT DICKSON DD, WALTER C.D.ROBINSON of Lawrence Co PA & MISS THAMAR E. GLENN of New Lisbon

M: at Smith's Ferry PA on 16th inst SAMUEL DARBY & MISS MATTIE WORKMAN both of Wellsville

M: 8th inst by REV J M DUNDASS, DANIEL FALLON & MISS ELLA WARRICH, both of vicinity of Hanover

M: same day by same, THOMAS M. GEORGE & ANNA MISS ANDERSON both of Maysville Oh

M: same day by same, GEO E McDONALD of Bayard & MISS MILLIE S. HOSTETTER of Minerva

M: 22nd inst by EDWARD PETTIT ESQ., MARCUS B. MORLAN & MISS HANNAH ARMSTRONG, all of this co

PIONEER ASSN: preliminary meeting to be held in Salem Jan 12 at Town Hall. The following are among the persons of Centre Tp whose names have been sent for publication: PETER YOUNG, JOSHUA BOWMAN, WM. FILSON, JACOB HARBAUGH, FISHER A. BLOCK-SOM, DAVID SHULTZ, MARTIN SHULTZ, ABEL LODGE, J.B.NELSON, JACOB ARTER & ISAAC HASTING

A man named PERRIN cut his throat last Thurs night at Franklin

JAMES TOLLERTON, SR., an old & respected citizen of Salem, while engaged in feeding his stock, fell dead on Wed. last

The only child of C.H.GILMAN & wife, formerly of this place, a little daughter 17 mo old, died at Youngstown on Sat 18th inst

The colored people of the ME persuasion in Wellsville are endeavoring to build a church for themselves.

GEORGE HAMILTON, son of W.W.HAMILTON, formerly of this place, has been bound over to the Common Pleas Court of Wayne Co in $500 bail for robbing a car on the Pittsburgh, Ft.Wayne & Chicago RR. The property stolen consisted of silver plated ware which was being shipped to a merchant of Bucyrus. Young HAMILTON is in jail at Wooster.

GEORGE SLOAN of Hanover, this co, died at his residence on Tues morn last of heart disease ae 73y. One of the early settlers of the county & always identied largely with its business interests, he was probably more generally & favorably known than any other individual in that section of the county. A christian gentleman of strict honor, affable & courteous, his life will be remembered as a bright example & his loss mourned by all who knew him.

1871

Jan 2,9,16,23,30	Feb 6,13,20,27	Mar 6,13,20,27
Apr 3,10,17,24	May 1,8,15,22,29	Jun 5,12,19,26
Jly 3,10,17,24,31	Aug 7,14,21,28	Sep 4,11,18,25
Oct 2,9,16,23,30	Nov 6,13,20,27	Dec 4,11,18,25

Mon 2 Jan 1871 (Vol 4 no 39) (from WRHS microfilm)

M: on 21st ult by REV J N SWAN, THOMAS CREIGHTON of Calcutta Oh & MRS SARAH McCULLOUGH of Berlin Iowa

M: 22nd ult by REV J.S.GRIMES, WILLIAM H. RECK & MISS JOSEP-HINE EWING all of Alliance

M: 5th Oct by J.W.KEMP, GEORGE SULTNER of Hanover O & MISS KATE LIBER of New Garden OH

M: 22nd ult by REV WM LYNCH, H.M.GRONER & MISS MARTHA ZIMMER-MAN both of this county

M: 29th ult by REV A B KIRTLAND, ALBERT ZIMMERMAN & MISS LOUISA HENRICK all of this co

M: 22nd ult ABRAM MOORE of Salineville & MISS MAGGIE CAMERON of Carroll Co

M: at American House, Enon Valley PA on 27th ult by Rev B MILLER, J.F.LAUGHLIN & MISS SALLIE MULLEN both of Leetonia

M: 22nd ult by REV ROBT HAYS, ISAIAH G. McCORMICK & MISS LAURA V. TODD both of this co.

D: 11th ult MRS. CARRAHER of East Liverpool ae 35y

D: 15th ult MRS. MICHAEL STRAIN of E.Liverpool

D: 15th ult NELLIE CURBY D/O PIERCE & LOUISA CURBY of E.Liv. ae 15mo

D: 15th ult MRS JANE BELL SHENKEL, daughter of JAMES & ANN LEIGH of East Liverpool ae 18y 8m.

D: on 22nd ult in Stark Co, WM. GARRIGUES in his 82nd year

D: at the Infirmary on 25th ult, OLIVER HUCHISON ae 74y

D: 22nd ult MARGUERETTA AGNES BOYCE D/O CHARLES R. & FRANCIS M. BOYCE of Wellsville ae 4y 6m 17d

D: 15 Nov of typhoid fever, JEROME NALL of East Palestine

D: 30th ult LEONORA HOLLOWAY D/O LEONARD & ADA ae 6m 15d
(also) SUDDEN DEATH: the infant child of LEONARD & ADA HOLLOWAY of this place was discovered dead in bed Fri morning
On retiring to bed on Thurs eve, the child appeared to be in possession of its usual health. Fri morn when Mrs H arose to prepare her husband's breakfast it seemed to slumber sweetly.Shortly after, on going to the bedside, she found the child cold in death.

D: 1st inst SUSAN WILLIAMS of Madison Tp ae 22y

D: 31st ult at res of her son in law, DAVID SCHAEFER in Fairfield Tp, ELIZABETH BARNES ae 75y

One day last week a little child of RUFUS MARTIN of Elkrun Tp fell against a hot stove & was severely burned. One eye will be sightless.

HENRY BRINKER while assisting in butchering at JOHN WORMAN'S last Tues slipped & fell upon a stone & was seriously infured in the back. MR. BRINKER is about 60 years of age & resides in Salem Tp near Burger's church. He is in a critical situation & doubts are entertained of his recovery.

DEATH OF JAMES HALL: the mutations of time invade every family circle & rend assunder all social ties. Upon the morning of the New Year death claimed the mortal tenement of an old & respected citizen of New Lisbon. Mr. JAMES HALL, who had attained the age of 71y. The illness that has just terminated fatally was of a week's duration & was painful in the extreme. MR HALL was a scrupulously honest man, kind & genial in all his ways, modest & retiring a true friend & good citizen. He will be buried by the Odd Fellows Fratern-ity of which he was an honored member, tomorrow (Tues) afternoon at 2 o'clock from his residence (in next issue, resolutions of respect on his death from Buelah Lodge No 182, IOGT)

Mon 9 Jan 1871 (Vol 4 no 40) (from WRHS microfilm)

M: on 29th ult by REV J D BROWNLEE, JOSEPH McCLELLAN & MISS MARY AUGHINBAUGH of Wellsville

M: at the Prot.Episc.Church, Salem on 26th ult by REV GEORGE S. VALLANDIGHAM of New Lisbon, JAMES C. JOHNSON & MISS LOVINA MORLAN

M: at same place & time & by the same, HARVEY KIDD & MISS ELLA MATTHEWS all of Salem

M: 30th ult by REV J. HUSTON, ROBERT ROBSON & MISS BESSIE THOMPSON all of Salineville

M: 22nd ult by Rev A.BAKER, JOSEPH E. DERR of Jones Co Iowa & MISS SUSANNA SHAW of Hanover this co.

M: 25th ult at the res of the bride's parents by REV JONAS LOWER, T.F.CALLENDER & MISS SAMANTHA A. SWITZER both of Hicksville, Defiance Co Oh

M: 5th inst by REV D V HYDE, ERRETT L. CROOK & MISS AMANDA J. HOLLOWAY, all of Fairf Tp

D: in Col'ana on 30th ult, VALENTINE WILHELM ae 57y 9m 9d

D: in Oct 1870, at the residence of her husband in Rosavio de Santa Fe, Argentine Republic, South America, MARTHA KENNAN w/o WILLIAM C. KENNAN and daughter of MRS. D. PEARSON of Wellsville ae 37y, also, ANNABELLA, daughter of the above, ae 1 month

D: in Salem 1st inst RACHEL HOOPS w/o JESSE ae 37y

D: 25th ult at West Point, Madison Tp, MRS. MARGARET SCROGGS, ae 84y

D: 28th ult in Salineville, NANCY CARRUTHERS w/o J.G. ae 40y 4m 3d

D: in Goshen Tp 19th inst SIDNAH G. KEELER, mother of JOSEPH MEEKS of Leetonia ae 57y

D: at his residence in Salem on 4th inst, MAHLON ALLISON ae 63y

D: 8th inst in Hicksville, Defiance Co Oh SARAH ANN SWITZER after an illness of 3 days, ae 45y 3m 25d

There are 3 churches in Leetonia: the Methodist, Lutheran & Catholic

A post office has been established at "Teegarden's" on the Niles & New Lisbon Railway with URIAH TEEGARDEN as postmaster

323 couples were married in CCO last year...

DEATH OF ALBERT T. HILLMAN: we are pained to announce the death of ALBERT T. HILLMAN, which sad event occurred at the residence of his parents 1 mi north of New Lisbon on Mon eve 2nd inst. His age was 21y 5m. He was employed in the carriage manufacturing establishment of WILLIAM MYERS until some months since, when failing health admonished him to withdraw- He was a most estimable young man, a universal favorite with his acquaintances & his death will be deeply deplored by all who knew him. His parents & relatives have the sincere sympathy of all.

Mon 16 Jan 1871 (Vol 4 no 41) (from WRHS microfilm)

M: 3d inst by GEORGE W. BORING ESQ., PATRICK McKENNA & MISS ISABELLA FIGGINS all of Salineville

M: 12th inst by REV LYNCH, MR. PHYLONZO CARR of Mt Union & SARAH HOLLOWAY of Salem

M: same day by same, SAMUEL HUES & ANNA HOOPS both of Salem

M: 29th ult by J.KANNAL ESQ., EDWARD FERRALL & EMMA HEACOCK

M: Nov 4th by REV J J JACKSON, ROBERT WILLIAMS & MARY A. PATTERSON

M: 29th ult by same, JOHN W. CONKLE & MAGGIE A. DAVIS all of New Waterford

M: 22nd ult by same, ALONZO BIRMAN & MARIA GRONER

M: 8th inst by REUBEN WATT ESQ., J.F.BENSON & LIZZIE UNDER-WOOD, both of this co

M: 7th inst by H.C.ROBBINS, ESQ., ANDREW HOUSE & MISS NANCY ANN MILLER both of this co

D: 7th inst in Salem infant daughter of ROBERT McCAMMON ae 5 weeks

D: 31st ult in Salem, JAY LOCKARD, eldest son of W.E. & M.E. ae 5y 10m ;3d

D: 9th inst in Salem, MRS. LOUIS GIFFORD, ae ----y

D: 8th inst in Wellsville, ANNIE PFOFFENBAUGH D/O JOHN & ROSA ae 2y 6m 12d

D: 12th inst infant child of WM. & KATE BAXLEY of this place ae 5 weeks

D: 12th inst ELLA MARY PATTERSON, eldest dau of DR. W.E. & ARABELLA of Dungannon ae 5y 4m

D: 8th inst in Salineville, ELIZABETH T.JONES W/o THOMAS ae 22y 11m 22d

D: 8th inst in Salineville, MARTHA E. WALLACE d/o MRS. ANN WALLACE ae 6y 4m

D: 9th inst in Salineville, NICHOLAS JAMES RANDOLPH S/O RESIN & CAROLINE ae 3y 4m 21d

DR. JOSEPH SAMPSELL & WIFE gave a brilliant party Wed eve last at res on Washington St

We learn from Salem Journal that MRS S.J.FAGUE, on 31st ult, appeared before the Mayor of that place & swore her life against her husband, stating that on several occasions her life had been threatened & she lived in constant fear; the Mayor bound FAGUE over in sum of $100 for appearance at court

SAMUEL COBURN one of the old pioneers of Col Co died on 8th inst near Calcutta. He was ae 91y

A little girl ae about 6y by the name of MARTHA WALLACE was burned to death at Salineville last Sunday by her clothes taking fire at a stove

PIONEER MEETING held Thurs last, calling it the Columbiana County Pioneer Association, elected GEN JACOB B ROLLER of Centre Tp, Pres; a Vice Pres from each twp in the county; J K RUKENBROD of Perry Secy & JAMES BROWN of Perry, Treas.

MRS. JANE BENNER, an elderly lady residing about 3 mi S of town, was badly burned last Sun. It appears that while in the act of lighting a pipe she fell into the fire place where a brisk fire was burning at the time & in an instant was a mass of flames. Her screams attracted the attention of other inmates of the house who rushed to her rescue & smothered the flames & saved her life. Succor came not too soon. Although badly burned, she will recover.

Mon 23 Jan 1871 (Vol 4 no 42) (from WRHS microfilm)

M: 19th inst by ELDER WILLIAM BAXTER, THOMAS T. NEWHOUSE & MISS CATHARINE ANN MORLAN both of this co

D: in Butler Tp on 11th inst CATHARINE CARL widow of the late DANIEL CARL

D: 11th inst in Salem, _____KAUFMAN ae 3y

D: at Nashville Tenn, HENRY PHILIPS ae 27y. His remains were interred in the Philip's Church Cemetery in Salem Tp on 13th inst

D: 13th inst in Salem, JOHN PHILLIPS ae 70y

D: on 17th inst in Salem Tp, at res of ISAAC PHILLIPS, MRS. KELLEY ae about 85y

D: 17th inst JENNIE McLEARN D/O JOHN of Salem ae 6y

D: 12th inst near Hanover, CHARLES WANEY son of SARAH WANEY ae 7y 6m 24d

D: 14th inst CHARLIE WHITESTONE S/O RICHARD & CATHARINE of Franklin

D: 14th inst in Carroll Co ELLEN FITZPATRICK D/O HUGH ae 8y

D: 3d inst near Norristown Carroll Co WILLIAM KENMUIR ae 65y

D: 16th inst in Hanover Tp AARON HIVELY S/O JOHN & ELIZABETH ae 15y 6m 2d

D: 19th inst at Union Hotel,New Lisbon, GEORGE BOWMAN ae 40y

D: 19th inst in Salem Tp, MARY SWITZER W/o MARTIN ae 66y 8m 20d

D: on ....inst in Hanover, THOMAS LEONARD HOLE S/O DR. S.J.- & MARY ANN ae about 2y

D: 19th Nov 1870, THOMAS F. MILBURN ae 4y 6m. On 7th Dec 1870, JOHN L. MILBURN ae 8m 10d. Both children of LOT R. & ANN MARIA MILBURN of Hanover Tp

D: 21st inst of scarlet fever, JENNIE JOHNSON PATTERSON D/O DR. W.E. & ARABELLA PATTERSON of Dungannon ae 1y 2m

JAMES NEVIN, an old & respected citizen of Unity Tp, met with serious & well nigh fatal accident last week; he had driven into the woods some distance from his house, with his horses & sled to load some fire wood & caught his leg between the sled & a piece of timber, breaking it just below the knee in such a manner that the bone protruded through the flesh. His family became alarmed at his long absence & went in search of him, finding him lying in the snow almost perished. Medical attendance was procured & he is improving as rapidly as could be expected.

HENRY ATEN of Wellsville still lives adjoining the farm he settled in 1800. He is 99 years of age. His son, C.M.ATEN ESQ., of this place, is ae 66y. Their joint ages are 165y

PIONEER ASSOCIATION: BY LAWS & CONSTITUTION on p3

On Sat last a short distance east of E Palestine a young man about 24y was run over by the cars & instantly killed. His head was severed from his body & his right arm torn and mangled in a horrible manner. His body could not be identified, though it is thought he was a man named ROOT a miner from the Syracuse coilleries. This is the 5th or 6th person killed near EP within last 3 yrs

"Fairyland Schottish" is the title of a new & beautiful piece of music composed by HOMER HARRIS of this place

Mon 30 Jan 1871 (Vol 4 no 43) (from WRHS microfilm)

DEATH OF COLONEL G.I.YOUNG: (long obit) COL.G.I.YOUNG, editor of the Buckeye State of this place, occurred at Columbus Fri 27th inst where he was serving in House of Representatives from this county. Had been in poor health some time... had been probate judge of Mahoning Co, Military Secretary to Gov Todd, chief of a department at Washington...his remains reached here Sat Eve under escort of members of the Legislature. He was buried with Masonic & Odd Fellow ceremonies on Sun, with 8 members of the Legis. as pallbearers. His father & mother & a wife & young daughter survive him. He was about 38y of age. [M: in Canfield by REV W G MARSH on 27th ult, Hon.G.I.Young, Probate Judge & SUSAN BINGHAM, both of Canfield --Buckeye State 3 Apr 1856] [Ed.note: He was Garrison Ivester Young, and his wife is buried at Lisbon, but no stone exists for GI.,BUT is on veteran burial list]

M: 16th inst byREV D V HYDE, JOHN WILLISTON & MISS LOUISA LIBER both of this county

M: 28th ult by REV. LOCK, T.R.BRADSHAW & MISS RETTIE A.-McKENZIE both of East Liverpool

M: 19th inst by Rev J.M.CARR, ED.M.FORD of New York & MISS ALICE A. HUNTER of Wellsville

D: near Columbiana on 26th inst JACOB COBLENTZ at an advanced age. He had been entirely blind for several years prior to his death. He was one of the early residents of New Lisbon & was esteemed an excellent citizen.

D: in Washington Co Missouri, Nov 1870 at the res of her son in law, HARVEY J. SMITH, MRS. NANCY McCOY WEST, relict of the late GEORGE WEST. She was born in Columbiana Co Oh/ Buckeye & Patriot please copy.

D: 27th inst in Hanover Tp, PATRICK McGEE ae 67y

D: on ...inst in Carroll Co, JOSEPH McBRIDE ae 46y

D: 29th inst ISABELLA BAKER W/o THOMAS of Elkrun Tp ae 56y

MIDDLETON TOWNSHIP: TO THE PIONEERS OF COLUMBIANA CO OHIO, IN CONVENTION ASSEMBLED: BY URIAH THOMAS....2 1/2 columns devoted to early history of CCO; among items of interest:

URIAH THOMAS was born Sec 26 St.Clair Tp on 16 June 1813, son of ENOS THOMAS, who settled in St.Clair Twp sometime between 1794 & 1797, coming from Redstone Fort in Pa. About 1796 THOMAS FAWCETT settled on bank of Ohio River a mile below E Liv & in 1798 erected the first gristmill in co. In 1798 JOSEPH McKINNON & family came from VA across the Ohio River & settled in St.Clair, now Liv Tp, the ledest son was MICHAEL who now lives in Liv Tp & was 89 yr old Aug 1 1870; the third mill in the township was erected by ROBERT JACKMAN on north branch of the little Beaver on section 2 near the present site of FREDRICKTOWN. The last Indian killed in the county was the noted White Eyes. He was shot by WILLIAM CARPENTER near a spring in Madison Tp in sight of BOUGH'S old mill on the west fork of Little Beaver below West point, on Sun afternoon May 31, 1799, and was buried Mon June 1, 1799, by Indians, assisted by a family by the name of WALKER who lived in the vicinity.

GOLDEN WEDDING: we learn from Salem Journal that THOMAS & ELIZABETH SPENCER aged respectively 74 & 76, celebrated their golden wedding at their residence in Salem last Wed eve the 25th inst. 40 nephews & nieves were present. They are in remarkably good health.

Mon 6 Feb 1871 (Vol 4 no 44) (from WRHS microfilm)

M: 29th ult by REV J M BRAY, LEVI SUMMERS & MISS CELESTIA STAUFFER both of Co

M: 31st ult by REV R CUNNINGHAM, A.C.YENGLING, M.D. & MISS KATE DEEMER, DAUGHTER OF DR. D. DEEMER all of Col'ana

REV JOHN MOFFETT pastor of the Second Presbyterian Church of Wheeling W VA was stricken with paralysis a few days ago. Rev M commenced studying for the ministry while a resident of this place, some years ago, when the late Rev A O Patterson occupied the pulpit of the Pres Ch & will be remembered by many of our citizens   45

D: in Yellow Creek Tp on 9th ult, LAURA ATKINSON, youngest d/o JOHN & MARY ANN ae 6y 3m 2d

D: 15th ult AMASETT CAREY WILSON ae 1y 6m 25d

D: 31st ult JOHN KERNS of Hanover Tp ae 89y

D: 3d inst WILLIAM HOOKER s/o JOHN & BARBARA of Elkrun Tp age 10y 6m 12e

NORTH GEORGETOWN this county has 2 stores, 1 drug store, 1 grocery, 4 shoemaker shops, 2 cabinet shops, 1 tailor shop, 1 flouring mill, 1 sawmill, 2 cheese factories, 2 blacksmiths shops & 2 physicians. It is a flourishing little village.

Mon 13 Feb 1871 (Vol 4 no 45) (from WRHS microfilm)

D: 31st ult at her residence near Fairfield, MRS. PHOEBA ROGERS ae 74y

D: 5th inst in Col'ana GEORGE LAMB ae 64y 8m 20d

D: 30th ult in Knox Tp WILLIAM CREW ae 24y

D: in Washington Tp on 2nd inst of scarlet fever, FLORA E. HART d/o ALEXANDER & MARGARET HART ae 5y 2m 19d

D: in Wellsville 22nd ult, EMMA A. HAMMOND w/o THOMAS G. ae 31y

D: 8th ult in Franklin Tp LAWRENCE J. WARRICK S/O JONATHAN & CATHARINE ae 2y 8d

D: 3d inst DAVID ALVA GAMMEL S/O JACOB & MARGARET J. ae 6 weeks

D: 10th inst ALEXANDER McALLISTER of Frankln Tp ae 80y

D: 11th inst a twin son of JAMES & MARY HAMILTON of Robbinsville, Centre Tp, ae 10 days.

PERKINS the Wellsville burglar, reconsidered his pleas of not guilty & on Fri plead guilty to indictment; Judge FREASE sentenced him to 7 yrs in Penitentiary

M: in New Lisbon on 9th inst at res of bride's parents, by Rev Dr. DICKSON, GEORGE W. McMILLEN of Marshaltown Iowa & MISS GEORGIANA CROWL of New Lisbon...at 2 o'clock that afternoon they took the cars for their western home.

M: Dec 15, 1870 by REV G.ZEIGER, AMOS BOWMAN & MISS REBECCA KILPPINGER all of this co

M: 5th inst by REV GEORGE VOGLESONG, JAMES L WOODS Of Salem & MISS WESSIE VOGLESONG of Hanover

M: 25th ult by SAMUEL WILLIAMS, ESQ., JAMES HOOPS & MISS ALPHARETTA A. WINDELL all of this co

Mon 20 Feb 1871 (Vol 4 no 46) (from WRHS microfilm)

M: on 14th inst by REV G W JOHNSON, JAMES H. WATSON & MISS MARY ROSENBERRY all of Alliance

M: 6th inst by SAMUEL WILLIAMS,ESQ., LEWIS CULLENBERGER 7 MISS NANCY JANE CAMPF

M: 16th inst by REV W LYNCH, JACOB W. SMITH & SUSAN C. EWALT all of Salem

D: 10th inst AMELIA F. STANLEY W/o JONATHAN in 39th yr

D: 12th ult in Col'ana MRS. ARABELLA LINDSAY a native of Ireland ae 83y 6m

D: 12th ult near Col'ana MRS. ELIZABETH CALDWELL ae about 70y

D: 20th ult near Col'ana, MRS. ANNA HARTMAN ae 22y

D: in Fox Tp Carroll Co on 31st ult, DANIEL STOUT in 82nd yr

D: 8th inst at Hanover Station, MRS. ANN STOUT ae 62y

D: in Salineville on 11th inst ROBERT WILLIAM WHEATLEY S/O MICHAEL ae 3y 5m

D: 9th inst in Washington Tp, MARY FOGO in 82nd yr

D: in Chicago Ill on 12th inst MARTHA E. SHIMP W/o PETER ae 45y

D: 15th inst at res of his father, THOAMS KENNETT ESQ., in Salem, EDWARD KENNETT ae about 25y

Court Proceedings:
MARY A. WEAVER vs LOMINA WEAVER: DIVORCE GRANTED

WILLIAM T. GILES, editor & publisher of the Freeport ILL Bulletin, a native of New Lisbon, was here on visit

We learn from the Salem Journal that JOHN CRUTZINGER, living in Greenford, Mah Co, whilst grinding bark at his tannery, a few weeks ago, was in some manner caught by a cylinder which revolved at the rate of 90 revs per minutes which resulted in breaking a leg & otherwise injuring him. The limb was amputated but the operation of which together with the other injuries reveived, caused his death on last Tuesday.

TACY WILSON of Salem had a paralytic stroke on last Wed which in all probability will prove fatal. (see 27 Feb)

The First Presbyterian Congregation of Leetonia will erect a commodious house of worship in the spring.

Mon 27 Feb 1871 (Vol 4 no 47) (from WRHS microfilm)

M: 8th inst by M H ENDLY of Maple Creek, Dodge Co., Nebraska & MISS E. AZDELL of East liverpool

M: 16th inst by REV WM. DALZELL, WILLIAM GILMORE & MISS LANER J FIFE, all of this co

M: 21st inst at res of bride's father, ALVAN McCURDY & MISS ISABELLA ANDREWS

M: 20th inst at the Catholic Church in Wellsville by FATHER McGUIRE, JAMES McGUERN & MISS ELLEN RYAN

M: 16th inst by Rev WILLIAM HASTINGS, WILLIAM H. MOORE, of Marshall Co Iowa & MISS ELLA FORBES of Wellsville Oh

D: 18th inst in Salem, MISS NANCY WALKER ae ----y

D: 20th inst in Salem infant child of Mr. CLAYTON ae 1mo

D: 20th inst in Salem MONROE MATTHEWS ae 32y

D: 20th inst in Salem, TACY WILSON ae 80y (see 20 Feb)

D: 20th inst in Wellsville, WILLIAM ANDERSON ae 83y

D: 20th inst in Elkrun Tp, SARAH LONGSHORE W/o VINCENT ae ----y

D: 17th inst in Col'ana MRS ANNA M. WELK ae 84y 7m 27d

D: 15th inst JOSEPH LAFUSS S/O DONIE LAFUSS of Hanover Tp ae 10y

D: 24th inst MARY MICHELL W/o JOHN of Hanover Tp ae 46y

D: 18th inst CLARA RICHARDS D/O HARRIET & W.K. ae 10mo

D: in Winchester OH, CATHARINE L. THOMAS ae 20y 11m 24d

PIONEER MEETING: those who gave info: FISHER A. BLOCKSOM, Ae ABOUT 87/88; GENERAL ROLLER; BENJAMIN BLACKBURN said he was 81y old & occupied & lived on his present farm in Unity Tp since year 1800; suggestion by H.H.GREGG made that effort should be made to collect & preserve the early NEWSPAPERS.

WILLIAM KEMBLE, an old citizen of Elkton, has purchased property in Col'ana & will remove there in spring

Mon 6 Mar 1871 (Vol 4 no 48) (from WRHS microfilm)

The German Language: MRS. M. HELLER & MISS A. SHAEFFER from Germany, will receive pupils for instruction in the German language. New Lisbon...

M: Th Feb 23d by REV DR. BAILEY, PROF. M.C.STEVENS, Superintendent of the Salem Union Schools & MRS. S.M.COOPER of Lafayette Ind

M: 28th ult at Union Hotel by Rev T.A.SCOTT, W.T.WILSON & MISS M.E.ANDRE, of this co

D: 12th ult in Col'a MRS. ARABELLA LINDSAY, a native of Ireland, ae 83y 6m

D: 2nd inst in Dungannon, GEORGE A. LEBUS, S/O ANTHONY N. & CATHARINE, ae 9y 4m 17d

D: 1st inst ELIZABETH RAMSEY W/o WM. of Centre Tp ae 52y

D: 27th ult infant child of JAMES & LIDDIA HOSTETTER of Hanover Tp ae 2mo

D: 28th ult in Dungannon ELIAS DEARR RISDEN S/O JOHN W. & ISABELLA RISDEN ae 7 mo

D: 12th ult near Col'ana MRS. ELIZABETH CALDWELL ae 70y

D: 25th ult at res of ALFRED HEACOCK in Salem, MRS. ELIZABETH W. FARQUHAR in 92nd yr of age

D: 28th ult FRANKIE J. CALLAHAN S/O JOHN of Salem in 3d yr

D: Tues 14th ult of paralysis, MRS. ELIZABETH STEWART W/o DANIEL, formerly of Col Co, ae about 43y

D: 2nd inst in Carroll Co EDWARD RUTLEDGE ae 75y 6m

D: in city of Milwaukee Feb 27, little WILLIE McDONALD only child of D. & A.J., ae 2y 7m

We have received the VILLAGE ECHO published at Chicago & East Fairfield O by PROF F.A.SHOEMAKER It bears the same relation to a newspaper that an echo does to sound. It is devoted entirely to home interests & spelling schools.

Mon 13 Mar 1871 (Vol 4 no 49)(from WRHS microfilm)

The wife of JOHN SHEELY of Summitville, this co., ran away from her husband last week, taking with her a little daughterMrs S is 50y of age & reported "smart for her age."

JOHN W. MORRISON, prominent lawyer of this place, was severely injured in Pittsburgh by a train running over his arm...which had to be amputated. His father & brother hastened to his side. He is getting along as well as the circumstances will allow. (issue of 20 Mar states that HARVEY MORRISON reports his brother is getting along very well & will recover.)

Legal notice DAVID HECK & MARY M. HECK his wife, who reside in Porter Co Indiana, take notice that HIRAM HECK of Col Co filed petition against them & Thomas CROOK & others about sale of land in sec 12 Unity Tp.

M: 7th inst by REV WM BAXTER, WILLIAM H ADAMS & MISS ELIZABETH A LODGE both of this co

M: 2nd inst at Presby parsonage by RE DR DICKSON, THOS. BENTON BLAIR & MISS MARTHA ALICE McLAUGHLIN both of this co

M: 28th ult by REV J C EASTON, REV. A.J.YOUNG of Hookstown PA & MISS R. MARION STEWART of Wellsville

M: 6th ult by REV McCLELLAN, MR. C. EWING & MISS MID. ANDERSON both of Wellsville

D: in Salem on 6th inst ANDREW STANLEY in 33d yr

D: 5th inst near Winona, CATHARINE COPPOCK, relict of JOHN Ae 92y

D: 28th ult WILLIAM URQUHART in 45th yr

D: 2nd inst JESSIE MAY DEVERS ygst ch/o JOHN & SARAH ae 2y

D: 12th inst in New Lisbon infant child of G,.S. & LINNA MOORE.

D: in Salineville Nov 25, 1870, EDDIE MEREDITH S/O WILLIAM & NANNIE ae 1y 6m 9d

D: 7th inst ELIZABETH ARTER W/o SIMON of Salem Tp ae 65y

MRS. ELIZABETH MARSH died at the residence of her son in Bloomington Ill on Fri eve last week. She removed from Homeworth CCO to Bloomington last Summer.

MAN KILLED NEAR COLUMBIANA: we learn from the Columbiana REGISTER that on last Wed a brakeman on the coal train named ANDREW DAVIDSON was killed about 1/2 mi E of that place. He was engaged in setting a brake when the brakewheel came off throwing him between the cars, the greater portion of the train passing over his body. The body was horribly mangled, the right leg being cut nearly or quite off, the abdomen being so lacerated that the intestines protruded from the wounds. He had been on the road for about 14y in the capacity of brakeman. He leaves a wife, but no children, in Alliance where he resided.

Mon 20 Mar 1871 (Vol 4 no 50) (from WRHS microfilm)

M: 15th inst by REV WM BAXTER, JACOB H. CASTNER of Crestline & MISS ANNA R. ATTERHOLT of this place

M: same day by same, J.H.BIRDSON of Alliance & Miss M.J.-LUTHER of this co.

M: 9th inst by REV C.E.BUTLER, JOHN ANDREW & MISS MARY FURNISS of Wellsville

D: 1st inst of paralysis, ELIZABETH A. RAMSEY w/o WILLIAM of Hanover Tp ae 55y

D: in Wellsville Feb 9, PATRICK McQUADE ae about 60y

D: 12th ult near Col'ana MRS. ELIZABETH CALDWELL w/o JAMES ae 65y

D: in New Lisbon on 17th inst MARY E. JOHNSON d/o JAMES M. & NANCY ae 21y 2m

D: near New Albany Mah Co on 14th inst GEORGE POW ae 70y

The office of the NEW LISBON JOURNAL has removed to DORWART'S building opposite BRIGGS & BURNS dry good store just above the post office & nearly opposite our old quarters.

DR. WILLIAM BLECKER [BLECHER] an old & prominent citizen of Mansfield, died in that city last Wed. He was at one time a member of the Ohio Legis. & has filled several other offices of Honor. Several years ago he resided in New Lisbon.

DR. JAMES GRAHAM of Cincinnati & REV. JOHN B. GRAHAM of WVA were in town last week on account of their sick mother

ADAM DIEHL a former engineer on the C & P RR COMMITTED SUICIDE
in Cleveland last Wed.week, by shooting himself

Mon 27 Mar 1871 (Vol 4 no 51) (from WRHS microfilm)

M: 16th inst by REV J N SWAN, ANDREW A. DRUMMOND & MISS HANNA S. KETCHUM all of this co

M: 23d inst by WM.M.CRAWFORD ESQ., JOHN SHAFFER & MISS ZULICA M. UNDERWOOD, both of Middleton Tp

M: 21st inst in Col'ana by REV JJ JACKSON, JOHN STOUFFER & MISS MOLLIE HUFFMAN

M: Tues 14th inst by REV J H LEPER, S.McLEAN & MISS ADELINE VANFOSSEN both of Madison Tp

M: 23d inst by REV DR. DICKSON, NEW LISBON, DANIEL SHARPNACK & MISS ALVIRA WILSON both of Salem

D: 13th inst MAHLON HOLE of West Tp in 79th yr

D: in Carroll Co THOMAS JOSEPH HALPLY HASSLY S/O CHARLES HASSLY ae 11m 2 weeks

D: 11th inst in Hanover Tp GEORGE SHERKS ae 62y

D: in Hanover Tp JAMES MACKENTIRE ae 45y

D: in Franklin Twp on 25th inst, JAMES HAMILTON S/O JOHN & HANNAH ae 3y 4m

D: in Leetonia MINERVA LESHER D/O M & R ae 11m

D: in Col'ana 22nd inst HATTIE SHEETS W/O SAMUEL ae about 55y

D: in Phila Pa Mar 17th & buried in Salem Oh Mar 22nd, LOTTIE L. CASSELBERY W/O WILLIAM D., ae 46y

OBIT: on Mar 1, ELIZABETH A. w/O WILLIAM RAMSEY ESQ., in 52nd year of her age. Mrs. ELIZABETH RAMSEY was worthy of more than mere passing mention. She was the daughter of HUGH KING for many years a ruling Elder in the Presby Church of Bethesda, of which church Mrs R became a member when about 17y old. She was married to WILLIAM RAMSEY ESQ., OCT 1 1839 &
was THE MOTHER OF 11 CHILDREN , 8 sons & 3 daughters, 5 of the former & 2 of the latter survive her. Mrs R was characterized by a large measure of strong common sense which experience has pronounced to be of all forms of knowledge the most important & profitable. She was an earnest & consistent member of the church, appreciating the value & duty of personal godliness & realizing the obligations which devolved upon her, as a member of the church & a mother in Israel. Her children were to her objects of special prayer & while she aimed to bring them up in the nurture & admonition of the Lord, she took them with her to the throne of grace, praying with them & taught them early the way of God, by prayer & supplication. Mrs. R was a general favorite with her acquaintances. Her friendships were not hastily formed nor soon forgotten. Her attachments were strong & lasting.- In all the relations of wife, mother & friend, she had few superiors. "Her children arise up & call her blessed, her husband also, & he praiseth her. Give her of the fruit of her hands, let her own works praise her in the gates."

Country belle eloped: FRANK CULLER employed by JOHN CRONICK, living in Maho.Co., as a hired servant, became sweet on one of MR CRONICK'S 3 daughters, the youngest, MATTIE ae 17; a few evenings ago, they eloped to Enon Valley PA & were legally married; she is now working out by the week to earn money to buy furniture.

REV J F JONES, who has had pastoral charge of the ME Church here for last 3y has been appointed to Greensburgh PA. REV EDWARD BIRKIT has been assigned to New Lisbon

The wife of ANDREW DAVIDSON, the brakeman lately killed near Col'ana, upon hearing of the sad fate of her husband, became deranged & has not yet recovered her senses.

Mon 3 Apr 1871 (Vol 4 no 52) (from WRHS microfilm)

The letting for the building of a Meeting House at Church Hill advertised for Sat. last, has been postponed until Sat the 8th inst

M: 23d ult by Friends ceremony, MORRIS HEACOCK of Salem & SIDNEY S. LIVEZEY of Frankford PA

M: 23d ult at Smiths Ferry PA by JOHN McFALL ESQ., THOMAS KERR & MISS SARAH ELLEN LOYD both of Wellsville

M: 16th ult by REV JOHN PATTERSON, SAMUEL FISHER of Clarkson & MRS MATTIE BOWER of Washington PA

M: 28th int at the Union Hotel in New Lisbon by E.GARSIDE, ESQ., JOHN LIPPINCOTT & MISS MARY J. HENDRICKS all of this co

D: 29th ult at Farmersburg Ind., CORDY IRWIN D/O JAMES formerly of this co, ae 2y 23d

D: 1st inst SOLOMON SITLER SR., of Salem Tp ae 71y

D: 1st inst at the Infirmary, SUSANNAH BARNES, ae 80y

D: 2nd inst at the Infirmary, ELIZABETH SCROGGS ae 72y

GEORGE M. LEE, an attorney of Cincinnati, formerly of New Lisbon, died on Thurs last at the Longview Insane Asylum, near Cincinnati where he had been an inmate for the last 2 yrs

The family of REV. A.T.SCOTT the popular divine of the UP Church of this place was visited by a fine healthy girl last Sun morning. The Reverend gentleman is the happiest man in town

Legal Notice: JOHN PRICE, now residing in the state of California, is hereby notified that JENNETT PRICE, did on 1 Apr file petiton charging him with extreme cruelty, gross neglect of duty & willful abandonment of said Jennett & family for the past 4 yrs. Asks alimony, custody care & control of her children & the right to use, manage & dispose of her separate property without interference & for general relief.

BRAKEMAN KILLED: Last Tues morning at half past 1 o'clock, FRANK ALLMAN a brakeman on the Pittsburgh Ft Wayne & Chicago RR was killed on the road near Sewickley. The dec'd was the front brakeman on a freight train & was relieved by another brakeman about Osborns Station. He then started back over the train to get into the caboose but before arriving at the rear car he fell from the train. He was missed at Sewickley & a search being instituted his body was found upon the track fearfully mangled. It appears that no less than 3 trains passed over the remains. The body was fearfully mutilated, in fact, literally cut to pieces. Deceased had been on the road but for a couple of months and was about 19y of age. His residence was with his stepfather at Middletown, near East Fairfield, this county, to which place the remains were sent for interment.

Mon 10 Apr 1871 (Vol 5 no 1) (from WRHS microfilm)

M: 4th inst at res of officiating minister by REV.T.A.SCOTT, MATTHEW W. ADAMS of New Lisbon & MISS SARAH BROWN of Hanover.

M: 27th ult at Smith;s Ferry PA aby JOHN McFALL ESQ., JAMES POE & MISS MATTIE PRENTISS both of Wellsville

M: 13th ult by JOSIAH ROHRBAUGH,ESQ., ENOS ANGLEMIRE & MISS ABBY GALBRAITH all of this co

M: by same on same evening, SOLOMON LEAF of Columbiana & MISS MARIA LONGECKER of Leetonia

D: in Memphis Tenn on 25 Feb SAMUEL GRACY S/O WILLIAM & MARGARET of Franklin Tp CCO ae 25y 11m 19d

THOMAS LAUGHLIN, ESQ., an old & highly esteemed citizen of St.Clair Twp., died a few days ago.

One day last week LINDLAY MORRIS, deputy sheriff took ELLEN ROGAN, a girl 17 yrs of age, to Newburgh. No known cause for her insanity.

KING DORWART of Memphis Tenn. sent us Southern papers.

Mon 17 Apr 1871 (Vol 5 no2) (from WRHS microfilm)

M: on 6th inst in Alliance by REV.J.S.GRIMES, GEORGE W. JEN-KINS & MISS ALICE SHOEMAKER, both of CCO

M: 4th inst by REV HENRY B FRY, EDWIN BASSETT of Allegheny City PA & MISS SARAH R. GUY of Salem

M: 30th ult by REV J N SWAN, DANIEL M. SMITH & MISS KATE E. SMITH all of this co

M: 6th inst by SAMUEL POLLOCK,ESQ., PETER FREED & MRS. CLEM. TAYLOR, of New Garden

M: 6th inst in Salem by Rev H B FRY, ROBERT O. CAMPBELL & MISS ELIZA J. LLOYD of Mah Co

D: 5th inst in Wellsville, LULU DELL MORROW D/O W.C. & P.A.,ae 1y 4m

D: 31st ult near Washingtonville, MRS. MADALINE BUCHER ae 87y

D: in Salem 28th ult HARRIET CLARKE D/O JAMES ae 26y 3m 1d

D: 12th infant child of JOHN & REBECCA NEEDHAM of this place

D: 12th inst infant child of JOHN C. & SARAH FILSON of Centre Tp

TERRIBLE ACCIDENT: on Fri eve last CHARLIE EARHART, intelligent & sprightly little son of GEORGE EARHART of this place, ae about 5y, was so terribly burned that death ensued during the night. He had gone to an unoccupied pig pen on this father's premises to play. The pig pen contained a quantity of dry straw to which, it is supposed, he applied a match. In an instant he was completely enveloped in flames. His screams attracted the attention of his mother who ran to his assist-ance, but too late to be of any use, for before she could reach him all his clothing was consumed. The unfortunate youth died during the night.

FATAL ACCIDENT: about 4 o'clock on last Mon eve, PERRY DERODES, a young man about 16y, son of DAVID DERODES, Who resides about 6 mi nE of town, accidentally shot himself with a revolver, the ball entering his thigh & passing upward a considerable distance into his body. He lingered until about 12 o'clock Mon night, when death relieved him from his suffering.

Mon 24 Apr 1871 (Vol 5 no 3) (from WRHS microfilm)

M: 19th inst at the Presby parsonage by REV DICKSON, JOHN DOUGLASS & MISS MARTHA LOCH, both of New Lisbon

M: 6th inst by R H GARRIGUES,ESQ., GEORGE A. SIMPSON & MISS ELLA LEACH all of Salem

M: 20th ult at bride's res in Ravenna by REV H J WHITE, CHARLES ROWELL of Edinburgh, Portage Co & MRS MARGARET NEY formerly of this co

M: 20th inst at res of bride's mtoher in Butler Tp by REV W LYNCH, S.D.AMERMAN, MD, of Alliance & MISS SADIE A. COFFEE

D: 15thinst at res in Salem, ZADOK S. FRENCH ae 63y 3m 8d

D: 13th inst in Wellsville PETER AUSTIN in 63d yr

D: near Meages' Mill Mar 31, MARY McGARVEY D/O JOSEPH & JANE ae 15Y

D: 2nd inst LENA D. WELLINGTON D/O JASON & MARTHA of Franklin Tp ae 4y 7m

D: 1st inst PHEBE J. McFERRAN D/O ALBERT & NANCY ae 15y 6m

D: 20th inst ELIZABETH McQUOID of Wayne Tp ae 73y

D: in Dungannon 3d inst GEORGE SANOR of Gillford ae 83y

D: 3d inst JAMES McCORMiCK of Carroll Co ae 84y

SANFORD C. HILL, well known throughout W.Pa & Ohio died at his residence in East Liverpool on Mon last. Hill's almanacs are among our earliest recollections

JOHN SAXTON, of the Canton Repository & Republican & the oldest editor in the state died Mon morn 17th inst; was for more than half a century editory & pub of the Repository

MAN KILLED: JAMES BLACK was almost instantly killed at Wampum Furnace on Sat a week ago while driving a cart; it is supposed that he was kicked to death by the horse he was driving. He leaves a wife & large family of children

Mon 1 May 1871 (Vol 5 no 4) (from WRHS microfilm)

M: 5th ult by REV J M CARR, E.FINCH & MISS SALLIE CONNELL all of Wellsville

M: 19th ult by same, CAPTAIN A.S.SHEPHARD & MISS HENRIETTA RIDDLE all of Wellsville

M: 20th ult by REV J D BROWNLEE, JAMES McKENZIE of Saline-ville & MISS CHRISTINA SMITH of Wellsville

M: 19th ult by EDWARD PETTIT ESQ, ALBERT MONTGOMERY & MISS MARY WOLLAM all of this co

M: 25th ult by ELDER HENRY KURTZ, JOHN COPE & MISS LOUISA GUY all of this co

M: 8th ult in Rochester PA by REV W DARBY, DANIEL BRICKER & MISS MOLLIE MURPHY both of Salem

M: 11th ult by REV J M BRAY, JOSIAH W. BRUCE of Mah.Co. & MRS. MARY E. BANKS of this co

D: 24th ult JOSEPH OSBORN S/O JOSEPH & EMMA of Wellsville ae 11y 7m

D: 22nd ult ALICE REBECCA WORMAN D/O JOHN & MAGDALENA of Salem Tp ae 10m 19d

D: 21st ult of consumption, FOSTER WHINERY ae 15y

D: 5th ult of consumption, REBECCA HARLAN W/O EDWARD of Knox Tp ae 55y 5m

D: at the Infirmary on 18th ult, ALEX. BINGHAM ae 78y

D: at the Infirmary on 29th ult DANIEL KUNTZ ae 76y

D: in New Lisbon 25th ult EDDIE WALLACE VOGAN infant child of G.W. & M.J. ae 3 weeks

D: in New Lisbon on 1st inst LOUISE KENNEDY ae 46y

VENGEANCE JUSTIFIED: trial at Frederick Maryland of HARRY BLACK for the homicide of COL.W.W.McKAIG at Cumberland last Oct; our readers will feel some interest in the case, as Col McKAIG's father was at one time a citizen of New Lisbon. The deceased had seduced the sister of the accused, a beautiful & highly accomplished young lady & kept up his criminal association with her even after he had been M:, taking her from her home in Baltimore. The fact becoming known to young BLACK, he sought out the seducer & they quarreled, drew pistols & MCKAIG was killed. Jury found him "Not Guilty"...

FRANK GEISSE of Wellsville, a brakeman on the Atlantic & Great Western RR, was instantly killed a few days ago while in the discharge of his duties.

Mon 8 May 1871 (Vol 5 no 5) (from WRHS microfilm)

M: in New Lisbon on 3d inst by H.E.FROST ESQ., DAVID WHITACRE & MISS MARY BURNS all of New Lisbon

M: 27th ult by REV J N SWAN, ALEXANDER McINTOSH & MISS MARTHA H. FIFE, all of this co

M: 4th inst by REV D V HYDE, JOHN F. FOLEY & MISS ELIZABETH CARNS, both of this co

WILLIAM UNDERWOOD, whose age is now 84y, & who is the oldest man in Middleton Tp, split 120 rails in one day during the fore part of last week.

The Wellsville Union says that RICHARD HENDERSON, more generally known as SANTA ANNA, the HERMIT, died a few days ago at East Liverpool. Several days previous to his death he fell out of bed in a fit & lay for 2 days without anything to eat before he was found.

J.H.BENZE, of Beaver Pa aed 35y, who with his wife kept a millinery store, had in their employ a rather attractive young girl ae 18y named MERRIMAN with whom the said BENZE eloped last Sat night. At last account MISS MERRIMAN's big brother was in hot pursuit of the absconding parties.

Mon 15 May 1871 (Vol 5 no 6) (from WRHS microfilm)

M: 29th ult by REV WM BAXTER, ELDER C.E.VAN VOORHEES, of Knox Co & MISS ELLEN FARGESON of this co

M: 9th inst by same, CHAS. R. PROBERT of Cleveland & MISS SADIE J. TAYLOR, of Salem

M: 2nd inst by REV MAXWELL, JOS. MOFFIT & MISS J. DEGNAN all of Leetonia

D: 26th ult MRS. M.M.FRANCIS, W/O THOMAS of Salineville

D: 9th inst wife of WILLIAM TEEGARDEN of Salem Tp ae 68y

D: 12th inst ROSANNA STEWART W/O EMANUEL of Centre Tp ae 61y

BENJAMIN ALLEN, formerly of Columbiana, died recently in St.George, Kansas

On Sun morn last week, ENOS ELDRIDGE one of the oldest citizens of Salem, died after a long & painful illness caused by cancer in the face.

Mon 22 May 1871 (Vol 5 no 7) (from WRHS microfilm)

M: 2d inst EPHRAIM HARROLD & MISS MARY A. YARIAN both of Columbiana Oh

M: 11th inst by REV ROBT HAYS, A.J.McLAUGHLIN of Madison Tp & MISS MARTHA A. FIGLEY of Wayne Tp

M: 27th ult by FATHER EDWARD VATMAN, J.L.GRUBER & MISS MARY A. ROLLER all of this co

M: 18th inst by J.McVICKER ESQ., WALL CALVIN & MISS MARTHA ANN BOOHECKER of Leetonia. (also) We learn from the COLUMBIANA REGISTER that on evening of marriage of WALTER CALVIN & MISS BOOHECKER at Grafton, near Leetonia, some of the Grafton boys congregated to serenade the happy pair with tin horns & cow bells, & demanded $10 as a quietus, but Mr C couldn't see it in that light. He gave the boys $3 with which they were not satisfied & thereupon broke in his windows & doors & then dispersed. The next morning Mr C preferred charges against the boys before ESQUIRE ABBOTT, who upon examination, let the boys go "Scott free."" This ruling of the justice will have a very bad effect on the boys. (29 May 1871 issue)

D: 16th inst, MARY DICKEY of Elkrun Tp ae 49y 6m

D: 20th inst in New Lisbon, MRS. CATHERINE WHITACRE ae 82y

A fight occurred at the negro picnic above Wellsville on Thurs in which A.D. BATCHELOR was stabbed severly. We have no particulars.

We learn from Wellsville Union that dwelling house of WILLIAM O. FRAZER in Madison Tp was on Sat 13th inst entirely destroyed by fire from sparks from chimney. He was in Wellsville at the time; house was 2 story frame, valued at about $2500, had no insurance.

DEATH OF THOMAS STARR: This gentleman died very suddenly at his residence in this place Wed eve last about 6 o'clock. He was sitting on the door step, caressing his little granddaughter & remarking that he felt unwell stepped into the house & laid down upon a bed & expired in a few minutes. His death was attributed to an abcess of the lungs. He was a man of many admirable virtues. We believe we strain nothing when we say that MR STARR had not an enemy in the town. No man knew him without respecting him. His family in their bereavement has the hearty sympathies of those who appreciated his worth. He was about 70y of age. His remains were followed to the grave on Fri afternoon by numerous mourning relatives & a large concourse of sorrowing citizens. He lived & died a faithful zealous & consistent member of the United Presbyterian church.

Mon 29 May 1871 (Vol 5 no 8) (from WRHS microfilm)

M: 23d inst by REV H FRY, WILLIAM J. STREET & MISS MARION EMILY ASK, all of Salem

D: 21st inst THOMAS McLARAN & on 24th inst, WILLIAM MOORE, both old & much respected citizens of Wellsville

D: at his late residence in Columbiana, JOHNSON CAMPBELL ae 67y 8m

D: 22nd inst MARGARET LOUDEN, WIDOW OF JOHN, Dec'd of Wayne Tp ae 64y

DR. ENOCH C. CLOUD formerly of Columbiana & lately city editor of the OHIO STATESMAN, died in Columbus last Tues morn.

Mr. MARMIAN VALLANDIGHAM, son of the REV.DR.GEO.S.VALLANDIGHAM of this place, who has been confined to his room for several months past from an abcess in the back, was operated upon by DR. McCOOK of Pittsburgh a few days ago. The operation was delicate & difficult but was successfully performed.

The SALEM REPUBLICAN says the golden wedding of Mr. RICHARD GARDNER & WIFE in that place on last Wed was a very pleasant affair. Several valuable presents were made on the occasion—. In the company were 3 sons, 3 daughters, 42 grandchildren & 4 great grandchildren.

MR. CASS KELLY, a fireman on the Main line, C & P RR met with an accident at Hanover last Sat. & received injuries which resulted in his death.

DALLAS G. CRUM, of Unity Tp, the young man who was so severely injured recently by falling from the cars near Leetonia, has since died from the effects of his injuries.

KILLED BY A TRAIN: WILLIAM McINTOSH, of Wellsville, was knocked down & run over by a train near the railway shops of the C & P Road at Cleveland last Fri Mornin. Death must have been almost instantaneous for his body was badly crushed.- His remains were sent to Wellsville for interment, where the deceased lived & where his widow now resides. He was a man about 35y of age.

Mon 5 June 1871 (Vol 5 no 9) (from WRHS microfilm)

M: in Salineville on 10th ult by GEORGE W. BORING ESQ., DANIEL TOLSON & MISS DORLISHA A. WERE

M: 25th ult by REV CUNNINGHAM, FRANK P. DEEMER & MISS LAURA F. PEEPLES, all of Col'ana

M: 11th ult at East Birmingham PA by REV DAVID HESS, L.D.BRU-BAKER & MISS M.A.BUZZARD all of Col'ana

M: same day in Republic Ohio by REV ECKMAN, EMANUEL BRUBAKER of Columbiana & MISS REBECCA TROXEL of Republic O

D: 8th Apr, SUSAN CULBEY ae 26y

D: 24th ult in Franklin Tp, MAGDELENA WILLYARD ae 85y

D: 28th ult in Summitville, HANNAH WATSON W/O DAVID

D: 30th ult MRS. DAVID ASTRY of Fairf Tp ae 61y

D: 4th ult in New Alexander GEORGE HARRISON S/O THOMAS & M.E. ae 5y 8m 17d

D: on ---ult, MARY MILLER ae 5y 3d

D: 29th ult, JOHN GARDNER S/O THOMAS K. & LUCINDA of New Garden ae 2y 10m. (also) at New Garden on Mon last an interesting & sprightly little son of THOMAS K. GARDNER was scalded to death by falling into a bucket of hot water, during the absence of the family from the house.

Memorial day: list of graves decorated in Lisbon

Mon 12 June 1871 (Vol 5 no 10) (from WRHS microfilm)

M: in Providence May 23d by REV.J.ALDRICH, CHARLES H. PIERCE of Wellsville & MISS MARY A.M.HULL of Providence

M: 1st inst by REV M A MILLER, JAMES HAGMAN of E.Liv & MISS CATHARINE PATTERSON of Carrollton

M: 7th inst by REV DR DICKSON, J.T.BREWSTER & MISS SUSAN HARBAUGH, both of New Lisbon

M: 8th inst at the Presby church, Salem, by REV H B FRY, R.P.TRIMBLE of the firm of WRIGHT & TRIMBLE, & MISS FANNIE CRISSELL youngest daughter of CHAS CRISSELL all of Salem

M: 14th inst at Pyburn's Bluff, Tenn, by A.F.PAYNE,ESQ., R.K.BAIRD, formerly of Salem OH & MISS MARY PYBURN

D: at his res near Calcutta on 10th ult of softening of the brain, ROBERT KENNEY in his 79th yr

D: 28th ult in Dayton, NETTIE KURTZ W/O HENRY J. KURTZ Mrs. K formerly resided in Columbiana where she was highly esteemed by all who knew her.

D: 3d inst in Butler Tp, OLIVE STRATTON W/O WILLIAM ae 36y

D: 4th inst MARY A. LOWERY W/O ROBERT T. of Salem ae 61y

THE COLUMBIANA REGISTER says that REV.A.B.WAY, formerly a leading clergyman of Alliance, some time since became entirely too sociable with some of the good looking sisters & had to quit preaching. He was not inclined to work with his hands & to raise funds, he forged notes in amount of 2000 or 3000 dollars. Last week he heard he was about to be arrested, feigned illness, then took off for Utah or Canada...he leaves a wife & family behind.

GOLDEN WEDDING of ISAAC & ESTHER BOONE was celebrated last Tues eve at res in Salem. 105 guests present including 5 children & 8 grandchildren. The marriage certificate was presented, bearing the names of 32 witnesses, only 8 of whom are now living & only 1 of whom was present.

DR. WILLIAM H. LYON, a prominent physician of Salem, died very suddenly on morn of 4th inst. He had written a prescription for a lady & she had just stepped out of the office when he fell to the floor, dead.

ISAAC WILSON, colored cook at the Park House, Col'ana, had his watch stolen Tues night last week by a man who was traveling as a dead beat thru the country.

QUINN DAY, a colored barber of Salem, was arrested last Mon on charge of carrying concealed weapons. He had a hearing before a magistrate & in default of bail was placed in prison where he remained until Fri when he was released.

EDWIN STANTON BREWER, SON OF THE LATE MAJOR ANSON L. BREWER, passed the exam & admitted a Cadet at West point. Good for Edwin!

Mon 19 June 1871 (Vol 5 no 11) (from WRHS microfilm)

M: 13th inst in Col'ana by REV.R.CUNNINGHAM, ISADORE BISHOP & MISS HATTIE HUFFMAN all of that village

M: 13th inst by REV IN SWAN, JOHN KERR of Gavers & MISS ELLEN B. REID of West Point OH

D: 2d inst wife of EPHRAIM HUSTON ae 55y

D: 4th inst THOMAS LEEK of Liverpool

D: 8th inst in Wellsville of consumption, ANNA ANDREWS, ae 18y 5m 13d

D: 17th inst MRS. JOHN FORBIS of Wayne Tp ae 70y

D: 17th inst BELLE McCULLOUGH D/O JAMES of Wayne Tp ae 48y

D: 17th inst LOULA ELLA CALDWELL D/O FRANK of Elkrun Tp

DEATH OF HON. CLEMENT L. VALLANDIGHAM: Hon Clement L. Vall-andingham, accidentally shot himself last Fri night about 9 o'clock at a hotel in the town of Lebanon, this state. He was in Lebanon as one of the counsel of THOMAS McGEHAN. It appears that no one was present with Mr V when the accident occurred, but ex Lt.Gov McBURNEY who has been associated with him in the defense of McGehan. McBurney had expressed some doubts as to the theory that MYERS had shot himself, & V. picked up a pistol from the table, saying he would show him in a half second. Two pistols were on the table, one unloaded, & by mistake he took up the loaded one. He put it in his pocket & drew it with the muzzle next his body. Just as it was leaving his pocket it was discharged, the ball entering, it is said, near the same place Meyers was shot. He at once ejaculated "Oh murder," and said he had taken the wrong pistol. He lingered until Sat morn at 10 o'clock when he expired. Mr V was born in New Lisbon & was about 50y of age. Forgetting his faults, we can truly say that when the bells have tolled their farewell peals, when the pall, the hearse & the funeral procession have passed & gone, the good qualitites of the man will not be forgotten by the party with which he was so prominently identified, and that he will live in history as a remarkable man. (next week: the funeral: probably the largest ever held in Ohio; procession was about 2 miles in length; among pall bearers were HON. A.G.THURMAN, HON.S.S.COX, HON.GEO.E.PUGH, HON. GEO.McCOOK, HON JUDGE GILMORE, GEN.O.C.MAXWELL, JOHN HOWARD, SAMUEL CRAIGHEAD, ELIHU THOMPSON, D.K.BOYER, W.H.GILLESPIE & D.A.HOUK. Buried by the Masonic fraternity.)

Court proceedings:
MARY ANN WILSON vs THOMAS B. WILSON: in divorce, decree granted.
MARY B. JOHNSTON vs JOHN P. JOHNSTON: ditto
URIAH TEEGARDEN vs MATILDA TEEGARDEN: IN DIVORCE: decree granted for gross neglect of duty

Mon 26 June 1871 (Vol 5 no 12) (from WRHS microfilm)

SAMUEL BUCK died at Conneaut Ohio last week, ae 84. Over 60y ago he was jilted by the girl he loved & retired to a house he built for himself & furnished in good style where he dwelt alone until he died. Out of doors he wore the garb of man & permitted himself to be addressed as Mr. Buck. In the house he always wore his long hair parted in the middle & put on female attire, & in this guise would only appear as Miss Buck. Many fine dresses he had worn were found in his hermit house after he died.

MRS. PATTON, W/O JAMES, living about 5 mi NE of Leetonia, committed suicide on Mon morn by hanging herself in the barn. No cause is assigned for the rash act. Her brother committed suicide by taking poison some 9 yrs ago, & her sister made an attempt on her life by cutting her throat with a knife but she recovered.

MRS. HAUGH, an elderly & much respected lady of Wellsville, died last Thurs.

Post office established at SPRUCE VALE, with WILLIAM HUDLE-STON as postmaster.

MAN KILLED IN WELLSVILLE: Mon eve last JOHN GRONER, prop'r of the Missouri House, was killed by DANIEL SMITH. Smtih & ALBERT WELCH had a fight a short time previous & Groner & some other members of the household had succeeded in ejecting him. Smith went to a nearby barber shop & washed the blood off himself, came back & killed Groner., by wound on side of head. (over two columns of testimony by witnesses) (also) DAN SMITH, charged with the killing of JOHN GRONER, proprietor of the Missouri House in Wellsville, on eve of 19th inst was brought to town last Wed. Before taking him to jail, he was excorted to the barber shop of Mr. SHERROW to be shaved. Quite a crowd gathered to see the prisoner; he bore himself cooly & walked away with his escorts unconcernedly as if he was uninterested in the matter.

M: 20th inst by REV WM BAXTER, DAVID GASKILL & MISS ANNA R. GREEN, both of this co

M: 21st inst at Glasgow PA by ROBERT McKEAGE ESQ., B.E. SHEETS & MISS MAGGIE McLEAN of New Lisbon

D: MISS HATTIE CLARKE of Salem OH, died 28 Mar ae 26y (poem)

D: 8th inst in Salineville of consumption, MARY C. CLARK w/o JAS. in 41st yr

D: in Brush Creek Tp, Jeff Co Oh on 10th inst, WM. KERR in 71st yr of age

D: 17th inst ARENA MICHAELS infant D/O HARMON & MARY ae 5m 9d

D: 18th inst at late res near E.Fairfield, JOSEPH BELL ae 63y

The brick work of the ME Church at Salineville is completed & the roof is nearing completion.

Mon 3 July 1871 (Vol 5 no 13) (from WRHS microfilm)

M: 21st ult by Friends ceremony, LORENZO AIKEN of Col Co & MISS ESTHER STRATTON of Maho Co

M: 12th ult in Salem by SAMUEL HARDMAN ESQ., JAMES BEATTY & MISS SARAH E. ADAMS

M: 8th ult in Salem by same, ALEXANDER CAVIN & MISS MARY J JOHNSON

M: 27th ult in Leetonia by REV.S.BAECHLER, WILLIAM F. STOLL & MISS WILHELMINA ZIEGER

M: 12th ult at Glasgow OH by REV J N SWAN, FRANK FOSTER of New Salem OH & MISS ANNA C. SHAFFER of Glasgow

M: 13th ult by same, JOHN MARCH JR. & MISS CARRIE N. BOOTH all of this co

M: 20th ult by ELDER J.M.HORN, HENRY COX & MISS ELIZABETH TEMPLIN

M: 28th ult by H.E.FROST ESQ., JOHN LOCKARD & MISS MARY GROVES both of Leetonia

D: 19th ult at his late res in Salem, JOSIAH JOHNS in his 71st yr

D: 24th ult in Col'ana, SUSAN ETTA HUM D/O REUBEN & ELIZABETH ae 8y 7m 3d

D: at his res in Sandy Twp., Stark Co June 25, 1871, WILLIAM PROUSE ae 83y 1m 6d. MR. PROUSE was the 4th son of MICHAEL & ELIZABETH PROUSE & was born near Muddy Creek, Lancaster Co PA May 20th 1788. He first came to Ohio in 1809, lived near New Lisbon a short time & then went to Canton OH

A biography of HON CLEMENT L. VALLANDIGHAM will be prepared immediately. Such of his friends as may have letters or may be acquainted with facts or incidents illustrating his character will confer a favor by sending them as soon as possible to the REV. JAMES L. VALLANDIGHAM, Newark, Del. It is also in contemplation to erect a monument in teh City Park of Dayton. A letter from Dayton says Mrs. V is slowly recovering.

D: 22nd ult near Salem, DR.J.W.COFFEE, after a lingering illness, ae about 58y

DEATH OF ALICE S. MYERS: it is with profound regret that we announce the death of ALLIE, youngest daughter of WILLIAM & NANCY MYERS of this place, which occurred on 27th ult from scarlet fever. She was an unusually lovely, handsome & interesting little girl & a general favorite with all. She was ae 7y 10m 20d. (poem)

DEATH OF JAMES GRAHAM of New Garden: we are pained to announce the death of JAMES GRAHAM of New Garden which occurred at his residence in that place on Wed morn last. Mr G was not only a successful merchant, but in all his social relations he won the affectionate regard of all who knew him. He was a kindly genial & good man. The memory of his good deeds & unostentatious benevolence will live long in the minds of men. He had been in ill health for several weeks previous to his demise. [in next week, Resolutions of respect on death of JAMES GRAHAM, brother of Sandy Lodge F & AM at Hanover]

Mon 10 July 1871 (Vol 5 no 14) (from WRHS microfilm)

M: in Waseca on 17th ult by REV SAMUEL RICHARDSON, FRANK Y. HOFFSTOTT of St.Peter Minn & MISS KATIE RYAN of Waseca Minn

M: 4th inst by REV DR.DICKSON, JEFFERSON FREED & MISS ANN METZ both of this co

M: 28th ult at the Reformed parsonage by REV G M ALBRIGHT, JAMES WEIKERT & MISS ELLEN M. ROHRE both of Washingtonville

M: 6th inst by same, at same place, ALPHEUS FARMER & MISS SUSANNA BINGHAM both of this co

M: 25th ult by H.A.HUNTER ESQ., WILLIS CARTER & MISS JANE BROWN both of Salineville

D: 19th ult LUCINDA JANE HARRISON D/O THOMAS & MARY E. ae 17y 1d

D: 6th inst in Pittsburgh PA, ANGIE E. HARBAUGH W/O LEWIS D. in 29th yr of age.

NEW LISBON IN EARLY TIMES: we reprint the following amusing story from HARPER'S MAGAZINE of Feb 1866: (mentioned are: E.M.STANTON, A.W.LOOMIS, JUDGE SPAULDING , JUDGE COFFIN, C.L.VALLANDIGHAM, McCOOK FAMILY.)

Mon 17 July 1871 (Vol 5 no 15) (from WRHS microfilm)

M: 6th inst in Wheeling WVA by Rev FISHER, HOMER C. WELLS of Wellsville OH & MISS KATE BAGULY of Wheeling

M: 14 th ult inKyger OH by REV G W ISAMINGER, W.P.WELLS of Steubenville OH & MISS ELLA SAUNDERS of former place

M: 2nd inst by G.W.BORING, ESQ., JAMES CORDINGLEY & MISS MAGGIE STITT, all of Salineville

M: 13th inst by REV MAXWELL, W.C.DeJANE & MISS M J NICHOLS all of Leetonia

D: 1st inst MARY IDA CAMPBELL D/O WILLIAM & MARY of Middleton ae 12y

JACOB LAYMAN, who was so severely injured a few weeks ago by a fractious horse, at the Salem depot, was buried on Fri last.

D: on 9th inst MRS. KESIAH ALLISON of Fox Tp Carroll Co Oh ae 60y

DEATH OF JOSEPH E. VANCE: It is with sorrow that we announce the death of JOSEPH E. VANCE of this place, which sad event occurred on Sabbath the 16th inst at 11 o'clock am. He was one of our most prominent citizens. In deportment he was gentle yet dignified, mild & unassuming, though firm when firmness was necessary; his politeness was from the heart, not that mere conventional form which passes for politeness with the world, but a living principle springing from a bosom alive to every just & kind feeling, to every tender & generous emotion. He was a lawyer by profession, but of late years, owing to failing health, he had withdrawn from the bar. His age was 60y. The funeral will take place from the Presbyterian Church tomororrow (Tues) at 2 pm. (also, from24 July) "The funeral of JOSEPH E. VANCE on last Tues took place from the Presbyterian church & was largely attended. At 2 o'clock the body was conveyed to the church where religious services were conducted by REV. GEO.S.VALLANDIGHAM of the Episcopal Church & from thence was taken to the SPRINGER GRAVEYARD and consigned to his last resting place by members of the masonic order, of which the deceased was a member.-" (bur. Lisbon Cem)

SAD ACCIDENT: we learn from the WELLSVILLE LOCAL that on Sat last a youth named ROBERT GLENN, ae about 17y, son of GEORGE & CAROLINE GLENN, residing about 3 mi from the mouth of Yellow Creek, took down a gun for some purpose & playfully pointed it toward his little brother, just to scare him. The little fellow told him to desist & he turned the gun toward a pet chicken belonging to his little sister EMMA, ae 8, who began to plead with him not to hurt her pet. At this, he put a cap on the gun & not knowing there was a load in it, thought he would snap the cap at her to scare her. He pulled the trigger & in a moment the poor little girl's brains were scattered all over the ceiling. The agony of the entire family is intense, and the foolish boy is nearly beside himself. She was buried the next day.

Mon 24 July 1871 (Vol 5 no 16) (from WRHS microfilm)

NOTICE: WILLIAM SULLIVAN whose residence is unknown is notified that BRIDGETTA SULLIVAN filed on 19 July 1871 for divorce for extreme cruelty & gross neglect of duty. M.E. Taggart her atty.

M: 15th inst by REV. WM BAXTER, RICHARD CLIFTON & MISS ANN APPLEGATE both of this co

M: at Methodist parsonage, New Lisbon July 18 by REV E. BIRK-ETT, WILLIAM CAPPELL & MISS MAGGIE HOWARD both of this place

D: last Fri morn 14th inst after a brief illness of brain fever, ERILA THERESA ERICKSON youngest dau of FRANK & ALBER-TINA of Col'ana ae 2y 5m

D: 9th inst ALTON STREET infant s/o ZADOK H & NANNIE B of Salem

D: Tues 11th inst in Salem, MRS. HARRIET SHINN W/O WM. ae ---y

D: Tues morn 13th inst near Salem, JOHN NICKUM ae 56y

D: 17th inst of apoplexy, JACOB F. SCHILLING ae 72y

D: 17th inst at the Infirmary, FINDLEY McGREW ae 82y

D: 21st inst ELIZA JANE ATKINSON D/O JOHN & ANN of this place ae 6y

Memoriam: JOSEPH E. VANCE, from New Lisbon Lodge No 65 F & AM

DANIEL DOWNER of East Liverpool was run over by the cars on Tues morn & instantly killed. His head was entirely severed from the body. Downer was intoxicated at the time & was lying on the track enjoying a drunken sleep. (also) we learn from the Wellsville Union that a man named Downer was run over & his head cut off by the noon freight train Tues last Week.- When found he had a bottle of whisky in one pocket & a handy billy in the other.

Mon 31 July 1871 (Vol 5 no 17) (from WRHS microfilm)

M: 3d inst in Leetonia by DANIEL ABBOTT ESQ., FREDERICK ADAMS & MISS MAGGIE A. DEEMER both of New Lisbon

M: 27th inst by REV DR. DICKSON, CHARLES CUSHMAN of Hillsdale PA & MISS HELEN WINES of New Lisbon

D: 19th inst in Wellsville ALICE E. MONAGHAN D/o WILLIAM & MAGGIE A., ae 3y 8m 9d

D: 15th inst in Damascus, PHILIP POORMAN ae 69y

D: at Ypsilanti Mich on 9th inst of consumption, NATHAN H. BASSETT formerly of Salem

D: 28th inst CLARA STOCK D/o SAMUEL & ELIZABETH of Centre Tp ae 4y

D: 28th inst ELIZABETH FORBES of Wayne Tp ae 42y

JACOB R. SLACK, a prominent grocery merchant of Steubenville, committed suicide by hanging himself last Wed.

MISS MARY ORR (BURFORD) adopted daughter of S.W.ORR, ESQ., of this place is very ill & it is thought she cannot recover (also) ROBERT BURFORD of Cincinnati is in town due to dangerous illness of a sister.

RAPE IN WELLSVILLE: we learn from the Union that on Sat last TOM SWEARINGEN of Wellsville was arrested & taken before J.M.JENKINS on charge of rape made by a young girl named VAUGHN. He escaped & went to Cleveland, where he was again arrested. The Cleveland officers turned him over to Wellsville officers hancuffed, got as far as Yellow Creek, when he jumped off the train & made his escape to the Virginia side of the river, by being rowed over by some(one) in waiting with a skiff for that purpose.

Statistics in probate court: no of deaths,births,marriages etc

THOMAS MURRAY of St.Clair Tp was arrested & put in jail on charge of cruelty preferred by his wife; domestic matters have been going wrong for some time.

MISS BELLE HERRON, eldest dau of REV.S.T.HERRON, formerly of this place but now of Corning Iowa, is in town on a visit to friends.

Mon 7 Aug 1871 (Vol 5 no 18) (from WRHS microfilm)

On Mon last, about noon, JAMES MELLVANE, a laborer at the blast furnace in Leetonia, was helping to load a heavy iron pipe on a wagon, the ropes broke, letting the pipe fall on him, killing him instantly. He was a M: man, about 56y of age, and leaves a wife & 8 children.

M: 1st inst at the Reformed Parsonage by REV GM ALBRIGHT, JOHN EVANS & MISS MARY FINNEGAN both of Robbinsville, this co

D: 27tyh ult infant child of L.& V. SIMPSON of Salineville ae 2m

D: in East Fairfield 27th ult JAS.H.BROWN ae 64y 11m

D: 25th ult in Butler Tp, LEMUEL HARRIS S/o ROBERT ae 26y

D: 29th ult MARGARET BILGER d/o GEORGE ae 26y 3m 10d

D: 30th ult HENRY M. GIBSON S/o AG & M of Salem ae 9y

D: 26th ult SALOME METZGAR, 2nd dau of JOHN & M.E. of Col'ana

D: in Lawrence Kans of cholera infantum, LEE AMOS FROST S/o WILLIAM G & E.A. ae 1y 2m 27d

D: 5th inst CLEMENT B. FIGLEY S/o WILLIAM & BIANCA of New Lisbon ae 2y 9m 22d (also,p1: Death never occasions keener sorrow than when it robs a family circle of a bright & beautiful child, nor inflicts a sharper pain that when it suddenly bereaves a father & mother of a little one that has just reached an age when it s brightness & intelligence are most interesting. Mr & Mrs. WILLIAM FIGLEY have just been bereaved in the death of their little son CLEMENT. Bright, intellignet, beautiful , loving he naturally commanded a large share of his parents affeciton, & their sense of loss in his death is necessarily great. But pure on earth he is pure forever.

D: 3d inst PHOEBE ANN WELKER W/o JAMES of Elkrun Tp ae 37y

DR. C.B.TIFFANY formerly of Wellsville died near Port Homer, Jeff Co Oh last Thurs

ROBERT BURFORD of Cincinnati is in town due to dangerous illness of a sister.

Mon 14 Aug 1871 (Vol 5 no 19) (from WRHS microfilm)

SHOCKING ACCIDENT: telegram rec'd Sat by MAHLON BRIGGS of this place with sad intelligence of the death of his 2 sons, 2 grandchildren & a hired man near Eddyville, Iowa. The sons, WM.G. & GEORGE W., and MAHLON & ANNA, children of Wm & a hired man died this morning from the effects of damp in a coal bit. They had a coal mine on their land.

Dispatch announcing the death of MRS. VALLANDIGHAM, widow of HON.C.L.VALLANDIGHAM at Cumberland MD was rec'd by the friends at this place yesterday.

D: near Valley Post Office, on 25th ult, LEMUEL J. HARRIS ae 26y 8m 1d

EDWARD F. YOUNG, JR. a brakeman on the PF & CRR was arrested near Waterford last week on a charge of wife desertion: he had been spending several days in the woods in theat vicinity to escape the officers but on Fri night last he was taken & conveyed to Pittsburgh to answer the complaint. Whether he was lodge in jail or how the matter was disposed of we have not heard. He had been M: but a short time to a very respectable young lady & we have heard no cause for his so suddenly sundering the marriage tie without the interference of a divorce court. Col.Register.

Accident: A daughter of ANDREW SIMON, res. 3 mi N of town met with a severe accident on last Wed. She was out buggy riding when the horse stumbled & fell, throwing her from the buggy.- In the fall, Miss Simon received several bruises, besides a broken shoulder blade. Dr. Springer was called & set the broken bone, & we are able to announce that the patient is getting along finely.

Mon 21 Aug 1871 (Vol 5 no 20) (from WRHS microfilm)

M: 10th inst by REV W LYNCH, JESSE W. WAY & MISS MARIETTA CARNS, all of Salem

D: Th Aug 10th in Wellsville, MRS. MARGERY McBANE ae 67y

D: 13th inst at res in Wellsville, MRS. MARGERY SMITH ae 49y

D: 6th inst MISS ANNA BRUCE D/o REV. WM. & M.A. of Wellsville

D: 15th inst WILLIE G. NACE S/o GEO.S. of this place ae 11y

D: 17th inst ANDREW JOHNSTON S/o ROBERT & JANE of this place ae 1y 6m

D: 13th inst MARTHA ESTERLY D/o JACOB B. & MELINDA of Columbiana ae 10y 7m

D: 9th inst in Salem CHARLES SHEEN ae 32y

THOMAS FREDERICK of Vineland formerly of New Lisbon has been spending several days here with rels & friends

MAHLON BRIGGS furnishes us with further particulars regarding the death of his 2 sons, 2 grandchildren & a hired man near Eddyville, Iowa. The coal pit was used during the summer as a watering place for stock, the water being drawn up by horse power in the half of a barrel used for a bucket. On day of accident, 2 sons of WM.G.BRIGGS, MAHLON ae about 20y & CHARLEY, ae about 14, and a hired boy went to draw water from the pit which is about 20 feet deep. The bucket wouldn't draw, Charley went down & fainted away. Mahlon called to his father at the house & then went down for his brother; Charley got out safely, and the father went down, and became powerless; the boy went for George W. Briggs & a hired man, but while absent, Miss Briggs came to the pit & went down. George Briggs went down with the hired man & met the same sad fate. Five persons lost their lives, only one got out alive.

HENRY C. DAY of Ravenna was found dead in the water closet of the St.Charles Hotel at Toledo. The Blade says the cause in unknown but it is suspected that he may have been his own slayer by taking poison.

The new ME Church of Salineville will be ready Dec 1.

Mon 28 Aug 1871 (Vol 5 no 21) (from WRHS microfilm)

Letter reprinted from Clement L VALLANDIGHAM to his sister MARGARET on the death of her late husband, JOHN ROBERTSON DATED 12 DEC 1869, to MRS M.E. ROBERTSON, New Lisbon P1

SAMUEL PETTIT an aged & respected citizen of this township died at his res 1 mi N of town yesterday morn. He was ae 79y

SIMON SPIKER & HIS SON QUINCY will open a new business selling agreicultural implements.

M: 15th inst by REV J N SWAN, ANDREW B. BUNTING & MISS MARY McGILVARY both of Wellsville

M: 21st inst at res of JOSEPH mCGARVEY in Wayne Tp by REV WRIGHT, SAMUEL WARREN & MISS ROSAAN McGARVEY all of co

M: 17th inst by REV R CUNNINGHAM, GEORGE H. DONGES & MISS LOUISA NOGAL all of Col'ana

D: Tues 22nd inst MRS. MARY MARCH of Madison Tp ae 88y

D: in Canton of the ult, of cholera infantum, EVA J. ARTER D/o GEORGE & HARRIET ae 4m 19d

EMMA HERRON of Leetonia who has been an inmate of the Newburg lunatic asylum for 6y was pronounced incurable & was last week sent to the county infirmary.

On Sunday last week the wife of GEO. WILLI of Salem fell dead whilst preparing dinner. Her husband had stepped out about 20 min before & on return found her a corpse.

OLIVER TORRENCE for many years a well known conductor on the C & P Panhandle & Ft.Wayne road,died at his res in Rochester Pa on 12th inst of inflammatory rheumatism. The deceased was a brother of Milo Torrence of this place.

Sunday was almost as quiet as the day, nearly a century ago, when "OLD ABE LODGE" from Loudon Co VA first paddled his canoe up the placid waters of the Little Beaver & tied up near where the Market St bridge crosses the stream, to make his camp for the night.

Our young friend JAMES WARD has committed matrimony with ELLA HENDERSON: congrats.

RELCIT: MRS. ELIZABETH HEPHNER of this place presented us with a copy of the OHIO PATRIOT pubished by her father WILLIAM D. LEPPER dated 28 Aug 1812, 59 yrs ago today.

Mon 4 Sep 1871 (Vol 5 no 22) (from WRHS microfilm)

M: 20th ult in E.Liv by FATHER MAGUIRE, WILLIAM DUNN & MISS BERTHA BENNETT

M: on 20th ult in E Liv by REV JOHN HODGKINSON, N.T.ASHBAUGH & MISS LYDIA BOUGHTON

M: 15th ult by REV ROBT HAYS, WILLIAM HUNTER of Wash.Tp. CCO & MRS MARTHA CRAWFORD of Irondale OH

M: 23d ult by SAMUEL HARDMAN ESQ, BENJAMIN S. ELTON & MISS ELIZA ANN McDONALD

M: in Montpelier VT 9th inst by REV MR LORD, SPENCER BORDEN of this city & MISS EFFIE A. BROOKS, D/o THE LATE J.J.BROOKS of Salem OH

D: in E.Liv Aug 21st infant dau of THOMAS & LEVINA ARBUCKLE ae 11m

D: 24th ult ESTHER KERNS of Hanover ae 86y

D: in New Lisbon on 2nd inst, MARY ORR (BURFORD), adopted daughter of S.W.ORR ae 28y

DR. D.B.HART for several years a practicing physician at West Point, this co, removed to Akron to embark in the drug business.

The barn of SIMEON SUMMERS, living 1 mi W of Salem was struck by lightning & took fire last Mon night.

PIONEER MEETING: FISHER A. BLOCKSOM chm & C.M.ATEN Secy, to ascertain how many would attend the Pioneer Celebration & free dinner given by the people of Salem on Sep 7 at 11 am. About a dozen persons agreed to attend: FISHER A. BLOCKSOM, C.M.ATEN, ANDREW ROACH, WILLIAM DORWART, MATHIAS NACE, HENRY TRUNCIK, H.H.GREGG, JOHN RAMSEY, ROBERT WHITACRE, SIMON SPIKER, BELUS LOUNSBERRY, ANDREW C. RAMSEY.. They exhibited early copies of the OHIO PATRIOT which had been turned in, dated 27 Mar 1819; 23 Dec 1826 and 19 May 1827. JACOB HEATON drew up invitation to dinner, & announced that the following would be asked to deliver addresses suitable to the occasion: GEN. JACOB ROLLER, FISHER A. BLOCKSOM, BENJ. BLACKBURN, GEO.BURNS, SR., MORRIS MILLER, BENJ. HAWLEY, JOHN STANLEY.

Mon 11 Sep 1871 (Vol 5 no 23) (from WRHS microfilm)

M: 6th inst at Indianapolis, by REV C P MARTINVALE, JOHN HALL of New Lisbon & MISS V.A.TEDROWE of Indianapolis.

M: 31st ult by JAMES DOYL ESQ, JOHN H. FUHR & HENRIETTA HIESTAN D/o JOHN of Knox Tp CCO

M: 7th inst at house of bride's father by REV DR DICKSON Of New Lisbon, JOHN PATTERSON & MISS HARRIET A. ENDLY both of co

D: 5th inst in Salem Tp infant child of A.SNIDER ae 2m

D: 3d inst in Salem of cholera infantum, LEONA E. HOLE d/o JACOB & AMELIA E. ae 6m 12d

D: in Salem 30th, REV. JOHN B COX ae 52y

COL.CO.PIONEER ASSN.: dinner on 7th inst at Salem gotten up by JNO.DELLENBAUGH of the American House. JOHN LARWELL of Wayne Co, now in 80th yr, came from Wooster; he settled in CCO in 1802 & learned trade of a papermaker at mill on Little Beaver; FISHER A. BLOCKSOM came to New Lisbon in 1805. ZADOK STREET instroduced a resolution denouncing the recent proceedings on the sale & transfer of the FRIENDS GRAVE YARD at Salem for business purposes & the digging up the bones of the early Pioneers of the town & carting their remains around etc.

ROBERT HENDERSON, SON OF PETER HENDERSON of this township, died of lockjaw Fri eve. ae 14y 5m. Unusually bright & intelligent lad of much promise.

CHRIST DORWART who has been absent in the west for over a year, returned to town last week, looking as robust & healthy as ever.

The little son of MR.KINSEY of East Liverpool was killed on Fri afternoon last by the caving in of a sand bank.

The United Brethren Church near Simpkins School House, Middleton Tp, will be dedicated Sun the 24th inst

Mon 18 Sep 1871 (Vol 5 no 24) (from WRHS microfilm)

M: at ME parsonage New Lisbon by REV E BIRKETT on 7th inst, JESSE WILSON & MISS SUSAN HISCOCK both of co

M: by REV A I YOUNG, ANDREW BLYTHE of E.Liv. & MISS AMANDA LEIPER of Hookstown PA

M: 29th ult G.W.HAUN of E.Liv & MISS NANNIE E. CURFMAN of New Cumberland WVA

M: 9th inst at Mt.Jackson PA by REV McCLELLAN, JACKSON COTTEN & MRS. MARY BOONE, both of Salem

M: 7th inst by REV S M HICKMAN, WILLIS CADWALLADER of Salem & MISS MINNIE HANNA of Pittsburgh PA

M: 12th inst at the Presby parsonage by REV DR DICKSON, RUFUS CALDWELL & MISS M.A.BROWN both of co

D: in St.Louis MO on 2nd inst RACHEL CUNNINGHAM formerly of E.Fairfield CCO ae 78y

D: on ---inst at Smiths Ferry PA, ANN ORMES W/o JOHN & dau of ENOCH HARPER of this township (see death of ENOCH HARPER, colored, in 2 Oct issue)

MRS SARAH THOMAS an elderly lady residing 2 mi W of town died very suddenly last Mon.

Partition notice: SUSAN M. FARMER W/o ISAAC P.; JESSIE N. JONES W/o JOHN R. JONES of Col.Co.Oh, VIRGINIA LEPPER W/o CHARLES W. of Cuya.Co Oh; ANN G. GILMAN W/o JOHN M. and HETTY CORNWELL, widow of JOHN CORNWELL dec'd, of city of St.Paul Minn, and MARY CORNWELL, widow of PETER CORNWELL dec'd....petition filed by DAVID W. CORNWELL demanding partition of lot 183 on Market St in New Lisbon, & for assignment of dower to MARY CORNWELL.

Mon 25 Sep 1871 (Vol 5 no 25) (from WRHS microfilm)

M: at res of bride's parents Thur 7 Sep by REV S M HICKMAN, WILLIS CADWALLADER of Salem & Miss MINNIE HANNAH of Pittsburgh PA

M: 6th inst M. CALLAHAN & MRS ANNIE CALLAHAN both of Salem

M: at res of bride's father in Butler Tp 14 Sep by SAMUEL WILLIAMS JP , SAMUEL COPPOCK & MISS CELESTA FULTZ

M:. 10th inst by SAMUEL HARDMAN JP, JEREMIAH WILCOX & MRS ELIZA J. WISNER all of Salem

M: 20th inst at res of CATHARINE BRINKER by REV G M AL-BRIGHT, JOHN SHIVE & MISS KATE FISHER both of co

M: 5th inst by REV WM BAXTER, SAMUEL J. WHITE & MISS LAURA VATTLES, both of Niles, Trumbull Co

M: 12th inst at the Presby Pars by REV.DICKSON, RUFUS CALDWELL & MISS M.A.BROWN both of co

M: 20th inst by REV DICKSON, WILLIAM E. CLUNK & MISS J. WILSON both of New Lisbon

D: 23d Sept in New Lisbon, JACOB SHAWKE ae 83y 11m 23d
(also) IN MEMORIAM: JACOB SHAWKE was born near Lebanon PA Sept 30, 1788, and died in New Lisbon Sept 26,1871 ae 83y 11m 23d. He came to Ohio in 1804 & settled in New Lisbon in fall of 1806. The son of JACOB SHAWKE, an officer in the REVOLU-TIONARY WAR, himself a soldier of the War of 1812. He gallantly volunteered as a private in the late civil war but could not be mustered into service on account of his advanced age, much to his regret. A member of no particular church, he led a life consistent with Christ's teachings. He died surrounded by all his family, except one daughter who preceeded him. The venerable partner of his joys & sorrows, now in greatly impaired health, still survives him.

New UP Church of Wellsville is progressing; roofers are putting on the slate

ALBERT MORRIS, formerly a resident of this place, now of Osage Mission, Kans, has been raising some tall vegetables.

Mon 2 Oct 1871 (Vol 5 no 26) (from WRHS microfilm)

M: 21st ult by REV J M BRAY, WILLIAM OLDHAM & MISS TILLIE BALL both of Salem

M: 20th ult in Cleveland by DR.SHEPHARD, T.J.FORNER & MISS OMA MAYLONE both of Wellsville

M: 14th ult by REV ROBERT HAYS, ISAAC FALLOON & MISS ELLEN CUAIL (sic: QUAIL) both of Salineville

M: 20th ult by same, ALEX McGREGGOR & MISS MARY A. ROSE both of Wellsville

M: 24th ult in Col'ana by REV S BAECHLER, G.S.SNYDER & MRS. MARY HARMAN

M: at res of bride's parents in St.Clair Tp on 28th ult by REV WM DALZELL, G.F.RAUCH & MISS LOUISA J. WELCH

D: 17th ult in Hudson, Bates Co Missouri, OLIVE JESSIE STAPLETON only dau of WILLIAM & M.E. ae 3y 2m

D: 25th ult in Butler Tp, child of JOHN DILWORTH ae 2y 8m

D: 21st ult SARAH JANE HOLLABAUGH ae 5m 13d

EASY ROBERTS, a pious & wealthy citizen of Salineville, arrested on charge of dealing in counterfeit money on 23d ult by secret service; he is Supt. of one of the extensive coal mines operated by the Cleveland Iron Co. Bound over to US District Court in $10,000 bond.

DEATH OF ENOCH HARPER: The death of this old & respected <u>colored</u> citizen occurred last Fri morning. Mr. HARPER in early life was a slave in Louden Co VA. Obtaining his freedom, he removed to this place about the year -----, and continued to reside here up to the time of his death, where he by industry & economy secured a competence of this world's goods & reared a large & respectable family. At the time of his death MR HARPER was aged about 63y. He bore a character for uprightness & integrity that commended him to all that knew him. His remains were followed to the grave by a large number of people (see death of daughter in Sept 18th issue)

TERRIBLE RAILROAD ACCIDENT: on Mon night about 10 o'clock, JOHN STAFFORD, an Englishman employed in the coal mines at Robbins station on the Niles & New Lisbon RR, while lying on the track near Franklin Square was run over by a down extra train & instantly killed. His 2 legs were cut off & his body otherwise horribly mangled. He had been to Leetonia to procure a draft to send for his wife in England. Before starting for Leetonia, he was censured by the bank boss for his intemperate habits, when he replied "he hoped God would strike him dead if he tasted liquor for a year." While at Leetonia he drank to intoxication, started to return by walking on the track & on reaching the spot where he met his death, not knowing what he was doing, lay down on the track & hence the result. No blame is attached to the engineer.

WEDDING of CLARENCE F. SMALL of the firm of S.SMALL & SONS and MISS KATE E. LODGE, eldest dau of ABEL LODGE of the banking firm of ZEPERNICK & LODGE was solemnized Wed eve 27th ult at res of bride's parents on East Walnut St by REV WM BAXTER of the Disciple Church. For weeks previous, little else was talked of in fashionable circles but the upcoming event. Now on wedding tour of all Eastern cities & Niagara Falls.

MRS. JANE WALKER of Allegheny PA on Thurs morn last while visiting relatives at Calcutta was stricken down & died in less than 2 hours.

<u>Mon 9 Oct 1871</u> (Vol 5 no 27) (from WRHS microfilm)

REV. JAMES HENDERSON, formerly pastor of the ME Church in Wellsville, died a few days ago at Zanesville, of congestion of the lungs.

MRS. MARY HELMAN, widow of the late WILLIAM HELMAN dec'd died suddenly at her residence on Market St last Tues morn. She was ae 82y.

SCALDED TO DEATH: at Leetonia last Wed about 1 o'clock, a little boy 3 yr old, son of MR. APLET while walking backwards in the house, fell into a wash boiler full of hot water & was so badly scalded that he died about 9 o'clock the same eve.

D: Aug 27 near New Lisbon, SAMUEL PETTIT in his 80th yr

D: 7th inst wife of FRANK DALES of Centre Tp ae 37y

DEATH OF SAMUEL CROOK: Sameul Crook died at his residence in Fairf.Tp Thur 5th inst ae about 76y. His life was one of even character and steady industry. He was ever the good & worthy citizen & esteemed by all who knew him. Buried Fri.

M: 22nd ult by REV S A HUGHES, J.O.JONES & <u>MRS</u> E. McLERAN both of Salem

M: in Liscombtown on 6th ult WARRICK MARTIN of Liscombtown (formerly of Wellsville OH) & MISS MARY CUTTS of Bureau Co Illinois

M: 12th ult by REV J M CARR, LEWIS WALKER & MISS REBECCA LAWRENCE

M: 24th ult by JETHRO MANLEY, WILLIAM MASSEY & MISS MARY HILL both of E.Liv.

M: 19th ult by REV J R DUNDAS, JAMES N. McCORMICK & MISS LINNIE J. VANFOSSEN all of Hanover O

M: 20th ult by same, ISRAEL BEBOUT of Kansas & MISS SARAH McLONEY of Hanover O

M: 21st ult by same, DANIEL COLESTOCK of Allegheny City & MISS MARY E. <u>COULAN</u> of Hanover

M: 28th ult in Middleton Tp by WM M CRAWFORD ESQ., JOHN C. THEAKSTAN & MISS ELIZABETH HEWITT

M: 28th ult by REV H H8ILBISH, ISAIAH METZ & MISS SARAH HARMEN all of this co

M: 28th ult in Leetonia by REV S BAECHLER, J.M.MYERS of Canfield & MISS ROSANNA SUMMERS of Leetnia

M: 3d inst by REV A CRAMER, WM. DONBART & MISS KATE BERGEN-WALT all of Col'ana

FAMILY REUNION: children & grandchildren of DR. AARON CONNELL met at his res in Summitville on 27th ult, having been separated for more than 20 yrs. The no. present was 34, being father & mother, 6 sons, 2 daus, 1 son in law, 5 daus in law, & 18 grandchildren.The next morning they all took the cars for Wellsville where they spent a day & night with the oldest son, ALFRED. DR. CONNELL can boast of what few men can, namely that he furnished 7 sons for the war of the Great Rebellion, of whom 2 were killed.

Premium list for the fair.; CONTINUES NEXT WEEK

<u>Mon 16 Oct 1871</u> (Vol 5 no 28) (from WRHS microfilm)

Front Page: the Chicago Fire

M: 4th inst at res of bride's father by REV P J McGUIRE, WILLIAM BECK of Mansfield OH & MISS MAGGIE J. MARTIN of Wellsville. We congratulate our friends Bill & Maggie.

M: 5th inst at the Cowan House, by REV E BIRKETT, CHARLES SMITH & MISS ORSINA BAIRD both of Salineville

M: 5th inst at res of bride's father in Salem, MR. MELL H. HUDSON of Kansas City MO & MISS MARY E. THOMAS

M: 13th inst in Salem by ---, WASHINGTON MOSSMAN of Jamestown PA & MISS JENNIE MORRISON of Salem

DAVID HOSTETTER died at the residence of his Son HIRAM near Minerva last Tues, ae 85y. Deceased located in that neighborhood over 50 yrs ago & has resided there ever since. He was a <u>halfbrother</u> of WILLIAM HOSTETTER of this place.

NEWSPAPER: D.G.STEEN & W.H.WATSON have issued a prospectus for a new paper at Leetonia to be called the LEETONIA GAZETTE. It will commence when subscriptions reach 500.

The New ME Church at Salineville will be dedicated on 29th inst. Distinguished clergymen from a distance will be present to assist in the ceremonies.

<u>Mon 23 Oct 1871</u> (Vol 5 no 29) (from WRHS microfilm)

M: 17th inst at res of bride's father by REV R CUNNINGHAM, NOAH E. NOLD, one of the proprs of the COLUMBIANA REGISTER & MISS LIZZIE KRIDLER, both of Col'ana

M: 5th ult by ESQ. WATT, ROBERT LAWRENCE & MISS MARTHA SMITH all of E.Palestine

M: 10th inst by REV. R. CUNNINGHAM, ISRAEL DEEMER & MISS HANNAH ZEIGLER both of Col'ana

M: 6th inst by REV JAMES P. IRWIN, B. RENKENBERGER of Mah.Co.-& MISS ELMIRA CLOSE of this co

M: 11th inst by REV JOSEPH HOLLINGSHEAD, GEORGE W. MARKS & MISS LEE ANN ALLISON both of East Livberpool

M: 25th ult by REV S. COON, W.T. COPE & MISS SALLIE ROBBINS both of Salineville

M: 3d inst by JOSEPH CREW ESQ, WILLIAM HARDINGER & MISS LAVINA GREEN all of Butler Tp CCO

M: 12th inst by REV DUNDAS, T.J.HENSCHILLWOOD of Alliance & MISS H E KING of Homeworth this co

M: 17th inst at res of bride's parents near New Lisbon by REV T A SCOTT, THOMAS A. WALTER & MISS MARY L. SWITZER

D: 12th inst, ORSINA SMITH W/o CHARLES J. of Salineville, ae about 20y. Six yrs ago the writer knew Orsina well & dearly.-On the morning of the 5th inst. she was a bride, living in the affections of a fond husband & the dark side of life began to assume a brighter hue when Death suddenly clasped her in his icy embrace. (signed R E C, New Lisbon)

D: Thurs eve 19th Oct at his res in Centre Tp, BENJAMIN LODGE in 77th yr. Mr. LODGE was one of our substantial old pioneers, honest & upright in his dealings, & he prospered accordingly. He came to ColCo when it was almost a wilderness & helped to clear out the forest & improve the country & now leaves it covered with a bountiful supply of Nature's productions. In the fall of 1808, 63 yrs ago, Mr. Lodge's father came from Loudon Co VA near what is now called Wheatland & bought some land & settled in the NE corner of Salem Tp, his son Benjamin, the subject of this obit, being then in his 14th yr. The Pioneers, the men who settled in the dense forests & helped to clear out the country, will soon have passed away, leaving the fruits of their toil & hardships to be enjoyed by those who survive them & we should all fee grateful to those men of iron constitutions who suffered & toiled for our benefit in the early settlement of the country.

D: 22nd ult MISS NANCY McCONNER of East Fairfield ae 30y

D: 16th inst MARTHA HANNAH DAWES W/o BENJAMIN F. of Salem Tp ae 32y

DANIEL J. SMITH, confined in jail for the murder of WILLIAM GRONER proprietor of the Missouri House in Wellsville last spring, has been indicted by the grand jury for murder in the 2nd degree. The trial will not come off this court.

With the present issue of the JOURNAL our editorial management terminates. It is a conceded fact that no paper in Eastern Ohio exceeds the circulation of the JOURNAL. JAMES K. FREW, the proprietor, who has considerable newspaper experience, will assume the editorial control in the next issue. GEORGE B. CORBETT

The bell for the new courthouse arrived on Tues. It weighs something over 2200 pounds & cost over $900. It contains in moulded letters the following inscription:

Cast By
A.FULTON'S SONS & CO.
Pittsburgh, Pa.
———
County Commissioners
SAMUEL BURGER
ANDREW ARMSTRONG
JOSHUA LEE

REV.J.L.VALLANDINGHAM, brother of the late CLEMENT L. is preparing a book of 500 pages which will contain full details of the personal, professional & political career of the deceased statesman. The book will have an engraving of his birthplace in New Lisbon and of his residence in Dayton. It will be ready for the press some time in November.

Election of JP in Salem Tp on 10th resulted in election of JESSE HAWLEY & A.A.THOMAS.

Mon 30 Oct 1871 (Vol 5 no 30) (from WRHS microfilm)

M: Mon 23d inst by FATHER McGUIRE at Summitville, JAMES HANLY & MISS MARGARET J. FICKESS both of Liverpool

M: 25th inst at res of E.BRUBAKER by Rev H.H.HILBISH, REV A P JONES of Huron Co Oh & MRS ELIZABETH REINHART of Col'ana

M: 26th inst by H.E.FROST ESQ, C.V.FARR & MISS W.J.LOW of E.Fairfield

M: at Lima Oh by REV KELLEY, assisted by REV JOHNSTON at the res of bride's father, GEN.ARMSTRONG of Allen Co Oh, WM. RAMSEY ESQ of Col Co & MRS. E.E. McKIBBEN of the former place

COURT PROCEEDINGS:
SAMANTHA BLACK vs WILLIAM H. BLACK: divorce granted, alimony & custody of child
FANNY SANOR vs JOHN SANOR, trial to court, decree for $500 alimony
EDWARD BOYLE vs SARAH BOYLE: dismissed at pltf costs
MATILDA RICHEY vs GEORGE RICHEY: ditto
MARY ANN TAYLOR vs BUCYRUS TAYLOR, continued
JEREMIAH SEVIHART vs NANCY: DIVORCE CASE, dismissed (SWIHART?)
MARY L. BARTH vs SAMUEL T. BARTH: continued
PHEBE B. PAXON vs JOHN W. DICKINSON, BASTARDY; trial to jury, ordered to pay $500 to plaintiff
DAVID CORNWELL vs SUSAN M. FARMER etal, dismissed at pltf costs

D: Fri 20th inst at res of her son in law F.GORE, in Wellsville of lung fever, MRS. MARTHA MONTGOMERY ae 61y 5m

D: 18th inst at his res after a lingering illness, DAVID McCALLA ae about 62y

Leetonia is to have 2 newspapers: The TIMES & GAZETTE This brings to 11 the number in county

Mon 6 Nov 1871 (Vol 5 no 31) (from WRHS microfilm)

M: at ME Parsonage Oct 31 by REV E BIRKETT, THOMAS E. LUCAS & MISS CATHARINE MARSDEN all of New Lisbon

D: 13th inst in Beaver PA, DAVID IKIRT, formerly of Col Co, ae 67y

FORMER CITIZEN OF COLUMBIANA CO MURDERED IN KANSAS: Intelligence has been recd of the murder at Cotton Wood Falls, Kans on 23d ult of JAMES FISHER, formerly of Elkrun Tp, this co. From what we can learn, it appears that MR FISHER was confined to his bed with fever & the individual who committed the deed was watching with him & knowing that FISHER was in possession of $400, he attacked the defenseless man while in bed, secured the money & left him for dead. In the morning he was visited by several neighbors when he revived sufficiently to relate what had occurred, & immediately expired. The neighborhood was aroused, pursuit instanity instituted & in a short time the villain was apprehended & is now in jail.

COURT PROCEEDINGS:
ELIZABETH SHAW vs JAMES SHAW, divorce granted & custody of youngest child given to petitioner

Mon 13 Nov 1871 (Vol 5 no 32) (from WRHS microfilm)

CHARLES BRUFF a son of COLONEL JOSEPH BRUFF of Damascus, a brakeman on the P FtW & C RR was run over on Wed morning by the cars at Pittsburgh & rec'd injuries from which he died the following morning.

On Thurs last JOHN HARVEY (a colored man in Salem) was arrested after a search of house revealed large stock of stolen merchandise from E A LEASE & CO, DAVID McCALLA & others

M: Nov 6 by REV J D BROWNLEE, HENRY A. BUNTING & MISS MARY McINTOSH both of Wellsville

M: 5th inst by H.E.FROST ESQ, WILLIAM WALKER & MISS SARAH ELLEN SHEEHAN all of this place

M: 2nd inst at res of bride's parents in Pittsburgh PA by REV A B LEONARD, CHARLES B. CALLAHAN formerly of Salem & MISS MARY E. LUPTON of Pittsburgh

M: 1st inst at Mt Gilead by REV MILTON McMILLEN, ALLEN W. EDDY of Salem & LILLIE B. JONES of Cardington, Morrow Co Oh

MRS NEWTON DIXON of Marshall Co Iowa & a former resident of Columbiana, while on a visit to her old friends, rec'd the sad news of the serious illness of her daughter. She hastened to take the first train home, expecting to arrive in time to see her daughter alive, but before she departed a second dispatch came announcing her daughters's death which occurred on the 6th inst

NEWSPAPER: The Salem JOURNAL says the Leetonia TIMES is now in full blast; the first number will be issued as soon as material & machinery arrives.

Item from Cleveland Herald says that MISS AMANDA HANNAH of Greeley Colo, formerly of New Lisbon, is the first and only lady who has ever made the ascent to the summit of Pikes Peak.

The new courthouse bell was hung last week; If CAPT BECK cannot ring it it will be bad...for the Captain.

Mon 20 Nov 1871 (Vol 5 no 33) (from WRHS microfilm)

M: 2nd inst by REV H LONG, T.C.FITZPATRICK of Washingtonville & MISS MARY J. GILBERT of Col'ana

M: 18th inst by ANDREW ARMSTRONG ESQ, DAVID EVANS of Mineral Ridge & MISS REBECCA J. RITCHEY of Elkton

D: Fri Nov 10 at East Palestine, EDWARD P. YOUNG ae 54y 2m 23d

D: Fri Nov 10 at his late res in Madison Tp, JOHN FRASER in 66th yr

REV.DR.DICKSON is making plans to remove to New Albany Ind, where he rec'd call from Presbyterian church there.

Long list of teachers & towns

Estate: ENOCH HARPER; MRS. ELIZA HARPER, exr

Mon 27 Nov 1871 (Vol 5 no 34) (from WRHS microfilm)

M: 9th inst at Mechanicstown OH by REV J A SIMPSON, WILLIAM KERR & MRS ELIZABETH SMILEY both of New Lisbon

M: 16th inst at Reformed Parsonage, North Lima, by REV H HILBISH, DAVID DELLAR & MISS APPA PIPER both of Col'ana

M: 16th inst by WM. WATT ESQ., LEVI GEORGE & MISS REBECCA WARD both of Middleton Tp CCO

D: 4th inst at Homeworth, ANNIE LITTLE W/o ANDREW ae 33y

D: 24th inst MARY McGAFFICK D/o ANDREW & MARY ANN of Saline-ville ae 21y

NEWSPAPER: THE WELLSVILLE LOCAL is no more. It has been in existence just one year. Mr MARTIN gives notice in the last issue that about 1 Dec he will issue a new paper in East Liverpool, to be called the East Liverpool GAZETTE & hopes to take his patronage with him. Success, DAVE.

NEWSPAPER: Mr PORTER will retire from the SALINEVILLE NEW ERA & be succeeded by Mssrs REESE & CLARK. Success.

NEWSPAPER: MR. ATTERHOLT retires from the management of the COLUMBIANA REGISTER It will be published hereafter by Messrs HOLLOWAY & NOLD

If you want a nice article of job work, leave your orders at the DORWART building opposite BRIGGS & BURNS store, which is just opposite the Journal office

FISHER MURDER: more facts on murder of JAMES FISHER, near Osage, Missouri on 18th inst in a Kansas paper. MARTIN GOSS the supposed murderer of FISHER had formerly lived on his farm & was attending him while sick. While asleep he was struck a violent blow on the head, they struggled, left Fisher for dead; Mr F died next day at home of ARCH MILLER where he was taken for treatment, he having no family. Prisoner in jail at Emporia for 1st degree murder

Mon 6 Dec 1871 (Vol 5 no 35) (from WRHS microfilm)

M: 23 Nov by REV J C MALOY, EDWARD O'ROURKE of Fort Wayne IND & MISS ADA ABRAHAMS of Wellsville Oh

M: in Pittsburgh 19th Nov by DR. MAYER, DAVID MANNIST of Wellsville & Miss TILLIE CITRON of New York

M: at parsonage 23 Nov by REV A DALE, FRED ELLENBERGER of Bradie's Bend & MISS KATE KING, formerly of New Lisbon

M: at Weddel House, Cleveland on 18th inst by REV N C GRANT, W.C.PURVIANCE & MISS LIBBIE JONES both of Damascus

M: at Presby parsonage Nov 22 by REV H B FRY, EDWARD BOON & MISS MARY HILL both of Salem

D: Sabbath eve Nov 19, ISABEL DICKSON at res in Wellsville

D: Fri 17th inst in East Liverpool, ETTIE HELENA DAVIDSON ae 10m 5d

The new Presbyterian CHURCH at Leetonia will be dedicated next Sabbath, 10th inst. Rev I G HALL of Kenton will preach; the installation of the pastor elect, REV A B MAXWELL, will take place the same day

JOHN HARVEY, the negro burglar of Salem, escaped from jail here Tues eve last by sawing the iron bar on the cell door

INQUEST: on 30 Nov 1871 in Salem Tp by A B KING, CORONER to discover manner & by whom JOHN G KUHN whose body was found near the RR bridge on the P & FTWRW in Leetonia on 30 Nov came to his death. Inquest showed he was struck by an express train on said RR; the dec'd was hard of hearing & RR gave all the proper signals.

NEWSPAPER: THE EAST LIVERPOOL POTTERS' TIMES has been resur-rected & will appear regularly hereafter.

Mon 11 Dec 1871 (Vol 5 no 36) (from WRHS microfilm)

M: 16 Nov by REV A T YOUNG, at res of bride's mother, WILLIAM ANDERSON of E.Liverpool & SARAH McDONALD of Hanover Tp, Beaver Co PA

M: 23d ult at res of bride's parents, WILLIAM J. TILBROOK of East Liberty PA & ARETA C. HAMILTON D/o COL.T.S.HAMILTON of Unity Tp CCO

M: Thur 30th inst at res of bride's parents by REV G W RIGGLE, assisted by REVS TURNER & CROSS, FRANK CROXALL & MISS ANNIE KERR both of this place

M: 30th inst by REV J M CARR, JOHN BEAN & MISS MARY HARDMAN both of Wellsville

D: at his res in Oceola Iowa on Sat 18 Nov ae 64y, THOMAS R. THURSTON formerly of Col Co

D: Sun last 26th inst at his res in Wellsville of consumpt-ion, JOHN MINER in the ----yr of his age

D: in Pittsburgh PA on 25th PATRICK BUTLER formerly of Wellsville

DEATH OF O.M.SPRINGER: it is our painful duty this week to chronicle the sad intelligence of the death of MARCUS O.-SPRINGER, only son of DR. SPRINGER of this place who died Tues eve last in Chicago where he had been for some months attend-ing lectures at the Medical College. The College bldg having been burnt during the late fire, the Institution was moved into the hospital bldg & it is supposed Mr Springer there contracted some disease which resulted in his death. The remains were brought to New Lisbon & interred on Thurs afternoon. The dec'd leaves a wife and one child. The afflict-ed family & friends have the sympathy of the community.

MRS RIDDLE, W/o JUDGE J.A.RIDDLE of Wellsville died in that place on Tues night last

Mon 18 Dec 1871 (Vol 5 no 37) (from WRHS microfilm)

M: Dec 5, S.M.HOLLOWAY & MISS LIZZIE SARAN. Nov 30th, HENRY T. AUFFMAN & MISS PHEBE TURRINGTON. Dec 6th, WM. SELL & MISS SUSAN GRIMES, all of CCO, by D.V.HYDE

M: Nov 16 by REV A C McCLELLAND of Pittsburgh, ISAAC N. ENGLE of Industry PA & MISS AUSTIE A. RICH of East Palestine OH

D: Thurs Morn Dec 12th at his res in West Point, WILLIAM TREFFINGER, in 26th yr of his age

D: in New Lisbon Dec 11th, MRS. A.B. ORR W/o S.W.ORR

PARTITION: JAMES ROHER, EMMA ROHER, LYDIA ANN BETZ & JONAS BETZ h/h & MARY A. WEIKERT & HIRAM h/h Of CCO, and REBECCA ROHER, ----BOSTON (INFANT CHILD & HEIR OF ALCAZENA BOSTON DEC'D) and JOSEPH BOSTON of Maho Co Oh, petition filed vs them by REUBEN L. INGLEDUE on real estate lot 8 in village of Washingtonville

The China wedding of Mr & Mrs FARQUAR of Salem was celebrated Mon eve last

A.B.WAY, the absconded Alliance preacher, has returned. His forged papers having all been taken up by his friends, he feels safe.

P.C.YOUNG, ESQ., late editor of the BUCKEYE STATE, returned to New Lisbon Tues last after an absence of 2 months in the west. He looks well, & contemplates returning west to settle during coming spring

REV WM DOUTHET well known in this community died at the res of his nephew JOSEPH DOUTHET near New Castle PA on 6th ult in 83d yr of his age. The deceased was a United Presbyterian minister & labored in that capacity for nearly 60 yrs.

There are 4 prisoners in jail here all from Salem. Among them was EDDY THOMPSON, a child 9 yrs of age, charged with assault-ing a school teacher. Eddy started out young. He paid the penalty of a small theft in prison once before.

ACCIDENT: JOHN MARSDEN of this place a brakeman on the Niles & New Lisbon RR met with with a serious accident on Fri last at Washingtonville. He was engaged in coupling cars when he was caught between the bumpers & his body severely crushed, thereby endangering his life. Mr M died from the effects on Sat morning & an inquest was held, post mortem exam made by DR. GILMOR, found that the viscera & right kidney were sufficiently contused to cause death. The dec'd was in the 18th yr of his age & was a promising young man to his parents & was the main support of the family. (also) The funeral sermon of JOHN MARSDEN was preached in the ME Church on Sabbath eve by REV.BIRKETT

Resolutions of respect for MARCUS O. SPRINGER from the Concordia Lodge No 38 IOOF

Mon 25 Dec 1871 (Vol 5 no 38) (from WRHS microfilm)

M: 17th inst at Portland Methodist Church, Louisville KY by REV J P GOODSON, ADAM RICHARDS, formerly of New Lisbon & MRS. MARIA WRIGHT of the former place

M: by REV J N SWAN at the res of the bride Dec 14, LAUGHLIN McBANE & MISS KATIE McBANE, dau of ALEX McBANE all of cco

M: Thurs Dec 14 at res of bride's father by REV J ARTHUR, ALEXANDER GRANT & MISS BELL McVANE

M: on Christmas morning at the Cowan House New Lisbon by REV T A SCOTT, C.C.ALEXANDER & MISS SALUTHA LONG both of Col'ana

M: 14th inst by REV J J ESTILL, CALVIN WEYL & MISS FLORENCE SNIDER all of this co

M: 23d ult by ESQ HAWLEY, assted by MARTIN DICKINSON, BENJAMIN HOWEL & MISS NANCY CUSTARD all of this co

M: 30th ult OSCAR F. McCLAIN of Carroll Co & MISS HANNAH M. JOHNSON of Homeworth

M: 17th inst at Unionville by REV S. BACHLER, F. VANSKIVER & MRS MARY KEYSER

M: Dec 16th by REV T A SCOTT, TAYLOR B. REED & MISS SUSANNA BLAKE all of this co

D: near Salineville on Thurs Dec 14, JAMES MAPLE in 79th yr

D: Oct 30 in Fair. Tp MAGDELENA WISLER W/o ANTHONY ae 72y

D: 6th inst in Butler Tp WM.HENRY GOLDY S/o SP & BE ae 14y 4m 20d

D: 13th inst after a short illness of inflammatory rheumat-ism, MISS LINN COPE D/o HENRY of Wellsville

D: in Col'ana Dec 11, MARY BELL DEEMER, D/o J & M, ae 3m 28d

D: 22nd inst ROBERT CHAMBERLAIN S/o JOHN & ELMIRA of Elkrun Tp ae 22y 8m

D: Dec 18 HARRY GEISSE THOMAS S/o H G & ANNIE E. THOMAS of Wellsville ae 2y 1m 15d

1872

Jan 1,8,15,22,29	Feb 5,12,19,26	Mar 4,11,18,25
Apr 1,8,15,22,29	May 6,13,20,27	Jun 3,10,17,24
Jly 1,8,15,22,29	Aug 5,12,19,26	Sep 2,9,16,23,30
Oct 7,14,21,28	Nov 4,11,18,25	Dec 2,9,16,23,30

Mon 1 Jan 1872 (Vol 5 no 39) (from WRHS microfilm)

D: 26th ult, LINDSEY CANON of Elkrun Tp ae 92y 8m 11d

M: at res of bride's father 27th Dec by REV BIRKETT, JAMES R. MITCHELL of Beaver Falls & Miss MARY L. ROGERS of New Lisbon.

M: 21 Dec at the Cowan House by REV G M ALBRIGHT, FRANK CARLL & MISS MARY LYNN both of Mah Co

M: Dec 20 by REV C TAGGART, asstd by REVS J D SHANKS & G.W.RIGGLE, T.F.ANDERSON of E.Liv & MISS HATTIE J. HUSTON of Calcutta

M: 28th ult by REV T A SCOTT, JOSEPH CRAWFORD & MISS CHRIST-INA A. PHILPOT all of Centre Tp

M: 13th inst at res of bride's parents by REV J R DUNDASS, ISAAC KIBLER & MISS NANCY J. LINN both of this co

M: by Rev J.HUSTON Dec 28, JOSEPH F. HENRY & SUSANNAH ROGERS both of CCO

M: 28th inst by REV J S KENNEDY, I.N.WHITE of CCO & MISS ------McGOWAN of Steubenville Oh

DROWNED: We learn from the WELLSVILLE UNION that on last Mon while a large number of persons were enjoying their Christmas sports by skating upon the river at that place, two boys, LAFAYETTE BENNET of East Liverpool ae about 17 & FRANK PARLINGTON of Wellsville, ae 12, broke through the ice & were drowned. PARLINGTON was the first to break through & BENNET, at a distance of several rods, hearing his cries, ran to his assistance but finding him beyond reach of the hand, he instantly drew off his coat & plunging it within the boy's grasp was endeavoring to draw him out of the water, when the treacherous ice gave way & both went down to rise no more.- The bodies were recovered after a search of some 4 hours.

SUICIDE: We learn that JOHN A. MOORE, living between Washing-tonville & salem committed suicide on Sat 23d ult by hanging himself in his barn. No cause is assigned for the rash act, except that Mr. MOORE has been considered partially insane for some months.

SUDDEN DEATH: THE COLUMBIANA REGISTER of last week says on Sabbath eve, 24th inst, MRS. ELIZABETH COLE W/O HENRY died suddenly after partaking of a hearty supper & assisting in the evening's work & enjoying her usual health up to within a few moments of her death.

NEWSPAPER: We have rec'd the second number of the SALINEVILLE MINER, formerly the NEW ERA. It has been enlarged to 32 columns & makes a very creditable appearance.

"Town Talk"...Two children of DR. RHODES died last week at Leetonia from small pox or varioloid"

Mon 8 Jan 1872 (Vol 5 no 40) (from WRHS microfilm)

M: at Brighton PA by REV R P BORN, GEORGE P FREY & MISS LIZZIE NAASER both of Wellsville

M: Dec 25 by LEVI KING ESQ,, GEORGE D. SMITH of Salem & CLESTIA BYDER of Reding, all of CCO

M: at American House, Salem, Dec 11 by REV H B FRY, DAVID M. MARSHE Oof New Garden & MISS ANNIE ARTER of Hanover

M: 28 Dec at res of bride's parents in Salem by REV H B FRY, OSBORN R. COOK, ESQ. & MISS KATE M. SEATON

M: 25th ult by REV ROBT HAYS, WM. CLOSE & MISS ELIZABETH A. JOHNSON D/O THOMAS, both of Washington Tp CCO

M: Dec 25 by REV DV HYDE, EMMET BURSON & MISS SARAH RICHEY both of CCO

D: Dec 18 at Alliance CLARA MAY BRADSHAW infant d/o THEODORE & ADDIE

D: Dec 31 MRS. JONATHAN GLECKLER, dau of WM. MARLATT in Col'ana of consumption ae 33y 6d

D: Jan 1, WM. WHAN of Elkrun Tp ae 91y

D:1st inst ELIZA ANN DONNELY W/O CHARLES of Centre Tp ae57y

D: 2nd inst REUBEN GODDARD of Wayne Tp ae 78y

D: 9th inst GRACE EVABEL COULSON youngest d/o GEORGE H. & M.E. of Hanover Tp ae 1y 6m 23d

REUBEN GODDARD of Wayne Tp, ae about 75y, was found dead on Fri morning near an old cabin that he sometimes lived in. On Tues morn he left the residence of his son in law, DAVID McDIVITT, supplied with some provisions & was not heard of until found dead. The provisions were still in his coat pocket which leads to the suppostion that he had been dead for some time. He was in the habit of staying amongst his friends while not at his own cabin which accounts for his absence for so long a time without being looked after.

JAMES STEWART an old gentleman living by himself near Robbins coal bank, was found dead in his house on Fri morn last. Mr S was in New Lisbon the day before, apparently in good health.

ad: D.C.DELANO, Photographer

ACCIDENT: we are informed that DR. CAREY, of Salem, was seriously & probably fatally injured on Mon by being thrown out of his buggy & dragged some distance on the ground. He was driving from his residence to his office when his horse became frightened & ran away with the above result.

ELOPEMENT: Two miles SE of this village live, or did live, 2 families named VAUGHN & SHOEMAKER, the former consisting of JOSEPH, ae 72, his son ROBERT, ae 40, and his (ROBERT's) wife; the latter consisting of WM. SHOEMAKER & two daughters, one ae 16 and the other about 10. This JOSEPH VAUGHN, who has a wife living in some part of the world, set to work to seduce SHOEMAKER's eldest daughter, by first persuading her that she would be better feed & clothed than with her father & also learn to sew & finally persuaded her to go & live with his son & daughter in law, where they, the lovers of 72 & 16, lived together as man & wife for a couple of weeks, when he removed her to some unknown parts. They returned on the 23d of Dec & on that night, Joe, Bob & wife loaded their few traps into a one horse wagon & with an old horse skedaddled, & have not since been heard from.

Mon 15 Jan 1872 (Vol 5 no 41) (from WRHS microfilm)

D: in Salem on 8th inst after a lingering illness, ELLA TEMPLE D/O EDWIN & MENEMA ae 18y

D: Dec 11 at the res of her son in Knox Tp, JUDITH CRISINGER ae 89y 3m 7d

D: Dec 5 near Homestead Iowa from congestion of the brain, SAMUEL CRISENGER ae about 64y

D: Dec 31 at Logansport Ind, EMMA DOUGHLASS, dau of JOSEPH M. & ARVILLA SPRINGER formerly of this place ae 21y

M: on 28th ult by JOSEPH CROW JP, B.F.ILER & SEYRENE WHIT-ACRE, all of Butler Tp CCO

M: 18th ult by G.W.BORING ESQ, CHARLES DUNLAP & MISS SARAH A COCKBURN all of Salineville

M: 25th ult by same, WILLIAM J. FINNEGAN & MISS MAGGIE HECKATHORN all of Salineville

M: 4 Jan by REV J O. MELOY of Rochester Pa, to MISS KATE FRAZER of Wellsville Oh [note: exactly as reads, apparently no groom listed unless the minister is]

M: at res of bride's parents Jan 4 by REV J T McCLURE, SANFORD H. NEVILLE of East Liverpool & MISS ELLA STEVENSON of Wheeling WVA

ARREST OF REV. A.B.WAY: Alliance Jan 7, the arrest of A.B.WAY, the well known forger, caused considerable excite-ment at this place this evening; arrest order issued Xmas day & put in hands of Portage Co Sheriff, but Way made his escape thru a back window at his residence & with assistance of our law abiding & worthy Mayor made his escape & has been away until this afternoon. He returned home some time last night to spend a few hours with his family when advised by a prominent one horse lawyer that he had better not tarry long; the atty made haste to the livery stable & had a span of horses to make way with their bird. Notice was at once given R.W.TEETERS who had sworn out the warrant & he hastened & got 3 horses under saddle, got the city marshal & two special deputies & sent them in pursuit of the refugees.-The arrest was made about 5 mi north of this place. WAY will be taken to Portage Co Jail in the morning.

[CORRECTIONS] It is astonishing how many people are being resurrected now a days. H.G.BOOTH, who rumor said died of smallpox a short time ago, is now flying around town as lively as a cricket. JIMMY STUART, reported found dead on Friday last, was in town a day or two afterwards, looking for the man who killed him. And WM. PATTERSON, who was supposed to have been killed on the railroad about 3 weeks ago, returned home on Wed., sound as a dollar.

JAS.H.SLACK who died of smallpox in Steubenville, was not so much of a printer as a grocer. The printer, EDWARD C. SLACK, still lives you can tell your folks. "Papers should be sure they have the facts."

DR. CARY, of Salem, whom we mentioned last week as having been thrown from a buggy on New Year's day & seriously hurt, we are informed, died from the effects of his injuries on Wed morn last.

DEATH OF JAMES STARR: we are once more called upon to record the death of another old citizen of New Lisbon. On last Fri morn the 12th inst, MR. JAMES STARR died at his res on Market St, at the advanced age of 75y. The dec'd was one of our most industrious & conscientious citizens. In his business relations he ever exhibited the strictest integrity. He was a member of the United Presb.church & as such was ever faithful in the performance of his duties. His remains were followed to the grave on Sat by a large number of relatives & friends.

Mon 22 Jan 1872 (Vol 5 no 42) (from WRHS microfilm)

M: Tues aft 9th inst at the Monongahala House, Pittsburgh, by REV I N BAIRD, CHAS.C.SNIDER of the firm of STEELE,SNIDER & CO. & MISS ANNA WEBB, both of Salem

M: 1st inst by REV J W DAVIS, JAMES M. TAYLOR of E.Liv & MISS MARY E. GROSCOST of Brighton Tp, Beaver Co PA

M: Mon Jan 1 by REV E.R.SQUIRE, CHARLES D. VANCE of Pittsburgh & MISS CARRIE L. PURNELL of Allegheny City

M: 1st inst by REV D V HYDE, JOSIAH B STANLEY & MISS MARTHA HAWKINS both of Mah Co Oh

M: 14th inst by REV D V HYDE, CLARKSON BECK & MISS REBECCA J. STANLEY both of this co

D: 14th inst in Salem, infant child of JACOB & MARTHA KRING

D: 13th inst in Salem, MARTHA KRING W/O JACOB ae 30y

D: 12th inst in Salem MRS SHANNON W/O JOHN P. ae 41y

SCALDED TO DEATH: WILLIE BARR a little child of WILLIAM & MARY BARR of Elkrun Tp, ae 11m, was severely scalded a few days ago by pulling a cup of hot coffee off the table & spilling it on its breast, from the effects of which it died on Wed last.

We are informed by the Columbiana REGISTER that "on Tues Jan 9, a little son of WILLIAM ENGLISH of Elkrun Tp was scalded so severely that it died on the 10th inst. The circumstances as reported : the mother of the child had just taken a pot of beef from off the stove & taken the beef out & let the pot containing the liquid in which the beef was coooked stand on the floore; and the child, which was about 2y 3m old was playing in the room & by some means spilled the contents of the pot over itself which produced the fatal result. The accident was a sad one to the parents & relatives of the lost one & it is hoped will serve as a warning to others never to place vessels of any kind containing boiling fluid withintthe reach of small children-The above reads as though it might have originated from the death of WILLIAM BARR's child, of the same township, who died on the same day, under similar circumstances, an account of which we give in another item.

HENRY HESSON & wife f'ly of this place, now of Huntington Ind, are visiting friends

Mon 29 Jan 1872 (Vol 5 no 43) (from WRHS microfilm)

D: 16th inst PETER EASTON S/O WALTER & SUSAN of Robbins Station ae 8 weeks

D: 18th inst in Middleton, ORPHAN BOULTON, W/O LEVI, ae 80y 6m 15d

D: 22nd inst in New Lisbon infant child of JOHN R. JONES of Allegheny City Pa

D: 13th inst in Chicago, ELMA HOWEL formerly of Salem in 72nd yr of his age

NEWSPAPER: Salineville will make one more effort for a newspaper. This time it is to be printed at home. The WELLSVILLE-UNION-SALINEVILLE-MINER had too far to travel it seems to be a success.

Mon 5 Feb 1872 (Vol 5 no 44) (from WRHS microfilm)

COURT:
OVERTON STANLEY vs MARGARET: DIVORCE GRANTED
DANIEL BONSALL vs ELIZABETH DECREE FOR DIVORCE
REBECCA ESTEP vs WILLIAM: DECREE FOR DIVORCE

S.M.HALVERSTADT of Weeping Water Falls, Neb, formerly of this co., called & renewed his subscription

Court: JOHN HARVEY the Salem dry goods operator plead guilty to larceny & sentenced to 4y in Pen. John Barnhard, charged with larceny of 2 watches at Salineville, plead not guilty, trial next week

HENRY HARLOW who broke jail here 2y ago was recaptured by Sheriff MORRIS last week & returned; caught at Greeneville Pa where he was stopping with his mother.

Mon 12 Feb 1872 (Vol 5 no 45) (from WRHS microfilm)

D: Tues 6th inst JOHN RAHMANN of Wellsville

D: 15 Jan GEORGE ASHFORD at East Carmel ae 72y

D: Jan 29, MRS. ELIZABETH TEGARDEN ae 38y 9m 11d

D: 4th inst JOSEPH EWEING of Hanover Tp ae 94y

D: 5th inst ELECTIOUS EELLS of Middleton Tp, twin brother of ERASTUS EELS, in 64th yr

D: 8th inst SAMUEL STEWART Of Salem Tp ae 79y 9d

D: 4th inst infant son of ALEXANDER & MATILDA BEVINGTON of this place

GEORGE M. LEE, an attorney of Cincinnati, formerly of Col Co, died in Longview Insane Asylum near Cincy a few days ago where he had been an inmate for the last 4y

Mon 19 Feb 1872 (vol 5 no 46) (from WRHS microfilm)

M: Feb 11 by JETHRO MANLEY, JOHN POWELL & MISS ELIZABETH FRANCIS GRAFTON both of E.Liv

M: Jan 31 at Glasgow PA by ROBT McKAGE, JP, JAMES H. MERTON of McKeesport PA & MRS HATTIE McSKIMEN of Wellsville

M: at Col'ana on 8th inst by REV WM C SMITH, WM. McCALL of Pittsburgh & MISS MARY LAPSLEY of Col'ana

D: 8th inst in Hanover Tp, WILLIAM HENRY MATHER ae 82y

D: 9th inst in Dungannon, MRS. CONNOR, ae 80y

D: 14th inst in Norristown Carr.Co, JOHN B.CONLIN in 29th yr

D: at the Infirmary Feb 13, ORINDA ALBRIGHT ae 23y

D: Wed 7th inst near Hammondsville OH, JAMES H. McKINNEL formerly of this co

D: Mon 12th inwst CAPT. B.F.WAY at his res in Welllsville

D: 5th inst in Perry Tp APELINE KISER ae 17y

D: 5th inst MATILDA HILLYARD ae 32y

D: in E.Liv Sat 10th inst MRS. OGDEN W/O DR.B.B.OGDEN

D: Fei 9th inst near New Lisbon JAMES YOUNG ae 60y

D: 18th inst near Col'ana at res of JOSEPH TAYLOR, SETTA MURPHY in 31st yr

D: 16th DAVID STEWART S/O EMANUEL of Centre Tp ae about 30y

D: Sabbath morn 18th inst at res of his father in Elkrun Tp, JOHN STERLING in 45th yr; funeral tomorrow

D: in Huntington Ind, Tues Jan 30, MARY ELIZABETH W/O JOHN S. PROVINES ae 34y 11m 10d; MRS. PROVINES was a daughter of JOHN WILEY ESQ., a pioneer of this county who died at res of Mr P about a year ago. She was born in Dark Co Ohio & her parents emigrated to this country when she was an infant of 6 weeks. On 25 Aug 1853 she married JOHN S PROVINES & the issue of this union is 6 children, 4 of whom are living: the oldest, ALLIE, ae 14y, JOHN W. ae 11; ROSELLA ae 9 & MARY the babe, ae 1, and these children bereft of care of a kind & watchful mother are left to survive her & to them her loss is irreparable. Mrs P was raised in Presby faith but united with the ME church about 4y since & that church had not a purer, truer, more exemplary & devoted member than she. Thus she died in the prime of life, fully prepared to be ushered into the presence of her Creator & before she had yet laid aside the mourning robes for her lamented father. The sympathies of the public are with her bereaved family. Huntington Democrat.

OBIT: DEATH OF JABEZ BEAUMONT: from the Oregon MO Sentinal: on Mon Jan 22, 1872, JABEZ BEAUMONT, an old & respected citizen of Holt Co, died at his residence in this city after 5 wks illness. The dec'd was a native of Gothrop, Yorkshire, England, born in 1814. At the tender age of 4y he came to America with his mother & brothers, his father having preceded them to this country the year before. After 2y sojourn in Maryland & 4y in Pa, and some time in VA, the Beaumont family removed to what was then known as the Great New West and settled in NEW LISBON, COLUMBIANA CO OHIO, where they remained 19 yrs. It was at New Lisbon where the dec'd devoted himself to the study of law & where he was admitted to the bar of Col.Co. sometime between 1834 & 1838. From that time till 1853, when he came to Missouri, Mr B practiced law in New Lisbon & served his fellow citizens of that town & county many years as Justice of the Peace.- Mr. B has resided in Holt Co for upward of 18y, where by his persevering, prudent consistent course of life, he won the respect of all & amassed a considerable fortune. He was a strong believer in the validity of the christian religion as taught in the Bible, though he never attached himself to any religious denomination. He was temperate in everything & his liberality to schools, churches, and other useful & benevolent institutions was proverbial. He retained his counsciousness to the very last & died with great serenity of mind. He requested his older brother, JOSEPH, who was present during the latter portion of his sickness, that his remains might be taken to WESTON, PLATTE CO., MISSOURI & placed along side of those of his sainted brother THOMAS, the late DR. BEAUMONT of West, which request was faithfully complied with by the bereaved relativees. The deceased was never married & consequently leaves no family to mourn his loss. He was an invalid for about 5 weeks, suffering from an effection of the lungs terminating in death. Thus has departed from among us one of the most respected residents of our town. All speak of him in the highest words of praise. Peace to his ashes! (Ed)

With this issue I withdraw as Editor; it will be under control of J.K.FREW. FRANK MILLER

WILLIAM LEE, one of the original proprietors of Leetonia & for whom the town was named, died at Randolph PA last week. MR LEE was the contractor for the building of the Niles & New Lisbon Railroad & a member of the Leetonia Iron Company.

The Baptist Church of Salem was dedicated yesterday

DANIEL STEWART of Youngstown committed suicide the other day

Mon 26 Feb 1872 (Vol 5 no 47) (from WRHS microfilm)

M: 22nd inst at Cowan House by H.E.FROST ESQ., SAMUEL RORHL & MISS ALICE HAWKINS all of CCO

M: same day at same place & by the same, JOSEPH Q. WOODS & MISS AMANDA HOPPES all of this co

M: 13th inst by REV J P McGUIRE, H.M. McCREARY & MRS LIZZIE K O'DONNELL both of Wellsville

D:: 20th inst JOHN SHAWK of Centre Tp formerly of Beaver Co PA, ae 74y

REV GEORGE JOHNSON of Presby ch has moved to New Lisbon with his family

We learn from a report that MICHAEL DRISCOL who was committed to jail at the the late term of court charged with committing a rape, & who with others made his escape a few weeks ago, was killed in attempting to jump from a railroad train. The Leetonia Reporter says that his death occurred in New Jersey & that his body was brought to Pittsburgh & burried a week ago last Sat. The mother of Michael committed suicide in Pittsburgh by jumping from a 3d story window some time ago, when she heard of his arrest & imprisonment.

The trial of REV. G.H. LOWMAN of Wellsville commenced last Fri, charges of falsehood, fraud & dishonesty are preferred against Mr LOWMAN by Rev John Mc Carty of the Steubenville Conference

J.B.ROACH of Monticello Ind, who has been visiting in New Lisbon, left for home last week

Mon 4 Mar 1872   (Vol 5 no 48) (from WRHS microfilm)

M: 15th inst at the American House, Wooster, by REV MR PEPPER, A.J.STRAWN & MISS LYDIA J. THOMAS both of Salem

M: 8th inst by REV C SMITH, WM McCALL of Pittsburgh & MISS MARY LAPSLEY of Col'ana

M: at Mr KENTNER'S res Feb 22 by REV H B FRY, S.L.COOK of Salem & MRS ANNIE ARNOLD of Canfield

M: Jan 7 by REV W L NELSON, JOHN A SUMMERS & MISS CATHA-RINE S. SANOR both of CCO

M: Jan 16 by same, at Rochester OH, GEORGE HEITZMAN & MISS RACHEL WOLF all of CCO

M: 16 Feb, JEFFERSON MILBURN & MISS MARY ANN SOMMER at the res of W.L.NELSON, Rochester CCO

M: 14th at res of brides' mtoher by REV A B MAXWELL, FRANK KNOWLDS of Col'ana & MISS ORIE MEEKER of Leetonia

D: 1st inst wife of WM KIMBLE of Col'ana, formerly of Elkton ae 65y

D: 2nd inst SADIE BARLOW D/O RICHARD & ELIZABETH of Centre Tp ae 5y 3m

D: at res in Butler Tp Feb 24 GEORGE BURNS ESQ, ae 78y

D: Feb 11 JOSEPH C. BRUFF infant S/O JOSEPH & ANNA M. BRUFF ae 9y

D: Feb 25, ANNA L. BRUFF ae nearly 32y

D: at his res on So Walnut St, Wellsville of consumption, EDWARD MORGANS in 83d yr

D: 25th inst EMMIT SUMMER S/O SOLOMON & MARY ANN of West Tp ae 12y

D: Jan 28, VIOLA CHARLOTTE OTT, D/O JOSEPH & MARY ANN of Hanover Tp ae 3m 13d

HORRIBLE DEATH: on Fri last HARPER RUSSELL, switchman at the RR Depot at this place, in attempting to step on the engine while in motion was caught by the machinery & his body literally torn to pieces killing him almost instantly. He was buried Sunday at half past 2 pm. Wellsville Union.

C.H.KEIPER intends to remove to Cloud Co Kan shortly, offers house goods for sale.

PETER LOWREY, charged with adultery with CATHARINE McCART-NEY, residing near New Garden, had a hearing before Esq FROST Fri, resulting in his being required to give bail for his appearance at court in sum of $200 in default of which he was committed to jail.

Mon 11 Mar 1872   (vol 5 no 49) (from WRHS microfilm)

D: in Col'ana Mar 1, MARTHA DEEMER W/O JOHN ae 39y 4m 15d

D: 5th inst EMANUEL STEWART of Centre Tp ae 69y 5m

EMMET KANNAL stopped to see us; he is goind a good drug business at Renssalear Ind.

DEATH OF WILLIAM R. SMILEY: Just as we go to press this morning, we receive the sad intelligence of the death of WILLIAM R. SMILEY who died at the residence of his father in this place, this morning, in 24th yr of his age, after a lingering illness of more than 2y. Mr S had rec'd a good education & was a young man of much promise. Atthe time of his death he held the office of County Surveyor & previous to his election to that office had been engaged in Teaching, most of the time as Principal of Cold Run Academy. He was a member of the UP Church of this place, & an upright & exemplary young man. He leaves a wife & one child & many friends to mourn his loss.

M: 7th Mar by REV WM BAXTER, CLINTON GARRETT & MISS RATIE UNDERWOOD both of this place

M: 7th inst at res of bride's fther by REV G M ALBRIGHT, EMARR T. SITLER & MISS LUCINDA PEPPEL, both of Salem Tp

M: in Pittsburgh on Feb 27 before ALDERMAN McMASTERS, J.B.SMITH of Goshen & JENNIE STRAWN of Salem

M: Feb 21 by REV C P CONE, D.W.FOSTER & MISS MARY H McCREARY all of Wellsville

M: Feb 28 by same, FRED S. STOFFEL & MISS ROSE E. HOLLAR both of Wellsville

M: by REV J M CARR Feb 22, H.C.WOOSTER & MISS MARY C. GILMOR both of Wellsville

MAN KILLED: on Sat Mar 2 about 5 pm while the gravel train of the C & P RR Co was backing onto a side track in the shop year, a laborer on the train, giving the name of THOMAS KELLY, in attempting to leave the train while in motion, fell between the cars, the wheels passing over his neck & breast, crushing him so that when assistance reached him he was dead. An inquest was held by MAYOR LONG & the verdict of the jury was in accordance with the above facts. No papers were found in his possession nor anything to give a clue where he came from except that when he hired on the train he told the conductor he came from Pittsburgh Pa & said he was a stone cutter by trade. -Wellsville Union

A colony consisting of about 100 families from Ohio have purchased 8000 acres of land from the LL & G RR Co at Divide Station, Anderson Co KANS & will settle there during the coming spring.

Mon 18 Mar 1872   (Vol 5 no 50) (from WRHS microfilm)

M: 14th inst by REV T A SCOTT at his res in New Lisbon, ALLEN T. CALLAHAN & MISS NANCY WARD

M: 3d inst by REV W LYNCH, E.H.DUFFIE & MISS R.A.McGILL all of Salem

M: Feb 29 at res of JESSE HAWLEY ESQ, JONATHAN H. LONGSHORE & MISS MARY BARNS both of Col Co

D: Thur Mar 13 THERESA PRITCHARD W/O D.A. ae 37y; she was a daughter of ex-sheriff HOSTETTER of this place & was an esteemable woman. She leaves a family of small children & many friends to mourn her loss. The funeral took place from the res. of her father on Wed & was attended by a large number of friends & acquaintances

D: at the Infirmary Mar 5, MARY EIDENIRE ae 81y

D: at her home in Wellsville Thur May 5, MRS. MARGARET McBRIDE in 93d yr

D: at East Liverpool Sun morn 3d inst MR. WOSHER PETERSON

D: 5th inst at her res in Salem SARAH WILSON ae 82y

D: 4 Mar ROSIE MARILLA BURBICK, D/O ARTHUR & ELIZABETH of Yel Ck Tp ae 1y 11m 18d

D: 10th inst JAMES S. HOSTETTER of Hanover Tp ae 46y (also) JSH whose death we chronicle this week, went a short time ago to the assistance of a neighbor whose hay stacks were in danger of burning & in his efforts to save the property, rec'd injuries which caused his death.

D: at New Alexander, FRANKLIN ZEHERNICK S/O CARRY & LOVINA ae 1y 1m 22d

D: in Carroll Co JOHN A. BRIGHT S/O JOHN & MARY JANE ae 4mo

LEGAL NOTICE: LYDIA H. HAVILAND, JOSEPH HAVILAND, SAMSON WALKER, LEWIS B. WALKER, MARY C. JONES, HENRY C. JONES, who reside in CCO; SARAH LIPSEY, EDMUND LIPSEY, who reside in Mahoning Co Oh; ELI H. ROGERS, LINDLEY M. ROGERS, who reside in Warren Co Ohio; JONATHAN S. ROGERS who res in Vermillion Co Ill; ESTHER W. ALLMON, JESSE ALLMON, res in Marshal Co Iowa; ROBERT M. HAINES res in Powsheik Co Iowa; JOSEPH W. HAINS, BENJAMIN L. HAINES, ELI J. HAINES, MATILDA T.-HAINS, THOMAS C. HAINES & JAMES O. HAINES, who reside in Marion Co Oregon....take notice that ROBERT M. HAINES of Col Co filed for partition of lot 33 in town of Damascus

An affray in a grocery store at Dungannon on Mon afternoon involving HENRY SULTNER & JOSEPH SMELTZ, came to blows; a pocket knife was produced & SULTNER had been cut across the side of the neck, laying the jugular vein bare. The knife was found to be quite dull, which saved the life of SULTNER. SMELTZ claimed the knife as his, he was arrested.

Mon 25 Mar 1872 (Vol 5 no 51) (from WRHS microfilm)

M: 10 Mar by ELDER HENRY KURTZ at his res in Col'ana, JOHN B. METZLER & SUSANNAH BASINGER of Maho Co Oh

M: at Presby parsonage Salem, Mar 9 by REV H B FRY, DANIEL FRAZIER & MISS E.A.SEYFORT

M: also Mar 15 at res of MR.MURPHY on East Broadway St by REV H B FRY, ALBERT H ROBINSON of Sharon Pa & MISS MARY MURPHY of Salem

M: 21st inst at res of bride's father by REV G M ALBRIGHT, OLIVER GRIMES & MISS ELMIRA WIRT both of Salem Tp

M: 19th inst by REV S S McKOWN, at his res near Guilford, GALEN FISHER & MISS NETTIE OBRINE.

D: 8th inst in Butler Tp, SOPHIA FRENCH D/O DAVID & ELIZA M in 10th yr

D: at res near Clarkson on 18th inst JAMES GASTON ae 79y

D: 5th inst in E.Liv., MAGGIE McBETH ae about 15y

D: 16th inst MARGERY HUDSON infant d/o JAMES & ELIZA ae 8mo

D: 8th inst JAMES HOGE of Washington Tp ae 55y 11m

D: in Wellsville Sun 17th inst after a short illness, MRS. SARAH BENWOOD

D: at his res in Wellsville Mar 21 ABRAHAM LEGGET ae 56y

JOSEPH VALLANDIGHAM arrived home last week. He has been at Troy NY for over a year.

REV S Y KENNEDY, the new pastor of the ME of this place, occupied the pulpit yesterday & will remove to town this week.

REV DICKSON preached in the Presby.ch yesterday. He will remove with his family to New Albany Ind. tomorrow

The Pittsburgh M.E.Conference made these appointments in our vicinity:

DAMASCOVILLE	J M BRAY
NEW LISBON	S Y KENNEDY
ELKTON	J D LEGGET
HANOVERTON	JOHN WRIGHT
SALINEVILLE	A J LANE

Mon 1 Apr 1872 (Vol 5 no 52) (from WRHS microfilm)

MISS JESSIE UNDERWOOD, the young lady of Middletown referred to in the Journal of last week as having the measels or smallpox died of the latter disease on 27th ultimo, & was buried the same night. The father & grandmother of the dec'd are now suffering with the same terrible malady.

M: at Mr EISMAN'S res in Salem Mar 19 by REV H B FRY, WM. ALFRED & MISS MARY L MYERS

M: Mar 25 by H E FROST ESQ, JOHN D COLE & MISS LIZZIE RAMAGE all of this place

M: 21 Mar at parsonage near Enon Valley PA by REV JOHN B MILLER, HENRY BRIGHT & MISS ELMANDA S. CRESS both of E.Palestine CCO

M: Mar 11 in Beaver PA by REV JOHN DAVIS, JOHN Q.A. FOWLER of East Liverpool & MISS MAGGIE DOUGLASS of New Lisbon

M: by Rev JJ ESTIL at his res in Franklin Square CCO, Mar 26 inst at 9 o'clock, ALBERT GONGAWARE & MISS RACHEL KINNEY both of Leetonia

D: WALTER OLIVER BROWN S/O M.A. & JENNIE of Hanover Tp ae 11m 12d

D: MARY EIDENIRE D/O PHILLIP of Hanover Tp ae 30y

D: Feb 20 at res of HIRAM BELL of Col'ana SARAH CAREY in 30th yr

D: 22nd ult HOWE RANK, infant son of AMOS & REBECCA RANK of Salem ae 1y

D: 18th Mar JOHN THURMAN WRIGHT S/O JOHN & MARY J of Hanover Tp ae 4m 13d

D: Mar 29 in Hanover JAMES R. WILEY ae 63y

D: 28 Mar MARGARET O'DONNEL D/O PETER of Dungannon ae 32y

NEWSPAPER: Salineville is again talking newspaper. We are informed that the Alliance LOCAL has been sold to parties in that place. By all means let us have another paper in this county. There is only ten and another is badly needed.

The Columbiana REGISTER says that on Mon eve last MRS. KECK wife of PETER KECK residing 2 mi north of Col'ana was kicked by a cow & was at last accounts in a very critical condition

Mon 8 Apr 1872 (Vol 6 no 1)

A deranged man named SEACHRIST, from Columbiana, who was wandering about town all day Fri., singing & preaching, was taken to jail Sat. by the sheriff & marshall.

M: at the Myers House, Janesville Wisc., on 20th ult by REV.H.C. TILTON, AMOS FIFE of West Point, CCO, & MATILDA G. CROW, of Monroe, Green Co., Wisc.

D: 31st ult, MARTHA JANE STOCKMAN, d/o W.A. & MARY of Centre Tp., ae 16y 8m 10d.

D: 5th Apr in New Garden, SUSAN NELSON w/o THOMAS ae 70y.

D: 5th inst ROBERT ESTILL of New Lisbon, ae nearly 69y.

D: at Capiome, Nemaha Co.,Kan., on 29 Mar, MRS. ELIZABETH HOSTETTER, widow of JOSEPH,ESQ., late of Paris Tp, Stark Co., ae 62y.

D: 19th inst at res in Leetonia of typhoid fever, JACOB N. KANDALL, ae 42y.

D: 5th inst at Bayard, JAMES RILEY WITNEY, infant son of STEPHEN & ETTIE WITNEY, ae 1y 1m.

D: at res in Wellsville Mar 21, ABRAHAM LEGGETT, ae 50y.

D: 29th ult in Salem, MRS. SARAH STEELE, w/o NELSON of the firm of STEELE, SNYDER & CO., merchants, ae 43y.

D: Jan 27th at res of her grandfather, JOHN McDEVITT, near Wellsville, MISS MAGGIE McGILLVARY, ae 16y 6m.

LEGAL: LYDIA H. HAVILAND, JOSEPH HAVILAND, TAMSON WALKER, LEWIS B. WALKER, MARY C. JONES, HENRY C. JONES, who reside in CCO; SARAH LIPSEY & EDMUND LIPSEY, who reside in Mahoning Co; ELI H. ROGERS, LINDLEY M. ROGERS, who reside in Warren Co Ohio; JONATHAN S. ROGERS, who resides in Vermillion Co Ill; ESTHER W. ALLMON, JESSE ALLMON, who reside in Marshall Co Iowa; ROBERT M. HAINES, who resides in Powsheik Co Iowa; JOSEPH W. HAINS, BENJAMIN HAINES, ELI J. HAINES, MATILDA T. HAINS, THOMAS C. HAINES & JAMES O. HAINES, who reside in Marion Co., Oregon...take notice that ROBERT M. HAINES of Col.Co. filed for partition of lot 33 in town of Damascus.

JOHN E. HESSIN, of Manhattan, Kans, former res of New Lisbon, visited friends & relatives here last week.

Obit: WILLIAM R. SMILEY, a young man. In his 15th year he was appointed assistant teacher of the New Lisbon Union Schools. In his 18th year, he acted as principal of Cold Run Academy, after which he became principal of New Lisbon Union Schools, which he filled nearly 2 years; the last he superintended was Canfield Union Schools. Ill health caused him to leave; he was elected Surveyor of Col.Co. til his death. At age 18, he joined the UP Church of New Lisbon. He leaves a widow, one child, father & mother.

The following Justices of the Peace were elected:

CENTRE TWP	JOHN M. DICKINSON
KNOX TWP	ISAAC WEAVER, JR.
ST.CLAIR TWP	WM.B.SHANNON
ELKRUN TWP	C.V.CROW
FRANKLIN TWP	JOHN WILLIARD & EDWARD WELSH
WEST TWP	JOSEPH COULSON & LEVI KING

Officers of the New Lisbon Silver Cornet Band: Pres, GEO.F. SHIELDS; V.P., C.L.FROST; SEC, H.E.FROST; TREAS, JACOB H. ARTER; LEADER, C.F.SMALL.

Mon 15 Apr 1872 (Vol 6 No 2) (from WRHS microfilm)

M: 9th inst at res of bride's father by REV G M ALLBRIGHT, WILSON S. RAMSEY & MISS SUSAN E. FRANTZ, both of Centre Tp

M: at res of bride's mother in Salem on 11th inst by MAYOR FAWCETT, GEORGE A. RUGGY & MISS KATE S. WALKER

D: 9th inst SARAH E. LONGSHORE wife of D.W.C.LONGSHORE of Elkrun Tp ae 32y

D: Th eve 4th inst REV ROBERT CUNNINGHAM of Col'ana ae 48y

D: in Middleton Tp Mar 27 MISS MARY UNDERWOOD ae 15y

D: Fri morn Mar 28 at Achor, JOHN YOUNG ae 74y

ABNER WINES, who for the last year or two has been employed in the Buckeye office, departed for St.Louis last week

JACOB H ARTER left last week on a visit to Kansas with a view of making his future home in that state

L.H.EELLS has sold out his furniture business at Hanover & has gone exclusively into the undertaking business. He will keep on hand a large supply of coffins of all sizes & styles & is prepared to attend funerals at short notice

22 Apr 1872

M: 11th inst at res of bride's mother by JOSEPH FAWCETT, Mayor, GEORGE ROGER & KATE WALKER, all of Salem.

M: 11th inst at res of bride's parents in Salem by REV.WM.- LYNCH, DAVIS T. RUTH & FLORENCE E. DAVIS.

M: 11th inst at res of bride by REV.H.Q.GRAHAM, JOHN FOLEY of Leetonia & MARTHA LEMMON, of Westmoreland Co Pa.

M: 10 Apr at res of bride's father, GASTON HOUSE, Wellsville, by REV.J.D.BROWNLEE, BAZIL ROUGH & NANCY GASTON, both of Wellsville.

D: in Norristown, Carroll Co 16 Apr, ANDREW MEGAVENRY, ae 70y.

D: 12th inst at Leetonia, CHARLEY WOLF, infant son of HARRY & RADY WOLF, ae 9m.

D: 15 res of her son in law, WM.MILLER, in Leetonia Apr 2, MRS. JULIA F. WELLMAN.

D: Mar 29 in Hanover, JAMES B. WILEY, ae 63y.

D: at res of her son in law, MR.A.NOGAL, in Columbiana on Mar 30, SARAH TURNER, in 85th yr.

D: 20th inst, wife of HENRY WILLIAMS of Elkrun Tp, ae about 35y

D: 19th inst, ABRAM GASKILL of Centre Tp, ae 72y.

D: 14th inst MARY PATTERSON, widow of JOSHUA PATTERSON, late of Wayne Tp, ae 76y.

D: 16th inst, FRANK R. HOLLOWAY, s/o LEONARD & ADA of this place, ae 3m 8d.

D: 13th inst, MRS. A.G.ADAMS, w/o JAMES C. ADAMS, near Bunker Hill, Ind, formerly of this place, ae 49y 11m 10d.- (obit) The remains of MRS. A.G.ADAMS w/o JAMES A., formerly of New Lisbon, were brought to this place last Tues & laid beside her 3 children in the "Springer Graveyard."

Mon 29 Apr 1872 (Vol 6 no 4) (from WRHS microfilm)

M: in Walla Walla Wash Territory on 5 Jan, J.M.PARKER & MISS LAURA B GLENN formerly of New Lisbon

M: by JOHN M DICKENSON ESQ, on 27th inst JNO ELIJAH BROOKS & ELIZABETH MAY GARTHWAITE of Salem

M: 18th inst by REV W LYNCH, WILLIAM JENNINGS of Salem & MISS LEAH MINARD of Maho Co

D: Mar 18 of pleurisy, HENRY SHEETS at Wellsville ae 79y 5m

D: Apr 19 of congestion of the lungs, IRA A. SHEETS infant son of W.H. & ELLA M. at Wellsville, ae 10mo

D: at her res in Beloit Wisc. on Wed 10th inst in 70th yr, MRS. SILA BROOKS W/O DeLORMA BROOKS

D: Fri morn in Salem, GEORGE STEINBECK, a native of Hesse Darmstadt, Prussia, in 60th yr

D: 17th inst in Butler Tp, MRS MARGARETTA FOUTZ W/O JOSHUA & DAU OF B & C. SPROWL ae 23y 8m 11d

D: 20th inst at res of her father in Parkersburgh W VA MRS MARGARET THEISSE, D/O ALEXANDER & MARY GAILEY ae 20y 4m

DEATH OF CAPT. CLINTON J POWERS: following from Pittsburtgh Dispatch; the dec'd resided in this place with his parents for several years & friends here regret to hear of his death: CAPT. CLINTON J POWERS of the 4th U.S.Cavalry died at res of his father (B? paper is creased) J.POWERS Esq, ae 27y; graduated at West Point with high honors in 1865 & assigned to 4 USC; joined his regt in Texas, but sickness compelled him to come home; died Sunday afternoon after a brief illness. He was shortly to have married a lady in Antonio Tx, dau of a prominent physician; funeral today from St.Peter's church

Mon 6 May 1872 (Vol 6 no 5) (from WRHS microfilm)

M: by REV H B FRY at the Presby parsonage, Salem Apr 20, JOHN S. MATHEWS of Goshen & MISS OLIVE C BOWMAN of Ellsworth

M: 22nd inst by REV C L WINGET, at the res of the officiating minister in Salem, DAVID S. HOOPS & MISS MARY E. JOHNSON all of this co

M: 2 May by REV WM BAXTER, ALBERT G. PHILLIPS & MISS MARY J. WINDLE both of this co

M: 4th inst by REV D V HYDE, JOHN BAIN & MISS CHRISTIANA WELKER all of this co

M: 29th ult by REV ROBT HAYS, ANGUS LAMOND of Wellsville & MIS ALOINA CURREN of Wayne Tp

D: 26th ult in Salem, MISS SARAH SCIPLE

D: 29th ult in Salem MISS MARY ELIZABETH HUDSON

D: 26th ult in Salem MISS ELLA ROBINSON

D: near Franklin PA MRS. M'KINSTRY ae about 90y, f'ly of Salem

D: 2nd inst MARY DONNELLY WIDOW OF JOHN of Elkrun Tp ae 89y

D: 24th ult very suddenly of inflammation of the bowels, AMOS E. BUSS of Brown Twp., Mahoning.

D: at res of Henry BULLOCK, in East Liverpool, Fri Apr 26, HENRY KIRBY ae 24y 4m

D: at his res in Calcutta on Sat Apr 27, MORGAN FULK ae 76y

D: at res of JAMES AZDELL in East Liverpool on Mon morn Apr 29, JOHN H BRYAN ae 30y 8m 21d

D: at his res on Robison St, East Liverpool Mon night Apr 29, JOHN HENSHALL ae 59y

D: 27th ult CATHERINE FREED of West Tp ae 76y 7m 19d

D: 2nd inst at Titusville Pa, SOPHIA McENTEE dau of EMANUEL STEWART late of Centre Tp ae 28y 10m 25d

H.B.DORWART & HIRAM WHERRY killed a black snake yesterday over 6 feet in length

SAMUEL STEVENSON, an old & well known citizen of Wellsville, died suddenly at his residence in this place on Thurs.

JEHU W. STEWART has removed to the old homestead on the Salem Rd; he has resided at Titusville Pa for several years

13 May 1872

Death of another old citizen: MORRIS E. MORRIS died at res of his grandson, MR.J.L.STRAUGHN, near town on May 10th, at the advanced age of 95y; he was born in Shorpshire, England, in 1778, and removed to Adams Co.Pa. where he married in 1805, and in the same year, immigrated to New Lisbon. He was a soldier in the War of 1812, was by occupation a brick maker & farmer, & an industrious hard working man. Was a member of the Presbyterian Church of New Lisbon.

M: 6th inst at res of THOMAS FARMER by REV C.L.WINGET, GEORGE E. FARMER & MARY E. BAKER.

M: 2nd inst at res of bride's father in Columbiana, by REV.DR.I.N.BAIRD, C.C.BAKER & WILHIE FITZPATRICK;(also), CHARLES C. BAKER of the Salem Journal was married on 2nd to WILHIE FITZPATRICK of Columbiana.

M: 2nd inst at res of bride's parents in Salem by REV.WM. LYNCH, RICHARD POW & ELLA WEBB.

M: 18th ult in Washingtonville by REV.N.WEAVER, J.C.RYAN, ESQ., & EMMA A. ROYER, of Michigan.

M: 1st inst at res of bride's parents in Salem, by Society of Friends, JOSEPH R. MITCHELL of Baltimore, MD & SARAH E. TRAGO.

M: 2nd inst by REV.WM.LYNCH, G.W.FISHER & EDITH CADWALADER, all of Salem.

M: 15 Apr at res of CHARLES BOONE by Rev.H.B.FRY, HENRY SHAFFER & SALLIE E. LEE, both of Salem.

M: 9 May by REV.WM.BAXTER, EDWARD SNYDER & JOSEPHINE McGAFFIC.

Found drowned: last Thurs. CORONER KING called for an inquest on the body of a young man found drowned in a creek about 2 miles west of town, near the res of MR.BROUGHTON. He proved to be MARSHAL SEARS, an inmate of the County Infirmary, & had been fishing. MR. STEVENSON, Supt. of the Infirmary, says he was subject to fits & it is supposed he fell in during an attack. He was buried in the cemetery east of town.

Washingtonville Cornet Band, under the leadership of JAMES STEPHENS, went to New Lisbon today. An excellent band.

COURT: ABIGAIL STEVENS vs JAMES W. STEVENS, dismissed by plaintiff at her costs.

20 May 1872

COURT: JOHN E. NEIL vs ELIZABETH NEIL, petition for divorce, granted.
ANNA MARTTA vs SAMUEL MARTTA, decree for divorce.

M: May 12 in Columbiana by REV.W.DARBY, OSBORN LYON & MARY DERHODS.

M: 9th inst at res of MR.WILLHELM, near Unionville, by REV.S.BAECHLER, JOHN GINTHER & MARY A. GRACE, both of co.

M: 14th inst by same at res of MR.HAAS in Columbiana, CHRISTIAN B. HAAS & SYBILLA LIPP, both of Mahoning Co.

M: at res of bride's father in Salem, May 13, by REV.C.L.-WINGET, HIRAM CAMERON & RUTH BENNET, all of co.

THOMAS THOMPSON, better known in this community as Tommy, was married 23 Apr to MARTHA PARKINS at Rensselaer, Ind.

The trial of DANIEL J. SMITH for the murder of JOHN GRONER at Wellsville, starts on Wed.

MRS. JAMES C. VANFOSSEN, of Madison Tp, has been declared insane, & an application made to admit her to the asylum.

27 May 1872

M: 16th inst by REV.WM.LYNCH, at res of bride's parents in Salem, FRANK JAY CRANK & PHOEBE J. WEST.(see June 10)

M: 16 May by REV.J.C.MELOY, J.M.MAYLONE & EMMA J. DAVIDSON, all of Wellsville.

D: 18th inst, PHILIP F. GEISSE of Wellsville, ae 58y 5m 50d

D: 22nd inst ELIZABETH LOWER w/o ELIAS of Columbiana, ae 52y 8m 23d.

D: 19th inst in Salem, JOEL HOLLOWAY ae 86y.

D: at the house of his grandparent, HANNAH MORRIS in Butler Tp, May 17, FRANKLIN WIDDOES HARRIS, in 10th yr.

D: May 24, BAILEY F. RANDOLPH, of Achor, CCO, ae about 50y

D: 20th inst near Salem, WILLIAM DARLINGTON ae 61y.

JOHN ROBINSON, formerly a res of this place, now of Allegheny City, called to see us.

Man killed, coroner's inquest: LUCIEN H. GAGE, a res of Jefferson, Ashtabula Co.,Oh, had a wife & 2 children; he left home about the 3rd of the month, was traveling with ROSSTON, SPRINGER & HENDERSON'S show; got into a fracas with some of the showmen at Carrollton of Fri a week ago, & received injuries which resulted in his death at the Union House in this place, last Wed. eve. He & some other men had for some time been following the show with a lifting machine, shooting gallery & blowing machine, to which the showmen objected. To drive them off, they were attacked. A blow to the right side of the head caused his death. One of them was THOMAS, or BOB RIVERS, being the boss canvassman.

3 June 1872

M: May 21 by REV.H.B.FRY, assisted by REV.A.B.MAXWELL, HOMER C. BOYLE & MAGGIE BOYLE, both of Salem.

M: 30 May by REV.T.A.SCOTT, at res of bride's father in Elkrun Tp, J.LESLIE of Loudon Co.,VA & JOSEPHINE SMITH.

M: 23d ult in Columbiana by REV.W.DARBY, W.R.KNOWLES & KATE BEARD.

M: 23d ult by REV.T.P.JOHNSTON, SYLVANUS HISEY & ANNA BARCLAY, all of Columbiana.

D: 24th ult near Damascus, MARY STANLEY w/o BENJAMIN.

D: 31 May, JANE WHITACRE w/o JOHN of this place, ae 63y.

D: 25th ult infant child of WM.HAWKINS, ae 4m.

D: June 30(?), JOHN MARQUIS of Centre Tp, ae 95y.

D: Nov 25, MARTHA JANE HELMAN of St.Clair Tp, ae 28y.

The Golden Wedding of MR. & MRS. PETER YOUNG, of this place, was celebrated at their residence last Thurs.

10 June 1872

M: May 28 at their own house in Salem, by R.H.GARRIGUES,-ESQ., CHARLES TROESCHER & MISS MAGDALENA HAMMEL.

M: May 16 by REV MELOY, J.M.MAYLONE & EMMA DAVIDSON, all of Wellsville.

M: 6th inst at Reformed Parsonage by REV.G.M.ALBRIGHT, J.L.WADDLE & REBECCA ANGLEMYRE, both of Leetonia.

M: 16th inst by REV.WM.LYNCH at res of bride's parents, F.JAY CRANK of Pittsburgh PA & PHEBE WEST of Salem (see May 27)

D: 30th ult in Salem, MRS. AMANDA E. SHARPNACK w/o JOHN H. in 35th yr.

D: 8th inst JOSEPHINE JOHNSON d/o JAMES M. & NANCY of New Lisbon, in 17th yr.

D: 8th inst NANCY FIGGINS w/o JOHN of Salineville ae 69y.

D: 8th inst SARAH JAGGAR d/o BENJ.G.& ELIZABETH of this place, in 11th yr.

D: 6th inst SOPHIA MARIA TRUNICK d/o JOHN & NANCY of Centre Tp, ae 2y 2m.

D: at res in Calcutta, May 24, MRS. JANE HAMILTON, ae 79y 10m.

REUNION: a reunion of the RANKIN FAMILY, of whom ROBERT RANKIN, well known to all the old residents of this county, was a brother, was held in New Lisbon at res of one of the sisters, MRS. ELIZABETH CHARTERS. One brother, PETER RANKIN, of Jackson Mich, & 4 sisters, MRS. BARBARA DALLAS, of Irondale, Jefferson Co Ohio, MRS. MARGARET BLAIR, of Butler Co Pa, MRS. JANE McINTOSH, of Wayne Tp, CCO, & MRS. CHARTERS are the surviving members of the family. Their ages are respectively 77,75,73,69 & 66 years.

HENRY ATEN, ESQ., of Wellsville, will soon be 100 years old.

17 June 1872

M: at Squirrel Creek ranche, May 23, by REV.W.F.WARNER, LOUIS O. HOWELL, of El Paso Co., Colorado & K.AUGUSTA WILSON, of New Lisbon.

M: June 12 at Salineville by REV.A.J.LANE, JOHN McGILLIVRAY & SALLIE E. POTTS, d/o ISAAC W. POTTS.

M: May 20 at res of bride's parents in Salineville by REV.A.J.LANE, J.G.DESSELLEM & MARY A. PUMPHREY.

D: June 2 in Salineville, MATILDA STARKEY d/o LEVI G. & NANCY, ae 1y 9m.

D: June 6, JOHN KRONK, in 52nd yr.

D: 16th inst in this place, JAMES B. HARTMAN of Pittsburgh, ae 25y.

ERASTUS EELLS started last Wed. on a visit to Iowa.

Mon 24 June 1872

Death of JOSEPH MAUS. We record the death of another old citizen of New Lisbon, MR. JOSEPH MAUSE, who died suddenly at his residence a short distance west of town last Fri.- MR.MAUS removed to this place in 1818, 54 years ago, & has resided here ever since. He was at one time Sheriff of Col.Co., a farmer by occupation & a good citizen & neighbor. The funeral took place Sat. evening, a large number of relatives & friends attended. (also) Died 21st inst, JOSEPH MAUS of Centre Tp, ae 82y.

M: June 4 by REV.WM.LYNCH, JAMES WILSON & MRS.MARY COY, both of Salem. (see July 1)

M: 15th inst at the Reformed parsonage by REV.G.M.ALBRIGHT, NOAH MELLINGER of Mahoning Co & MARY IDA KELLER of CCO.

M: 19th inst by REV.WM.HUNTER,D.D., JAMES VEERS of Portage Co & MARY FROST, d/o JAMES FROST of Hanover Tp.

M: 15 June at Salineville by REV.A.J.LANE, HENRY SALTER & LENA RUDER, both of Salineville

M: by same at same time & place, EARNEST RUDER & CLEMENTINE HEINSMAN, both of Salineville.

M: June 19 at res of HENRY AMPT, 365 Richmond St., Cincinnati, by REV.DR.TAYLOR, DR.J.S.ROBERTSON & LIZZIE M. ROWE, both of Germantown, Ohio; the Dr. & Lady arrived in town last Fri eve. We wish them a long happy journey.

M: at Smiths Ferry PA by REV.WALLACE, GEORGE POTTS & MAGGIE J. McCLELLAND, both of Salineville.

D: 16th inst LUCINDA SHIVE, w/o DAVID of Centre Tp, ae 24y 2m 1d.

D: at Salineville June 15, JOS. BLAZER in 56th yr.

D: 15th inst, wife of THOMAS McCLELLAN of Centre Tp, ae 67y.

On Monday a week ago, a boy named HARLOW was drowned while bathing in the Ohio River at East Liverpool.

MR. R.McVICKER of Fremont, Neb., paid a visit to his brother JOHN McVICKER ESQ., of this place last week. He & his lady will start early this week on a visit to Ireland.

The remains of a human being, supposed to have been an Indian, were discovered by some workmen in East Liverpool lately, while engaged in excavating a cellar. They indicated a once large frame.

REV.GEORGE N. JOHNSON was installed as pastor of the Presbyterian Church of this place last Friday.

1 July 1872

M: 22nd inst at the Union House by H.E.FROST ESQ, HUGH J. MADISON & HANNAH CRUMBY of Salineville.

M: 24th inst by REV.WM.LYNCH, JAMES WILSON & MARY COY, both of Salem. (see 24 June)

D: June 15 at his res in Hanover Tp, AARON W. DURHAMMER ae 46y 7m.

D: June 29, LOU MORRISON w/o HARVEY ESQ., of New Lisbon, ae 24y; she was a dau of JAMES M. JOHNSON of this place & was beloved by all her friends & acquaintances.

J.L.ROBERTSON & J.L.VALLANDIGHAM, ESQS., are visiting friends & relatives in this place.

MR.J.W.JOHNSON, who has resided for 4 years in Keokuk, Iowa, is visiting friends & relatives here.

Accident: GEORGE HEATON, a young man from Cool Springs, was picking cherries, fell from the tree upon a picket fence, 2 of the pickets entering his back a distance of about 4 inches, one of them going near his heart. He is in critical condition.

8 July 1872

M: 2nd inst at the Parsonage, New Lisbon, by REV.S.Y.KENNEDY, J.K.PICKETT & ANNA R. ENGLAND, both of Salem.

M: 3d inst at ME Parsonage, New Lisbon, by same, J.M.TOOT & LETTIE HOWARD, both of New Lisbon.

M: 6 Jly by JOHN M. DICKINSON, ESQ., JOHN MILLWARD of Pittsburgh & LOUISA SHAW, of CCO

M: at Smiths Ferry PA, July 3, by REV.WALLACE, THOMAS EVANS & LIZZIE BURTON, both of Salineville.

D: in Vicksburg, Miss, June 20, WILLIE K. DORWART, only son of KING & ANNA L. DORWART, ae 1y 1m 27d.

Last Fri morn, DAVID WITTER of North Lima, on awaking early, discovered that his wife was missing & he began searching for her, she having been suffering from mental derangement for some months past. He found her in the store room & beheld his wife a corpse, she holding in one hand a razor, and her throat cut from ear to ear. When found, the hand which held the razor was raised over the throat as though just in the act of making another cut. She attempted to take her life in a similar manner last Nov., but recovered; mental derangement is supposed to be the only cause. —Columbiana Ledger.

ANDREW WALKER, an old respected citizen of Wayne Tp, fell from a load of hay last Tues which resulted in his death the next morning; he was 82. He was returning from the field with his son, when the wagon jolted, he landed on his head & shoulders & was paralyzed by the shock.

15 July 1872

M: June 27 by REV.J.R.DUNDAS, EDEN REEDER & ELIZA HELEN SCHOOLEY, both of Hanoverton.

M: 2nd inst by same, DALLAS SOUTHWORTH & CORNETTA A. LOZIER of Stark Co.

M: 4th inst by same, JAMES M. ENGLISH & ELIZA HOMER, of Mt.Union Oh.

M: 11th inst at Cowan House by JOHN M. DICKINSON ESQ, SAMUEL MADISON & MARY CONNER, all of co.

M: 27th ult in New Garden by E.GARSIDE ESQ., ROBERT B. WOOD & HANNAH A. EWINGS, all of co.

M: 4 July by ELDER J.H.JONES, JAMES M. MARSHALL & ALICE TRIEP, all of Salem.

M: June 22 at res of bride's parents in Salineville, by MAYOR CARUTHERS, JOHN WHEATLEY & SUSAN WELBORNE.

M: July 3 at res of bride's mother by REV.A.J.LANE, GEO. SHECKLER & ISABELLA DONALDSON.

M: same time & place by same, JOHN DONALDSON & FANNIE COLVIN, all of Salineville.

D: June 25, MRS. MARGARET LYMAN, ae about 70y, native of Castle Dermott, County Kildare Ireland & for the past 13 years a res of New Orleans.

D: 12th inst PHEBE ANN BRICKER w/o ENOS of Salem Tp in 27th yr.

D: July 11 in Leetonia, UNDINE M. WESTON, infant daughter of BYRON & JESSIE, ae 9m 28d.

REV.CHARLES CALAHAN, of Centreville, Reynolds Co., Missouri, was outraged on June 23. He was formerly pastor of First Methodist Church in Wellsville for 4 years, some 18 years ago (c1854), and was chaplain of the 84th Regt.Ills.Vol.-Inf. He was beaten by some toughs because he said he knew who burned the courthouse there.

MRS. MARTHA BOOTH, an aged & highly respected lady of East Fairfield, died on 4th inst.

ERASTUS EELLS: long letter in this issue about his trip to Iowa. In it, he mentions: met at Iowa City by old friend & neighbor, DANIEL DORWART; saw JOSEPH LODGE; went to livery stable owned by CALEB WAY, formerly of New Lisbon; saw JACOB CROWL in Chicago; in Bryan, Ohio, visited Mr.F.LUCY, a brother in law, former resident of Franklin Tp., CCO, & visited the grave of his wife.

22 July 1872

Suicide at Wellsville: on Sat. 13th inst, JAMES MILLIGAN, an employee in the railroad shops at Wellsville, committed suicide by hanging himself in a coal shed in the rear of his residence; body discovered by his daughter; he was about 53, left 4 daughters.

M: by HARVEY McCOWN, ESQ., at his office near Enon Valley PA, on 14th inst, BARTLETT STROUSE & AMELIA FENSTERMAKER, both of Leetonia.

D: 9th inst MARY B. FREKSE, of Columbiana, ae 40y 5m 22d.

D: MARY ECKSTEIN, w/o DAVID H., of North Georgetown on July 10, ae 82y 10m.

D: 20th inst, JACOB BARNES of Elkrun Tp, ae 68y.

D: 19th inst, ―――, wife of JOEL JOHNSON of Salem Tp, ae about 50y. [note: this is his 3rd wife, ELIZABETH GEORGE, whom he married 12 Mar 1861. Buried Hart Cemetery.]

D: 18th, MARION WHITACRE, son of DAVID & MARY, ae 4m 2 wks.

29 July 1872

M: July 8 by REV.M.L.WORTMAN, CORNELIUS CHANDLER of Wellsville & JENNIE HART of Dungannon.

M: July 9 by same, WILLIAM E. MOORE of East Liverpool & MATTIE E. RILEY of Industry, Pa.

M: July 24 by REV.J.B.WALLACE, at Smiths Ferry PA, JASON LYTLE & LIZZIE MILLS, all of Maysville, CCO.

D: July 21st, 1862 [sic] at her res. in Wellsville, MRS. FORTUNE WAY, in 59th yr.

D: July 22 after a lingering illness, ELI DAVIDSON of Salem, ae about 70y.

D: 23d inst BENEZETTE F. THOMPSON, of this place, in 64th year of his age.

D: 19th inst in Butler Tp, MARY ETTA HOGUE, w/o LEE, ae 24y.

D: July 19 in Salineville, MRS. MARY WHITAKER in 80th yr

D: July 24 at Salineville, infant son of ALEXANDER & J.M. STITT

D: July 24 at Salineville, ANNIE FALOON d/o JOSEPH & MAGGIE, ae 2y 9m 24d.

D: July 22, MRS. MARY J. MORLEY of East Liverpool, ae 49y 3m 3d.

ROSSTON, SPRINGER & HENDERSON'S Circus in New Lisbon Aug 8.

Last Sat., as REZIN NEWHOUSE was coming into town driving a pair of young horses to a light spring wagon, with his little son & daughter, & his brother in law, MR.SMITH, of Mansfield, OH, they ran away; one child hurt.

Island Run in Beaver Co. PA, is the scene of oil well excitement.

5 Aug 1872

M: July 22 by FATHER E.W.J.LINDESMITH, JOHN BOYL & MARY LAWRY, all of Leetonia.

M: 25th ult in Girard by ELDER J.M.VANHORN, LORENZO T. McCARTNEY of Salem & AMANDA A. FERGUSON of Girard.

M: July 24 by REV.J.B.WALLACE at Smiths Ferry PA, JASON LITTLE & LIZZIE MILLS, all of Maysville, CCO.

D: 31st ult, FRANCIS ZEIGER of Leetonia, ae 72y.

D: 27th ult BENJAMIN HISEY of Fairfield Tp, ae 78y.

D: 34th ult at res of his parents at Columbiana, JOHN FLICKINGER ae 25y.

D: Aug 1 at father's res east of Leetonia in Fairfield Tp, NATHAN NICHOLS in 38th yr.

D: 31st ult MARY J. BAKER, w/o GEORGE of Salineville, ae 28y

D: 2nd inst CARRIE PRITCHARD, youngest d/o R.B. & JOANNA of this place, ae 4y 9d.

D: 22nd ult, HARRIET SWEANNY of Dungannon, ae 83y.

D: 3d inst in New Lisbon, RHODERICK WILSON, infant son of RHODERICK & MAGGIE, ae 9m.

D: July 25, MARY JANE SKINNER, consort of W.A.SKINNER, of Salineville, in 26th yr.

Sad accident: JACOB FISHER, of Springfield Tp., Mahoning Co, last Thurs was unloading hay, his mother driving the team; the chain broke, hit him on head, crushing his skull. He died in a few hours. —Columbiana Ledger.

JAMES R. GRAHAM, formerly a resident of New Lisbon, now of Davenport, Iowa, was here visiting his family.

12 Aug 1872

M: 1 Aug in Salem by SAML HARDMAN JP, B.F.CALLAHAN & A.A. CAVEN.

M: 9th inst at ME Parsonage, New Lisbon, by REV.S.Y.KENNEDY, HENRY E. SINSELL of East Carmel & MARY J. JONES of Columbiana.

Sudden death, on 28th ult, MISS LIZZIE TILL, a young lady who went from Wellsville to Cleveland for a visit a short time since, died suddenly there; called on a friend on King St., was taken ill & died. She lived in Wellsville as a domestic about a year previous to her departure for Cleveland; her father resided in East Liverpool, her mother having died some time since.

D: 31st ult, HARRY RENS, infant son of DALLAS & ARBANA of Salem, ae 4m.

D: 4th inst, WILLIE BROOKS, infant son of HON.J.TWING BROOKS, of Salem, ae 3y.

D: at the Infirmary July 25, DANIEL GOODWIN, ae 53y.

19 Aug 1872

M: 13th inst at New Lisbon by ESQ.FROST, CHARLES SMITH & AMELIA ROANERT, both of Salineville.

M: Aug 13 by REV.WM.P.TURNER, assisted by REV.G.W.RIGGLE, WILLIAM PETERSON & SUSAN ASHBAUGH, all of East Liverpool.

M: Aug 8 by REV.J.N.SWAN, assisted by REV.JOHNSON, JAMES AZDELL & NAN McPHERSON, all of co.

D: 2nd inst in Salem, ALICE JOHNSON,d/o WM.& MARGARET ae 8m.

D: Aug 11, CHARLES B. DRENNAN of Salem, ae 23y 9m.

D: 9th inst at Damascus, AXY HALL, ae about 60y.

D: 30th ult LEWELLA YENGLING d/o JOHN & MARY of Salem ae 5m.

D: 7th inst MINNIE R. JOHNSON d/o JAMES & VILLA of Salem, ae 10m.

D: 1st inst in Salem, ALVA T. WATSON & on the 3rd, ELVIN A. WATSON, twin children of NATHAN B. & ELIZABETH M. WATSON, ae 10m.

D: 10th inst in Salem, DAVID MILLER, formerly of Browns-ville, PA, ae 79y.

D: Aug 13 at East Liverpool, MRS. JANE KENNEY, ae 73y.

D: Aug 7, FREDERICK FRITZ, ae 68y.

D: 13th inst, GEORGIE SHAWK, s/o G.W. & E.M.SHAWK of Cleve-land, ae 8m; funeral at the res of MRS. SHAWK in this place last Thurs.

D.W.McLAIN, of Cincinnati, visited relatives & friends here last week.

JOHN FRASER, formerly of this county, but for 3 years a res-ident of Missouri, was shot & instantly killed a short time ago, while engaged in a fracas with a drunken desperado.

26 Aug 1872

M: 20 Aug by REV.WM.BAXTER, THOMAS YARWOOD & ELIZABETH LINDSAY, both of New Lisbon.

M: 15 Aug by JOSIAH ROHRBAUGH, ESQ., CHRISTINE DRUFUS & ANNA CLAUN, both of Leetonia. [correction Sep 2 says CHRISTIAN KRUFFS & ANNA CLUAN, both of Leetonia.]

M: 15 Aug by SAML HARDMAN JP, HENRY LAW & ROTCHET STAHL, all of Salem. [correction Sep 2 says TOCHET STAHL.]

M: 21st inst at Darlington, PA, by REV.H.N.POTTER, HARM B. DORWART & BELL D. CLECKNER, all of New Lisbon.

D: 16th inst ALFRED TRAIT s/o ALFRED & FRANCIS of Salem, ae 4m 9d.

D: 19th inst HARVEY D. MURRAY, s/o JOHN H. & MARY D., of Hanover Tp, ae 11m 8d.

D: 20 Aug in Minerva, IRENE C. DIBBLE d/o DR.B.S. & E.J. DIBBLE

D: 19th inst FRANKLIN GRONER s/o SIMON & MARY of Centre Tp, ae 14m.

D: at res in St.Clair Tp on 8th inst, DANIEL GONZALES ae 50y

D: 25th inst ENOS NOLD, S/O SAMUEL & VELINA of Salem Tp, ae 3m 1d.

JOSEPH SPRINGER will start soon on trip to California; several years ago he made the journey overland; this time, via the Union Pacific Railroad.

2 Sep 1872

M: 13th ult at New Lisbon by ESQ.FROST, CHARLES SMITH & AMELIA ROANERT, both of Salineville.

M: at res of bride's parents on 22nd ult by JOSEPH FAWCETT, Mayor of Salem, C.H.ELLIS & FRANK SHARP all of Salem.

D: 29th ult, MYRTHA GALBREATH d/o PARKER P. & CELESTIA A., of Fairfield Tp, ae 3m 9d.

D: 24th ult, DANIEL SWEITZER of Salem Tp, ae 75y 10m.

D: 14th ult NANCY MILBURN of Hanover Tp, ae 86y.

D: 20th ult HAMILTON ANDERSON s/o WM. & SARAH of Carroll Co, ae 1y 6m.

D: at Morengo, Iowa, on 26th ult, CHARLES D. HOSTETTER, aged about 71y; had been a resident of New Lisbon from 1824 to 1850; was favorably known.

D: Aug 17, MARGARET HASNESS, w/o ABRAM, of Oregon, Holt Co., MO, formerly of this place, ae 63y.

D: 30th ult, LIZZIE S. PARISH, d/o WM. & MAGGIE, ae 3m.

D: 1st inst infant child of JOHN & HARRIET PATTERSON, of Centre Tp

Death of a prominent citizen: on Thurs night last, LAUGHLIN McLEAN, highly respected citizen of Wellsville, died after a lingering illness; was born in this county, spent his whole life here & for 20 years was prominently identified with Wellsville business. For several years was a member of the firm of GUNN & McLEAN, a member of the UP Church. Wel.Union.

D: 22nd inst of typhoid fever, MRS. KRONK of this place; by her death, an entire family has passed away within a period of about 2 months, the husband going first, followed a few days ago by the only child, and lastly, the wife & mother. —Columbiana Register.

9 Sep 1872

EIGHT CHILDREN AT A BIRTH: The Cincinnati Lancet reports on 21 Aug, MRS. TIMOTHY BRADLEE of Trumbull Co Ohio gave birth to 8 children: 3 boys & 5 girls. They are all living & healthy, but quite small. MR. BRADLEE was married 6 years ago to EUNICE MOWERY, who weighed 273 pounds on the day of her marriage. She has given birth to 2 pairs of twins, and now 8 more, making 12 children in 6 years. MRS. BRADLEE was a triplet, her mother & father both being twins, and her grandmother the mother of 5 pairs of twins. [Ed.note: Trum-bull Co.marriage records show that TIMOTHY A. BRADLEY & EUNICE A. MOWRY were married on 4 Oct 1854, making it 16 years ago, not 6 years.]

M: 1st inst by JOSEPH CREW JP, MITCHELL LITTLE & MAGGIE E. WERNET, all of New Garden. [correction Sep.16 says MITCHELL SITTLE]

M: 31st ult by EST. ROHRBAUGH, at res of bride's father, ORLANDO HOLLOWAY & LOMIE STUCKMAN.

M: 29th ult by REV.J.M.CARR at res of bride's parents in Wellsville, ALEXANDER FORBES & RUTH A COOPER.

M: Sept 5 by REV.WM.FALCONER, assisted by REV.G.W.RIGGLE, GEO.MILLER of Pittsburgh, & BELLA MILLS of East Liverpool.

M: Sep 3 at res of bride's parents by REV.T.A.SCOTT, BENNETT LOCK of Leetonia (formerly of Sharon PA) & LILA J. EELLS, of New Lisbon.

D: at Leetonia 26th ult, MRS. HARRIET M. TOWNSEND in 31st yr

D: 27th ult in Salem, infant child of HENRY & HELEN SCHAFER.

D: 22nd ult at Salem, STEWART S. RUSSEL, infant son of STEWART & ANNIE S., ae 18m 15d.

D: 27th ult in Butler Tp, infant child of JACOB GOODBRAKE ae 3m

D: 31st ult in Salem, JACOB ALBERT VIEGLE s/o JOHN & LOUISA ae 1y 9m.

D: 31st ult in Butler Tp, JULIA A. PARISH d/o the late GEORGE HECKLER, ae 35y.

D: 30 Aug, infant son of MR.& MRS. CHARLES STERNE, of Salem, ae 4m.

D: 31 Aug, CATHARINE EBBERHART w/o CHARLES of Salem ae 31y

D: 31 Aug, FREDERICK W. STILSON of Salem, ae 52y.

D: Sep 3 at res in Salineville of asthma & general debility, MRS. NICHOLSON McGILLIVRAY, in 64th yr.

GEORGE LEONARD of East Palestine met death one night last week under very strange circumstances. A young man named SOLOMON MEEK & LEONARD went to Springfield to get whiskey. After filling their jugs & their bodies with the hellish beverage, they started home. MEEK says when they reached home, LEONARD was very much intoxicated; they got out of the buggy, unhitched the horses, led him to the barn & then laid down on the barn floor. His sister went out & found MEEK lying in the barn asleep, & LEONARD lying with his head out of the buggy, quite dead. -Col.Register

16 Sep 1872

M: 3rd inst by REV.S.BAECHLER at res of JESSE GILBERT in Middleton, IRA T.TULLIS & MOLLIE L. GILBERT.

M: 1st inst at Chambersburg by LEVI KING ESQ, REUBEN HAAS & EMMA ZIMMERMAN.

M: 3 Sep by REV.ROBT.HAYS, GEORGE DYSART & HARRIET SANDERS, both of Salineville.

D: 4th inst in Salem, HADLEY TANNER, ae about 40y.

D: 5th inst, infant child of JERRY LACEY of Salem, ae 8m.

D: 6th inst in Salem, CHARLES A. RUSSELL ae 28y.

D: at West Leetonia Sep.3, PETER HARRINGTON, ae 29y 6m.

D: 13th inst FRANK GASKILL of New Lisbon, ae 40y.

D: 7th inst MARY McALLISTER, widow of HECTOR of Franklin Tp, ae about 80y.

D: 7th inst, JOHN SMITH, s/o ALEXANDER & JANE, of Elkrun Tp, ae 9y.

D: 8th inst ELIZABETH RINEHART w/o SOLOMON of Centre Tp, ae 94y 7m 12d.

Sudden death of FRANK GASKILL: he went to work in good health, had pain in head; remarked to wife that he was dying, sorry to leave the children. Ruptured blood vessel.

FITZ BRADY has moved his barber shop to the south corner of the new Court House, and fitted it up in fine style.

JOSEPH S. LODGE ESQ., of Iowa City, called to see us Sat. on way to Soldiers & Sailors Convention in Pittsburgh Pa, stopping to see friends.

23 Sep 1872

Petition for divorce: WILLIAM McINTOSH vs ANN McINTOSH, filed 21 Mar 1872, for wilful absence.

D: 13 Sep, RHODA JANE GLENN, d/o JAMES & ANN of Salineville, ae 16m.

D: 21st inst, HATTIE BELL HUM, d/o R.W. & MARY, ae 9m 4d.

D: Sep 14, WILLIAM E. WARD s/o MAXIN & LYDIA A., ae 10m 4d.

M: 11 Sep by REV.J.C.MELOY, W.A.BURNETT & MRS. S.A.WALKER, all of Wellsville.

M: by REV J.B.WALLACE at Smiths Ferry PA Aug.11, JAMES M. FISHER & MARY A. JEROME, both of Steubenville.

M: by same Sept.3 at Smiths Ferry, JOSIAH SCOTT & CAROLINE M. MOORE, both of East Liverpool.

M: by same Sept 9 at Smiths Ferry, THOMAS EVANS of Hancock Co WVA, & MARTHA QUINN of CCO.

M: by same Sept 10 at Smiths Ferry, HERBERT SMITH & EMMA ABBOTT both of East Liverpool.

M: 5th inst at res of bride's father in Osage Iowa, JOHN KIMBLE of Columbiana & EMMA MORGAN of Osage.

M: 12th inst by ELDER HENRY KURTZ at his res in Columbiana, JACOB A. WARD & CATHARINE HECK, all of co.

M: 15th inst at Columbiana by JOSIAH ROHRBAUGH ESQ., ALBERT A. FARMER & ZILLA BELL TAYLOR.

M: Sept 3 by REV.C.P.GOODRICH, JNO.W.KNOWLES of East Liverpool & MRS. LOUISA C. MORRIS of Johnston, Trumbull Co Oh.

M: 19th inst by J.M.DICKINSON, ESQ., DAVID S. PEPPLE & MARY E. BRINKER.

M: 12th inst by EDWARD PETTIT JP, WILLIAM G. CRAWFORD & SALON J. MEIGHER, all of co.

EMMET KANNAL of Rensselaer, Ind., is here visiting.

DR.JAMES GRAHAM, a former resident of this place, now of Cincinnati, is here visiting.

REV.JOHN B. GRAHAM, of Holliday's Cove WVA, called to see us & to renew his subscription to the paper.

SAMUEL CLECKNER had one of his thumbs crushed last Monday morning while working in the coal mines west of town.

30 Sep 1872

Fire at the Lunatic Asylum at Newburgh, Cuyahoga Co Ohio. Eleven of the inmates at the Newburgh asylum, from this county, were returned on Saturday.

An aged colored woman of Salem, named BARRETT, was killed at the railroad crossing a mile west of that place on Thurs last by a passing train.

D: Fri Sep 20 at Leetonia, LIZZIE SINNING, d/o C.C. & ELIZABETH, ae 19y 6m 17d.

D: 19th inst at Leetonia, FREDERICK HOWENSTINE, a native of Switzerland, ae about 26y.

D: Sep 22, MARTHA ANNE EVANS, d/o ISAAC & MARTHA A. of Salineville, ae 9m 21d

D: 28th inst FRANKLIN ENTRIKIN, s/o GEORGE of Salem Tp, ae about 25y.

M: Sep 25 by REV.S.Y.KENNEDY, EDWARD M. JOHNSON & HELEN SMALL, both of New Lisbon.

M: same day by same at ME Parsonage, ROBERT CHISHOLM & ELLEN M. BEER, both of Homeworth.

M: Sep 18 at res of bride's parents in Salineville, by REV.S.M.COON, WILLIAM ROSE & EMMA HALL.

M: Sep 11 by REV.J.C.MELOY, W.A.BURNETT & MRS. S.A.WALKER all of Wellsville.

DAVID GALBREATH, residing near Winona, committed suicide last Tues by cutting his throat with a large knife. He was a tanner by occupation, and managed 3 establishments, one being the NELSON tannery in this place. Caused by temporary insanity & dyspepsia. He leaves no children.

Mon 7 Oct 1872 (Vol 6 no 27) (from WRHS microfilm)

M: Sep 14 by same, WM. SHINN & MISS MARY A. FOX all of Salem

M: 1st inst by REV T A SCOTT at res of bride's parents in New Lisbon, ROBERT ARMSTRONG of Sharon Pa & MISS MATTIE R. EELLS

M: Sep 19 by same at his res, IRA GASTON & MISS JOSEPHINE CONKLE all of this co

M: 2nd inst by REV S Y KENNEDY, O.W.HASKELL of W VA to MISS SARAH E. McGAVRAN of Guilford CCO

M: Sep 25 by same, ROBERT CHISHOLM & MISS ELLEN M. BEE, both of Homeworth

M: Sep 24 by REV W LYNCH, EMMET KANNAL of Indiana & MISS MARY E. DUCK of Salem

M: in 1st Presbyterian Church of Newton Hamilton PA, Oct 2, by REV S W POMEROY, JOHN E. HESSIN ESQ., of Manhattan Kans & CORDELIA POSTLETHWAITE of the former place

M: Sep 19 by REV R G TUNNISON, at Alliance, WILLIAM M. JOHNSTON & MISS ROSE ANN E. HOEY both CCO

D: in Leetonia Mon Sep 16 of cholera infantum, CARRIE MAY GRAFTON D/O EH & MINNIE ae 1y 20d

D: Sep 18 in Butler Tp CCO, LOUISA BOWMAN W/O JOHN ae 21y 11m 28d

D: 10th ult MRS JANE FOGG WIDOW OF THELATE EBENEZER of Salem ae 64y

D: 30th ult in Wayne Tp, GERSHOM CALVIN IRWIN S/O WILLIAM of Pittsburgh ae 21y

D: Sep 25, ELMER WOODWARD S/O PETER & ELIZABETH of Hanover ae 9m 8d

D: 28th ult HANNAH S. COULSON W/O SAMUEL of West Tp ae 59y 2m 26d

JOE H. GROSNER of Mansfield, formerly of this place, was married on 28th ult at Sharon PA to MISS BERTHA ALEXANDER of the latter place

CORNERSTONE LAID: yesterday a week ago the cornerstone of the new CATHOLIC CHURCH at Salineville was laid with Rt.Rev. RICHARD GILMORE, Bishop of Cleveland assisted by REVS P J McGUIRE & VATTMAN of Summitville & Dungannon. A stand was erected adorned with green & the national colors from which the Bishop preached a masterly sermon. The building will be a frame, 36 feet front, 60 feet back & has a high & healthy location in West Salineville

Mon 14 Oct 1872 (Vol 6 no 28) (from WRHS microfilm)

M: at Smiths Ferry PA Sept 26 by SQUIRE PETTIT, SILAS W. WASHBURN of E.Liv & MISS SARAH MARGARET BEEBOUT of Sloan's Station Ohio

M: 26th ult at Salem by JESSE HAWLEY JP, HENRY W. FARMER & MISS CATHARINE BAKER

M: in ME Ch, E.Liv Thur eve Oct 10 by REV W P TURNER, W.J.SMITH of Wash.Co.Pa. & MISS LIZZIE TAYLOR of E.Liv Oh

M: Sep 12 by REV J B WALLACE, at Smiths Ferry PA, ALFRED J JOHNSON & SALLIE FOUTTS both of E.Liv OH

M: Oct 8 by REV S M COON, W.W.McGILL & MISS LAURA E. MONTGOMERY all of Salineville

KILLED BY THE CARS: about 6 o'clock last Wed eve a man named WILLIAM COLE was discovered lying on the track of the P FT W & C RW at Leetonia. Upon going to the place, it was discovered that he had been run over by a train of cars & was dead. His head was laid open & the parts scattered in every direction. Near the body lay another man dead drunk & who the next day could give no account of the terrible accident- He didn't even know that a train had passed although when found his head was resting on one of the ties & close to the rail. CORONER A B KING was summoned & held an inquest upon the body of COLE. The jury found a verdict in accordance with the above facts. The deceased was a res of Allegheny City was a pudler by occupation & was employed at the Leetonia Rolling Mill. He leaves a wife but no children.

69

D: 7th inst in Salem, SARAH ELIZABETH STREET W/O S.T.STREET ESQ, in 32nd yr

D: Sept 23 JOSIAH KEITH of West Tp ae 78y

D: Oct ---, dau of WILLIAM & MARY KEGNEY of Franklin Tp ae 14y

D: Oct --- MARTHA JANE WINDER D/O L.H. & E.J. ae 1y 11m 24d

D: Sep 23d at Smiths Ferry PA HARRY HOWARD WALLACE S/O REV J B & MARY ae 1y 1m 24d

21 Oct 1872

M: 16th inst at res of MRS. FRANCES BYE, by REV.M.CARR, P.C.YOUNG ESQ., & ANNA E.L.A.ATEN, of Wellsville. [note: he was PETER CLEVER YOUNG]

M: 10th isnt at East Liverpool by REV.W.P.TURNER, W.J.SMITH of Washington Co PA & LIZZIE C. TAYLOR of East Liverpool.

M: 10th inst at res of WM.DANIEL by Friends ceremony before R.G.GARRIGUES, CHARLES O. HEGGEM & ELIZA R. BOE, both of Salem, & formerly of Norway.

M: Oct 7 by FATHER LINDERSMITH, JOHN EISENHAUER & MARY NAEBART.

M: Oct 10 by REV.MR.COYLE, ADAM FISHER & MARY ELLEN SHARLEY, both of co.

M: 17th inst by REV.G.W.JOHNSON at res of bride's parents, WILLIAM HAINES of Carroll Co & ALICE KURTZ of CCO.

M: Oct 17 at res of HENRY CROFTS by REV J.C.TAGGART, J.W. HICKMAN & EMMA McLEAN, both of co.

M: 16th inst by REV.H.B.FRY, A.D.ARRISON of Philadelphia & MARY BROWN of Salem.

M: at res of bride in Wellsville on Oct 17 by REV.J.B.WILKIN, GEORGE MACK & SARAH M. STEELE, both of Wellsville.

M: 3d inst by REV.H.H.HILBISH at his res in North Lima, SAMUEL VANSICK [sic: VANSYCKLE] & SUSAN WINDLE, both of Fairfield Tp.

M: at Canfield 10th inst by REV.ROGERS, B.G.BAKER of Columbiana & MARY JANE BEAN, of Green Village, Mahoning Co.

D: at the Infirmary Oct 17, ANTHONY LEWIS, ae 71y.

D: 16th inst A.S.WARD of New Lisbon, ae 62y.

D: 16th inst ISABELLA YOUNG of Franklin Tp, ae 82y.

D: 17th, ROBERT LOCH s/o WILLIAM & ESTHER of Elkrun Tp, ae 5y.

Mon 28 Oct 1872 (Vol 6 no 30) (from WRHS microfilm)

Church directory:
PRESBYTERIAN — REV GEORGE N. JOHNSON
UNITED PRESBY — REV T A SCOTT
DISCIPLE — REV WM BAXTER
METHODIST EPISCOPAL — REV S Y KENNEDY
PROTESTANT EPISC. — REC GEORGE S. VALLANDIGHAM

M: at res of bride's parents Salem, Oct 17, by REV W R SPINDLE, JOSEPH REITZELL & MISS SADIE E. STACKHOUSE

M: by Rev JOHN C. COIL, Oct 17 JOSEPH STEWART & MISS ELIZABETH BIGLER all of this co

M: 10th inst by REV B FRY, A D ARRISON of Philadelphia & MISS MARY BROWN of Salem O

M: 10th inst by Friends ceremony, CHARLES O'HEGGEM & ELIZABETH R. BOE both of Salem

M: Sabbath eve Oct 6 at his res in Salineville by REV A J LANE, THOMAS P FRANCIS & MISS MARY E. ERION of Mt.Vernon, Linn Co Iowa

D: 21st inst SARAH LOCH D/O ELIZABETH of Elkrun Tp ae 5y 8m 20d

D: 14th inst in Wayne Tp wife of CAPTAIN JAMES WORMINGTON ae 76y

D: Oct 14 at his daughter's res near Clarkson, MORDECAI CRAWFORD of Leetonia ae 69y 29d

D: at Leetonia Oct 11, JANE LUNAMAKER ae 55y 8m 20d

D: at Leetonia Oct 14 SARAH A. GILLESPIE W/O J.S. ae 26y 11m 6d

D: at Leetonia Oct 8 ROBERT BURESS ae 8y 10m 12d

D: in Salem on 18th inst JNO. SNOOK ae 74y 6m

D: on eve of 21st inst MRS MARTHA BEESON W/O EDWARD of Salem ae 47y

D: Sep 23 JOSEPH KEITH of West Tp ae 78y

D: 14th inst at his res near Damascus, JAMES RALEY in 72nd yr of age

D: 18th inst MALVINA BURFORD W/O DAVID of Salem ae —y

D: Thurs morn Oct 24th at Jethro, HARRY LLOYD S/O JOHN & CATHARINE ae 18mo

A new United Presbyterian congregation was organized at Leetonia on the 19th inst. Rev T A SCOTT of New Lisbon officiated

REV DAVID HARGEST lately from Wales, England, has been appointed to the charge of the Presby congregation at Oak Ridge in Yellow Creek Tp & Madison Church in Madison Tp, supplying the pulpits on alternate Sabbaths

Mon 4 Nov 1872   (Vol 6 no 31) (from WRHS microfilm)

COURT:
BRIDGETTA SULLIVAN vs W ILLIAM: divorce granted & custody of child given to petitioner

OBIT: Died at his residence in Salem on the morning of the 27th of Oct DANIEL WALTON ae 79y. He was one of the Soldiers in the war of 1812; was married to SUSAN BOSWELL in Philadelphia in 1814 by whom he had 13 children; 4 died in infancy, 8 are yet living, 4 boys & 4 girls. In 1833 he moved from Phila. to Ohio & settled in Goshen Twp., what was then called the "Beech." By perseverance, industry & frugality he succeeded in opening up a nice farm, planting orchards & fruit trees , doing the hard work of a pioneer & raised his large family of children. In 1845, himself, wife & daughter united with the Baptist church of Salem, where he has ever continued an exemplary & devoted member; his faith & trust in God was that of a confiding child in an earthly parent. In 1849 his first wife died. In 1853 he was again married to MARY COWN. She too united with the Baptist church & they were truly helpers to each other. She died just 7 weeks before him; both their remains rest side by side in our little Salem cemetery. Peace to their ashes. Salem Republican.

D: 27th inst DANIEL WALTON of Salem in 79th yr

M: 31 Oct at the Reformed Parsonage by REV G M ALBRIGHT, JOHN MEHAN & MISS MAGGIE SHIVE both of this co

M: 30th ult by REV S BAECHLER, at his res in Col'ana, MR CLAYTON F. LAU & MOLLIE A. BAECHLER

M: Oct 31 by REV W LYNCH, CHAS.S.BRADFORD, M.D. & MISS MARTHA J. PENNOCK both of Damascoville

D: 21st inst of typhoid fever, SUSAN HOLLOWAY W/O JOSHUA of Salem ae about 65y

D: Thur Oct 24 at her res near Mt.Union, MRS ELIZA CONKLE W/O PETER ae 31y 7m

D: at res of her father in Franklin Square, MARY FARMER W/O EMANUEL Oct 25 ae 27y

D: 1st inst THOMAS RICHEY EVANS S/O DAVID D. & REBECCA J. of Elkrun Tp ae 3d

Trial of D J SMITH for the murder of WILLIAM GRONER on 19 June 1871, commenced; found for manslaughter only. Testimony of witnesses printed...WM. GRONER, son of dec'd; PHILIP BRUNER, son in law of dec'd; THOS. LAWSON, of Wellsville; DR. HAMMOND; WM. BRIGHT of Wellsville; WILLIAM LUCAS of Connecticut, a wool manufacturer; WM. McINTOSH; HENRY SHAUB; QUIGLEY HAMILTON of Georgetown PA; W.D.ROSS; JOHN GREEN; ALEX. DENHAM; EDWARD KIRKPATRIC; WM. KIRKPATRIC; JAS.- McBRIDE; DANIEL SMITH, DEFDT

Mon 11 Nov 1872 (Vol 6 no 32) (from WRHS microfilm)

M: by REV GEORGE VOGLESONG at Hanover Nov 5, JOHN W. MILLER & SAMANTHA BAUGHMAN

M: Oct 31 in Pittsburgh by ALDERMAN McMASTERS, WILLIAM DUNN of Wellsville, OH & MISS MAGDALENE SIMPSON of Dundee Scotland

D: Oct 24 in Col'ana, HARRIET LUELLA THOMPSON ae 10y 8m 18d

D: 4th inst MRS JANE MONTGOMERY of Elkrun Tp ae 54y

D: 8th inst MARY JANE ATCHISON W/O JAMES of Elkrun ae 40y 5m 26d

D.J.SMITH was sentenced to the Penitentiary for 6 yrs

18 Nov 1872

M: 14th inst by REV.T.A.SCOTT, at res of bride's parents near New Lisbon, J.L.WELLINGTON & GUSSIE MORRISON.

M: by REV.J.C.MELOY, Nov 6, W.B.McCORD & HELEN L. GEISSE, all of Wellsville. [Ed.note: this is WILLIAM B. McCORD, b 20 Nov 1844, Editor of "History of Columbiana Co., Ohio and Representative Citizens", 1905; see sketch p450]

M: by REV.J.N.SWAN, at res of bride Nov 7, CLARENCE V. WILCOXIN & MARY McPHERSON, all of co.

M: by REV J.M.KENDIG at res of bride Nov.7, FRANKLIN SCHAUWEKER of Canfield & ALICE KEMBLE of Columbiana.

M: 2nd inst by JOSEPH FAWCETT, Mayor of Salem, EPHRAM MURPHY & ANNA E. SNYDER, both of Salem.

M: Nov 4 at home of bride's parents in Salem, by REV.W.R. SPINDLER, HOWARD B. DOLE & FLORA WALTON.

M: Nov 7 at res of bride's parents by REV.A.B.MAXWELL, assisted by REV.ROGERS of Canfield, RILY M. GILBERT & ANNIE E. KING, all of Leetonia.

M: Oct 10 at res of bride's parents by REV.T.A.McCURDY, JAS.F.BRICE of Wellsville & ANNIE E. ADAMS, of Steubenville.

D: Nov 11 at his res in Wellsville, ALLAN McDONALD ae 81y.

D: 9th inst at Salem, JACOB RITTER, ae 93y 6m.

D: 12th inst SARAH ANN BINSLEY w/o JOSHUA of Wayne Tp ae 34y.

D: 17th inst in New Lisbon, MRS. SARAH A. VOGAN w/o J.W. ae 51y 7m 18d.

25 Nov 1872

M: 10th inst by REV.WEAVER at his res in Greenford, JOHN ROYER & ANNA HARMON of Mahoning Co.

M: 17th inst by JOSIAH ROHRBAUGH ESQ., ISAAC HURTMAN & ANNAMELIA KYSER both of CCO.

M: Nov 7 by R.A.GARRIGUES ESQ., WILLIAM RIDOUT & LIZZIE HAZEL.

M: 14th inst at res of WM.TEES, New Brighton, PA, by REV. CRICHLOW, W.E.LEASE of Salem & LIZZIE BENKOWSKI of Mt.Vernon, OH.

M: 3 Sep by REV.ROBT.HAYS, ANDREW B. BINSLEY & ELLA J. HAYS, both of Wayne Tp.

M: same day by same, GEORGE DYSART & HARRIET SANKERS, both of Salineville.

M: at res of JOHN HUDSON, Middleton Tp, by JOSEPH KANNAL ESQ., JAMES ROHOR & SUSAN CROSS, both of co.

M: 7th inst by REV.ROBT HAYS, CASPER TRITT of Greenvillage, Mahoning Co, & ANNA M. FARMER, eldest daughter of GEORGE W. FARMER of Salineville.

M: Nov 14 by REV.JNO.R.DUNDAS, D.D., JNO. SINGER of Alliance & MARY JOHNSON of Summitville.

M: Nov 14 by REV.JOHN LONG, S.ADDISON BATCHELOR of Wellsville & SALLIE P. KAYE of Pittsburgh PA.

D: at his res in St.Clair Tp Oct 15 of consumption, CHARLES HAMBLE ae 27y.

D: 19th inst MRS. JANE BENNER of Centre Tp, ae 73y.

D: 12th inst SARAH ANN BINSLEY w/o JOSHUA of Wayne Tp, ae 34y.

2 Dec 1872

M: 21st inst by REV.WM.LYNCH, JAMES WOODRUFF & MARY F. BEAR, both of Salem.

M: at res of bride's parents on Nov 21 by REV.C.A.BUCKS, J.L.CLARK of New Lisbon & MARY E. WHITE of Shannon, Carroll Co., Ill.

D: 22nd inst of typhoid fever, MRS. ELIZABETH STRICKLER w/o DANIEL of Columbiana, ae 26y 9m 9d.

D: 29th ult ELIZABETH BRICKER d/o PHILIP & MARY of Salem Tp, ae 16y 8m.

D: Near Teegarden's Mill Nov 13, PETER COFFIELD, ae 36y.

D: near Leetonia Nov 20, MARY GINTHER, ae 3y 10m.

9 Dec 1872

M: 25th ult at Pittsburgh by REV.I.N.BAIRD, of Allegheny City, THOMAS COPE & RETTIE GREENAMYER both of Columbiana.

M: 21 Nov by REV.JOHN A. CLEMMENT at his res in Knox Tp, SAMUEL HESTAND & CLEMENTINE SUMMERS, both of co.

M: 21st Nov by same, at res in Knox Tp, GALEN W. SUMMERS & JANE CONSER, both of co.

D: 1st inst in Fairfield Tp, MRS. ELIZABETH HISEY w/o JOSEPH, ae 80y.

D: at the Infirmary, Nov 20, ELIZA J. STEEL, ae 19y.

D: 9th ult in Butler Tp, DEBORA M. FRENCH w/o BARZILLAI, in 46th yr.

D: 19th ult in Salem Tp, HANNA MARTIN ae 72y

D: 17th ult near Winona, Butler Tp, MRS. ARAMINTA MERRILL ae 32y

D: 1st inst, LAURETTA MERRILL d/o ARAMANTA MERRELL, deceased, ae 14y.

D: 2nd inst HETTIE FAWCETT of Salem in the ---y of her age.

D: 2nd inst in Salem, JANE DENNIS in 85th yr.

Burned to death Sat morn last, a little son of WM.S.MENDELL, foreman in JUDGE RIDDLE's tannery, while playing about the grate with other children, got too near the fire & clothes ignited; died the following day. Was but 2y 4m old. Well.Un.

Chinese at Beaver Falls, PA: "65 more almond eyes, pig-tailed shufflers arrived at Beaver Falls. This addition makes the total number now employed there 155. They are strike breakers, to work at cutlery works of the Harmony Society when the Englishmen struck." [Refer to Beaver Falls Area Centennial, Historical Salute to the Centuries, 1868-1968 for more detail]

Mon 16 Dec 1872 (Vol 6 no 37) (from WRHS microfilm)

D: 12th inst LEONARD LOUY of this place ae 77y

M: Thurs Nov 28 at res of PETER DAVIDSON in Wellsville by REV J D BROWNLEE, THOMAS DICKSON & MISS MAGGIE FRASER all of Wellsville

M: 12th inst at res of bride's parents near New Lisbon by REV G N JOHNSTON, W.D.KINTY & MISS NANNIE BROWN all of Centre Tp

D: Sat morn 30 Nov at his res near Wellsville, JOSEPH H BLACKBURN ae about 65y

D: Mon Dec 9 HATTIE MELVINA BURFORD infant d/o D.B.BURFORD ae 6m21d

D: 7th inst EMMA A. COPE D/O SAMUEL of Fairfiel Tp ae 20y 2m 3d

S.W.ORR, ESQ., of Kingston MO, formerly a res of this place, has been spending several days in town

WM. KYLE, an employee in Farmer's coal bank at Salineville was killed on Wed last by the falling of a large piece of slate.

TERRIBLE DEED: A MAN MURDERS HIS TWO CHILDREN WITH A HATCHET: FLIGHT, CAPTURE & IMPRISONMENT OF THE MURDERER

We give particulars of a brutal & revolting murder committed in the county. ERBEN PORTER, residing 12 1/2 mi east of Columbiana, last Thurs morn, murdered his two little girls ae 1 & 3 yrs. He was living with his father in law, HENRY FLICKINGER who with his wife, had gone to a neighbor's to assist in butchering early that morning. There were in the house at the time of the murder, PORTER, his 2 children & 2 brothers in law, aged about 12 & 15 y, & MRS PORTER. The children were playing & Porter suddenly smote them dead. Mrs P was upstairs, the brothers in law raised an alarm; Porter left the house, going towards Leetonia & had telegraphed MARSHALL ROLLER of that place to come & arrest him; report says the family has been afraid of him for a long time; last winter he drove his wife & a small child out of doors on a cold night & the latter was badly frozen & afterwards died from the effects. The dead girls were named MINNIE & ADELINE. The Pittsburgh paper says that Porter was married some 4y ago to a lady in Col'ana Co but was divorced. He disappeared from his 2nd wife in April last & did not reappear until October. There is nothing to indicate that he was either drunk or crazy when he committed the deed.

23 Dec 1872

THE PORTER MURDER: last week we gave the brief story of this unnatural & brutal murder. MRS. PORTER testified that she saw him go upstairs & took a hatchet out of a chest. Shortly, "I heard MINNIE utter a pitiful cry...I said, ERB, what have you done? He left the house; I opened the door & found my children lying on the floor dead. I raised the alarm to the neighbors. He left home about first April last, didn't return til mid October; said he was in Illinois. He threatened to take my life & the childrens' lives about 3 months ago. MINNIE was 3 yrs old on 22 Nov last & ADELAIDE 1yr old on 23 Oct last." The funeral of the children took place in Col'ana on Sabbath week, at the ME Church. A correspondent of the Cleveland Leader interviewed PORTER in jail in Warren, stating "I was born in Columbiana Co in the year 1840, in the part of the county that was afterward annexed to Mahoning Co.; have always lived in this county; was a soldier in the late war, first enlisted in 24th Ohio Regiment, Co.C, serving 3y 1m 9d; afterward enlisted in 70th Ohio Veterans, til the close of the war; was slightly wounded at battle of Chickamauga; was married to MISS YOUNG, of my county, prior to going into the army, but was divorced shortly after my return. I've been married to MISS FLICKINGER about 4 years, she being a lady of nearly 25 years of age; had no children by the first wife, but 3 by my present wife, one of them having died sometime since. I did not know how the children were killed. Have been living with my father in law for the last 2 months; has been some disagreement with wife's parents, also wife's brother; think they have not used my wife right. Had a fight with wife's uncle." The reporter describes him as a man of thought, with black hair, heavy black moustache & a keen eye. He is either an innocent man with an iron nerve to thus bear the shocking news coolly, or one of the most horrid & willful of murderers to thus coolly do the deed laid to his charge. [IRWIN G. PORTER & SARAH JANE YOUNG married on 28 Jan 1860 by GEO.LAMB, JP]

M: Dec 12 by REV.GEO.N.JOHNSON, JOHN W. FREEMAN & MARY F. LEE of this place.

M: by Rev.J.N.SWAN at res of bride Dec.12, ALEXANDER SHAW & MISS SMITH, d/o DANIEL SMITH, all of CCO.

M: 4th inst by REV.W.DARBY, W.M.BUSHONG & L.E.TODD, all of Columbiana.

D: 16th inst O.L.LODGE of Wellsville, ae about 51y.

D: 17th inst at Wellsville, MISS MARY QUINLAND.

LUNDY BRIDENSTINE, a jeweller of Minerva, was found dead in his store on last Fri. forenoon, with a bullet hole in his breast. At his feet lay a small pistol, in one chamber, was the shell of an exploded cartridge. It is supposed that the shooting was accidental, there being no evidence to show any reason for suicide.

D: at Leetonia Dec 8, JOHN CLARK s/o JOHN & LYDIA, ae 2y 9m 9d.

Legal: AGATHA LING, widow of LAWRENCE LING dec'd, residing in state of Michigan, CATHARINE BAGALEY & JOHN her husband, MARY PEIFFER & PERCILA her husband, CAROLINE DIVELLE & STEPHEN her husband, TRACY WILLIAMS & DAVID her husband, residing in Williams Co., Ohio; LINORA ELIZA LING & AMELIA SOPHIA LING, minor children of DENNIS LING dec'd, residing in Penna., will note that petition was filed by JOSEPH LING, demanding partition of real estate, lot 8 in Hanover & lots 216 & 217 in PTTER, BROWN & ARTER'S addition to the town of Hanover.

30 Dec 1872

Terrible accident: last Tues, the res of MRS.McLENEN on Brush Creek, about 6 miles from this place, was discovered to be in flames; after the fire, some charred human bones were discovered among the debris, showing that the lady had been consumed. The deceased was 90 years of age. —Salineville Index.

M: 17th inst by J.M.DICKINSON, JP, PATRICK FLEMING & JULIA FARRALL.

M: 26th inst by J.M.DICKINSON JP, GUSTAVIS M. FLICKER & AMELIA EUNGWIRTH, all of co.

M: Dec 24 at res of bride's parents by REV.J.J.JACKSON, ISAIAH FLICKINGER & MANT M. TULLIS, both of Columbiana.

M: at res of bride's parents Dec 23 by JETHRO MANLEY ESQ., JOHN EARDLY & SARAH HILL both of East Liverpool.

M: at res of bride's parents Dec 25 by same, STEPHEN SMALL of Beaver Falls PA & ELIZA E. RIGBY of East Liverpool.

D: at Leetonia Dec 18, MARY REBECCA DILDINE d/o JOHN C. & ESSIE LURETTA, ae 3y 8m 10d.

D: at Leetonia, Dec 19, infant of JOHN & SARAH WHITEFOOT.

D: Dec 22 at Infirmary, BARBARA PALMER ae 72y.

D: 24th inst at Salineville, JOHN McGAVERN, in 75th yr.

Relatives of MARTIN MEACHAM, recently deceased in California, and a native of Ohio, are inquired for. His neighbors think he was from Columbiana Co., that he had a brother, a doctor, and a sister. Further information from J.A.MYERS, Clerk of Court, or the Journal office, New Lisbon.

From the Freeport Ill. Bulletin, we learn of the death of MATTIE J. GILES, D/O E.& C.C.GILES, of Holden, MO., formerly of this place.

1873

Jan 6,13,20,27	Feb 3,10,17,24	Mar 3,10,17,24,31
Apr 7,14,21,28	May 5,12,19,26	
Jly 7,14,21,28	Aug 4,11,18,25	Jne 2,9,16,23,30
Oct 6,13,20,28	Nov 3,10,17,24	Sep 1,8,15,22,29
		Dec 1,8,15,22,29.

Mon 6 Jan 1873 (Vol 6 no 40)

M: on 2 Jan by REV WM BAXTER, J.H.KAISER & MISS MARY E. STOCK, both of this co.

M: 20th Dec 1872 by REV.THOMAS P. JOHNSON, HARVEY LIST & MISS MOTTIE TRENT of Col'ana.

M: in Canton on 26th ult by REV.FATHER GAMBER, J.S.V.LAWLER, editor of the Carroll Co Chronicle & Miss EMMA McGREGOR, daughter of the editor of the Stark Co Democrat.

M: on New Year's Eve by REV.R.H.McCLELLAND, at the res of the bride's parents , R.F.TAGGART of Palestine Oh & MISS HARRIET EVELYN BREWSTER, of North Beaver Tp, Lawrence Co Pa.

M: 31st ult by REV.W.R.SPINDLER, JOHN B. PARK & MISS ANN HOLE all of Salem.

D: Mon night 30 Dec 1872, infant child of GEORGE McCORD of Wellsville, aged 3m.

D: Mon night 30 Dec 1872, in Wellsville, JOSEPH STOFFEL aged about 18y.

D: 31st inst at his late residence on Broadway, ABRAM M. SHANE of Salem, aged 37y.

Mon 13 Jan 1873 (Vol 6 no 41)

M: Dec 31st by REV.W.DARBY, PROF.F.M.ATTERHOLT & MISS MARY E. BEARD, all of Col'ana.

M: 4th inst by REV.S.BAECHLER, ALLEN F. RICKERT of Medina Co. & Miss SARAH LEHMAN of CCO.

M: 25th ult at East Middleton by REV.C.L.WIGNET, LEVI ASTRY & MISS ANNA GILBERT, all of this co.

M: 25th ult at East Middleton by REV. C.L.WIGNET, EDWARD DALZEL & MISS EMILINE FARMER, both of this co.

D: at Leetonia Dec 31, 1872, CAROLINE ELDER w/o PERRY ELDER aged 24y.

D: at Leetonia on Dec 25, 1872, JULIA CARROLL w/o JOHN CARROLL aged 44y.

D: at Leetonia Dec 30, 1872, infant son of HENRY & HANNAH CARY, aged 2y.

D: 1st inst infant child of H.C.JONES ESQ., of Salem.

D: 2nd inst MARY MEAD relict of the late JOHN MEAD aged about 86y.

D: Sun morn last NELLIE QUINN infant dau of THOMAS & EMMA QUINN of Salem, aged 4m.

D: 8th inst MARY STORY w/o GEORGE STORY aged 35y.

Mon 20 Jan 1873 (Vol 6 no 42)

M: 14th inst at his own residence in Leetonia by REV.A.B.-MAXWELL, WILLIAM STRATTON & MISS REBECCA DAVIS.

M: Dec 12th by same, F.FARR & MISS SUSAN SHOEMAKER.

M: Nov 14th 1872 by J.KING ESQ, DAVID FIGLEY & MISS ROSE WEAVER, all of this co.

D: 13th inst at res of his son in law, REV.A.B.MAXWELL, in Leetonia, MINER MERRICK, aged 81y.

D: 15th inst JESSE BRICKER s/o J.F. & LYDIA BRICKER of Salem Tp, aged about 20y.

D: in Salineville Dec 1,1872, JOHN E. STABLEY in 21st year.

D: Dec 18, 1872 ELIZABETH BOYLE of Salineville ae 1y 18d.

D: Jan 11,1873 LOUIS EDWARD BOYLE of Salineville ae 3y 4m 3d

Mon 27 Jan 1873 (Vol 6 no 43)

Railroad accident: on Tues as the mail train going west was crossing the New Garden road, it ran into JOHN MYERS who was coming into town, inflicting such severe injuries that death ensued on Tues night about 2 o'clock. Aged about 67y, he lived 2 miles west of Scrable, leaves a wife & 3 grown children. (long description of accident & injuries)

M: 23d inst by REV.D.V.HYDE, W.B.NEYE & MISS ADDIE CROOK all of this co.

M: 23 Jan by REV.ROBT.HAYS, GEORGE W. TODD & MELISSA J.-McCORD d/o JESSE McCORD, all of Wayne Tp.

M: New Year's Day at res of bride by REV.T.B.ANDERSON, REUBEN E. PRICHETT of CCO & MISS ALICE R.A.DORAN, of Lawrence Co Pa.

M: Thur Dec 12, 1872 at res of bride's father, GEN.J.C. VAUGHAN in Thomasville, GA by REV.BISHOP PEARCE, WILLIAM M. NIXON, formerly of Salineville & MISS LUA VAUGHAN.

M: at res of WM.RURDAL, Salem Tp., Jan 19, by REV.C.L.-WINGET, ROBERT GURNEY & MISS TEVERA FOX.

M: Tues 21st inst by REV.M.A.PARKINSON, at res of bride's parents in Carrollton, S.J.CAMERON, editor of Free Press, & MISS SARAH E. CRUMRINE.

D: at the Infirmary Dec 30, 1872, OLIVER RENEKER aged 20y

D: at the Infirmary Jan 20, JACOB TOBEY, aged 70y.

D: 18th inst LOUIS JOHNSON s/o JOHN W. & ETTIE JOHNSON of Coal Creek Iowa, aged 4y 3m.

D: at Washingtonville Wed morn 15th inst EMMA ROLLER d/o JOS. ROLLER ae 12y 3m

D: at Leetonia Jan 10, infant d/o ALBERT & LAVINA ZIMMERMAN.

D: 20th ELIZABETH McLAUGHLIN w/o JACOB McLAUGHLIN of Elkrun Tp aged 68y.

D: 19th ult WILLIAM HARRISON of Franklin Tp ae 37y.

D: 24th inst MYRA E.C.STOKESBERY d/o ISAAC & ANNA STOKESBERY, of this place, aged 20y 5m.

Yesterday morning a week ago, JOSEPH SCOTT of Middleton Tp was found dead in the United Brethren Church at Hazelville. He was stricken down while kindling the fires & was quite dead when found.

Mon 3 Feb 1873 (Vol 6 no 44)

M: 21st inst by REV.J.S.GRIMES,D.D., W.P.McCOOK of Stark Co & MISS A.D.AILES of CCO.

M: Thur 23d Jan by REV LEGGET, BENJAMIN BURSON & MISS EMMA HUSTON both of Middleton Tp.

D: Tues morn Jan 21st in Liverpool Tp, CCO, of consumption, MISS MELISSA J. McCAIN, aged 22y 6m 22d.

D: at his res in Hanover Tp Jan 14th, AARON WINDER aged 58y 5m 20d.

D: 31st ult RACHEL KERR widow of JOHN KERR of Wayne Tp ae 67y.

D: 30th ult SARAH JANE McCORD, w/o ALEXANDER T. McCORD of this place, aged 30y 10m.

Mon 10 Feb 1873 (Vol 6 no 45)

M: 29 Jan at res of bride's father by DR.HUNTER of Pittsburgh, WM.H.BAYNE, Editor of the Batesville, Ark., Republican, & MISS LOU WOODRUFF of Salem.

M: at New Alexander Jan 30th by ELDER C.L.WINGET, S.P.WISEMAN & MISS SAMANTHA LOWER all of CCO.

M: Feb 6 by REV W.P.TURNER, CHAS. KNOBELOCK of Pittsburgh & MISS EMMA HULME of East Liverpool.

D: Jan 22 at Cleveland O, by REV JABEZ HALL, J.C.CATLETT of Wellsville OH & JULIA F. ABBEY of Glastenbury Conn.

M: Jan 3 by S.SMILEY ESQ, ROBERT CRUMBLY & MISS MARIBAH RABISKA of Carroll Co Oh.

D: on Jan 29th at her res in Salem, MRS. MARGARET BEAUMONT aged 64y 8m.

D: 2nd last at Salem R.J.WALLACE s/o JOHN W. WALLACE,19th yr

D: 28 Jan MARGARET HARRISON w/o WM.H.HARRISON of East Liverpool.

D: Feb 1st ALEXANDER SMITH of Salineville in 20th yr.

D: same day REBECCA MARY WILLIAMS d/o JOHN K. & N.P. WILLIAMS, aged 5m 18d.

D: same day ALFRED MADISON s/o JOHN & HANNAH MADISON of Salineville aged 24d.

Mon 17 Feb 1873 (Vol 6 no 46)

M: by Elder KURTZ at his res Feb 6, B.KYSER & MISS ELIZABETH TYSON, both of CCO.

M: 6th inst at res of JOHN LONG, in Leetonia, by REV.L.-BAECHLER, JOHN J. OEHRIE & MISS CAROLINE E. HAAG.

M: in Leetonia on 3d inst by REV.J.COIL, WALTER GRIM & MISS MARY J. HACKETT of Warren, Trum Co Oh.

M: on eve of Jan 23d by JOHN A. CLEMENT at his res in Knox Tp, L.BAUM & MISS H. McCOLLY both of CCO.

D: 8th Jan RACHEL SCHOOLEY w/o RICHARD SCHOOLEY of Hanover Tp in 33d year.

D: 14th inst PERCY C. GARRETT infant son of CLINTON & RATIE GARRETT of Robbins, aged 3m.

D: in East Rochester Feb 7, REV.E.B.ORT, M.D., in 37th yr.

REV.GEORGE S. VALLANDIGHAM, pastor of the Episcopal Church of this place, died suddenly in Cincinnati last Thurs. morning. He was 56y old & a native of New Lisbon.

Mon 24 Feb 1873 (Vol 6 no 47)

M: 12th Feb by REV.S.Y.KENNEDY, JOHN HETZEL of Harden Co Oh & MISS MARY J. CARLILE of New Lisbon.

M: by REV.G.N.JOHNSTON on 20th inst at res of bride's mother in New Lisbon, G.W.ENDLY of Indianapolis Ind, & MISS ALICE B. THOMPSON.

D: on 17th inst PHILIP SHOUVER of Fairfield Tp ae 77y.

DEATH of JOHN FOULKS: We are called upon to announce the death of another old citizen of Col.Co. The subject of this notice, we believe, was the oldest citizen in the county, except CAPTAIN JAMES WORMINGTON of Wayne Tp., who is in his 103d year. MR.FOULKS died at his residence in Elkrun Tp on Sat. morning, aged 97 years. His funeral today at 1 o'clock.

Mon 3 Mar 1873 (Vol 6 no 48)

M: by REV.WM.BAXTER on 25th Feb, DAVID DeROADS of Franklin Square & MISS ELIZABETH FRAZER of New Lisbon.

M: Thurs Feb 13 at res of bride's parents in Mt.Union Oh, by REV. WM.COX,D.D., assisted by REV.E.BURKETT, REV.J.R.THOMPSON of the Pittsburgh Conference & MISS MARY V. COX, youngest daughter of the officiating minister.

M: Thur Feb 27 by REV.WM.P.TURNER, ISAAC HUFF of W.Va. & MISS MARY FOWLER of East Liverpool.

M: at Smith's Ferry Pa Feb 13 by JOHN McFALL ESQ., ANDREW L. WEAVER & MISS MARY DONALDSON both of Salineville.

M: 25th inst by REV.W.R.SPINDLER, STEPHEN A. BAKER & MISS MARY E. STEIN, all of Salem.

M: also by the same at the same time & place, B.T.CATTELL & MISS LAURA I. CARSON.

D: at his res in Wellsville Tues morn Feb 25, JOHN T. SWEARINGEN aged 66y.

D: 20th inst RACHEL HOWARD w/o CHARLES HOWARD, Salem, aged about 30y.

D: at the Infirmary Jan 24th ADAM ECKSTEIN aged 49y.

D: Sat 22nd inst JOSEPH SAXON of Salem aged 66y.

D: Feb 3, MARY HIME w/o DANIEL HIME of West Tp ae 62y.

D: Dec 13 CHARLES MULHERIN SR of Franklin Tp aged 72y.

D: Feb ---, PRISCILLA JOHNSTON of East Tp., Carroll Co., aged 80y.

D: Feb 25th, -----SWITZER of Dunganon aged 67y.[deaths v1 p262: FLORIAN SWITZER,married,70y, b Germany]

D: Feb 24th WM.S.WANEY of Franklin Tp aged 56y 11m 9d.

Mon 10 Mar 1873 (Vol 6 no 49)

M: Feb 27 by REV.S.Y.KENNEDY, E.B.ENTRICAN of Salem Tp & MISS MARY J. HARBAUGH of New Lisbon.

M: Sat eve Feb 21st at res of bride's father by ELDER H.P. BORTON, AUSTIN FULTY & MISS ELIZABETH M. KING, both of Butler Tp.

M: Feb 27 at res of bride's parents by REV.H.B.FRY, WILLIAM S.DOTTARAR & MISS MARY J. COOK all of Salem.

D: Feb 4, MARY ALICE McARTOR d/o O.D. & MINNIE McARTOR aged 2m 21d.

D: 26th ult MISS EMELINE BROWN of Pittsburgh Pa at res of F.I.MELANY of Butler Tp CCO, aged about 45y.

D: Mar 1 in Salem, IDA M. McCALLA aged 17y 5m.

D: 7th inst SAMUEL MATHEW GAMBLE s/o R.G. & NANCY ANN GAMBLE of Elkrun Tp aged 2y.

OBIT: JOHN McCOY, a res of Wellsville & an employee of the C & P Railroad was killed near Ravenna on Wed night a week ago. He fell while passing from car to car & was killed instantly. His remains were brought to Wellsville on Fri. & interred on Sat. Deceased had been in the employ of the company about 6 months & had been married about the same length of time. He was a member of the Presbyterian Church.

The old court house bell was sold on Thurs for $100. Mr. ERASTUS ELLS, a member of the Union School Board, was the purchaser. It will, in a short time, be removed to the school building. This is just as it should be. The bell has done service in our town for over 40 years; it is a good bell & should be kept here. [SEE 23 Oct 1871 for the new bell]

Mon 17 Mar 1873 (Vol 6 no 50)

The body of LEWIS EVANS was found last Tues in a creek near Youngstown. As yet, nothing definite has been developed, but it is thought he was murdered.

M: at ME Church, Keasawqua, Iowa, Feb 27, by REV.W.J.-SPAULDING, F.M.MILLER, County Superintendent of Public Schools & Miss NANNIE SNYDER d/o JACOB SNYDER, formerly of New Lisbon.

M: in Salineville Mar 11 by J.C.BAIRD JP, GEORGE KNOLL & MRS. ANN WALLACE.

M: Feb 27 by REV.MENDENHALL of Fort Wayne Ind, CYRUS YOUNG of Zanesville Ind, formerly of Col.Co., & MISS HATTIE YOUNG of Roanoke, Ind.

D: 11th inst WILLIAM CHARLES BAXTER of Salem aged 24y.

D: 11th inst DRUCILLA TEST w/o ZACHEUS TEST aged about 43y.

D: 7th inst SAMUEL MATHEW ADAMS s/o R.G. & NANCY ANN ADAMS, of Elkrun Tp, aged about 2y.

D: at the res of her husband in Liverpool Tp. on Sun Mar 2nd, MARGARET KOUNTZ w/o THOMAS BRADY in her 66th yr.

Mon 24 Mar 1873 (Vol 6 no 51)

On Sat., WM. POTTER stabbed & killed GEORGE SHEETS in a dispute growing out of a debt of 25 cents at Staunton VA.

SAMUEL WOODS, an aged citizen of Fairfield Tp, died suddenly at his res a short time ago.

M: on 11th inst in Locust Grove Church by ELDER S.B.TEEGAR-DEN, J.C.HENDRICKS & MISS MARY V. MUSSELMAN.

M: 6th ult at res of JOHN SATTERTHWAIT by ESQ. GARRIGUES, ROBERT TOLLERTON & MISS MARY E. THOMAS all of Salem.

M: at parsonage by REV.B.LONGHEAD, Mar.8th, SETH COLWELL & MISS JANE HOPPES both of CCO.

M: 13 Mar by R.H.GARRIGUES ESQ, R.P.HARPER & MISS M.J.STOCK-WELL.

M: 13th inst by JOSEPH FAWCETT, Mayor of Salem, ISAAC RHODES & MISS LIZZIE FLITCRAFT, both of that vicinity.

M: Sun eve Mar 16 at Wellsville by REV.J.M.CARR, JOHN G. WILLIAMS of Wadsworth, Nevada & MISS LUCINDA J. MILLIGAN of Wellsville.

M: at East Rochester Oh Mar 13 by JOSEPH COULSON ESQ, GEORGE WHITACRE & MISS MARY A. HOLDEMAN.

D: in Leetonia on 6th inst at res of JOSEPH MEEKS, CYNTHIA D. MEEKER aged 65y.

D: 11th inst ANNA IRENE BURSON infant d/o LANDON & DELL BURSON of Elkrun Tp.

D: 14th inst ISABELLE PAINTER w/o REUBEN PAINTER of Butler Tp aged ----y.

D: in Salem 17th isnt JACOB PAINTER aged ----y.

D: JOHN PATTERSON of Hanover Tp aged 50y.

D: ELIZABETH McQUILKEN of Franklin Tp aged 72y.

D: at East Liverpool on Fri eve 14th inst, JOHN ROSS, recently from England.

D: on eve of Mar 13th of cerebro-spinal meningitis after an illness of less than 20 hours, WILLIE SUPER RICHARDS, only child of REV. & MRS. F.RICHARDS of Chicago, aged 3y lacking 2d.

D: 8th inst MRS.ANNIE E.PORTER w/o DAVID PORTER JR.,in 26th year

D: in Salem 8th inst MRS.MELISSA SLUSSER aged 29y.

D: in Salem 12th inst WILLIAM J. SUMMERVILLE s/o ESAU S. SUMMERVILLE aged 4y 10m.

D: at the Infirmary 17th inst CATHARINE LILLY aged 75y.

OBIT: on Fri morn a week ago, an aged gentleman named ELIAS EYSTER, residing near Washingtonville, was found dead in the water closet. His death was caused by heart disease.

OBIT: we regret to announce the death of MRS. BROWNLEE, w/o REV. J.D.BROWNLEE, pastor of the United Presbyterian Church of Wellsville, which occurred in that place the latter part of last week.

Mon 31 Mar 1873 (Vol 6 no 52)

GEN. SHERMAN's famous horse, LEXINGTON, on which he rode from the Atlantic to the sea, died in Madison Wis. on 12th inst.

M: at res of bride's father on 16th inst by REV.J.STOTHARD, NEVIN E. BURNS, formerly of New Lisbon & MISS LILLY F. THOMPSON of River Falls, Wis.

M: 20th inst at Salineville by REV.S.M.COON, HUGH McCULLOUGH & MRS. M.E.McCRACKEN.

D: Fri morn 21st inst FANNY E. LEASE only dau of C.F. & S.B. LEASE of Salem aged 2y 1m.

D: 12th inst at his res in West Leetonia, PETER SCULLY ae 64y

D: Fri Mar 21, MRS. ISA BROWNLEE, w/o REV.J.D.BROWNLEE of Wellsville, aged 28y.

D: at Columbiana Mar 22, JOS.WOLFE in his 75th yr.

D: 20th inst HOMER H. GAVER s/o HIRAM & REBECCA GAVER of Centre Tp aged 30y 1m 6d.

D: near Howville, Ind. Mar 1, in 25th yr, MRS.NANCY J. CRAWFORD, w/o JAMES G.CRAWFORD, formerly of Williamsport, CCO.

Mon 7 Apr 1873 (Vol 7 no 1)

SAMUEL POULSON, a resident of Cadiz,Oh, committed suicide by hanging at that place.

M: on 20th Mar by REV.ROBT HAYS, JOHN McPHERSON & MISS KATE L. CAMERON, all of this co.

M: same day by same, JAMES P. WYCOFF of Salineville & MISS ELLEN SHAFFER of Jefferson Co.

M: 20th ult at Salineville by REV.S.M.COON, HUGH McCULLOUGH & MRS. M.E.McCRACKEN.

M: 27th ult by Friends ceremony, JONATHAN STANLEY & HANNAH EARL both of Salem.

D: 30th ult ISAAC EMERSON HOKE s/o JONAS & REBECCA HOKE of Salem Tp ae 1y 8m.

D: Mar 29th LAURA KING d/o ROBERT KING of Franklin Tp ae 20y 8m 9d.

D: Mar 27th HERMAN McARTOR, s/o M.P. & MARGARET McARTOR of Middleton Tp, aged 6y 6m.

Mon 14 Apr 1873 (Vol 7 no 2)

M: 3d inst by EDLER S.B.TEEGARDEN, ASBERRY CHANDLER & MISS MARY K. FERRALL all of this co.

M: Apr 5th by W.L.NELSON ECC, JEREMIAH E. MYERS & TRESSA WETHERSPOON all of West Tp CCO.

D: 6th inst near Salem, HARRY WILSON ae 16y 6m.

D: 14th inst at Damascus, ISABELL F. PAINTER w/o REUBEN PAINTER in 41st yr.

D: 31st ult in Calcutta of diptheria, CHARLES F. SINCLAIR, aged 9y 8m 12d; also on the 1st inst, WILLIE E. SINCLAIR, aged 4y 9m 27d, sons of A.F. & M.A.SINCLAIR. Since the above was put into print we have learned of the death of another child in the same family.

D: 14th inst THOMAS LOUDEN of Wayne Tp aged about 57y.

OBIT: JENNIE DYER, who attempted suicide at Salem some time ago, succeeded in putting an end to her wretched existence at a sporting house in Pittsburgh yesterday morning, a week ago, by taking a large dose of morphine.

JAMES L. SMITH ESQ., a prominent lawyer of this place & well known throughout the county, died at his residence Wed.after noon. His funeral took place on Fri & was largely attended.

MRS. SARAH CONNEL w/o DR.CONNEL of Salineville died on last Mon., at the age of about 61y. She leaves a husband & 4 children to mourn her loss.

Mon 21 Apr 1873 (Vol 7 no 3)

KILLED, on Mon eve a young man named H.E.SIMSELL, employed as brakeman on the P.Ft.W.&C.RR while coupling cars near Alliance, fell between the rail & a car passing over him crushed him so as to break his neck & otherwise fatally injure him. Coroner DEWALT was notified & held an inquest on Tues, when the jury returned a verdict of accidental death. Deceased resided near New Waterford & was about 25y of age.

M: Apr 10th near North Benton, Mah.Co. by REV.WM.DICKSON, DANIEL D. VANFOSSAN of New Lisbon & Miss SADIE EHRHART of this place.

M: Apr 12th by ELDER C.E.VANVOORHES, GEORGE W. ARMSTRONG & MISS LYDIA MORRIS.

M: at res of bride's parents by REV.R.G.THOMPSON on Thurs eve Mar 27th, GEORGE HANNA formerly of New Lisbon, & MISS CLARA VON GOHREN of Greeley Colo.

M: by REV.H.B.FRY, at the Presbyterian parsonage, Salem, Apr 10th, GEORGE WILLS & MISS CELIA HAYS.

M: Mar 20th by ISAAC WEAVER, ISAAC HESTAND & MISS LYDIA GRASS, all of this co.

M: Apr 8th at New Lisbon by H.E.FROST,JP, JOEL JOHNSON & MRS. MARIA L. ALTHAR, all of this co.

M: 27th ult at res of bride's father by REV.C.L.WINGET, MARCUS O. CROOK & MISS MARANDA FARMER , all of CCO.

M: 10th inst at res of bride's father by same, THOS.L.STANLEY & MISS A.E.BRICKER, all of this co.

M: Thur Apr 17 at res of groom by REV.S.M.COON, PETER McGILLIVRAY & MISS V.M.ADAMS, all of Salineville.

M: Apr 8th by REV.W.WILSON, JACOB STUCKRATH,JR., of this place & MISS VIRGINIA BELL STERLING of Phila.,Pa.

The solemn question arises every now & then. Who was the first white child born in Ohio? Here now is a Bucyrus person furnishing the Cincinnati Commercial with a list of five "first white children", the latest in date being JOHANNA MARIA HECKENELDER, born at Salem [Salem mission in Tuscarawas Co] April 1781, & who has generally been considered "primus." The Bucyrus groper among musty records produces a white male baby in Wyandot Co. in 1775; a white he-baby on the headwaters of the Miami River in 1774; a white male child at Gnadenhutten July 4th, 1773; and a baby, sex unknown, found with its mother by BOUQUET's expedition in 1764, on the banks of the Muskingum.

D: 11th inst at Smith's Ferry Pa, MRS.SUSAN SMITH aged about 91y.

D: 9th inst at Leetonia, CORNELIUS J. BRANNON, s/o WILLIAM & MARY BRANNON aged 9d.

D: Apr 11th STEPHEN CLARK of Washington TP aged 69y.

D: Apr 13th JANE ANN SMITH d/o WM.& ANN SMITH of Salineville aged 4 weeks.

D: 13th inst JOSHUA WARD of Elkrun Tp aged about 58y.

Mon 28 Apr 1873 (Vol 7 no 4)

MRS.BOOTH, an aged lady of this place, died at her res on N.Market St last Tues eve. The funeral was Fri. when the body was taken to Salem & placed in a vault.

M: Apr 21st by JOSEPH COULSON JP, JONATHAN C. BALL & MRS. SARAH E. BROWNLEE, all of CCO.

M: 8th inst by WEBSTER STREET JP, FRANKLIN T. DALES & MISS ANNIE WHITACRE.

M: Wed eve Apr 16th at bride's res in Salem, by REV.THOS.N. BOYLE, BENJAMIN F.DAWES & BARBARA THARP.

M: Thur eve Apr 17th at res of bride's parents in Salem, by same, HARRY H. JOHNSTON & MISS ELLEN NIBLO.

M: Apr 20th by JETHRO MANLY ESQ, JOSEPH W. CROXALL & MISS LIZZIE POWELL both of E.Liv.

M: at Iola, Kans on 7th inst by REV.H.W.STRATTON, R.S.LONG, of Wellsville OH & MISS F.M.SHEASLEY of Greenville, Pa.

D: ALICE GARWOOD, on Mon eve Apr 21st, at Salem, in 91st yr

D: WILLIAM FITZPATRICK of Franklin Tp, aged 24y.

D: 13th inst SARAH VIRLINDA SWEARINGEN d/o ELIMELECH & MARIA SWEARINGEN aged 29y 9m.

D: Tues 15th inst ALEXANDER WARD of Fairfield Tp aged about 70y.

D: at her res in Wellsville Apr 5th of typhoid pneumonia, MRS. MARY McBETH in her 68th yr

Mon 5 May 1873 (Vol 7 no 5)

D: Apr 20th at Green Hill, LYDIA C. WICKERSHAM aged 65y.

D: Sat morn Apr 26 at Wellsville at res of GEORGE GUNN, WILLIAM NOBLE aged 39y 1m 3d.

D: 27th ult FRANK GEORGE s/o W.E.GEORGE of Middleton Tp aged 11y.

D: 24th ult WM.B.JOHNSON of Salem, s/o THOS.M. & MARTHA B. JOHNSON, aged 18y 9m 3d.

D: Apr 25th, LIZZIE MILLER w/o LEANDER MILLER of Hanover Tp aged 24y 9m.

CAPT. JAMES WORMINGTON died suddenly at his res in Wayne Tp on last Tues. He was born in London Sept 21, 1770 & was at the time of his death over 102 years of age. We have in our possession the data for an extended & full sketch of the Captain's life, which for want of time we defer until our next issue.

M: 29th ult at Reformed parsonage by REV.H.HILBISH, JOHN SHINGLER & MISS MALINDA SHAWECKER all of Col'ana.

M: at Salem Apr 24th by REV.THOMAS N. BOYLE, NATHAN PLATT & MISS REBECCA WEBB both of Salem.

M: at Cannelton PA May 1st by I.F.MANSFIELD ESQ, J.C.BARTON & MISS S.A.PETERS, of Middleton, CCO.

Mon 12 May 1873 (Vol 7 no 6)

M: 23d ult by SAMUEL HARDMAN JP, MR. EBERHARDT & MISS LOUISA HACK, all of Salem.

M: by REV.WASHINGTON DARBY, LEVI ARNOLD & MISS ELLEN TULLIS, all of Col'ana.

M: 25th ult at New Garden by E.GARSIDE ESQ, THOMAS M. PICK-ENNY & MRS. LYDIA ILER all of this co.

D: Thur May 1st MATTIE DELL HOLLOWAY d/o J.G. & JULIA HOLLOWAY of Col'ana aged 9m 15d.

D: 1st inst THOMAS C. ALLEN of Col'ana aged 41y.

D: 1st inst at his res in Washingtonville, JOSEPH BOSTON aged 38y 16d.

D: 7th inst WILLIAM GRIFFITH of Butler Tp, aged 78y. The dec'd was confined to his bed for over 4 yrs by paralysis.

CAPT. JAMES WORMINGTON: died on 29th ult, aged 102y 7m 12d; mar. at Clarkson, MRS. ELEANOR McMILLAN & had 1 daughter.-This daughter married & had one child, a daughter now married to ANDREW BINSLEY of Wayne Tp. [1850 census, Wayne Tp p248: JAMES, 75mEng, farmer $1200 real estate; ELLEN, 61f IRE & FRANCIS, 16m OH, farmer]

Mon 19 May 1873 (Vol 7 no 7)

M: May 15th at New Lisbon by HENRY E.FROST ESQ, JOHN CALDER-HEAD & MISS SARAH SHAW all of this co.

M: May 6th at res of NATHAN COBURN of Salem, by REV.H.B. FRY, CHARLES L. WHINERY & MISS LYDIA A. CARLE.

M: May 16th at res of bride's parents by REV.G.N.JOHNSTON, SANSOM I. HEWIT & MISS MARY H. CRAWFORD, both of CCO.

M: May 1st at Hanover by ELDER SAMUEL FOX, SAMUEL HALSTEAD of Wellsville & MISS LUCINDA SINCLAIR.

D: May 2 in Salem, EMMA GARRETSON d/o DR.ELI GARRETSON in 27th yr

D: May 14th at res of her father, SAMUEL LIEHM in Wellsville, MRS. FANNIE DOUGLASS w/o JOHN DOUGLASS, of consumption.

D: May 11th MRS. NANCY B. HOPKINS, Wellsville, aged 45y.

Mon 19 May 1873

D: May 1st at New Garden of consumption, ENOCH LUCAS ae 80y

D: May 13th MRS. REBECCA COPELAND of Col'ana in 83d yr

D: May 12th SARAH G. THOMAS of Salem in 76th yr.

D: May 13th MRS. MARY BRICKER of Salem Tp aged 81y.

M: one of the most notable events of the past week, in New Lisbon, was the marriage in the German Church on Thurs eve of ROBERT SCHAWECKER & MISS AVINA SCHAFFER. REV.BAECHLER of Col'ana performed the ceremony, witnessed by a large audience. The ceremony over, the invited guests repaired to the residence of A.J.VOLKERS where a sumptuous repast was partaken of.

The social event of last week took place Tues eve at res of MR. & MRS. DORWART, the occasion being the marriage of their daughter, MRS. SARAH C. HUTCHINSON & THOMAS MUIR of Oneida, Knox Co Ill. Quite a number were present to witness the ceremony, performed by REV.G.N.JOHNSTON of the Presbyterian Church. On Thurs the happy pair started for their western home.

Court proceedings:

JONATHAN VAUGHN vs ANNA M. VAUGHN, pet.to divorce; dismissed

Fri morn a week ago a young man named SAMUEL F. PETERSON of Springfield Tp., Jefferson Co.OH committed suicide by hanging himself in the stable with a halter strap.

Mon 26 May 1873 (Vol 7 no 8)

D: May 24th HANNAH DALES w/o CHARLES DALES of Centre Tp ae 35y

OBIT: death of MARY J. SCOTT, died at res of her parents in this place on Sat., aged about 30y. MISS SCOTT was an estimable young woman, possessed of more than ordinary mental attainments & esteemed by all her acquaintances. She took a lively interest in the education of children & spent nearly 9 years of her young life as a teacher in the New Lisbon Union School. At an early age she connected herself with the United Presbyterian Church, of which she was an active member; she was the only daughter of kind & affectionate parents, the sister of indulgent brothers & in her death a light went out that only the grace of God can supply.

Mon 2 June 1873 (Vol 7 no 9)

M: 25th ult by JOSIAH ROHRBAUGH ESQ, JOHN J. NITREWER of Mah.Co. & MISS ANNIE W. WANSETLER of CCO.

M: Thur May 29th at res of bride's parents in Wellsville by REV. HOLLINGSHEAD, WM. CLARK & MISS LAURA McCAULEY.

D: on 13th ult at res of ANDREW FLICK near Salem, OLIVE LIPSEY of Damascus aged 22y 10m.

D: Sun night 25th ult JOHN J. SMITH of Wellsville ae 22y 10m

D: Sat 25th ult ELIZABETH W. GORDON w/o JOHN GORDON

D: May 21st GEORGIANNA VANFOSSEN d/o JAMES C. & MARTHA J. VANFOSSEN of this place aged 1y 8m 13d.

D: May 31st MARY ANN WADINGTON w/o JOHN WADINGTON of Salem Tp, aged 34y.

Mon 9 June 1873 (Vol 7 no 10)

M: at res of bride's father in Bellaire OH by ELDER J.M.VAN HORN, assisted by REV. G.M.BOYCE, W.H.BAXTER of Wellsville & MISS LIZZIE C. LONG of Bellaire.

M: May 29th at Salem by REV.H.R.FRY, JOHN M. WALKER & MISS LIZZIE H. HINSHILLWOOD.

D: Sat May 31st at 6 1/2 o'clock pm at his res in Liverpool Tp, WILLIAM CHRISTY STEWART aged 56y.

D: June 4th ELLIS COPE of Fairfield Tp aged 61y.

D: 2nd inst in Salem, JANNETTA L. RUSSELL d/o W.W. & M.A.-RUSSELL aged 4y 11m 15d.

D: 26th May in Butler Tp JOHN ELLIOTT aged 65y.

Mon 16 June 1873 (Vol 7 no 11)

M: by REV JOHN COIL on 3d inst, P. BUHECKER & MISS REBECCA JOHNSON all of Leetonia

Mon 16 June 1873 (Vol 7 no 11)

M: Thur June 12th at res of bride's parents by REV G.W. RIGGLE, M.M.HUSTON & MISS SUSIE SMITH, all of E.Liv.

M: Tues June 10th at Hanoverton by SAMUEL FOX, ESQ., M.V. LIGHTEAN of Chicago Ill & MISS AGGIE MILNER of H'ton.

M: June 5th by REV.S.Y.KENNEDY at M.E.Parsonage in New Lisbon, JOHN DEEMER & MRS. ELIZABETH M. PRESTON both of Col'ana [she was born a BUSHONG -ed]

M: in Salem on 10th inst by REV W.R.SPINDLER, ALBERT M. MORE-LAND & MISS MARTHA M. RICHARDS all of Salem.

D: at Leetonia 13th isnt ELIZABETH BALL d/o CHARLES & MARGARET BALL aged 11m 13d.

D: Tues 10th inst AUSTIN CALHOON of Wellsville ae 15y.

SUPPOSED MURDER: On Wed morn near Irondale the body of THOMAS EVANS of that place was found on the Cleveland & Pittsburgh RR Tracks in a horribly mangled condition. It is probable that he was foully dealt with. Suspicion at once attached to a party named PATRICK DOUGHERTY with whom he had last been seen. Search was made for him, he was arrested & confined in the lockup at Irondale.

The TRIAL of ROBERT W. CHAMBERLAIN for the murder of GEORGE McCONNAUGHY in Jan. last, came to an end last Tues; counsel asked for verdict of murder in 2nd degree, JUDGE PAINE consented & gave the case to the jury. The latter retired & after brief consultation, rendered a verdict of guilty in the 2nd degree. The Judge sentenced him to imprisonment in the penitentiary for life.

Mon 23 June 1873 (Vol 7 no 12)

M: Wed June 18th by REV GEORGE N. JOHNSTON, W.S.POTTS & MISS LIZZIE WISDEN of this place.

M: 10th inst at res of bride's parents by REV J.J.SLUTTS, W.F.INGRAM & MISS SARAH E. SCATTERGOOD both of New Garden.

D: June 15 of consumption, S.I.THOMPSON of New Waterford, aged about 56y.

D: Mon June 19th of consumption, JOSEPH F. RANDOLPH of East Fairfield, aged 35y.

D: Thurs 10th inst, ------HUSTON, w/o ALEXANDER HUSTON of Middleton Tp, aged 86y. [probably MARY RHINEHART whom he married 28 Oct 1824]

D: Mon 16th inst MRS.GORBY relict of SAMUEL GORBY dec'd of Middleton Tp, aged 83y.

D: at the res of her son in law MILTON RAILEY near Hanover on 7th June, MARY ARMSTRONG relict of JAMES ARMSTRONG, aged 84y 4m 72d.

Mon 30 June 1873 (Vol 7 no 13)

M: 20th June by SAMUEL HARDMAN JP, JAMES W. LEACH & MRS. CATHARINE PIDGEON all of Salem.

M: 10th inst near East Palestine by REV.MR.GOGLEY, JOHN McCALLA of Salem & MISS HANNAH BAYLES of Beaver Co Pa.

M: 24th June by REV H.B.FRY, C.B.GRUWELL of Iowa & MISS R.A.PENROSE of New Garden Oh.

D: June 25th, REV.WILLIAM FULTON pastor of Fourth U.P. Church, Allegheny, aged 36y; buried in Wellsville.

D: Mon morn June 30th WILLIAM BAKER of Elkrun Tp aged 65y

OBIT: DR. GEORGE McCOOK an old & highly respected citizen of New Lisbon, died at his res in this place last Mon eve. He was born in Cannonsburgh, Washington Co Pa June 1795, and first came to New Lisbon in 1818, where he commenced to practice medicine.

D: Sat June 28th at her res in New Lisbon, MARY SAVACOOL aged 75y.

Mon 7 July 1873 (Vol 7 no 14)

M: on 24th ult at res of bride's father by REV.G.M.ALBRIGHT, JAMES KENNEDY of Pittsburgh & MISS ELIZABETH WILLIARD of Franklin Tp.

M: Sun June 15 by REV.WILLIAM VANCLEVE, OLIVER COPE of CCO & MISS MARY IRWIN of Salem, Ill.

M: July 2nd by ESQ.FROST, PARK P. MICHINER & MISS LARENA J. VANHORN both of West Tp., this co.

M: by REV G.N.JOHNSON at the parsonage in New Lisbon on 2nd inst, JOHN ROSETTE & MISS LETHA SHELTON all of Ohio.

M: by same at res of JAMES HENDERSON on 3d inst, HENRY A. FOUTS of Poland & MISS MARGARET C. WOLLAM of New Lisbon.

M: by same at res of bride's father on 31st ult WILLIAM C. BARCUS & MISS ADALINE SPENCER both of Salineville.

D: May 26th HARRY A. McARTOR s/o O.D. & MINNIE McARTOR aged 2y 5m 8d.

D: June 9th at Bunker Hill,Ind, JAMES C. ADAMS ae 54y 8m 4d

D: July 5th, JAMES McCULLOUGH of Wayne Tp ae 81y 8m.

D: July 2nd ELIZABETH TODD w/o JOHN TODD of Wayne Tp ae 36y

D: July 5th ELLIS FRANK JOHNSON of this place ae 31y.
Obit: Death of ELLIS FRANK JOHNSON, on Sat 5 July, of the firm of J.M.JOHNSON & SON, died at the res of his parents in this place of consumption, aged 31y. (issue of 14 July)

Mon 14 July 1873 (Vol 7 no 15)

M: 6th inst by REV.W.DARBY, JOHN HARROLD & ELIZABETH WILDER-SON

M: Sat 5th inst by DR.JAMES HILLICK at res of bride's parents, IRA McARTOR & MISS LIZZIE J. FERRALL all of Col'ana

M: 25th ult at Enon Valley PA by ---, JAMES McDERMOTT & MISS NANCY McLEAN both of New Lisbon Oh.

M: at the Reformed Parsonage by REV.G.M.ALBRIGHT, SOCRATES BIERD of Youngstown & MISS ANNA SHELENBERGER of Canfield.

D: 5th inst WM. EDWARDS of Middleton Tp aged 70y.

D: 11th inst RAYMOND CLAYTON NOSS s/o W.J. & MAGGIE NOSS of this place, aged 2m 15d.

Mon 21 July 1873 (Vol 7 no 16)

M: 24th June by REV.J.GORDON CARNICHAN, Meadville PA, WM.B. RUNDLE of Wellsville Oh & MISS MARIA R. STUART d/o the late ARCHIBALD STUART.

M: at the Presbyterian parsonage, Salem, on 3d inst by REV.H.B. FRY, SAMUEL SHINN & MISS JENNIE WEAVER all of CCO.

D: at Leetonia 8th inst CORA D. TANNAHILL d/o JAMES & MARGARET TANNAHILL, aged 1y 8m 14d.

D: 7th inst at Westville, MRS. ELIZABETH ANN BUSHONG, formerly of Columbiana, aged 29y. [nee TOMBAUGH, she was widow of ALEXANDER BUSHONG -ed.]

There was great excitement at Salt Lake City recently over the announcement that ANN ELIZA WEBB YOUNG, w/o BRIGHAM YOUNG, had forever left him, carrying off furniture & personal effects. She will institute suit for divorce & alimony for a large sum. (article Jly 28th says she was his 17th bride!)

DAVID KURTZ, an old & prominent citizen of Minerva, died of apoplexy last Sat morn; he had arisen from the breakfast table when he suddenly fell to the floor and expired without a struggle. MR.KURTZ was a brother in law of MRS. THOMAS CORBETT of this place & was held in high esteem in the community in which he had so long resided.

A son of MRS. SMITH of New Springfield, aged about 10y, died suddenly on Thurs a week ago. His death, it is supposed, was the result of an overdose of currants which he had eaten the evening previous.

Wouldn't it be well to have the grass in SPRINGER'S GRAVE YARD mowed? If the grass is designed for a lawn, the grass is too long; if for a hay field, the crop should be cut.

JOHN PETTIT a young man of Smith's Ferry Pa, formerly of New Lisbon, died at the res of his parents in that place on Sat eve the 12th inst.

Mon 28 July 1873 (Vol 7 no 17)

D: on 18th inst at Col'ana, MRS. CAROLINE FLORENTINE HAUPT-MANN, aged 22y 7m 18d.

D: 21st inst ELMIRA THOMPSON d/o the late B.F.THOMPSON of this place aged 37y.

D: Thurs 24th inst ANNA M. SMITH d/o JAMES L. & MRS. E. SMITH of this place, aged 24y.

D: at the Infirmary July 15th, JOHN LINDSAY aged 69y.

Mon 4 Aug 1873 (Vol 7 no 18)

M: 27th ult at New Lisbon by H.E.FROST ESQ, MONTERVILLE ROOT & MISS MARIA EWING.

M: 22nd ult at res of bride's parents by REV.MR.SWAIN, F.C.McDONALD, Editor of the Niles Independent, & MISS ANGIE ZEHRING of Germantown, Oh.

M: 24th ult at res of bride, by REV.J.N.SWAIN, PHILLIP FRAZER of Wellsville & MISS LIZZIE A. McBANE of Madison Tp.

M: 26th ult by REV.W.DARBY, GEORGE E. TODD of New Waterford & MISS ALBINA FITZPATRICK of Middleton, Oh

M: 21st ult in Sharon Pa by REV.R.V.GRAVES DD, JOSEPH C. CHAIN & MISS S.B.BAIRN both of this co.

M: 28th ult by FATHER LINDESMITH, PATRICK BIGGINS & MISS MARY WOODS both of Leetonia.

M: 31st ult by same, MICHAEL MACHAN & MISS MARY RIEL both of Leetonia.

D: 23d inst at Leetonia, WM.J.BRANNON s/o WM. & MARY BRANNON aged 2m 14d.

D: 24th inst in New Garden, LAURA BELL JONES aged 15y 10m.

D: 27th ult at St.Catharines, Ont.,Canada, MRS. ANNIE McGREGOR w/o WM. McGREGOR & d/o REV.G.A.LOWMAN. With her husband, Mrs.M. resided in China for a number of years, where he carried on business, but she went to Canada to be retored to health. She was a granddaughter of MICHAEL ARTER of Hanover & a niece of JOSEPH ARTER of this place. The remains will be taken to Wellsville for burial on 27th.

D: at Leetonia on 31st ult PATRICK HAUGHTON s/o THOMAS & MARY HAUGHTON aged 19d.

D: in Hanover Tp, ANNA MAY MILLER d/o ANDREW & ELIZABETH MILLER ae 3m.

Mon 11 Aug 1873 (Vol 7 no 19)

M: July 31st at American Hotel, Canton, by ELDER S.S.CHAP-MAN, HENRY PERDUE & MISS OLIVE CROWL both of Minerva.

M: 5th inst by JOSIAH ROHRBAUGH ESQ, ARHART SHAFFER & MISS LIZZIE BILGERS both of this co.

M: at res of bride's father on 7th inst by REV G.M.ALBRIGHT, WILLIAM GRONER of Boone Iowa & MISS SOPHIA BRICKER of CCO.

D: July 3d at Moorestown NJ, ELISHA HUNT aged about 94y.

D: at Philadelphia on 30th ult ADAM D. ARRISON formerly of Salem aged 29y.

D: Aug 1st of consumption, ALSADA HARMAN d/o LEVI & RACHEL HARMAN, of Col'ana, aged 19y 11m 9d.

D: 7th inst at res of her aunt, MRS. H.MARTIN, MARTHA C. THOMSON d/o the late DR. JOHN THOMSON of this place.

D: near Parkersburg WVa on 8th inst ALEXANDER GAILEY formerly of this place in his 66th yr.

Death of Mr. JAMES C. BURNS. It was with no little surprise that our community was this morning apprised of the death of MR.BURNS. Up to last Thurs we understand, Mr.B was actively at work at the sash factory, where he has been operating for years. He died in the 59th yr of his age.

JACOB FITZPATRICK, of Fairfield Tp, was fatally wounded in falling from a load of hay.

Mon 18 Aug 1873 (Vol 7 no 20)

M: at res of bride's mother by REV.J.P.IRWIN, DANIEL STRICK-LER of Col'ana & MISS LORETTA SYKES of Canfield.

M: July 31st by REV.S.M.COON, WILLIAM A. SALTSMAN of Saline-ville & MISS ALICE RUSSELL of Carroll Co.

M: Aug 7th by REV.H.HILBISH, JOHN L. VANSYCLE & MISS AMANDA HOLLOWAY both of Col'ana.

M: Aug 5th by REV.SCOTT, S.B.FISHER of Carrollton & MISS SOPHIA D. HENRY of Leesville, Carroll Co.

M: Aug 7th by REV J.A.E.SIMPSON, JOHN A. ROGERS & MISS SARAH PHILPOT all of Carroll Co.

M: in Salem on 3d inst by REV.H.FRY, SAMUEL SHINN & MISS JENNIE WEAVER all of CCO.

M: Aug 14th at the Adams House by J.M.DICKINSON ESQ, WOOSTER SALTSMAN & MISS MELINDA SALTSMAN, of Salineville.

D: at his res in E.Liv. on 14th ult, W.WARICK aged 71y 3m.

D: Aug 14th at his res in New Garden, C.LIBER ae 65y 7m 27d.

D: 8th inst at Salem, ANNA L. SNYDER w/o CHARLES C. SNYDER & d/o ISAAC & ANN WEBB aged about 25y.

D: 10th inst at Salem, VESTA GERTRUDE HOLE d/o ROBERT & CAROLINE M. HOLE, aged 21m.

D: June 26th, JAMES CARMAN of Carroll Co, aged 101y 3m 28d

D: at res of DR.WILSON of Alliance on 14th inst, ESTHER JOHNSON w/o JOHN W. JOHNSON, formerly of this place, but now of Keokuk, Iowa, about 23y of age.

D: one of the oldest citizens of Minerva, FERDINAND BOORY died on 6th inst in 55th yr

GEORGE BURNS, s/o late JAMES BURNS of this place, for some years a resident of Chicago, is about to remove his family here & take a position at the planing mill, so long & successfully operated by his father.

Mon 25 Aug 1873 (Vol 7 no 21)

M: Aug 11th by FATHER LINDESMITH, MATHEW HALEY & MISS BRIDGET COLLANS.

M: Aug 13th by same, MICHAEL GILLOOLY & MRS. MARGARET DALY

M: 31st ult by JETHRO MANLEY, JAMES LOGAN & MISS ELIZABETH ROW, both of E.Liv.

M: last Thur by J.M.DICKINSON ESQ, at Robbins Station, JAMES WOODRICH & MISS FANNY LEE. Mr.D. says a large party attended the wedding & after the ceremony was performed the white folks had a lively dance. That being over, the colored folks— it was a colored wedding — sung the JOHN BROWN song and ended with a rich Virginia hoe-down.

D: at Wellsville on 16th inst, infant child of MRS. OELA C. ROOSE, aged 2y.

D: 15th inst, same place, JAMES PATTERSON ae 60y 9m 28d

D: in Yellow Creek Tp Aug 4th, MARGARET McGILVERY in 81st yr

D: Aug 14th ANNA M. WAY of Leetonia in 51st yr

D: at the Infirmary on 13th inst, CATHARINE MESSIMORE ae 67y

D: 11th inst JAMES McGINNIS of Salineville ae 10y.

D: 18th inst near North Lima, JACOB SPAETH aged 81y 5m 14d.

D: 10th inst MRS.DR.N.K.McKENZIE of Wellsville.

Thur morning MRS. ELIZABETH MILLARD w/o JOHN B. MILLARD of Butler Tp who has been partially deranged for some time, went to Hanover & purchased some strychnine for the purpose of killing rats, as she represented to the druggist, & some laudanum that she often used with other things in an application for a pain in her side. On her way home she stopped at her brother's, GEORGE WATERS, a short distance south of New Garden & called, as she had frequently done, for some cold tea. MRS. WATERS suspecting nothing, gave her the tea & she stepped out on the porch, put some of the poison into her drink & drank it. This was about 9 o'clock in the morning.- Medical aid was called, but could be of no avail. She died about 5 pm.

On last Sabbath while on the way to camp meeting near Wellsville, a man named DAWSON from near Fredericktown was thrown from his buggy & so severely injured that he died on Wed. A lady was also thrown from a buggy & run over, but escaped with a few bruises.

WILLIAM McKEE, once a citizen of this vicinity & well known by many as a worthy man, died suddenly at his home in Leetonia of apoplexy last Mon eve aged about 70y.

Mon 1 Sep 1873 (Vol 7 no 22)

M: 28th ult at the Cowan House by H.E.FROST ESQ, JAMES CONLIN & MISS SARAH McGARVEY all of CCO.

M: 26th ult by ELDER BAXTER, E.H.McKEE & MISS IRENE TULLIS all of CCO.

M: 26th ult at his res in Middleton Tp by WM.M.CRAWFORD ESQ, WM.W.PICKFORD & MISS MARY A. HOLDERREED, both of Fairf.Tp.

D: 13th ult at Salem, MRS. PHEBE J. CRANK ae 26y.

D: 14th ult at Salem, C.LIBER in 66th yr. of his age.

D: 21st ult at Wellsville J.F.COOPER in 26th yr of his age

D: 22nd ult at Allegheny City Pa, MRS.W.G.FOSTER formerly of Wellsville aged 35y.

D: 23d ult at New Garden infant d/o THOMAS BARTRAM, ae 15m.

D: 21st ult MARCUS SMEDLEY MONTGOMERY s/o WM. MONTGOMERY JR. of Elkrun Tp aged 3y 25d.

D: 25th ult infant child of GEORGE HAWKINS of Centre Tp.

D: Aug 29th MARY A. RUSSEL w/o W.W.RUSSEL of Salem ae 38y.

ROBERT T. HILLMAN, an old citizen of this vicinity, died at his res near New Lisbon on 26th ult in 62nd yr. He was a native of New Jersey & came here in 1833.

Mon 8 Sep 1873 (Vol 7 no 23)

A Canton lawyer, grossly insulting a young daughter of Mr. & Mrs. GEORGE McGUIRE, was severely cowhided by the mother.- Mr. McG attended, revolver in hand, to see that the work was well done.

M: Thur Aug 28th, by ELDER H. KURTZ at his res in Col'ana, DAVID KIBLER & MRS. KATHRINE SMITH, both of Mah.Co.

M: Aug 24th at res of bride's parents by REV.S.WAGNER, E.W.NICHOLS & MISS MATTIE D. BAKER.

D: of consumption in Forest, Hardin Co Oh, LETITIA D. SHAFFER d/o EMANUEL P. & JULIA A. HARMAN ae 25y 8m 17d.

D: PATRICK O'HARE of Carroll Co., ae 83y.

D: 2nd inst in Adams Co Ind, MARTIN SCHERER, a former res of this county, aged 73y.

D: 3d inst at res of his son, near Maysville, Hanover Tp, WILLIAM BURTON ae about 83y.

D: 30th ult JOHN SOUDER of Middleton Tp ae 75y.

D: 1st inst at her res in this place, RACHEL E. FILSON aged nearly 72y.

Mon 15 Sep 1873 (Vol 7 no 24)

M: 4th inst by REV.H.HILBISH, WILLIAM W. HUM & MISS ADELIA METZ all of CCO.

M: 13th inst by H.E.FROST ESQ, at his office, GEORGE NOBLE & MISS ELIZABETH BARROW.

M: at Salineville Sep 7th by REV.J.W.McABEE, LOUIS N. BRITT of Wheeling WVa & MISS SARAH E. TOMS of the former place.

M: 7th inst by same, TOBIAS ROTHGEIB & MRS. ELIZABETH WEIGHTENHOUSER all of Beaver Tp., Mah.Co.

M: 6th inst by ELDER H.KURTZ, FRANK W. FETTERS & MISS FLORENCE L. YOUNG, all of CCO.

D: at Salem on 4th inst MARGARET DECOURSLAY ae 79y

D: Sat Sep 6 in St.Clair Tp, JENNETTE CULLER d/o PHILLIP & MARY CULLER ae 11y 11m 6d.

D: 30th ult SAMUEL WISNER of Williams Co formerly of Salem ae 68y.

D: 13th inst PRESTON BECK of Hanover Tp ae about 75y.

D: 9th inst JOHN BINSLEY of Franklin Tp in 78th yr

D: Sep 5th at Salem, MARY COOK in her 85th yr

D: Sep 6th at Salem, MARTHA GAILEY aged 91y.

Mon 22 Sep 1873 (Vol 7 no 25)

M: 7th inst by JOSEPH CREW ESQ, J.C.VAUGHN & MISS IDA TRESCOTT all of Salem.

M: 20th inst by H.E.FROST ESQ, at his office, WILLIAM WARR & MISS MARY A. NOBLE all of this co.

M: Sep 9 by REV.W.DARBY, ALBERT MATHER & MISS RACHEL E. WRIGHT of Beloit, Mah.Co.

D: 13th inst at Massillon, ELIZABETH THOMPSON w/o JOSEPH THOMPSON, formerly of this place, aged 67y.

D: 10th inst near E.Lewistown, infant dau of FRANK & MARGARET ROHRBAUGH in 4th yr of her age.

D: 13th inst at Salem, ELIZABETH PROCTOR d/o DAVID PROCTOR JR, ae 2y.

D: at New Albany on 10th inst, MRS. NANCY BROWN ae 36y.

D: 9th inst MRS. HARDMAN of Wellsville in 88th yr

D: Sep 15th MARGARET McLANE w/o MATHEW McLANE of Wellsville in 62nd yr.

D: 22nd ult near Cannon's Mills, ALLIE SMITH, d/o MRS. & MR. M.S.SMITH, nearly 8 yrs of age.

Mon 29 Sep 1873 (Vol 7 no 26)

M: Sep 4th by REV ROBT HAYS, WM.M.TODD of Centre Tp & MISS NANNIE McDIVITT of Elk Run Tp, both of this co.

M: by REV.JAS.SWAN, Sept 23d JAS.A.GREEN & MISS LIZZIE DAVIDSON, all of CCO.

M: 25th inst by J.M.DICKINSON ESQ, ALBAN W. FURNEY & MISS MOLLIE A. MELLINGER all of this co.

M: 28th Sep by REV.G.M.ALBRIGHT, DAVID REDFOOT & MISS SARAH RAVER, of Leetonia.

M: 18th by same, DAVID BURNSIDES of Wash.Tp & MISS BELLE McINTOSH of Madison Tp, both of this co.

M: 25th inst at the Reformed parsonage by the same, WILLIAM S. ANGLEMYER & MISS MARY ZIMMERMAN, both of Leetonia.

M: 23d inst at res of bride's father by same, THOMAS E. BRINKER & MISS AMELIA J. WORMAN all of this co.

M: 34th, by Elder WM.BAXTER at St.Charles Hotel, Pittsburgh, DAVID A. PRITCHARD & MISS AUGUSTA McELROY both of this place.

D: 27th inst at New Lisbon, WILLIAM CARLILE ae about 22y.

On 23d inst the venerable HENRY ATEN of Wellsville, completed one century of his life. A family reunion, appropriately took place on that day, attended by over 20 of Mr.A's descendants. He has lived at Wellsville 67 yrs & is still active & favored with a retentive memory.

JOHN SPRINGER SR., formerly of this place, was killed last Thurs. morning by a railroad accident at Bunker Hill, Ind.

A son of Prof. I.P.HOLE, of Hanover, aged about 14y, recently fell from a tree & died of injuries received on the 24th inst

Mon 6 Oct 1873 (Vol 7 no 27)

M: 25th ult by REV.C.BAECHLER, ENOS BRICKER & MISS SUSANNA SIMON, all of this co.

M: 30th ult by JOSEPH CREW ESQ, WILLIAM KOUNTZ & MISS HANNAH BAUMAN all of this co.

D: at Salem on 17th ult, MISSOURI SUMMERVILLE d/o ESAU & EVALINE SUMMERVILLE, aged 2y.

D: 26th ult MAHLON HOLE s/o I.P. & MARY HOLE, of Hanover, aged 13y.

D: 10th ult GEORGE WILLIAMS of Salem in 16th yr

D: Sep 29th HOWARD J. HAWKINS s/o T.G. & K.Q.HAWKINS of Elkton aged 8m 21d.

D: 1st inst, ---- CROSS, w/o THOMAS CROSS of Centre Tp, aged 61y 11m. [probably CUSIAH CROSS d 1873 ae 61y 11m at Centre Tp., death records 1-38]

D: 27th ult JOHN McGARY near Dungannon, aged 80y.

D: at his res in Franklin Tp Sep 30th, RICHARD CARNEY ae 87y

SAD & FATAL ACCIDENT: a private letter brings us intelligence of a sad accident which occurred at Hudson, MO on 26 Sept. In the morning of that day, HARRY STAPLETON s/o WM. STAPLETON, formerly of this co., aged about 12y, rode a horse to a neighbor's with a halter & on returning home, the horse ran away, throwing him off & dragging him by the halter strap, which was fast on his arm, about a quarter of a mile. Died the same day.

FATAL ACCIDENT: WILSON HOFFMAN, a young man about 19y of age, living at Homeworth, in climbing for hickory nuts, fell from a tree a distance of 30 feet to the ground & was instantly killed.

Mon 13 Oct 1873 (Vol 7 no 28)

M: at res of JACOB BUSH in Green Village Oh by REV H.B.FRY, on 2nd inst, ISAAC N. BURBECK, formerly of New Lisbon & MISS CATHARINE ROBBINS of Green Village, Mah.Co.Oh.

M: by same at Presbyterian parsonage on 1st inst DAVID FAWCETT & MISS HATTIE BOSSERT all of Salem.

M: 2nd isnt by REV.G.W.RIGGLE, D.A.NAUGLE & MISS LIZZIE ANDERSON both of E.Liv.

M: 2nd inst by REV.T.N.BOYLE, JAS. MANSBRIDGE & MISS E.L.-SPENCER all of Salem.

M: 2nd inst at res of bride's father, by REV.J.HOWARD STOUGH, ALBERT M. DILWORTH & MISS MARIA HALVERSTADT all of CCO.

D: in Salineville on 6th inst infant son of J.M. & REBECCA IRWIN, aged 2m.

D: in Salineville on 7th inst THOMAS HALL s/o JOHN & HELEN HALL aged about 2y.

D: 25th ult at Salem, HUGH STEWART in 59th yr.

D: on 6th inst HANNAH BARBER of Salem aged 20y.

D: on 4th inst MARY S. HAGUE of Salem in 34th yr.

D: Sep 29th, ESTHER SNYDER of Col'ana aged nearly 74y.

D: Sep 30th, JOHN SNYDER, s/o WILSON SNYDER & WIFE of Col'ana, in his 4th yr.

D: 5th inst MAVARINE CULLENBERGER d/o LEWIS & NANCY JANE CULLENBERGER of Butler Tp ae 9m 24d.

Mon 20 Oct 1873 (Vol 7 no 29)

DEATH OF R.G.WOODS: after a protracted contest between life & death, our brother, ROBERT G. WOODS, for the last 5 or 6 years editor & proprietor of the "Ohio Patriot", expired at his place of living, about 10 o'clock Mon eve, 13th inst.- The deceased was about 37y of age. (long obit)

M: at the res of bride's mother, MRS.HARRIET WILSON of this place by REV.G.N.JOHNSTON, M.A.McCOY, of Omaha Nebr & MISS ANNA WILSON.

M: 15th inst at Cleveland by REV.TWITCHEL, DONALD McGREGOR of that city & MISS EMMA MARTIN of East Liverpool.

M: 9th inst at Col'ana by ELDER H.KURTZ, JACOB A. WARD & MISS LYDIA YOUNG, all of that place.

M: by same on 11th inst, ELIAS MOORE & MISS SAMANTHA METZ all of Col'ana.

M: by REV.N.H.WEAVER, DILWORTH GREENAWALT of Washingtonville & MISS LIZZIE ZIMMERMAN of Greenford.

D: 14th inst at her res in Elkrun Tp, ELIZABETH CANNON, w/o the late LINDSEY CANNON, aged 84y 1m 28d.

D: near Franklin Square on 7th inst, MARY LANT in 65th yr.

D: at Leetonia on 10th inst, JACOB HISE in his 68th yr.

D: same date & place, MARIA FAHEY in 2nd yr of her age.

D: at Col'ana on 6th inst, MARY GANT ae 67y.

D: on -- inst, MRS. THOMAS HOLLINGSWORTH of Rensselaer Ind., formerly of this place.

D: 10th inst HENRY WALTER of Elkrun Tp aged 82y.

D: 13th inst RACHEL HAIFLEY of Salem in her 47th yr.

Mon 27 Oct 1873 (Vol 7 no 30)

M: Sep 16th by REV WM COX, FRANK B. HOGE & MISS LIZZIE H. COX, all of this co.

M: 21st at Wellsville by ELDER J.M.VAN HORN, GEORGE M. CLARK & MISS CRISSIE K. BAXTER.

D: 18th inst EMILY WATERS of Salem aged 26y.

D: at Wellsville on 17th inst, JAMES M. BRANNON aged 30y.

D: CATHARINE BARNES w/o WILLIAM BARNES of West Tp ae 38y 6m.

D: son of ELISHA & SUSAN EMMONS of Hanover Tp ae 4m 17d.

D: at Salem 6th inst HARRIET GOODLEY ae 70y.

D: 13th inst at Salem, HESTER GIBBONS ae about 54y.

D: 22nd inst SARAH DAVIS d/o WM.E. & MARIA E. DAVIS of Elkrun Tp aged 1y 4m 16d

D: 23d inst DAVID CALVIN CULLER, s/o JOHN W. & ISABEL JANE CULLER, of Elkrun Tp, aged 14m.

Mon 3 Nov 1873 (Vol 7 no 31)

M: at Wellsville by REV.J.N.SWAN, ALEXANDER SMITH of Allegheny PA & MISS MARY A. SMITH.

M: by REV A SWEENEY, ABRAM PITTINGER & MISS LIZZIE DAVIS, both of Carroll Co.

M: in Salem on 26th ult by R.H.GARRIGUES ESQ, JOHN H. KIRK-BRIDE & MISS HANNAH M. FARQUHAR.

M: in Salem 23d ult by REV.H.B.FRY, ALEXANDER S. ROBINSON & ANNIE B. McCRACKEN all of this co.

M: at North Lima by REV.W.HAUPT on 23d ult, JOHN CLAY of Mah.Co. & MISS LIZZIE ZOOK of Col'ana.

M: 23d ult by WM.CRAWFORD ESQ in Middleton Tp, GEORGE HUSTON & MISS MARTHA FARR.

D: on 28th ult at Wellsville, AGNES SMITH ae 38y.

D: CATHARINE BARNES w/o WILLIAM BARNES of West Tp in 39th yr

D: at North Lima 26th ult, NATHAN HAHN ae 68y.

D: 27th ult at res of his son in law SAMUEL ROLLER, of Elkrun Tp, JESSE HEATON aged 66y 7m.

ELIAS HOLE was found dead between Bayard & E.Rochester on 22nd ult with two bottles of liquor, one of which he had partly emptied in his stomach.

Mon 10 Nov 1873 (Vol 7 no 32)

M: 6th inst at Titusville Pa, RUFUS HERRON of New Lisbon & MISS JENNIE SHUGART of that place.

M: 20th ult by REV.J.D.LEGGETT, DIOGENES ROGERS & MISS MARY COPE, both of this co.

M: 10th ult at Winona by SAMUEL WILLIAMS ESQ, CHAS. WILLIAMS & MISS JANE ELLIS all of this county.

M: 29th ult by REV.FATHER GRACE, JOHN GUNNING of E.Liverpool & MISS MAGGIE McHENRY of Allegheny City.

M: Nov 2d by REV.M.WALLACE, JOHN DOVER of E.Liverpool & MRS. MOUNTFORD, recently of England.

Mon 17 Nov 1873 (Vol 7 no 33)

M: 6th inst at the Lutheran parsonage in Salem Tp by REV.J.-HOWAR STOUGH, DAVID SMITH & MISS SAMANTHA E. KENTY all of CCO.

M: 9th inst by JOSEPH CREW JP, CURTIS VOTAW & MISS ANNA A. BLACK all of CCO.

M: 13th inst at Parsonage by REV.G.M.ALBRIGHT, FRANK ZIMMER-MAN & MISS MARY E. KEYSER all of this co.

M: 23d ult by REV.C.H.TAYLOR DD, MISS MOLLIE A. STUART & WILLIAM P. SANDERS of St.Joseph Mo.

M: 31st ult in Salineville by REV.BEACH, ANDREW MOFFIT & MISS MARY THOMPSON.

M: 13th ult by WASH.BORING ESQ, JAMES BROWN & MISS LAURA STITT.

M: at same time by same, JOHN GREEN & MISS JANE STITT, all of Salineville.

M: 5th inst in Canton by REV.J.C.LAVERTY, GEORGE W. THOMAS of Bellfonte PA & MISS FLORENCE A. ARTER d/o DR.D.A.ARTER formerly of this co.

D: 11th inst at Wellsville, JOHN C. MILLER in 23d yr.

D: 1st inst at Columbus,Oh, F.G.ADY s/o J.H. & JULIA A. ADY in 18th yr, formerly of Wellsville.

Mon 24 Nov 1873 (Vol 7 no 34)

M: Thurs last by REV.S.Y.KENNEDY, ABNER G. WINES & MISS FRANCES CUSHMAN d/o DR. S.D.CUSHMAN all of this place.

M: 8th inst by JOSEPH COULSON ESQ, JAMES LYNN & MISS ELIZA-BETH KELLY, all of West Tp.

M: 15th by same, FRANK P. WHITACRE & MISS JOSEPHINE BURSON all of this co.

M: 13th inst by REV.HARGEST, GEO.COPELAND & MISS TAMAR G. McCURDY all of this co.

M: same time & place by same, JOSEPH F.SAINT & MISS EVELYN E. McCURDY, all of this co.

M: by same, same day, D.W.LOWRIE & MISS MINNIE CRAWFORD all of this co.

D: 17th inst MARY BOWMAN of Fairfield Tp ae 98y 2m.

D: at Salem 6th inst MARTHA COX aged 11y 9m.

D: 14th at Salem, SUSANNA KLING in her 48th yr.

D: in West Tp 31st ult, JOHN BOWER in his 85th yr.

D: 18th inst CYNTHIA ANN PIKE d/o THOMAS & LEAH PIKE of Elkrun Tp ae 29y 1m 5d.

D: 21st inst MISS ALICE BENNER of Centre Tp aged 54y 2m 21d

Mon 1 Dec 1873 (Vol 7 no 35)

M: 24th ult in Col'ana by REV.W.DARBY, WILLIAM BEARDSLEY & MISS ISABEL MORELAN.

M: 25th ult at Wellsville by REV.J.DAY BROWNLEE, SAMUEL A. MARTIN & MISS MARY L. FOGO all of Wellsville.

M: 20th ult by REV.THOS.N.BOYLE, PAUL METZGAR & MISS SARAH ADA GREINER.

M: 20th ult at Salem by same, SETH DUNN & MISS JOSEPHINE KIRKBRIDE of Salem.

M: 19th ult at Salem by SAMUEL HARDMAN JP, WALTER FLITCRAFT & MISS ELLA RITCHEY all of CCO.

M: at Vanwert Oh on 13th ult, IRA P. SCHISSLER, formerly of Wellsville, & MISS ALICE GRAHAM of the former place.

Mon 8 Dec 1873 (Vol 7 no 36)

M: 27th ult by REV.J.M.VANHORN, GEORGE L. APPLE & MISS MAGGIE R.R.RUSELL all of Wellsville.

M: 24th ult by REV.ROBT HAYS, JOHN HANNUM & MISS DELLA PATTERSON all of CCO.

M: 27th ult by REV.H.B.FRY, ARCHIBALD COOK & MISS BESSIE BRAINARD all of Salem.

M: 26th ult at Salem by REV.W.R.SPINDLER, CHARLES HOWARD of Salem & MISS JULIA GREEN of Mah.Co.Oh.

M: 26th ult at Washingtonville by REV.S.WAGNER, CHARLES C. CAMPBELL & MISS FLORA M. GRIM.

M: 26th ult by D.V.HYDE, JAMES BETZ & MISS LOUISA SHINN all of this co.

M: Nov 30th by JETHRO MANLEY ESQ, TIMOTHY RIGBY & MISS HELEN JOHNSON both of E.Liverpool.

M: Nov 37th by REV.WM.GASTON at Bellaire, WM.W.CUNNINGHAM of E.Liverpool & MISS JENNIE GORBLE of this place.

D: 1st inst JOHN McSHADDEN of Wayne Tp ae 85y.

D: 2nd inst MRS. EMELINE BRIGHT w/o WM.BRIGHT of Wellsville aged 37y 5m 27d.

D: 24th ult at Pittsburgh, MRS. AMELIA CITRON, mother in law of MR.D.MANNIST of Wellsville ae 55y.

D: 26th ult at Hanover, BENJAMIN SINCLAIR ae 76y.

D: Nov 4th GRANT SIMERSON DYKE s/o PHILLIP & CATHARINE DYKE of Elkrun Tp ae 8y 5m.

D: Nov 6th, MARY TRUNICK d/o EDGAR & KITTY TRUNICK of New Lisbon ae 2y 5m.

A frightful accident occurred at the res of HENRY TRUNICK last Fri eve; he had occasion to purchase a small quantity of benzine, which was in a bottle or vial & palced it on a mantel shelf for a short while. From some cause the fluid leaked or bursted the bottle & it got into the fire, causing a terrible blaze & fearfully burning a little daughter of ED TRUNICK's about 3y of age, so that it died on Sat. The grandmother was also badly burned.

FATAL ACCIDENT: We learn from the Carroll Free Press that WM.CAHILL of that co was shot on 25th ult while out on his own farm, by the accidental discharge of a rifle in the hands of a young man named ABLE. MR.CAHILL died from the effects of the shot on the next Friday.

Mon 15 Dec 1873 (Vol 7 no 37)

M: 27th ult by REV.J.C.MELROY, LEWIS OLDRIDGE & MISS LAURA PROSSER, all of Wellsville.

M: 6th inst at Cleveland by REV.WASHBURN, HARRY B. GARRIGUES & MISS DOLLY WEBSTER.

D: 5th inst CHRISTENA ZEIGLER w/o MICHAEL ZEIGLER of Col'ana, born in Wertenberg Germany on 23 Dec 1806.

D: JOHN LOCK of Sharon Pa fell dead in that place on Thurs last aged about 56y.

D: Dec 11th MART R. MILLER d/o SIMON & SAMANTHA MILLER of Washingtonville aged 19y 6m 12d.

TRIAL OF IRVIN G. PORTER for the murder of his children.- Trial Dec 8 thru Dec 12, 1873. The scene of the tragedy was at the house of JACOB FLICKINGER, the father in law of PORTER, about 2 1/2 miles east of Columbiana. (contd next issue)

Mon 22 Dec 1873 (Vol 7 no 38)

D: Dec 6 at E.Liverpool, ALICE JACKSON w/o SAMUEL P. JACKSON in her 37th yr.

D: Dec 17th at Wellsville, ALBERT EWING s/o T.H.EWING, in 10th yr

Mon 29 Dec 1873 (Vol 7 no 39)

D: 24th inst MARY ROLLER w/o JACOB ROLLER of Elkrun Tp ae 64y

D: 23d inst at res of his mother in Elkrun Tp, DR.DAVID B. YOUNG, aged 31y 8d.

D: 20th inst ELIZABETH J. WARD d/o J.& MARGARET WARD of Elkrun Tp ae 21y.

M: 25th inst by REV.I.N.WHITE, F.T.McLAIN of Ames, Story Co., Iowa & MISS MARY J. FLEMING of Gavers, CCO.

M: 24th inst by H.E.FROST JP, at the Union Hotel, JOHN C. ANDREWS & MISS ELLA KING, all of this co.

M: 23d inst in Salineville by REV.S.M.COON, JAMES C.SPRINGER of Wayne Co Oh & MISS RACHEL McHENRY of Carroll Co Oh.

M: 25th inst in New Garden by E.GARSIDE ESQ, THOMAS NELSON & MRS. MARGARET CARMAN all of CCO.

M: 25th inst by same at res of E.GARSIDE in New Garden, WM. BELAT & MISS LEVINA ALBRIGHT all of CCO.

Sad news reached the family of MRS. M. ROBERTSON of this place on Tues last by telegraph, of the death of her son, JAS.L.ROBERTSON, ESQ., of Napoleon, Henry Co., Ohio. The deceased was the oldest son of the late JOHN ROBERTSON & was about 30 yrs of age.

1874
Jan 5,12,19,26   Feb 2,9,16,23   Mar 2,9,16,23,30
Apr 5,13,20,27   May 4,11,18,25   Jne 1,8,15,22,29
Jly 6,13,20,27   Aug 3,10,17,24,31 Sep 7,14,21,28
Oct 5,12,19,26   Nov 2,9,16,23,30 Dec 7,14,21,28.

Mon 5 Jan 1874 (Vol 7 no 40)

M: 1st inst ALONZO CHANDLER & MISS EMMA NEIGH both of CCO.

M: by REV.J.MELOY on 24th ult MR.VAL.B.FINN of Philadelphia & MISS MELLIE GIESSE of Wellsville.

M: at his office in New Lisbon on 31st ult by H.E.FROST JP, FRANCIS M. COX & MISS VIOLA MINER all of CCO.

M: by Rev.S.WAGNER on 24th ult JOSEPH C. WOODS & MISS MARY WILKINSON both of Washingtonville.

M: 13th ult by REV.JOHN COLL, LOT MORRIS & MISS LYDIA A. LONGENECKER all of CCO.

M: by ELDER (T/J?) H.HARRIER, WM.W.BOYLE of Mahoning Co & MISS CHARITY HOOPES of CCO.

M: on Christmas Day by REV.H.B.FRY, JAMES COSTELLO of Atwater & MISS CLARA M. HAWKINS of Salem.

M: on Christmas Day by REV.REEVES, CICERO FARMER & MISS ELMA HARRIS, all of Salem Tp.

M: on New Year's Day by REV.ROBERT HAYS, DAVID L. CROMLEY & MISS MAGGIE SMITH all of Salineville.

M: on 1st inst at Allegheny City by REV.JOHN BAKER, EVANS GRAY, printer, formerly of this co., & MISS LOU BENNER of this place.

BEN WILLIAMS who was arrested at Salineville a short time since & who paid the penalty of $1.00 & 5 days in jail for living unlawfully with MRS.MARY McGURTY, has been taken to Clearfield Co., Pa. to answer a similar charge.

The LIVERPOOL GAZETTE says a marriage took place on the 2nd inst on the P & C road in a train running 30 miles an hour. REV.T.J.KENNEDY of Steubenville performed the ceremony by which S.J.HOLMES of East Liberty PA & MISS MALINDA CONNOR of Carroll Co. were united in wedlock.

Mon 12 Jan 1874 (Vol 7 no 41)

M: 3rd inst at New Garden by E.GARSIDE EDQ, F.J.WARD & MISS ELIZA J. PETTIT all of CCO.

M: 25th ult by REV.W.B.ROLLER, W.D.WEIKERT & MISS LOUISA RHODES all of this co.

M: 1st inst by REV.N.H.WEAVER, S.SLAGLE & MISS SOPHIA CHARLTON all of this co.

M: at Wellsville on 24th ult by JOHN M. JENKINS ESQ, ALFRED MARTIN & MISS MARIDA ALLABACH.

M: 1st inst at Salineville by REV.ROBERT HAYS, DAVID L.-CRUMLY & MISS MAGGIE SMITH all of this co.

M: Dec 18th at Rochester PA by REV.T.S.HODGSON, GEORGE P. FISHER & MISS MAGGIE SMITH both of this co.

D: 28th ult at Hanover, GEORGE SMITH aged 76y.

The last WELLSVILLE UNION states that ROBERT A. SHERRARD of Steubenville died at this place on 1st inst in 85th yr.

Also, the death of CAPT.STANDISH PEPPARD, the oldest steamboat man of Georgetown, Beaver Co, aged about 60y.

WM. RUTH, of Wellsville, came very near being lost on Tues last. Being drunk, he fell out of a skiff, but was rescued from perishing.

News came to town last Tues of the death of DR. GEORGE L. McCOOK at the res of one of his sisters, MRS.HANNA, in Illinois. He was a native of this place, read medicine with his father, went to Pittsburg nearly 25 yrs ago where he attained a large practice. He was about 48y of age. The body of the deceased was conveyed to Pittsburg & placed by the side of his wife & daughter who preceded him in death.

M: at same place by same on 23d ult ADAM CALHOUN & ADDIE GEORGE of East Liverpool.

M: at Achor on 1st inst by J. ENTWHISTLE, JOHN A. MOUGH & MISS M.E.EAKIN.

Mon 19 Jan 1874 (Vol 7 no 42)

M: 8th inst by REV.S.Y.GRIER, T.J.GARLICK of Wellsville & MISS MATTIE SHUTTER of New Cumberland, WVa.

M: same day by REV.J.N.SWAN, GEORGE FOWLER of Irondale & MISS MARY RANSOM of Madison Tp, CCO.

M: at Ohioville Jan 13th by SANFORD ALMY JP, GEORGE W. BRANNON & MISS MARY GREEN, both of Calcutta Oh.

M: Jan 8th by REV.S.M.COON, WILLIAM BENSON & MISS ROSA BRANNON all of CCO.

M: Jan 15th in Salineville by REV.S.M.COON, D.D.DALLAS & MISS MAHALA D. HALL.

D: 15th inst GEORGE McCORMICK of Wayne Tp aged 52y.

Mon 26 Jan 1874 (Vol 7 no 43)

M: 14th inst in Salem by REV.JOHN HAWKER, ELISHA W. KELTY & MISS ELLEN S. GOLDY.

M: at Smith's Ferry PA on 20th inst by A.J.PETTIT ESQ, COLUMBUS B. ARMSTRONG & MARY A. TRIMMEN both of Wellsville Oh.

M: at Smith's Ferry PA on 22nd inst by J.McFALL ESQ, JOHN ARB & HANNAH ALLETON both of East Liverpool Oh

M: at Smith's Ferry PA on 22nd inst by same, DAVID S. SIMPSON & ANNA S. PHILLIPS both of Salineville.

D: 22nd inst in this place JESSIE D. HINE d/o R.R. & P.L.HINE aged 5y 3m 13d.

D: 16th inst in Salem, NANCY BAUM, aged 73y.

D: 14th inst in Columbiana, NANCY YENGLING, aged 70y.

D: 15th inst in Salem, MRS. CATHARINE CALLAHAN aged 33y.

D: in Salineville on 17th inst MICHAEL DENNEN aged 69y.

OBIT: JOHN FASNACHT, long a citizen of this place, died at the infirmary on 14th inst in his 83d yr. He & his brother WILLIAM came here about 40 years ago. They were Germans, but somehow got into Napoleon's army, whose fortunes & misfortunes they accompanied in the fearfull winter campaign into the heart of Russia. They knew how to subsist on uncooked horseflesh & it used to be said they were not adversed to indulging on deceased swine even if not bled to death.

A MRS. LITTLE, living near New Garden, this co., smothered to death her little girl, 6 months old, a few nights ago, while returning home from an oyster supper in that neighborhood.

Mon 2 Feb 1874 (Vol 7 no 44)

A FRIGHTENED BRIDEGROOM: The ALLIANCE LOCAL says a young woman a few days since from the neighborhood of East Rochester presented herself to the Township Trustees for a temporary hospital, which in pity for her condition, was granted.- After her convalescence, TRUMAN ARNOLD, one of the trustees, started with the mother & child to deliver her to her home near East Rochester. When they arrived at Bayard Station, a well dressed gentleman & lady stepped aboard the train, who bore unmistakable evidence of being recently married. The woman in charge of MR.ARNOLD whispered to him that the "bridegroom was the father of her child!" Mr.ARNOLD craved the privilege of introducing the happy father to his child, which, after some show of reluctance, was agreed to. MR.ARNOLD then brought the bridegroom face to face with the woman and child, which produced quite a sensation, not at all tending to enhance the bliss of a honeymoon trip. At Rochester he suddenly disappeared from view, leaving the bride in the car to pursue her journey alone. [see NLJ 2 Mar 1874--I.BAIRD may be the man in question.]

DEATH OF DAVID ANDERSON: Died last Fri morning at his res. on Jefferson St. in 74th yr of his age. Native of York, Pa. Funeral last Sun from Presbyterian church.

M: 20th ult by A.J.PETTIT ESQ, COLUMBUS B. ARMSTRONG of Wellsville OH & MISS MARY A. TRIMMEN of Jefferson Co Oh

M: 15th ult at Brownsville PA by REV.J.H.COULTER, ALFRED MYRES of Sloan's Station OH & MISS SABINA H. BULGER of Brownsville PA.

M: 24th ult at Cannelton PA by I.F.MANSFIELD,ESQ, WINFIELD S. GILBERT & MISS DEURIA LATTA both of Fairfield OH.

D: 17th ult in Hanover, WILLIAM MILBOURN aged 60y.

D: 22nd ult at Salem, MRS. MATILDA B. PENNOCK, formerly of Perry Twp., late of Janesville, OH, in her 60th yr.

Mon 9 Feb 1874 (Vol 7 no 45)

M: 5th inst at the Reformed Parsonage by REV.G.M.ALBRIGHT, DAVID SHIVE & MISS RACHEL J. FIGLEY both of Centre Tp.

M: 27th ult in West Tp by REV.MR.WILSON, MR.F.DAVIS & MISS EMILY BURT.

D: 25th ult MARGARET DICKEY aged 61y.

D: 27th ult. SAMUEL BARD, aged ----y.

D: 1st inst at res of her mother in St.Clair Tp, of heart disease, ELLA HAMBEL, aged about 26y.

D: 29th ult, ELIZABETH A. FRAZIER w/o DANIEL FRAZIER ae 39y.

Mon 16 Feb 1874 (Vol 7 no 46)

M: 29th ult at Salem by REV.T.N.BOYLE, ALBERT BURTON & MISS ESTHER M. STRAWN.

M: 5th inst at Salem by same, JACOB WALKER & MISS ELLA LAMB.

M: 5th inst at Salem by REV.JOHN CLEMENT, JONAS GOODMAN of Salem & MISS MAGGIE WOOLF of Butler Tp.

M: 4th in New Lisbon by REV.WM.HUNTER DD, W.C.MILLER & MISS LIZZIE McGINNERY both of Sparta, Stark Co Oh.

M: 9th inst at Cannelton PA by I.F.MANSFIELD ESQ, LOGAN DYKE & MISS FANNIE M. BARTON all of Mt.Carmel OH.

M: 7th inst by R.H.GARRIGUES JP, JACOB KRING & MISS MARTHA D. McCLAIN.

M: 4th inst EZRA TAYLOR & MISS LUCY KING.

M: 10th inst at Pittsburgh PA by REV.S.R.FRAZIER, JOHN MEREDITH & MISS HESTER S. EDWARDS, both of Salineville OH.

D: 6th inst at Salem, EUGENE E. ASK, aged 19y.

D: 9th inst at Salem, ELIZABETH COY, aged 69y.

D: 1st inst at Mt.Pleasant, Huntington Co PA, MISS ELLA McKEE with consumption, aged 22y.

RACHEL FURGUSON, aged 99y, living in Mansfield, was burned to death Thurs. morning by her clothes catching fire.

MARY DAVIS, w/o JOHN DAVIS, both natives of Col.Co., died at her res. in Crawford Co. on 30th ult, aged 77y. MR.DAVIS is a brother of MRS.JOSIAH GASKILL of this place.

Mon 23 Feb 1874 (Vol 7 no 47)

M: by REV.J.M.KENDIG, on 10th inst, JAMES FOX of Salem & MISS ORA GRONER of Columbiana.

M: 12th inst by REV.T.N.BOYLE, ALBERT R. CATTELL & MISS UREE E. COBBS.

M: same day by same, JOSEPH WILKINS & MISS MARTHA CALLAHAN, of Salem.

M: 14th inst by JOSEPH CREW JP, WILLIAM WHITACRE & MELISSA WATERS, all of Salem.

D: 10th inst at Otter Creek, MO, MRS.C.L.CUTLER, formerly of Wellsville, aged 41y.

D: 21st inst ISAAC HASTINGS of Centre Tp aged 80y.

D: 15th inst at Robbins, SIDNEY MOSELY, colored, aged 20y.

D: 18th inst in East Liverpool, infant son of FRANK & MAGGIE EDWARDS.

The happiest man in Elkrun Tp. is CHRIS. BOWMAN. TWINS & mother doing well.

MRS. ANN JOBE of Cannonsburg PA died on 7th inst aged nearly 99y. She was married in 1791, not long after which she & her husband came to New Lisbon. She lived at Pittsburg when there was nothing but a fort or blockhouse.

Mon 2 Mar 1874 (Vol 7 no 48)

The ALLIANCE LOCAL says that I. BAIRD, a gay lothario, formerly of Salem, visited that place on Thurs last, on the solicitation of Constable TRAIL, & presented a young lady with $150 towards the support & education of a little urchin, who has the right to call him "daddy." [see NLJ 2 Feb 1874, the frightened bridegroom, who may be I.BAIRD]

We learned from the Pittsburgh papers that GEORGE NEEMES, who is well known to the citizens of New Lisbon, was united in marriage with MRS. ELIZABETH McENULTZ of that city last Thurs evening.

M: 25th Dec by ELDER S.S.McKOWN, WILLIAM H. PIKE & MISS MATTIE PETTIT all of CCO.

M: 17th ult by REV.R.A.CURRAN, DAVID M. BURGER of Minerva, Stark Co, & MISS MARY E. HINE of CCO.

M: 19th ult by REV.JOHN B. MILLER, FRANK I. GILBERT & MISS JENNIE M. ANDERSON, all of CCO.

M: 15th inst in East Liverpool by REV.TURNER, MR.SIMMS & MISS HARKER.

D: 24th ult JAMES ENNIS VIVIAN s/o JOHN & LOUISA VIVIAN of Centre Tp aged 3y 4m.

D: 15th ult at Robbins, SIDNEY MORSE aged 20y.

D: 18th ult at East Liverpool, infant son of FRANK & MARTHA EDWARDS.

D: 15th ult ISRAEL COPE of Fairfield Tp CCO aged 90y.

D: 20th ult R.R.DONALLY at Wooster, formerly of Salem.

D: 21st ult in East Liverpool, WILLIAM PETERSON, aged 23y.

D: 19th ult in Wellsville, JOHN BARR aged 54y.

OBIT: MRS. MARTHA E. MITCHELL died suddenly at her home in Cincinnati on 20th ult at age of 47y. She was the only daughter of JUDGE C.D.COFFIN, formerly for many years a prominent citizen of New Lisbon.

A terrible accident occurred at a sawmill near ENTRIKEN's about 4 miles North of town last Wed. by which MR.CAREY HAINES was sadly torn & mangled. By some means he came into contact with the saw when in motion & one shoulder, some of his ribs & backbone were fearfully mutilated, in addition to which severe internal injuries were sustained, resulting in death after much suffering, which took place on Sat.

A piece of brazen rascality occurred at Hanover lately. One JOHN BURTON is charged with seducing the wife & children of GEORGE MILNER from their home. Mrs.M. wanted to be divorced, but failed, then went off with BURTON. Community there brands BURTON as a great villain.

GEN.EDWARD C. WILSON, a native of Steubenville & brother of the late R.C.WILSON of this place, died suddenly at Philadelphia on 16th ult. He was a lawyer by profession & filled highly important positions in both a state & national capacity.

Mon 9 Mar 1874 (Vol 7 no 49)

WILLIAM OGLINE, the Canfield Landlord who was recently convicted at Pittsburgh being too much & not enough married to a Columbiana girl, was sentenced on Sat last to pay a fine of $200 & go to the workhouse for one year.

M: 6th inst by REV.S.Y.KENNEDY, JOHN MILLER & MISS MARTHA WEDLOCK both of New Lisbon.

M: 10th ult by J.A.CLEMENT at his res in Knox Tp, JOHN FULTS & MISS ELIZA A. STOFFER both of CCO.

D: 2nd inst HANNAH E. CROWL w/o H.B.CROWL of Centre Tp ae 23y

D: 21st ult in East Liverpool, WILLIAM PETERSON ae 23y.

D: 24th ult MARTHA DUYEREA McCURDY d/o SAMUEL & SARAH McCURDY of Madison Tp ae 13y 5m 27d.

D: 1st inst in Salem, MRS.HELEN RUSH w/o DR.R.B.RUSH ae ---.

D: 7th inst in Salem, MRS.SARAH ISEMAN w/o DAVID ae 66y 9m 20d.

D: 2nd inst in Salem at res of his mother, EDGAR W. JAMISON ae about 19y.

D: 2nd inst in Madison Tp, NANCY PATTERSON w/o ALEXANDER ae 74y.

D: 5th inst at Cliff Works, RESIN BARTIN ae 36y.

D: 25th ult FELIX KUSK, Hanover Tp, ae 35y.

D: 3d inst in Hanover Tp CAROLINE REESE ae 31y 15d.

The fatal accident resulting in the death of CAREY HAINES noticed last week falls severely on his wife & two little children, most especially as Mrs.H. has been rendered partly helpless by a recent attack of paralysis.

Mon 16 Mar 1874 (Vol 7 no 50)

M: 12th inst BY REV WM. BAXTER, JOSIAH NEVILLE & MISS SARAH MORLAN both of this co.

D: 20th ult in Leetonia, QUINCY RICE ANGLEMYER, infant son of LUKE & MAGGIE ANGLEMYER, aged 5m 20d.

D: 9th inst DANIEL ANISON FREEMAN s/o FREDERICK & HARRIET FREEMAN of Elkrun Tp ae 6 weeks.

D: 10th inst JOHN McGAFFICK s/o JOSPEH & JANET McGAFFICK of Wayne Tp ae 10m 16d.

D: 11th inst WILLIAM E. DAVIS of Elkrun Tp ae 50y 9m.

D: 5th inst at Wellsville, DONALD NOBLE ae 44y.

D: 11th inst at Wellsville, JOHN HERBERT ARMSTRONG ae 1y 5m 24d.

D: 5th inst at Col'ana, GRACE SNYDER infant dau of SOLOMON & SUSAN SNYDER.

M: 17th inst at Wellsville by REV.JAMES HOLLINGSHEAD, THOMAS G. HAMMOND & MISS MARY HENDERSON all of Wellsville.

M: 19th inst by REV.WM.BAXTER, WILLIAM CHAMBERLIN & MISS MATTIE HILTEBIDDLE both of this co.

M: 10th at res of bride's mother in Leavenworth Co Kan, by REV.IRWIN, M.J.WESLEY BROWN & MISS M.ELLA CORY.

D: 13th inst inst Salem MISS ELIZA J. COFFEE.

D: 19th inst CHARLEY RUPP s/o HENRY & ANN RUPP of this place ae 2y 10m.

D: 13th inst near Salem, AARON ANTRIM, one of the old settlers of this vicinity.

OBIT: MARY MORRISON w/o JAMES B. MORRISON, one of the venerable pioneers of Col.Co., & a lady respected by all who knew her, died Mar.19,1874, ae 76y 8m 24d.

Mon 30 Mar 1874 (Vol 7 no 52)

M: 26th inst by EDWARD PETTIT JP, GODFREY N. CRAWFORD & MISS MARY E. STUCKMAN all of this co.

M: 12th inst by REV.J.A.CLEMENT, RODNEY C. MILNOR & MISS LIZZIE STURGEON all of this co.

D: at Chambersburg on 20th inst WILLIAM HARWOOD ae 13y 3m.

D: 15th inst SARAH LONGENECKER of Salem Tp in 40th yr of age.

D: 21st inst in Hanover infant child of L.PARTHE, aged 14m.

Mon 5 Apr 1874 (Vol 8 no 1)

M: 19th ult at the parsonage of REV.MR.MILLER in Pittsburgh, CLARK SNYDER & MISS MARY MORRIS all of Salem.

M: 25th ult by REV.C.L.WINGET, SAMUEL WARNER & MISS MARY ALLEN all of this co.

M: 25th ult by REV.ROBERT HAYS, DANIEL SMITH of Yellow Creek Tp & MISS JESTEEN SHARP of Highlandtown.

M: 12th inst at Col'ana by REV.J.M.KENDIG, EPHRAIM METZLER & MISS ISADORE MARCH.

D: 29th ult at his res in Salem, CALVIN C. BRAINARD ae 62y.

D: 26th ult at Pittsburgh, JOHN W. MENTZER formerly of Salem ae 60y.

D: 30th ult MARY CONSOR w/o GEORGE CONSOR of Salem ae 52y.

D: 20th ult LUCINDA WILLIAMSON w/o THOMAS WILLIAMSON of Salem ae 50y.

D: 25th ult in Genesco Ill., JOSEPH ENTRIKEN formerly of Salem Tp, CCO ae 75y 4d.

D: 31st ult KITTIE COWAN d/o A.J. & SUSAN COWAN, ae 2y 5m.

OBIT: JOHN TEMPLIN of Mah.Co. ae about 60y, died very suddenly last Sat. week of heart disease. He arose in the morning feeling as well as usual, at his breakfast & after walking around for a short time, sat down on a chair & immediately dropped dead.

MRS. FREDERICK NEUSBAUM of Salem was found dead in bed Fri. night a week ago.

MISS JOSEPHINE WHINERY, sister of MRS.S.J.FIRESTONE of this place, died at Alliance last Sabbath evening.

Mon 13 Apr 1874 (Vol 8 no 2)

M: 18th ult at Freedom PA by REV.M.L.WORTMAN, J.G.HILLMAN & MISS S.A.NICKUM.

D: 7th inst JOHN FIGGINS of Salineville in 77th yr of age.

D: 30th ult in Hanover Tp JOHN HIVELY ae 61y 6m 26d.

D: 6th inst in New Garden wife of THOMAS NELSON ae 53y.

D: 2nd inst at East Liverpool infant son of EPHRAIM & DORCAS GASTON.

OBIT: Death of Capt.REUEL TALBOT: the sudden death of CAPT. TALBOT, by dropsy of the heart, a farmer residing about 1 1/2 miles west of New Lisbon on Sat.Afternoon. He was in 66th yr.

Mon 20 Apr 1874 (Vol 8 no 3)

M: 9th inst in Salem by REV.THOS.N.BOYLE, HOWARD GARRIGUES of Massillon & MISS ALICE L. HUTTON.

D: 8th inst in Salem JAMES L. HOLE infant son of L.C.& RACHEL HOLE, aged 18m.

D: 11th inst in Salem at his late res. AMOS FAWCETT ae 75y.

D: 19th inst in Salem, MRS. PHEBE SMITH.

D: 16th inst in Salineville, infant son of JOSEPH & SUSAN DAVIS aged 10m.

D: 12th inst in Col'ana, JESSE M. ALLEN aged about 68y.

D: 12th inst at Damascus, JOHN KILLE aged ----y.

There is a law in Switzerland compelling parents to plant 2 trees on the birth of each child. If such a law ere in force here, our friend JOHN W. MICK would have to plant 4 trees in honor of the arrival of those twins--girls--the other day.

MAJOR JOHN L. STRAUGHN is all smiles. He is at last the father of a sweet little girl.

JOHN RAKESTRAW, an old & respected citizen of Salem, was buried in that place last Sabbath.

Fatal Accident: a young son of a MR. BARNHART, Residing near Homeworth, fell into a boiling-pan at a sugar camp on 10th inst & was so badly scalded that he died in a few hours.

Mon 27 Apr 1874 (Vol 8 no 4)

M: 15th inst by REV.WILL T. ROBBINS, JOSEPH L. WHITLA of New Brighton PA & Miss SALLIE E. BATCHELOR of Wellsville.

D: 20th inst ADAM HOFFMAN of Elkton ae 51y 10m 8d.

D: 19th inst in Pittsburgh, WILLY ALBERT WEBER s/o J.A. & AUGUSTA WEBER aged 2 weeks & 2 days.

D: 10th inst in city of Quincy Ill. MRS. REBECCA R. WILLIAMS formerly of Slaem ae 60y 4m 26d.

D: 20th inst in Salem OLIVER A. THOMAS ae 43y.

D: 14th inst in Butler Tp MISS HANNAH BROWN ae 34y.

D: 22nd inst in St.Clair Tp, L.W.SMITH ae 22y 3m.

D: 20th inst in East Liverpool, CARRIE RIGBY d/o WM. & MARY RIGBY, ae 2y 4m.

D: 20th inst MAGGIE HAGEN d/o JAMES HAGEN of Dungannon ae about 25y.

D: 23d inst MAGGIE OTT d/o JOSEPH & MARY ANN OTT of Hanover ae 7m.

D: 25th inst REBECCA VAUGHN w/o W.H.VAUGHN of Hanover formerly of this place aged about 65y.

We have received a note from EMMETT KANNAL of Rensellear, Ind., from which we learned the particulars of THOMAS McCOY'S death. He died on Tues the 7th inst aged 70y 2d.

JACOB FOWLER, an old & estimable citizen & proprietor of the Brick works, East Liverpool, died on Mon last.

Mon 4 May 1874 (Vol 8 no 5)

M: 27th ult by SQUIRE McFALL of Smith's Ferry, CHAS. MONT-GOMERY & MISS LIZZIE GEARY, both of Wellsville.

M: 23d ult at Col'ana by REV.HILBISH, JOSHUA FLICKINGER & MISS MARY E. PERKINS d/o REV.L.B.PERKINS formerly of CCO.

M: 23d ult by REV.T.N.BOYLE, COL.J.H.REED of Macon MO & MISS ANNA STREET of Salem.

D: 23d ult at Salem WILLIAM SHINN ae 42y.

D: 18th ult in East Liverpool, MRS.SUSAN BLYTHE ae 90y.

Mon 11 May 1874 (Vol 8 no 6)

M: in Allegheny City PA on 30th ult by REV.D.C.PAGE, HIRAM T.DEMPSEY of Beaver Falls PA & MISS MARY ROBINSON of Allgheny City.

M: 30th ult by REV.COON, JOHN SHECKLER & MISS MARGARET GRACEY all of Salineville.

D: 30th ult in Wellsville JANE FOGO in 80th yr.

D: 1st inst in Wellsville HUGH BEAN in 74th yr.

D: 6th inst SAMUEL FUGATE of Hanover Tp ae about 83y.

D: 2nd inst at Milford, NY,NY, LYMAN BROOKS, formerly of Salem in 80th yr.

D: 4th inst MIROM NELSON s/o JEROME B. & ANN NELSON of this place aged 10y 6m 2d.

D: 8th inst REBECCA A. TORRENCE w/o H.M.TORRENCE of this place aged 43y 7m 25d.

OBIT: MRS.NANNIE MILLER w/o FRANCIS MILLER & d/o JACOB SNYDER formerly of this place, died in Keosauqua Iowa on 21st ult aged 22y.

DEATH OF A PIONEER: MICHAEL McKIBBON SR. died in East Liverpool on 2nd inst aged 93y. He joined the Presbyterian Church where now stands the village of Calcutta in 1812 & adorned his profession until called hence.

Mon 18 May 1874   (Vol 8 no 7)

M: 7th inst in Salem by REV.H.B.FRY, JONATHAN MARTIN & MISS LIZZIE A. SIPLE both of this co.

M: 12th inst in Salem by REV.T.R.BOYLE, JOSEPH O. GREINER & MISS ADELLA J. CAMPBELL.

M: 7th inst in Fairfield by REV.TEEGARDEN, DAVID F. DICKEY & MISS MOLLIE E. COPE.

M: 23d ult by REV.HAYS, WILLIAM F. ARBUCKLE of Madison tp & MISS NANCY C. TODD of Wayne Tp.

D: 9th inst ROBERT PATTERSON of Butler Tp in 72nd yr.

D: in Knox Tp 11th inst, DANIEL REDMAN ae 52y 5m.

HON.S.W.GILSON died at his res in Canfield on morning of 12th inst having suffered from spinal affection for over a year past.

COE SCOTT of East Liverpool, while spading garden last Mon., fell dead off his feet. He was aged about 70y.

The remains of DANIEL HARBAUGH were brought home last Tues & interred the following day.

HON.DAVID HARBAUGH of Detroit Mich. was in town last week in attendance at the funeral of his brother, the late DANIEL HARBAUGH.

Mon 25 May 1874 (Vol 8 no 8)

M: 14th inst in New Garden by E.GARSIDE, JOHN FERN of Stark Co & MISS JENNIE E. GARDNER of Hanover Tp.

M: 14th inst by REV.T.J.HAYS, ROBERT SKYLES & MISS SARAH J. McCONAUGHEY both of Col'ana.

M: 29th ult by REV.J.COIL, ORVILLE JONES & MRS. LOUISA APPLEGATE all of this co.

M: 14th inst by REV.N.H.WEAVER, DAVID WEIKART & MISS SADIE CHAPEL both of Washingtonville.

M: 14th inst by REV.J.COIL, D.COPE of ---- & MISS ISABELLA SHEETS of Leetonia Oh.

D: in Hubbard O. on 21st inst PETER SPRINGER, formerly of New Lisbon, aged 69y.

Court proceedings:
SABINA WYLIE vs LEWIS C. WYLIE: Divorce granted & custody of children to plaintiff.
MARY N. ROSE vs WILLIAM ROSE: Divorce granted. Custody of children to petitioner & maiden name restored.

DEATH OF THOMAS G. HUSTON: we are called upon this morning to chronicle the death of THOMAS HUSTON of Homeworth, this co., which sad event occurred on the 20th inst. MR.HUSTON was Recorder of this co. for 2 terms. He was aged about 66y.

Our old friend, JOSEPH McLAUGHLIN, of Elkrun Tp, determined not to remain single. Accordingly, last Mon. he proceeded to Lawrence Co Pa. & was united in wedlock to MISS CAROLINE McCARTNEY formerly of West Point.

Mon 1 June 1874 (Vol 8 no 9)

Court proceedings:
VIRGINIA A. DELLENBAUGH vs JOHN A. DELLENBAUGH. Divorce granted & maiden name, VIRGINIA A. GROSSMAN, restored.

M: 22nd ult at Winona, ELISHA STEER, of Concord, Belmont Co Oh to ELLA GILBERT of Winona.

M: 14th ult at Irondale,OH by REV.E.W.BROWN, LEVI LARVAN of Newark OH & MISS BARBARA OGLE of Salineville.

M: 22nd ult by REV.J.N.VAN HORN, THEODORE GILBERT of Gallia Co Oh & MISS SAMANTHA GRAFTON of Wellsville OH.

D: 10th ult in Middleton Tp, JAMES NEVIN ae 92y.

D: 28th ult ARTHUR McCORD of Wayne Tp ae 66y.

D: 28th ult WARNER PETERS SR. of Centre Tp ae 77y.

FISHER A. BLOCKSOM JR. & WIFE were made happy last week by the arrival of a ten pound boy baby. FISHER sits & grins at it & wonders when it will have teeth & what makes it so bald-headed & whether it looks like him. It is supposed he will recover.

JAMES ARBUCKLE, formerly of East Liverpool, was recently murdered & robbed of $1500 in Arkansas.

DEATH OF WARNER PETERS, SR.: Our citizens were startled to learn Fri. morn that WARNER PETERS SR. who lived a mile & half south of town had died suddenly the night before. He was aged 77y.

Mon 8 June 1874 (Vol 8 no 10)

M: 28th ult by REV.ROBERT HAYS, THOMAS E. ENDLY of Indianapolis Ind & MISS MARJORY ROSE of Madison Tp CCO.

M: 27th ult by Friends ceremony, BARCKLEY MARIS of Salem & MISS ANNA PIM of Carroll Co Oh.

D: 29th ult MARY H. PAINTER of Salem in 81st yr.

D: 31st ult at Col'ana, HARVEY HOLLOWAY ae 16y 10m 17d.

DEATH OF ABIJAH McLEAN: on last Thurs morn ABIJAH McLEAN, another of our old citizens, died at his res. in this place. He had been bedfast for some time & his death was not unexpecteed. Mr.McLEAN was well known throught the co., he had been county surveyor, treasurer & auditor. He was buried on Fri with Masonic honors. He was aged 67y.

JOHN McCORMICK, an old & respected citizen of Wayne tp died yesterday morning aged about 68y.

Mon 15 June 1874 (Vol 8 no 11)

M: 4th inst by S.Y.KENNEDY, FRANK D. WARD & MISS ELLA R. EDDY.

M: 25th ult by FATHER LINDESMITH, THOMAS J. MEYERS & FIDELAS JACK all of Leetonia.

M: 4th inst by REV.H.B.FRY, WILLIAM KOLL & MISS JENNIE THOMAS both of Salem.

M: 27th ult at Alliance by REV.E.L.FRAZIER, A.B.HOFFMAN & MISS ELLA ERWIN both of Col'ana.

M: 4th inst at Canfield by REV.J.B.ZUMPE, REV.J.H.HARTMAN of Tamaqua PA & MISS MARY A. BERGER of No.Georgetown this co.

M: at same time & place by same, WILLIAM BOWMAN & MISS ROSANA BERGER, both of Knox Tp this co.

D: 7th inst SARAH COBURN widow of JOHN of Wayne Tp ae 78y.

D: 25th ult at Salineville, EMMA MULLER ae 11y 2m 11d.

D: 29th ult near Woodstock, Richland Co Wisc, SILAS HART formerly of this co., in his 44th yr.

D: 10th inst at Salineville, JAMES ADAMS in 75th yr.

The SALEM ERA informs us that on night of 3d inst a basket was left inside of JOHN YENGLING's gate, containing a beautiful male infant. The little fellow appeared to be about 6 or 8 weeks old & had a card pinned to his clothing containing the name "JIMMIE HUNTER."

Mon 22 June 1873 (Vol 8 no 12)

M: 18th inst by REV.HOLLINGSHEAD, HOMER McLAUGHLIN of East Liverpool & MISS CORNELIA BOTTENBERG of Wellsville.

M: 11th inst by REV.BOYLE, S.P.COULTER of Parker's City, PA & MISS MARY E. ARCHBOLD of Salem.

D: 11th inst in Salem, WALTER JAMISON infant son of MRS. G.T.JAMISON aged 17m 22d.

D: 3d inst in Salem infant son of THOMAS CALDWELL ae 6m.

D: 17th inst EMMA S. HALVERSTADT of Salem Tp ae 13y 9m 7d.

DR.GEORGE MENDENHALL, one of the leading physicians of Cincinnati, died a few days ago of paralysis. DR. MENDENHALL was for some years a resident of this county.

LUTHER B. CALVIN of Mahoning Co & MRS. LEAH YODER of Col.Co.- were married yesterday at Locust Grove Church 3 miles north of Washingtonville.

Mon 29 June 1874 (Vol 8 no 13)

ANNA GAFFNEY, a middle-aged woman of intemperate habits, died suddenly at Ironton OH Tues morning from the effects of arsenic administered by herself.

M: 17th inst by REV.BOYLE, STEPHEN B. RICHARDS & MISS GERTRUDE WHINERY both of Salem.

M: 18th inst by JOSEPH CREW ESQ, ANDREW J. CLEMENT & MISS AMZIE M. EDWARDS all of this co.

M: 22nd inst at Salineville by REV.S.M.COON, GEORGE B. SMITH of CCO & MISS RACHEL M. DORRANCE of Jeff.Co.Oh.

D: 16th inst in Salem SARAH KELLEY aged 50y.

D: 18th inst in Wellsville MRS. MARTHA M. PHILLIPS aged 70y.

D: 25th inst in Wayne Tp MRS. MARTIN ARMSTRONG ae 82y.

A physician murdered in Mahoning Co: the little town of North Benton in Mah.Co. was the scene of a bloody tragedy on last Tues. An insane man named EDWARD HARTZELL shot DR.- HIRAM A. CONRAD. DR.CONRAD was but 37y of age.

Mon 6 July 1874 (Vol 8 no 14)

M: at Minerva on 18th ult by REV.R.A.CURRAN, WILLIAM A. LIV- INGSTON & MISS FLORA LEITH both of Bayard this co.

M: 25th ult by REV.FRY, WILLIS WEAVER & MISS ANNA R. KUHN both of Salem.

M: 25th ult by REV.BOYLE, O.B.MILLER & MISS MARY E. KIRK- BRIDE both of Salem.

M: 7th inst by REV.G.N.JONSON, DANIEL HAHN & MISS ELLA BECK both of Knox Tp.

M: 27th inst by same, ALEXANDER MILLER & MISS ELIZABETH BURNETT both of Salineville.

M: 15th ult by same, JAMES McCLELLAND of Wisconsin & MISS ANNIE E. McCLELLAND of this co.

M: 25th ult by REV.ROBT HAYS, JOHN TODD & MISS MARY JANE FIGLEY both of Wayne Tp.

M: 28th ult by REV.I.T.ALLEN, JOSEPH KIRK & MISS ELIZABETH JOHNS both of this co.

D: 28th ult in Salem MRS. HANNAH HALL ae 78y.

D: 18th ult in New Waterford, LEWIS WALKER, s/o JACOB & SARAH, aged 34y 3m 14d.

D: 29th ult at the Infirmary, DANIEL McGREGOR ae 36y

SUDDEN DEATH: MRS. JACOB ENDLY, residing about 3 miles south of town, died very suddenly of heart disease last Thurs.- night. MRS. ENDLY was the daughter of the late JUDGE DANIEL HARBAUGH. Her age was about 64y.

Mon 13 July 1874 (Vol 8 no 15)

DAVID YOUNG, father of the editor of the BUCKEYE, died at his residence in Middleton Tp yesterday.

JOSEPH VALLANDIGHAM, of the PATRIOT office, has succombed to the charms of one of New Lisbon's fairest daughters. He was married on May 23d to MISS SUSAN A. LIVINGTON, eldest daughter of GEORGE LIVINGSTON.

M: 4th inst by JOHN KANNAL ESQ, SELL McMILLAN & MISS LOU BARNET both of this co.

M: 2nd inst at the Reformed Parsonage by REV.G.M.ALBRIGHT, EMANUEL UNDERWOOD & MISS ANNA KOUNTZ both of No.Georgetown.

Mon 13 July 1874 (Vol 8 no 15)

D: in Dungannon on 27th ult MRS. MARY McARDIE native of Drumadonald, Ireland, ae 78y.

D: at Alliance on 7th inst, infant dau of CLINTON & RACHEL GARRETT ae 6m.

D: 28th ult in Washingtonville JOHN DETWILER ae 64y.

Mon 20 July 1874 (Vol 8 no 16)

M: 8th inst by REV.A.J.PETTIT, SAMUEL MORLEY JR. & MATTIE E. BRANDON both of E.Liverpool.

M: 9th inst by REV.HILBISH, WARREN STOKESBERRY of Knox Co OH & MISS LUCY A. CREPS of Mahoning Co.Oh.

M: 25th ult by REV.L.M.DUNDAS, JOSEPH SHATER & MISS ELIZA- BETH THOMAS both of this co.

M: 11th inst by REV.G.N.JOHNSON, MATTHEW W. HEALD of East Carmel & MISS SARAH E. DICKEY of New Lisbon.

M: 9th inst by same, JOHN STEELE & MISS ALICE LEIREY.

M: same time WM.STEELS & MISS SARAH DUMBLETON all of this co.

M: 14th inst by same, WILSON H. VANFOSSEN & MISS SOPHRONIA VOGAN all of New Lisbon.

M: 17th inst by REV.A.B.MAXWELL, B.P.HOLMES & MISS FANNIE A. ABBOTT both of Leetonia.

M: 7th inst by WM.DICKSON, CHARLES WARRINGTON of Salem & MISS LUCINDA ALLISON of Beloit OH.

M: 8th inst by REV.J.P.ERWIN, JAMES R.HAWKINS of Salem & MISS ELIZABETH J. RUSSELL of Milton OH.

M: 1st inst by SAMUEL HARDMAN ESQ, JOHN B. HIDDLESTON & LIZZIE MOUNTS all of Salem.

D: 6th inst at res of her parents, MR.& MRS. ISAAC WEBB in Salem, MISS HATTIE M. SNIDER of consumption in 35th yr.

D: 5th inst in Knox Tp, MARY LOUISA BOWMAN d/o JOHN & LOUISA BOWMAN ae 3y 1m 6d.

D: in Hillsboro Oregon 18th ult JOSEPH BOYCE M.D., formerly of Wellsville OH, ae 71y.

D: 13th inst at his home in E.Palestine, BROWN TAGGART ESQ.

D: 15th inst ELIZABETH EVERETT w/o Z.S.EVERETT of Centre Tp ae 64y 10m.

Mon 27 July 1874 (Vol 8 no 17)

D: 15th inst CATHARINE DELLER w/o NICHOLAS DELLER of Butler Tp aged ---.

D: 19th inst at the infirmary, MARGARET BLACKBURN ae 70y.

DEATH OF JOHN WATSON: from the Davenport Iowa Democrat we learn that JOHN WATSON, formerly a resident & one of the early settlers of New Lisbon, died at that place on 22nd inst aged 79y 4m 2d. Deceased was born in York Co PA 20 Mar 1795, where he resided with his parents until 1804 when the family settled in this place. He was married 4 July 1816 to Miss MAGDALENA HELMAN. In 1855 he moved to Davenport.

JOHN BREWSTER, formerly of this place, now of Wheeling WVA was married to a young lady in that city one day last week.

FRANK ZIMMERMAN, assisted by his wife, one day last week added another girl to our population----& it is said to be a fine girl, too.

Mon 3 Aug 1874 (Vol 8 no 18)

DEATH OF MRS. STEPHEN A. DOUGHTON: MRS.S.S.A., w/o STEPHEN A. DOUGHTON, died Fri evening last after a lingering illness-She was his 2nd wife & aged about 40y.

DEATH OF WILLIAM KEMBLE: Another old & respected citizen of this co. has passed away! WILLIAM KEMBLE died at his residence in Col. last Sat morning in 75th yr of his age.

M: 30th ult by REV.M.F.LAUFIER, WILLIAM WAGELY & MISS ELIZA VOLKERS both of New Lisbon.

M: 21st ult by JESSE HAWLEY ESQ, JOHN CHAMBERLIN of Iowa & SARAH HALL of this co.

M: 20th ult by J.S.CALVERT ESQ, JOSEPH BAKER of Beaver Co Pa & MISS KATE HUDSON of Wellsville Oh

D: 25th ult at the Infirmary, RICHARD WILLIAMS ae 74y.

D: 26th ult at the Infirmary, JAMES STEWART ae 69y.

Mon 10 Aug 1874 (Vol 8 no 19)

DEATH OF JACOB WILHELM: We are once more called upon to chronicle the death of another of Col.Co's respected citizens. JACOB WILHELM, died at his residence near Cool Springs, Fairfield Tp, 3 Aug 1874, aged 80y 1m 16d. He came to this co. from Wortenberg Germany in 1794, with his father, who settled in that part of the co. since struck off to Mahoning. Of his family of 9 children, 5 sons & 2 daughters are living, 5 of them in this county.

M: 4th inst by H.E.FROST ESQ, MACLEAN LONGSHORE & MISS ANN NEILL all of this co.

M: 28th ult by REV.ROBT HAYS, DAVID M. HUNTER & MISS LIZZIE OGLE both of Washington Tp.

M: 26th ult by J.A.CLEMENS, JESSE FRESHLY & MISS SAMANTHA RUFF both of Knox Tp

M: 23d ult by D.M.CAREY ESQ, WILLIAM H. MERCER & MISS DEBORAH E. BROWN, both of this co.

M: same time by same, GEORGE S. WOOLF & MISS IDA WINDLE both of this co.

M: 26th ult by REV.KENDIG, ALEX. GREENLEE & MISS EMMA VANSKIVER both of this co.

M: 8th inst FRANK SNYDER of New Lisbon & MISS SALLIE McDEVITT of Salineville.

D: 3d inst in Middleton, Fairfield Tp, MARIA BROWN w/o LEWIS BROWN, at an advanced age.

D: 16th ult in Martinsburg WVA MRS. JULIA B. HALDEMAN w/o JOSEPH S. HALDEMAN formerly of Salem OH.

D: 6th inst at East Palestine MARGARET TAGGART ae about 35y.

D: 3d inst at East Liverpool CORRA E. HUSTON infant dau of MARCUS M. & SUSAN HUSTON, aged 4m 1d.

Mon 17 Aug 1874 (Vol 8 no 20)

M: 13th inst by E.GARSIDE ESQ, EPHRAIM EWING & MISS CAROLINE HINER of Hanover Tp

M: 5th inst by REV.W.L.DIXON, GEORGE W. YANT of Hanover & MISS ADDIE WESTFALL of Carroll Co.

M: 14th inst at the Union House, New Lisbon by HENRY E. FROST JP, D.W.REEDER & MISS CARRIE ULRICK all of this co

M: 13th inst by REV.ROBT HAYS, GEORGE P. HUSTON & MISS SADIE MONTGOMERY both of Calcutta Oh

D: 9th inst at Salem PRICILLA COFFEE aged about 50y.

D: 11th inst at Franklin Square, SIBEL COY aged 25y.

D: 11th inst near Leetonia JACOB HENRY infant son of MARTIN & BARBARA HENRY aged 11m.

D: 7th inst near Summitville, THERESA McMULLEN aged about 22y.

D: 10th inst CARLISLE SHEPHERD, infant son of CAPT. & MRS. SHEPHERD of Wellsville, aged 9m 19d.

D: 8th inst EMIL ALBERT HERWIG, infant son of ERNST & ROSANA HERWIG, of Wellsville, aged 2m 3 wks 4d.

Mon 24 Aug 1874 (Vol 8 no 21)

MRS. MARY STEWART w/o JAMES STEWART, one of the oldest res. of Wellsville died last Wed.

WILTON LINN & his brother THOMAS of Hanover have received information that a wealthy uncle in California has died & willed to them $50,000, to be delivered when THOMAS is of age, which will be in about 4 yrs.

M: 17th inst by REV.J.A.MILLER of Allegheny, FRANK GRAHAM of Pittsburgh & MISS CLARISSA A. DOUGHTON of New Lisbon.

M: 20th inst at the Cowan House, this place, by J.M.DICKIN-SON ESQ, DANIEL ROGEN & MRS. JANE McPHEE.

M: 18th inst by REV.THOMAS D.PITTS, I.L.JAMES of Wellsville & MISS ALICE J. PRESLEY of Steubenville.

M: 12th inst by REV.GEORGE VOGLESONG, MR. LOU C. WHITE of Wellsville & MISS EMMA H. VOGLESONG of Hanover, dau of the officiating clergyman.

M: 20th inst by REV.G.W.RIGGLE, MONTERVILLE MACKALL & MISS MARY A. KINNEY both of Calcutta OH.

M: 20th inst by JOHN BRINDLEY ESQ, JOHN TWADDLE & MISS MARGARET A. ARB all of East Liverpool.

D: 12th inst in Knox Tp, JOHN CRISSINGER aged 70y

D: 12th inst in Salem, ELIZA A. REED w/o S.F.REED ae 25y 20d

D: 13th inst in Salem, PERCY R. SHARPNACK s/o D.H.SHARPNACK ae 1y 7m.

D: 15th inst in Butler Tp EMMA SPROWEL ae 21y 13d.

D: 18th inst ANDREW MYERS, adopted son of ERASTUS EELLS of New Lisbon, aged 20y.

D: 22nd inst MUZELLA ULERY d/o JOHN S. & EMELINE ULERY of Centre Tp, aged 6m 21d.

Mon 31 Aug 1874 (Vol 8 no 22)

M: 25th inst by REV.KENDIG, MAHLON B. ERWIN & MISS ANGIE FLICKINGER both of this co.

M: 26th inst by REV.BUTTS, THOMAS M. LAYING & MISS KATE C. HILLERMAN, d/o J.H.HILLERMAN all of Pittsburgh Pa.

M: 27th inst at res of bride's father by REV.G.M.ALBRIGHT, EDGAR SMITH & MISS REBECCA BRICKER both of this co.

D: 28th inst WILBERT A. HUFFMAN s/o SARAH HUFFMAN of Elkton aged 5m 3 wks.

D: 29th inst MRS. AMFIELD C. WARD of New Lisbon ae 81y.

D: 30th inst HANNAH MASKREY of this place aged 34y.

JOSEPH HOLLOWAY, an old resident of Col'ana died on the 22nd inst. He was about 70y of age.

MARY KENTNER w/o ELI, formerly of Salem, died at Jamesport Missouri on 17th inst.

Mon 7 Sep 1874 (Vol 8 no 23)

M: 25th ult by ESQ.SMART, ELIAS LOWER of Fairfield Tp & MRS. CAROLINE ROW of Unity Tp this co.

M: 3d inst THOMAS T. BARRETT of Tuscarawas Co Oh & MISS ELIZABETH R. CADDIS of Salineville

D: 19th ult of cholera, IDA MAY CLARK d/o J.LYTTLETON & MARY E. CLARK, aged 5m 22d.

D: 3d inst at res of J.ROSS JUNKIN in Wellsville, MRS. NANCY McBEAN aged 70y.

D: 2nd inst in Salineville, JAMES McMILLEN aged about 64y.

D: 4th inst DAVID W. HALVERSTADT aged 33y 7m 11d.

Died in Berlin, Mahoning Co last Wed evening, MRS. ANNA ROWLAND at the advanced age of 100y 9m.

Mon 14 Sep 1874 (Vol 8 no 24)

M: 5th inst by H.E.FROST ESQ, FRANK BROWN & MISS SIDNEY J. WOOD both of this co.

M: 3d inst by REV.H.HILBISH, J.W.DONBART & MISS CATHARINE MITCHELL all of this co.

M: 3d inst by ELDER J.M.VAN HORN, EZEKEL DURBIN & MISS THERESA MOORE both of Wellsville.

M: 3d inst by REV.I.J.DELO, J.W.SHONTZ & MISS EMMA NOLD both of Leetonia.

M: 3d inst by REV.S.M.COON, GEORGE PAISLEY & MRS. SALOME B. BELL all of Salineville.

D: 1st inst in Salem MARY HOLLOWAY relict of JOEL aged 82y.

D: 7th inst in Salem MRS.M.A.WEBSTER relict of LARY WEBSTER aged 40y.

D: 3rd inst in Salem ELLA BRAINARD of typhoid fever ae 17y

D: 8th inst MRS. ROSANNA HAMILTON w/o J.Q.HAMILTON M.D. of Wellsville, ae 41y.

D: 6th inst in Salineville, JAMES SALTSMAN in 65th yr

Mon 21 Sep 1874 (Vol 8 no 25)

M: 16th inst at the res of bride's parents by REV.G.N.JOHN-SON, D.W.BONNELL of Hubbard OH & MISS MATTIE E. GOLLOWAY of this place.

M: 10th inst at house of MARTIN POLAND by REV.G.N.JOHNSON, ALEX.N.McCORD & MISS CYNTHIA B. POLAND all of this co.

M: 12th inst by same, B.A.YOUNG & MISS JENNIE ARMSTRONG both of this co.

M: 17th inst by REV.WILLIAM BAXTER, ALLEN WATSON & MISS MARY E. KIBLER.

M: 17th inst by same, FRANK SNYDER & MISS SARAH J. McDEVITT

M: 16th inst at Oak Ridge parsonage by REV.DAVID HARGEST, JAMES M. SMITH & MISS ELIZA J. GRANT all of this co.

M: 17th inst at Dungannon by REV.VATTMAN, GEORGE J. PIERO & MISS EMMA G. THOMPSON both of this place.

M: 15th inst by same, JOHN SMITH & MISS TILLIE HICKMAN of Wellsville CCO.

M: 11th inst by REV.B.F.WOODBURN, ALF.K.SCANDRETT & MISS ALICE ATTERHOLT both of Allegheny City [PA]

M: 15th inst W.F.KIRK of Salineville & MISS SAMANTHA CARAHAN of Carrollton OH.

D: 9th inst NELLIE LEMON d/o MR.& MRS.JESSE LEMON of Salem ae 6y.

D: 1st inst CHRISTIAN CRAMER of Col'ana ae 53y 25d.

D: 16th inst in Salineville, MISS ALSIGNA SALTSMAN in 22yr

D: 18th inst in East Liverpool, THOMAS THOMPSON.

D: 10th inst at Denver Colo of typhoid fever, MRS. MARY E. McCARTY aged 31y. She was the daughter of JAMES SHURTZ of Alliance OH.

D: 13th inst in Cleveland, MARGARET GLASS of this twp ae 71y

D: 15th inst PERRY MOORE BOWMAN s/o CHRIS. & A.A.BOWMAN of Elkrun Tp ae 7m.

D: 16th inst MINNIE EVERETT McCLELLAND d/o ALBERT & MARGARET McCLELLAND of Centre Tp ae 8y.

D: 19th inst in New Lisbon, MRS.LINNIE MARBLOW w/o SAMUEL MARBLOW ae 21y.

MRS. HANNAH STARKEY, living in Youngstown, will be 100 yrs old in Dec. next

A few days ago SAMUEL WARNER of North Lima, dropped dead in his cornfield while cutting off corn.

Mon 28 Sep 1874 (Vol 8 no 26)

M: 18th inst by REV.D.V.HYDE, EDWARD L. SHINN & MISS ELMIRA BETZ.

M: 17th inst by same, ALONZO C. McCONNER & MISS MARY A. SHINN

M: 16th inst by same, HOMER BRINKER & MISS MARY E. STOCK.

M: 21st inst by FATHER LINDERSMITH, EDWARD McNAMARAH & BRIDGET BARRET

M: 22nd inst by same, JOHN QUINN & MISS MARY MUNK.

M: 15th inst by REV.HILBISH, AUGUSTUS CORTRIGHT of Allegheny PA & MRS. EMMA SCHAFFER of Col.Co.

M: 22nd inst by J.M.DICKINSON JP, JOHN ADAMS & MISS ROSE M. NOBLE.

M: 22nd inst by EDWARD PETTIT ESQ, LYMAN LAMBORN of New Lisbon & MISS SARAH SCADDEN of Elkrun Tp.

M: 17th inst by REV.SMITH, G.A.FOX of CCO & MISS ELMIRA COMBS of Stark Co.

M: 27th inst by E.GARSIDE ESQ, HARRY ANTHONY & MISS SARAH E. AMON, all of this co.

M: 23d inst by REV.COON, GEORGE S.SHARP & MISS REBECCA J. FRASER all of this co.

D: 23d inst in Salem, SAMUEL GEER ae 74y.

D: 18th inst in Salem BESSIE McCARTY d/o T.J. & A.C.McCARTY ae 2y

D: near Angola Ind, GULIELMA WEAVER in 87th yr, formerly of Salem.

D: 25th inst at the Infirmary, WILLIAM SIDDALLS ae 58y.

D: 22nd inst HENRY STOKESBERRY of Centre Tp ae 61y.

D: 27th inst AMANDA E. MORRON w/o JOHN A. MORRON of this place ae 41y.

MRS. WINIFRED BARD, for many years a res of Middleton Tp, died on 1st inst at her res in Gallia Co. of heart disease.- She was 83y of age.

Mon 5 Oct 1874 (Vol 8 no 27)

M: 22nd ult by REV.D.V.HYDE, EZRA C.STANLEY & MISS MARY F.F.HAWKINS all of this co.

M: 23d ult by REV..B.FRY, JOHN H. MILLER & MISS ROSA D. BOW-MAN all of Salem.

M: 24th ult by REV.JOHN HAWKER, MARSHALL STAMP of Fairfield & MISS LEAH A. DAVIS of St.Clair.

M: 24th ult by REV.T.N.BOYLE, LEMUEL L. CLIZBE & MISS JENNIE LAUBIE all of Salem.

M: 24th ult by JOSIAH ROHRBAUGH ESQ, APTLE ESTERLY & MISS LOUISA EYSTER both of New Waterford, this co.

M: 29th ult in Salem by REV.THOMAS NBOYLE, HILL TOLERTON & MISS REBECCA WHEELER.

M: 24th ult by REV.J.N.SWAN, D.S.McBANE of Akron O & MISS MARY ELLIOT of Madison Tp, CCO.

M: 29th ult by JOHN ROBINSON ESQ, DAVID LINDERSMITH & MISS MALINDA GOLAHER.

D: 25th ult in Col'ana ALONZO WILL s/o CHRISTIAN WILL ae 4y

D: 26th ult MARTHA COOK w/o STACY COOK of Salem ae ---y.

D: 26th ult MRS. ELIZABETH DETRICK of Salem ae ---y.

D: 1st inst MELLIE E. COULSON w/o GEORGE H. COULSON of Hanover Tp ae 27y.

D: 29th ult at Winona CASPER WILLIAMS aged about 80y.

D: 21st ult at Delhi, Hamilton Co OH, ALEXANDER MACKENZIE aged 66y.

MRS. ANNA J. BEGES, one of our oldest & most highly respected citizens, died on last Tues. of paralysis in 78th yr. She was the wife of the late DAVID BEGGES.

Mon 12 Oct 1874 (Vol 8 no 28)

M: 7th inst by REV.WM.BAXTER, HENRY S. BURNETT & MISS ALICE WARD both of New Lisbon.

M: 8th inst at res of bride's mother by REV.G.N.JOHNSTON, MARTIN THOMAS of Madison Tp & MISS EMMA S. MILLER of this place

M: 6th inst by REV.DAVID HARGEST, A.BYRON JENKINS of Wellsville & MISS JENNIE E. WILCOXON all of this co.

M: 6th inst in Salem by REV.THOS.N.BOYLE, JOSEPH BAKER & MISS MARY A. GALBRAITH.

M: 27th ult at the Cowan House by REV.WM.BAXTER, GEORGE WELCH & MISS AMERICA FARMER both of East Liverpool.

M: 3d inst by REV.JOHN LONG, ANDREW RATTERY & MISS LIZZIE WILSON both of Wellsville.

M: 1st inst by REV.J.C.MELOY, JOHN E. McGLENNEN & MISS ELIZA KOUNTZ d/o JACOB KOUNTZ ESQ of Wellsville.

D: 2nd inst in Salem CORA CHAPLIN of typhoid fever aged 20y

D: 8th inst at res of her grandfather, JAMES DORRANCE, of this place, ANNA V. FRANTZ, of Clear Springs, Washington Co, Maryland, aged 16y.

D: 8th inst MARION RITCHIE of Fairfield Tp ae 54y.

D: 10th inst HATTIE A.L. FREDERICK d/o BYRON FREDERICK of Centre Tp, ae 16y 3m 12d.

D: 5th inst in Hanover JACOB MOORE SR. aged 92y.

REUNION: A reunion of the McINTOSH FAMILY was held at the residence of MR.D.A.McINTOSH of this place on last Tues. The family consists of 6 persons, 5 brothers & 1 sister, all of whom were present. The eldest of the family is D.D.McINTOSH of Wayne Tp, aged 70y. The next in order of age is MRS.JAMES PEDEN aged 66, & ALEXANDER McINTOSH, aged 64. ANDREW resides near Beloit, Mahoning Co., aged 59; W.S. of Pittsburgh, aged 54, the youngest being PHILIP, who resides near Foxburgh, PA. The united ages of the family is 372 years. The two eldest were born in Scotland, the others being natives of Yellow Creek Tp., this co.

Mon 19 Oct 1874 (Vol 8 no 29)

M: 15th inst at the Reformed parsonage by REV.G.M.ALBRIGHT, FRANK BADGER & MISS ANNA BAKER, both of this co.

M: 13th inst by REV.THOS.N.BOYLE, SAMUEL McCARTER of Carroll Co & MISS MARY E. BOONE of Salem.

M: 13th inst by ELDER J.M.VAN HORN, H.A.LICHENBERGER & MISS AMELIA H. BAXTER both of Wellsville.

M: 14th inst by REV.THOS.N.BOYLE, GEORGE POW & MISS HELLEN STEELE both of Salem.

M: 30th ult at Port Allegheny PA by WM.WILKINS ESQ, THOMAS THAYER & MISS JULIA MARTIN of Madison Tp this co.

M: 12th inst at Pittsburgh PA by WM.P.TURNER, EDWARD COOK of East Liverpool & MISS ROXANNA F. BRICK of Mineral Point OH.

D: 13th ult in Wellsville SAMUEL L.COLLINS ae 87y.

D: 3d inst ANN BOURNE w/o ENOCH BOURNE ae 37y 2m 8d.

D: 15th inst at Elliotville OH FRANK DAVIDSON s/o WM.& MARTHA DAVIDSON ae 2y.

D: 14th inst at Yellow Creek OH, WILLIAM J. POTTER in 34th yr of his age.

Mon 26 Oct 1873 (Vol 8 no 30)

M: 15th inst by REV.J.N.SWAN, L.A.CRAWFORD of Steubenville & MISS MAGGIE McBANE of Wellsville.

M: 20th inst by REV.G.N.JOHNSON, WILLIAM A. HALL of Cleveland & MISS MAGGIE E. DORRANCE of this place.

M: 21st inst by same, JAMES R. DORRANCE & MISS H. LOU DORWART all of this place.

M: 17th inst by REV.W.R.SPINDLER, ABEL MEAD & MISS DELLA PHILLIPS all of Salem.

M: 22nd inst by ELDER P.N.JONES, J.M.ESSICK & MISS SUSAN F. ZEPERNICK, all of CCO.

M: 22nd inst by EDWIN PETTIT, JP, THOMAS NUZEM & MISS NANCY D. CALDWELL all of this co.

The wedding of JOHN W. JOHNSON of this place & MISS MARY E. TAYLOR of Massillon will take place in Massillon next Thurs eve.

WILLIAM OGLINE of Canfield who was convicted of adultery with MISS HANNAH WALLACE of Columbiana a few months ago, sentenced to 12 months imprisonment in Allegheny Co workhouse, PA, is again at liberty, having received a pardon.

Mon 2 Nov 1874 (Vol 8 no 31)

M: 29th ult at res of JAMES B.ESTEP in Massillon by REV.E.L. FRAZIER, assisted by REV.O.EBERT, JOHN W. JOHNSON & MISS MARY E. TAYLOR.

M: 27th ult at the Reformed parsonage by REV.G.M.ALBRIGHT, LEONARD F.BRINKER & MISS MARY S. HALVERSTADT all of this co

M: 21st ult at res of HIRAM BELL in this co by REV.G.N.JOHNSTON, FLETCHER LOWELL & MISS RHODA M. LUDLAM both of Milville NJ.

M:22nd ult by REV.JACKSON, JONAH MORROW of Salineville & MISS C.L.JOHNSON of Harlem Springs.

M: 23d ult by REV.J.C.MELOY, SHERWOOD BOYD & MISS ELIZABETH SIMMONITE all of Wellsville.

M: 28th ult in Wellsville by same, ROBERT S. McCLELLAND & MISS ELLA CULP both of Somerset Jeff.Co.Oh.

M: 27th ult near Calcutta by ELDER J.M.VAN HORN, EMMETT H.FIRRAL & MISS EOLINE V.JACKMAN.

D: 26th ult VIRGIL H. BURSON of Elkrun Tp ae 28y.

D: 21st ult in Salineville JOHN H. SALTER ae 52y 2m.

D: 25th ult SARAH JANE JOHNSON ae 22y.

D: 23d ult ELIZA N. WARD of New Garden CCO ae 65y 4d.

MRS. MARY TETERS, relic of the late JOHN TETERS died at Alliance on 21st ult aged 84y. Deceased was the only daughter of JOB COOK, who settled in Col.Co. near Salem in the year 1797 and was among its first settlers.

THOMAS SPENCER one of Salem's oldest citizens, died on Wed the 28th ult after a few hours illness.

Court proceedings:
ISAAC G. RITTENHOUSE vs ROSANNA RITTENHOUSE: DIVORCE, dismissed at defd. costs.
GEORGE M. SMITH vs ALCINDA SMITH. Divorce granted.

Mon 9 Nov 1874 (Vol 8 no 32)

Court proceedings:
AMELIA KINSEY vs ZEBULUM KINSEY: Divorce granted.
SARAH GUY vs EDWARD GUY: action for divorce, dismissed for non-prosecution.
HENRY B. CAMP vs ADA CAMP: Divorce granted.
SUSAN R. TAYLOR vs JESSE TAYLOR: Divorce granted.
FRANKLIN INGLEDUE vs MARGARET INGLEDUE: Divorce granted.

M: 3d inst by SAMUEL HARDMAN JP, ANDREW POTTER & MARY SHARP, d/o THOMAS SHARP.

M: 5th inst by REV.J.J.ESTELL At res of bride's mother at Franklin Square, JAMES C. McINTOSH & MISS SADIE McKELVEY of Leetonia.

M: 29th ult at res of bride's father by REV.J.M.KENDIG, WM.A.MOORE & MISS CELESTIA RUMMEL.

M: 1st inst by REV.E.A.BRINDLEY, J.A.WILLIAMS & MISS EMMA K. WELLS both of Wellsville OH.

M: 25th ult by REV.JAMES H. HOLLINGSHEAD, GEORGE ALLABACK of Wellsville & MISS MARY F. GREER of W.Va.

M: 27th ult at Delaware OH by REV.J.VOTE, A.J.BISHOP of Wellsville & MISS EMMA M. BORNE of Kenton OH.

M: 29th ult by REV.HINGELY, S.L.EDWARDS of Walton, Boone Co., KY & MISS ELLA N. PETTIT, d/o A.J.PETTIT ESQ, of Smith's Ferry Pa.

M: 4th inst by JOHN WEAVER ESQ., THOMAS J. BROWN & MISS RACHEL TOLSON all of Salineville Oh

D: 24th ult in Pittsburgh, MINNIE HANNA CADWALLADER w/o WILLIS CADWALLADER formerly of this place in 22nd yr.

D: 29th ult CLARKSON HARRIS, of Butler Tp, ae 38y.

D: 5th inst in Salem Tp of consumption, MRS.SARAH TROTTER w/o JOHN TROTTER aged about 66y.

D: 28th ult KATE COY w/o GEORGE W. COY of Salem Tp ae 31y.

Wellsville Police Court: the somewhat notorious house of MRS. MAY was "pulled" and the woman above was fined $5 & costs on a charge of keeping a house of ill fame.

FRANKLIN STALLCUP, ESQ., of Alliance, son in law of JAMES CLARKE, of this place, died last Sat.

Mon 16 Nov 1874 (Vol 8 no 33)
(pages are missing in this issue)

Mon 23 Nov 1874 (Vol 8 no 34)

D: 3d inst SUSANNAH COSS relict of the late PETER COSS of Wayne Tp aged 84y 7m.

D: 15th inst MISS MAGGIE HOEY d/o ELIZABETH HOEY of Salineville ae 22y.

D: 18th inst MRS. MARGARET CRAWFORD of Madison Tp ae 85y 8m.

M: 19th inst by JOHN M. DICKINSON ESQ, DAVID PHILIPS & MISS MARY A. PROSSER all of this co.

M: 12th inst by REV.C.L.WINGET, LLOYD F.KLYNE & MISS ELLA M. WEAVER.

M: 14th inst in Knox Tp by REV.J.CLEMENT, GEORGE TEEGARDEN & MISS SUSAN BARTCHY.

M: 20th inst by HENRY E.FROST JP, F.M.GROOMS & MISS FLORA M. DALES all of this co.

Mon 30 Nov 1874 (Vol 8 no 35)

M: 24th inst at Col'ana by REV.T.N.BOYLE, ARAGO ESTON of Burnside Conn & MISS DELLA FITZPATRICK of former place.

M: 26th inst by REV.JOHN LONG, GEORGE W. FURNISS & MISS MARY E. HENDRICK both of Wellsville.

M: 26th inst at Rochester PA by REV.HUDSON, SAMUEL HENDERSON & MISS SARAH C. FRENCH, both of Wellsville OH.

D: 23d inst at the Infirmary, GEORGE BELTZ ae 78y.

D: 21st inst in Salem, BESSIE C. ECKSTEIN infant dau of C.W. & MARY ECKSTEIN, ae 10m.

M: 16th inst ESTELLA MAY FISHER d/o REV.SANFORD G. & LOUIE J. FISHER of Washington, Kansas, formerly of East Liverpool, aged 3y 5m.

D: 26th inst in East Liverpool, WILLIE UPDEGRAFF s/o JACOB & ELIZABETH UPDEGRAFF aged 12y.

D: 28th inst in East Fairfield, WILLIAM STOKESBERRY ae 63y.

Sudden death in Salem: SAMUEL MONTGOMERY died very suddenly at his res. in Salem last Mon.morning. He was in his 62nd yr and was born in County Tyrone, Ireland.

Mon 7 Dec 1874 (Vol 8 no 36)

KILLED ON THE RAILROAD: Thurs afternoon, WILLIAM M. GROFF, the well known coal merchant of Wellsville, met with a sudden & lamentable death on the railroad track below town. He was 46 yrs of age.

Two children of GEORGE SKINNER of Cleveland, formerly of Wellsville, died of scarlet fever last week.

M: 3d inst in New Garden by E.GARSIDE ESQ, MURDOCK JEHU & MISS EMMA WOLF all of this co.

M: 25th ult in New York by REV.DR.KITCHEL, F.D.KITCHEL of East Liverpool O & MISS FLORA McD. PORTER of New York City

M: 3d inst by REV.JAMES H.MEEK, near Carrollton Oh, REV.J.B. WILKIN & MAGGIE J. LONG.

D: 28th ult at Salem EMMA GORE w/o H.GORE ae 34y 10m 10d.

D: 25th ult at Salem JANE BEAN w/o ISRAEL BEAN ae 80y 8m 22d.

D: 25th ult in Salem MRS. ELIZABETH ARMSTRONG aged 15 years.

D: 25th ult in Middleton, Fairfield Tp, ARMELA GARRETSON ae 87y.

Mon 14 Dec 1874 (Vol 8 no 37)

M: 3d inst by REV.D.S.KENNEDY, CHARLES A. ATWELL of Sewickley & MAGGIE McKOWN d/o JAMES McKOWN.

M: 19th ult by REV.JOHN A. CLEMENT, JONAS KING & MISS EMMA BROTHERS both of Homeworth this co.

M: 19th ult by REV.D.V.HYDE, J.M.CARTER & MISS MARY E.-HAWKINS both of this co.

M: 6th inst by REV.THOS.N.BOYLE, JOHN ZIMMERMAN & MRS. MARY TEEGARDEN both of this co.

M: 6th inst in Salem by MAYOR DUNLAP, J.PRATT GAGER & ROSA A. WALKER.

M: 2d inst in Salem by REV.W.R.SPINDLER, JACOB CUSTARD & MRS. NANCY MILLER all of this co.

JOHN KEMBLE, of Hanover Tp, an old citizen of Col.Co., died on the 5th inst.

ROBERT SHEARER, who was stricken with paralysis some weeks since, died at his res in this place about 11 o'clock Wed. He was 47y 9m of age.

JESSE W. REEDER, a well known citizen of Hanover Tp, was kicked in the stomach by a horse on Fri of last week, from the effects of which he died the next day.

Mon 21 Dec 1874 (Vol 8 no 38)

DAVID OHL, of Mecca Trumbull Co, was instantly killed on Mon last week by a limb falling from a tree. He leaves a large family.

D: 10th inst FLORENCE REED d/o MR.& MRS. JAMES REED of Salem ae 3y.

D: 16th inst of diptheria at Portland, Mich., LENA J. WHITNEY d/o W.C. & MATTIE J. WHITNEY ae about 3y 6m.

D: 19th inst dau. of JOHN M. & HANNAH JOHNSON of Elkrun Tp ae 1y 3m.

D: 11th inst at Leetonia PATRICK MADIGAN ae 28y.

D: 20th inst in New Lisbon after a long & painful illness, ANNIE KERNS w/o RICHARD KERNS ae 27y.

D: 15th inst in Salem, SANFORD W. VOGLESONG of St.Louis,MO, son of CATHARINE VOGLESONG of Hanover O, aged 40y 15d.

D: 19th inst MISS LUCINDA FERRELL of Fairfield Tp ae 29y.

WILLIAM PIKE a former res. of this county, died on 28th ult at Page City, Iowa.

Tomorrow (Tue) eve, the engagement of M.B.ADAMS of this place & MISS EMMA ERNWEIN, an accomplished & beautiful daughter of M.ERNWEIN Esq., merchant of Carson St.,Pittsburgh, will end in marriage of the parties at the residence of bride's parents

Mon 28 Dec 1874 (Vol 8 no 39)

M: 17th inst at res of bride's father by J.M.KENDIG, assisted by REV.G.M.ALBRIGHT, REV.G.H.ALBRIGHT & MISS LIZZIE A. WORMAN both of this co.

M: eve of 22nd inst at res of bride's parents, No.1705 Carson St., Pittsburgh PA by REV.A.F.HERZBERGER, M.B.ADAMS of New Lisbon OH & MISS EMMA ERNWEIN of former place.

M: 17th inst by REV.M.J.SLUTZ, HENRY STANGEE & LYDIA MURRAY.

M: 24th inst by REV.G.M.ALBRIGHT, MAHLON J. NICHOLS & MISS MARIA SWITZER both of Salem Tp.

D: 21st inst EVAN THOMAS of Elkrun Tp, in 90th yr of age.

D: 20th inst NANCY BELL LEACH d/o BENJ. & MARY LEACH of Salem ae 4y 6m.

D: on 29th inst at the Infirmary, CHALKLEY KELLEY aged 64y. The above was an inmate of the infirmary more than 40 years.

D: in Freeport, Ill. on Fri. Dec 4, of typhoid fever, MRS. CHRISTIANA WIMER, w/o WILLIAM WIMER, aged 65y 6m. MRS. WIMER was a native of Lancaster PA & moved to New Lisbon O when about 17y of age, where she remained until 1856 when in company of her husband & family, she went to Ill. & lived near Freeport 11 years. Mrs.M. leaves a large family. Since the above was put in type, a son has died, and others of the family are dangerously ill.

SUDDEN DEATH: JOHN BURBICK, of Greenford, Mah.Co. while in attendance at a literary society on the evening of the 19th inst, fell over & expired without a struggle. He was a son of DAVID BURBICK of Wayne Tp this co. & was aged 34y. He leaves a family.

A MRS.LEE, a married woman of Franklin Square, eloped last week with a man named PAT HUGHES who is said to have a wife & family somewhere in the state of New York.

CHURCH DIRECTORY:

UNITED PRESBYTERIAN:	REV.W.G.NEVIN
METHODIST EPISCOPAL:	REV.S.Y.KENNEDY
FIRST PRESBYTERIAN:	REV.G.N.JOHNSTON
CHRISTIAN CHURCH:	REV WILLIAM H. BAXTER
FIRST REFORMED CHURCH:	REV.G.M.ALBRIGHT
TRINITY (PROTESTANT EPISCOPAL) CHURCH:	(none listed)

NEW LISBON CORPORATION OFFICERS:

MAYOR:	HENRY E. FROST
COUNCIL:	E.B.SMILEY
	EDWARD WHITACRE
	GEORGE FLUGAN
	WILLIAM MYERS
	STEPHEN A. DOUGHTON
	RICHARDSON ARTER
CLERK:	H.CLAY CORBETT
TREASURER:	C.F.SMALL
FIRE WARDEN:	T.H.WHITE
MARSHAL:	JOHN W. SPRINGER

1875

Jan 4,11,18,25	Feb 1,8,15,22	Mar 1,8,15,22,29
Apr 5,12,19,26	May 3,10,17,24,31	Jne 7,14,21,28
Jly 5,12,19,26	Aug 2,9,16,23,30	Sep 6,13,20,27
Oct 4,11,18,25	Nov 1,8,15,22,29	Dec 6,13,20,27

Mon 4 Jan 1875 (Vol 8 no 40)

M: 27th ult by REV. WM. BAXTER, WILLIAM MORGAN & MISS AMELIA K. DEEMER, both of co

M: 24th ult at Wellsville by REV.T.A.McCURDY, ELDRIDGE PIERCE & MISS HARRIET S. COPE.

M: 23d ult by same, JOHN DENHART & MISS EUPHEMA L. STEWART, d/o JAMES STEWART ESQ., of Wellsville.

M: Oct 1st by JOSEPH KENNAL JP, JOHN O'KANE & MISS ELIZA JANE DICKEY, all of this co

M: 9th ult by same, WILLIAM C. FARR & MISS HATTIE BURSON, all of this co.

M: 25th ult in Salem, JAMES BENNETT & MISS MARY A. BUNNELL d/o J.H.BUNNELL of Canfield.

D: 27th ult in Salem, JOSIE M. DAVIS d/o MILTON DAVIS ae 13y 4m

D: 24th ult in Allegheny City PA, ANNIE PITCAIRN w/o ALEXANDER PITCAIRN & mother of JOHN PITCAIRN of this place, ae 77y. MRS. PITCAIRN was a native of Scotland & came to this country in 1842.

D: 20th Nov at Salem, LIZZIE L. ARMSTRONG, ae 18y 7m 5d, & the only dau of SIMON ARMSTRONG, late deceased & LIZZIE his wife.

D: 12th ult, MRS. MARY HUM, w/o JACOB HUM of Columbiana ae 77y

D: 31st ult, MRS. THEODORE McCOWN PEEK w/o D.W.PEEK & d/o SAMUEL McLANE of Wellsville, in her 22nd yr.

D: 24th ult at Wellsville, MRS. AMELIA PARSON in 74th yr

D: 2nd inst at Salem, JOSEPH TAYLOR, ae about 70y.

We learn that one day recently, while parties were removing bodies from an old family burying ground near Homeworth, the petrified remains of an old lady were exhumed.

The wife of DANIEL J. SMITH & d/o HON. JOSIAH THOMPSON died at her home near East Liverpool last Mon night after a short illness.

Mon 11 Jan 1875 (Vol 8 no 41)

ELIZABETH HOLLINGER of Elkrun Tp was found dead in her bed last Thurs morning. She was ae 71y & was in her usual health the night previous to her death.

M: 31st ult by EDWARD PETTIT JP, FRANK NUZUM & MISS VIOLET WELKER, both of this co.

M: 31st ult by REV.T.N.BOYLE, GEORGE RICHARDS & MISS ANNA A. ANTRIM, both of Salem.

M: 24th ult by E.P.SHAW ESQ, W.W.WEEDON of CCO & MISS CARRIE VANFOSSEN of Wayne Co Ill.

M: 24th ult by REV.S.Y.KENNEDY, HENRY McMILLAN of Leetonia & MISS HESTER FREEMAN of this place.

D: 1st inst in Salem, J.M.LYSETT ae 28y 6m.

D: 28th ult LIZZIE WILLIAMSON, ae 22y 6m.

D: 3d inst in East Palestine, MRS. LOU SUMMERVILLE w/o ADAM SUMMERVILLE, ae 24y.

D: 1st inst at Leetonia, PETER BURK s/o JOHN & MARY ae 1y

D: 3d inst NATHAN PHILLIPS of Elkton ae 61y 11m.

D: 3d inst WARREN McLANE s/o JAMES & EUPHEMA of Madison Tp ae 4y

Mon 18 Jan 1875 (Vol 8 no 42)

A CENTENARIAN: GEORGE MOOR, aged 100y, died on 8th inst at his res in Harrison Tp., Carroll Co Oh.

JOHN GOODWIN, one of the oldest citizens of East Liverpool, died suddenly last Fri.eve. He had been identified with the business interests of that place for years.

The remains of JAMES ARBUCKLE, who was murdered on a trading-boat in Texas last year, have arrived at Rochester PA, where his family resides. Mr.A. was formerly a resident of East Liverpool.

M: 12th inst by REV.WM.BAXTER, THOMAS WELCH & MISS CARRIE CRAWFORD, both of co.

M: 31st ult at Prospect Bank Farm, Chase City, VA, by REV.THOMAS DREW, WILSON J. FIFE of New Lisbon & MISS MARGARET GILLESPIE, d/o GEORGE GILLESPIE.

M: 3d inst at East Liverpool, by JOHN BRINDLEY JP, JOHN BROUGHTON & MRS. ANN BUXTON.

M: 7th inst by JACOB DESSELEM JP, JOHN MALEY & MISS MAGGIE McPHEE, all of this co.

M: 10th inst by REV.W.L.NELSON, LAURTES STOUFFER & MISS ANNIE WOLF.

M: 4th inst at East Liverpool by JOHN BRINDLEY JP, ALBERT WEBBER & MISS FLORA ROBINSON.

M: 14th inst by J.M.DICKINSON ESQ, WILLIAM S. MALONE & MISS EMMA RUPP.

M: 5th inst at Cleveland, J.F.LACOCK & MISS IDA IRWIN, both of Salineville.

M: 6th inst in Leetonia by REV.A.B.MAXWELL, E.P.LEVAN & MISS ANNIE HOLLOWAY, both of this co.

M: 10th inst in Leetonia by same, WILLIAM N. BAKER of CCO & MISS MAGGIE BEAN, of Mahoning Co.

M: 13th inst near Columbiana by the same, M.L.BOSSART of Salem Tp & MISS MINTIE HOLLOWAY.

M: 4th inst in Columbiana by REV.WINGET, THOMAS PIFER & MISS MARY HUSTON.

M: 12th inst in East Liverpool by REV.RIGGLE, MESSRS M.H.-FOULTS & GEORGE H. MARTIN & MISSES SABINA & EMMA BLOOR.

D: 5th inst at Salem, MARY KOLL d/o DANIEL ae 26y 10m 18d.

D: 9th inst at Salem, DORA BELL WILLIAMS d/o WEST & HARRIET ae 1y 8m.

D: 10th inst at Salem, ISRAEL BUMBAUGH ae 76y.

D: 9th inst in Elkrun Tp., SARAH MORRIS, widow of the late JONATHAN MORRIS, ae 83y 2m 17d.

D: 12th inst in Salineville of diptheria, FRANKIE HOFFEE ae 4y 11m.

D: 5th inst in Strasburg, VA, HENRY KEISTER, youngest brother of ISAAC KEISTER of Columbiana.

D: 6th inst in New Garden, SUSANNAH CATHARINE GARSIDE w/o E. GARSIDE ESQ., ae 45y 9m 23d.

Mon 25 Jan 1875 (Vol 8 no 43)

M: 14th inst by REV.THOS.N.BOYLE, R.A.PEARCE of Hanover & MISS MAGGIE McCORD of Salem.

M: 19th inst by REV.WM.BAXTER, R.C.WILSON & MISS KATIE CLUNK, both of this co.

M: 30th Dec 1874, by HENRY WILHELM, JP, JOSEPH BURBECK of New Lisbon, CCO & MISS MARY A. METZGAR of New Albany, Mahoning Co.

M: Thur Jan 7 by REV.RICHARD LEA of Pittsburgh, JOHN O'NEAL of Steubenville & MISS CELIA BATCHELOR of Wellsville.

M: Jan 14th by REV.ROBT.HAYS, JOHNSON McINTOSH of Southern Iowa & MISS ANNA McINTOSH, eldest d/o DANIEL G. McINTOSH of Glasgow, Oh.

M: 7th inst by REV.S.S.McKOWN, at his res near Gillford, CALDWELL W. HOLLOWAY & MISS MARY E. HART.

M: at same time & place by the same, JOHN MITCHEL & MISS JULIA A. O'BRINE all of this co.

D: 15th inst in Salineville of croup, JOSEPH GRANT RODGERS, s/o J.M. & M.C.RODGERS, ae 6y 3m 3d.

D: 23d inst, MARGARET JOHNSTON w/o W.H.JOHNSTON of Centre Tp.

D: 8th inst at Leetonia, S.J.KERR ae 52y 1m 10d.

D: 9th inst at Wellsville, MRS. ANN CAMERON of Oak Ridge, ae 62y.

DEATH OF MRS. SUSANNAH CATHARINE GARSIDE: MRS. GARSIDE, w/o EDWIN GARSIDE of New Garden, was the eldest daughter of ABRAM & NANCY GARDNER; was born in Mifflin Co Pa Mar.13, 1829, came to this co with her parents in 1855 & has been a resident of the same until her death.

DEATH OF OLD CITIZEN: Wed. morning last death removed from the sphere of life one of the most worthy & respected citizens of New Lisbon. For more than 50 years ROBERT JOHNSON was a resident of this vicinity & during that time taught to his neighbors how possible & advantageour it is to lead a blameless life. He was born in Washington Co PA in or about the year, 1799, & in 1832 removed to this co., locating in Elkrun Tp.

Intelligence has been received of the death of ROBERT SHEARER, father of the late ROBERT SHEARER of this place, at his res at Wellsburgh, WVa. He was sick at his place of business on Sat. & died Mon., the 18th inst, ae 75y. Deceased was at one time a resident of New Lisbon & was well known in this community.

Mon 1 Feb 1875 (Vol 8 no 44)

DAVID STERLING, formerly of New Lisbon, is dangerously ill at his res. in Brooklyn, Iowa.

MARGARET HUM, of Fairfield Tp, who had a leg broken a short time ago, died on 31st ult, ae 67y.

On Sabbath last, JOHN SIMPSON, an old & highly respected citizen of Washingtonville, aged some 80 years, was buried.

M: 21st ult by EDWIN PETTIT ESQ, J.M.POLAN & MISS IDA M. WHITACRE, all of this co.

M: 27th ult by REV.G.N.JOHNSTON, WILLIAM LODGE & MISS JULIA GREEN, both of New Lisbon.

M: 26th inst by REV.G.M.ALBRIGHT, EDWARD W. COOKE & MISS DELLA BRICKER, both of Salem.

M: 28th inst by same, PAUL BRICKER & MISS LIBBY TRESH, both of Salem.

M: 27th ult by REV.JOHN HARKER, PROF.JULIUS LUQUIENS of Boston & MISS EMMA CLARK, of Salem.

D: 27th ult in New Lisbon, JOHN CALEB WHITACRE, s/o JONATHAN & HANNAH WHITACRE, ae 4y 6m.

D: 22nd ult in Salem, CHARLES C.McCAIN, in 35th yr.

Mon 8 Feb 1875 (Vol 8 no 45)

THOMAS CROXALL, a valued & highly esteemed citizen of East Liverpool, one day last week accidently fell upon the ice & received such an injury as to result in his death in a short time.

DEATH OF ABEL LODGE: Another old citizen of New Lisbon has gone. On last Mon, Feb.1st, ABEL LODGE died at his res in this place, ae 78y 6m 11d. Born at Wheatland, Loudon Co VA Aug 21, 1796 & moved to this place on Oct.19,1809 with his father JONATHAN LODGE. He married May 21st 1821 & had a family of 2 sons & 6 daughters, all of whom are now living except one son, O.L.LODGE, who died at Wellsville the past year. The surviving son is JOSEPH LODGE, a prominent business man of Iowa City, Iowa.

MRS. SARAH BECK, of Gillford, widow of PRESTON BECK, died Fri. morning 29th ult.

Court proceedings:
HANNAH J. KEELEY vs JAMES M. KEELEY, decree for plaintiff for divorce & custody of children. Deft to pay costs.
THOMAS WARNER vs PHOEBE J. WARNER, divorce granted to plaintiff at his costs.
NANNIE C. WESTFALL vs ELI B. WESTFALL, divorce granted. Custody of children to plaintiff, & maiden name restored.

Death has been visiting our venerable people. In addition to the departure of ABEL LODGE, we chronicle the decease of MRS. SUSAN SEACHRIST at the Infirmary, aged abt 80y. Also, the death of JANE VAUGHN of Centre Tp ae 75y. AND, on last Mon. morning, JACOB LONGENECKER, a highly respected citizen of Salem Tp., was found dead in his bed. He was aged about 70y.

On last Sat. the body of MRS. H. KINNEAR was brought from Allegheny City to this place for interment. The deceased was a daughter of MRS. SCINTHIEL, formerly of East Carmel, but now a res of this place.

Mon 15 Feb 1875 (Vol 8 no 46)

M: 2nd inst in New Garden by E.GARSIDE ESQ., FRED H. CONSOR & MISS KATE BELAT both of this co.

M: 10th inst in Buffalo NY by REV.G.G.SMITH, MR.A.A.McCOY, of Buffalo, & MISS ADDIE L. WILSON of New Lisbon.

M: 11th inst in New Garden by E.GARSIDE ESQ., OLIVER P. PAXON & MISS CORDELIA DAY, all of this co.

M: 6th inst by REV.S.Y.KENNEDY, WILLIAM CYRUS WELKER & MISS JENNIE SIMKINS, both of Elkton, this co.

M: 4th inst by REV.J.A.CLEMENT, PERRY SANOR, of West Tp & MISS MARY WILSON, of Hanover Tp.

D: 10th inst in Salem of pneumonia, PETER FISHER.

D: 2nd inst in Salem, JAMES WILSON, ae 27y.

D: 8th inst MRS. ISABEL ADAMS of Centre Tp ae 79y.

D: 9th inst JAMES HOGE of Wayne Tp, ae 90y 3m.

D: 9th inst THEODORE FRANCIS EHRHART & on the 10th, HATTIE ALCINDA EHRHART, children of REUBEN & LOUISA EHRHART, aged respectively 5y 10m & 1y.

D: 3d inst at the Infirmary, CATHARINE McBEAN, ae 72y.

Mon 22 Feb 1875 (Vol 8 no 47)

D: 5th inst in West Tp, SOPHIA HOLE in 84th yr.

D: 1st inst in Hanover, FANNY SWEARINGEN d/o HARRY & JENNIE, ae 21m.

D: 7th inst in Franklin Tp, HUGH LAUGHLIN, ae 63y 1m 22d.

D: 14th inst in Salem, SAMUEL R. HEYCOCK, ae 66y.

D: 31st ult MARY JANE McGARY d/o DANIEL McGARY of Millport

D: 18th inst CATHARINE MILLER widow of JACOB MILLER of Centre Tp, ae 68y 2m.

D: 20th inst at res of JOSEPH RICHEY ESQ, of Centre Tp, LEVI RICHEY ae 70y.

D: 16th inst DUNDENA McCASKEY d/o EMPSY & MARY McCASKEY of Madison Tp, ae 19y.

D: 12th inst in Canton, MRS. BEGGES w/o DAVID J., ae abt 50y

Information has been received of the death of JAMES McKENZIE, of Yellow Creek Tp, which occurred Fri. evening.

CAPT. ALEXANDER FRAZIER died on the cars last Wed. while en route from New Orleans to his home in Wellsville, where his parents live. He had been in poor health for some months.

Mon 1 Mar 1875 (Vol 8 no 48)

In 1850, THOMAS STRINGER, a prominent merchant & mill owner of Ashland, caught the gold fever & went to California, leaving behind him his wife & 4 children. After a while he sent letters back to the wife telling of his success & writing in the most cheering way of the time when he would return home with enough to give her every comfort which money can buy. Time passed on & suddenly the whole community was electrified with the news of his murder. The poor wife accepted it as true, and sent money on to defray the funeral expenses. His children grew up, married & were settled. The patient wife, after a life of excessive toil, passed away from earth. Last week, the son, E.T.STRINGER, who is a resident of Ashland, accidentally heard of THOMAS STRINGER, living in western Missouri, but formerly of Ashland County.- His suspicions were aroused & he at once set out in search of the man whom he believed to be his father. At last account he had found the man & recognized him as his father, but, as yet the recognition has not been mutual. This Mr.STRINGER has a family in the west & it remains to be seen whether this is the "murdered" THOMAS STRINGER, or not. [see April 5th]
CONTINUED
[April 5, 1875 NLJ:] From the "Union Democrat", Sonora, California: "In June 1854, THOMAS STRINGER was murdered in this county, near Jamestown. He owned what is known as the Cold Spring Ranch, & leased it to M.C.KEYES & another party. KEYES & his wife conducted the house which was a stopping place for teamsters in those days. STRINGER lived at the place, sometimes hauling lumber to a tunnel nearby.- He was missing a few days, & after a search, the team he went from the house with was found in the woods, tied to a sapling, where they had stood several days harnessed to the wagon; when found the animals were famished. Nearby lay the body of STRINGER in a decomposing condition.

M: 11th ult in Cleveland, by REV.SAMUEL MOWER, FRANK BARD & MISS DORA STRAWN, both of Salem.

M: 18th ult at Salem, by REV.H.R.FRY, DAVID WHINERY & MISS ARABELLA COFFEE.

M: 11th ult at Salem, by same, EDWIN D. WINDLE & MISS AMY WHINERY.

M: 18th inst at Salem by MAYOR DUNLAP, J.S.TEST & MISS MATTIE E. WHINERY, all of this co.

M: 13th inst WILLIAM F. KING of Gillford & MISS EVA TALER of Iona, Mich.

D: 26th ult WILLIE POLLOCK s/o JOHN S. & MARY A. of Elkrun Tp ae 4 weeks.

D: 26th ult, ELIZABETH SHEROW w/o WILLIAM SHEROW of this place, ae 61y 7m 13d.

JAMES PAUL, at one time a res of New Lisbon, died at Ottawa, Kans., recently.

ROSS MOORE, a young man well known in New Lisbon, fell dead in his school room one day last week. Cause, heart disease. He was teaching in Beaver Co., a few miles east of Liverpool.

<u>Mon 8 Mar 1875</u> (Vol 8 no 49)

M: 4th inst by REV.W.G.NEVIN, W.B.JONES of Youngstown & MISS MARY M. HARRIS of New Lisbon.

M: 18th ult by JOSIAH RHORBAUGH ESQ., CHARLES TRAIL & MISS IRENE SNYDER, both of Columbiana.

M: 25th ult in Washington Tp by REV.S.B.STEVENSON, J.B.HAYS & MISS MAGGIE THOMPSON.

D: 19th ult at Germantown, Ohio, CLEMENT S. ROBERTSON s/o DR. JOHN S. & LIZZIE M. ROBERTSON, ae 2m 3 wks 3d.

D: 25th ult at Harlan, Ind., DAVID ASTRY s/o JONAS ASTRY,SR. formerly of CCO, ae 29y 5m 9d.

D: 3d inst at Clear Springs MD, MRS. IDA V. LUTHER, youngest dau of JAS. & MARY DORRANCE of New Lisbon, ae 19y 8m.

D: 1st inst JOHN GREENAWALT of Salem Tp ae 85y 23d.

D: 3d inst ANTOINETTE SHAFFER d/o WILLIAM & MARY SHAFFER of Elkton ae 6y 3m 6d.

D: at the Infirmary on 5th inst, GEORGE WHITE ae about 80y.

HENRY EATON, an old res of Yellow Creek Tp, died Thurs.

<u>Mon 15 Mar 1875</u> (Vol 8 no 50)

A divorce case is pending in Guernsey Co Common Pleas court, in which the plaintiff, HANNAH HAGUE, is 74, & the defendant, JEHU HAGUE, is 72 years of age. The complaint is based on a charge of ADULTERY.

M: 3d inst in Salem, by REV.J.HAWKER, J.S.GOLDY & MISS D.C.JOHNSON, all of this co.

M: 4th inst in Washingtonville by REV.S.WAGNER, HENRY TROTTER & MISS MARY J. RHODES.

M: at same time & place by same, FRANK INGLEDUE & MISS AMANDA MEGARGE all of this co.

M: 4th inst in Columbiana by REV.C.L.WINGET, DANIEL BUSHONG & MISS MARY WHAN, all of this co.

M: 9th inst near Wellsville by REV.DAVID HARGEST, ROBERT C. VANCE of Washington Co PA & MISS MARY E. McGOUGH of Yellow Creek Tp.

D: 9th inst ELLEN JANE BINSLEY w/o ANDREW BINSLEY of Wayne Tp ae 21y.

D: 7th inst in Hanover Tp, RICHARD SCHOOLEY ae 93y 6m.

D: 6th inst at New Alexander, CCO, AMELIA ZEPERNICK, ae 71y.

<u>Mon 22 Mar 1875</u> (Vol 8 no 51)

M: 10th inst at Salem by REV.S.B.TEEGARDEN, ISAAC F. WILLIAMSON of Iowa & MARY JANE DUNN, of this co.

M: 11th inst in Leetonia by REV.M.J.LAUFFER, HENRY KEUGELE & MISS MELINDA SUMMERS.

D: 10th inst at his res in Madison Tp, ISAAC FIFE SR in 82nd yr of age. MRS. ELIZABETH FIFE, wife of ISAAC FIFE SR., died 29th May 1873, in her 76th yr.

D: 14th inst in St.Clair Tp, CYNTHIA REDDICK w/o SAMUEL REDDICK ae 42y 5m 18d.

D: 10th inst in Middleton Tp, JOHN HILL, at an advanced age.

D: 24th inst WILLIAM S. COLLINS of Wayne Tp.

D: at Upper Sandusky, ANSON GRISELL, formerly of this place.

D: 16th inst, infant daughter of ANDREW & ELLEN JANE BINSLEY of Wayne Tp, ae 6 weeks 2d.

D: 6th inst WILLIAM SEYMOUR WRIGHT, s/o DANIEL & SARAH A. WRIGHT of Madison Tp ae 6y 8m 15d.

D: 8th inst, HENRIETTA WRIGHT, daughter of the above parents, ae 4y 9m 25d.

A lady named SHULTZ was accidently drowned near East Palestine on 13th inst.

We are informed that MR. AUGUSTINE, son in law of MR.J.T. BREWSTER, died a day or two ago in Iowa.

REV.GEO. HARDESTY, known to some of our citizens, died at Malvern on Mon. last. He was for many years an earnest minister in the Methodist Church. His wife was MISS HILLERMAN, a native of this place. [GEORGE HARDESTY & HANNAH J. HILLERMAN m 7 Dec 1836 in CCO]

JACOB HEATON & wife celebrated their woollen wedding (40th) at their home in Salem on the 12th inst.

The many friends of MISS LAURA SHIELDS d/o GEO.SHIELDS will regret to learn of her death, which took place at the res of her grandfather yesterday evening.

<u>Mon 29 Mar 1875</u> (Vol 8 no 52)

It is with regret that we record the death of WM.M.ASHTON, ESQ., which occurred at his home near Clarkson, this co., on Fri. of last week.

M: 17th inst at Alliance by REV.J.L.SMITH, JOSEPH HOFFMAN & MISS MARY NICHOLS, both of this co.

M: 17th inst by REV.J.HAWKER, DAVID ASTRY & <u>MRS.</u> MARY A. RAKESTRAW.

M: 18th inst by REV.C.G.PALMER, FRANKLIN P. LOWER & MISS MARY COLE, both of this co.

M: 17th inst at Wellsville by REV.J.DAY BROWNLEE, JOHN T. THOMAS of Cuyahoga Falls, Summit Co.,Oh & <u>MRS.</u> MARY ANN MORGAN<u>S</u> of Wellsville.

M: 11th inst at Sloans Station by REV.J.N.SWAN, GEORGE W. CAMPBELL of Jefferson Co & MISS CATHARINE ARNOLD.

M: 11th inst by JOHN WEAVER ESQ., DAVID SIMPSON & MISS ELIZABETH A. BEADLIN, all of Salineville.

M: 10th inst by REV.G.N.JOHNSTON, JAMES LOWRIE & MISS MARY E. DICKEY, all of Elkrun Tp.

M: 18th inst by REV.WM.M.TAYLOR, PERRY W. WELKER of Petersburgh, OH & MISS BINA HISEY of near Columbiana.

D: 22nd inst of diptheria, LETTIE A. BUELL d/o SAMUEL & RACHEL BUELL, ae 7y 2m 20d.

D: 12th inst in Columbiana, CATHARINE FESTER w/o JONATHAN FESTER ae 38y 10m 8d. [note: there were FESLERS and FETZERS in Columbiana; she was probably a FES<u>LER</u>]

D: 20th inst LIZZIE McMILLAN w/o SMITH McMILLAN.

D: 21st inst MORRIS WARD s/o DAVID & PHEBE WARD.

D: 13th inst MRS. HANNAH DALES w/o GEORGE DALES of E.Rochester, CCO

D: 9th inst MARY ETTIE McMILLAN d/o JOHN & MAGGIE McMILLAN of Madison Tp ae 4m 16d.

D: 15th inst MRS. MARTHA WALKER of Wellsville in 83d yr

D: 10th inst at Franklin Square, WM.E.MARSHALL ae 52y 4m 28d

D: 11th inst at Leetonia, HARRY WARD s/o DENNIS & AMELIA WARD ae 8m 19d.

D: 16th inst at Leetonia, EDWIN INMAN s/o THOMAS B. & MARY E. INMAN ae 1y 9m 13d.

D: 15th inst at Leetonia VIOLET BURNS d/o CHARLES & MARIA BURNS ae 1y 2m.

D: 16th inst in Columbiana, BERTHA ALLEN only daughter of JOHN E. & AMANDA ALLEN, ae 4y 6m.

D: 21st inst, IDA BELL SPRINGER d/o REUBEN & NANCY SPRINGER of St.Clair Tp., ae 16y 1m 19d.

WILLIAM WATSON, an old citizen of this place, died at his res Sat. evening, ae 79y.

We received a notice of the death of DANIEL KURTZ, which occurred at his res near Bayard, West Tp., on 4th inst. Deceased was a native of New Lisbon, in his 55th yr.

Mon 5 Apr 1875 (Vol 9 No.1)

MRS. MATILDA SAPP, of Ravenna, OH, celebrated her 100th birthday on 10th ult, by a family reunion attended by 48 of her descendants.

M: 25th ult at res of bride by REV.THOMAS HILLOCK, assisted by REV.HARMON REEVES, R.J.GRANT of Shanadore City, Schuykill Co PA, & MISS CHRISTENA BAKER of East Fairfield, CCO.

M: 25th ult by REV.J.J.HAYS, R.E.NEVIN of Enon PA & MISS ANNIE E. CAMPBELL of New Waterford, OH.

M: 1st inst by REV.W.BEDALL, WILLIAM H. CRAWFORD & MRS. LYDIA A. MEHEN, both of this co.

D: 30th ult HARVEY S. DRUMMOND s/o ANDREW & HANNAH DRUMMOND of Madison Tp, ae 2y.

D: 26th ult SARAH ESTELLA GARSIDE d/o JOHN & RACHEL GARSIDE, ae 4y 7m 2d.

D: 31st ult of consumption, ELIZA VAUGHN w/o W.G.VAUGHN, of Centre Tp, in her 50th yr.

JAMES BROWN, an old & respected citizen of Salem, died at his res last Sat.morning.

LAURA PITCAIRN d/o JOHN & CATHARINE PITCAIRN, died at res of her parents this morning, ae 22y.

COL. JOSIAH T. HERBERT, of East Liverpool, died suddenly at St.Louis last Tues. His funeral took place at East Liverpool on Thursday.

WILLIAM GARRETSON s/o HIRAM GARRETSON of Cleveland, died on 29th ult at Gaylord Institute, Mass., ae 18y.

Mon 12 Apr 1875 (Vol 9 no 2)

M: 27th ult at Rochester PA by REV.T.C.HODGSON, WILL G. BENT-LEY & MISS EVA L. BEAN, both of Salem.

M: 25th ult by REV.JOHN HAWKER, DANIEL WILLIAMS & MISS NANCY McDONALD.

M: 30th ult at Franklin Square, by same, J.WILLIAM COOK & MISS MIRIAN R. HEATON, all of this co.

M: 20th ult by SAMUEL HARDMAN JP, NATHAN CLIPPINGER & MISS SOPHIA RATHGEB, all of Salem.

M: 25th ult near New Albany by REV.H.B.FRY, JOHN D. WEBB & MISS HATTIE E. BARNES.

M: 30th ult by REV.ROBERT HAYS, PETER CLAGER of Wayne Tp & MISS CATHERINE HIGGINS of Osnaburg, Stark Co.

D: 31st ult at the Infirmary, LOUISA WELDON, ae 30y.

D: 5th inst at the Infirmary, PERRY FICKES ae 60y.

D: 25th ult in New Britain, Volusia Co., Fla., JOSEPH P. STELLER, formerly of Salem, ae 35y 11m 5d.

D: 28th ult, E.A.MILLER infant son of DANIEL & IDELLA MILLER of Salem, ae 30d.

D: 22nd ult in Salem of diptheria, LETTIE A. BUELL d/o SAMUEL & RACHEL BUELL, ae 7y 2m 20d.

D: 8th inst, REASON WELCH of Wayne Tp, ae 57y.

D: 8th inst, at res of her father, JAMES CLARK ESQ., of Centre Tp, ANNA STALLCUP, ae 31y.

D: 11th inst JACOB FREED, of Fairfield Tp., ae 75y.

Obituary: we condense the following from an obituary notice in the Salem Republican, of JAMES BROWN,SR., whose death was announced last week. MR. BROWN was born in Glasgow, Scotland, May 1st, 1799. His family emigrated to America in 1809 & settled at Germantown, Pa. He was married Apr. 7th, 1821 to MISS ELLEN WYLLEY, with whom he lived 43 years. MRS. BROWN died in Salem in 1864. In the fall of 1834, MR. BROWN removed with his family from Philadelphia, & settled for a time near New Lisbon. In 1839 he removed to Salem where he died.

Mon 19 Apr 1875 (Vol 9 no 3)

M: 25th ult by REV.I.N.WHITE, ANTHONY CLAGER & MISS ROSE E. McLANE, all of Wayne Tp., this co.

M: 8th inst at New Waterford by REV.J.Z.MOORE, GEORGE J. CHURCHILL & MISS SADIE A. BOIES.

M: 10th inst at Enon Valley PA, JOSEPH DUCK & MISS MINNIE FINK, both of Salem.

M: 6th inst by REV.J.H.HARRIER, ROSCOE CLEMENSON & MISS MARTHA E. STANLEY, all of this co.

M: 8th inst by same, JOHN B. STANLEY & MISS JULIA A. FISHER, both of this co.

M: 20th ult by REV.S.W.SWICK, JEREMIAH B. ZIMMERMAN & MISS SOPHIA ANGLEMYER, both of Leetonia.

M: 7th inst by REV.S.B.STEVENSON, MR. JAMES, of Carrollton & MISS CAROLINE WILLIAMS, of Salineville.

D: 17th inst, MRS. ELIZABETH CALDWELL, w/o THOMAS CALDWELL of Elkrun Tp, ae 46y 3m.

JAMES CLARK, an old & respected citizen of Salineville, died at his res at that place on 6th inst, ae 57y.

A young man named WILLIAM YOUNG fell into a well at Steubenville Wed.morning & was instantly killed, his neck being broken & his skull badly crushed.

Mon 26 Apr 1875 (Vol 9 no 4)

M: 11th inst at Allegheny City PA, ADAM KLING & MISS RUTH HARRIS, both of Salem.

M: 15th inst by REV.G.M.ALBRIGHT, WM.CARNS & MISS NANCY GAUS, both of this co.

M: 18th inst by REV.S.WAGNER, J.M.WHITELEATHER & MRS. ANNA WOOLF, both of North Georgetown.

M: 14th inst by REV.E.CURTIS, L.N.GIBBONS of Wellsville & MISS AGNES PATTERSON, of Newburgh.

D: 3d inst HANNAH RICHARDS w/o THOMAS RICHARDS of Hanover Tp ae 70y.

D: 10th inst at Gallipolis, JOHN WILLIAMS, ae 7y 10m 20d.

D: 18th inst CARRIE DAVIDSON d/o KENNETH F. & NANCY DAVIDSON of Wellsville in her 9th yr.

Golden Wedding: Fri, 23 Apr, was the 50th anniversary of the marriage of MR. & MRS. MAHLON BRIGGS, & in honor of that day, friends from the cities & country around, gathered for the affair.

Mon 3 May 1875 (Vol 9 no 5)

M: 20th ult by REV.I.N.WHITE, HENRY CRAWFORD & MISS SARAH J. SHIVERS, all of this co.

M: 22nd ult in East Liverpool, by REV.RIGGLE, FRANK CRAWFORD & MISS EMMA DURBIN, both of this co.

M: Sat 24th ult by REV.G.W.RIGGLE, P.W.PAUL, of Darlington, Beaver Co.,Pa., & MISS ANNA B. CURRY, of East Liverpool.

M: Fri Apr 22nd, SAMUEL MORLEY & MRS. SARAH HULSE, both of East Liverpool.

D: 10th inst JOSEPH BONSALL of Burlington, Iowa, formerly of Salem, ae 40y.

D: 21st ult at Leetonia, MARGARET E. McMANNUS ae 10m 20d.

D: 21st ult at Leetonia, JOHN HALEY s/o PATRICK & MARY HALEY, ae 11m 8d.

D: 23d ult at Leetonia, PATRICK McNAMARA s/o MICHAEL & MARY McNAMARA, ae 6m 12d.

D: 22nd ult of heart disease, MRS. MARY C. KERR w/o SAMUEL C. KERR, of Salem, ae 43y.

D: in Cleveland Wed.Apr 28th, MR. T.W.ABRAHAM, formerly of Wellsville, ae 38y.

D: at her home near East Liverpool on Tues Apr 27th, MRS.- ELIZABETH FISHER, ae 72y.

D: Mar 18th, HARVEY MORGAN ELLIOT, ae 9y 7m 3d; also, on Apr 5th, MARY ELIZABETH ELLIOT, ae 7y 8m 27d, children of LAUGHLIN & MATILDA ELLIOT, of Smith's Ferry, Pa.

D: 2nd inst MRS. LYDIA BRICKER w/o DAVID BRICKER of Salem Tp, ae 70y.

ELIJAH P. DAVIDSON, aged 89y on the 24th, was beaten up & murdered in Leetonia. Suspect SAMUEL MEAD was jailed. [a 2 column article]

Mon 10 May 1875 (Vol 9 no 6)

M: 29th ult by REV.LONG, JAMES H. COOK, of Salem & MISS ELIZABETH KENREICH, of Green Tp., Mahoning Co.

D: 3d inst near New Waterford, HENRY KOCH, ae 47y 8m.

D: 30th ult at New Waterford, SEYMOUR KETCHUM, ae 72y.

D: 7th inst, JAMES STERLING of Elkrun Tp, in 80th yr.

D: 8th inst CHARLEY MARTIN s/o SAMUEL & JANE MARTIN of Centre Tp, ae 5m.

D: 8th inst, CHARLES MELGRIM of Centre Tp, in 81st yr.

D: 1st inst at East Liverpool, EDDIE NEVILLE s/o SANFORD & ELLA NEVILLE, ae 2y.

Mon 17 May 1875 (Vol 9 no 7)

M: 6th inst by REV.J.M.KENDIG, FRANK BRINKER & HATTIE HOFFEE, both of Salem Tp., CCO.

M: 4th inst by REV.C.L.WINGET, GEORGE M. SMITH of Salem & MISS REBECCA GREER, of Columbiana.

M: 5th inst near Wellsville by REV.DAVID HARGEST, CHARLES R. DALES of Centre Tp & MISS MARTHA J. TURNER, of Yellow Creek Tp.

M: 11th inst at St.John's Church, Summitville, by REV.B.B.- KELLY, JAMES HANLON & MISS SUSAN GALLAGHER, all of Saline- ville.

M: 10th inst by REV.J.C.TAGGART, GEORGE L. THOMPSON & MISS LOUISA RALSTON, both of East Liverpool.

M: 8th inst by REV.E.A.BRINDLEY, J.T.McBRIAR of Freedom,PA & MISS DORA ROWE of East Liverpool.

D: 9th inst MRS. M.A. BRUBAKER w/o L.D.BRUBAKER of Columbi- ana, ae 22y 14d.

D: 8th inst at Wellsville, PENINA BELL KOUNTZ, eldest daughter of J.G.JR. & MARY L. KOUNTZ, ae 4y 8d.

Mon 24 May 1875 (Vol 9 no 8)

M: 20th inst at res of bride's parents by REV.W.G.NEVIN, MATHIAS T. NACE & MISS ELLA F. EELLS, all of New Lisbon.

M: 19th inst at res of bride's parents by REV.G.N.JOHNSTON, GEORGE H. HUSTON & MISS MAGGIE McDONALD, all of New Lisbon.

M: 13th inst by REV.C.B.HENTHORNE, J.MORRIS WEBB of Chester Co PA & MISS LUCINDA EDWARDS, of CCO.

M: 11th inst at Columbiana by REV.J.Z.MOORE, REV. W.B.CAMP- BELL & MISS FANNIE A. McCUNE.

M: 11th inst by REV.I.N.WHITE, JOHN M. ALCORN of Beaver Co PA & MISS SERINDA BRADY of CCO.

M: 16th inst at East Liverpool by REV.E.A.BRINDLEY, MR.C.- HOYTE & MRS. ANNA J. FAY.

D: 14th inst at Salem, ELIZABETH GARWOOD d/o JOHN W. & ASENETH GARWOOD, in her 20th yr.

D: 18th inst JACOB KAUFFMAN of Salem ae 79y.

D: 20th inst MISS RUTH SWEARINGEN d/o ELIMELECK & SARAH SWEARINGEN, ae 60y 4m 3d.

D: 20th inst CASSANDRA ANN FARMER, w/o WILLIAM FARMER of Fairfield Tp ae 66y 22d.

D: 21st inst G.F.ADAM of this place, ae 73y 6m. DEATH OF G.F.ADAM: We are again called upon to announce the death of another of our old citizens. G.F.ADAM, who died Fri after- noon, was born in Wurtenberg, Nov.27th, 1802, came to America in 1826 & to New Lisbon in 1829.

D: 17th inst in Salineville, MISS ELIZABETH HOEY,in 84th yr

D: 19th inst at Salineville, MRS. ROSANNA WILLIAMS, ae about 74y

D: 24th inst in Madison Tp, LAURA E. KETCHUM d/o WILLIAM H. & SARAH E. KETCHUM, ae 7y 3m.

Court proceedings: MARTHA BROWN vs LEANDER BROWN, divorce granted.

SAMUEL LAMBORN, an old resident of New Lisbon, died last Mon. & was buried Tues., aged 71y.

Mon 31 May 1875 (Vol 9 no 9)

Golden Wedding: MR. & MRS. WILLIAM HOSTETTER will celebrate the 50th anniversary of their marriage on 16th of June.

Court proceedings:
JANE BUNTING vs OLIVER C. BUNTING, divorce granted & plain- tiff's maiden name restored.
WILLIAM H. RICHARD vs HARRIET RICHARD: divorce granted
JACOB WELCH vs MARCELLA WELCH: divorce granted
LAURA FORNAY vs JOHN FORNAY: divorce granted
HARRIET LEIGH vs JOHN LEIGH: divorce granted

M: at res of bride's parents in Smith's Ferry PA by REV.- STIFFEY, HENRY S. BEAUMONT & MISS JENNIE HAMILTON.

D: 12th inst in New Alexandria, MARY HOUTS ae 81y 11m 27d.

D: 23d inst at the Infirmary, JOHN M. COLLIER, ae 75y.

D: 18th inst in Salem, DEACON RICHARD CAUFFMAN, ae 78y 8m 16d

D: 28th inst in Salem, EMMA MARSHALL d/o JOHN MARSHALL ae 20y

D: 26th inst at East Liverpool, EMMA MOODY w/o BENJAMIN MOODY, ae 32y.

Mon 7 June 1875 (Vol 9 no 10)

JOHN MONTGOMERY, an old & highly esteemed business man of Salineville, died at that place on Wednesday.

M: 19th ult in Washingtonville by REV.W.W.LANG, J.W.DUBBS & MISS MINNIE FARMER.

M: 20th ult at res of bride's parents by same, J.T.WHARTON & MISS MATTIE E. BETZ.

M: 9th ult at Enon Valley PA by REV.ALBERT DILWORTH, GEORGE W. BALLENTINE & MISS ELLA N. WALKER, both of Washingtonville

M: 3d inst at Hanoverton by REV.GEORGE VOGLESONG, assisted by REV.C.B.HENTHORN, WILLIAM H. KAUFFMAN of Salem & MISS GEORGIA VOGLESONG.

D: 31st ult at Marshalltown, Iowa, LAVINA F. HANNA d/o THOMAS HANNA, ae 31y.

D: 1st inst, CATHARINE ELIZABETH McBANE, d/o JOHN A. McBANE of Wellsville, after a lingering illness.

D: 25th ult near Wellsville, MISS KATE E. McBANE.

D: 9th ult, MR. W.P.BENWOOD of Wellsville, ae 35y.

D: 3d inst ALICE A. SITLER d/o S.H. & ELIZABETH SITLER of Salem Tp, ae 12y 3m 29d.

D: 5th inst in New Lisbon, LEE A. WHITNEY, infant s/o WATSON C. & MATTIE J. WHITNEY of Portland, Mich., ae 1y 5m.

Mon 14 June 1875   (Vol 9 no 11)

The Columbiana Register announces the funeral of MRS. DAVID ESTERLY, and also of JOHN DEEMER, last Tues.

M: 10th inst at res of bride's parents, E.L.RANDOLPH ESQ., of this place & KATIE HOOVER, only dau of DR.Z.L.HOOVER of Bloomington, Ill.

M: 4th inst by REV.S.M.COON, JAMES R. RUSSELL & MISS MARY GARRET, all of Salineville.

D: 9th inst LUCINDA RANDELS w/o JOHN deceased, ae 67y 9m 23d

D: 7th inst WILLIAM HOLLAND, of Hanover ae 74y 2m 13d.

D: 9th inst LYDIA GRONER d/o SIMON & MARY GRONER of Centre Tp ae 2y 30d.

D: 31st ult at Wellsville, ELLA WILLIAMS d/o BAZIL E. WILL-IAMS, in 17th yr.

D: 5th inst MRS. ANN SMALLEY of Wellsville ae 78y.

D: 8th inst, ALEXANDER LUCAS of Centre Tp, a native of Strausburgh, Germany, aged 47y.

Mon 21 June 1875   (Vol 9 no 12)

HENRY WOLF, a soldier of the war of 1812 & the oldest member of the Presbyterian Church in Freedom, PA, died lately, in his 91st year.

WILLIAM UNDERWOOD, a citizen of Middleton Tp, died Tues June 15th at res of his son, MAHLON UNDERWOOD, ESQ., in 89th yr.

DEWALT WILLIARD & wife, of this place, reached the 55th anniversary of marriage last Fri. Mr. W. is in his 85th year, & his wife but a few years younger.

M: 15th inst by REV.G.N.JOHNSTON, ROBERT CARSON & MRS. MARY AUSTIN, both of Wellsville.

M: Thur. May 20th at res of bride's parents near New Water-ford, by REV.W.W.CURRY, assisted by REV.J.M.WALLACE & W.G.NEVIN,   REV. WM.M.HUNTER & MISS EMMA NEVIN.

D: 25th ult in Madison Tp, NANCY JANE KETCHUM d/o WILLIAM H. & SARAH E. KETCHUM, ae 1y.

D: 31st ult in Elkrun Tp, FANNY DYKE w/o JAMES L. DYKE, aged about 20y.

D: 30th ult at res near Patmos, WILLIAM C. STRATTON, in 62nd yr of his age

D: 26th ult at East Liverpool, EMMA MOODY w/o BENJAMIN MOODY, ae 33y.

D: 12th ult at Columbiana, MRS. KEZIAH GETZ w/o JACOB GETZ ae 64y 11m 16d.

D: 10th ult near Middleton, CARL BETRAM WOODS s/o JOHN L. & F.T.WOODS, ae 7y 10m 24d.

D: 11th ult at North Lima, MRS. CATHARINE WANSETLER ae 71y 2m 6d.

D: 28th ult at Salem, EMMA MARSHALL ae 20y.

D: 15th ult at res of his daughter in Salem, JOHN BRICKER, 84y 8m.

D: 7th ult in New Alexander, DENT LIVINGSTON RITZ, s/o JAMES E. & CATHARINE O. RITZ, ae 1y 24d.

Mon 28 June 1875   (Vol 9 no 13)

M: 15th inst by REV.DR.NESBIT, REV.R.STEWART ROSS, of Unionville, PA & MISS MARY C. ZIMMERMAN, of this co.

M: 5th inst by SAMUEL HARDMAN JP, JULIUS A. ZANG of Alliance & MISS ADA M. PURDY of Salem.

M: 17th inst at Ravenna by REV.H.WEBB, HOMER H. WOOLF of Atwater & MISS CARRIE V. CRUMRINE, d/o DAVID CRUMRINE.

M: 16th inst in Salem by ELDER HARMON REEVES, JOHN B. MARSH-ALL & MRS. LOUISA THOMPSON.

M: 17th inst at Salineville by REV.G.W.JOHNSTON, BENJAMIN ROBERTS & MISS MARTHA SHEAN, all of Salineville.

M: 17th inst by same, FRANK GODDARD & MISS CLARA PRESSEY, all of Salineville.

M: 3d inst by REV.ROBT.HAYS, JAMES McPHERSON of Washington Tp & MISS EMMA J. PATTERSON, eldest dau of DAVID PATTERSON, of Wayne Tp.

M: 22nd inst at res of bride by REV.A.R.CHAPMAN, assisted by REV.W.G.NEVIN,   CAPT. R.C.TAGGART & ANNA F. COPPOCK, all of CCO.

M: at ME parsonage in Elkton by REV.W.BEDALL, J.W.HAINES & MISS JENNIE RANSOM, both of this co.

M: 24th inst by REV.A.R.CHAPMAN, WILLIAM DeSHERROW of New Lisbon & MRS. M.A.TANNER of Salem.

M: 24th inst by same, W.H.YOUNG, of Achor & MISS ELIZA J. TAYLOR, of East Carmel, all of this co.

M: 23d inst by REVS. HAYS & WHITE, at res of bride's parents in Wayne Tp, STACY WALLACE & MISS VIRGINIA A. BROWN.

M: same time & place HUGH FRASER & MISS MARY ELLA BROWN.

M: 21st inst at Salineville by JOHN WEAVER ESQ., THOMAS CROOKS of Alliance & MISS ELIZABETH E. KYLE of former place

M: 15th inst at Cleveland by REV.MENDANHALL, I.B.CAMERON of Salineville & MISS D.A.IRWIN of Cleveland.

D: 22nd inst SARAH ELIZABETH McCORD d/o ARTHUR & ELIZABETH McCORD, of Wayne Tp, ae 7y 9m.

D: 11th inst near Wellsville, MISS JANETTE O. McBANE.

D: 7th ult at Lagrange, Ind., HESTER STOCKMAN formerly of New Lisbon, ae 74y 8m 10d.

D: 21st inst GRACE BISHOP d/o & only child of ISADORE & HATTIE BISHOP, of Columbiana, ae 3y 2m 18d.

D: 20th isnt ALICE McCAN of Leetonia ae 54y 2m 25d.

D: 27th inst at res of J.L.FORBES, MISS MAGGIE CARLILE ae 26y

D: 25th inst MRS. YOUNG, w/o SAMUEL YOUNG of Hanover Tp, ae about 30y.

Mon 5 July 1875   (Vol 9 no 14)

M: 10th ult by REV.H.B.FRY, JOB COOK & MISS EMMA SMILEY, d/o DR. SMILEY, both of Salem.

M: 17th ult by MAYOR STOKLEY, JAMES R. TOWNSEND of Salem,OH & MISS SALLIE S. STRATTON of Philadelphia.

M: 22nd ult by REV.J.C.TAGGART, W.E.McGAVRAN & MISS ALLIE DEVERS, all of East Liverpool.

M: 1st inst by REV.G.W.JOHNSON, NELSON WALLACE & MISS ELIZABETH McDEVITT, all of Salineville.

D: 19th ult at Homeworth, RENNIE THOMAS, only son of JEFF & MARY J. THOMAS, ae 4y 1m 8d.

Mon 12 July 1875 (Vol 9 no 15)

During the celebration of the 4th at West Unity [Williams Co] OH, a man named PETER KRINDLE was killed by the premature discharge of a cannon. He leaves a family.

The wife of WILLIAM MAXWELL of Hicksville, aged about 50y, recently hung herself in the upper story of the house.

M: 6th inst at Smith's Ferry PA by REV.G.A.LOWMAN, MR.B.M.-ALLISON & MISS MARY A. BUNTING, both of Wellsville.

M: 7th inst at New Lisbon by H.E.FROST JP, SAMUEL MARQUIS & MISS LIZZIE DURANT.

D: 3d inst in Madison Tp, MRS. HULDAH COOPER, ae 85y.

D: 5th inst in Madison Tp, MRS. AMY CLARKE, ae 46y.

D: 30th ult in Fairfield Tp, NOAH WORMAN ae 57y 7m 26d.

Mon 19 Jly 1875 (Vol 9 no 16)

M: 12th inst by REV J.M.KENDIG, WILLIAM H. MILLER & MISS REBECCA C. SAMPSELL, both of Columbiana.

D: 12th inst, near New Waterford, MR.SHIVERS TODD in 38th yr.

D: 14th inst EPHRAIM HOLLOWAY of Centre Tp ae 62y 9m.

D: 14th inst FRANCES YOUNG w/o J.M.YOUNG of Centre Tp ae 35y.

D: 18th inst ANDREW BARNES of Elkrun Tp in 76th yr.

Mon 26 Jly 1875 (Vol 9 no 17)

M: 15th inst at Enon Valley PA by REV.MR.LAFFERTY, ROBERT PAYNE & MISS VIRGINIA RANDALL, all of Leetonia.

M: 5th inst by REV.R.G.FERGUSON, SAMUEL G. RITTER of Butler & MISS LOU SMITH of Wellsville Oh.

D: 13th inst HANNAH E. WOODS d/o J.F. & JANE WOODS of Fairfield Tp, ae 3y 3m 22d.

D: 17th inst in Salem, ALVIRA L. SHARPNACK w/o DANIEL SHARPNACK in 38th yr.

D: 15th inst of consumption, ROBERT B. STEVENSON of Butler Tp ae 39y

D: 21st inst at Wellsville, MISS SADIE SAMPSON, ae 30y.

D: 20th inst, MRS. SUSANNA APPLE of Wellsville ae 45y.

Mon 2 Aug 1875 (Vol 9 no 18)

ALPHONSO HOLLY, the first male white child born in the Western Reserve, died at his res in Cleveland on Sun.morning, ae 75y.

On Mon eve, July 19th, a man named GOTTFRED WAGNER, committed suicide by haning in the Portage Co jail, where he was incarcerated for an attempted assasination.

M: 4th ult at Rouseville, Pa., by REV.MERRITT, MR.W.SINCLAIR of Salem & MISS MAGGIE McCALL.

M: 13th ult at Hanover Station by REV.O.EBERT, THOMAS E. SWEARINGEN & MISS KATE E. MILLER.

M: 22nd ult at Cannelton PA by P. MANSFIELD ESQ, JAMES GILLESPIE & MISS ELSIE HUFF, both of Achor.

M: 3d ult by REV.MAXWELL, FRED. NEUSBAUM of Salem & MISS ———— ENGLISH of Leetonia.

M: 29th ult by REV.D.JONES, LEONARD CLECKNER of New Lisbon & MISS ANNA McCLELLAND of New Brighton, Pa.

D: 20th ult, MRS. LYDIA KYSER w/o JACOB KYSER of Columbiana ae 36y 9m 9d.

D: 22nd ult in Columbiana, JOSHUA FAULK ae 58y 5m 6d.

D: 20th ult in Columbiana, MARION KINNEAR s/o HAMILTON KINNEAR ae 6m.

D: 25th ult, MARY SNOOK, relict of JOHN SNOOK, ae about 77y

D: 23d ult at Freedom,PA., ROBERT COOPER HILLMAN, only child of J.G. & S.A.HILLMAN, ae 7m 18d.

D: 26th ult MARY J. WILSON infant d/o RODRICK & MAGGIE WILSON ae 9m.

D: 21st ult, infant child of FRED & MARGARET ANN ADAMS, of this place.

D: 17th ult in Wilmington, Del., R.ISABELLA MARKS, w/o REV.LAFAYETTE MARKS & eldest daughter of the late SAMUEL QUIGLEY, M.D., of Calcutta, Oh.

Mon 9 Aug 1875 (Vol 9 no 19)

M: 18th ult at Smith's Ferry PA by SQUIRE PETTIT, RESIN BAKER & MISS JENNIE STIGLEMAN, both of New Lisbon.

M: 26th ult by REV.J.C.TAGGART, CHRISTOPHER BARNS & MISS M. BELLE RALSTON, all of East Liverpool.

D: 30th ult at Leetonia, EVA MARY PEPPEL, d/o DANIEL & MARY PEPPEL, ae 3m.

D: 30th ult in Salem, MISS MARY ANN WALKER in 62nd yr

D: 2nd inst in Salem, CHARLES B. SCHAFFER, infant s/o HENRY & SARAH E. SCHAFFER, ae 6m 7d.

D: 25th ult at Leetonia, CAROLINE WEIGAND, d/o ANDREW & CAROLINE WEIGAND, ae 2y 26d.

D: 2nd inst wife of MARTIN GILLESPIE of Achor, this co.

D: 26th ult at Salineville, MR.FRANCIS J. ANDREW, ae 41y.

D: 6th inst ELIZABETH SHAWKE, w/o the late JACOB SHAWKE of this place, aged 80y 13d.

D; 5th inst NETTIE JANE ADAMS, d/o MAGGIE & FRED. ADAMS ae 2y

Mon 16 Aug 1875 (Vol 9 no 20)

We are peained to learn of the sudden death of MR.W.K.RAMSEY, s/o WM. RAMSEY of Hanover, which occurred on Fri eve of brain fever. He was a young man of much promise & leaves a wife & 3 small children. The funeral took place yesterday morning & was largely attended; 111 carriages formed the procession to the burying place.

D: 13th inst, W.K.RAMSEY of Hanover Tp, ae 28y.

M: 8th inst at East Liverpool by REV.E.BINGLEY, JAMES COWAN & MISS ELDORADO A. SCOTT.

D: 8th inst ELIZABETH IREY, mother of EDEN IREY of Hanover Tp., ae 73y.

D: 7th inst at Salem, JOHN McCLYNCHEY ae about 50y.

D: 8th inst at Rosemont, Philadelphia, JENNIE ATEN BARTHOLO-MEW, w/o A. BARTHOLOMEW of Wellsville, in 32nd yr.

D: 13th inst, ELIZABETH ELLEN CRAWFORD, d/o SUSAN CRAWFORD of this place, ae 2y 3m.

D: 12th inst MARY ELIZABETH McDERMOTT d/o JAMES & NANNIE McDERMOTT, of this place, ae 11m 19d.

D: 14th inst ISAMENA M. CLARKE w/o SAMUEL CLARKE of this place, ae 64y.

Mon 23 Aug 1875 (Vol 9 no 21)

M: 18th inst by REV.WM.BAXTER, ISAAC BARRICK & MISS AMY C. COULSON, both of this co.

M: 12th inst near Baden, Beaver Co., MICHAEL WARD & MISS MATTIE SHAFFER, both of this co.

M: 12th inst by REV.J.Z.MOORE, at Columbiana, URBAN F. WEBB & MISS EMMA R. SINSELL.

D: 16th inst ANNIE ELTON SCROGGS d/o J.J. & M.Y.SCROGGS ae 2y

D: 29th ult MAGGIE BURCAW w/o WILLIAM BURCAW ae 23y 14d

D: 18th ult at res of JAMES SHIELDS of this place, ELMIRA HAMPSON, ae 40y.

D: 14th ult D.S.NOBLE of Wellsville in 36th yr of her age

D: 4th ult in Yellow Creek Tp, JOHN A. McLEAN s/o CHARLES McLEAN, in 20th yr.

D: 9th inst FLORIEN TUCKER infant s/o W.A. & HANNAH C.-TUCKER of Salem, ae about 5m.

D: 20th inst LOIS LLOYD STRAUGHN infant d/o JOHN L. & MARY E. STRAUGHN, ae 16m.

D: 16th inst at Salineville, JOSEPH STITT ae 11y 3m 12d.

D: 21st inst at res of L.H.GREEN, RALPH GREEN ae 2y 11m.

WILLIAM C. ADAMS s/o the late MATTHEW ADAMS & brother of MARTIN ADAMS of this place, died at his res in Windham, Portage Co., on 15th inst, aged about 70y.

Mon 30 Aug 1875 (Vol 9 no 22)

M: 19th inst in Alliance by REV.J.M.THOMAS, FRANKLIN COPE of CCO & MISS JESSIE ROLLIE of Stark Co.

M: same time & place by same, ALLEN B. COPE & MISS WILMA GEIGER, both of CCO.

M: 19th inst near Fairfield by ELDER HARMON REEVES, GEORGE LOWER & MISS ADA S. BRADFIELD.

M: 8th inst in Knox Tp by REV.J.A.CLEMENT, WINFIELD SHEATZLEY & MISS SARAH A. KIMES.

M: 26th inst by REV.S.M.COON, THOMAS C. TOLSON & MISS ELLEN BROWN, all of Salineville.

D: 25th inst at the Infirmary, ANNIE BELL ae 2y 6m.

D: 16th inst at Columbiana, JACOB B. TODD, ae 22y 7m 19d.

D: 20th inst at Salem, MARY L. TALMAGE, ae 25y 5m.

D: 18th inst at Salem, RICHARD NELSON BARCLAY s/o J.M. & SETTA BARCLAY, ae 6m.

D: 21st inst at Salem, ALPHEUS ALEXANDER FRAZIER, ae 19m on the 23d inst, and ROBERT ALLEN FRAZIER, ae 19m 2d, twin children of DANIEL & ELIZABETH ANN FRAZIER.

D: 22nd inst at res of JOSEPH L. LOWRY ESQ., in Pittsburgh, GEORGE HINCHLIFFE, formerly of Salem, in 40th yr.

D: 24th inst JANE JOHNSON w/o JAMES HENRY JOHNSON of Franklin Tp, ae 63y.

D: 26th inst in New Lisbon, EDNA BONBRIGHT, youngest d/o WILLIAM & KATE BONBRIGHT, ae about 3y 3m.

D: 13th inst in East Liverpool, MRS. BURFORD, w/o A. BURFORD, ae 58y.

D: 15th inst in East Liverpool, MRS. S. BAILEY ae 75y.

D: 14th inst in Leetonia, CATHARINE RYAN ae 40y.

D: 16th inst in Leetonia, ISABELLA MOFFET d/o JOSEPH & SUSAN MOFFET, ae 2y.

D: 20th inst in Leetonia, DANIEL CARY s/o EDWARD & MARY CARY ae 11m 8d.

D: 28th inst REBECCA MARY McLAUGHLIN d/o A.J. & MARTHA A. McLAUGHLIN of Madison Tp, ae 2y 4m 18d.

Mon 6 Sep 1875 (Vol 9 no 23)

M: 26th ult at Columbiana by REV.J.M.KENDIG, THOMAS T. TODD & MISS JENNIE C. SHEETS, both of Unity Tp.

M: 2nd inst by J.M.DICKINSON JP, WILLARD F. COYLE & MISS CANES T. BRINKER.

D: 26th ult at Columbiana, JACOB ESTERLY ae 83y 4m 19d.

D: 26th ult, ROLAND TEST infant s/o JOHN B. & MARY LOUISA TEST of Salem, ae 1y 5m 23d.

D: 26th ult in Salem, MRS. MARY A. HUDSON w/o JOHN ae 49y

D: 28th ult at res of THOS.KELLY in Salem, an infant child aged about 4 mo.

D: 29th ult at res of his father in Salem, GEORGE W. KLING, ae 18y.

D: 29th ult at New Albany, SAMUEL COX, father of MRS. AARON WILSON of Salem, ae 84y.

D: 29th ult near Washingtonville, FREDERICK BIGLER ae 73y. [ed.note: this is probably FREDERICK BILGER]

D: 25th ult in Green Tp., Mahoning Co., SUSAN COOK w/o JACOB COOK, ae 73y.

D: 4th inst DEBORA A. HAWKINS w/o THOMAS HAWKINS of Elkrun Tp ae 69y.

D: 5th inst ELMER WALLACE HASSIN s/o JONATHAN & ELIZABETH HASSIN ae 13y.

D: 5th inst HARRY D. KERR s/o WILLIAM & ELIZABETH KERR of Center Tp ae 6m.

Mon 13 Sep 1875 (Vol 9 no 24)

M: 17th June, in San Francisco Calif., by REV.J.W.HEMPHILL, J.T.BOONE, JR., of Salem & MISS LAURA M. STATELER, of San Francisco.

M: 2nd inst by REV.ISAAH H. REITER, D.D., J.M.WALTER of Washingtonville O & MISS ANNA WEAVER of Miamisburg, Oh.

M: 25th ult by H.P.BOSTON JP, JOHN M. STANLEY & MISS MARY A. GREENAWALT of Knox Tp., CCO.

M: 9th inst by REV.D.HYDE, WILLIAM TARR & MISS EMMA LODGE, all of this co.

D: 29th ult at New Albany, Mahoning Co., SAMUEL COX, ae 84y

D: 5th inst at Salem, LEWIS RIGHTER ae 49y 11m 19d.

D: 6th inst at Salem, wife of LEWIS RIGHTER ae 45y 3m 11d

D: 1st inst, D.H.ECKSTEIN of North Georgetown, ae 72y 3m 3d.

D: 31st ult MARY HILLIARD d/o JOHN & SARAH HILLIARD of Perry Tp ae 1y 11m 3 wks

D: 1st inst at Leetonia, WALTER BARR s/o WILLIAM & MARGARET BARR, ae 11m 21d.

D: 3d inst at Leetonia, OAKLEY BOUGH, s/o JOHN H. & EUPHEMA S. BOUGH, ae 3y 17d.

D: 31st ult at Leetonia, MARY O'CONNER, ae 64y.

D: 21st ult near Teegarden's Mill, ANN BURLEY DALZELL d/o EDWARD & EMELINE DALZELL, ae 1y 9m.

D: 3d inst at Salem, JOHN ADAM KLING, ae 50y 8m.

D: 8th inst REV.G.D.KINNEAR of Columbiana, ae 68y.

D: 12th inst MARY C. McMICHAEL, w/o R.H.McMICHAEL of Centre Tp ae 49y.

D: 12th inst at the Infirmary, SARAH JONES ae 70y.

D: 11th inst ADA MARY LOUDEN d/o JONATHAN & LAURA LOUDEN of Wayne Tp., ae 1y 10m 10d.

DEATH OF MRS. THOMAS HAWKINS, of Elkrun Tp: Again we have to record the death of another of the old, honored & respected citizens of the county. MRS. THOMAS HAWKINS, of Elkrun Tp, died Sat the 4th inst & was buried on Sun.afternoon. MRS. HAWKINS, whose maiden name was DEBORAH ANN WARRING, was born at Norwalk, Conn., Apr.22d, 1806. In Apr 1830, she married JOHN JOHNSON, of Washington Co., Pa. He lived but a few years, and on Nov.24,1839, she married THOS.HAWKINS, who survives her. Three children are living of the 7 with which they were blessed. MRS. HAWKINS was a member of the Methodist Church & the funeral was conducted by REV.D.V.HYDE.

Mon 20 Sep 1875   (Vol 9 no 25)

ARCHY L. STEWART of Beaver Falls PA & MISS KATE H. THOMPSON, of this place, were married Wed. morning.

M: 13th inst by E.A.BRINDLEY, at res of MR.BUXTON, WILLIAM MOUNTFORD & MISS ELIZA GORDON both of Salineville.

M: 16th inst by REV.G.N.JOHNSON, WILLIAM RODEBAUGH & MISS MARIETTA POLAND, all of this co.

M: 11th inst by REV.ROBT.HAYS, JOSEPH Y.WHITACRE of Fox Tp., Carroll Co., & MISS CASSANDRA GRAFTON, d/o WILLIAM GRAFTON of Wayne Tp., this co.

M: 15th inst by same, JAMES McBANE of Liverpool Tp & MISS MAGGIE N. McINTOSH of Madison Tp.

D: 9th inst at Hanover, JAMES HENRY RAY, s/o JOSEPH B. & MARY C. RAY, ae 2y 1m 29d.

D: 9th inst at Hanover O, daughter of MR. & MRS. S.A.WOOLF of Salem, ae 1 week 4d.

D: 21st ult at Tom's Brook, VA, JOHN JACOBS, ae 67y 2m 5d.

D: 15th inst at the Infirmary, JAMES ELLIS (colored) ae 60y

D: 14th inst at Salem, SALLIE ANGLEMYER, ae ----y.

D: 8th inst at Salem, ELIZABETH SPENCER, ae 81y.

D: 16th inst FRANK DOBSON, infant s/o AARON & FRANCES DOBSON, ae 1y 3m 8d.

Mon 27 Sep 1875   (Vol 9 no 26)

M: 5th inst by REV.J.A.CLEMENT, BENJAMIN BIERY & MISS LUSETTA SHIVELY, all of Knox Tp.

M: 13th inst by same, PHILLIP CONSOR & MISS AMANDA HUMPHREY, all of this co.

M: 22nd inst by J.M.DICKINSON ESQ., HENRY MORNINGSTAR & MISS MARY JANE HOOKER, all of this co.

M: 15th inst by REV.J.J.ESTILL, JACOB O. DETWILER & MISS ELIZABETH RITTER, all of this co.

M: 20th inst by REV.J.Z.MOORE, DANIEL W. MOORE of East Palestine, & MISS LUELLA CONKLE, of New Waterford.

M: 21st inst by REV.DAVID HARGEST, WILLIAM FIFE & MISS LUCINDA McKEE of Yellow Creek Tp.

D: 19th inst at Columbiana, FREDDY W. SHAFFER s/o THOMAS J. & JANE SHAFFER, ae 4y 8m 7d.

D: 17th inst at Leetonia JAMES CLARK s/o ANTHONY & MARY CLARK, ae 1m 12d.

D: at res of her son JOSEPH at Salem, EVALINE STANSBURY ae 73y

D: 13th inst at Salem, HOMER J. HANNEY, s/o ROBERT & LYDIA ANN HANNEY, ae 17m 11d.

D: 18th inst in Berlin Twp., JOSEPH LEONARD ae 72y.

D: 20th inst in Salem, HARRY FISHER s/o GEORGE & E.B.FISHER, ae 9m 19d.

D: 16th inst JOHN BATTIN of Salem, ae 75y 7m 14d.

D: 25th inst LEAH PATTERSON, d/o MRS. JEANNETTE PATTERSON, of Hanover Tp, ae 17y 7m 9d.

Mon 4 Oct 1875   (Vol 9 no 27)

M: 16th ult by SQUIRE BUSKY of Canfield, DAVID H. PICKETT of Salem & MISS KATE ANN MATHERS of Stark Co.

M: 27th ult at res of JOHN DICK, EDWIN MILLARD & MISS ALICE SNIDER.

M: 21st ult at Leetonia, CHARLES KOLL & MISS HONORA HOGUE, all of this co.

M: 24th ult by REV.E.HINGLEY, J.H.SIMMS & MISS SYNDONIA HARKER, both of East Liverpool.

D: 23d ult at Columbiana, MRS. A. STURGEON ae 49y 1m 12d.

D: 25th ult in Unity Tp, REBECCA HARROLD ae 82y 3m.

D: 25th ult at Leetonia, MAGGIE NAUGHTON, d/o THOMAS & MARY NAUGHTON, ae 1y 3m.

D: 9th ult at Leetonia, KATE GARTHWAIT, d/o WALTER & MATILDA GARTHWAIT ae 3y 7m.

D: 22nd ult at Leetonia, WALTER GARTHWAIT, s/o the above parents, ae 1y 8m 20d.

D: 8th ult at Franklin Square, JOSEPHINE B. JORDEN, w/o DR.D.JORDEN, of New Brighton, Pa., ae 18y 5m 7d.

D: 29th ult at Leetonia, MARGARET MASTERSON d/o OWEN & ELIZABETH MASTERSON, ae 10m 24d.

D: 20th ult at Leetonia, WILLIAM HUGHES ae 66y.

D: 1st inst HOMER FRANCIS RAMSEY s/o WILSON C. & SUSAN E. RAMSEY, of Centre Tp, ae 4m.

D: 29th ult WILLIAM JACKSON in 28th yr.

D: 30th ult MRS ELIZABETH BAGSHAW in 59th yr

DEATH OF DAVID BOWER, a prominent merchant in this place who has been in ill health during the past year, died at his res Sat.eve last, ae 64y. As an exemplary Christian, courteous business man, kind & obliging citizen, he earned & maintained the confidence & esteem of all who knew him.

MRS. DAVID PRITCHARD presented MR.PRITCHARD with a handsome boy a few days ago. Both doing well & long may they wave!

FREDERICK FLUGAN, an aged & respected citizen, died at his res in New Lisbon last Mon, ae 81y. He was a native of Germany & came to this co in 1836, where he continued to reside to the day of his death. He served 14 years in the English & German cavalry service.

Mon 11 Oct 1875   (Vol 9 no 28)

M: 23d ult in Columbiana by JOSEPH KANNAL ESQ., ALLEN DEYSER & MISS MARY EIGHMAN.

M: 30th ult in Beaver Pa by REV.LYNCH, J.C.KERR & ELLA JOHNSON, both of East Liverpool.

M: 22nd ult by REV.M.PARKISON, HUGH F. HALL of Salem & MISS ANNETTA F. BARNES of Shippingport, Beaver Co Pa.

D: 5th inst, infant child of CALDWELL & MARY E. HOLLOWAY of Salem Tp.

D: 22nd ult at Salineville, ELLAS STITT, s/o WILLIAM & MARGARET STITT, ae 3y 2m 23d.

D: 27th ult at Salem, CATHARINE MOORE w/o ROBERT MOORE ae 73y

D: 2nd inst in Greenvillage, MARY COCHIL infant d/o DANIEL & MARTHA COCHIL, ae 6m 25d.

D: 3d inst at Salem, EMMA SHEEN d/o JAMES & EMMA SHEEN ae 11y

D: 9th inst at Salem, ELMER A. HOLLOWAY s/o JOSEPH & LYDIA S. HOLLOWAY, at Jeffersonville, Ind., ae 24y.

D: 9th inst MERVIN GREEN s/o LEVINA GREEN of this place ae 1y

CHARLES MONDAY, of this place, who was so terribly wounded by falling from a tree near Mt.Union, died from the effects of his injuries last Mon.evening.

LEMUEL TOMAN, living 3 miles north of Columbiana, met with an accident last Mon. which resulted in his instant death. He was assisting a neighbor to tear down an old cider press, & was crushed by falling timber which produced instant death.

Mon 18 Oct 1875 (Vol 9 no 29)

M: 5th inst by REV.P.RAETHER, JOHN MUNTZ & MISS CATHARINE KUHL d/o JOHN KUHL of Gillford, this co.

M: 7th inst at Columbiana by REV.C.L.WINGET, SAMUEL B. CARTER & MISS ETTIE A. RICHARDSON, all of this co.

M: 2nd inst by REV.M.A.PARKINSON, GEORGE CARSON & MISS MARY MARKER, both of Wellsville.

M: 30th ult by same, GARRET V. DEVER of Wellsville & MISS RACHEL A. PAISELY of Knoxville, Oh.

D: 9th inst at Wellsville, WILLIAM CLARKE MAYLONE ae 21y.

D: 8th inst at Salineville, ROBERT WILLIAM HEPPLEWHITE, s/o JOHN & MOLLIE, ae 3y 3m 4d.

D: 8th inst at Salineville, ELIZABETH J. DONALDSON, d/o JOHN & FANNY DONALDSON, ae 6m 12d.

D: 11th inst at Salineville, ROBERT DONALDSON, in 19th yr.

D: 10th inst at Salineville, JAMES HETHERINGTON s/o RICHARD & JANE, ae 2y 5m 10d.

D: 12th inst HENRY ETHELBERT MORRIS s/o GEORGE & MARY JANE MORRIS, of Centre Tp, ae 11m 25d.

Mon 25 Oct 1875 (Vol 9 no 30)

M: 7th inst by REV.J.J.ESTILL, JOSEPH T. McKEE & MISS MARGARET BYERS, both of New Lisbon.

M: 14th inst by J.B.RITCHEY ESQ., WILLIAM H. BAKER & MISS LYDIA A. KING, both of Gillford, this co.

M: 14th inst by REV.S.B.TEEGARDEN, JAMES H. CALVIN & MISS MARY M. ROLLER.

M: 16th inst by SAMUEL HARDMAN JP, FERDINAND NEWMAN of Canton, OH & MISS ALICE K. VEIGLE of Salem.

M: 14th inst near Greenford, Mahoning Co., by REV.LANG, ALDEN GREENAMYER & MISS LORETTA W. CALLAHAN.

M: 5th inst at res of JONAS SLAGLE ESQ., by Rev.W.W.LONG, MR. M.L.ROLLER & MISS KATIE B. SLAGLE.

M: 13th inst by same, G.C.DONALDSON of Carroll Co. & MISS LIZZIE JOHNSTON, of Washingtonville, this co.

M: 20th inst at res of bride's parents by REV.D.HARGEST, JOHN F. WOOD of Brazil, Clay Co., Ind., & MISS SUE H. GILMORE, of Madison Tp, CCO.

D: 14th inst in Wellsville, MRS. HANNAH PEEPLES ae 49y 4m 4d.

D: 17th inst in Columbiana, ELIZABETH REED, ae 85y.

D: 5th inst in Middleton Tp, MARY C. RODGERS ae 87y 3m 16d.

D: 14th inst at Centerdale, Iowa, JANE B.LAMBRON [LAMBORN], formerly of Salem, ae about 48y.

D: 19th inst at Winona, MATTIE ENGLAND, ae 20y.

Trial of SAMUEL MEAD, for the murder of ELIJAH DAVIDSON.- (result of the case: He is found guilty, sentenced to be hung; escaped jail & is captured about a year later & killed in a shootout with the law. 3 column story)

Mon 1 Nov 1875 (Vol 9 no 31)

M: 20th ult by REV.J.M.KENDIG, GEORGE E. RUSSELL of Crestline, OH & MISS MARY E. GREENAMYER of Columbiana.

M: 21st ult by REV.J.GRANT, DAVID B. BURFORD & MISS LIZZIE THOMAS, both of Salem.

M: 21st ult in Salem Tp by ELDER HARMON REEVES, MR. NER GAUNT & MISS BELLE FOUTS, of this co.

M: 27th ult at Columbiana by REV.C.L.WINGET, SAMUEL B.-CARTER & MISS ETTIE A. RICHARDSON, all of this co.

M: 27th ult by REV.J.D.LEGGET, BEN.F.METZ & MISS GEORGIE HILLERMAN, all of Malvern, Oh.

M: 19th ult by REV.W.LEA, WILLIAM B. HOLLAR of Wellsville & MISS LAURA L. RANKIN d/o R.J. & F.B.RANKIN.

M: 21st ult by REV.E.A.BRINDLEY, COSTELLO ROBB & MISS ---- GORBY, all of East Liverpool.

M: 21st ult by JOHN BRINDLEY ESQ., RALPH SCRAGG & MRS. MARIE G. GARCIE, both of East Liverpool.

D: 13th ult in Canfield, MRS. ELIZABETH SWANK, in 87th yr.

D: 21st ult in Salem, BENJAMIN TEST ae about 20y.

D: --- inst, ELIZABETH PARSONS, of Centre Tp, ae 83y 8m 14d.

MEAD TRIAL: found guilty in first degree (4 cols)

Mon 8 Nov 1875 (Vol 9 no 32)

M: 21st ult at res of bride by P.W.SMITH ESQ., JOHN WILSON & MRS. JANE MARLANEE, all of this co.

M: 28th ult by same at res of bride's father, ALVEN C.-HUSTON & MISS PHOEBE BURSON, all of this co.

M: 3d inst at Cleveland, by REV.E.P.GARDNER, HENRY O. SITTLER of Leetonia & MISS IDA LIVINGSTON of New Lisbon.

M: 29th ult at New Lisbon by REV.G.N.JOHNSTON, JEFFERSON CLAPSADDLE & MISS REBECCA M. CRAWFORD, both of this co.

M: 2nd inst by same, at res of bride's parents, JAMES ATTERHOLT & MISS SARAH H. FLEMMING, all of this co.

M: 3d inst by same at res of bride, A.J.RUFFINGTON of Washington Co Pa & MRS. CAL RANDOLPH of New Lisbon.

M: 30th ult at Columbiana by REV.C.L.WINGET, LEWIS K. BELL & MISS CORNELIA MORRIS, all of this co.

D: 14th ult at Bunker Hill, Miami Co., Ind., WILLIAM MARLNEE in 58th yr.

D: 29th ult in Wellsville, MRS. SOPHIA RILEY in 30th yr.

Last Thurs. a boy named WILLIAM HESS, about 12y old, while attempting to jump on the cars near the Wellsville car shops, on the C & P RR, fell between the cars & was instantly killed.

On Thurs last another of Salem's Aged & respected citizens, JOHN W. THOMAS, was called from the cares of this world. The deceased was born in Pennsylvania & was 82 yrs old. He emigrated to this county in 1823.

SAMUEL MEAD'S letter to Judge FREASE before attempting suicide.

CHARLES ANDERSON, indicted for rape on the daughter of FERDINAND OVERLANDER of East Palestine, plead guilty & was sentenced to Ohio Penitentiary for 15 yrs.

Mon 15 Nov 1875 (Vol 9 no 33)

SAMUEL MEAD sentenced to be hung on Fri Feb 25, 1876.

On last Fri., MR. & MRS. STOCKDALE JACKMAN, of St.Clair Tp., celebrated their 25th anniversary.

M: 6th inst by J.M.DICKINSON JP, SYLVESTER G. COWGILL ESQ. & MISS SADIE C. HOFFMAN, all of this co.

M: 2nd inst by SAMUEL HARDMAN JP, I.A.HALVERSTADT & MISS E.A.PEPPEL, both of Salem Tp.

M: 6th inst at Salem by REV.J.GRANT, JOEL F. BARBER & SARAH A. CRONIC

M: 21st ult at Salem by same, L.T.KERR & ALIVA CLIPPINGER.

M: 7th inst by REV.E.HINGLEY, FREDERICK DEIDRICK & MISS FANNIE BURFORD all of East Liverpool.

D: 24th ult at Salineville, JAMES SMITH ae 49y 11m 1d

D; 22nd ult at Leetonia, LILY THACKSTON d/o WILLIAM & VIRGINIA THACKSTON, ae 1y 5m 17d.

D: 28th ult at Leetonia, MARY E. McCLUSKEY d/o DAVID & THERESA McCLUSKEY ae 1y 1m.

D: 27th ult at his res 3 mi south of Leetonia, ANDREW BRINKER in 49th yr.

D: 22nd ult at East Fairfield, JOHN LOW, ae 74y 4m 17d.

D: 4th inst at Columbiana, WILSON SNYDER ae 27y 1m 12d.

D: 3d inst at Columbiana, MRS. REBECCA NEWHOUSE ae 87y.

D: 30th ult THERESA BETHSHEBA KIDDEY, & on the 7th inst, ELIZABETH EVALINE KIDDEY, twin daughters of CHARLES & MARIA KIDDEY, of Wellsville, aged respectively, 5 & 13 days.

D: 10th inst at Wellsville, WILLIE WELLS s/o W.G. & ESTHER WELLS, ae 4y.

D: 6th inst at Moline, Ill., ELIZABETH KERNS, formerly of Salem Tp., ae 78y 10m 6d.

D: 9th inst at Salem, ANN NICKUM, ae about 62y.

D: 2nd inst at Steubenville, HARROLD M. WARRICK, only child of J.F. & M.J.WARRICK, ae 5y 3m 10d.

D: 2nd inst at East Liverpool, ZEBULON HENRY KINSEY, ae 29y.

D: 3d inst at Salineville, MARY A. PERKINS, ae 13y 7m, & on 10th inst, ANNIE PERKINS, ae 10y 8m, daus of ELI & SARAH PERKINS.

D: 8th inst at Salineville, DAVID CUMMINGS ae 24y 2m 14d.

DEATH OF IRVIN G. PORTER, the child murderer. IRVIN G. POR-TER, who murdered his two children near Columbiana on 12th Dec 1872, & who was tried here, convicted & sentenced to life imprisonment in the penitentiary, died in that institution on Sabbath of last week. Shortly after his incarceration, he became a raving maniac & was confined in an iron cell. He never recovered his senses. He was sick but a few days.

MRS. LARWELL, relict of the late HON. JOHN LARWELL of Wooster, Oh, is on a visit to MRS. STRAUGHN. MRS. L. is a sister of the late JOSEPH STRAUGHN, & long a resident of Salem. The LARWELLS settled in Columbiana Co. as early as 1802, and in 1807, went to Wooster.

Mon 22 Nov 1875 (Vol 9 no 34)

Born in Denver, Colo., on 13th inst, MRS. M.A.McCOY, nee ADDIE WILSON, of a daughter.

MISS ALICE STEVENS of Salem, died at Newburgh on 13th inst. She was 20y, & died of congestion of the brain which was brought on by close & unremitting study while a student of Ann Arbor College, Michigan.

M: 10th inst at Oak Ridge Parsonage by REV.D.HARGEST, JAMES McMILLEN of Maidson Tp & MRS. ELIZABETH ANDREWS of Manchester VA.

M: 4th inst at Elkton by REV.W.BEDALL, GEORGE CHAMBERLAIN & MISS SARAH JANE CROFT, both of this co.

M: 18th inst by REV.D.V.HYDE, DAVID REES & MISS MARY A.-GASKILL, both of this co.

M: 21st ult at Columbiana, by REV.J.I.SWANDER, M.W.BLACKBURN & MISS SADIE E. HAYS.

M: 4th inst at the res of the bride's parents by REV.J.W.-SWICK, H.B.CROWELL & MISS AMANDA M. CHANDLER, both of co.

M: 10th inst by same, JOHN W. TAYLOR of New Baltimore, Stark Co., & MISS MAGGIE BOWMAN, of CCO.

D: 11th inst at Elkton, EDDIE BURSON s/o J & L BURSON ae 6y.

MRS. MARY PARKER, widow of the late JUDGE PARKER of Mans-field, died last week, ae 77y. MRS. PARKER was a res of New Lisbon for many years. At the time of her marriage to JUDGE PARKER, she was the widow of JUDGE GEORGE ENDLY. She was the mother of MRS. SARAH WOODBRIDGE of Youngstown.

JANE SMITH had VALENTINE JACK arrested for bastardy at Leetonia last week. A hearing had before MAYOR SCHWITZER & JACK was bound over in sume of $300 for appearance at court.

JOHN McLAUGHLIN, a former res of Columbiana, died at Orrville a short time ago.

The wife of WILLIAM WHITACRE of Pittsburgh, formerly of this place, died one day last week. She was the only daughter of ROBERT HANNA, of Cleveland.

Mon 29 Nov 1875 (Vol 9 no 35)

JOHN COVER, of Milton Tp., Mahoning Co, on the 18th, put his toe upon the hammer of his rifle & blew into the barrel to see if it was loaded. His toe slipped off & the gun dis-charged, the ball passing up through the mouth into the brain, killing him instantly.

M: 11th inst by REV.A.R.CHAPMAN, WILLIAM BURCAW & MISS SARAH E. DONNELLY, all of this co.

M: 18th inst at res of bride's parents, by REV.L.WAGNER, CHARLES GILLMAN of Mineral Ridge & MISS MARY E. KING of Washingtonville.

M: 30 Sept by REV.S.W.SWICK, WILLIAM WHAN & MISS MARY E. WILLETTS, both of this co.

M: 18th inst at Columbiana by REV.J.KENDIG, JERRY P. RIPPLE of Mahoning Co & MISS LAURA E. HUFFMAN of CCO.

M: 18th inst at Salem, BARCELIOUS G. BUELL & MISS MAGGIE A. WHITACRE.

M: 11th inst at Salem by REV.J.GRANT, DANIEL ISEMAN & MRS. ---- CAMPBELL all of Salem.

D: 14th inst ANNETTA JANE HASSIN d/o J.N. & L.N.HASSIN, of Madison Tp, ae 9m 7d.

D: 28th inst at res of his father in Wayne Tp, FRANK EWING, ae 22y.

D: 19th inst JAMES RALPH HUNTER youngest son of JAMES H. & ANNA E. HUNTER, ae 2y 4m.

D: 26th inst at Wellsville, MRS. HANNAH STEVENSON, in 74th yr

JOHN WILLETS, a well known & highly esteemed citizen of this township, died at his res near the Saltworks last Sat. morn-ing, ae 62y.

MRS. JENNIE McGINNIS, w/o GEORGE W. McGINNIS of Elkrun Tp, has been declared insane & was taken to Newburgh.

Last Sat. evening, MR. & MRS. T.C.BOONE of Salem, celebrated their 25th wedding anniversary.

MARGARET McKEE, w/o TOOLEY McKEE, has instituted suit against him, laying the damages at $3000

JAMES HUESTON is now in 88th yr, lives in Calcutta, CCO; he remembers CAPT. BRADY & ADAM & ANDREW POE.

Mon 6 Dec 1875 (Vol 9 no 36)

WM. KIDD & family of Salem, moved last Sat. to Hopewood, Almedia Co., California.

VALENTINE JACK, failing to give security of $500 for the maintenance of a bastard child born to him by MARY MYERS of Salem Tp, now domiciles in the Hotel de Fountain.

On Fri eve as the 4 o'clock train was leaving the Salem station, it struck an old man named McCARTNEY, inflicting such injuries as to cause his death.

WM. TAYLOR, for many years a butcher at Salem, dropped dead in a water closet last Thurs. morning.

M: 25th ult at Columbiana by REV.J.M.KENDIG, WILLIAM M. WOOD of New Orleans, LA & MISS JULIA BRITLAUCH, adopted daughter of A.MILLER of Columbiana.

M: 25th ult at res of bride's parents, 3 mi south of Alliance, by PROF.J.A.BUSH, WILLIAM H. HILL of New Alexander & MISS SARAH S. BARBER.

M: 4th inst in Knox Tp by REV.J.A.CLEMENT, JOHN F. WHITACRE & MISS FLORA M. WILSON, all of this co.

M: on — inst at res of bride's parents in Salem Tp by ELDER HARMON REEVES, FRANKLIN A. FILSON & MISS LYDIA FARMER.

M: 2nd inst by REV.S.STEVENSON, WILLARD L. HOWELL of Fremont Centre, Mich., & MISS MARY E. CRUMLEY of Salineville.

In Memoriam: Mt.Nebo Grange No 644, P of H, of CCO, for ANDREW BRINKER who died Oct.26th, 1875.

D: 26th ult in Knox Tp, HENRY ZIMMERMAN, ae 73?y (or 78y?)

DEATH OF ZACHARIAH RAGAN, D.D., on 27th ult at Steubenville; was Chaplain in US Army at Fort Russell, took ill, thought vacation at home would help, was stricken down on Sat. The deceased was well known in New Lisbon, having served as Pastor of the Methodist Protestant Church of New Lisbon (now occupied by MARY LAMBORN as an oyster saloon)

Mon 13 Dec 1875 (Vol 9 no 37)

ALEXANDER PATTERSON, an old & highly respected citizen of Madison Tp, died at res near the "Round Knob" Thurs morning.

BENJAMIN TEST died at res in Winona last Friday.

M: 6th inst by D.M.CAREY ESQ., SAMUEL WHITE of New Brighton PA & MISS LUCY SHARP, of Salem.

M: 25th ult at Beaver Falls PA by REV.J.I.FRASIER, REUBEN R. SALYARDS of Salineville & MISS MATTIE LYTEL of Maysville Oh

D: 7th ult at Salem, ELLA PARKER d/o SHELDON PARKER in 3d yr.

D: 28th ult at Winona SARAH J. JOHNSON w/o WILLIAM JOHNSON ae 27y.

D: 1st inat at Columbiana, BETHUNA ALMARINE TODD only child of G.E. & ALBINA TODD, ae 1y 5m 13d.

D: at Wellsville, BERTHA L. BRUNER only child of PHILIP BRUNER, ae 6y 9m.

D: 28th ult at Wellsville, CLYDE ROSS McGREGGOR, s/o CHARLES & CHARLOTTE McGREGGOR, ae 3y 5m 13d.

D: 8th inst at Wellsville, MISS MAGGIE PEEPLES, ae about 21y.

D: 9th inst REBECCA J. WALLACE of Elkrun Tp, in 35th yr.

OLD MAN FOUND DEAD: J.L.EVANS, found in JOSHUA BOWMAN'S woods, having been dead for 4 days. Fell over 9 foot precipice, & broke his neck. He was going to Gillford to visit his daughter MRS. KING; had been visiting his son, J.L.EVANS, JR., of Gillford. He was 78y old.

Mon 20 Dec 1875 (Vol 9 no 38)

STUART G. McKEE, well known printer & editor of Alliance, in company with MISS MOLLIE McGREE, has fled from that place to parts unknown, leaving behind a wife & family.

M: 7th inst at Pittsburgh PA by REV I.C.PERSHING, HENRY NIXON & MISS LILL SCAIFFE, both of Salineville.

M: 2nd inst at Leetonia by REV.J.W.SWICK, WILLIAM SYLVA & MISS MAGGIE WAGSTAFF, both of Leetonia.

M: 11th inst by WM.JOHNSON JP, JAMES A. BURTON & MISS FRANCIS McGRAHAM, all of this co.

M: 14th inst by REV.D.V.HYDE, FRANK WINDLE & MISS LIZZIE STURGEON, both of Columbiana.

D: 13th inst at Salineville, CORA LELA POWELL, d/o JAMES & ANGELINE POWELL, ae 2y 15d.

BURNED TO DEATH: we learn from the Index that last Wed.-morn, a little daughter of ARTHUR PLUNKET, of Salineville, was so badly burned she survived but a few hours. Her clothes caught fire at the grate; her parents were absent from home, & only younger children were there who could not help her.

Mon 27 Dec 1875 (Vol 9 no 39)

Suit has been commenced in Common Pleas Court of Carroll Co., by MISS FRANC WHEDON against FRANKLIN FOSTER of Minerva, for breach of promise, claiming $15,000 damages.

MARTIN EAHOLTZ & wife celebrated their crystal wedding on Christmas evening.

M: 22nd inst in Philadelphia by REV.WM.P.BREED, JOHN ROBINSON of New York City & MISS MARY MOORE of Phila.Pa.

M: 25th ult at Columbiana by REV.C.L.WINGET, WILLIAM MEGARGE & MISS TILLIE STRABLEY, all of this co.

M: 23d inst by REV.E.HINGELY, AMOS DAWSON of Smith's Ferry PA & MISS MARIA HARKER of East Liverpool.

D: 14th inst MRS. MARY FREW w/o PHILIP H. FREW of Lawrence Co Pa, ae 22y.

D: 28th ult at Lagrange Oh, GEORGE WALLACE brother of W.H.WALLACE ESQ., of Hammondsville, in 70th yr.

D: 16th inst, infant s/o REV.J.B. & MAGGIE J. WILKIN of Wellsville.

D: 22nd inst CHARLES BRINKER s/o DANIEL BRINKER JR., dec'd, of Salem Tp, ae 18y 5m.

	1876	
Jan 3,10,17,24,31	Feb 6,14,21,28	Mar 6,13,20,27
Apr 3,10,17,24	May 1,8,15,22,29	Jne 5,12,29,26
Jly 3,10,17,24,31	Aug 7,14,21,28	Sep 4,11,18,25
Oct 2,9,16,23,30	Nov 6,13,20,27	Dec 4,11,18,25.

Mon 3 Jan 1876 (Vol 9 no 40)

JOHN H. SHAW Esq, the Auditor of Carroll Co, suddenly & unexpectedly died Tues morn at about 4 o'clock.

M: 23d ult by REV G.M.ALBRIGHT, SIMON SHIVE & MISS ALICE BATES both of this co.

M: 30th ult by REV M F LUFFER, WILLIAM CLEMEN of Peppen, Prussia & MRS. CHARLOTTE VOLKERS of New Lisbon.

M: 23d ult in Salem by REV W R SPINDLER, ABEL LLOYD & MISS LUNCINA CRONICK.

M: 23d ult in Middleton by REV.C.L.WINGET, IRA KANNALS & MISS ANNIE PHILLIPS all of this co.

M: 23d ult by REV P H JONES, PATTERSON H. McDONALD of East Rochester OH & MISS LUEMMA J. MARSHALL of Carroll Co.

M: 28th ult by JOHN TRAVIS ESQ, EDWIN BENNETT & MISS MARY A. STEVENSON all of Madison Tp

M: 27th ult by J.M.DICKINSON JP H.W.BROWN & MISS JENNIE CLUNK.

M; 29th ult by REV JOHN ALFORD, J.E.GOLLADAY of New Lisbon & MISS MAGGIE DUNCAN of Beaver PA

M: 25th ult at Cliff Mine by REV VAN HORN, A.MARSH of Dorsetshire England & MISS MATTIE RIDINGER of East Liverpool

M: 28th ult by REV JOHN LONG, WILLIAM H. BARKER & MISS LOUISA ROBINSON all of E.Liverpool

M: 30th ult by REV H B FRY, G.B.COOPER of Wellsville & MISS IDA BARNABY of Salem.

M: 30th ult by REV J D BROWNLEE, JAMES C. AUGHINBAUGH & MISS JESSIE V. HAMILTON all of Wellsville

D: 31st ult SARAH C. FREDERICK w/o BYRON FREDERICK of Centre Tp ae 42y.

D: 3d ult in West Liberty Iowa, SARAH D. BATTIN formerly of Salem ae 71y 10m 12d.

D: 9th ult in Cleveland ELIZA PROBERT dau of EDWARD SMITH of Wellsville

D: 21st ult near Winona MARGARET ENGLAND ae 56y

D: 25th ult at Damascus JOEL YATES aged 66y 11m 20d

D: 27th ult in Wellsville ELIZABETH BURBECK w/o ARTHUR BURBECK

Mon 10 Jan 1876 (Vol 9 no 41)

M: 2d inst by REV G.M.ALBRIGHT, ARNOLD HARROLD & MISS MELISSA WIRTS both of this co

M: 30th ult by REV W.R. SPINDLER, HERMANN MAYERHOEFER of Pittsburgh PA & MISS ELLEN DEMING of Salem Oh

M: 29th ult by REV WM DALZELL, S.M.DALZELL of Niles OH & MISS ELNORA KING of Sharon PA

M: 23d ult at Alliance O by REV E L. FRAZIER, M.C.PETERSON of East Liverpool & MISS ELVA E. GASKILL of Alliance

M: 3d inst by H.E.FROST JP, JOHN PARKS & MISS ELLEN BRADBURY both of New Lisbon

D: 6th inst NANCY P. GREEN w/o JAMES G. GREEN of Wayne Tp ae 27y

D: 7th inst at res of her son in law PORTER HARBAUGH of New Lisbon, MRS. MARY G. BROWN ae 74y.

MRS. KATE G. WOODS of Norfolk VA is in town, called here to attend the funeral of her mother MRS. JOHN BROWN of E.Palestine

Mon 17 Jan 1876 (Vol 9 no 42)

M: 14th ult at Webster Iowa by REV M.V.BLOODGOOD, H.A.TOLERION of Salem OH & MISS FLORA E. JOHNSON.

m: 6th inst by REV HARMON REEVES, MERVIN HENDRICKS & MISS EMMA BETZ

m: 4th inst by REV.GRANT, ALBERT BARNES & MISS IDA BARINGER

m: 24th ult at Salem by same, DANIEL CAMPBELL & MISS EMMA SWARTHY

m: 11th inst at Salem by REV H.B.FRY, assisted by REV.S.M.-VERNON of Pittsburgh, R.B.RUSH M.D. & MISS MARY A. CONCLE

m: 6th inst at New Brighton PA by REV A.WILSON, GEORGE H. MACKALL of Achor & MISS MARY J.BIDDELL of New Brighton PA

M: 30th ult by J.H.CREW ESQ, BENJAMIN F. CRIST & MISS SARAH E. HARDINGER all of Butler Tp

D: 12th inst Infant son of PRESTON SMITH of E.Liv. ae 10y

D: 11th inst at Salineville infant son of JOHN M. & N.A.-HUNTER ae 11m 25d.

Mon 24 Jan 1876 (Vol 9 no 43)

MILLIARD GRIM, a res. of Washingtonville, hung himself yesterday evening in his bedroom at that place.

JAMES LAWRENCE SR., an old citizen of Lee Tp., Carroll Co, departed this life on the 11th inst.

M: 13th inst by REV J.Z.MOORE, JOHN W. HOLLOWAY & MISS CHRISTIANA H. CAMPBELL both of CCO

M: 16th inst by REV. BEDALL, F.P.ADDIS & MISS MARY HUSTON all of this co

M: 11th inst at the res of the bride's parents by rev J.W.SWICK, LAWRENCE CHANDLER & MISS ELLA ATTERHOLT both of this co.

M: 23d inst by J.M.DICKINSON JP, JAMES CROUCH & MISS JENNIE WHAN all of this place.

D: 6th inst at Leetonia CLARENCE N. FARMER s/o SAMUEL J. & MARY A. FARMER ae 6y 4m 24d

D: 7th inst near Leetonia, SARAH ZIMMERMAN ae 43y 8m 9d

D: 9th inst at Leetonia son of A.W. & MARY LEWIS AE 3 wks

D: 15th inst at East Liverpool MRS.G.PEPIN in her 59th yr

D: 12th inst at Indianapolis IN LENA MAY LEWIS d/o C.H. & ANNIE LEWIS formerly of this place ae 8m 3d

D: 13th inst at Salem BESSIE BUMBAUGH d/o JOHN & RACHEL BUMBAUGH ae 14m

D: 18th inst at her home in Elkrun Tp, MRS. MARIA BELL widow of JOSEPH BELL

FAMILY REUNION: ON Wed 19th inst the children, & grandchildren of HENRY STOCK met by chance at the res of his son SAMUEL STOCK, near town. The gathering was a happy one. It is equally true that it called up sad recollections of the dear departed. There were present the venerable HENRY STOCK now in his 82nd yr, WILLIAM STOCK & FAM., SAMUEL STOCK & FAM., JASON STOCK, REBECCA W/o JACOB SPRINGER, MARIA W/o BENJAMIN HOYLES of Wood Co Oh & ELIZABETH W/o JAMES TROTTER of Washington Co. HENRY STOCK came to this co aobut the year 1805 & has resided here ever since. He was married to MINERVA STALCUP who died about 40y ago. He has 2 sisters living whom he has not seen for 21 yrs. The afternoon was spent very quietly & pleasantly.

MISS MOLLIE McGREW is out with a letter of denying the charge of eloping with one S.G.McKEE of Alliance, as published in a number of our exchanges. She asserts that she left home for the west several months ago, is at present teaching school in Richland Center, Wis. and she knows nothing whatever as to the whereabouts of Mr.McKEE.

MRS. HANNAH HUSONG w/o F.T.HUSONG died at Akron last Wed morn of consumption ae 42y 1m 25d. The dec'd was the dau of M & N. BRIDENSTINE of Col.Co.

Mon 31 Jan 1876 (Vol 9 no 44)

Front page story on History of schools of New Lisbon.

MRS. ALLISON of Washingtonville, this county, is 86 yrs of age & occasionally walks from that place to Leetonia.

M: 26th inst at res of ROBERT SHAW by REV G.N.JOHNSTON, GEORGE GROOMS & MISS JENNIE HELTZEL all of this co.

M: 11th inst by REV H.P.BORTON, MISS LIZZIE SHRIVER & OSBORN SHREVE all of this co.

M: 20th inst by D.M.CAREY JP, LEWIS FEHL & MISS ANNIE STARKE all of this co.

D: 7th inst at Leetonia, KETURAH ABLETTE ae 29y 24d.

D: 23d inst at Col'ana, MISS ANNA E. ROBERTSON d/o D. & MARTHA ROBERTSON, in 24th yr.

D: 26th inst ELIZABETH BARNES w/o THOMAS BARNES of Elkrun Tp ae 43y 13d.

D: 26th inst at the Infirmary, JOHN WAY, aged about 63y.

Mon 6 (sic) Feb 1876 (Vol 9 no 45)

M: 27th ult at Salem by C.L.WINGET, M.P.CANS & MISS E.C.CARPENTER all of CCO

M: 23d ult by REV.WM.BAXTER, JAMES CLUNK & MISS JENNIE LAMBORN all of this co

D: 27th ult OLIVER HECK of CCO ae 46y.

D: 28th ult of typhoid fever, MISS ELLA M. BELL of Col'ana

D: 30th ult PATRICK MELON of Centre Tp ae 70y.

D: 2nd inst wife of JESSE SMITH of Smith's Ferry PA ae about 57y.

Suicide by hanging: EDWIN BENNETT residing 1 1/2 miles NE of West Point, this co, committed suicide on last Fri morning by hanging himself in the barn. BENNETT was a carpenter by trade about 39y years of age & was married about 5 weeks ago.

Suicide by shooting: on last Fri, JOSEPH VALE a son of JOHN T. VALE ESQ., of East Carmel this co, armed with a revolver, went to the barn & committed suicide by shooting himself.- Deceased was about 35y of age & unmarried.

DEATH OF MRS. ANN BARBARA GLASS: MRS. ANNA BARBARA GLASS, consort of JOHN GLASS deceased & mother of ELDER LEWIS GLASS, died at the res of her son JACOB GLASS in West Tp on 19th ult at the advanced age of 94y 5m27d. The posterity of these parents, as accurately as could be ascertained, is 9 children, 70 grchildren, 157 gt grch & 21 gt gt grch. Her remains were deposited in the New Alexander Cemetery. The funeral service was conducted by Revs. CARSON, SHIVELY & CLEMENT.

Mon 14 Feb 1876 (Vol 9 no 46)

M: 2nd inst at Salem by REV.J.GRANT, WALLACE W. WELKER & MISS ANNIE M. WEST.

M: 25th ult at Wellsville by REV.VAN HORN, CURTIS W. ATKINSON of that place & miss LIZZIE M. BARNARD of Woodstock, Ontario.

M: 29th ult by JOHN WEAVER ESQ, MARTIN DEVINE & MRS. HONORA HANLEY all of Salineville.

D: 5th inst near North Benton, LEORA K. BLACKBURN d/o B.J. & MARY BLACKBURN ae 2y 4m.

D: 30th ult at Leetonia infant daughter of SAMUEL & MARY HAVIC ae 3y.

D: 2nd inst at Leetonia infant son of JOHN & MARGARET HARRIGAN.

D: 3rd ult at Erie PA CLIFFORD LOCKE youngest brother of E.B.LOCKE of Leetonia ae 7y 8m

D: 24th ult at Leetonia MARY MOORE d/o JAMES & MARY MOORE ae 3y 5m 5d.

D: 7th inst at Wellsville MRS. AGNES McKINNELL ae 76y.

D: 4th inst at Colorado Springs WILL A. SMITH of Wellsville ae 21y.

D: 3d inst HOMER WILSON VAUGHN s/o WILLIAM S. & LYDIA VAUGHN of Yellow Creek Tp ae 2y 8m.

D: 27th ult at Rochester PA JAMES ADAMS HENDERSON only child of SAMUEL & ELIZABETH HENDERSON of Wellsville ae 9m 4d.

D: 11th inst MARY HANLIN d/o JAMES & MARY HANLIN of St.Petersburgh PA & grandchild of PATRICK FINDLEY of Wellsville whom the mother was visiting, aged 2y.

Court proceedings:
SUSAN J. FOWLER vs WILLIAM FOWLER decree for divorce & $1000 alimony.

Mon 21 Feb 1876 (Vol 9 no 47)

M: 17th inst by REV.G.N.JOHNSTON, LEONARD McLAUGHLIN & MISS NANNIE VAN FOSSEN all of this co.

M: 15th inst by REV DAVID HARGEST, EDWIN L. MARTIN & MISS CLARA M. McCASKEY all of Madison Tp.

D: 16th inst FRANK WILES of New Lisbon ae 58y.

D: 6th inst at Salem NATHAN H. ARMSTRONG ae 73y.

D: 9th inst at McKeesport PA, LIZZIE MILLER youngest d/o FRANK & SUE MILLER formerly of New Lisbon, ae 1y 9m 5d.

D: 9th inst at Salem MRS. NANCY OZENGER w/o A. OZENGER after a lingering sickness ae 30y.

D: 1st inst at Springfield OH, MRS. H.J.CREIGHTON formerly MISS HELEN BEAUMONT of Salem.

D: 14th inst at East Liverpool, EMMA CROXALL d/o MRS. EMMA CROXALL, widow of THOMAS CROXALL, in 17th yr of her age.

D: 15th inst at East Liverpool, HARRIET WILSON ae 57y.

D: 17th inst at Wellsville, JOHN DUNCAN, aged ---y.

Birthday celebration: on last Tues, the 15th inst, the children, grandchildren & great-grandchildren of MRS. TABITHA CRAIN widow of JOHN CRAIN, met at the residence of MADISON VIERS of Salem Tp. to celebrate her 87th birthday.- MRS. CRAIN has long been a resident of Salem Tp., having with her husband settled on the farm where she now resides more than 60 years ago.

Court proceedings: WILLIAM R. GRANGER vs MINA GRANGER, divorce granted to plaintiff.

A terrible accident occurred near Youngstown last Mon evening. MRS. RACHEL APPLEGATE, aged 84y, was sitting near the fire in her room when by some means not explained, her clothing caught fire & she was enveloped in flames when discovered by a person who happened to enter a room. By throwing bedclothes around her the fire was extinguished but she was already horribly burned; and after a night of great agony, she died Tues. morning.

Mon 28 Feb 1876 (Vol 9 no 47)

M: 16th inst by REV.A.B.MAXWELL, E.S.HALIBURT of Erie PA & MISS FANNIE HARPER of Leetonia O.

M: 24th inst by REV G.M.ALBRIGHT, THOMAS E. LODGE & MISS CLARA E. BRINKER all of this co.

M: 15th inst at Salem by ELDER CAMERON, WILLIAM MOTE of Indiana & MISS LYDIA E. COFFEE of this co.

M: 22nd inst at Salem by MAYOR DUNLAP, NATHANIEL RALPH & MISS ELNORA OLIVER.

M: 25th inst at Salineville by JOHN WEAVER ESQ., JOHN C. McDANIEL of Carroll Co & MISS MAGGIE M. LEISHMAN of Salineville.

D: 22nd inst, infant son of J.B. & E.W.WILSON of Elkrun Tp

D: 17th inst at the Valley P.O., ARTHUR HOOPS s/o WILLIAM & LUCINDA HOOPS, aged 4 mo.

D: 4th inst at Colorado Springs, WILL.A.SMITH of Wellsville aged 21y.

D: 9th inst at Canfield, L.L.BOSTWICK in his 71st year.

D: 11th at Clarkson, MRS. R.A.FLOWERS aged about 22y.

D: 9th inst at Salineville, BERNARD O'DONNELL ae 14y 6m.

MRS. MICHAEL HENRY, an old & highly respected widow lady of Columbiana, died at that place last Thurs.

Mon 6 Mar 1876 (Vol 9 no 49)

M: 1st inst at res of bride's parents by REV.G.N.JOHNSTON, WILLIAM C. FLUGAN & MISS CLARA MILLER, all of this place.

M: 2nd inst by EDWARD PETTIT JP, JOHN L. CALDWELL & MISS MARY J. CRAWFORD, all of this co.

M: 23d ult at Pittsburgh PA by REV.ANDERSON, JOHN L. DOUGLASS of Wilkesville, Vinton Co Oh & MISS S. AMANDA RAYL of East Liverpool Oh.

D: 25th ult at Salineville, MRS. MARY JANE WILLIAMS, w/o JOSEPH B. WILLIAMS, in her 38th yr.

D: 29th ult at East Liverpool, MISS JULIA HUMRICKHOUSE.

D: 14th ult in Sullivan Co., Ind., JOSEPH CANAAN, formerly of this co., aged 76y.

Mon 13 Mar 1876 (Vol 9 no 50)

M: 6th inst by REV.LEW, JAMES TOMPKINS of Salem & MISS EMMA C. MYERS of Steubenville.

M: 2nd inst at Ohioville, Beaver Co.,Pa., by SANFORD ALMY ESQ., JAMES COCHRAN & MISS NANCY GREEN, both of East Liverpool OH

D: 9th inst MARY EMMA BRINKER, w/o HOMER BRINKER & d/o SAMUEL & ELIZABETH C. STOCK, aged 19y 7m 10d.

D: 2nd inst at the Infirmary, GEORGE DARRY, aged 65y.

D: 1st inst at Leetonia, LUCY W. BAYARD, ae 5y 2m 8d.

D: 4th inst at Leetonia, MRS. KATIE DENNEY in her 29th yr.

D: 6th inst at East Liverpool, SARAH ANN SMITH, d/o HENRY SMITH ae 8y 3m.

D: 29th ult at Vanport, Beaver Co Pa, JAMES DOUDS s/o JOHN & ELIZABETH DOUDS, formerly of East Liverpool, Oh.

D: 7th inst at Leetonia, JESSIE LOCKE, infant d/o E.B. & LILA LOCKE.

D: 8th inst at Omaha Neb., MOSES McLAUGHLIN, father of W. McLAUGHLIN of this place & formerly a resident of this county, aged about 87y.

D: 23d ult at Salineville, MAGGIE BURNIP, aged 6y 3m, and on the 25th ult, WILLIE BURNIP, aged 4y, children of MATTHEW & MARGARET A. BURNIP.

D: 3d inst at Columbiana, BENNETT G. BAKER, ae 36y 10m 18d.

WILLIAM CARTWRIGHT SR., a prominent citizen of East Liverpool, died last Tues. of paralysis.

Mon 20 Mar 1876 (Vol 9 no 51)

Alliance has a centenarian in the person of DENNIS QUINN, who was born June 10th, 1775.

JAMES McCANAHEY, formerly of Alliance, has been murdered in Cheyenne Co., Neb.

M: 9th inst at New Waterford, by J.Z.MOORE, SANFORD C. BOOTH & MISS EMMA TODD.

M: 7th inst at Pittsburgh by REV.WM.P.TURNER, WM.HENRY CARY of East Liverpool & MISS CHARLOTTE M. REASNER of Cannonsburgh PA

M: 16th inst by REV. WILLIAM BAXTER, STANTON BAKER & MISS VELINA HOLLOWAY both of this co.

D: 6th inst JOHN EDWARD LUCAS infant s/o THOMAS F. & KATE LUCAS.

D: Wed morn Mar 15th in her 26th yr, MRS. VIRGINIA A. WALLACE w/o STACY WALLACE & d/o DAVID & SUSAN F. BROWN. Born in Columbiana Co., was married on 26th June last. (long obit)

D: 7th inst at Centerdale, Iowa, JOSEPH BALL, formerly of Salem, aged 73y.

D: 10th inst at Wellsville, MARY RYAN, a native of the parish of Callen, Kilkenny Co., Ireland, & wife of PATRICK FENNELLY, aged 55y.

D: 13th inst at Salem, STACY COOK, aged 86y.

J.W.STITT, s/o JAMES STITT of Salem, died in Heren Texas on 12th Feb of consumption.

Mon 27 Mar 1876 (Vol 9 no 52)

M: 16th inst at Salem by MAYOR DUNLAP, NICHOLAS DELLER & MISS SINA E. ILER of Butler Tp.

M: 4th inst in New Garden by E.GARSIDE ESQ, JOSEPH J. WINDLE & MISS SUSANA KIRK, all of this co.

M: 22nd inst at the Cowan House in this place by J.M.DICKINSON ESQ., JOHN W. DETWILER & MISS MATTIE A. GRONER, all of this co.

M: 20th inst by WILLIAM GILSON JP, EMERY CLECKNER & MISS SARAH HANLEY, all of Salineville.

M: 15th inst at Newport, KY, by REV.G.BROWN, J.P.HANNA of Pittsburgh & MRS. A.H.THOMAS.

M: 15th inst by REV.WM.T.BEATTY, CHARLES S. BAILEY & MISS KATE L. McCARTY, of Smith's Ferry PA.

M: 14th inst at res of ISAAC HUGHES, J.B.BRUBACHER of Elk Point, Dakota Territory, & MISS REBECCA E. CARPENTER of New Lisbon, OH.

M: 23d inst by REV.S.M.DAVIS, JNO.W.RUSSELL & MISS LUCY SWEARINGEN, all of Wellsville.

D: 19th inst at Columbiana, GEORGE E. WEAVER s/o HENRY B. & LUCENA WEAVER aged 4m 12d.

D: 13th inst at Columbiana, MRS EMMA FERRELL, w/o EDMOND FERRELL, aged 30y.

D: 17th inst JOHN E. BRADFIELD of Scioto Co Ohio, formerly of Col.Co., aged ----y.

D: 26th inst NANNIE CAMERON d/o DAVID CAMERON of Wayne Tp, aged 19y. (see also 3 Apr)

Mon 3 Apr 1876 (Vol 10 No 1)

M: 12th ult near Centerview, VA, by REV.THOMAS W. GREER, J.L.TAYLOR, formerly of Carroll Co Oh & MISS MARY HARVEY of Charlotte Co VA

M: 30th ult at the res of the bride by REV.O.V.W.CHANDLER, CHARLES W. CLARK & MISS LIZZIE H. McCARTY, both of Steubenville.

M: 30th ult at res of bride's father by HENRY E. FROST, JP, THEODORE SANDERS & MISS EMMA SPENCE.

D: 26th ult NANCY BELL CAMERON d/o DAVID CAMERON of Wayne Tp, aged 22y. (see also 27 Mar)

D: 18th ult at Salem, MRS. ANNA L. DAVIS, ae 78y 3m 25d.

D: 20th ult in Salem Tp, ZEPHAS DICKINSON, aged 84y.

D: 21st ult at Salem, ADA E. BAKER d/o MARY JANE BAKER ae 2y 10m.

D: 28th ult, at Salem, infant d/o ELIAS LACY.

D: 22nd ult in Goshen Tp, SARAH MATHERS w/o THOMAS MATHERS ae 63y.

D: 21st ult MRS. MURRAY mother of JOHN MURRAY of Hanover Tp., aged 82y.

D: 1st inst ALEXANDER TODD of Wayne Tp ae 91y.

D: 26th ult MERVIN McCORD, s/o JAMES & MARY McCORD of Wayne Tp, ae 3y 1m 14d.

The late ROBERT HARRIS: ROBERT HARRIS, late station agent of the Niles & New Lisbon Railway, died at the res. of his parents in this place of pneumonia Tues morning last aged 21y 5m 15d.

ANDREW McPHERSON, s/o ANDREW McPHERSON SR., of Madison Tp., died at Pioche, Nevada on 15th ult from injuries received from a horse. He was aged 40y.

Mon 10 Apr 1876 (Vol 10 no 2)

M: 4th inst by REV.A.R.CHAPMAN, EDWARD WALLACE & MISS MATILDA PATTERSON all of this co.

M: 22nd ult at Humboldt, Neb., S.M.PHILPOT & MISS WINNIE A. MOON.

M: 29th ult at Columbiana by REV.C.L.WINGET, EVERETT FARMER & MRS. SARAH McKEE all of this co.

M: 23d ult at the res of bride's parents by REV.JOSEPH HORNER of Pittsburgh, CHARLES HORNER, of the same place & MISS HATTIE E. MASON, d/o JOHN MASON ESQ., of CCO.

M: 28th ult at New Albany Oh by REV.H.B.FRY, JOHN B. SHEPHERD & MISS ISABELLA AULD.

D: 28th ult in Middleton Tp, WILLIAM FARR, ae 80y 3m.

D: 2nd inst at Iowa City, REV.ALCINOUS YOUNG, formerly pastor of the M.E.Church of this place, in his ----yr.

D: 2nd inst in Wellsville, WILLIE C. FORY, s/o SAMUEL & MARGARET FORY, aged 13y.

D: 3d inst at Wellsburg WVa, JAMES R. ABRAHAM brother of T.J.ABRAHAM of Wellsville, aged 64y.

D: 5th inst WILLIAM GAUZE of Centre Tp ae 58y 6m.

D: 4th inst, LYDIA A. VANCE w/o FRANK VANCE of this place ae 28y 6m.

D: 30th ult near Greenvillage, HIRAM T. CALLAHAN, ae 26y.

D: 19th ult at Salem, LENORA MAY BEESON, d/o O.J. & SIDNEY A. BEESON, ae 8y.

D: 3d inst at Salem, EFFIE BEESON, d/o O.J. & SIDNEY A. BEESON, ae 18m.

D: 8th inst JAMES WOODS of Fairfield Tp, ae 67y.

D: 8th inst GEORGANNA WOODWORTH, d/o P.H.WOODWORTH of Centre Tp, ae 9y 1m 14d.

MRS. LAURA N. HAYS d/o JACOB STEWART of Wellsville, died morning of 1st inst at Missouri City, MO. Her remains were brought to Wellsville for interment.

GEORGE T. RIDDLE, a well known business man of Wellsville, on Mon. last, deserted a wife & 5 children, to follow the fortunes or misfortunes of a young widow named HUNTSMAN, an unscrupulous adventuress. The guilty pair have gone to Canada.

Mon 17 Apr 1876 (Vol 10 no 3)

M: 12th inst by J.M.DICKSON, JP, EDWARD BUTLER of this place & MISS ELIZABETH FRANCIS of Salem.

M: 11th inst near Wellsburg WVa, THEODORA DARE of East Liverpool & MISS LAURA BUCKEY.

M: 16th inst at Salem by D.M.CAREY, JP, EDGAR FRENCH & MISS EMMA VANCYOC all of this co.

D: 11th inst ELIZABETH BOUGH of New Lisbon ae 95y 8m 11d.

D: 11th inst at the Infirmary, RACHEL BEARD of Middleton Tp, aged 63y.

D: 6th inst at Allegheny City, infant d/o JOHN & NELLIE BOWER aged 3m.

D: 12th inst at East Liverpool, SAMUEL CRAWFORD in 76th yr.

D: 11th inst LEVADA C. REED infant d/o A.C. & S.V.REED of Wellsville.

D: 14th inst infant child of JONAS & SARAH BRIDENSTEIN of this place, aged 10d.

THOMAS SWEET, who was recently severely injured in a coal bank, died at his res at this place on Wed eve ae 45y.

JAMES WOODS, residing about 2 miles east of Columbiana, died on the 7th inst, aged 67y.

Mon 24 Apr 1876 (Vol 10 no 4)

M: 13th inst at Columbiana by REV.C.L.WINGET, EDWIN MEESE & MISS OLIVE FOUTZ both of Salem.

M: 5th inst at Salem by REV.W.R.SPINDLER, HOMER LEONARD of Trumbull Co & MISS LOUISA KINNAMAN of Mahoning Co.

M: 11th inst at Enon Valley, PA, CHARLES M. WATSON & MISS ANNIE CRAINE all of this co.

M: 18th inst at Smith's Ferry PA by JOHN McFALL ESQ., FRED. SHACKLETON & MRS. ISABELLA JACKSON, both of East Liverpool.

M: 16th inst by REV.E.A.BRINDLEY, JAMES LEIGH & MISS SARAH THACKERAY, both of East Liverpool.

M: 19th inst at res of RUTH BYE near New Garden by S.T.TEEGARDEN, MR. O.H.WHITELEATHER & MISS LIL A. BYE.

M: by the same ceremony, J.G.BYE & MISS ANNA WOOLF.

WILLIAM GRAHAM, aged nearly 100 years, and the father of 17 children, died in Beaver Co. a few days ago. He voted for THOMAS JEFFERSON & at every election since. He also served in the War of 1812.

D: 16th inst SARAH ELIZABETH COBURN of Wayne Tp ae 47y.

D: 18th inst at Infirmary, ARIEL RUSSELL of Knox Tp ae 71y.

D: 10th inst at Leetonia, JAMES McINTOSH, ae 28y 10m 9d.

D: 16th inst MRS. ANN RANDEL, one of the oldest citizens of Butler Tp, CCO.

D: 20th inst JOSEPH GREEN, s/o WAVERLY & LUCY GREEN of this place, aged 7m.

D: 19th inst MRS. CHARLOTTE SCHLEY of Wayne Tp, ae 86y.

D: 22nd inst EMILY MARY MARTIN d/o SAMUEL & JANE MARTIN of Centre Tp, ae 2m.

D: 20th inst in Hanover, SARAH SWEARINGEN w/o ELIMELECH SWEARINGEN, ae 81y 9m 12d.

D: 17th inst MISS MARY J. BLYTHE of East Liverpool

Mon 1 May 1876 (Vol 10 no 5)

DEATH OF HENRY ATEN, SR. A Centenarian Gone. We learn from the "Union" that at about 3 o'clock Fri morning, the 28th ult, HENRY ATEN, the oldest man probably in Ohio, breathed his last breath at the home of his daughter, MRS. CATLETT of Wellsville, where he had made his home for a number of years past. MR. ATEN was born in Northumberland Co PA Sep.23,1773- He located at Pittsburgh in 1800, in 1804 he married MARY MORGAN & in 1806 came to this county.

JAMES BLACKBURN, formerly of East Palestine, died near MT.JACKSON, Lawrence Co Pa a few days ago. He at one time represented Col.Co. in the Ohio Legislature & cast his vote at Unity Tp. polls for 60 consecutive years. Aged 86y.

WALTER LOCKARD of Hanover Tp was brought to town Thurs.-morn. by CONSTABLE WEST, having been bound over to court under the bastardy act.

M: On 30th ult at Albia Iowa, by REV.CLARK, M.V.COUSINS of the above place & MISS FANNIE BENNETT d/o H.BENNETT ESQ., formerly of West Point, this co.

D: 29th ult ANASTACIA MEISTER w/o JOHN MEISTER of Wayne Tp, ae 83y.

D: 28th ult MARY L. IKIRT, w/o GEORGE P. IKIRT of Madison Tp, aged 23y.

ANOTHER PIONEER GONE: MRS. ELIZA GRAHAM of this place, relict of the late GEORGE GRAHAM, departed this life on Thurs night, Apr 28th, aged 88y. She was the mother of REV.JOHN B. GRAHAM of Holiday's Cove WVA, DR.JAMES GRAHAM of Cincinnati, GEORGE GRAHAM of Terre Haute, IN & MRS. DR.-FRIES of Cincinnati.

JAMES HENDERSON of this township, one of the old pioneers, died at the res of his son Wed last. He was 96 yrs of age.

AN ATROCIOUS CRIME ! A YOUNG WOMAN OUTRAGED ! Eleven of the fiends bound over to court. On the 16th ult in Salem Tp, near Franklin Square Station, a young woman aged 21y, accompanied by a young man, passed the depot at Leetonia, going west, when they were grossly insulted by a gang of ruffians congregated at the station. They followed & soon there were 15 to 20 ruffians. They stoned & clubbed the young man & he fled for his own safety. They caught the girl, some of the villans holding her while others committed upon her person their hellish designs. NELSON McCANN forced them to stop. Her name was DRUSILLA HANNAH. She was found 4 days later at her brother in law's near Alliance. Fifteen were arrested & held for a preliminary hearing:

JOSEPH DOLAN	FRANK MEEK
WILLIAM FAIRFIELD	TIM RYAN
JOHN McGUIRE	JOHN TOOLE
JOHN HELDT	JOHN BALL
PETER FLEMING	"DOC" McILLVAINE
GEORGE NANGLE	PATRICK GAFFNEY
WILLIAM JACK	JOHN HUGHES
JOHN RIPPLEY	ADAM SUMMERVILLE

On last Tues, a preliminary trial was held at Franklin Square, & the little village was thronged with people from all the surrounding towns to hear the case. Trial opened at 10 o'clock & continued until 4 pm. First witness was Miss DRUSILLA HANNAH, aged 21y, lives Alliance; has parents in New Castle. NELSON McCANN & FIRMAN ALBRIGHT testified against the ruffians. CHARLIE BROWN, the young man who was her escort, substantiated the statements of the girl. Each was bound over in the sum of $800 at the May term of court with the exception of WILLIAM JACK, JOSEPH DOLAN, JOHN RIPPLEY & JOHN HUGHES, who were acquitted. [another column, same page says: DRUSILLA HANNAH & CHARLIE BROWN, the criminating witnesses in the Franklin Square rape case, were brought to town last Fri & placed in prison. They are held in order that they may not be tampered with & spirited away, and thus thwart the ends of justice.] 2 full columns of testimony.

Mon 8 May 1876 (Vol 10 no 6)

M: 2nd inst at Salem by REV.W.R.SPINDLER, JOSEPH T. SMITH & MISS CALLIE H. PYLE, all of this co.

M: 2nd inst at Salem, JOHN WOODRUFF & MISS F. GRANT.

M: 4th inst by REV.G.M.ALBRIGHT, ADAM MILLER & MISS MARY E. MITCHEL, both of Gillford, this co.

M: 25th ult by REV.A.T.BELL, JOHN HICKMAN of St.Clair OH & MISS MARY A. JORDAN, of Washington Co Pa.

M: 9th inst at the res of bride's parents by REV.J.S.BROAD-WELL, DR. N.E.WRIGHT & MRS. LIZZIE A. SMITH, all of Berea,Oh.

D: 1st inst in Elkrun Tp, MR.G.A.BLAIR in his 79th yr.

JOSEPH THOMPSON, well known in this vicinity, & at one time Representative from this co. in the State Legislature & also sheriff of this co., died at the res of his son in law, W.L. YOUNG of this place at about 9 o'clock this morning, aged 82y.

SUDDEN DEATH: On last Sat. morning, says the Columbiana "Register",CHRISTIAN HIVELY of that place. He leaves a wife and 2 children. He was about 33y.

Mon 15 May 1876 (Vol 10 no 7)

DICK BURNETT was the first of "Judge Lynch" in the Black Hills country. They hung Dick for stealing a horse & shooting a man while on a drunk. He was raised in Steubenville.

M: 14th inst by REV.A.R.CHAPMAN, SAMUEL McGOWAN & MISS JENNIE ARTER, all of this place.

D: 9th inst in Elkrun Tp, HANNAH MONTGOMERY, aged 70y.

D: 11th inst in Elkrun Tp, JAMES BOUGH, aged 44y.

SUDDEN DEATH: HENRY JAMES BOUGH, an unmarried man, aged about 40y, died suddenly last Thurs. morning.

Mon 22 May 1876 (Vol 10 no 8)

BENJAMIN ANTRIM, an old citizen of Salem, died last Sunday morn. He had been confined to the house by sickness for the past year.

DEATH OF JOSEPH THOMPSON (long obit) He was born in Loudoun Co VA near a posttown called Wheatland, on 10 Feb 1794, & moved to Ohio with his father whose name was also JOSEPH.- The family settled in the northern part of Middleton Tp. They arrived in Ohio in December 1804.

EDWARD CRAWFORD, residing near Williamsport, aged about 80y, fell from his chair a few days ago & immediately expired.

On last Thurs afternoon, R.W.TAYLOR, JR., Editor of the "Buckeye State", & MISS HELEN VANCE, one of New Lisbon's fairest daughters, were united in the bonds of matrimony.- The ceremony was performed by REV.A.R.CHAPMAN, Pastor of the ME Church & witnessed by many relatives & friends.

M: 18th inst by REV.WM.BAXTER, N.B.BILLINGSLEY & MISS MARY WALLACE, d/o J.H.WALLACE ESQ, all of this place.

M: 19th inst by J.M.DICKINSON, JP, ROBERT STEWART & MISS MARTHA FORD, all of this place.

M: 13th inst by REV.L.B.KING, F.SMITH of Salem & MISS EMMA R. WEST of Hanover.

D: on —th inst at Columbiana, DAVID GLOSSER in 75th yr.

D: 14th inst at the Infirmary, JAMES MORGAN of Hanoverton, aged 77y.

D: 21st inst at res of her brother JOHN McINTOSH of Wayne Tp, MARGARET McINTOSH, aged 80y.

D: 15th inst MRS. SUSAN R. GIBBONS of Wellsville ae 65y 5m 21d

D: 15th inst ALBERT MARTIN s/o JAMES MARTIN ae 32y.

Mon 29 May 1876 (Vol 10 no 9)

M: 18th inst at Columbiana by REV.A.E.WARD, ELI BRICKER & MISS EMMA LONG, all of this co.

M: 17th inst at Columbiana by D.ROBERTSON JP, WILLIAM A. DOTY & MISS SUSAN HARMON all of this co.

M: 16th inst by REV.MURPHY, CHARLEY MULHERRIN of Summitville & MISS KATE DEVINNEY of Chillicothe, Oh.

M: 25th inst by REV.A.R.CHAPMAN, A.B.CRUBAUGH of Mt.Union & MISS JENNIE PARSONS all of this co.

M: 26th ult near Pittsburgh PA by REV.F.R.HOTRING, MICHAEL FISHER of East Liverpool & MISS ISABELLA HICKMAN of Allegheny Co PA.

D: 22nd inst WILLIE E. MANNING infant s/o J.W. & J.M.MANNING of Salineville aged 1y 26d.

D: 22nd inst ELIZA J. SWITZER d/o JAMES & CATHARINE SWITZER of Elkrun Tp, ae 22y 3m 3d.

Mon 5 June 1876 (Vol 10 no 10)

DEATH OF JOSEPH J. SCROGGS: JOSEPH J. SCROGGS died at his res at Westport Tues eve May 30th. At his death, CAPT. SCROGGS was 41y 6m of age & leaves a widow & 4 children. He was a native of West Point & the son of REV. SCROGGS of that place. He was active with the UP Church & was buried Thurs from his late residence & his remains were deposited in the family burying ground at Calcutta.

M: 25th ult by JOHN BRINDLEY JP, EDWARD LEIGH & MISS NANCY CLAYPOOL, both of East Liverpool.

M: 25th ult by same, THOMAS FARMER & MISS JENNIE LAUGHLIN, all of East Liverpool.

M: 29th ult by REV.W.R.SPINDLER, ALEXANDER McCORMICK & MISS MARGARET DICKENBAUGH, all of Salem.

M: 31st ult by REV.A.R.CHAPMAN, WILLIAM HAINSON & MISS ELIZABETH VERNER of East Liverpool.

M: 10th ult at Smith's Ferry by SQUIRE PETTIT, DAVID ORR & MRS. ELIZA THOMPSON, both of Waterford, Oh.

M: 30th ult at the Wilbur Meeting House by Friends ceremony, CHARLES GAMBLE & MARTHA HALL.

D: 31st ult WILLIAM ROBERT THOMPSON s/o WILLIAM & ISABELLA THOMPSON ae 3m.

D: 30th ult MRS. SAMUEL D. WILSON of Salem ae 27y 6m 15d.

D: 2nd inst THOMAS HAWKINS of Elkrun Tp ae 94y 3m.

D: 26th ult in Franklin Tp, EDDIE JOSEPH CARY s/o BERNARD & SUSAN CARY ae 11y.

Mon 12 June 1876 (Vol 10 no 11)

Court proceedings: EDITH COOK vs ALEXANDER W. COOK decree for divorce & alimony.

A reunion of the FREDERICK family took place on last Wed at the res of MRS. LYDIA WALTERS. 47 Persons were present & partook of an excellent dinner prepared for the occasion. The guests were J.C.PIKE & wife, WILHELMINA CALDWELL & dau., B.F.FREDERICK & wife, CHARLES CROOK & wife, R.G.EELLS & wife, JOHN A. MYERS, wife & dau, JASON GREEN & wife, BYRON FREDE-RICK, PEGGY GREEN & ELIZABETH FREDERICK, each over 80 years of age, DAVID WALTER, wife,son & dau., HARRISON WALTER, wife & children, W.C.SHERBINE, wife, son & dau., THOMAS WALTER, wife & children, MISS ALCY WHITACRE, 2 daus of IVAN LODGE of Iowa, & MRS. CATHARINE ADAMS. All the Frederick family, B.F. & 6 sisters were present except THOMAS who resides in Baltimore. We understand this family will hold a reunion picnic this fall.

M: 8th inst by REV. WM. BAXTER, ALFRED DOZZLE of Massillon & MISS KATE HARPER of this place.

M: 18th ult by REV.J.CLEMENT, GEORGE D. SUMMER of West Tp & MISS ELIZABETH A. FISHER of Knox Tp.

M: 31st ult in Allegheny City by REV.J.C.MELOY, PROF. J.B.-LUTTON of Pulaski PA & MISS NANNIE JEFFERY of Wellsville Oh.

M: 3d inst by REV.ROBERT HAYS, GEORGE SOWERS & MISS MARY O. BIRCH, both of Salineville.

M: 4th inst in Augusta, Carroll Co by ELDER O. EBERT, JOSEPH HARRISON of New Alexandria & MELINDA COULSON of Hanover Station.

M: 5th inst by FATHER LINDERSMITH, JOSEPH DOWLING & HANNAH McMANIMON.

D: 8th inst MRS. JANE LOUDEN of Wayne Tp ae 71y 11m.

D: 6th inst wife of WILLIAM ROSE of Wellsville ae ---y.

Mon 19 June 1876 (Vol 10 no 12)

Court proceedings: CATHERINE McLAUGHLIN vs JOHN McLAUGHLIN, divorce granted to petitioner on payment of costs.

A reunion of the TEEGARDEN family was held at res of URIAL TEEGARDEN, SR., of Salem Tp. last Tues. Eight children of the late REV. WILLIAM TEEGARDEN were present. Their united ages in round numbers footed up to 560 years & their average height was 6 feet. The members of this family were widely separated, one or more being residents of the following states: Ohio, Indiana, Wisconsin & California. The time was spent in pleasant & social intercourse in which was related for the entertainment of each other, reminiscences of their lives since their separation. In the evening, they repaired to the Hart Church cemetery & paid a tribute of memory of father & mother, by decorating their graves with choice flowers.

SUICIDE: the people of Knox Tp were startled Sat. eve by the report that a young man named STACKHOUSE, living in West Tp, had committed suicide by shooting himself thru the heart. It appears that he had been paying attention to a young lady named HEACOCK, who was teaching school a short distance east of North Georgetown, & boarding with a Mr.MERCER. Sat. eve when he called & while seated in the kitchen, she handed him a note, whereupon he drew a revolver & shot himself through the heart & died very shortly after. He was taken home yesterday.

M: 8th inst by REV.J.W.JOHNSON, WILLIAM MAYRES & MISS ESTELLA DAVIS, all of Salineville.

M: 14th inst by J.M.DICKINSON, ESQ., ISRAEL BEAN & MISS MARY J. COCKSTON, of Salem.

M: 15th inst by REV.A.R.CHAPMAN, JOSEPH PARK of Canton & MISS MARY McCREADY of New Lisbon.

M: 15th by REV.FRY, WALTER BRAIN & MISS IDA CRUMRINE, all of Salem.

M: 13th inst by STANTON THOMAS JP, near Winona, WALTER GALBRAITH of Guthrie Co Iowa & MISS JENNIE PORTER of Salem.

M: 11th inst by REV.E.A.BRINDLEY, GEORGE GLASS of New Castle PA & MISS SARAH CARTRIGHT of East Liverpool.

M: 15th inst at res of MRS.G.F.ADAM by REV G.N.JOHNSTON, DR.W.S.MILLER of Findlay Oh & MISS LOU ADAM of this place.

D: 11th inst in Columbiana, DANIEL A. STOUFFER ae 61y 10m 16d.

D: 8th inst LYDIA LEAF w/o JOSHUA LEAF of Col'ana, ae 72y 8m.

D: 8th inst MRS. REBECCA RUPERT ae 82y 9m 29d.

D: 15th inst SARAH JANE MARSDEN, d/o JOB & HANNAH MARSDEN of Centre Tp ae 15y 1m.

Mon 26 June 1876 (Vol 10 no 13)

M: 8th inst at Salem by SAMUEL HARDMAN JP, HOMER H. WILSON & MISS MARY ALICE MORGAN, all of this co.

M: 22nd inst MARY KNOWLES d/o ISAAC W. KNOWLES of East Liverpool & REV.DANIEL STAFFORD of Pittsburgh ME Conference.

M: 18th inst by REV.ROBERT McMAHON, of Calcutta, WILLIAM HAMILTON & MISS NANCY McBANE all of this co.

M: 8th inst by REV.A.R.CHAPMAN, FRANK HOLLINGER & MISS MARIA BURSON, all of this co.

M: 15th inst by REV BRAY, LEVI HICKMAN & MISS ALLIE HENRY, all of this co.

M: 19th inst by REV.H.STURGEON, at the res of bride's parents, HUBER TRIFFINGER of West Point,CCO & MISS TILLY J. HARTSHORNE of Beaver Co Pa.

D: 22nd inst LOUANA ELIZA ARTER d/o ALPHEUS & MARY A. ARTER of this place, aged 1y 2m 26d.

D: 20th inst JAMES S. WARD of New Lisbon ae 30y.

D: 20th inst MISS HATTIE REED of East Liverpool ae 26y.

D: 18th inst at Columbiana, SADIE FISHER d/o ELI & LIZZIE FISHER ae 1y 11d.

D: 20th inst in Butler Tp., SARAH DUTTON in her 85th yr.

D: 26th inst THOMAS HICKLING of Centre Tp, ae 43y.

Mon 3 July 1876 (Vol 10 no 14)

M: 19th ult at E.Liverpool by REV.J.C.TAGGART, GEORGE H. McCOY & MISS ANNIE M. GONZALES both of this co.

M: 28th ult by REV.G.M.ALBRIGHT, WILLIAM WILSON & MISS MATTIE ALDRIDGE, both of New Lisbon

M: 29th ult at the ME parsonage by REV.A.R.CHAPMAN, EUGENE SULIOT & MISS ANNIE COURTNEY all of this co

M: at Pittsburgh on 15th ult, by REV.R.PHELEN, WILLIAM M. VANHORN & MISS MARY M. BROWN.

D: 25th ult at the res of her father, MRS. ELIZABETH KENNEDY ae 35y 17d

D: 28th ult at New Galilee PA of cholera infantum, BIRDIE PORTER, infant son of S.H. & ELLA PORTER of E.Liverpool

D: 30th ult infant child of FRED & ----ADAMS, of Centre Tp.

A son of MR. BLACKMORE of Smith's Ferry, aged 13y, was drowned on last Sat. afternoon.

On Tues morn last week, HUGH MAGEHAN, a laborer on a gravel train on the New Castle & Franklin Railroad, in an attempt to get on an engine, missed a step & fell under the wheels & was run over & instantly killed.

Wickedest boy in Columbiana Co: FRANK McCARTNEY, aged about 15y, living at Robbins for sometime, was arrested Mon last for stealing a gold watch from DAVID PORTER of Butler Tp. He has twice escaped from the Reform Farm & boasts he was one of the party who fired the buildings that resulted so disastrously; he also is indicted in Summit Co; next trip will be to the Penitentiary.

CCOLUMBIANA REGISTER says that a child of DANIEL COURTNEY, near Beloit, Mahoning Co, was stolen from his residence on Sunday; Mr. C. & wife were visiting at neighbors while the 2 children slept, oldest about 4y, youngest 20 months; gone but a short time; on return they found the oldest child asleep & the youngest one gone. Suspicion rests on a band of gypsies camped near by.

L.C.AXE of New Garden says "its a girl..."

BORN: at Deer Lodge, Montana Territory, June 9, 1876, to the wife of CAPTAIN JAMES H. MILLS, editor of the North-West, a daughter. CAPTAIN MILLS is a native of New Lisbon.

We learn from the East Liverpool GAZETTE that MISS HATTIE REED, of that place, died on Thurs last week. She was a young lady greatly esteemed for her amiable disposition & cultivated qualities of mind.

Mon 10 July 1876 (Vol 10 no 15)

M: 22nd ult by REV.CLEMENTS, J.T.MATHER of Mah.Co. & MISS E.P.JACKSON of this co.

M: 29th ult by same, LABAN SOMERS & MISS NETTIE SHISLER both of this co

M: 4th inst at Salem by Rev H B FRY, SETH MOORE & MISS ISIDORE BOWMAN

M: 4th inst at same place by same, JOHN McKINSEY & MISS ADA WEAVER

M: 1st inst at same placeby REV P J WARD, MR. MULLEN of Mecca & MISS WEALTHY REEDER of Salem

M: 28th ult by JOHN BRINDLEY JP, DAVID LEIGH & MISS ELLA STANLEY both of East Liverpool

M: 5th inst by REV A W BUTTS, WILLIAM STIVER of Penna. & MISS ANNA JONES of E.Liverpool

D: 28th ult LIZZIE HEATON d/o R.G. & ANNA HEATON ae 18m

D: 28th ult near Damasucs DANIEL R. PETTIT ae 59y

D: 23d ult at Salem REBECCA FOGG ae ----y

D: 15th inst MISS HATTIE CREW ae ----y

A boy named THOMAS RAFFERTY, attempting to board a train at New Brighton, fell under the wheels & was instantly killed.

GEORGE WEBSTER was killed at New Castle PA Tues morn while engaged at one of the guns firing salutes in honor of the Centennial Fourth. He was struck by a rammer. THOMAS HARDY, a thumber, & a companion, were wounded. HARDY it is thought seriously; his recovery is doubtful.

CHILD LOST & FOUND: from the Alliance Review we learn that 2 weeks ago yesterday evening, a child of DANIEL COURTNEY, residing near Beloit, aged about 20 months, mysteriously disappeared from his dwelling while he & wife were away; on following Tuesday, about 9 o'clock, the family of NATHAN BALL, a neighbor, were startled by hearing the wail of a child in an adjoining lot. They hastened there & found the lost child, stripped on nearly every vestige of clothing & bruised & torn in a most shocking manner. It is supposed the abductor, fearing discovery, returned it where it might be found. There is no clue yet.

CENTENNIAL SKETCH OF NEW LISBON: (long article) among names mentioned in text are: FISHER A. BLOCKSOM (1805). ARTICLE continues to list businesses & businessmen in 1876...

"One hundred years from now the newspapers will be publishing extracts from this issue of THE NEW LISBON JOURNAL, showing how the first Centennial was celebrated."

MRS. BUSHONG fell from a horse at Columbiana last Tues., injuring herself slightly.

DR. J.C.HEATON of Alliance died last Tues. at Des Moines Iowa of hemorrhage.

ROBERT T. LOWERY of Salem died very unexpectedly last Monday of cholera morbus after a few days illness.

Mon 17 July 1876 (Vol 10 no 16)

CHURCH DIRECTORY:

UNITED PRESBYTERIAN: REV W.G.NEVIN
METHODIST EPISCOPAL: REV.A.R.CHAPMAN
FIRST PRESBYTERIAN: REV G.N.JOHNSON
CHRISTIAN CHURCH: REV. WILLIAM H. BAXTER
FIRST REFORMED CHURCH: REV G.M.ALBRIGHT
TRINITY (PROTESTANT EPISCOPAL) : none listed

M: 4th inst at Pittsburgh PA by REV S P WOOLF, T.S.ARNOLD of the True Press of Columbiana OH & MISS MAGGIE J.C.BERRY of Pittsburgh PA

M: 4th inst FRANK W. GEORGE of E.Liverpool & MISS ANNA Z. SWALLOW of Monroe Co

D: 18th ult CHARLES STACKHOUSE ae 22y 3m 21d

D: 8th inst MRS. SARAH LEMMON w/o JESSE LEMMON of Salem

D: 15th inst NELLIE GERTRUDE WOODWORTH d/o HARRY & MARIA of Elkrun Tp ae 4m

D: 15th inst ANNA BELL McMILLEN d/o JOHN & MARY JANE of Wayne Tp ae 21y 7m 13d. Funeral yesterday, largely attended with over 100 buggies & carriages in the procession; services by REV.JAMIESON.

Last Thurs a severe storm hit Freedom, on the Ohio River, about 5 miles above Rochester. The residence of THOMAS LIGHTHILL was washed away, while containing MRS. LIGHTHILL & her 4 children. All were drowned & the bodies probably washed into the Ohio.

JOHN GRONIN of E.Liverpool, recently injured on the railroad, died at that place last Tues aged 59y.

JOHN KLEINOGLE of E.Liverpool died suddenly at that place last Mon morn. He was a potter & leaves a wife & 5 children

On Wed eve last, ROBERT DAILEY & NANCY SMITH of St.Clair Tp were brought to jail on a mittimus of JAMES B. McCOY, JP of Fredericktown, charged with adultery. On Thurs morn they were brought before the Probate Court on a writ of habeas corpus & released.

An old man named SHARP living in Steubenville was accidentally run over by the 11 o'clock train on the C & P road Sat morn & almost instantly killed.

Mon 24 July 1876 (Vol 10 no 17)

M: 12th inst at Leetonia by A.B.MAXWELL, WILLIAM P. WALKER & MISS MARTHA TETLOW both of Washingtonville

M: 18th inst at Smith's Ferry PA by ESQ McFALL, JOSEPH WELCH of Madison Tp & MISS JOSIE WELCH of East Liverpool

M: 13th inst by REV H B FRY, MORRISON JUSTICE of Austintown, Mah.Co. & MRS. ELIZABETH BOWMAN of Salem

D: 7th inst at Leetonia MINERVA APPLEGATE aged 70y

D: 19th inst at res of WM. ASTRY, 1 mi west of Franklin Square, WILLIAM WEAVER aged 85y

D: 11th inst MARGARET HOFFSTOTT of Calcutta in 75th yr

D: 13th inst FRANCIS GILES w/o HENRY GILES (colored) of this place aged 28y

D: 23d inst JOHN MASON of Centre Tp in 62nd yr

Court last week on trail of the remainder of the Leetonia boys indicted for rape, committed on the person of DRUSILLA HANNAH last April; unexpectedly the counsel made a proposition to counsel for the state that PATRICK GAFFNEY, GEORGE NANGLE & JOHN HELDT would enter a plea of guilty if the cases against PETER FLEMING & DOC. McILVANE would be nollied, which was accepted. The 3 who pleaded guilty were sentenced to the penitentiary for 3 years each, & the other two, together with the two witnesses, DRUSILLA HANNAH & CHARLEY BROWN, were discharged from jail.

WILLIAM DRAKE, a former resident of Wellsville & a railroad employee was accidentally killed on the Pan Handle road near Steubenville a few days ago.

MRS SARAH SMELTZ nee DENNIS of Wellsville was arrested & fined for disorderly conduct last week.

THOMAS CARTWRIGHT of East Liverpool died very suddenly at that place on 7th inst aged 53y.

ISAAC MYERS died at his residence on West Walnut St last Thur night after a short illness aged 73y.

A reunion of the NEWHOUSE family took place at the res of GIDEON NEWHOUSE IN Fairfield Tp on 12th inst; the occasion was the coming together of a family long separated & all present were in their happiest mood.

DEATH OF GEN. WILLIAM ARMSTRONG: we are sorry to learn from the Cleveland Plain Dealer of 21st of the death of GEN. WILLIAM ARMSTRONG of Allen Co Ohio aged about 70y. The father of Gen.A. was one of the very early settlers of Col.Co., having settled in Wayne Tp on 20 Apr 1805, coming in on the old Moravian Trail which passed but 2 or 3 miles south of New Lisbon. The farm on which the father settled is now owned & occupied by COL.MARTIN ARMSTRONG, a brother of Gen.William, where no doubt the deceased was born. In year 1835/36 and 1836/37, Gen A was elected & served as a member of the House of Rep. of the Ohio Legislature from Col Co & a few years after moved to Allen Co where he was elected to the position of Treas of the county & in 1867 was also elected to lower house of Legislature. He was always faithful to his trusts.

Mon 31 July 1876   (Vol 10 no 18)

M: 25th inst in New Lisobn at res of ROBERT MORROW ESQ, by REV A R CHAPMAN, MARQUIS W. BENSON & MISS SENETH M. TRUNICK

M: 27th inst by same, WILLIAM I. SCHUKERT & MISS MARY I. BROWN.

M: 13th inst by REV J W SWICK, SOL.E.NOLD of Leetonia & MISS CORA E. OSWALD of Canal Dover OH

M: 31st inst at the Friends' Meeting house, Flushing, Belmont Co Oh, WILLIAM L. ASHTON of Col.Co. & MISS ELIZA F. HOLLOWAY d/o JACOB HOLLOWAY of Flushing.

M: 27th inst by E.GARSIDE ESQ, at res of bride's parents near Hanover, EPHRAIM EWING & MISS LENA GRIM all of this co.

D: 25th inst WILLIAM LEONARD ALLISON s/o JOHN & ALEZON ALLISON of Elkrun Tp ae 6m

D: 23d inst WILLIAM THOMPSON s/o JOHN of Calcutta ae 22y

JOHN HARDING, a prominent citizen of Austintown, was killed Thursday by having his head strike the barn as he was riding through the doors on a load of hay.

DAVID HUM, an old & respected citizen of New Lisbon, died at his res on Jefferson St last Tues. He was among the oldest of the pioneer inhabitants of our town & had been in ill health for a long time before his death. His funeral on Thursday, remains conveyed to Columbiana & deposited in the family burying ground. JOHN HUM, A brother of the deceased, died at his residence near Columbiana on Wednesday morning.

Birthday party last Thurs for JOSIE d/o W.M.HOSTETTER on 11th birthday.

DANIEL DORWART, of Iowa City, formerly a resident of New Lisbon & brother of our townsman WM. DORWART, has been spending several days in this place. He is a sprightly, jovial gentleman & is having a lively time among his old acquaintances. He has been absent for 22 years & expresses surprise at the extent of improvements in New Lisbon during that time. From here he will go to Lancaster PA, his native place & after visiting relatives & friends in that seciton, will see the great Centennial Exposition.

W.H.NIGHT a well known citizen of Middleton Tp fell from his chair on last Mon & expired immediately. Aged about 81y.

JOEL JOHNSON an old resident of Salem Tp, died very suddenly at his res Fri morn; he had been in ill health for some time but was able to travel about in his buggy. On morning of his death he was about the house attending to his ordinary business when he was suddenly seized with a pain in the stomach of which he complained at the time, and throwing up his arms, dropped to the floor & expired. He was about 78y

PETER F.BAILEY of Minerva who lost his right arm in consequence of the accidental discharge of a gun & a fortnight ago was taken to the Northern Ohio Hospital for the insane, having become insane from anxiety about his family, died at Newburgh a week ago. His remains were interred at Minerva last Sabbath.

Mon 7 Aug 1876   (Vol 10 no 19)

PETER FIELDS, of Berlin Tp, Mah.Co. committed suicide by cutting his throat on Mon last week & died the next day. He had been ill for some time & was supposed he has been laboring under mental depression at the time.

M: 3d inst by REV J H CONKLE, WILLIAM P. COOPER & MISS MARY E. COLE both of Wellsville

M: 27th ult at Salem by MAYOR DUNLAP, LEA S. BENNETT & MISS LIZZIE A. STRATTON

M: 27th ult at Salem by same, SAMUEL L. WHINERY & MISS LAURA M. STRATTON all of this co

M: 20th of 6th month in Phila by Friends ceremony, JOSEPH B. PHILLIPS of Iowa & ANNIE WRIGHT of Plainfield, York Springs, Adams Co PA

D: 27th ult at Salem ELIZABETH REEVE relict of the late JOSHUA REEVE in 71st yr

D: 27th ult at Cannon's Mill, MR. M.S.MOORE ae 80y

D: 30th ult MRS. AINSWORTH at her res in Liverpool Tp

D: 21st ult WILLIAM SMITH near Highlandtown CCO in 80th yr

D: 27th ult MISS ELIZABETH McCOY near Highlandtown this co in her 74th yr

D: 27th ult FRANCES M. BEESON d/o RICHARD & NANCY S. of Allegheny City Pa ae 47y

The SALEM REPUBLICAN says the funerals of two old & very excellent people of Damascus took place last Monday: JOHN STANLEY JR., who started a woolen mill in taht place on the spot where the Baptist Church now stands. It is said to be the first manufactory built in Salem. He was in his 81st yr. MRS. REBECCA CARR the 2nd person, was also widely known & much respected. She was in her 57th yr.

MISS MARY TAGGART of East Palestine sister of M.E.TAGGART of Leetonia died at Phila. last Sunday. She was on a visit to the Centennial when stricken down with typhoid fever which resulted in her death. Her remains were interred at East Palestine.

Serious accident: last Fri, at JEHU RALEY's about 1 1/2 mi S of East Fairfield in Elkrun Tp; they were repairing a wagon shed, one of the sleepers having rotted off, when THOMAS RALEY, son of JEHU, was assisting, the sleeper being too short, fell over, carrying young Raley down; it fell upon his head, mashing the upper jaw bone & he is now in very critical condition.

DIED on Fri last 28th July at his res near East Fairfield, ELIJAH FARR an old & respected citizen of CCO, in 79th yr; was native of Loudon Co VA but for many years a res & citizen of our co having settled on the NE corner of Elkrun Tp where he continued to live until old age & death removed him to the quiet & peace of eternity.

TWO MORE PIONEERS GONE: Last week we noted the deaths of Messrs. JOHN & DAVID HUM, brothers, promising to give further notice this week. In 1806, JACOB HUM, father of the subjects of our sketch, then consisting of his wife & 3 sons, JOHN, DAVID & our fellow townsman JACOB HUM, the former a lad about 4y old, & the latter but a mere babe, settled on the property now owned by Mr.ROTHWELL on Sec 14 where he resided until his death. At the time of their locating in the township there were few improvements & was a wilderness. The subjects of our sketch, which were the oldest of a family of 5 sons & 1 daughter soon became of great assistance to their parents in clearing up & improving their home & are justly entitled to be classed amoong the early pioneers of the township. John, the oldest of the two, has ever since his first arrival in the township been a resident of the immediate neightborhood where his father located & has for a large portion of the time been a consistent memeber of the church & highly respeceted. He died on 26th ult, aged 74y 3m 26d. DAVID lived for many years in the same neighborhood but for a period of about 30y has been a resident of New Lisbon where he died on 25th ult. He was a member of the ME church for 50 yrs, and was aged in his 73d yr. (Col.Register)

DR.JESSE GARRETSON, formerly of this place, a half brother of the late HIRAM GARRETSON, died in Cincinnati on Sunday of last week.

Mon 14 Aug 1876   (Vol 10 no 20)

ATTEMPTED SUICIDE: on Thurs afternoon last the notorious TOM SWEARINGEN of Wellsville, while under the influence of liquor, attempted to cut his throat with the large blade of a pen knife. His sister, witnessing his apparent attempt at destruction, rushed to him & snatched the instrument from him. The gash made in his throat was between 2 & 3 inches long but not sufficiently deep to cause any very serious injury. DRS.HAMMOND & RUSSELL made the necessary repairs.

M: 8th inst by REV A R CHAPMAN, JAMES BRADY & MISS NELLIE F. HERBERT all of this co

M: 27th ult by REV P J WARD, P.BUTLER of VA & MISS MARY McDONALD of Salem

D: 6th inst in her 7th month ANNA MELINDA HUFFMAN infant child of SAMUEL & REBECCA HUFFMAN of Glasgow

D: 10th inst RENA SHARP d/o GEO.S. & REBECCA SHARP of Wayne Tp ae 1y 9d

D: 7th inst at E.Liverpool MISS MARY HILBERT D/O Mr & Mrs MARTIN HILBERT in 19th yr

D: 7th inst infant daughter of JOHN & MARY REESE of Centre Tp

D: 7th inst at Salem WILLIE STRINGFELLOW infant son of WILLIAM & MARY STRINGFELLOW ae 7m 9d

D: 9th inst at Salem WILLIE W. ECKSTEIN infant son of C.W. & MARY ECKSTEIN ae 6m

D: 18th inst MARGARET DOBSON w/o JOSEPH DOBSON of Wayne Tp & first daughter of THOMAS BEVINGTON of Beaver Co PA, a soldier of the Revolutionary War, ae 73y 4m

D: 10th inst CHRISTENA HAMPSON w/o R.A.HAMPSON of New Lisbon ae 39y 4m 8d

D: 9th inst at Salem MINERVA THOMPSON ae 4y

D: 11th inst MARY MARGARET HOWELL d/o BENJAMIN & NANCY M. HOWELL of Salem Tp ae 6m

D: 10th inst of cholera infantum JESSIE PATTERSON infant dau of WILLIAM & ELLA PATTERSON of Wellsville

MISS CARRIE STULL ae 16y d/o JOHN M. STULL of Warren OH & MISS CLARA BROWN, ae 14 of Greenville PA were drowned on 7th inst at Chautauqua Lake NY while bathing

JOHN W. EDWARDS a former res of Ellsworth, Maho.Co., was drowned on the 7th of last month by the burning of the propeller St.Clair

The Wellsville UNION says a MISS WELSH of Bellair entered complaint before JUSTICE STEWART on Mon last against ----FITZGERALD of Wellsville charging him with fornication and bastardy. FITZGERALD was arrested, had a hearing before the Justice & was held in bail to answer at Court. The defendant in the case has been married only a few months.

From the SALEM ERA: MAMIE, a bright & interesting 3y old dau of ROBERT THOMPSON of Salem met with an accident last Tues afternoon which resulted in its death. It was playing around the house & accidentally fell backwards into a bucket of hot water, so severely scalding itself that death ensued at 3 o'clock the following morning.

On 31st ult a child of JESSE FESLER of Salem Tp aged about 14m was severely scalded by the accidental overturning of a teapot & the spilling of the boiling contents upon its person. It lingered until last Tues night when death put an end to its suffering.

MRS.AARON KINES of Alliance was instantly killed by the cars last Tues afternoon. In attempting to cross the RR near the station at that place, she was run over by a train of cars & her head completely severed from her body. She was a sister in law of MR.YERKES HOWELL of Salem.

HARRY WATSON of the Leetonia Reporter is about to start a new paper at East Palestine.

PHEBE JOHN, relict of JOSIAH JOHN, died at her residence in Salem on Mon morn last after 2y illness. She was 57y old.

JOHN B. DAILEY formerly of New Lisbon, died at his res in Mansfield on morning of 6th inst, ae 48y. He leaves a wife & 4 children.

Mon 21 Aug 1876   (Vol 10 no 21)

JOHN STANLEY, formerly a furnace hand at Leetonia, was found dead in his room at New Castle PA Sat eve 13th inst. His body was in an advanced stage of decomposition. Persons passing an old vacant shanty just across the creek & above the bridge from New Castle were attracted by a very foul smell & on investigating found the body with his throat cut from ear to ear. At the coroner's inquest is was ascertained that during the last few days of life STANLEY had roomed with JOHN ARMSTRONG at the place near the bridge. Jury verdict that STANELY came to his death at the hands of JOHN ARMSTRONG. At last accounts, he had not been arrested.

D: 13th inst MARGARET ARMSTRONG D/O HAMILTON ARMSTRONG of Knox Tp ae 39y 10m 16d

D: 15th inst at Fairview Maryland, MARY DORRANCE w/o S.GILMORE DORRANCE & daughter in law of JAMES DORRANCE of this place.

D: 20th inst ELIZABETH EWING w/o SAMUEL EWING of Wayne Tp ae 53y 2d.

JACOB ESTELL of Franklin Square had 73rd birthday last Wed

The Columbiana True Press learns from the Dalton Gazette that there is living at this time in Congress, Wayne Co, MRS. SARAH KUFFEL the oldest daughter of ADAM POE. She is now a very aged woman but is very active doing her own cooking & other household work. She can thread a needle without glasses.

The Terra Cotta works at Leetonia are turning out a fine lot of ornamental work. They manufacture flower vases of every description, ornaments for yards and the best kind of stoneware.

Mon 28 Aug 1876   (Vol 10 no 22)

D: 10th inst MARGARET DOBSON w/o JOSEPH DOBSON of Wayne Tp ae 73y 4m 8d

D: 13th inst at New Waterfrod, WILLIAM HARRIS PENGILL s/o T.W. & S.J.PENGILL ae 5m 18d.

M: 17th inst by REV DAVIS, HOMER HARRIS of New Lisbon & MISS MAGGIE A. MARTIN of Wellsburg WVa

M: 17th inst by REV J.F.CALLAHAN, GEORGE F. DURKE of New Brighton PA & MISS MOLLIE M. WILLIAMS of Columbiana

M: 21st inst by REV A W BUTTS, J.N.GALLAGHER of Phila. to MISS IDA F. LITTLE of E.Liverpool

M: 10th inst at Col'ana by REV A E WARD, FRANK DEMING of Salem & MISS JENNIE HAMPSON of New Lisbon

M: 15th inst at Enon Valley Pa by Rev ---, PHILIP DEMMER & MRS. ELLA WALKER all of this co

M: 15th inst at Darlington PA by REV J W RIGHTER, JOSEPH DAVIS & MISS JENNIE ZEIGLER both of Unity Tp this co

M: 6th inst in Knox Tp by REV J A CLEMENT, WILLIAM D. DOWLIN of Hanoverton & MISS EMMA WEKER of Hardin Co Oh

M: 1st inst by REV J M BRAY, JAMES SPENCER & MISS CATHERINE BABCOCK, both of W Va

M: 22nd inst by same at the bride's res., DAVID BOOTH & MISS ELIZA HAYS d/o HARRISON HAYS all of this co

M: 24th inst by REV A R CHAPMAN, JOHN S. EDWARDS & MISS NANCY C. CRUBAUGH all of this co.

Reunion of FREDERICK family at the old homestead north of New Lisbon; over 125 present; history of the FREDERICK FAMILY prepared by MRS.CLEMENTINE SMITH of Kansas was read by JOHN A. MYERS. A full account of the affair will appear in the Journal in a few weeks.

The Salem Republican says that about a week ago a little child of ENOCH HOULETT rec'd a scratch in the hand from a rusty nail which has since resulted in lockjaw & the child is not expected to live.

From the Salem Era we learn that the HOULETT boy, mentioned elsewhere died from the effects of the wound last Tues.

MRS. ALEVENIA McINTOSH died suddenly of apoplexy at the res of her daughter MRS. M.B.JOHNSTON at E.Liverpool on Mon last in 80th yr.

The Leetonia Reporter says that STANLEY who was recently murdered at New Castle PA was employed as a section hand at Leetonia on the A & GW RR & boarded with JAMES McANULTY. On 5th inst before going to NC he placed some $200 in a pocket; he was about 60y of age & is said to have been a quiet sober industrious man.

We learn from Salem Republican that a trial of considerable interest is going on at Winona, JOB WARREN vs REBECCA WARREN, an aged Quaker couple. He sues for divorce & she files cross petition for alimony alone. Testimony before Squire THOMAS

We regret to learn of the death of MRS. CATHERINE HARBAUGH w/o DAVID HARBAUGH of Detroit Mich which sad event occurred in that city last Sat. night. She was a daughter of the late DAVID BEGGS ESQ of this place & was a most estimable lady

Mon 4 Sep 1876 (Vol 10 no 23)

M: 17th ult at Washingtonville by REV G WAGNER, J.C.KLING & MISS FLORA E. HILLIS both of Salem

M: 24th ult by REV J ESTILL, JOHN M. ALBRIGHT & MISS LEIVINA CHURCHILL of Guernsey Co Oh

M: 17th ult at Salem by Squire PEEPLES, of Franklin Square, OSCAR BETZ & MISS SALLIE NICHOLS both of this co

M: 20th ult by ---at Glasgow PA, H.B.RALSTON of Wellsville & Miss ANNIE WEAVER d/o JOHN WEAVER of Salineville

M: 31st ult by REV.S.S.McKOWN, WILLIAM D. CALDWELL of Elkrun Tp & MISS HORTENSE L. DeFORD of Carroll Co

D: 27th ult ELIZABETH UNKEFER of Unity Tp ae 80y

D: 22nd ult DANIEL ISEMEN of Salem ae 55y

D: 26th ult at E.Liverpool MISS NANCY BLACKBURN

D: 6th ult at Homeworth, MARY BAKER w/o HIRAM BAKER

D: 27th ult at Salem MISS EMMA E. TALMAGE in 24th yr

D: 29th ult at Salem MRS. ANN RAMSDEN widow of the late RICHARD RAMSDEN ae 75y 4d

D: 25th ult at West Chester PA MISS MAY T. HIDDLESON d/o MRS SARAH HIDDLESON of Salem in 19th yr

D: 11th ult SOLOMON YARIAN of Unity Tp ae 52y 7m 22d

D: 20th ult ELIZABETH EWING w/o SAMUEL EWING of Wayne Tp ae 53y 2d

THE FREDERICK FAMILY UNION on 23day last month held first family union, on old homestead farm 1 1/2 mi North of this place known as the Frederick Farm; rain forced them inside to MRS. GEORGE WALTERS barn; B.F.FREDERICK called meeting to order; JOHN A. MYERS ESQ, read the following history prepared by MRS. CLEMENTINE SMITH (FORMERLY FREDERICK) of Cherokee Co Kansas.

THE FREDERICK FAMILY

During last half of 18th century, 2 brothers NOAH & CHRISTOPHER FREDERICK emigrated from Germany to Lancaster PA; NOAH married a Miss MARGARET ---- & by her had 3 children, 2 sons, 1 da. u; from the oldest son, THOMAS, the family here is descended. He was born near the waters of the Big Sweetalla in region of Lancaster. When about 7y his father was killed by Indians while plowing & his two boys taken prisoners. The wife & daughter being in the barn, saw the Indians & escaped. The daughter in after years was married to a Mr. SHOFFT. Of his children nothing definite is known except that one daughter MARGARET was married to a MR. GLESSINGER & died in or near Dungannon, CCO, where her descendants still reside. The Indians were Shawnees, & the boys were separated, the last Thomas knew of his brother; Thomas was taken to western portion of Ohio & eastern Indiana; the name Kee-Saw-So-So was given to him & when of age his ears were pierced. After the treaty with the French & Indians, he was given up & delivered to Fort Duquesne, present city of Pittsburgh. From there he went to Phila. & apprenticed himself to a shoemaker named BENJAMIN STONE, a Quaker & as Thomas was ignorant of his real name, Stone bestowed his own upon him. After learning the trade he found that he was near Sunburg, Northumberland Co PA, in the same region from which he had been taken prisoner. There he met a man who had interested himself in behalf of the captives & after conversation, was convinced that Stone had been taken from that portion of the country about the time of the killing of NOAH FREDERICK. He requested Stone to tell him all he could remember; he recalled a dog & horse which he described & of a whirlwind that took off the roof of his father's barn while the children were playing. This the man recollected to have happened to Noah Frederick's barn a short time previous to his being killed. He believed he could take him to his mother & accordingly took him to Noah Frederick's wife who was married a second time & living near. She at first could scarcely believe him to be her long lost son. She said her son Thomas had a large gathering on the back of his neck which his father had opened with a razor. The scar was found on Stone's neck as described & that convinced her that he was in reality her son. After that he resumed his proper name of Thomas Frederick. After Thomas was married & had children old enough to remember, he was visited by his father's brother CHRISTOPHER who then lived near Lancaster. He told Catherine...Thomas' 2nd child...that her father was the only relative he had in this country & as he was unmarried, he wanted his nephew Thomas & his children to inherit his property. This is the last positive knowledge we have of him, but there is reason to believe he after married & he or his children moved to Virginia. Thomas Frederick & his family removed from Yankmanstown, Northumberland Co Pa in 1804 to Col.Co.Oh & settled on section 12, Centre Tp where he resided til his deah on 3 May 1808. His wife ANNA MARGARET FREDERICK died Feb 28, 1826. They both lie buried in the family burying ground which is on the NE corner of the section & about 1/2 mi from their residence.

Remarks were made by REV.J.CLARKE TAGGART of E.Liverpool & who paid a high tribute to his venerable grandmother. Remarks made by JOHN C. PIKE, Z. FREDERICK of Mahoning Co, MRS. MARIA PIKE, MRS. CLEMENTINE SMITH & NOAH FREDERICK, of E.Liverpool. Another reunion will be held 24 Aug 1877.

Last Sat GEORGE GREENAWALT of Franklin Square was so severely injured by being thrown from a grain drill while driving thru Washingtonville on his way home, that he died from his injuries yesterday morning. Mr G was a worthy & highly esteemed gentleman whose death is universally deplored.

Salem Era says a reunion of the children, grandchildren & great grandchildren of NICHOLAS GEE, numbering 106 was held on 24th ult at Ellsworth upon the old homestead where Nicholas settled in 1816. There was a reunion 40 years ago, all of whom except 6 attended the present one, of these 5 have died & one was absent. Our esteemed citizen, FIRMAN GEE of the Victor Stove Co at Salem, is one of the children.

Mon 11 Sep 1876 (Vol 10 no 24)

Essay written for the Pioneer & Historical Assn (from the Ohio Patriot) by H.H.Gregg. Sometime in autumn of 1808, WILLAIM D LEPPER came from Hanover PA & established the Ohio Patriot; paper was first printed in a log house on Beaver St, which was built by old George Duck for his son George who was soon after elected sheriff of the county. The house is located on lot no 192. In June 1826 Mr Lepper stated he started the German paper DER PATRIOT AM OHIO on 1 Dec 1808 & not meeting enough support discontinued it & on 7 Nov 1809 the first numnber of the Ohio Patriot was issued.(no paper in Cleveland til 1818) Some of the incidents related by Hon.- FISHER A.BLOCKSOM, who will be 94 yrs old the 11th of this month, (tells of trails in area, delivery of mail,stages)

In 1876, the following newspapers being are published in the county:

SALEM REPUBLICAN, J.K.RUKENBROD ed
SALEM ERA, ED.F.RUKENBROD, ed
WELLSVILLE UNION, W.B.McCORD, ed
TRIBUNE, EAST LIVERPOOL, SIMMS & BRADSHAW eds
POTTERS' GAZETTE, EAST LIVERPOOL, D.B.MARTIN ed
INDEPENDENT REGISTER, COLUMBIANA, GEN.E.S.HOLLOWAY, ed
COLUMBIANA TRUE PRESS, L. ARNOLD ed
LEETONIA REPORTER, W.H.WATSON, ED.
SALINEVILLE INDEX, J.W.LACOCK, ed
NEW LISBON JOURNAL, J.K.FREW, ed
BUCKEYE STATE, ED.F.MOORE pub & GEO.B.CORBETT ed
OHIO PATRIOT, POTTS & MURPHY eds

M: 27th ult in Knox Tp by REV J A CLEMENT, THOMAS G. SYNE & MISS MARTHA JH. HENRY both of West Tp

M: 3d inst at Leetonia by REV A B MAXWELL, JAMES C. WEIKART & MISS MARY CHAPPLE both of Washingtonville

M: 23d ult at Steubenville by REV W M GRIMES, DR. J.M.MURDOCH of Wellsville & MISS MATTIE D. JENKINS of Harrison Co OH

D: 4th inst EVA THOMAS d/o EMMA THOMAS of Elkrun Tp ae 2y 6m

D: 13th ult AUGUST SHAFFER s/o FRED & CLARA SHAFFER of Cedar Rapids Iowa formerly of New Lisbon of scarlet fever aged 3y

D: 29th ult at Cedar Rapids, FREDDIE SCHAWECKER s/o ROBERT & ELVINA late of this place of scarlet fever aged 2y

D: 19th ult in Knox Tp LULA ESTELLA KELLY d/o E. & D. KELLY ae 8m 13d

D: 9th inst JOHN TAGGART of East Palestine ae 64y

Pioneer meeting held at East Liverpool; the following is a list of the members present & their age:

WILLIAM BIGGS	77	WILLIAM DAVIDSON	67
MRS. DAVIDSON	66	C.M.ATEN	71
H.H.GREGG	66	JAMES SCOTT	57
GEO.POE	86	JAMES LITTLE	69
S.W.SNODGRASS	69	KEZIE RAMSEY	59
MARTHA McCLUE	65	JAMES KELLY	66
GEORGE ANDERSON	62	M.MILLER	77
J.ARTER	80	R.HUSTON	77
H.MORELAND	74	G.BUCHHEIT	68
J.LOGAN	74	J.W.GASTON	68
B.B.OGDEN	70	J.J.IKIRT	50
D.BOYCE	52	A.G.McCREADY	57
W.MORROW	57	W.BLOOR	52

WILL MOORE, a young man aged about 21y, died at East Liverpool last Sabbath

JOHN TAGGART, an old & highly esteemed citizen of East Palestine died in that place last Sat. He was the father of M.E.TAGGART of Leetonia & REV.J.C.TAGGART of E.Liv

Mon 18 Sep 1876 (Vol 10 no 25)

GEORGE STEWART, of Massillon, master of a boat running on the canal, was drowned near Cleveland last Mon; his remains brought home for interment

M: 14th inst by REV G H ALBRIGHT at the res of the bride's parents, L.S.DEEMER & MISS MARY I. BRICKER

D: 6th inst at the Infirmary JOHN KIRKENDALL of Elkrun Tp aged 94y

D: 6th inst at Salem after a short illness TAMAR HIDDLESON ae 78y ;10m

D: 7th inst at Leetonia EDWARD CUFF ae 38y

D: 11thinst at New Waterford CORA LYNNE MALONEY d/o DR.J.M.- & LAURA E. MALONEY ae 9m 26d

D: 5th inst at No.Georgetown FRANKLIN WHITELEATHER ae 23y

D: 13th inst in Madison Tp infant dau of JOSEPH & ELLEN MONTGOMERY

The Republican announces the death of WILLIAM GARWOOD an old & much respected citizen of Salem who died Mon last aged about 71y; he was one of the pioneers of Salem.

MRS. CHRISTIANA M. BOLLMYER died at Warren Trum.Co. Tues morn Sep 12 & was buried at New Lisbon last Wed. Mrs. B was the mother of J.F.BOLLMYER who was assassinated on the streets of Dayton in 1862 by a man named Brown. She was 66y and was at one time a res of New Lisbon.

Salem Era says that FRANK HUNT son of JOHN HUNT of Salem met with an accident last Sun morn which resulted in his death in the afternoon; it seems there were quite a number of boys at Alliance designing to board some eastern bound freight train & get a free ride home. Frank had succeeded in getting on but finding his companions not so fortunate, jumped off to rejoin them. In doing so he came in contact with the4 upright switch bar & was thrown under the wheels which passed over one of his legs bruising & lacertaing it in a terrible manner. The conductor was notified & brought him to Salem.

Mon 25 Sep 1876 (Vol 10 no 26)

D: 6th inst at Hanover E.F.ARTHUR aged about 26y

D: 16th inst at Salem MISS ANNA REEP aged 19y

D: 21st inst DAVID BURBECK of Wayne Tp ae 65y

D; 23d inst at the Infirmary GEORGE STEVENS of St.Clair Tp ae 39y

M: 19th inst by REV GEO N JOHNSTON, JAMES MOORE of Saline-ville & MISS LIZZIE J. FORBES all of this co

M: 12th inst by REV J H LEPER, F.A.WITT ESQ, of Col'ana & MISS MARY B. CALVIN of Calcutta bot h of CCO

M: 14th inst by REV M F LAUFFER, SAMUEL BAILEY & MISS BARBARA BAILHARTZ all of CCO

M: 7th inst by PROF J.A.BRUSH at Mt.Unon, WILLIAM W. WEAVER & MISS ELIZA J. PENTZ both of No Georgetown Oh

M: 14th inst by REV A H WARNER, W.A.BOOTHE of Pittsburgh & MISS SALLIE H. BAELZ of Salem

M: 13th inst at Salem by REV WM. ROSS, ALPHONSO ZIMMERMAN & miss EMMA WEST

M: 19th inst at Salem by REV H B.FRY, M.THOMAS HINSHILLWOOD & MISS KATE WELKER

M: 20th inst by REV S.M.DAVIS, GEORGE N. BRUNER & MISS AGNES A. PARSONS all of Wellsville

M: 5th inst at Bridgewater PA by REV J HOLLINGSHEAD, THOMAS BUTLER of Wellsville & MISS MARY E. WOODRUFF of the former.

M: 4th inst at Rochester PA HERMAN C. McILVAIN of Roch PA & MISS ELLA DANIELS of Wellsville O

M: 19th inst at Leetonia by REV M J INGRAM, WILLIAM NICHOLS & MISS LEAH KELLER both of Franklin Square CCO

Fatal accident: we learn from GEORGE CROWL of accident last Tues in Canfield Tp on farm of PETER CLINE, while threshing machine in operation, the boiler exploded; ISAAC RHODES, NOAH CUMMINGS, & DAVID FOX were instantly killed; JERRY FOX & M. WARD were severely injured & recovery is considered impossible.

W.H.WATSON has disposed of the Leetonia Reporter & retires; succeeded by JAMES A. HAMILTON & JOHN F. MARCHAND, both newspaper men, the former a son of WILLIAM HAMILTON, at one time auditor of CCO.

GEORGE H. EHRHART a respected citizen of New Lisbon died at his res on Sat morn of congestion of the bowels, aged 38y

Mon 2 Oct 1876 (Vol 10 no 27)

M: 21st ult at Kensington OH by REV L B KING, LEE C. HAWKINS of Elkton & MISS MARY J. HUDD of former place

M: 2nd ult at Canfield by REV A B MAXWELL, W.J.McKINNEY & MISS HANNAH MYGATT

M: 26th inst by REV J H BLACKFORD, ANGUS McBANE of Jeff Co Oh & MISS BELLA FRASER Of CCO

M: 28th ult near Fredericktown by REV W M GRIGGSBY, BAXTER HUSTON & MARY E. WOLLAM

M: same time & place by same, ALFRED FREAZEL & MISS ELIZABETH J. THOMPSON all of CCO

D: 21st ult in Middleton tp MAGGIE R. FITZSIMONS d/o THOMAS B. & MARY F. ae 11y 2m 16d

D: 22nd ult at Middleton Tp JIMMIE B. FITZSIMONS s/o THOMAS B & MARY F. ae 13y 9m 8d

Mr & Mrs W.E.CURRY of E.Liv celebrated 25th anniversary last Monday

Mon 9 Oct 1876 (Vol 10 no 28)

M: 28th ult by REV WM BAXTER, NATHAN WILCOXEN & MISS ELIZABETH A. SPRINGER all of this co

M: 28th ult by REV WINGET, THOMAS RICHEY & MISS ROSE HYDE both of this co

M: 4th inst by REV T A McCURDY, D.S.ACHE of Allegheny City & MISS ELLEN E. SMITH of Wellsville

M: 28th ult near Millport OH by REV DAVID HARGEST, W.A.CHAIN & MISS MAGGIE A. COPELAND all of this co

D: 3d inst at Jethro of hemorrhage of the bowels THOMAS H. MURRAY in 27th yr

D: 16th ult NANCY PHILIPS w/o JESSE PHILIP of Fayette Co Iowa ae 58y 8m 26d

D: 1st inst MARY ALICE ARMSTRONG d/o COLUMBUS & MARY A. ARMSTRONG of Wellsville ae 1y 10m 8d

Body of a 12 yr old boy found floating in the Ohio River at E.Liverpool on Sat 30th ult; in pocket was a shoe buttoner, & a medal inscribed "JOHN INGRAM Co G, 4th Mass Cav, Farmington Mass

ROBERT EELLS & MISS LYDIA RICHARDSON of Middleton tp were married Tues 26th ult.

Baby show held (to raise money for Ladies Cemetery improvement society); winners were: 1st in Class 1, ANNIE McKEE, entered by MISS JENNIE WILSON; 2nd premium to CHARLES PRIDE, colored; 1st premium in class 2 to MARY WHITACRE entered by MISS ELLA GREEN; 2nd premium to WILLIE BLOCKSOM. 1st premium was silver cups, 2nd, napkin rings.

MARTIN KINDIG one of the oldest citizens of Washingtonville died at his res in that place on last Mon aged 66y

An old & respected lady named MAUTZENBAUGH died at the res of DR.J.BASSART in Washingtonville on 28th ult aged 88y

REUNION OF THE DESCENDANTS OF JONAH & JOANNA ROBINSON last Thurs at Madison Church which is situated on the section of land they entered & occupied about 1802. People there from Pittsburg, Indiana & different parts of the state. GEORGE ROBINSON presented the old family bible & other papers from which the following points were elicited:
    JONAH ROBINSON was born in New Jersey in 1750. He moved to Bedford Co PA about 1797. In 1800 he moved to where the town of Wellsville now stands & worked the place in corn 1 or 2 years. From there with 11 children he moved to The Homestead in Madison Tp; neighbors were Indians, beavers & panthers. He died in year 1814; his wife survived about 26 yrs. Their children, all but two lived to a ripe old age. Three are still living, KINSEY ROBINSON, JACOB ROBINSON, & MATILDA HASSON, the youngest, who is 71y. A patched quilt made in NJ by JOANNA ROBINSON is supposed to be 100 yrs old. They had 13 children, 68 grch, 259 gr grch & 160 gr gr grch, totalling 490, 135 of whom were present. (report by DAN CRAWFORD)

Mon 16 Oct 1876 (Vol 10 no 29)

M: 5th inst near Salem by REV H B FRY, HENRY BARNES & MISS MARY TROTTER both of this co

M: 5th inst in Knox Tp by REV J A CLEMENT, J.F.FRIFOGEL & MISS S.E.ZURBRUGG all of this co

M: 26th ult by REV A. McGUAGHEY, JOHN R. ELLS & MISS LYDIA M. RICHARDSON both of this co

M: 10th inst in Beaver Co PA b76 JUSTICE MANSFIELD, KERSEY BOOTH & MISS MARY E. HAYS both of Middleton Tp this co

M: 11th inst by ELDER TEEGARDEN, OTHELLO STURGEON & MISS ADDIE BONSALL both of Salem

M: 5th inst by REV S M DAVIS, at Presb.Parsonage, Wellsville, SIMEON LARKINS & MARTHA W. COMLEY both of Salineville

D: 24th ult at Bellaire, Wash Co PA SUSAN HAWKINS sister of WILLIAM FARMER of Fairf.Tp, this co, aged 69y 26d

D: 21st ult in Indiana, FREMONT VOTAW s/o AARON & RUTH ANN VOTAW of Winona this co ae 19y 9m 5d

D: 4th inst in Middleton Tp SAMUEL EDWIN FRITZSIMONS youngest child of THOMAS B. & MARY F. ae 2y 6m 15d

D: 12th inst at Clear Spring MD MARY A.P.FRANTZ, oldest dau of JAMES & MARY DORRANCE of New Lisbon in 44th yr of age

D: 14th inst at the res of MRS.EVA McPHERSON of St.Clair Tp, ANNIE C. McLAUGHLIN d/o JOHN & MARIA McLAUGHLIN of Madison Tp ae 25y

D: 10th inst at Sloan's Station, Jeff Co, MRS. ELIZA McCOY ae 18y 1m 2d

D: 8th inst of lung fever, MARY J. MEIGH w/o FRED. MEIGH of E.Liverpool

MICHAEL KARNS while in a state of intoxication was walking on the RR track near Massillon & instantly killed by the locomotive on Thurs night 5th inst

JOSEPH DENNIS of E.Liverpool has two bibles, one dated 1599 the other 1622; have been in DENNIS family ever since the years of publication.

GYPSY WEDDING performed by MAYOR DICKINSON of this place last Tues eve, on the farm of ANDREW BRINKER. Accompanied by Mrs D & 15 or 20 citizens, they went & found from 40 to 50 of them camped there; the parties were JOSEPH WELLS & MISS MARETTA JEFFREY of the US we suppose. A sumptious dinner was served with many apologies for the lack of wine, which couldn't be found anywhere in town.

HENRY WALSER, formerly a citizen of Hanover Tp, after passing thru many of the vicissitudes of life, lately died at Dallas TX

On last Thurs eve a very sad accident occurred to one of our town boys, which resulted in his death: SYLVESTER WILT, about 13y, was in Boardman Tp, Mah Co, where his father has been teaming for the Col'ana Lumber & Coal-Co; meeting a young man who had been out gunning he asked to be allowed to shoot off his gun, which was refused. The young man sat down his gun & stepped into a field to drive out some cows when Sylvester attempted to pull the gun thru the fence & in doing so, it discharged, the ball entering his neck, lodging in his brain, killing him instantly. His remains were brought home last Fri 6th inst. Col'ana Register.

The Trinity Reformed Church, 5 mi west of Lisbon, will be dedicated to the worship of the Triune God on Sun 29th inst; sermon by REV JOHNSON of New Lisbon, REV G.W.WILLIARD, president of Heidleburg College at Tiffin & others. G.M. ALBRIGHT, pastor

LEWIS McCLYMONDS native of New Lisbon but at present of Cleveland, has become brother in law to his brother WALTER, having just married the latter's wife's sister of Massillon

Mon 26 Oct 1876 (Vol 10 no 30)

M: 5th inst by REV W D NELSON, F.M.FRANKY of Alliance & MISS AGLINE WHITACRE of this co

M: 12th inst at New Middleton by H.B.FRY, WILLIAM A. KELLY of Iowa & MISS MARY HECKLER

M: 18th inst at Wellsville by REV MR.DAVIS, JAMES LUKE & MISS LAURA McKENZIE

M: 17th inst by REV G N JOHNSTON, at the home of the bride, JOHN McKARNES & MISS LYDIA H. GREEN all of this co

D: 17th inst at East Liverpool of consumption, ZILLAH DAULEY w/o DANIEL DAULEY aged 25y

D: 17th inst ELIZABETH LODGE widow of ABEL LODGE ae 76y 3m

D: 13th inst at East Liverpool of scarlet rash, JESSE WILBER CHAMBERS s/o MARTIN V.B. & MARTHA J. CHAMBERS in 3d yr of age

D: yesterday after a brief illness MAHALA FROST of Hanover Tp in 51st yr

In the matter of cremation, or disposing of dead bodies by burning, Washington Co.Pa is in advance of any other place in this part of the country. Dr.LEMOYNE an eminent citizen of that place, has erected a suitable establishment for that purpose on a locality called GALLOWS HILL — WHERE "OLD CRAWFORD" was hung 50 years ago for the murder of his son...intended to be used for consuming the body when he quits living & others to use. It is said to be much cheaper than the present mode of burial.

MARY BRICKER w/o DR. BRICKER, north of town, died on 22nd inst aged 36y

A.J.KING of West Tp writes to the Salem Republican that the late CATHERINE LOWER who died on the 16th inst at 93y of age, left 114 grch, 227 gt grch & 22 gt gt grch, these with her 16 children swell the number of her descendants to 379.

DR. HARDMAN of Salem, a man well known in public life, died on 17th ult at his res after several weeks illness.

GEORGE HOWARD an old citizen of this place died on 22nd inst in 76th yr; well known to everybody & always regarded as a genial, jovial sort of man & enjoyed life as well as most men

Mon 30 Oct 1876 (Vol 10 no 31)

M: 12th inst at res of bride's parents in Muskingum Co Oh by ELDER GRIMM, KIMSEY D. BELL of CCO & MISS L.E.McGINNIS

M: 5th inst in E.Palestine by REV S LOW, WILLIAM WATSON BURGESS & ALICE E. SHEETS both of Platte Co Neb

M: 9th inst by REV C L WINGET, MARION APPLEGATE of W Va & MISS CYNTHIA A KEMBLE of this co

M: 19th inst at res of bride's father, CCO, by REV LEEPER, assisted by REV.THOMPSON, JOHN A. SCOTT formerly of Fairview WV & MISS JENNIE THOMPSON

M: at New Middleton by REV H B FRY on 12th inst WM. KELLY of Iowa & MISS MARY HECKLER

M; 19th inst by same, ELLIOT ZEPERNICK & MISS CHARITY BRICKER both of Georgetown OH

M: 24th inst in Salem by same, JAMES LOWRY & MISS DORA SYFORT

M: 19th inst in Salem by STANTON THOMAS, inst at res of THOMAS COPPIC, near Winona, A.L.COPE & MISS RACHEL COPPIC both of this co

D: 22nd inst in Ohioville, LORENZE ORMS s/o B.F. & S. ORMS aged about 7y [colored?]

SUICIDE: of a former resident of Col.Co. at Philadelphia:- Last Fri Afternoon WILLIAM K. HASTINGS a former res of CCO but late of Jackson Co, this state, committed suicide by shooting himself in the forehead at Philad. The body taken to the morgue & a letter found: "My watch give to "Ike."- Live on & prosper. This terrible mystery will never be brought to light. I hope to God you may live to see the day. The truth is not now known & I am helpless" There was neither signature nor addresss to the letter. MR. HASTINGS was the son of the late ISAAC HASTINGS of this township.

MR. & MRS. JAMES DORRANCE of this place have during the last few months been sorely afflicted by deaths in his family. Not long since we chronicled the death of one of their daughters & in our last issue we were pained to note the decease of another...his eldest daughter...the sad occurrence having taken place in Maryland. In these afflictions Mr.D. & his family have the heartfelt sympathy of the community in which they are well known & highly respected.

JOHN GROOMS, Supt of the Co.Infirmary, was stabbed there by an inmate named HEADLY. About 2 yrs since, HEADLY's wife died at Wellsville leaving 2 children & the father concluding that he would be unable to support himself & children, went to the Infirmary. He cares for the heating engine. One of the children has since been sent out to work, another is at school. In an argument with Grooms, he stabbed him...not fatally, but charges will be brought.

WILLIAM W. & ROBERT WHITACRE, the former of Cleveland & the latter of St.Paul, sons of the late ROBERT WHITACRE, were in town last week visiting.

CHARLES AXE of New Garden, a boy about 13y, accidentally shot himself last Fri as he was coming from his grandfather's carrying a gun; it is thought the wound will prove fatal

Andersonville : complete history of Andersonville Prison by DR.R.R.STEVENSON, Surgeon in charge with an appendix containing the names of 13,000 Union soldiers who died there with dates and causes of death. Sent on receipt of $3. Trumbull Bros, Baltimore MD

Mon 6 Nov 1876 (Vol 10 no 32)

M: 31st ult at res of bride's parents by REV G M ALBRIGHT, FELIX SELL & MISS MARTHA E.M.FROST both of Hanover Tp

M: 19th ult by REV C L WINGET, J.D.LONGSHORE & MISS MARY E. MORLAN all of this co

M: 31st inst by Rev H.PALMER, JOSEPH KAHLER Of Colorado & MISS CAROLINE DEIDRICK of E.Liverpool

M: 1st inst in E.liv by REV J C TAGGART, J.W.JOHNSON & MISS MARY E. McKINNON

M: 19th ult by REV.J.E.HOLLISTER, ROBERT A. DUNLAP & MISS MARY E. SHECKLOR all of Salineville

D: 31st ult at his res in Elkrun Tp SIMON PIKE aged about 35y

D: near Spring Mountain, Cosh.Co.Oh of typhoid fever, MAGGIE E. WOLLAM d/o MARY & URIAH WOLLAM ae 19y 4m 19d

D: 1st inst in E Liv HENRY BULLOCK of consumption

JAMES McQUEEN died on Monday last in Keokuk Iowa; dec'd was born in Madison Tp, this co in 1826 & was 50y old at death

SUICIDE IN WELLSVILLE FROM FAMILY QUARREL: last Thurs a young man dangerously injured his sister then killed himself- It appears that JOHN BARR the young man had a dispute with his sister & struck her a blow with a cup, supposing he had dangerouly wounded her, in remorse he drew his revolver & shot himself in the head; after he had fallen to the floor he fired two more shots, one of which took effect in the head just below the right ear. His sister's injuries were not serious

FURTHER PARTICULARS ON SUICIDE OF JUDGE W.K.HASTINGS: WKH a former citizen of CCO who commited suicide at Phila Fri week, was buried at Jackson OH on Tues; Cincy Gazette gives more: 4 yrs ago he was apptd Common Pleas Judge; mental abberations from study; he left Jackson for the Centennial with his eldest daughter EMMA & others; he left his daughter at the hotel & went to the Navy Yard where he shot himself.- He leaves 4 children, was about 53y of age; his wife died 2 yrs ago.

PETITION FOR DIVORCE: GERTRUDE E. RIDDLE vs GEORGE T. RIDDLE, who res in unknown, filed 30 Aug 1876 charging adultery, & asking custody of the children named in the petition.

CHARLES AXE, of New Garden, the lad who accidentally shot himself which was noticed in last week's Journal, died from his injuries on the 27th ult

CAPTAIN JAMES DALES died at the res of his brother 6 miles west of town last Tues after a lingering illness. In early life CAPTAIN DALES was a popular steamboat commander & was widely known & highly esteemed from Pittsburgh to New Orleans. His death will be deeply regretted by a large cirlce of acquaintances. He was aged 56y.

MOSES HEADLEY who stabbed Supt. GROOMS at the Infirmary was arrested & confined in county jail.(he was later released & returned to the Infirmary, where he was closely watched)

Mon 13 Nov 1876 (Vol 10 no 33)

M: 2nd inst at Col'ana by Rev J.M.KENDIG, CHARLES O ORR, M.D. & MISS MAGGIE SNYDER all of this co

M: 2nd inst by same GEORGE J.M.MYERS & MISS SARAH H. RIPLEY both of Leetonia

M: 5th inst at Col'ana by REV A E WARD, JOSEPH YOUNG of E.Pal. & MISS ELIZABETH TODD of Clarkson

M: 28th inst by REV D. HARGEST, G.W.FREDERICK & MISS N.J.- PERRY all of this co

M: 2d inst by same, at the res of bride's parents HARVEY ROBINSON & MISS BELLE WILLIAMS all of this co

D: 10th inst MRS. NELLIE GRAFTON w/o WILLIAM of Wayne Tp ae 83y 10m 20d

D: 7th inst ABEL LODGE of Iowa at the res of his father EVAN LODGE of Elkrun Tp ae 41y

D: 8th inst MARY COONEY widow of THOMAS COONEY dec'd late of Franklin Tp in 88th yr

We learn from the Leetonia Reporter that on Mon last a man named JACOB HAAS residing about 5 mi east of Col'ana while feeding a threshing machine had one of his arms horribly mangled below the elbow by the spikes of the cylinder. The arm was also broken above the elbow. A physician was sent for to dress the wound & deeming amputation necessary proceeded to perform the operation. While in the act, MR. HAAS died whether from the effects of the anaesthetics administered or from the loss of blood we are unable to learn.

WILLIAM WILSON, a stone cutter was killed by a fall from a derrick at East Liverpool last Thursday.

Mon 20 Nov 1876 (Vol 10 no 34)

M: 13th inst at the ME Parsonage by REV A R CHAPMAN, JOHN CLECKNER & MISS FORGE SHEPPARD all of New Lisbon

M: 16th inst at Wellsville by REV J H CONKLE, CHARLES B. CUMMINS of Wellsville & Miss EMMA RIGGS (BIGGS?)

M: 13th inst at Wellsville by same SHEWELL L. ATEN & MISS MARY A. SCHROEDER both of Wellsville

M: 14th inst at Industry PA by REV A M PARKINSON, DAVID G. PAISLEY of Wellsville & MISS HATTIE V. BRADY of Knoxville Jeff Co Oh

M: 1st inst at Salem by REV H B FRY, assisted by REV DR. DAVIDSON, PHILIP MERTZ of North Benton & MISS MARY ENGLE of Salem

M: 31st ult by REV G M ALBRIGHT, FELIX SELL & MISS MARTHA E.M.FROST both of Hanover Tp

M: 2nd inst by REV M T LAUFFER, GEORGE BEILHARTZ & MISS LOUISA E. GENTHER all of this co

M: 31st ult by REV J RUTHRAUFT, H.B.SHELTON & MISS MOILLE E. GREENAWALT both of this co

M: 8th inst at Rochester Pa by REV SNODGRASS, CHARLES THOMAS & MISS CLARA GIBB

D: 16th inst at Wellsville MRS. ELIZABETH McGILLIVARY d/o JOHN McDEVITT

D: 12th inst at East Liverpool JOHNNY WILHELM McKINNON

MTS.T.M.T.McCOY who has been on a visit to Scotland returned home last week.

Mon 27 Nov 1876 (Vol 10 no 35)

M: 18th inst by REV MAXWELL, THOMAS H. McCREADY & MISS LIZZIE BARD all of Leetonia

D: 8th inst FRANK WILLIAMS s/o MR. & MRS WESLEY WILLIAMS of Salem ae 12y

D: 13th inst in Salem Tp SARAH DUNLAP w/o JOHN DUNLAP ae 69y 3m 1d

D: 14th inst in Salem EVERT KIRTLAN s/o MR & MRS WM. KIRTLAN ae 14y 4m 9d

D: 27th inst at East Liverpool wife of WILL ORR aged 29y

D: 24th inst ANNA SPRINGER infant dau of PETER V & ELIZA SPRINGER of this place

D: 21st inst MARY HICKOX w/o H.S.HICKOX of New Lisbon ae 67y

MRS. HICKOX w/o S.H.HICKOX of this place died suddenly last Tues eve of heart disease. Shortly after retiring Mr.H. discovered something unusual in her actions, called in some of the neighbors but she died in a few minutes. The aged couple located in New Lisbon about 3 yrs ago & by their exemplary deportment won the respect & esteem of all who knew them.- Mr.H. is entirely deaf which makes his loss unusually severe. On Fri morning Mr H & a daughter started with the remains of the deceased for New Haven Conn the place of their former residence

THOMAS POST of Bradford, McKean Co Pa formerly of Salem met with a serious accident on the 18th inst which resulted in his death. He had removed to the above named place about 5 weeks ago & on morning of the accident was engaged with others in raising a heavy iron pipe from an oil well. Its weight was fully a thousand pounds & in its ascent which was rapid it turned out of its course & struck the walking beam. The force of the colision snapped the rope & the pipe fell with full weight & unimpeded force upon Mr POST's shoulder, crushing him to the earth. He lived 8 hours after the accident. The dec'd was in his 27th yr & leaves a wife & two children. He was buried at Salem on Tues afternoon.

Subscription list (only those out of area)
STERLING, D.   BROOKLYN IOWA
GRONER, WILLIAM,   BOONE IOWA

Mon 4 Dec 1876 (Vol 10 no 36)

M: 30th ult by REV E CAMERON, ZACHARIAH MORRIS & MISS IDA R. SCOVIL all of this co

M: 30th ult by REV A R CHAPMAN, HENRY C. POTTS & MISS LAURA A. BENSON all of this co

M: 23d ult by REV J H BLACKFORD, ALEXANDER McBANE & MISS MAGGIE McINTOSH both of this co

M: 23d ult at E.Liverpool by FATHER P J McGUIRE, MICHAEL MURRAY of Jethro & MISS JENNIE PHILLIPS of Salineville

M: 23d ult by same, JOHN BUCHEIT & MISS ELLA WEBBER both of Liverpool

M: 28th ult by same, JOHN HICKS of Akron & Miss MAGGIE McSHANE of Jethro

D: 27th ult NANCY C. BARGER w/o W H BARGER of Centre Tp ae 34y

D: 28th ult GEORGE W. GOODEREL of Wayne Tp ae 34y

D: 24th ult at the Infirmary L.B.BAGLEY ae 38y

D: 9th ult in Madison Tp WILLIAM A. POWERS s/o E & F POWERS ae 28y

D: 13 ult at Wellsville WILLIE H. GAMBLE s/o THOMAS & SARAH H. GAMBLE ae 3y 10d

D: 1st inst MARTHA STEWART wife of ROBERT STEWART of this place, colored, aged about 18y

D: on 2nd inst at Wellsville MRS. ELIZA SINCLAIR w/o O.C.SIN-CLAIR Ae 36.

D: 2nd inst JACOB M. MOWRY of Salem Tp ae 43y 5m

By notice in another column it will be seen that JACOB M. MOWRY a well known & highly esteemed citizen of Salem Tp died at his res Sat. About 10 days ago he was stricken with congestion of the brain, followed by inflammation & lingered in intense agony until the time of his death.

On Sat morning MRS. ELIZA SINCLAIR w/o O.C.SINCLAIR ESQ. of Wellsville died after a short but painful illness. She was the daughter of GEORGE JOHNSTON of Hancock Co WVA & sister of REV G N JOHNSTON pastor of the Presby.church at New Lisbon

The United Presbyterian congregation of New Lisbon has extended a unanaimous call to REV A H ELDER late of McKees-port PA to become thier pastor.

DEATH OF SAMUEL HOOVER, SR. SAMUEL HOOVER SR., father of our fellow townsman WILLIAM A. HOOVER died at the res of the latter Tues morn in 85th yr. Mr HOOVER located in New Lisbon in 1828 & for many years carried on the tailoring business successfully & was always a quiet & industrious citizen.- After the death of his wife about 25 yrs ago he resided in various parts of Ohio, then removed to Illinois where he married again. After the death of his 2nd he broke up housekeeping & since has spent a part of his time in Ill. & part in Adams Co Pa, the place of his nativity. Within the last year or two he has made his home at the res of his son in this place. He was buried with Masonic honors.

FOUR PERSONS KILLED...last Thurs morn two miners named GEORGE DAVIS & JOHN DURHAM were engaged in dividing a keg of powder at res of former in Salineville when it exploded leveling the building owned by SIMEON SHECKLER. The victims were GEORGE DAVIS & WIFE, JOHN DURHAM & his little child, aged 15 mo. None were killed outright. At last accounts DAVIS was still living but with no hopes for his recovery.

MARY F. GILMORE of East Liverpool has been sent to the insane department of the Allegheny City poor house, having lost her reason because a burglar broke into the house where she was employed...she & her mistress searched for him & found him; she lost her reason as a result. People say they hardly think that true...she has always acted kind of queer.

Matrimonial: last Thurs at res of LEMUEL SCOVIL in Elkrun Tp, the marriage of his eldest daughter MRISS IDA B. to ZACHARIAH MORRIS.

The following criminals convicted were sentenced as follows
ELLIS, THOMAS W., BURGLARY - 3 YRS HARD LABOR OHIO PEN
GASKILL, GEORGE   "   "
CORBETT, DANIEL   "   "
GILLIGEN BROTHERS   "   "
BROWN, ----   "   "
McCARTNEY, FRANK - GRAND LARCENY   2 YRS "   "

MR. & MRS. H.W.BROWN of New Lisbon celebrated the 10th anniversary at res on West Walnut st last Tues.

Mon 11 Dec 1876 (Vol 10 no 37)

M: 30th ult by REV J H HARRIER, DAVID LEWIS of Maho Co & MISS MARGARET COBBS of this co

M: 5th inst by WM. M. CRAWFORD ESQ, JAMES S. BOWLES & MISS MARY AINSWORTH all of this co

M: 4th inst by REV J J ESTILL, JOHN W. COWICK of Penna & MISS JEMIMA EDWARDS of this co

M: 30th ult by REV S. WAGNER, WILLIAM CAYGILL ESQ of Nebraska & MISS REBECCA LODGE of this co

D: 4th inst MARY J. STREET w/o JOHN STREET of Cleveland formerly of Salem, aged 37y 1m 10d

D: 7th inst GERTIE ANN CROOK infant dau of MARCUS & MARANDA CROOK of Centre Tp ae 10d

D:4th inst MURRAY HUSTON s/o JOHN & MARY HUSTON of CentreTp

D: 4th inst of diptheria LIDA GERTRUDE KNOWLES d/o R.B. & EMMA KNOWLES of E.Liverpool ae 2y 7m

D: 6th inst of typhoid fever EDWARD GARDNER second son of DR. GARDNER of E.Liv.

D: 3d inst at Unionville, this county, MRS. OSBORN FARMER

DAVIS, the 4th & last victim of the Salineville explosion died last Sunday

THOMAS DUNCAN, an old & highly esteemed citizen of Wells-ville died last Mon morning after a brief but very painful illness

CAPT.ALEXANDER SNODGRASS after an absence of 11 yrs returned to town last week; was in war of rebellion; now resides in Wymoming Territory

MR & MRS JOHN COPE near Columbiana, celebrated their crystal wedding on the 28th ult

JOHN YEOMANS, a former citizen of East Liverpool, lately living in Akron, died in that place Wed. last week

REV.DAVID STREET is new pastor of Presby church at Salem

MRS REED, an old lady of 82 yrs living in E.Liverpool was severely burned last Fri by her clothes catching fire while standing before the grate. She lived but 14 hours.

Mon 18 Dec 1876 (Vol 10 no 38)

M: 28th ult by ELIJAH SHINN ESQ, E P ALRIDGE of Salem Tp & MISS SILVIA E. ARNOLD of North Benton Mah Co

M: 3d inst in Hanover by REV L B KING, ELBRIDGE G. WHITACRE & MISS MARY E. LIBER both of New Garden

M: 7th inst by REV J M BRAY, JAMES WHAN & MISS HANNAH M. BINGHAM all of this co

M: 7th inst by REV W A DAVIDSON, JOHN THOMAS & MISS NELLIE BISSELL both of Salem

M: 7th inst by same FRANK SIPLE & MISS FANNIE KIRKBRIDE both of Salem

M: 3d inst in Allegheny by REV W H GILL, ANDREW J. DONNELLE & MISS ELLA IRWIN both formerly of Salem OH

M: 14th inst at Wellsville by REV J H CONKLE, JOSEPH F. MOORE & MISS MAGGIE E. STEWART both of Wellsville

D: at East Fairfield MRS. SARAH PATTEN w/o JOSEPH PATTEN ae 71y 7m 20d

D: 14th inst SUSAN A. SMITH d/o CALVIN & NORA SMITH of Centre Tp ae 12y 1m

Mr & Mrs AMOS STEELE of Salem celebrated their tin wedding on Mon eve last

DEATH OF HON. FISHER A. BLOCKSOM: last Thurs morn at his res on West Walnut St, aged 95y 3m 3d. Mr B was in his usual good health until within a few days of his death. Suffered from a severe cold; he was long identified with the interests of New Lisbon being one of its first settlers & probably the oldest man in the county at the time of his death. The dec'd was born in Sussex Co Delaware Sept 11, 1782 & commenced the study of law with MR.FINNEY at Wilmington in 1802 with whom he remained about a year or til that gentleman removed to Phila. He then finished studies under MR BROOME of same place & was admitted to the bar April 1805. He emigrated to Ohio in 1805 & located in New Lisbon where he has since resided. He traveled thru this section of country with Gen LEWIS CASS long before the era of railroads, riding along a path in search of a location. He represented this district in the State Leg. from 1826 to 1832 & to state senate in 1847 & 1849 & was elected Pros.Atty of CCO 4 times, serving 8 yrs in all. He was in 1812 apptd deputy postmaster general. He cast his first vote in 1803 & voted for Madison in 1808. He was probably the oldest lawyer, oldest Mason & oldest Democrat in Ohio. He was buried Sat. with Masonic honors.

MRS. S. ELIZA TOWNER eldest daughter of ELDER P.K.DIBBLE died at the res of her husband in Mason City Missouri on 6th inst

REV.J.BAILEY accepted the call of the United Pres Church of Wellsville

MRS. MOLLIE A. THOMAS wife of REV.T.B.THOMAS of Wilkesbarre PA & daughter of WM. ANDERSON ESQ of Homeworth was brought home Thanksgiving a corpse & interred in the cemetery near Homeworth

Mon 25 Dec 1876 (Vol 10 no 39)

M: 19th inst by ---, D.M.CARTER & MISS JENNIE SCOTT both of Middleton Tp

D: 12th inst in Madison Tp ISABELLA SMITH w/o DANIEL SMITH SR. in 63rd yr

D: 24th inst of lung fever HARRY M. STRAUGHN infant son of JOHN L. & MARY E. STRAUGHN aged 3 weeks.

Subscription list (out of area)
COBURN, MINNIE C., ULMANS' RIDGE MO
ANDREWS, JOHN, PEWOMA, MICH

MISS EMMA SPRINGER of Delaware Oh d/o DR.GEORGE SPRINGER formerly of New Lisbon, now of Leipsic, is visiting in town the guest of MISS JULIA ADAM

REV.G.M.ALBRIGHT pastor of the Reformed Church north of town is leaving for Reformed Church in Columbus City Iowa.

DEATH OF MISS HATTIE K. STARR: Died at the res of her mother in New Lisbon on Dec 19 after a painful illness, HATTIE K. STARR ae 36y. For several months she had been confined to bed; member of United Presby Church; funeral Wed.

ADDITION:

Fri 28 June 1867 (Vol 1 no 11)

Divorce notice: JOHN FINDLEY, res. unknown, notified that HANNAH M. FINDLEY filed on 31 May 1867 petition for divorce, for willful absence over 3 years. Hearing at next term of court. J.L.SMITH, her atty.

INDEX

ABBEY, JULIA F. 73
ABBOTS, D.W. 34
ABBOTT, DANIEL 52
ABBOTT, EMMA 68
ABBOTT, ESQ. 39,49
ABBOTT, FANNIE 87
ABLE, MR. 82
ABLETTE, KETURAH 105
ABRAHAM, JAMES R. 108
ABRAHAM, JOHN Q. 1
ABRAHAM, T.J. 108
ABRAHAM, T.W. 97
ABRAHAMS, ADA 57
ABRAMS, NETTIE E. 10
ABRAMS, WILLIAM 10
ACHE, D.S. 116
ADAM, FRED 15
ADAM, G.F. 4,97,110
ADAM, GEORGE M. 15
ADAM, JULIA 120
ADAM, LOU 110
ADAMS, A.G. 63
ADAMS, ANNIE E. 70
ADAMS, CATHARINE 110
ADAMS, FRANCES 4
ADAMS, FRED 99,110
ADAMS, FREDERICK 52
ADAMS, H.NELSON 5
ADAMS, H.P. 8
ADAMS, HANNAH 32
ADAMS, ISABEL 94
ADAMS, JAMES 63,77,86
ADAMS, JOHN 11,89
ADAMS, LUELLA 27
ADAMS, M.B. 27,92
ADAMS, M.W. 15
ADAMS, MAGGIE 99
ADAMS, MARGARET 99
ADAMS, MARTIN 100
ADAMS, MATTHEW 32,48,100
ADAMS, NANCY A. 74
ADAMS, NETTIE J. 99
ADAMS, R.G. 74
ADAMS, RICHARD 9
ADAMS, RUTH 11
ADAMS, SADIE 18
ADAMS, SAMUEL 30,74
ADAMS, SARAH E. 51
ADAMS, V.M. 75
ADAMS, W.J. 22,39
ADAMS, WILLIAM 46,100
ADDIS, F.P. 105
ADY, F.G. 81
ADY, J.H. 81
ADY, JULIA A. 81
AIKEN, LORENZO 51
AIKEN, SAMUEL 8
AILES, A.D. 73
AINSLEY, PETER 20
AINSLEY, MARY 119
AINSWORTH, MRS. 112
ALBERT, ANNA 5
ALBERT, ANNIE 23
ALBERTS, JOSEPH 34
ALBERTS, LEVINA 34
ALBRIGHT, DANIEL G. 22
ALBRIGHT, ELIZABETH 22
ALBRIGHT, FIRMAN 1,109
ALBRIGHT, G.H., REV. 92,93,96
ALBRIGHT, G.M., REV. 3,10,11,
  26,27,29,33,42,38,39,51,52,54,
  58,61,62,63,64,65,70,77,78,79,
  81,83,87,88,90,104,105,106,109,
  110,111,115,117,118,120
ALBRIGHT, JOHN M. 114
ALBRIGHT, LEVINA 82
ALBRIGHT, ORINDA 60
ALCORN, JOHN M. 97
ALDRICH, J., REV. 50
ALDRIDGE, ALFRED 34
ALDRIDGE, HENRY 8
ALDRIDGE, MATTIE 110
ALEXANDER, BERTHA 69
ALEXANDER, C.C. 58
ALFRED, WM. 62
ALLABACH, MARIDA 82
ALLABACK, GEORGE 91
ALLBRIGHT, MARGARET 3
ALLEN, AMANDA 95
ALLEN, BENJAMIN 49
ALLEN, BERTHA 95

ALLEN, DAVID 21
ALLEN, I.T., REV. 87
ALLEN, JESSE M. 85
ALLEN, JOHN E. 95
ALLEN, MARY 85
ALLEN, THOS.C. 9,10,12,13,14,
  18,24,76
ALLETON, HANNAH 83
ALLISON, ALEZON 112
ALLISON, ALICE A. 34
ALLISON, B.M. 99
ALLISON, HANNAH C. 30
ALLISON, JOHN 20,34,112
ALLISON, KESIAH 51
ALLISON, LEE ANN 55
ALLISON, LUCINDA 87
ALLISON, MAHLON 43
ALLISON, MARY 20
ALLISON, MRS. 105
ALLISON, NANCY 34
ALLISON, WILLIAM L. 112
ALLMAN, FRANK 48
ALLMON, ESTHER 62
ALLMON, JESSE 62
ALMY, SANFORD 83,107
ALRIDGE, E.P. 119
ALTAFFER, JOHN P. 25
ALTERHOLT, LIZZIE C. 24
ALTHAR, MARIA L. 75
ALTMAN, MAGGIE 9
AMBLER, JACOB 21
AMERMAN, S.D. 48
AMON, SARAH E. 89
AMOS, FRANK 19
AMPT, HENRY 65
ANDERSON, ANNA 42
ANDERSON, CHARLES 102
ANDERSON, D. 38
ANDERSON, DAVID 83
ANDERSON, GEORGE 115
ANDERSON, HAMILTON 67
ANDERSON, HANNAH M. 34
ANDERSON, JENNIE 84
ANDERSON, LIZZIE 80
ANDERSON, MID 46
ANDERSON, REV. 106
ANDERSON, SARAH 67
ANDERSON, T.B., REV. 73
ANDERSON, T.F. 58
ANDERSON, W. 9
ANDERSON, W.G. 10
ANDERSON, WM. 2,7,9,12,46,57,
  67,120
ANDRE, JESSE 28
ANDRE, M.E. 46
ANDREW, FRANCIS J. 99
ANDREW, JOHN 47
ANDREWS & AUGHENBAUGH 40
ANDREWS, ANNA 50
ANDREWS, ELIZABETH 103
ANDREWS, ISABELLA 46
ANDREWS, JOHN 82,120
ANDREWS, JOSEPH, REV. 9,11
ANDREWS, REV.MR. 24
ANGLEMIER, MADISON H. 7
ANGLEMIRE, ENOS 48
ANGLEMYER, LUKE 84
ANGLEMYER, MAGGIE 84
ANGLEMYER, QUINCY 84
ANGLEMYER, SALLIE 101
ANGLEMYER, SOPHIA 96
ANGLEMYER, WILLIAM S. 79
ANGLEMYRE, REBECCA 64
ANTHONY, HARRY 89
ANTRIM, AARON 84
ANTRIM, ANNA A. 92
ANTRIM, BENJAMIN 109
ANTRIM, JOHN 7
APLET, MR. 55
APPLE, GEORGE L. 81
APPLE, JAMES E. 33
APPLE, LIZZIE MAE 33
APPLE, MARY J. 33
APPLE, SUSANNA 99
APPLE, WM. 33
APPLEGATE, ANN 52
APPLEGATE, LOUISA 86
APPLEGATE, MARION 117
APPLEGATE, MINERVA 111
APPLEGATE, RACHEL 106
ARB, JOHN 83

ARB, MARGARET 88
ARBUCKLE, JAMES 86,93
ARBUCKLE, JOSEPHINE 2
ARBUCKLE, LEVINA 53
ARBUCKLE, THOMAS 53
ARBUCKLE, WILLIAM F. 86
ARCHBOLD, MARY E. 87
ARMBRUST, ADAM 20
ARMBRUST, ANNIE 20
ARMSTRONG, AARON C. 10
ARMSTRONG, ANDREW 7,30,56
ARMSTRONG, COLUMBUS 83,116
ARMSTRONG, DANIEL 25
ARMSTRONG, ELIZABETH 91
ARMSTRONG, GEN. 56
ARMSTRONG, GEORGE 11,75
ARMSTRONG, HAMILTON 113
ARMSTRONG, HANNAH 42
ARMSTRONG, JAMES 77
ARMSTRONG, JENNIE 89
ARMSTRONG, JOHN 12,84,113
ARMSTRONG, LEVINA 25
ARMSTRONG, LIZZIE 92
ARMSTRONG, LOT G. 25
ARMSTRONG, MARGARET 113
ARMSTRONG, MARTIN 112
ARMSTRONG, MARTIN, MRS. 87
ARMSTRONG, MARY 13,77,116
ARMSTRONG, NATHAN H. 106
ARMSTRONG, ROBERT 69
ARMSTRONG, SIMON 92
ARMSTRONG, WILLIAM, GEN. 112
ARNOLD, ANNIE 61
ARNOLD, CATHARINE 95
ARNOLD, E.J. 10
ARNOLD, F.L., REV. 11
ARNOLD, J.W. 29
ARNOLD, JOSEPHINE 37
ARNOLD, L. 115
ARNOLD, LEVI 76
ARNOLD, SILVIA 119
ARNOLD, T.S. 111
ARNOLD, TRUMAN 83
ARRISON, A.D. 69
ARRISON, ADAM 78
ARTER, ALPHEUS 110
ARTER, ANNIE 58
ARTER, D.A., DR. 81
ARTER, ELIZABETH 46
ARTER, EVA J. 53
ARTER, FLORENCE A. 81
ARTER, GEORGE 53
ARTER, HARRIET 53
ARTER, HETTIE 34
ARTER, J. 115
ARTER, JACOB 43,63
ARTER, JENNIE 109
ARTER, JOHN 6
ARTER, JOSEPH 78
ARTER, LEONARD 34,36
ARTER, LOUANA 110
ARTER, MARY 110
ARTER, MICHAEL 78
ARTER, POTTER & BROWN 72
ARTER, RICHARD 7
ARTER, RICHARDSON 92
ARTER, SIMON 46
ARTER, T.G. 18
ARTHER, JOHN 7
ARTHUR, E.F. 115
ARTHUR, J., REV. 9,22,31,58
ASHBAUGH, N.T. 53
ASHBAUGH, OLIVER 36
ASHBAUGH, SUSAN 67
ASHFORD & BOWER 15
ASHFORD, GEORGE 60
ASHTON, WILLIAM 112
ASHTON, WM.M. 95
ASK, EUGENE E. 83
ASK, MARION E. 49
ASTRY, DAVID 95
ASTRY, DAVID, MRS. 50
ASTRY, JONAS SR. 95
ASTRY, LEVI 72
ASTRY, WILLIAM 111
ATCHISON, JAMES 70
ATCHISON, MARY J. 70
ATEN, ANNA 69
ATEN, C.M. 44,54,115
ATEN, HENRY 35,44,65,80
ATEN, HENRY SR. 108

ATEN, JENNIE 99
ATEN, LOUIS 15
ATEN, SHEWELL L. 118
ATKINSON, ANN 52
ATKINSON, CURTIS 106
ATKINSON, ELIZA J. 52
ATKINSON, ELIZABETH 11
ATKINSON, GEORGE 11
ATKINSON, JOHN 45,52
ATKINSON, LAURA 45
ATKINSON, MARY ANN 45
ATTERHOLT, ALICE 89
ATTERHOLT, ANNA R. 47
ATTERHOLT, ELLA 105
ATTERHOLT, F.M. 72
ATTERHOLT, GEORGE 12
ATTERHOLT, HENRY 7,28
ATTERHOLT, JAMES 102
ATTERHOLT, LIZZIE C. 24
ATTERHOLT, MATTIE J. 31
ATTERHOLT, MR. 57
ATWELL, CHARLES 91
AUFFMAN, HENRY T. 57
AUGHENBAUGH & ANDREWS 40
AUGHENBAUGH, CLAYTON 40
AUGHINBAUGH, JAMES C. 105
AUGHINBAUGH, MARY 43
AUGHINBAUGH, WM.H. 21
AUGUSTINE, A.L. 34
AUGUSTINE, MR. 95
AULD, ISABELLA 108
AUSTIN, MARY 98
AUSTIN, PETER 48
AVERY, S.A. 37
AWTHUR, DAVID 41
AWTHUR, LOUISA M. 41
AXDELL, JANIE 41
AXE, CHARLES 117,118
AXE, L.C. 111
AYRES, NEWTON 20
AZDELL, ANDREW O. 6
AZDELL, E. 46
AZDELL, ELLIE A. 6
AZDELL, JAMES 64,67
AZDELL, JOHN M. 8
AZDELL, MARIA 20
BABCOCK, CATHARINE 114
BACKLER, REV. 38
BADGER, FRANK 90
BADGER, JOHN 31
BADLEY, FRANK M. 4
BAECHLER, C., REV. 76,80
BAECHLER, MOLLIE 70
BAECHLER, S., REV. 31,51,54,
  55,58,64,68,70,72,73
BAELZ, SALLIE 115
BAGALEY, CATHARINE 72
BAGALEY, JOHN 72
BAGLEY, L.B. 119
BAGSHAW, ELIZABETH 101
BAGULY, KATE 51
BAHRENS, CHARLES, REV. 21
BAILEY, CHARLES S. 107
BAILEY, HARDING 18
BAILEY, J., REV. 120
BAILEY, JOSEPH 31
BAILEY, KEARSEY 32
BAILEY, PETER F. 112
BAILEY, REV.DR. 46
BAILEY, S. 100
BAILEY, SAMUEL 115
BAILHARTZ, BARBARA 115
BAIN, JOHN 63
BAIR, JOHN 7
BAIRD, ALICE A. 23
BAIRD, D.R. 31
BAIRD, I.N., REV. 1,2,3,4,5,
  6,7,11,13,14,19,23,24,27,28,
  42,59,64,71,83,84
BAIRD, J.C. 74
BAIRD, ORSINA 55
BAIRD, R.K. 50
BAIRD, REV. 10
BAIRD, SARAH A. 42
BAIRN, S.B. 78
BAKER, A., REV. 41,43
BAKER, ADA 107
BAKER, ANNA 90
BAKER, B.G. 69
BAKER, BENNETT G. 107
BAKER, C.C. 64

Name	Page	Name	Page	Name	Page	Name	Page
BAKER, CALLIE	25	BARNES, ZILLA A.	24	BEAN, EVA	96	BELL, SAMUEL	3
BAKER, CATHARINE	69	BARNET, LOU	87	BEAN, HUGH	85	BELL, WILLIAM	24
BAKER, CHRISTENA	96	BARNETT, EDWARD P.	14	BEAN, ISRAEL	91,110	BELTZ, GEORGE	91
BAKER, DANIEL	10	BARNETT, MARK	3	BEAN, JANE	91	BENEDICT, ELIZA J.	8
BAKER, FREDERICK	5,27	BARNHART, MR.	85	BEAN, JOHN	57	BENKOWSKI, LIZZIE	70
BAKER, GEORGE	66	BARNS, CHRISTOPHER	99	BEAN, MAGGIE	93	BENNER, ALICE	81
BAKER, GIDEON	7	BARNS, MARY	61	BEAN, MARY JANE	69	BENNER, JACKSON	4
BAKER, HIRAM	8,114	BARR, CHARLES	4	BEAN, NORA	2	BENNER, JANE	44,71
BAKER, ISABELLA	45	BARR, J.W.	4	BEAN, PIUS	3,10,42	BENNER, LOU	82
BAKER, JEPTHA	7	BARR, JOHN	84,118	BEAN, U.	12,36	BENNER, MARTIN	33
BAKER, JOHN, REV.	28,82	BARR, MARGARET	100	BEAR, CATHARINE	9	BENNER, NANCY C.	31
BAKER, JOSEPH	88,90	BARR, MARY	59	BEAR, MARY F.	71	BENNET, LAFAYETTE	58
BAKER, LORENA J.	24	BARR, MATILDA	4	BEARD, KATE	64	BENNET, RUTH	64
BAKER, MARY	9,64,66,107,114	BARR, RICHARD	4	BEARD, MARY E.	72	BENNETT, ANNA Y.	28,29
BAKER, MATTIE D.	79	BARR, WALTER	100	BEARD, RACHEL	108	BENNETT, BERTHA	53
BAKER, ORETTA S.	7	BARR, WILLIAM	59,100	BEARDMORE, MARY	37	BENNETT, EDWIN	104,106
BAKER, RESIN	99	BARRET, BRIDGET	89	BEARDMORE, W.	37	BENNETT, FANNIE	108
BAKER, STANTON	107	BARRETT, ---	68	BEARDSLEY, WILLIAM	81	BENNETT, H.	108
BAKER, STEPHEN A.	73	BARRETT, THOMAS T.	88	BEATTY, JAMES	51	BENNETT, ISAAC	10
BAKER, THOMAS	25,45	BARRICK, ISAAC	99	BEATTY, MARTHA	27	BENNETT, JAMES	92
BAKER, WILLIAM	3,9,77,93,102	BARROW, ELIZABETH	79	BEATTY, PHENIAH	1	BENNETT, LEA	112
BALDWIN, HANNAH M.	11	BARTCHY, SUSAN	91	BEATTY, WM.T., REV.	107	BENNETT, SAMUEL H.	3
BALDWIN, JAMES	25	BARTH, MARY L.	56	BEAUMONT, HELEN	106	BENNETT, WILLIAM	1
BALKER, GERHARD	1	BARTH, SAMUEL	12,56	BEAUMONT, HENRY S.	97	BENNETT, ZELPHA	23
BALL, A.	23	BARTHOLOMEW, A.	99	BEAUMONT, JABEZ	60	BENSON, ISAAC	37
BALL, CHARLES	77	BARTHOLOMEW, AARON	41	BEAUMONT, JOSEPH	60	BENSON, J.F.	44
BALL, ELIZABETH	77	BARTHOLOMEW, EDWIN	41	BEAUMONT, MARGARET	73	BENSON, LAURA A.	118
BALL, HATTIE	5	BARTHOLOMEW, EMMA	39	BEAUMONT, SUE S.	33	BENSON, MARQUIS	112
BALL, JOHN	109	BARTHOLOMEW, GEORGE	39	BEAUMONT, THOMAS, DR.	60	BENSON, WILLIAM	83
BALL, JONATHAN C.	75	BARTHOLOMEW, JANE	41	BEBOUT, ISRAEL	55	BENTLEY, THOMAS M.	5
BALL, JOSEPH	107	BARTHOLOMEW, JENNIE ATEN	99	BECK, ALBERT	21	BENTLEY, WALTER G.	40
BALL, KATE	23	BARTIN, RESIN	84	BECK, CAPT.	56	BENTLEY, WILL	96
BALL, MARGARET	77	BARTON, FANNIE M.	83	BECK, CHARLES	25	BENWOOD, MARY A.	10
BALL, NATHAN	7,111	BARTON, J.C.	76	BECK, CLARKSON	59	BENWOOD, SARAH	62
BALL, OWEN C.	28,29	BARTON, JOHN	10	BECK, CORNELIA	34	BENWOOD, W.P.	98
BALL, THOS.	7	BARTRAM, THOMAS	79	BECK, ELIZABETH	21	BENZE, J.H.	49
BALL, TILLIE	54	BASHAW, GEORGE M.	38	BECK, ELLA	87	BERGENWALT, KATE	55
BALLENTINE, GEORGE	97	BASINGER, SUSANNAH	62	BECK, FERDINAND	13,25	BERGER, MARY A.	86
BANE, HENRY	41	BASSART, J., DR.	116	BECK, FRANCES	2	BERGER, ROSANA	86
BANE, THOMAS L.	41	BASSETT, EDWIN	48	BECK, JAMES M.	26	BERRY, MAGGIE	111
BANKS, MARY E.	48	BASSETT, NATHAN	52	BECK, LYDIA	25	BERRY, MARY ANN	26
BANKS, REV.	8	BASTEL, ISABEL	24	BECK, PRESTON	79,94	BERTOLETE, J.B.	27
BANNING, HENRY C.	16	BATCHELOR, A.D.	49	BECK, SARAH	94	BERTOLETT, ANNA M.	22
BARBER, ANNA	23	BATCHELOR, CELIA	93	BECK, WILLIAM	55	BERTOLETT, DR.	22
BARBER, BENJAMIN	9	BATCHELOR, CLARA	32	BEDALL, REV.	105	BESLEY, THOMAS	16
BARBER, GEORGE W.	3	BATCHELOR, E.M.	33	BEDALL, W., REV.	96,98,103	BESSON, JOHN O.	11
BARBER, HANNAH	80	BATCHELOR, S.ADDISON	71	BEE, ELLEN M.	69	BESTER, CORA E.	1
BARBER, JOEL F.	103	BATCHELOR, SALLIE	85	BEEBOUT, SARAH M.	69	BESTER, E.L.	1
BARBER, SARAH S.	104	BATCHELOR, WM.H.	33	BEECH, ELIZABETH	36	BESTER, MARY	1,3
BARCH, PHILIP	9	BATES, ALICE	104	BEECH, WM.	36	BETTERIDGE, WALTER	31
BARCLAY, ANNA	64	BATES, NANCY A.	37	BEEN, JAMES	7	BETTIS, MILTON	4
BARCLAY, J.M.	100	BATTERSHELL, WILLIAM	7	BEEN, MOSES	7	BETZ, ELMIRA	89
BARCLAY, JAMES	35	BATTIN, COBURN	4	BEER, ELLEN M.	68	BETZ, EMMA	105
BARCLAY, RICHARD N.	100	BATTIN, DAVID	8	BEESON, EDWARD	70	BETZ, FREDERICK	42
BARCLAY, SETTA	100	BATTIN, JOHN	101	BEESON, EFFIE	108	BETZ, JAMES	81
BARCUS, JOHN	22	BATTIN, ROBERT	4	BEESON, FRANCES	112	BETZ, JONAS	39,57
BARCUS, MARY E.	20	BATTIN, SARAH	105	BEESON, I.N.	14	BETZ, LYDIA ANN	57
BARCUS, WILLIAM C.	77	BATTON, DR.	24	BEESON, JOHN	7,11	BETZ, MATTIE	97
BARD, EZEKIEL	7	BAUGHER, NATHAN	42	BEESON, LENORA	108	BETZ, OSCAR	114
BARD, FRANK	94	BAUGHMAN, HENRY	7	BEESON, MARTHA	70	BETZ, WILLIAM	1
BARD, JAS.H.	20	BAUGHMAN, SAMANTHA	70	BEESON, MARTIN	4	BEVINGTON, ALEXANDER	60
BARD, LIZZIE	118	BAUM, JOHN	28	BEESON, NANCY	112	BEVINGTON, MATILDA	60
BARD, SAMUEL	83	BAUM, L.	73	BEESON, O.J.	108	BEVINGTON, THOMAS	113
BARD, WINIFRED	89	BAUM, NANCY	83	BEESON, RICHARD	112	BIDDELL, MARY J.	105
BARE, PETER	13	BAUMAN, HANNAH	80	BEESON, SIDNEY	108	BIERD, SOCRATES	77
BARGER, NANCY	119	BAXLEY, KATE	44	BEGGES, ANNA J.	90	BIERY, BENJAMIN	101
BARGER, W.H.	119	BAXLEY, WILLIAM	8,44	BEGGES, DAVID	90,94,114	BIGGINS, PATRICK	78
BARINGER, IDA	105	BAXTER, AMELIA	90	BEGGES, MRS.	94	BIGGS, EMMA	118
BARKER, ELIZA	39	BAXTER, CRISSIE	80	BEHNER, BARBARY	6	BIGGS, WILLIAM	115
BARKER, WILLIAM H.	105	BAXTER, E.A.	7	BEHRNER, BARBARA	115	BIGLER, ELIZABETH	69
BARLOW, ELIZABETH	61	BAXTER, ELDER	79	BEILHARTZ, BARBARA	115	BIGLER, FREDERICK	100
BARLOW, RICHARD	61	BAXTER, HENRY	40	BEILHARTZ, GEORGE	118	BILES, JOHN	10
BARLOW, SADIE	61	BAXTER, JOHN L.	7	BELAT, CHARLES	12	BILGER, ANNA	23
BARNABY, CLARKSON	10	BAXTER, MARY	35,40	BELAT, DAVID	2,12	BILGER, FREDERICK	100
BARNABY, IDA	105	BAXTER, REV.	6,36	BELAT, KATE	94	BILGER, GEORGE	52
BARNARD, LIZZIE	106	BAXTER, W.H.	76	BELAT, WM.	82	BILGER, KATE	14
BARNES, ALBERT	105	BAXTER, WILLIAM	5,7,14,20, 24,36,44,74,80	BELATT, SUSAN	13	BILGER, MARGARET	52
BARNES, ALFRED	28	BAXTER, WM., REV.	1,2,3,10,13, 21,25,27,28,29,31,32,33,38,39, 40,46,47,49,51,52,54,55,61,63, 64,67,69,72,73,84,89,90,92,93, 99,106,107,109,110,111,116	BELDEN, G.W.	14	BILGERS, LIZZIE	78
BARNES, ANDREW	99			BELDEN, JUDGE	6	BILLINGSLEY, AMOS C.	5
BARNES, ANNETTA	101			BELDEN, MRS.	6	BILLINGSLEY, N.B.	109
BARNES, CATHARINE	80,81			BELL, A.T., REV.	109	BILLINGSLEY, RACHEL	39
BARNES, ELI H.	28	BAYARD, LUCY W.	107	BELL, ALMIRA J.	3	BILLINGSLEY, W.J.	6
BARNES, ELIZABETH	43,105	BAYLES, HANNAH	77	BELL, ANNIE	100	BINFORD, ROBERT	30
BARNES, HATTIE	96	BAYNE, LIZZIE	39	BELL, ELLA M.	106	BINGHAM, ALEX	49
BARNES, HENRY	116	BAYNE, WM.H.	73	BELL, HIRAM	62,90	BINGHAM, HANNAH	119
BARNES, JACOB	6,66	BEACH, REV.	81	BELL, JAMES	12,37	BINGHAM, SUSAN	45
BARNES, LOUISA	28	BEADLIN, ELIZABETH	95	BELL, JOSEPH	51,105	BINGHAM, SUSANNA	51
BARNES, MARGARET	35	BEALL, REASIN	7	BELL, KIMSEY	117	BINSLEY, ANDREW	70,76,95
BARNES, SUSANNAH	47	BEAN, ELIZABETH	3	BELL, LEWIS K.	102	BINSLEY, E., REV.	99
BARNES, THOMAS	105			BELL, MARIA	105	BINSLEY, ELLEN	95
BARNES, WILLIAM	80,81			BELL, PHEBE R.	24	BINSLEY, JOHN	79
				BELL, SALOME	12,89		

BINSLEY, JOSEPH	32	BOLLMYER, CHRISTIANA	115	BOWMAN, A.A.	89	BRANNON, GEORGE W.	83
BINSLEY, JOSHUA	70,71	BOLLMYER, J.F.	115	BOWMAN, AMOS	45	BRANNON, JAMES M.	80
BINSLEY, SARAH A.	70,71	BONBRIGHT, EDNA	100	BOWMAN, CHRIS	84,89	BRANNON, MARY	75,78
BIRCH, F.R.	27	BONBRIGHT, KATE	100	BOWMAN, CHRISTIAN	7	BRANNON, ROSA	83
BIRCH, MARY	110	BONBRIGHT, WILLIAM	100	BOWMAN, ELIZABETH	111	BRANNON, WILLIAM	75,78
BIRDSON, J.H.	47	BONNELL, D.W.	89	BOWMAN, GEORGE	44	BRANTINGHAM, CYRUS	35
BIRKETT, REV.	58	BONSALL, ADDIE	116	BOWMAN, ISIDORE	111	BRATT, ANGUS	32
BIRKIT, EDWARD, REV.	47,52, 54,55,56	BONSALL, ALBERT	16	BOWMAN, JACOB	7	BRATT, EMMA	32
BIRMAN, ALONZO	44	BONSALL, DANIEL	7,60	BOWMAN, JOHN	37,69,87	BRATT, SARAH A.	32
BISHOP, A.J.	91	BONSALL, ELIZABETH	60	BOWMAN, JOSHUA	7,43,104	BRAWDY, AARON	14
BISHOP, ANNA	38	BONSALL, ISAAC	21	BOWMAN, LOUISA	69,87	BRAY, J.M., REV.	2,3,38,41,
BISHOP, GRACE	98	BONSALL, JOEL	10	BOWMAN, MAGGIE	103		45,48,54,62,110,114,119
BISHOP, HATTIE	98	BONSALL, JONATHAN	10	BOWMAN, MALANCTHON	12	BREADEN, JANE R.	39
BISHOP, HOWELL S.	11	BONSALL, JOSEPH	96	BOWMAN, MARY	81,87	BREADEN, MARTHA S.	39
BISHOP, ISADORE	50,98	BONSALL, WILLIAM	32	BOWMAN, OLIVE C.	63	BREADEN, WILLIAM J.	39
BISHOP, SAMUEL R.	39	BOOHECKER, MARTHA A.	49	BOWMAN, PERRY M.	89	BREED, WM.P., REV.	104
BISSELL, J.G.	2	BOON, EDWARD	57	BOWMAN, ROSA D.	89	BREENE, MARY J.	20
BISSELL, MARY	2	BOONE, CHARLES	64	BOWMAN, SAMUEL	12,41	BREIDENSTINE, H.	37
BISSELL, NELLIE	119	BOONE, EMMA	16	BOWMAN, SOPHIA H.	30	BREIGHTON, JAMES P.	18
BLACK, ANDREW	31	BOONE, ESTHER	50	BOWMAN, WILLIAM	86	BRETZ, FANNY G.	11
BLACK, ANNA	81	BOONE, HANNAH C.	27	BOYCE, AMY A.	24	BRETZ, JACOB	11
BLACK, GEO.	28	BOONE, ISAAC	50	BOYCE, CHARLES R.	43	BREWER, ANSON L.	12,50
BLACK, HARRY	49	BOONE, J.T., JR.	100	BOYCE, D.	115	BREWER, CHARLES	12
BLACK, JAMES	48	BOONE, JAMES	9,13	BOYCE, DAVID	28	BREWER, EDWIN S.	50
BLACK, MARIAN	31	BOONE, JAMES, MRS.	13	BOYCE, FRANCIS M.	43	BREWER, ROBERT	12,36
BLACK, MATTHEW	38	BOONE, MARY	54,90	BOYCE, G.M., REV.	76	BREWER, SARAH A.	40
BLACK, ROBINS	9	BOONE, MAYOR	30	BOYCE, JOHN	24	BREWSTER, HARRIET E.	72
BLACK, SAMANTHA	56	BOONE, T.C.	103	BOYCE, JOSEPH, DR.	87	BREWSTER, J.T.	29,50,95
BLACK, WILLIAM H.	56	BOORY, FERDINAND	78	BOYCE, MARGUERETTA	43	BREWSTER, JOHN	87
BLACKBURN, B.J.	106	BOOTH, CARRIE N.	51	BOYCE, S.F.	21	BREWSTER, M.E.	34
BLACKBURN, BENJ.	46,54	BOOTH, DAVID	114	BOYD, SHERWOOD	90	BREWSTER, MARIAH J.	29
BLACKBURN, JAMES	108	BOOTH, H.G.	59	BOYER, ADA	41	BRICE, JAS.F.	70
BLACKBURN, JOHN A.	11	BOOTH, JEREMIAH	8	BOYER, CAROLINE	41	BRICK, ROXANNA	90
BLACKBURN, JOSEPH H.	71	BOOTH, KERSEY	116	BOYER, D.K.	50	BRICKER, A.E.	75
BLACKBURN, LEORA	106	BOOTH, MARTHA	66	BOYER, DAVID	41	BRICKER, CHARITY	117
BLACKBURN, M.W.	103	BOOTH, MRS.	75	BOYER, JERRY	12	BRICKER, DANIEL	48
BLACKBURN, MARGARET	87	BOOTH, SANFORD	107	BOYER, SAMUEL	31	BRICKER, DAVID	97
BLACKBURN, MARY	106	BOOTHE, W.A.	115	BOYL, JOHN	66	BRICKER, DELLA	93
BLACKBURN, NANCY	114	BORDEN, SPENCER	53	BOYLE, ALLEN	29	BRICKER, DR.	117
BLACKBURN, REBECCA A.	11	BORING, G.W.	32,40,51,59	BOYLE, EDWARD	56	BRICKER, ELI	42,109
BLACKFORD, J.H., REV.	116,119	BORING, GEORGE W.	42,44,50	BOYLE, ELIZABETH	72	BRICKER, ELIZABETH	71
BLACKLEDGE, LEVI	7	BORING, MARY	24	BOYLE, HOMER C.	64	BRICKER, ENOS	29,66,80
BLACKLEDGE, R.	7	BORING, WASH.	81	BOYLE, LOUIS E.	72	BRICKER, HENRY	7
BLACKMAN, IVAN	17	BORN, R.P., REV.	58	BOYLE, MAGGIE	64	BRICKER, J.F.	72
BLACKMORE, MR.	111	BORNE, EMMA	91	BOYLE, REV.	87	BRICKER, JESSE	72
BLAIR & SEYMOUR	18	BORTON, H.P.	74	BOYLE, SARAH	56	BRICKER, JOHN	98
BLAIR, G.A.	109	BORTON, H.P., REV.	105	BOYLE, T.N., REV.	83,85,86, 89,91	BRICKER, LUCINDA	26
BLAIR, JOHN	32	BOSSART, J., DR.	116			BRICKER, LYDIA	72,97
BLAIR, MARGARET	65	BOSSART, M.L.	93	BOYLE, THOMAS N., REV.	75,76,	BRICKER, MARY	71,76,115,117
BLAIR, THOS.B.	46	BOSSERT, HATTIE	80		80,81,85,90,91,92,93	BRICKER, PAUL	93
BLAKE, NANCY J.	18	BOSSERT, MATTIE A.	14	BOYLE, WM.W.	82	BRICKER, PHEBE ANN	66
BLAKE, SUSANNA	58	BOSTON, ---	57	BRACKEN, LINDLEY	5	BRICKER, PHILIP	71
BLAKE, THOMAS B.	35	BOSTON, ALCAZENA	57	BRADBURY, ELLEN	105	BRICKER, REBECCA	88
BLANCHARD, FREDERICK	23	BOSTON, H.P.	100	BRADFIELD, ADA S.	100	BRICKER, SOPHIA	78
BLAZER, JOS.	65	BOSTON, JAMES B.	18	BRADFIELD, BENJAMIN	7	BRIDENSTEIN, JONAS	108
BLEAKLY, WM.	33	BOSTON, JOSEPH	57,76	BRADFIELD, J.E.	21	BRIDENSTEIN, SARAH	108
BLECHER, WILLIAM	47	BOSTWICK, CHARLES E.	21	BRADFIELD, JOHN E.	107	BRIDENSTINE, LUNDY	72
BLECKER, WILLIAM	47	BOSTWICK, L.L.	106	BRADFIELD, MARY	21	BRIDENSTINE, M.	105
BLIZZARDS, A.C.	20	BOSWELL, ELLEN	26	BRADFIELD, SETH	30	BRIDENSTINE, N.	105
BLOCKSOM, A.J.	22	BOSWELL, SUSAN	70	BRADFORD, CHAS.S.	70	BRIGGS & BURNS	47,57
BLOCKSOM, FISHER A.	43,46,54, 111,115,120	BOTTENBERG, CORNELIA	86	BRADLEE, TIMOTHY	67	BRIGGS, ANNA	53
		BOUGH, ELIZABETH	108	BRADLEY, TIMOTHY	67	BRIGGS, CHARLEY	53
BLOCKSOM, FISHER JR.	86	BOUGH, EUPHEMA S.	100	BRADSHAW, ADDIE	58	BRIGGS, GEORGE W.	53
BLOCKSOM, J.F.	42	BOUGH, HENRY JAMES	109	BRADSHAW, CLARA	58	BRIGGS, JOHN	7
BLOCKSOM, WILLIE	116	BOUGH, JAMES	109	BRADSHAW, MR.	115	BRIGGS, MAHLON	53,96
BLOODGOOD, M.V., REV.	105	BOUGH, JOHN H.	100	BRADSHAW, T.R.	45	BRIGGS, WILLIAM G.	53
BLOOR, EMMA	93	BOUGH, MARQUIS H.	40	BRADSHAW, THEODORE	58	BRIGHT, AMY	30
BLOOR, SABINA	93	BOUGH, OAKLEY	100	BRADWAY, MARY J.	5	BRIGHT, ANNA E.	16
BLOOR, W.	115	BOUGH'S MILL	45	BRADY, CAPT.	103	BRIGHT, EMELINE	81
BLYTHE, ANDREW	54	BOUGHTON, LYDIA	53	BRADY, FITZ	68	BRIGHT, HENRY	62
BLYTHE, EVALONA	38	BOULTON, LEVI	59	BRADY, HATTIE	118	BRIGHT, JOHN	62
BLYTHE, HANNA B.	38	BOULTON, ORPHAN	59	BRADY, JAMES	7,113	BRIGHT, MARY J.	62
BLYTHE, JOHN W.	9,38	BOUQUET'S EXPEDITION	75	BRADY, MAHALA	18	BRIGHT, WM.	70,81
BLYTHE, MARY	108	BOURNAM, LYDIA M.	14	BRADY, MARGARET	74	BRINDLEY, E.A., REV.	2,91,97,
BLYTHE, MISS	26	BOURNE, ANN	90	BRADY, SERINDA	97		101,102,108,110
BLYTHE, MRS.	26	BOURNE, ENOCH	90	BRADY, STEPHEN	7	BRINDLEY, JOHN	88,93,109,111
BLYTHE, SOLOMON	1	BOUTWELL, HETTIE	6	BRADY, THOMAS	74	BRINKER, ANDREW	5,103,104,116
BLYTHE, SUSAN	85	BOVARD, CHARLES W.	30	BRAIN, WALTER	110	BRINKER, CANES T.	100
BOE, ELIZA R.	69	BOVARD, MAY J.	30	BRAINARD, BESSIE	81	BRINKER, CATHARINE	28,29,54
BOE, ELIZABETH R.	69	BOWDEN, JOSEPH	28	BRAINARD, CALVIN	85	BRINKER, CHARLES	104
BOIES, ANNA	25	BOWDEN, MARY L.	28	BRAINARD, ELLA	89	BRINKER, CLARA	106
BOIES, SADIE	96	BOWEN, B.F., REV.	35,37	BRAINARD, EMMA	37	BRINKER, D., DR.	2
BOISE, ELIZABETH	27	BOWER & ASHFORD	15	BRANDEBERRY, ---	36	BRINKER, DANIEL JR.	104
BOISE, JOHN	27	BOWER, ALICE	5	BRANDEBERRY, B.	7	BRINKER, FRANK	97
BOISE, MATTHEW	27	BOWER, DAVID	101	BRANDEBERRY, JACOB	7	BRINKER, HENRY	43
BOISE, NOBLE	27	BOWER, JOHN	81,108	BRANDEBERRY, LEVI	12	BRINKER, HOMER	89,107
BOISE, SAMUEL	27	BOWER, MATTIE	47	BRANDEBERRY, PHILIP	7	BRINKER, ISRAEL	12,36
BOISE, SARAH	27	BOWER, NELLIE	108	BRANDON, MATTIE	87	BRINKER, JACOB	10,28,29
BOISE, T.W.	27	BOWERS, EVADELL	41	BRANDY, ABRAM	23	BRINKER, JOHN H.	28,29
BOISE, WARREN	27	BOWERS, MICHAEL	41	BRANNEN, MARY	3	BRINKER, LEONARD F.	90
		BOWLES, JAMES	119	BRANNON, CORNELIUS	75	BRINKER, MARY E.	68,107

BRINKER, ROBERT 2
BRINKER, SARAH 5
BRINKER, THOMAS E. 80
BRITINSTINE, JONAS 38
BRITLAUCH, JULIA 104
BRITT, LOUIS 79
BRITTON, J.W. 27
BRITTON, MARTHA E. 30
BROADWELL, J.S., REV. 109
BRONSON, JOHN H. 31
BROOKS, DELORMA 63
BROOKS, EFFIE A. 53
BROOKS, GEORGE L. 6
BROOKS, J.H., REV. 16
BROOKS, J.J. 53
BROOKS, J.TWING 67
BROOKS, JNO.E. 63
BROOKS, JOHN 25
BROOKS, JOSEPHINE 38
BROOKS, LYMAN 85
BROOKS, SILA 63
BROOKS, THOMAS 9
BROOKS, WILLIAM 10
BROOKS, WILLIE 67
BROOME, MR. 120
BROOMLEY, PHOEBE 23
BROTHERS, EMMA 91
BROUGHTON, JOHN 93
BROUGHTON, MR. 64
BROUGHTON, WM. 12,36
BROUSE, ELIZABETH 37
BROWN, ABAGAIL 41
BROWN, CALEB, REV. 22
BROWN, CHARLEY 112
BROWN, CHARLIE 109
BROWN, CLARA 113
BROWN, DAVID 107
BROWN, DEBORAH E. 88
BROWN, E.W., REV. 86
BROWN, ELLEN 100
BROWN, EMELINE 74
BROWN, ENOCH 8
BROWN, FRANK 89
BROWN, G., REV. 107
BROWN, H.W. 119
BROWN, HANNAH 85
BROWN, HARMON 7
BROWN, JAMES 1,39,44,52,81,96
BROWN, JAMES SR. 96
BROWN, JANE 51
BROWN, JENNIE 62
BROWN, JOHN 19,41,78
BROWN, JOHN, MRS. 105
BROWN, JOSHUA 29
BROWN, LEANDER 97
BROWN, LEWIS 88
BROWN, M.A. 54,62
BROWN, M.J.W. 84
BROWN, MAGGIE 40
BROWN, MARIAH 22,88
BROWN, MARTHA 97
BROWN, MARY 8,12,18,69,98,
105,110,112
BROWN, MATHEW 7
BROWN, MR. 115,119
BROWN, NANCY 79
BROWN, NANNIE 71
BROWN, NATHAN 7
BROWN, POTTER & ARTER 72
BROWN, S. 29
BROWN, SARAH 48
BROWN, SUSAN 4,107
BROWN, T.B. 6
BROWN, TAMSON H. 8
BROWN, THOMAS J. 91
BROWN, VIRGINIA 98
BROWN, W.K., REV. 1,2,3,4,5,
6,11,19,37
BROWN, WALTER O. 62
BROWN, WILLIAM 18
BROWNLEE, ISA 74
BROWNLEE, J.D., REV. 35,37,38,
43,48,56,63,71,74,81,95,105
BROWNLEE, MRS. J.D. 74
BROWNLEE, SARAH E. 75
BROWNLEE, WM.R. 17
BROWNSON, R.SPENCER 7
BRUBACHER, J.B. 107
BRUBAKER, E. 56
BRUBAKER, EMANUEL 50
BRUBAKER, L.D. 50,97

BRUBAKER, M.A. 97
BRUCE & LUKE 1
BRUCE, ANNA 53
BRUCE, JENNIE H. 1
BRUCE, JOSIAH W. 48
BRUCE, M.A. 53
BRUCE, WM., REV. 53
BRUFF, ANNA L. 61
BRUFF, ANNA M. 61
BRUFF, CHARLES 56
BRUFF, JOSEPH 56,61
BRUNER, BERTHA 104
BRUNER, GEORGE N. 115
BRUNER, PHILIP 70,104
BRUSH, J.A. 115
BRYAN, JOHN H. 64
BRYON, JOHN 7
BUCHEIT, JOHN 119
BUCHER, MADALINE 48
BUCHHEIT, G. 115
BUCK, ADALINE 14
BUCK, JAMES D. 14
BUCK, JOHN F. 14
BUCK, SAMUEL 50
BUCKEY, LAURA 108
BUCKIUS, LAURA 35
BUCKIUS, S. 35
BUCKLEY, COL. 13
BUCKMAN, HARDING 5
BUCKS, C.A., REV. 71
BUEHECKER, MARGARET 33,34
BUEL, URIAH 20
BUELL, BARCELIOUS 103
BUELL, LETTIE 95,96
BUELL, RACHEL 95,96
BUELL, SAMUEL 35,95,96
BUHECKER, P. 76
BULGER, SABINA H. 83
BULL, R.B., REV. 30
BULLOCK, ENOCH 34
BULLOCK, HENRY 63,117
BUMBAUGH, BESSIE 105
BUMBAUGH, ISRAEL 93
BUMBAUGH, JOHN 105
BUMBAUGH, RACHEL 105
BUNNELL, J.H. 92
BUNNELL, MARY 92
BUNTING, ANDREW 11,53
BUNTING, HENRY A. 56
BUNTING, JANE 97
BUNTING, JOSEPHINE 42
BUNTING, MARY A. 99
BUNTING, MRS. 11
BUNTING, OLIVER 97
BURBECK, ARTHUR 105
BURBECK, DAVID 115
BURBECK, ELIZABETH 105
BURBECK, ISAAC 14,36,80
BURBECK, JAMES 14
BURBECK, JOSEPH 93
BURBECK, SARAH A. 4
BURBECK, WM. 12,36
BURBICK, ARTHUR 61
BURBICK, DAVID 92
BURBICK, ELIZABETH 61
BURBICK, JOHN 92
BURBICK, ROSIE 61
BURCAW, GEORGE 19
BURCAW, MAGGIE 100
BURCAW, SUSAN 19
BURCAW, WILLIAM 32,100,103
BURCHARD, DAVID T. 32
BURCHFIELD, AQUILLA 12
BURESS, ROBERT 70
BURFORD, A. 100
BURFORD, D.B. 71
BURFORD, DAVID 70,102
BURFORD, FANNIE 103
BURFORD, HATTIE M. 71
BURFORD, MALVINA 70
BURFORD, MARY 52,53
BURFORD, MRS. 100
BURFORD, ROBERT 52,53
BURGER, DAVID M. 84
BURGER, MAGDALENE 29
BURGER, SAMUEL 27,29,56
BURGES, JNO.H. 31
BURGESS, WILLIAM W. 117
BURK, JOHN 93
BURK, MARY 93
BURK, PETER 93

BURKE, HUBBARD & CO 17
BURKETT, E., REV. 73
BURLINGAME, CHARLES 26
BURNET, WILSON S. 2
BURNETT, DICK 109
BURNETT, E.F. 5
BURNETT, ELIZABETH 87
BURNETT, HENRY S. 90
BURNETT, JOHN 37
BURNETT, LOUISA 28
BURNETT, W.A. 68
BURNIP, MAGGIE 107
BURNIP, MARGARET 107
BURNIP, MATTHEW 107
BURNIP, WILLIE 107
BURNS & BRIGGS 47,57
BURNS, CHARLES 95
BURNS, G.W., REV. 8,12
BURNS, GEO.SR. 54
BURNS, GEORGE 18,61,78
BURNS, HUGH 4
BURNS, JAMES 78
BURNS, MARIA 95
BURNS, MARY 4,49
BURNS, MR. 26
BURNS, NEVIN 74
BURNS, VIOLET 95
BURNS, W.G., REV. 20
BURNSIDES, DAVID 79
BURSON, ANNA I. 74
BURSON, BENJAMIN 73
BURSON, DELL 74
BURSON, EDDIE 103
BURSON, EMMA C. 17
BURSON, EMMET 58
BURSON, GEORGE 17
BURSON, HATTIE 92
BURSON, J. 103
BURSON, JOSEPH 7
BURSON, JOSEPHINE 81
BURSON, JULIANA 42
BURSON, L. 103
BURSON, LANDON 74
BURSON, MARIA 110
BURSON, PHILENA A. 4
BURSON, PHOEBE 102
BURSON, REBECCA 17
BURSON, SARAH C. 5
BURSON, VIRGIL 90
BURSON, WM.P. 18
BURT, DAVID 21
BURT, ELIZABETH 21
BURT, EMILY 83
BURT, KATE 21
BURT, REV. 31
BURT, SYLVESTER, REV. 1
BURTON, ALBERT 83
BURTON, JAMES A. 104
BURTON, JOHN 84
BURTON, LIZZIE 65
BURTON, ROBERT 7
BURTON, WILLIAM 79
BURWELL, ELIZABETH 42
BURWELL, LOUIS 42
BURWELL, MARY 6
BURWELL, WILLIE 42
BUSH, J.A. 104
BUSH, JACOB 80
BUSH, JAMES 30
BUSHNELL, SYLVIA S. 9
BUSHONG, A.A. 26
BUSHONG, ALEXANDER 77
BUSHONG, ALPHEUS A. 26
BUSHONG, ANDREW 26
BUSHONG, BARBARA 26
BUSHONG, DANIEL 95
BUSHONG, DAVID 26
BUSHONG, ELIZABETH A. 77
BUSHONG, ELIZABETH M. 77
BUSHONG, J.J. 14
BUSHONG, JACOB 26
BUSHONG, JOHN 1
BUSHONG, MRS. 111
BUSHONG, W.M. 72
BUSKY, SQUIRE 101
BUSS, AMOS E. 63
BUTLER, C.E., REV. 47
BUTLER, EDWARD 108
BUTLER, JOHN SR. 39
BUTLER, P. 113
BUTLER, PATRICK 57

BUTLER, THOMAS 116
BUTTS, A.W., REV. 41,88,111,114
BUXTON, ANN 93
BUXTON, MR. 101
BUZZARD, M.A. 50
BYDER, CLESTIA 58
BYE, FRANCES 69
BYE, HEZIKIAH 35
BYE, J.G. 108
BYE, LIL A. 108
BYERS, ANNA B. 13
BYERS, MARGARET 102
CABLE, LYDE 8
CABLE, PHILIP 8
CADDIS, ELIZABETH 88
CADWALADER, EDITH 64
CADWALLADER, MINNIE 91
CADWALLADER, WILLIS 54,91
CAHILL, WM. 82
CAKE, E.B. 18,22,23,27,29,
34,35,37,40,41,42
CALAHAN, CHARLES, REV. 66
CALDER, DANIEL 7
CALDERHEAD, JOHN 76
CALDWELL, BROOKS 33,34
CALDWELL, ELIZABETH 45,46,47,96
CALDWELL, FRANK 50
CALDWELL, JAMES 47
CALDWELL, JOHN L. 106
CALDWELL, LOULA E. 50
CALDWELL, NANCY 90
CALDWELL, RUFUS 54
CALDWELL, SARAH M. 36
CALDWELL, THOMAS 25,87,96
CALDWELL, WILHELMINA 110
CALDWELL, WILLIAM 9,32,114
CALHOON, AUSTIN 77
CALHOUN, ADAM 82
CALHOUN, W.J. 17
CALLAHAN, ALLEN T. 61
CALLAHAN, ANNIE 54
CALLAHAN, B.F. 66
CALLAHAN, CATHARINE 83
CALLAHAN, CHARLES B. 56
CALLAHAN, FRANKIE J. 46
CALLAHAN, HIRAM 108
CALLAHAN, J.F., REV. 114
CALLAHAN, JOHN 46
CALLAHAN, JUDSON 39
CALLAHAN, LORETTA 102
CALLAHAN, M. 54
CALLAHAN, MARTHA 83
CALLAHAN, MARY A. 23
CALLAHAN, THOMAS 23
CALLAHAN, ZADOCK 17
CALLEN, THOMAS 8
CALLENDER, T.F. 43
CALLIHAN, JAMES 7
CALVERT, J.S. 88
CALVIN, ALLEN 10
CALVIN, JAMES H. 102
CALVIN, LUTHER 32,87
CALVIN, MARY B. 115
CALVIN, WALL 49
CALVIN, WALTER 49
CAMERON, ANN 93
CAMERON, DAVID 107
CAMERON, E., REV. 118
CAMERON, ELDER 106
CAMERON, HIRAM 64
CAMERON, I.B. 98
CAMERON, JNO. 10
CAMERON, KATE 9,75
CAMERON, LUCINDA 7
CAMERON, LYDIA A. 32
CAMERON, MAGGIE 43
CAMERON, NANCY B. 107
CAMERON, NANNIE 10,107
CAMERON, S.J. 73
CAMP, ADA 91
CAMP, DAVID 7
CAMP, HENRY B. 91
CAMPBELL, ADELLA 86
CAMPBELL, ANNIE 96
CAMPBELL, CHARLES C. 81
CAMPBELL, CHRISTIANA 105
CAMPBELL, DANIEL 105
CAMPBELL, EDWARD F. 38
CAMPBELL, GEORGE W. 95
CAMPBELL, JOHN 7,15,38
CAMPBELL, JOHNSON 49

CAMPBELL, LUCY 38
CAMPBELL, MARGARET 29
CAMPBELL, MARY 37,51
CAMPBELL, MRS. 103
CAMPBELL, ROBERT O. 48
CAMPBELL, W.B., REV. 97
CAMPBELL, WILLIAM 51
CAMPF, JACOB F. 41
CAMPF, NANCY JANE 45
CANAAN, JOSEPH 107
CANDLES, JOSEPH, MRS. 4
CANNON, ELIZABETH 80
CANNON, JOHN 7
CANNON, LINDSEY 58,80
CANS, M.P. 105
CAPPELL, WILLIAM 52
CARAHAN, JOHN L. 1
CARAHAN, SAMANTHA 89
CAREY, D.M. 88,104,105,108
CAREY, DR. 59
CAREY, SARAH 62
CARL, CATHARINE 44
CARL, DANIEL 44
CARLE, LYDIA 76
CARLILE, DANIEL 39
CARLILE, FREDDIE 39
CARLILE, HATTIE 28,29
CARLILE, MAGGIE 98
CARLILE, MARY J. 39,73
CARLILE, WILLIAM 80
CARLISLE, DANIEL 33
CARLISLE, ELIZABETH 1
CARLISLE, FRANK W. 33
CARLISLE, LIZZIE 30
CARLISLE, MARY J. 33
CARLL, FRANK 58
CARMAN, JAMES 78
CARMAN, MARGARET 82
CARNEY, RICHARD 80
CARNICHAN, J.GORDON, REV. 77
CARNS, ELIZABETH 49
CARNS, MARIETTA 53
CARNS, MILTON 23
CARNS, SAMANTHA 31
CARNS, WM. 96
CAROTHERS, WILLIAM M. 4
CARPENTER, E.C. 105
CARPENTER, REBECCA 107
CARPENTER, WILLIAM 45
CARR, ADDISON 16
CARR, CHARITY A. 2
CARR, J.M., REV. 45,48,55,57,61,67,74
CARR, JAMES 31
CARR, M., REV. 69
CARR, PHYLONZO 44
CARR, REBECCA 112
CARR, THOMAS 13
CARRAHER, MRS. 43
CARROLL, JOHN 72
CARROLL, JULIA 72
CARRUTHERS, J.G. 43
CARRUTHERS, NANCY 43
CARSON, GEORGE 102
CARSON, J.E., REV. 7,9
CARSON, KIT 12
CARSON, LAURA I. 73
CARSON, REV. 106
CARSON, ROBERT 98
CARTER, D.M. 120
CARTER, HATTIE A. 24
CARTER, J.M. 91
CARTER, J.WILLIS 24
CARTER, SAMUEL B. 102
CARTER, THOMAS 20
CARTER, WILLIS 51
CARTNEY, MARY A. 23
CARTNEY, P. 10
CARTNEY, PIERCE 36
CARTRIGHT, SARAH 110
CARTWRIGHT, THOMAS 112
CARTWRIGHT, WILLIAM SR. 107
CARUTHERS, MAYOR 66
CARY, BERNARD 110
CARY, DANIEL 100
CARY, DR. 59
CARY, EDDIE 110
CARY, EDWARD 100
CARY, HANNAH 72
CARY, HENRY 72
CARY, LAVINIA 38

CARY, MARY 100
CARY, SUSAN 110
CARY, WM.HENRY 107
CASE, CHAS.C. 17
CASE, WM.R. 17
CASS, LEWIS, GEN. 120
CASSELBERY, LOTTIE 47
CASSELBERY, WILLIAM D. 47
CASSEY, MR. 26
CASTNER, JACOB H. 47
CATLETT, J.C. 73
CATLETT, MRS. 108
CATTELL, ALBERT R. 83
CATTELL, B.T. 73
CAUFFMAN, RICHARD 97
CAVANAH, JUDGE 19
CAVEN, A.A. 66
CAVENAUGH, MARY J. 19
CAVIN, ALEXANDER 51
CAVIT, GEORGE 23
CAYGILL, WILLIAM 119
CHAIN, ALICE R. 10
CHAIN, H. 10
CHAIN, J.C. 22
CHAIN, JOSEPH 18,78
CHAIN, W.A. 116
CHALFANT, REV. 32
CHAMBERLAIN, ELMIRA 58
CHAMBERLAIN, GEORGE 103
CHAMBERLAIN, JOHN 58
CHAMBERLAIN, ROBERT 58,77
CHAMBERLIN, AARON 19,20
CHAMBERLIN, CATHARINE 20
CHAMBERLIN, GEO. 37
CHAMBERLIN, JOHN 88
CHAMBERLIN, THOMAS 8
CHAMBERLIN, WILLIAM 84
CHAMBERLIN, WILLIE 20
CHAMBERS, JESSE 117
CHAMBERS, MARTHA 117
CHAMBERS, MARTIN 117
CHAMPION, JAMES C. 41
CHANDLER, ALBERT 20
CHANDLER, ALONZO 82
CHANDLER, AMANDA M. 103
CHANDLER, ASBERRY 75
CHANDLER, CORNELIUS 66
CHANDLER, ELI 12,36
CHANDLER, LAWRENCE 105
CHANDLER, LOU M. 41
CHANDLER, O.V.W., REV. 107
CHANDLER, RACHEL 24
CHAPEL, SADIE 86
CHAPLIN, CORA 90
CHAPMAN, A.R., REV. 98,103,107,109,110,111,112,113,114,118
CHAPMAN, JOHN B. 40
CHAPMAN, S.S. 78
CHAPPLE, MARY 115
CHARLTON, SOPHIA 82
CHARTERS, ELIZABETH 65
CHARTERS, WM. 12,36
CHESSMAN, H.WARREN 12
CHESSMAN, M.L. 18
CHILD & WILLARD 2
CHILDS, T.P., REV. 7,10,12,18,21,27,28
CHILEY, SAMUEL 23
CHISHOLM, ROBERT 68,69
CHURCHILL, GEORGE 96
CHURCHILL, LEIVINA 114
CILWORTH, MARY C. 24
CITRON, AMELIA 81
CITRON, TILLIE 57
CLAGER, ANTHONY 96
CLAGER, PETER 96
CLAPSADDLE, ELIZABETH 21
CLAPSADDLE, JEFFERSON 102
CLAPSADDLE, JOHN 21
CLAPSADDLE, SAMANTHA 11
CLARK, ANTHONY 101
CLARK, CHARLES W. 107
CLARK, ELIZA 17
CLARK, EMMA 93
CLARK, GEORGE M. 80
CLARK, GRACE 17
CLARK, HATTIE 17
CLARK, HENRY J. 5
CLARK, IDA MAY 89
CLARK, J.L. 71
CLARK, J.LYTTLETON 2,17,89

CLARK, JAMES 24,51,96,101
CLARK, JOHN 72
CLARK, LYDIA 72
CLARK, MARY 19,24,51,89,101
CLARK, MR. 57
CLARK, REV. 108
CLARK, S.S. 14,22
CLARK, STEPHEN 19,75
CLARK, WILLIAM 14,17,76
CLARKE & McVICKER 30
CLARKE, AMY 99
CLARKE, HARRIET 48
CLARKE, HATTIE 51
CLARKE, HENRY 34
CLARKE, ISAMENA 99
CLARKE, JAMES 48,91
CLARKE, SAMUEL 99
CLAY, JOHN 81
CLAYPOOL, NANCY 109
CLAYTON, MR. 46
CLECKNER, ANNIE A. 28
CLECKNER, BELL D. 67
CLECKNER, EMERY 107
CLECKNER, JANE 32
CLECKNER, JOHN 23,118
CLECKNER, LEONARD 99
CLECKNER, SAMUEL 68
CLEMEN, WILLIAM 104
CLEMENS, J.A. 88
CLEMENSON, ROSCOE 96
CLEMENT, ANDREW J. 87
CLEMENT, J.A., REV. 94,100,101,104,106,110,111,114,115,116
CLEMENT, JOHN A.,REV. 71,73,83,84,85,91
CLEMMER, MARCIA 40
CLEVELAND, SUSIE P. 14
CLIFTON, RICHARD 52
CLINE, MARY E. 37
CLINE, PETER 116
CLIPPINGER, ALIVA 103
CLIPPINGER, NATHAN 96
CLIZBE, LEMUEL 89
CLOSE, ELMIRA 55
CLOSE, WM. 58
CLOUD, ENOCH C., DR. 49
CLOY, WM. 41
CLUAN, ANNA 67
CLUNK, ANTHONY 11
CLUNK, JACOB 12,36
CLUNK, JAMES 28,29,106
CLUNK, JOSEPH 36
CLUNK, KATIE 93
CLUNK, REBECCA 18
CLUNK, WILLIAM E. 54
COALE, BENJAMIN F. 36
COALE, CHASE 27
COBB, ELI 3
COBBS, MARGARET 119
COBBS, SELINA 5
COBBS, UREE E. 83
COBLENTZ, JACOB 45
COBURN, JOHN 86
COBURN, MINNIE 120
COBURN, NATHAN 76
COBURN, SAMUEL 13,44
COBURN, SARAH 86,108
COCHIL, DANIEL 101
COCHIL, MARTHA 101
COCHIL, MARY 101
COCHRAN, JAMES 107
COCHRAN, WM.H. 20
COCKBURN, SARAH A. 59
COCKSTON, MARY 110
COFFEE, ARABELLA 94
COFFEE, ELIZA J. 84
COFFEE, J.W. 51
COFFEE, LYDIA 106
COFFEE, PRICILLA 88
COFFEE, SADIE A. 48
COFFIELD, PETER 71
COFFIN, C.D. 84
COFFIN, JUDGE 51
COFFMAN, SAMUEL 27
COIL, JOHN, REV. 69,73,76,86
COLBY, H.S., REV. 25
COLE, ELIZABETH 58
COLE, JOHN 58
COLE, JOHN D. 62
COLE, LUCRETIA 20
COLE, M.A. 10

COLE, MARY 95,112
COLE, WILLIAM 69
COLESTOCK, DANIEL 55
COLFLESH, CATHARINE J. 19
COLL, JOHN, REV. 82
COLLANS, BRIDGET 78
COLLIER, JOHN M. 97
COLLINS, D.W., REV. 18
COLLINS, MARY ANN 35
COLLINS, MATHEW 7
COLLINS, SAMUEL L. 90
COLLINS, WILLIAM S. 95
COLTON, MR. 7
COLVIN, FANNIE 66
COLWELL, SETH 74
COMBS, ELMIRA 89
COMLEY, MARTHA W. 116
COMPTON, JOHN D. 40
CONCLE, MARY A. 105
CONDLES, JOSEPH, MRS. 4
CONE, C.P., REV. 61
CONGDON, MRS. 28
CONKLE, ELIZA 70
CONKLE, HANNAH L. 4
CONKLE, J.H., REV. 12,33,112,118,119
CONKLE, JOHN W. 44
CONKLE, JOSEPHINE 69
CONKLE, LUELLA 101
CONKLE, MARTHA A. 18
CONKLE, MOLLIE A. 1
CONKLE, PETER 70
CONLAN, MARY E. 55
CONLIN, JAMES 79
CONLIN, JOHN B. 60
CONN, HENRY V. 10
CONN, JAMES P. 16
CONN, SAMUEL H. 10
CONNEL, DR. 75
CONNEL, ELIZABETH 20
CONNEL, G.W. 41
CONNEL, SARAH 75
CONNEL, THOMAS M. 31
CONNELL, AARON, DR. 55
CONNELL, ALFRED 55
CONNELL, MARIA E. 5
CONNELL, SALLIE 48
CONNER, CHARLES 21,30
CONNER, MARY 66
CONNOR, MALINDA 82
CONNOR, MRS. 60
CONRAD, HIRAM, DR. 87
CONSER, JANE 71
CONSOR, B.T. 19
CONSOR, FRED 94
CONSOR, GEORGE 85
CONSOR, MARY 85
CONSOR, PHILLIP 101
COOK, ALBERT 41
COOK, ALESTA 41
COOK, ALEXANDER 110
COOK, ARCHIBALD 81
COOK, D.J., CAPT 42
COOK, EDITH 110
COOK, EDWARD 90
COOK, HATTIE 8
COOK, J.WILLIAM 96
COOK, JACOB 7,100
COOK, JAMES 4,97
COOK, JOB 90,98
COOK, LYDIA 4
COOK, MARTHA 90
COOK, MARY 74,79
COOK, O.R. 8
COOK, OSBORN R. 58
COOK, ROSILLIA 41
COOK, S.L. 61
COOK, STACY 90,107
COOK, SUSAN 100
COOKE, EDWARD W. 93
COOKE, MAGGIE J. 7
COON, S.M., REV. 55,68,69,74,75,78,79,82,83,85,87,89,98,100
COONEY, MARY 118
COONEY, THOMAS 118
COOPER, G.B. 105
COOPER, HULDAH 99
COOPER, J.F. 79
COOPER, PHINEAS 5
COOPER, RUTH A. 67
COOPER, S.M. 46

Name	Page	Name	Page	Name	Page	Name	Page
COOPER, THOS	16	COWAN, JAMES	99	CREW, NANCY	19	CUAIL, ELLEN	54
COOPER, WILLIAM P.	112	COWAN, KITTIE	85	CREW, WILLIAM	45	CUFF, EDWARD	115
COPE, A.L.	117	COWAN, MINERVA J.	6	CRICHLOW, REV.	70	CUFFEL, JULIA ANN	8
COPE, ALLEN B.	100	COWAN, SUSAN	85	CRISENGER, SAMUEL	59	CULBERTSON, ELIAS	12,36
COPE, AMY	35	COWGILL, SYLVESTER	103	CRISINGER, JUDITH	59	CULBERTSON, MARTIN	12,36
COPE, CALEB	7,28	COWICK, JOHN W.	119	CRISSELL, CHAS.	50	CULBEY, SUSAN	50
COPE, CHARLES F.	35	COWN, MARY	70	CRISSELL, FANNIE	50	CULLENBERGER, LEWIS	45,80
COPE, CHARLEY E.	28,29	COX, DR.	28	CRISSINGER, JOHN	88	CULLENBERGER, MAVARINE	80
COPE, D.	86	COX, ELLA J.	2	CRIST, BENJAMIN F.	105	CULLENBERGER, NANCY	80
COPE, ELLIS	76	COX, FRANCIS M.	82	CRIST, REV.	33	CULLER, DAVID	80
COPE, EMMA	35,71	COX, HENRY	51	CRITCHLOW, B.C., REV.	33	CULLER, FRANK	47
COPE, FRANKLIN	100	COX, JOHN V., REV.	54	CRITTENDEN, S.W., REV.	1	CULLER, ISABEL	80
COPE, HARRIET	92	COX, LIZZIE H.	80	CROCKER, C., MRS.	34	CULLER, JENNETTE	79
COPE, HENRY	58	COX, MARTHA	81	CROCKERTON, ANNIE	16	CULLER, JOHN W.	80
COPE, ISRAEL	84	COX, MARY V.	73	CROCKERTON, BARSHEBA	16	CULLER, MARY	79
COPE, JAMES S.	35	COX, REV.DR.	24,25,26,30,32	CROCKERTON, JOHN	16	CULLER, PHILLIP	79
COPE, JESSE	7,35	COX, S.S.	50	CROCKERTON, ROBERT	16	CULP, ELLA	90
COPE, JOHN	35,48,119	COX, SAMUEL	100	CROFT, SARAH JANE	103	CUMMINGS, DAVID	103
COPE, JOSEPH	8	COX, WM., REV.	24,25,27,73,80	CROFTS, HENRY	69	CUMMINGS, NOAH	116
COPE, L.D.	28,29	COY, ELIZABETH	83	CROMLEY, DAVID L.	82	CUMMINS, CHARLES	118
COPE, LINN	58	COY, GEORGE W.	91	CRONIC, SARAH	103	CUNAN, MICHAEL	19
COPE, LORANZO D.	35	COY, KATE	91	CRONICK, JOHN	47	CUNAN, SARAH J.	19
COPE, LOUISA	8	COY, MADISON	37	CRONICK, LUNCINA	104	CUNAR, MARGARET A.	5
COPE, MALINDA	8	COY, MARY	65	CRONICK, MATTIE	47	CUNNINGHAM, R., REV.	9,42,45,
COPE, MARGARET A.	35	COY, SIBEL	88	CROOK, ADDIE	110		50,53,55,63
COPE, MARY	2,35,81	COYLE, CATHARINE	13	CROOK, CHARLES	43	CUNNINGHAM, RACHEL	54
COPE, MATILDA	35	COYLE, JOHN F.	31	CROOK, ERRETT	43	CUNNINGHAM, WM.W.	81
COPE, MOLLIE E.	86	COYLE, REV.MR.	69	CROOK, GEO., REV.	12	CUPPOLD, LIZZIE	23
COPE, NATHAN	8,30,41	COYLE, WILLARD F.	100	CROOK, GERTIE	119	CUPPOLD, SAMUEL	23
COPE, OLIVER	40,77	CRABAUGH, ALICE	4	CROOK, MARANDA	119	CURBY, LOUISA	43
COPE, RUTH	28,29	CRAFT, ALVINA	10	CROOK, MARCUS	75,119	CURBY, NELLIE	43
COPE, SAMUEL	3,71	CRAIG, MARY C.	21	CROOK, MARGARET	22	CURBY, PIERCE	43
COPE, SOPHIE	35	CRAIG, ROBERT E.	5,21	CROOK, SALLIE E.	1	CURFMAN, NANNIE E.	54
COPE, THOMAS	4,35,71	CRAIG, SHERMAN P.	5	CROOK, SAMUEL	22,55	CURRAN, R.A., REV.	84,87
COPE, VIRLINDA	35	CRAIGHEAD, SAMUEL	50	CROOK, THOMAS	1,46	CURREN, ALOINA	63
COPE, W.T.	55	CRAIN, JOHN	106	CROOKS, THOMAS	98	CURREN, SARAH	22
COPELAND, B., MRS.	9	CRAIN, TABITHA	106	CROSS, CLEMENT L.	2	CURRY, ANNA	96
COPELAND, GEO.	81	CRAINE, ANNIE	108	CROSS, CUSIAH	80	CURRY, CATHARINE	28
COPELAND, MAGGIE	116	CRAMER, A., REV.	55	CROSS, FRANCES	7	CURRY, KATE	12
COPELAND, REBECCA	76	CRAMER, C.A.J., REV.	3	CROSS, REV.	57	CURRY, MAYOR	24
COPPIC, RACHEL	117	CRAMER, CHRISTIAN	89	CROSS, ROBERT S.	18	CURRY, W.E.	116
COPPIC, THOMAS	117	CRANK, F.JAY	65	CROSS, SUSAN	71	CURRY, W.W., REV.	98
COPPOCK, ANNA	98	CRANK, FRANK J.	64	CROSS, THOMAS	80	CURTIS, E., REV.	96
COPPOCK, CATHARINE	46	CRANK, PHEBE J.	79	CROSSER, JAMES	24	CUSHMAN, CHARLES	52
COPPOCK, EZRA	12	CRATON, JOHN	23	CROSSER, MARY	24	CUSHMAN, FRANCES	81
COPPOCK, JOHN	46	CRAWFORD, CARRIE	93	CROUCH, JAMES	105	CUSHMAN, S.D., DR.	81
COPPOCK, SAMUEL	54	CRAWFORD, DAN	116	CROUSE, CATHARINE	36	CUSTARD, JACOB	91
CORBETT, DANIEL	119	CRAWFORD, EDWARD	1,109	CROUSE, J., REV.	33	CUSTARD, NANCY	58
CORBETT, GEO.B.	115	CRAWFORD, ELIZABETH E.	99	CROW, C.V.	63	CUTLER, C.L.	83
CORBETT, GEORGE B.	56	CRAWFORD, ELLA	1	CROW, JOSEPH	59	CUTTS, MARY	55
CORBETT, H.CLAY	92	CRAWFORD, FRANK	96	CROW, MARY	16	DAHOFF, LYDIA	12
CORBETT, THOMAS, MRS.	77	CRAWFORD, GODFREY	84	CROW, MATILDA G	62	DAILEY, JOHN B.	113
CORDINGLEY, JAMES	51	CRAWFORD, HENRY	96	CROWELL, EDWIN M.	32	DAILEY, ROBERT	111
COREY, WILLIAM R.	6	CRAWFORD, J.Y.	30	CROWELL, H.B.	103	DAILY, MARTHA	26
CORNELL, MARY	38	CRAWFORD, JAMES	22,75	CROWL, ELIZABETH	34	DAILY, MARY E.	26
CORNWELL, AMERICA	5	CRAWFORD, JOHN M.	2	CROWL, GEORGE	29,116	DAILY, MR.	14
CORNWELL, D.W.	5	CRAWFORD, JOSEPH	58	CROWL, GEORGIANA	45	DAILY, THOMAS B.	26
CORNWELL, DAVID	2,5,54,56	CRAWFORD, L.A.	90	CROWL, H.B.	84	DALE, A., REV.	57
CORNWELL, HETTY	54	CRAWFORD, LIZZIE	22	CROWL, HANNAH	84	DALES, CHARLES	76,97
CORNWELL, JOHN	54	CRAWFORD, M.J.	30	CROWL, JACOB	66	DALES, FLORA M.	91
CORNWELL, MARY	54	CRAWFORD, MARGARET	91	CROWL, JOHN	34	DALES, FRANK	55
CORNWELL, PETER	54	CRAWFORD, MARGARY	22	CROWL, MAGDALENE	29	DALES, FRANKLIN T.	75
CORTRIGHT, AUGUSTUS	89	CRAWFORD, MARTHA	53	CROWL, MARY E.	2	DALES, GEORGE	95
CORY, M.ELLA	84	CRAWFORD, MARY	6,76,106	CROWL, OLIVE	78	DALES, HANNAH	76,95
COSS, PETER	91	CRAWFORD, MATTIE J.	3	CROWTHER, S., REV.	23	DALES, JAMES	118
COSS, SUSANNAH	91	CRAWFORD, MINNIE	81	CROXALL, EMMA	106	DALES, REV.	1
COSTELLO, JAMES	82	CRAWFORD, MORDECAI	70	CROXALL, FRANK	57	DALGLEISH, JOHN	17
COTTEN, JACKSON	54	CRAWFORD, NANCY J.	75	CROXALL, JOSEPH W.	75	DALLAS, BARBARA	65
COULAN, MARY E.	55	CRAWFORD, NOAH W.	1	CROXALL, MARIAH	32	DALLAS, D.D.	83
COULSON, AMY	99	CRAWFORD, OLD	117	CROXALL, SALLIE	13	DALY, MARGARET	78
COULSON, GEORGE H.	58,90	CRAWFORD, REBECCA M.	102	CROXALL, THOMAS	94,106	DALZEL, EDWARD	72
COULSON, GRACE	58	CRAWFORD, SAMUEL	108	CROXALL, WILLIAM	40	DALZELL, ANN BURLEY	100
COULSON, HANNAH S.	69	CRAWFORD, SINGERS	40	CROZIER, JOHN	7	DALZELL, EDWARD	100
COULSON, JAMES	23	CRAWFORD, SUSAN	99	CRUBAUGH, A.B.	109	DALZELL, EMELINE	100
COULSON, JOSEPH	4,19,21,22,63,	CRAWFORD, WILLIAM	9,42,47,55,	CRUBAUGH, ALICE	4	DALZELL, S.M.	105
	74,75,81		68,79,81,96,119	CRUBAUGH, DAVID	24	DALZELL, WM., REV.	23,27,40,
COULSON, M.E.	58	CREIGHTON, H.J.	106	CRUBAUGH, FREDERICK	33		41,42,46,54,105
COULSON, MELINDA	110	CREIGHTON, JOHN	12	CRUBAUGH, J.E.	13	DANIEL, WM.	69
COULSON, MELLIE E.	90	CREIGHTON, THOMAS	43	CRUBAUGH, NANCY	114	DANIELS, ELLA	116
COULSON, SAMUEL	69	CREIGHTON, VIRGINIA	5	CRUM, DALLAS G.	49	DANKS, J.A.	20
COULTER, J.H., REV.	83	CREIGHTON, VIRLINDA	31	CRUMBLY, ROBERT	73	DANKS, REV.	28
COULTER, S.P.	87	CREPS, LUCY A.	87	CRUMBY, HANNAH	65	DANNALS, SQUIRE	7
COURTNEY, ANNIE	110	CRESS, ELMANDA	62	CRUMLEY, MARY	104	DARBY, SAMUEL	42
COURTNEY, DANIEL	111	CRESSINGER, PETER	7	CRUMLEY, WILLIAM	26	DARBY, W., REV.	48,64,72,77,78,
COUSINS, M.V.	108	CREW, HATTIE	111	CRUMLY, DAVID L.	82		79,81
COUSOR, B.T.	19	CREW, HULDAH J.	9	CRUMRINE, CARRIE	98	DARBY, WASHINGTON, REV.	76
COVER, JOHN	103	CREW, J.H.	105	CRUMRINE, DAVID	98	DARE, THEODORA	108
COVERT, JAMES	18	CREW, JESSE	19	CRUMRINE, IDA	110	DARLINGTON, WILLIAM	64
COVERT, LEVARRA	18	CREW, JONATHAN	37	CRUMRINE, MICHAEL	36	DARRY, GEORGE	107
COWAN, A.J.	33,85	CREW, JOSEPH	4,55,67,79,80,	CRUMRINE, SARAH E.	73	DAULEY, DANIEL	117
COWAN, ANNIE E.	8		81,83,87	CRUTZINGER, JOHN	46	DAULEY, ZILLAH	117

DAVENPORT, ESTHER A.	29	
DAVIDSON, ANDREW	47	
DAVIDSON, CARRIE	96	
DAVIDSON, ELI	66	
DAVIDSON, ELIJAH	97,102	
DAVIDSON, EMMA	64	
DAVIDSON, ETTIE H.	57	
DAVIDSON, FRANK	90	
DAVIDSON, JOHN	5,31	
DAVIDSON, KENNETH	96	
DAVIDSON, LIZZIE	79	
DAVIDSON, MARTHA	90	
DAVIDSON, MATILDA	42	
DAVIDSON, MRS.	115	
DAVIDSON, NANCY	96	
DAVIDSON, PETER	71	
DAVIDSON, REV.DR.	118	
DAVIDSON, SARAH	11,16,31	
DAVIDSON, W.A., REV.	119	
DAVIDSON, WILLIAM	90,115	
DAVIS, AMOS	25	
DAVIS, ANNA	17,107	
DAVIS, CELESTIA	21	
DAVIS, CHARLES E.	36	
DAVIS, EDWARD B.	10	
DAVIS, ESTELLA	110	
DAVIS, F.	83	
DAVIS, FLORENCE	63	
DAVIS, GEORGE	119	
DAVIS, HENRY	7	
DAVIS, ISAAC	19	
DAVIS, J.W., REV.	59	
DAVIS, JAMES	14	
DAVIS, JANE	25	
DAVIS, JOHN	18,83	
DAVIS, JOHN, REV.	62	
DAVIS, JOSEPH	85,114	
DAVIS, JOSIE	92	
DAVIS, LEAH A.	89	
DAVIS, LIZZIE	27,81	
DAVIS, LYCURGUS	25	
DAVIS, MAGGIE A.	44	
DAVIS, MARIA	80	
DAVIS, MARY	31,83	
DAVIS, MILTON	38,92	
DAVIS, OLIVE	7	
DAVIS, PETER	21	
DAVIS, REBECCA	72	
DAVIS, REV.MR.	114,117	
DAVIS, S.M., REV.	107,115,116	
DAVIS, SARAH	80	
DAVIS, SUE	32	
DAVIS, SUSAN	85	
DAVIS, WILLIAM	24,80,84	
DAWES, BENJAMIN F.	56,75	
DAWES, MARTHA H.	56	
DAWSON, AMOS	104	
DAWSON, ELIZA	31	
DAWSON, ELLEN	21	
DAWSON, MR.	79	
DAWSON, REV.	21	
DAY, CORDELIA	94	
DAY, HENRY C.	53	
DAY, QUINN	50	
DEAN, BILLY	24	
DECOURSLAY, MARGARET	79	
DEEMER, AMELIA	92	
DEEMER, D., DR.	26,45	
DEEMER, FRANK P.	50	
DEEMER, ISRAEL	55	
DEEMER, J.	58	
DEEMER, JOHN	14,61,77,98	
DEEMER, KATE	45	
DEEMER, L.S.	115	
DEEMER, LEWIS J.	14	
DEEMER, M.	58	
DEEMER, MAGGIE A.	52	
DEEMER, MARTHA	61	
DEEMER, MARY B.	58	
DEEMER, SEMANTHA	38	
DEEVERS, JAMES	13	
DeFORD, HORTENSE	114	
DEGNAN, J.	49	
DEHOFF, JOSEPH	31	
DEIDRICK, CAROLINE	117	
DEIDRICK, FREDERICK	103	
DEJANE, W.C.	51	
DELANO, D.C.	23,59	
DELLAR, DAVID	57	
DELLENBAUGH, JOHN	54,86	
DELLENBAUGH, VIRGINIA	86	

DELLER, CATHARINE	87	
DELLER, NICHOLAS	87,107	
DELO, I.J., REV.	1,6,89	
DEMING, ELLEN	105	
DEMING, FRANK	114	
DEMMER, PHILIP	114	
DEMON, MARGARET	12	
DEMPSEY, HIRAM T.	85	
DENHAM, ALEX	70	
DENHART, JOHN	92	
DENNEN, MICHAEL	83	
DENNEY, KATIE	107	
DENNIS, JANE	71	
DENNIS, JOSEPH	116	
DENNIS, SARAH	36,112	
DERHODES, WILLIAM H.	24	
DERHODS, MARY	64	
DERODES, DAVID	48,73	
DERODES, PERRY	48	
DERR, JAMES	22,32	
DERR, JOSEPH E.	43	
DESELLUM, NANCY	42	
DeSHERROW, WILLIAM	98	
DESSELEM, JACOB	93	
DESSELLEM, J.G.	65	
DETRICK, ELIZABETH	90	
DETWILER, HATTIE	21	
DETWILER, JACOB O.	101	
DETWILER, JOHN	87,107	
DETWILER, W.J.	23	
DEVENEY, GRACE	33	
DEVENEY, WM.	33	
DEVER, GARRET	102	
DEVERS, ALLIE	98	
DEVERS, JESSIE MAY	46	
DEVERS, JOHN	46	
DEVERS, SARAH	46	
DEVERS, WILLIAM	16	
DEVINE, MARTIN	106	
DEVINNEY, KATE	109	
DEVORE, MARGARET	26	
DEWALT, CORONER	75	
DEWILTER, W.J.	23	
DEYSER, ALLEN	101	
DIBBLE, B.S., DR.	67	
DIBBLE, E.J.	67	
DIBBLE, IRENE	67	
DIBBLE, P.K.	120	
DIBBLE, R.H.	41	
DICE, EPHRAIM	41	
DICK, A.J.	19	
DICK, JOHN	101	
DICKENBAUGH, MARGARET	109	
DICKEY, C.B.	2	
DICKEY, CEDELIA	28	
DICKEY, DAVID F.	86	
DICKEY, ELIZA J.	92	
DICKEY, HAMILTON	13	
DICKEY, MARGARET	83	
DICKEY, MARY	49,95	
DICKEY, R.L.	5	
DICKEY, REV.	14	
DICKEY, SARAH E.	87	
DICKINSON, J.M.	68,72,78,79,	
	88,89,93,100,101,103,104,	
	105,107,109,110	
DICKINSON, JOHN	56,63,65,66,91	
DICKINSON, MARTIN	58	
DICKINSON, MAYOR	116	
DICKINSON, ZEPHAS	107	
DICKSON, ARNER	28	
DICKSON, BELLE	37	
DICKSON, ELIZABETH	4,14	
DICKSON, GEORGE	14	
DICKSON, ISABEL	57	
DICKSON, J.M.	108	
DICKSON, JAS.	16	
DICKSON, REV.	17,22,30,48,	
	54,62	
DICKSON, REV.DR.	45,46,47,50,	
	51,52,54,57	
DICKSON, ROBT., REV.	1,2,3,4,	
	9,10,14,16,18,19,20,21,23,	
	24,28,30,31,32, 35*,41,42	
DICKSON, THOMAS	71	
DICKSON, WM.	87	
DICKSON, WM., REV.	75	
DIEHL, ADAM	47	
DIEHL, WILLIAM	12	
DIEL, AMANDA	9	
DILDINE, ESSIE	72	

DILDINE, JOHN C.	72	
DILDINE, MARY	3,72	
DILFORD, J.L.	7	
DILLEY, L.S.	11	
DILWORTH, A.C.	39	
DILWORTH, ALBERT	80,97	
DILWORTH, BENJAMIN	28	
DILWORTH, JOHN	54	
DILWORTH, MARGARET	28	
DILWORTH, MARY C.	24,25	
DILWORTH, ROBT	1	
DILWORTH, S.C.	25	
DILWORTH, WILLIAM	1	
DINSMORE, –––	2	
DIVELLE, CAROLINE	72	
DIVELLE, STEPHEN	72	
DIXON, CYRUS	38	
DIXON, LIZZIE A.	10	
DIXON, NEWTON	56	
DIXON, SIMON	7	
DIXON, W.L., REV.	88	
DIXSON, ISABELLA	34	
DOBSON, AARON	4,101	
DOBSON, ANNIE M.	22	
DOBSON, ELIZABETH J.	24	
DOBSON, FRANCES	101	
DOBSON, FRANK	101	
DOBSON, HUGH	11	
DOBSON, JAMES	22	
DOBSON, JENNIE	22	
DOBSON, JOSEPH	113	
DOBSON, MARGARET	16,113	
DOBSON, RACHEL	11	
DOBSON, ROBERT	11	
DODGE, R.V., REV.	11	
DOLAN, JOSEPH	109	
DOLE, HOWARD B.	70	
DOLE, R.G.	27	
DONAHUE, CHARLES	39	
DONAHUE, REBECCA	39	
DONALDSON, ELIZABETH	102	
DONALDSON, FANNY	102	
DONALDSON, G.C.	102	
DONALDSON, H.W.	22	
DONALDSON, ISABELLA	66	
DONALDSON, JOHN	66,102	
DONALDSON, MARY	73	
DONALDSON, ROBERT	102	
DONALDSON, VIOLET	2	
DONALLY, R.R.	84	
DONBART, J.W.	89	
DONBART, WM.	55	
DONELLY, CHARLES	14	
DONGES, GEORGE H.	53	
DONGES, HENRY	39	
DONGES, MARGARET	39	
DONNELLE, ANDREW	119	
DONNELLY, JAMES R.	35	
DONNELLY, JOHN	63	
DONNELLY, MARY	63	
DONNELLY, SABELLA A.	35	
DONNELLY, SARAH	103	
DONNELLY, CHARLES	58	
DONNELY, ELIZA ANN	58	
DORAN, ALICE	73	
DORLAND, JAMES	7	
DORRANCE, JAS	90,95,113,116,117	
DORRANCE, MAGGIE	90	
DORRANCE, MARY	95,113,116	
DORRANCE, RACHEL	87	
DORRANCE, S.GILMORE	113	
DORSEY, REBECCA	38	
DORWART, ANNA L.	65	
DORWART, C.	28	
DORWART, CHRIST	54	
DORWART, DANIEL	66,112	
DORWART, H.B.	64	
DORWART, H.LOU	90	
DORWART, HARM B.	67	
DORWART, KING	6,48,65	
DORWART, MARY ELLEN	28	
DORWART, MR. & MRS.	76	
DORWART, SARAH C.	76	
DORWART, WILLIAM	54,112	
DORWART, WILLIE	65	
DORWART'S BUILDING	47,57	
DOTTARAR, WILLIAM S.	74	
DOTY, WILLIAM	109	
DOUDS, ELIZABETH	107	
DOUDS, JAMES	107	
DOUDS, JOHN	107	

DOUGHERTY, PATRICK	77	
DOUGHLASS, EMMA	59	
DOUGHTON, CLARISSA	88	
DOUGHTON, MR.	5	
DOUGHTON, S.S.A.	88	
DOUGHTON, STEPHEN	10,42,88,92	
DOUGLASS, ELVINA	25	
DOUGLASS, FANNIE	76	
DOUGLASS, FREDERICK	25,30	
DOUGLASS, JOHN	48,76,106	
DOUGLASS, MAGGIE	62	
DOUTHET, JOSEPH	57	
DOUTHETT, HANNAH	32	
DOUTHETT, WILLIAM, REV.	32,57	
DOVER, ELANOR	23	
DOVER, JOHN	81	
DOWLIN, WILLIAM	114	
DOWLING, JOSEPH	110	
DOWNARD, GEORGE	12,36	
DOWNER, DANIEL	52	
DOWNER, ZADOK	25	
DOYL, JAMES	54	
DOYLE, JANE	24	
DOYLE, JOHN	14	
DOZZLE, ALFRED	110	
DRAKE, WILLIAM	112	
DRENNAN, CHARLES B.	67	
DREW, THOMAS, REV.	93	
DRISCOL, MICHAEL	61	
DRUFUS, CHRISTINE	67	
DRUMMOND, ANDREW	47,96	
DRUMMOND, HANNAH	96	
DRUMMOND, HARVEY S.	96	
DRURY, LOUIE J.	11	
DUBBS, FRANCES	30	
DUBBS, J.W.	97	
DUCK, GEORGE	7,115	
DUCK, JOSEPH	96	
DUCK, MARY E.	69	
DUFF, JOHN	17	
DUFFIE, E.H.	61	
DULAN, MIKE	6	
DUMBLETON, SARAH	87	
DUNCAN, ANNA	38	
DUNCAN, CADDIE C.	30	
DUNCAN, EV	17	
DUNCAN, H.S.	17	
DUNCAN, HENRY S.	17	
DUNCAN, JOHN	106	
DUNCAN, MAGGIE	104	
DUNCAN, THOMAS	119	
DUNDAS, J., REV.	32	
DUNDAS, J.B., REV.	22	
DUNDAS, J.M., REV.	34,42	
DUNDAS, J.R., REV.	8,55,58,	
	66,71	
DUNDAS, L.M., REV.	87	
DUNLAP, CHARLES	59	
DUNLAP, HENRY	12	
DUNLAP, JOHN	118	
DUNLAP, LEWIS	40	
DUNLAP, M.V.	12	
DUNLAP, MAYOR	91,94,106,107,	
	112	
DUNLAP, ROBERT A.	117	
DUNLAP, SARAH	118	
DUNN, MARY JANE	95	
DUNN, MISS	9	
DUNN, SETH	81	
DUNN, WILLIAM	53,70	
DUNNAM, SAMUEL	18	
DURANT, LIZZIE	99	
DURBIN, EMMA	96	
DURBIN, EZEKEL	89	
DURHAM, JOHN	119	
DURHAMMER, AARON W.	65	
DURKE, GEORGE	114	
DURKEE, WILLIAM	41	
DUSTON, SAREPTA	32	
DUTTON, EDWIN	37	
DUTTON, SARAH	110	
DYER, JENNIE	75	
DYKE, CATHARINE	81	
DYKE, FANNY	98	
DYKE, GRANT S.	81	
DYKE, JAMES L.	98	
DYKE, LOGAN	83	
DYKE, PHILLIP	81	
DYSART, GEORGE	68,68	
DYSART, JAMES	38	
EAGLESON, J., REV.	16	

EAHOLTZ, MARTIN 104
EAKIN, M.E. 82
EARDLY, JOHN 72
EARHART, CHARLIE 48
EARHART, GEORGE 48
EARHART, JACOB 28,29
EARL, HANNAH 75
EARL, THOMAS 25
EARL, WILLIAM 42
EARLY, JACOB 34
EARLY, VALENTINE 35
EARSMAN, MARY C. 30
EASTON, J.C., REV. 46
EASTON, J.S., REV. 36
EASTON, PETER 59
EASTON, SUSAN 59
EASTON, WALTER 59
EATON, ALMIRA 17
EATON, HENRY 95
EATON, JOHN 7
EATON, S.M. 31
EATON, SAMUEL 17
EATON, WM., REV. 30
EBBERHART, CATHARINE 68
EBBERHART, CHARLES 68
EBERHARDT, MR. 76
EBERT, O., REV. 90,99,110
ECKLEY, E.R. 3
ECKLEY, WILLIAM H. 3
ECKMAN, REV. 50
ECKSTEIN, ADAM 73
ECKSTEIN, BESSIE 91
ECKSTEIN, C.W. 91,113
ECKSTEIN, D.H. 100
ECKSTEIN, DAVID H. 66
ECKSTEIN, MARY 66,91,113
ECKSTEIN, WILLIE 113
EDDY, ALLEN W. 56
EDDY, ELLA R. 86
EDDY, WILLIAM M. 11
EDGE, THOMAS G. 23
EDGERTON, ABBIE F. 18
EDMUNDSON, LAURETTA J. 9
EDWARDS, AMZIE M. 87
EDWARDS, FRANK 84
EDWARDS, HESTER S. 83
EDWARDS, JEMIMA 119
EDWARDS, JOHN 7,113,114
EDWARDS, LUCINDA 97
EDWARDS, MAGGIE 84
EDWARDS, MARTHA 84
EDWARDS, NANCY 8
EDWARDS, S.L. 91
EDWARDS, WM. 77
EELLS, CATHARINE 28
EELLS, ELECTIOUS 60
EELLS, ELLA 97
EELLS, ERASTUS 3,8,14,24,28,
60,65,66,74,88
EELLS, HANNAH 39
EELLS, L.H. 63
EELLS, LILA 67
EELLS, MATTIE R. 69
EELLS, R.G. 110
EELLS, ROBERT 116
EELLS, SARAH H. 28
EHRHART, DAVID 7
EHRHART, GEORGE H. 116
EHRHART, HATTIE 94
EHRHART, LOUISA 94
EHRHART, REUBEN 94
EHRHART, SADIE 75
EHRHART, THEODORE 94
EIDENIRE, MARY 61,62
EIDENIRE, PHILLIP 62
EIGHMAN, MARY 101
EISENHAUER, JOHN 69
EISMAN, MR. 62
ELDER, A.H., REV. 119
ELDER, CAROLINE 72
ELDER, PERRY 72
ELDRIDGE, CARRIE 18
ELDRIDGE, ENOS 49
ELLENBERGER, FRED 57
ELLIOT, LAUGHLIN 97
ELLIOT, MARY 90
ELLIOT, MARY E. 97
ELLIOT, MATILDA 97
ELLIOTT, CHARLES 20,41
ELLIOTT, EMMA 34
ELLIOTT, HARVEY M. 97

ELLIOTT, JOHN 76
ELLIS, C.H., REV. 2,10,67
ELLIS, JAMES 101
ELLIS, JANE 81
ELLIS, THOMAS W. 119
ELLS, JOHN R. 116
ELSER, CATHARINE 8
ELTON, BENJAMIN S. 53
ELTON, JOB W. 33
ELVERSON, WM.H. 23
EMICH, MARGARET 10
EMMONS, ELISHA 80
EMMONS, SUSAN 80
ENDLEY, DAVID 24
ENDLEY, HARRIET A. 24
ENDLY, EMMA E. 2
ENDLY, G.W. 73
ENDLY, GEORGE 103
ENDLY, HARRIET A. 54
ENDLY, JACOB 87
ENDLY, M.H. 46
ENDLY, THOMAS E. 86
ENDSLEY, A.J., REV. 35
ENGLAND, ANNA 65
ENGLAND, CORA M. 9
ENGLAND, GEORGE 34
ENGLAND, JAMES R. 9
ENGLAND, JOSEPH 6
ENGLAND, LIZZIE A. 9
ENGLAND, MARGARET 105
ENGLAND, MATTIE 102
ENGLE, AARON H. 24
ENGLE, ISAAC N. 57
ENGLE, MARY 118
ENGLES, LYDIA 23
ENGLISH, ELIZA 4
ENGLISH, JAMES M. 66
ENGLISH, LEVI C., REV. 10
ENGLISH, MISS 99
ENGLISH, WILLIAM 30,59
ENTRICAN, E.B. 74
ENTRIKEN, ---- 84
ENTRIKEN, BARTON 1
ENTRIKEN, BYRON 12,36
ENTRIKEN, ELIZABETH A. 20
ENTRIKEN, JOSEPH 85
ENTRIKEN, SAMUEL 33
ENTRIKIN, FRANKLIN 68
ENTRIKIN, GEORGE 68
ENTWHISTLE, J. 82
ERICKSON, ALBERTINA 52
ERICKSON, ERILA T. 52
ERICKSON, FRANK 52
ERION, MARY E. 69
ERNWEIN, EMMA 92
ERNWEIN, M. 92
ERWIN, ELLA 86
ERWIN, J.P., REV. 87
ERWIN, MAHLON B. 88
ESSICK, J.M. 90
ESTARBROOK, ARTEMUS 35
ESTELL, J.J., REV. 91
ESTELL, JACOB 113
ESTELL, ROBERT N. 30
ESTEP, JAMES B. 90
ESTEP, JOSEPH 8
ESTEP, REBECCA 60
ESTEP, WILLIAM 38,60
ESTERLY, ANNA 32
ESTERLY, APTLE 89
ESTERLY, DAVID, MRS. 98
ESTERLY, ELIZABETH 35
ESTERLY, JACOB 100
ESTERLY, JACOB B. 53
ESTERLY, LEVI 32
ESTERLY, MARTHA 53
ESTERLY, MELINDA 53
ESTILL, BYRON S. 14
ESTILL, ETTIE 14
ESTILL, J.J., REV. 9,18,58,62,
101,102,114,119
ESTILL, JAMES 14
ESTILL, JASON 12,36
ESTILL, JOHN A. 12
ESTILL, ROBERT 62
ESTON, ARAGO 91
ESTRY, ISAAC 30
EUNGWIRTH, AMELIA 72
EVANS, DAVID 56,70
EVANS, ISAAC 68
EVANS, J.L. 104

EVANS, J.L., JR. 104
EVANS, JOHN 52
EVANS, JONATHAN 7
EVANS, LEWIS 74
EVANS, MARTHA 68
EVANS, REBECCA J. 70
EVANS, THOMAS 65,68,70,77
EVERETT, ELIZABETH 87
EVERETT, Z.S. 87
EWALT, SUSAN C. 45
EWING, A.A. 3
EWING, ALBERT 82
EWING, C. 46
EWING, ELIZABETH 21,113,114
EWING, EPHRAIM 88,112
EWING, FRANK 103
EWING, JOHN D. 21
EWING, JOSEPH 60
EWING, JOSEPHINE 43
EWING, MARIA 78
EWING, ROBERT 12,36
EWING, SAMUEL 33,113,114
EWING, T.H. 82
EWINGS, HANNAH A. 66
EYSTER, ELIAS 74
EYSTER, LOUISA 89
FAGUE, S.J. 44
FAHEY, MARIA 80
FAIRFAX, ALLEN 7
FAIRFAX, ELIZABETH 7
FAIRFAX, HARRIET D. 38
FAIRFIELD, WILLIAM 109
FALCONER, JOHN JR. 8
FALCONER, WM., REV. 67
FALLON, DANIEL 42
FALLOON, ISAAC 54
FALOON, AGNES 18
FALOON, ANNIE 66
FALOON, H. 23
FALOON, JOSEPH 19,66
FALOON, MAGGIE 66
FARGESON, ELLEN 49
FARMER, ALBERT A. 68
FARMER, ALPHEUS 1,39,51
FARMER, AMERICA 90
FARMER, ANNA M. 71
FARMER, CASSANDRA 97
FARMER, CICERO 82
FARMER, CLARENCE 105
FARMER, EMANUEL 70
FARMER, EMILINE 72
FARMER, EVERETT 108
FARMER, GEORGE 27,35,64,71
FARMER, HENRY W. 20,69
FARMER, ISAAC P. 54
FARMER, JAMES 10
FARMER, JERUSHA 10,35
FARMER, L.R. 30
FARMER, LYDIA 39,104
FARMER, MARANDA 75
FARMER, MARIA 30
FARMER, MARY 70,105
FARMER, MAY BELLA 30
FARMER, MINNIE 97
FARMER, OSBORN, MRS. 119
FARMER, RICHARD 24
FARMER, SAMUEL 18,105
FARMER, SARAH 20
FARMER, SUSAN M. 54,56
FARMER, THOMAS 64,109
FARMER, WILLIAM 97,116
FARQUAR, MR & MRS 57
FARQUHAR, ELIZABETH W. 46
FARQUHAR, HANNAH 81
FARQUHAR, M.F. 25
FARR, C.V. 56
FARR, ELIJAH 113
FARR, F. 72
FARR, MARTHA 81
FARR, SAMANTHA 10
FARR, WILLIAM 92,108
FARRALL, JULIA 72
FARRAND, MINNIE 33
FASNACHT, JOHN 83
FASNACHT, WILLIAM 83
FAST, REV. 38
FAULK, JOSHUA 99
FAULKER, CONRAD 2
FAUTS, PAUL 4
FAWCETT, AMOS 2,85
FAWCETT, ANNA 41

FAWCETT, DAVID 80
FAWCETT, DEBORAH 39
FAWCETT, ELI 18
FAWCETT, ELLA A. 42
FAWCETT, HANNAH M. 2
FAWCETT, HETTIE 71
FAWCETT, JOHN 32
FAWCETT, JOSEPH 32,63,67,70,74
FAWCETT, LYDIA A. 18
FAWCETT, MARY J. 6
FAWCETT, MAYOR 63
FAWCETT, NATHAN 32
FAWCETT, SIMEON 41
FAWCETT, THOMAS 45
FAY, ANNA J. 97
FEARNS, JAMES 10
FEAZEL, ALFRED 116
FEHL, LEWIS 105
FEISER, FRANK 37
FENNELLY, MARY 107
FENNELLY, PATRICK 107
FENSTERMAKER, AMELIA 66
FERGUSON, AMANDA 66
FERGUSON, CURRY 22
FERGUSON, R.G., REV. 99
FERGUSON, SUSAN 22
FERN, JOHN 86
FERRALL, EDWARD 44
FERRALL, EMMETT 90
FERRALL, J.B. 24
FERRALL, LIZZIE 77
FERRALL, LYDIA 24
FERRALL, MARY K. 75
FERRALL, MIDE 21
FERRAND, FRANK P. 24
FERRELL, EDMOND 107
FERRELL, EMMA 107
FERRELL, LUCINDA 92
FESLER, FAMILY 95
FESLER, JESSE 113
FESTER, CATHARINE 95
FESTER, JONATHAN 95
FETTERS, FRANK W. 79
FETTERS, MARY 32
FETZER, FAMILY 95
FETZER, PHILLIP 34
FICKES, PERRY 96
FICKESS, MARGARET J. 56
FIELDS, PETER 112
FIFE, AMOS 62
FIFE, CATHARINE 5
FIFE, DAVID 7
FIFE, ELIZABETH 95
FIFE, ISAAC SR. 95
FIFE, J.H. 21
FIFE, JAMES 7
FIFE, JOHN 7
FIFE, LANER J. 46
FIFE, MARTHA H. 49
FIFE, MARY 32
FIFE, THOMAS R. 28
FIFE, WILLIAM 7,101
FIFE, WILSON J. 93
FIGGINS, ISABELLA 44
FIGGINS, JOHN 65,85
FIGGINS, NANCY 65
FIGLEY, BIANCA 52
FIGLEY, CLEMENT 36,52
FIGLEY, DAVID 72
FIGLEY, GEORGE 7,36
FIGLEY, JEMIMA 11
FIGLEY, JOHN 11
FIGLEY, MARTHA A. 49
FIGLEY, MARY JANE 87
FIGLEY, RACHEL J. 83
FIGLEY, WILLIAM 7,36,52
FILSON, FRANCIS E. 33
FILSON, FRANKLIN 104
FILSON, JOHN C. 34,48
FILSON, RACHEL E. 79
FILSON, S.A.G. 30
FILSON, SARAH 48
FILSON, WM. 43
FINCH, E. 48
FINDLEY, HANNAH 1,120
FINDLEY, JOHN 1,120
FINDLEY, PATRICK 106
FINERAN, MARTIN 18
FINK, MINNIE 96
FINK, REV. 31
FINLEY, EDWARD 4

128

FINN, VAL.B. 82
FINNEGAN, MARY 52
FINNEGAN, WILLIAM J. 59
FINNEY, MR. 120
FIRESTONE, DR. 26
FIRESTONE, JOHN 7
FIRESTONE, JUDGE 13
FIRESTONE, PERRY 7
FIRESTONE, S.J. 85
FIRRAL, EMMETT 90
FISHBURN, ELIZA 40
FISHER, ADAM 69
FISHER, ANNIE W. 13
FISHER, BRICE 7
FISHER, CHAS., REV. 23
FISHER, CHRISTIE 13,27
FISHER, CLARA J. 27
FISHER, DAVID 32
FISHER, E.B. 101
FISHER, ELENOR 31
FISHER, ELI 110
FISHER, ELIZABETH 97,110
FISHER, ESTELLA 91
FISHER, G.W. 64
FISHER, GALEN 62
FISHER, GEORGE 82,101
FISHER, HARRY 101
FISHER, HERMAN 31
FISHER, JACOB 66
FISHER, JAMES 56,57,68
FISHER, JEFFERSON 42
FISHER, JULIA A. 96
FISHER, KATE 54
FISHER, LAURA M. 6
FISHER, LIZZIE 110
FISHER, LOUIE 91
FISHER, MICHAEL 109
FISHER, PETER 94
FISHER, REV. 51
FISHER, RICHARDSON 19
FISHER, S.B. 78
FISHER, SADIE 110
FISHER, SAMUEL 13,27,47
FISHER, SANFORD G.,REV. 11,91
FISHER, SARAH 32
FITSIMONS, THOMAS 116
FITZGERALD, MR. 113
FITZPATRICK, ALBINA 78
FITZPATRICK, ALVERDA 8
FITZPATRICK, ALWILDA 8
FITZPATRICK, CHARLES 7
FITZPATRICK, DELLA 91
FITZPATRICK, ELLEN 44
FITZPATRICK, HUGH 44
FITZPATRICK, JACOB 8,78
FITZPATRICK, LAVOY W. 8
FITZPATRICK, NANCY 6
FITZPATRICK, SAMUEL S. 8
FITZPATRICK, SUSANNA 8
FITZPATRICK, T.C. 56
FITZPATRICK, WILHIE 64
FITZPATRICK, WILLIAM 75
FITZSIMONS, JIMMIE 116
FITZSIMONS, MAGGIE 116
FITZSIMONS, MARY F. 116
FITZSIMONS, SAMUEL 116
FLAUGHER, J.H. 5
FLEMING, MARY J. 82
FLEMING, PATRICK 72
FLEMING, PETER 109,112
FLEMMING, SARAH H. 102
FLICK, ANDREW 6,76
FLICK, BARBARA 29
FLICKER, GUSTAVIS M. 72
FLICKINGER, ANGIE 88
FLICKINGER, HENRY 71
FLICKINGER, ISAIAH 72
FLICKINGER, JACOB 82
FLICKINGER, JOHN 66
FLICKINGER, JOSHUA 85
FLICKINGER, MISS 71
FLITCRAFT, JOHN 6
FLITCRAFT, LIZZIE 74
FLITCRAFT, WALTER 81
FLOWERS, E.ANN 35
FLOWERS, R.A. 106
FLUGAN, FREDERICK 101
FLUGAN, GEORGE 92
FLUGAN, JAMES G. 3
FLUGAN, LEWIS 12
FLUGAN, LOUIS F. 36

FLUGAN, WILLIAM C. 106
FOGG, EBENEZER 69
FOGG, JANE 69
FOGG, REBECCA 111
FOGG, SAMUEL A. 40
FOGO, JANE 85
FOGO, MARY 46,81
FOLEY, JOHN 49,63
FOLGER, ROBERT 2
FOLLANSBEE, JAMES 35
FORBES, ALEXANDER 67
FORBES, ELIZABETH 52
FORBES, ELLA 46
FORBES, FRANCES 9
FORBES, J.L. 98
FORBES, LIZZIE J. 115
FORBIS, JOHN, MRS. 50
FORD, ED M. 45
FORD, MARTHA 109
FORNAY, JOHN 97
FORNAY, LAURA 97
FORNER, T.J. 54
FORNEY, ALBAN W. 2
FORY, MARGARET 108
FORY, SAMUEL 108
FORY, WILLIE 108
FOSTER & RIGBY 11
FOSTER, ABBY KELLEY 13
FOSTER, D.W. 61
FOSTER, FRANK 51
FOSTER, FRANKLIN 104
FOSTER, GEORGE 21
FOSTER, JAMES 11
FOSTER, W.G. 79
FOULKS, JOHN 73
FOULKS, WILLIAM 13
FOULTS, M.H. 93
FOUTS, BELLE 102
FOUTS, HENRY A. 77
FOUTS, ISAAC 21
FOUTS, JOSHUA 40
FOUTTS, JOHN 26
FOUTTS, M.H. 12
FOUTTS, NANCY 26
FOUTTS, SALLIE 69
FOUTZ, JOSHUA 63
FOUTZ, MARGARETTA 63
FOUTZ, MICHAEL 7
FOUTZ, OLIVE 108
FOWLER, GEORGE 83
FOWLER, JACOB 85
FOWLER, JOHN Q.A. 62
FOWLER, MARY 73
FOWLER, SUSAN J. 106
FOWLER, WILLIAM 106
FOX, DAVID 116
FOX, ELIZABETH 22
FOX, G.A. 89
FOX, JACOB 26
FOX, JAMES 83
FOX, JERRY 116
FOX, MARY A. 4,68
FOX, PHILIP 7
FOX, SAMUEL 76,77
FOX, TEVERA 73
FOX, ZIMRI 1
FRANCIS, ELIZABETH 108
FRANCIS, M.M. 49
FRANCIS, MARY 38
FRANCIS, THOMAS 49,69
FRANKY, F.M. 117
FRANTZ, ANNA V. 90
FRANTZ, MARY 116
FRANTZ, SOPHIA 23
FRANTZ, SUSAN E. 63
FRASER, BELLA 116
FRASER, HUGH 98
FRASER, JOHN 57,67
FRASER, MAGGIE 4,71
FRASER, MARY E. 41
FRASER, REBECCA 89
FRASIER, J.I., REV. 104
FRAZER, BELLE 38
FRAZER, DANIEL 26
FRAZER, ELIZABETH 73
FRAZER, KATE 59
FRAZER, PHILLIP 78
FRAZER, WILLIAM O. 49
FRAZIER, ALEXANDER 31,94
FRAZIER, ALPHEUS A. 100
FRAZIER, DANIEL 62,83,100

FRAZIER, E.L., REV. 86,90,105
FRAZIER, ELIZABETH A. 83,100
FRAZIER, ROBERT A. 100
FRAZIER, S.R., REV. 83
FREASE, JUDGE 45,102
FREAT, PETER 35
FREAT, SUSAN 35
FREAZEL, ALFRED 116
FREDERICK, ANNA M. 114
FREDERICK, B.F. 110,114
FREDERICK, BELLE 13
FREDERICK, BYRON 90,105,110
FREDERICK, CATHARINE 114
FREDERICK, CHRISTOPHER 114
FREDERICK, CLEMENTINE 114
FREDERICK, ELIZABETH 110
FREDERICK, FAMILY 110,114
FREDERICK, G.W. 118
FREDERICK, GEORGE 7
FREDERICK, HATTIE A. 90
FREDERICK, MARGARET 114
FREDERICK, NOAH 114
FREDERICK, SARAH C. 105
FREDERICK, THOMAS 53,110,114
FREDERICK, Z. 114
FREED, ALEXANDER 33
FREED, CATHERINE 64
FREED, GEORGE W. 30
FREED, JACOB 96
FREED, JEFFERSON 51
FREED, PETER 48
FREEMAN, DANIEL A. 84
FREEMAN, FREDERICK 84
FREEMAN, GEORGE 12,36
FREEMAN, HARRIET 84
FREEMAN, HESTER 93
FREEMAN, JOHN W. 72
FREESE, EVE 35
FREKSE, MARY B. 66
FRENCH, ANN 5
FRENCH, BARZILLAI 71
FRENCH, DAVID 62
FRENCH, DEBORA M. 71
FRENCH, EDGAR 108
FRENCH, ELIZA 62
FRENCH, JUDITH 10
FRENCH, OBADIAH 10
FRENCH, SARAH C. 91
FRENCH, SOPHIA 62
FRENCH, ZADOK S. 48
FRESHLY, JESSE 88
FREW, J.K. 60,115
FREW, J.S. 42
FREW, JAMES K. 1,2,56
FREW, MARY 104
FREW, PHILIP 104
FREY, GEORGE P. 58
FRIES, JUDGE 6
FRIES, MRS.DR. 108
FRIESE, EMMA B. 7
FRIFOGEL, J.F. 116
FRITZ, FREDERICK 67
FROST, C.L. 63
FROST, CATHARINE 3
FROST, E.A. 52
FROST, ESQ. 61,67,77
FROST, EZRA 3
FROST, H.E. 49,51,56,60,62, 63,65,75,78,79,82,88, 89,99,105
FROST, HARVEY 3
FROST, HENRY E. 2,76,88,91, 92,107
FROST, JAMES 65
FROST, JESSE 24
FROST, JOHN 11
FROST, LEE A. 52
FROST, MAHALA 117
FROST, MARTHA 117,118
FROST, MARY 24,65
FROST, MAYOR 14
FROST, WILLIAM G. 21,52
FRY, H.B., REV. 48,49,50, 57,58,61,62,63,64,69,74,75, 76,77,78,80,81,82,86,87,89, 94,96,98,105,108,110,111, 115,117,118
FUGATE, SAMUEL 85
FUHR, EVALYN V. 33
FUHR, JOHN H. 54
FULK, MORGAN 63

FULLER, ALEX R. 19
FULTON, A. 56
FULTON, WILLIAM, REV. 77
FULTS, JOHN 84
FULTS, WM. 14,20
FULTY, AUSTIN 74
FULTZ, CELESTA 54
FULTZ, LAVINA 33
FULTZ, WM. 7,9,19,22,23,25,34
FUNKHOUSER, MR. 34
FURGERSON, JOHN H. 20
FURGUSON, RACHEL 83
FURNEY, ALBAN W. 79
FURNISS, EMMA 32
FURNISS, GEORGE W. 91
FURNISS, MARY 47
GAFFNEY, ANNA 87
GAFFNEY, PATRICK 109,112
GAGE, LUCIEN H. 64
GAGER, J.PRATT 91
GAILEY, ALEXANDER 63,78
GAILEY, ANDREW 31
GAILEY, ANN 31
GAILEY, CHARLES 31
GAILEY, JOHN, REV. 5
GAILEY, MARTHA 79
GAILEY, MARY 63
GAILEY, MR. 42
GAILY, JOHN 20
GALBRAITH, ABBY 48
GALBRAITH, JACOB H. 40
GALBRAITH, MARY A. 90
GALBRAITH, WALTER 110
GALBREATH, CELESTIA 67
GALBREATH, DAVID 21,68
GALBREATH, JAMES 9
GALBREATH, MYRTHA 67
GALBREATH, PARKER 67
GALBREATH, SARAH W. 21
GALLAGHER, J.N. 114
GALLAGHER, SUSAN 97
GALLAHER, LIZZIE A. 28
GALLIGER, ISAAC 34
GAMBER, REV. 72
GAMBLE, CHARLES 110
GAMBLE, J.H. 27
GAMBLE, NANCY A. 74
GAMBLE, R.G. 74
GAMBLE, SAMUEL 5,74
GAMBLE, SARAH 119
GAMBLE, THOMAS 119
GAMBLE, WILLIE 119
GAMMEL, DAVID A. 45
GAMMEL, JACOB 45
GAMMEL, MARGARET J. 45
GANT, MARY 80
GARCIE, MARIE 102
GARDENER, CHARLES W. 3
GARDENER, SARAH 20
GARDNER, ABRAM 93
GARDNER, CHARLES W. 7,27
GARDNER, DR. 119
GARDNER, E.P., REV. 102
GARDNER, EDWARD 119
GARDNER, JENNIE 86
GARDNER, JOHN 50
GARDNER, LEVI 22
GARDNER, LIDE R. 12
GARDNER, LUCINDA 50
GARDNER, NANCY 93
GARDNER, REBECCA F. 7
GARDNER, RICHARD 37,49
GARDNER, RUTH 40
GARDNER, SUSANNA 22,93
GARDNER, THOMAS K. 50
GAREY, THOMAS M. 1
GARLICK, EMMA 38
GARLICK, T.J. 83
GARMAN, MAGDALINE 21
GARRET, MARY 98
GARRETSON, ARMELA 91
GARRETSON, DR. 18
GARRETSON, ELI, DR. 27,76
GARRETSON, EMMA 76
GARRETSON, GEORGE A. 3
GARRETSON, HIRAM 96,113
GARRETSON, JESSE, DR. 113
GARRETSON, LUCRETIA M. 18
GARRETSON, SARAH J. 27
GARRETSON, WILLIAM 96
GARRETT, CLINTON 61,73,87

GARRETT, PERCY C.	73	GIBBONS, L.N.	96
GARRETT, RACHEL	87	GIBBONS, SUSAN R.	109
GARRETT, RATIE	73	GIBBS, CAPT.	16
GARRIGUES, ESQ.	74	GIBBS, EMMA	37
GARRIGUES, HARRY B.	82	GIBBS, GEORGE W.	37
GARRIGUES, HOWARD	85	GIBBS, JOHN	28
GARRIGUES, R.A.	70	GIBSON, A.G.	52
GARRIGUES, R.G.	69	GIBSON, HENRY M.	52
GARRIGUES, R.H.	16,19,21,38,	GIBSON, J.S., REV.	18
	40,48,64,74,81,83	GIBSON, M.	52
GARRIGUES, WM.	43	GIESSE, MELLIE	82
GARRISON, THOMAS	7	GIFFORD, LOUIS	44
GARSIDE, E.	1,10,34,47,66,76,	GILBERT, ANNA	72
	82,86,88,89,91,93,94,107,112	GILBERT, ELLA	86
GARSIDE, EDWIN	22,34,93	GILBERT, FRANK I.	84
GARSIDE, JOHN	96	GILBERT, JAMES A.	30
GARSIDE, MARGARET E.	8	GILBERT, JESSE	68
GARSIDE, RACHEL	96	GILBERT, MARY J.	56
GARSIDE, SARAH E.	96	GILBERT, MOLLIE L.	68
GARSIDE, SUSANNAH	93	GILBERT, RILY M.	70
GARTHWAIT, KATE	101	GILBERT, THEODORE	86
GARTHWAIT, MATILDA	101	GILBERT, WINFIELD S.	83
GARTHWAIT, WALTER	101	GILES, C.C.	72
GARTHWAITE, ELIZABETH	63	GILES, E.	72
GARTSIDE, JOSEPH H.	19	GILES, FRANCIS	112
GARWOOD, ALICE	75	GILES, HENRY	112
GARWOOD, ASENETH	97	GILES, MATTIE J.	72
GARWOOD, DANIEL	3	GILES, WILLIAM T.	46
GARWOOD, ELIZABETH	97	GILL, W.H., REV.	119
GARWOOD, ISAAC	9	GILLESPIE, GEORGE	93
GARWOOD, JOHN	97	GILLESPIE, J.S.	70
GARWOOD, SYLVESTER S.	11	GILLESPIE, JAMES	99
GARWOOD, WILLIAM	115	GILLESPIE, MARGARET	93
GASKILL, ABRAM	63	GILLESPIE, MARTIN	99
GASKILL, ANNIE M.	1	GILLESPIE, SARAH	70
GASKILL, DAVID	51	GILLESPIE, W.H.	50
GASKILL, ELVA	105	GILLIGEN, BROTHERS	119
GASKILL, FRANK	68	GILLMAN, CHARLES	103
GASKILL, GEORGE	119	GILLOOLY, MICHAEL	78
GASKILL, ISRAEL	7	GILMAN, ANN G.	54
GASKILL, JOSIAH	83	GILMAN, C.H.	22,43
GASKILL, LEONARD	12,36	GILMAN, CHARLES H.	3
GASKILL, MARY A.	103	GILMAN, FANNIE	22
GASKILL, MILETUS	12,36	GILMAN, JOHN M.	54
GASTON, DORCAS	85	GILMAN, REBECCA	22
GASTON, ELIZABETH	42	GILMOR, DR.	58
GASTON, EPHRAIM	85	GILMOR, MARY C.	61
GASTON, IRA	69	GILMORE, ABEL S.	41
GASTON, J.W.	115	GILMORE, JUDGE	50
GASTON, JAMES	62	GILMORE, MAIMIE	25
GASTON, NANCY	63	GILMORE, MARY F.	119
GASTON, WM., REV.	81	GILMORE, RICHARD, REV.	69
GAUNT, NER	102	GILMORE, SALLIE	27
GAUS, NANCY	96	GILMORE, SUE	102
GAUZE, WILLIAM	108	GILMORE, WILLIAM	46
GAVER, HIRAM	13,75	GILSON, AGNES R.	5
GAVER, HOMER H.	75	GILSON, DAVID R.	10
GAVER, REBECCA	75	GILSON, MAGGIE A.	8
GEARY, LIZZIE	85	GILSON, S.W.	86
GEE, FIRMAN	115	GILSON, WILLIAM	107
GEE, NICHOLAS	115	GILTON, WM.W.	21
GEER, SAMUEL	89	GINTHER, JOHN	64
GEIGER, WILMA	100	GINTHER, MARY	71
GEISSE, ALFRED H.	19	GLASS, ANNA BARBARA	106
GEISSE, EMMA C.	7	GLASS, GEORGE	110
GEISSE, FRANK	49	GLASS, JACOB	106
GEISSE, HELEN L.	70	GLASS, LEWIS	106
GEISSE, LYDIA	20	GLASS, MARGARET	89
GEISSE, P.F.	20	GLECKLER, JACOB	1
GEISSE, PHILIP F.	64	GLECKLER, JONATHAN	58
GEISSE, REBECCA	19	GLENN, ALEXANDER	34
GEISSINGER, DANIEL W.	25	GLENN, ANN	68
GENTHER, LOUISA	118	GLENN, CAROLINE	52
GEORGE, ADDIE	82	GLENN, EMMA	52
GEORGE, ANN A.	17	GLENN, GEORGE	42,52
GEORGE, ELIZABETH	66	GLENN, JAMES	11,68
GEORGE, FRANK	76,111	GLENN, LAURA B.	63
GEORGE, JAMES	32	GLENN, RHODA J.	68
GEORGE, JOHN	37	GLENN, ROBERT	52
GEORGE, LEVI	57	GLENN, TAMAR	42
GEORGE, SARAH A.	36	GLENN, THAMAR	42
GEORGE, THOMAS	36,42	GLENN, WM.C.	33
GEORGE, W.E.	76	GLESSINGER, MR.	114
GEORGE, WILLIAM	2,8	GLESSNER, NOAH	41,42
GEPHART, LEWIS	31	GLOSS, MARGARET A.	22
GESS, GEORGE	34	GLOSS, SOLOMON	11
GETZ, JACOB	98	GLOSSER, DAVID	109
GETZ, KEZIAH	98	GOCHENAUR, DAVID	20
GIBB, CLARA	118	GOCHENAUR, ELCANY	20
GIBBINS, JACOB	41	GOCHENAUR, ELIZABETH	20
GIBBONS, HESTER	80	GOCHENAUR, JACOB	20

GODDARD, FRANK	98	GRANT, N.C, REV.	57
GODDARD, REUBEN	58	GRANT, PRES.	30
GODEN, MRS.	60	GRANT, R.J.	96
GODWARD, MARK	24	GRANT, REV.	105
GOERING, JOHN	36	GRASS, LYDIA	75
GOGLEY, REV.	77	GRATE, LOUISA W.	30
GOLAHER, MALINDA	90	GRAVES, R.V., REV.	78
GOLDEN, DAVID	12	GRAY, ENOCH	38
GOLDING, JAMES	7	GRAY, EVANS	82
GOLDY, B.E.	58	GRAY, JOHN, REV.	27
GOLDY, ELLEN	83	GRAY, LEANDER	39
GOLDY, J.S.	95	GRAY, W.S., REV.	7
GOLDY, S.P.	58	GREAVES, HENRY	8
GOLDY, WM.HENRY	58	GREEN, A.E.	28,29
GOLLADAY, J.E.	104	GREEN, ANNA R.	51
GOLLOWAY, MATTIE	89	GREEN, ELIZABETH	19
GONGAWARE, ALBERT	62	GREEN, ELLA	116
GONGUARE, SIMON	40	GREEN, F.M.	10,40
GONZALES, ANNIE	110	GREEN, HOLLAND	7
GONZALES, DANIEL	67	GREEN, J.W.	24
GOODBRAKE, AMELIA	6	GREEN, JAMES	20,23,79,105
GOODBRAKE, HATTIE	6	GREEN, JASON	110
GOODBRAKE, JACOB	6,68	GREEN, JOHN	70,81
GOODEREL, GEORGE W.	119	GREEN, JOSEPH	108
GOODERL, GEORGE	6	GREEN, JULIA	81,93
GOODERL, SUSAN	6	GREEN, L.H.	28,29,100
GOODLEY, HARRIET	80	GREEN, LAVINA	55,102
GOODMAN, JONAS	83	GREEN, LEWIS	28,29
GOODRICH, C.P., REV.	68	GREEN, LUCY	108
GOODRICH, W.J., REV.	21	GREEN, LYDIA	117
GOODSON, J.P., REV.	58	GREEN, MARY	83
GOODWIN, DANIEL	67	GREEN, MERVIN	102
GOODWIN, JOHN	93	GREEN, NANCY	105,107
GOODWIN, W.PERCY	35	GREEN, PEGGY	110
GORBLE, JENNIE	81	GREEN, RALPH	100
GORBY, MRS.	77	GREEN, SARAH	31
GORBY, SAMUEL	77	GREEN, THOMAS	7
GORDON, ELIZA	101	GREEN, WAVERLY	108
GORDON, ELIZABETH W.	76	GREEN, WILLIAM	16,19,22,30
GORDON, JOHN	76	GREENAMYER, ALDEN	102
GORE, EMMA	91	GREENAMYER, MARY	102
GORE, F.	56	GREENAMYER, RETTIE	71
GORE, H.	91	GREENAWALT, CAROLINA	33
GORE, PHEBE	14	GREENAWALT, DAN V.	33
GORMAN, CATHARINE	8	GREENAWALT, DILWORTH	80
GOSS, MARTIN	57	GREENAWALT, EMMA	33
GRACE, JOHN	39	GREENAWALT, GEORGE	115
GRACE, MARY A.	64	GREENAWALT, JOHN	95
GRACE, REV.FATHER	81	GREENAWALT, JOSEPH	33
GRACY, MARGARET	48,85	GREENAWALT, LEWIS W.	33
GRACY, SAMUEL	48	GREENAWALT, MARY	33,100
GRACY, WILLIAM	48	GREENAWALT, MOLLIE	118
GRAFF, A.D.	32	GREENAWALT, ROSA	33
GRAFF, FRANCIS M.	14	GREENLEE, ALEX	88
GRAFTON, ALONZO	35	GREENLEE, HARRIET	3
GRAFTON, CARRIE M.	69	GREENLEE, JOSEPH	3
GRAFTON, CASSANDRA	101	GREENWOOD, GEORGE B.	30
GRAFTON, E.G.	69	GREER, MARY F.	91
GRAFTON, ELIZABETH F.	60	GREER, REBECCA	97
GRAFTON, JAMES	31	GREER, THOMAS W., REV.	107
GRAFTON, JOHN	20	GREGG, H.H.	46,54,115
GRAFTON, MAY	20	GREINER, JOSEPH O.	86
GRAFTON, MINNIE	69	GREINER, SARAH A.	81
GRAFTON, NELLIE	118	GREY, CHARLOTTE A.	42
GRAFTON, SAMANTHA	86	GREY, FLETCHER W.	42
GRAFTON, THOMAS	13,35	GREY, JOHN A., REV.	35
GRAFTON, WILLIAM	101,118	GREY, ROBERT	8
GRAHAM, ALICE	81	GRIBBLE, PETER	35
GRAHAM, ANN M.	7	GRICE, CHARLES A.	3
GRAHAM, BARNEY	38	GRIER, MARY J.	18
GRAHAM, ELIZA	108	GRIER, S.Y., REV.	83
GRAHAM, FRANK	32,88	GRIFFITH, HATTIE R.	42
GRAHAM, GEORGE	108	GRIFFITH, WILLIAM	76
GRAHAM, H.Q., REV.	63	GRIGGSBY, W.M., REV.	116
GRAHAM, J.DALLAS	36	GRIM, ABRAHAM	7
GRAHAM, JAMES	36,51,66	GRIM, DANIEL	7
GRAHAM, JAMES, DR.	47,68,108	GRIM, FLORA M.	81
GRAHAM, JEFFIE	32	GRIM, LENA	112
GRAHAM, JOHN B., REV.	38,47,	GRIM, MILLIARD	105
	68,108	GRIM, PETER	7
GRAHAM, MARY E.	32	GRIM, WALTER	73
GRAHAM, NATHAN	36	GRIMES, J.S.,REV.	43,48,73
GRAHAM, WILLIAM	108	GRIMES, OLIVER	62
GRANGER, MINA	106	GRIMES, REV.	37
GRANGER, WILLIAM	106	GRIMES, SUSAN	57
GRANT, ALEXANDER	58	GRIMES, W.M., REV.	115
GRANT, ELIZA J.	89	GRIMM, ELDER	117
GRANT, F.	109	GRIMMESEY, ELLA	28
GRANT, J., REV.	102,103,106	GRIMMESEY, JOHN	5
GRANT, JOHN	7	GRISELL, ANSON	95
GRANT, MR.	30	GRISELL, C.D.	4

GRISILWOLD, A.J. 25
GROFF, WILLIAM 91
GRONER, DAVID 35
GRONER, FRANKLIN 67
GRONER, H.M. 43
GRONER, JOHN 51,64
GRONER, LYDIA 98
GRONER, MARIA 44
GRONER, MARY 67,98
GRONER, MATTIE A. 107
GRONER, ORA 83
GRONER, SIMON 67,98
GRONER, WILLIAM 56,70,78,118
GRONIN, JOHN 111
GROOMS, F.M. 91
GROOMS, GEORGE 105
GROOMS, JAMES JR. 12,36
GROOMS, JOHN 117
GROOMS, SUPT. 118
GROSCOST, MARY E. 59
GROSNER, JOE H. 69
GROSSMAN, VIRGINIA 86
GROVE, JENNIE 18
GROVE, P.LONSFORD 38
GROVES, JAMES 29
GROVES, MARY 51
GRUBER, ALVINA M. 40
GRUBER, FRANK 40
GRUBER, J.L. 49
GRUBER, JOHN L. 37
GRUWELL, C.B. 77
GULL, JOHN 28,29
GUNN & McLEAN 67
GUNN, GEORGE 76
GUNNING, JOHN 81
GURMANS, MAGDALINE 21
GURNEY, ROBERT 73
GUTHRIE, RICHARD 7
GUTHRIE, WILLIAM 7
GUY, EDWARD 91
GUY, LOUISA 48
GUY, REBECCA 8
GUY, SARAH 48,91
HAAG, CAROLINE 73
HAAS, CHRISTIAN B. 64
HAAS, JACOB 118
HAAS, MR. 64
HAAS, REUBEN 68
HACK, LOUISA 76
HACKETT, MARY J. 73
HAGEN, JAMES 85
HAGEN, MAGGIE 85
HAGER, SAMUEL S. 7
HAGMAN, JAMES 50
HAGUE, ANNA 21
HAGUE, HANNAH 95
HAGUE, JEHU 95
HAGUE, MARY S. 80
HAHN, DANIEL 87
HAHN, NATHAN 81
HAIFLEY, RACHEL 80
HAIFLY, AARON 4
HAINES, ANNA C. 37
HAINES, BENJAMIN L. 62
HAINES, CAREY 84
HAINES, ELI J. 62
HAINES, HARRY 14
HAINES, J.W. 98
HAINES, JAMES O. 62
HAINES, JOHN 30
HAINES, ROBERT M. 62
HAINES, THOMAS C. 62
HAINES, WILLIAM 20,69
HAINS, ELI 23
HAINS, JOSEPH W. 62
HAINS, MATILDA T. 62
HAINSON, WILLIAM 109
HAKE, JONAS 19
HALDEMAN, ADDISON 40
HALDEMAN, JOSEPH S. 88
HALDEMAN, JULIA B. 88
HALDEMAN, N.A. 41
HALES, LUCINDA 37
HALEY, JOHN 97
HALEY, MARY 97
HALEY, MATHEW 78
HALEY, PATRICK 97
HALIBURT, E.S. 106
HALL, ANNA L. 6
HALL, AXY 67
HALL, CHARLES F. 8

HALL, EMMA 68
HALL, HANNAH 87
HALL, HELEN 80
HALL, HUGH F. 101
HALL, I.G., REV. 27,39,57
HALL, JABEZ, REV. 73
HALL, JAMES 43
HALL, JOHN 54,80
HALL, MAHALA D. 83
HALL, MARTHA 110
HALL, REV. 40
HALL, SARAH 88
HALL, THOMAS 80
HALL, WILLIAM 36,90
HALLEN, DANIEL 21
HALLUM, ESQ. 39
HALLUM, GEO. 28,33
HALSTEAD, SAMUEL 76
HALVENSTADT, C.A. 41
HALVERSTADT, D.W. 24
HALVERSTADT, DAVID 89
HALVERSTADT, EMMA 87
HALVERSTADT, G. 32
HALVERSTADT, GEO. 31
HALVERSTADT, I.A. 103
HALVERSTADT, ISAAC 19
HALVERSTADT, J.S. 39
HALVERSTADT, JACOB S. 30
HALVERSTADT, LYDIA 31
HALVERSTADT, MARIA 80
HALVERSTADT, MARY S. 90
HALVERSTADT, PHEBE 31
HALVERSTADT, REBECCA 11
HALVERSTADT, S.M. 60
HAMBEL, ELLA 83
HAMBELL, JOHN 19
HAMBLE, CHARLES 71
HAMBLETON, ELIZA A. 22
HAMBLETON, LEWIS 22
HAMBRIGHT, ALSEA 36
HAMILTON, ANNIE T. 31
HAMILTON, ARETA C. 57
HAMILTON, BENJAMIN 25
HAMILTON, DAVID 31
HAMILTON, GEORGE 43
HAMILTON, HANNAH 47
HAMILTON, HATTIE 10
HAMILTON, HENRY 7
HAMILTON, J.G., DR. 89
HAMILTON, J.R. 26
HAMILTON, JAMES 45,47
HAMILTON, JAMES A. 116
HAMILTON, JANE 65
HAMILTON, JENNIE 97
HAMILTON, JESSIE V. 105
HAMILTON, JOHN 47
HAMILTON, JOSEPH 23
HAMILTON, MARY 31,45
HAMILTON, PHILIP 1
HAMILTON, QUIGLEY 70
HAMILTON, ROSANNA 89
HAMILTON, SARAH 1,19
HAMILTON, SUSAN E. 1
HAMILTON, T.S. 57
HAMILTON, W.W. 43
HAMILTON, WILLIAM 110,116
HAMMEL, MAGDALENA 64
HAMMOND, DR. 113
HAMMOND, DR. 70
HAMMOND, EMMA A. 45
HAMMOND, J.W. 3
HAMMOND, MARY V. 3
HAMMOND, SALLIE 3
HAMMOND, THOMAS 45,84
HAMPSON, CHRISTENA 113
HAMPSON, ELMIRA 100
HAMPSON, JENNIE 114
HAMPSON, R.A. 113
HANES, EBENEZER 7
HANK, RICHARD M. 9
HANLEY, HONORA 106
HANLEY, SARAH 107
HANLIN, JAMES 106
HANLIN, MARY 106
HANLON, JAMES 97
HANLY, JAMES 56
HANNA, GEORGE 75
HANNA, J.P. 107
HANNA, LAVINA 98
HANNA, LEVI 29
HANNA, MINNIE 54

HANNA, MRS. 82
HANNA, NETTIE 27
HANNA, ROBERT 103
HANNA, THOMAS 11,27,98
HANNAH, AMANDA 56
HANNAH, DRUSILLA 109,112
HANNAH, MINNIE 54
HANNAY, JOHN F. 2
HANNAY, THOMAS, REV. 38
HANNEY, HOMER J. 101
HANNEY, LYDIA 101
HANNEY, ROBERT 101
HANNUM, JOHN 81
HARBAUGH, ANGIE 51
HARBAUGH, CATHARINE 114
HARBAUGH, DANIEL 7,15,19,86,87
HARBAUGH, DAVID 86,114
HARBAUGH, DENNIS 15
HARBAUGH, JACOB 43
HARBAUGH, JONATHAN 41
HARBAUGH, LEWIS D. 51
HARBAUGH, MARY J. 74
HARBAUGH, PORTER 105
HARBAUGH, SUSAN 50
HARDESTY, GEO., REV. 95
HARDESTY, JOHN 27
HARDESTY, LORENZO D. 30
HARDING, JOHN 112
HARDINGER, SARAH E. 105
HARDINGER, WILLIAM 55
HARDMAN, DR. 117
HARDMAN, MAGGIE 27
HARDMAN, MARY 57
HARDMAN, MRS. 79
HARDMAN, SAMUEL 1,6,7,8,16,
17,18,19,21,22,24,26,27,29,
30,33,34,36,37,38,51,53,54,
66,67,76,77,81,87,91,96,98,
102,103,110
HARDMAN, SIMEON 6
HARDMAN, SQUIRE 27
HARDMAN, WM.H. 25
HARDY, THOMAS 111
HARGEST, D., REV. 102,103,118
HARGEST, DAVID,REV. 70,81,89,
90,95,97,101,106,116
HARKER, CHARLOTTE 23
HARKER, ELIZABETH 40
HARKER, JOHN, REV. 93
HARKER, MARIA 104
HARKER, MISS 84
HARKER POTTERY 29
HARKER, SYNDONIA 101
HARLAN, EDWARD 48
HARLAN, REBECCA 48
HARLOW, BOY 65
HARLOW, HENRY 60
HARMAN, ALSADA 78
HARMAN, EMANUEL 79
HARMAN, JULIA 79
HARMAN, LEVI 78
HARMAN, MARY 54
HARMAN, RACHEL 78
HARMEN, SARAH 55
HARMER, THOMAS 11
HARMON, ANNA 70
HARMON, SUSAN 109
HARPER, ELIZA 57
HARPER, ENOCH 54,55,57
HARPER, FANNIE 106
HARPER, KATE 110
HARPER, R.P. 74
HARRIER, J.H., REV. 96,119
HARRIER, T.H. 82
HARRIGAN, JOHN 106
HARRIGAN, MARGARET 106
HARRINGTON, PETER 68
HARRIS, A.H. 18
HARRIS, ALCINDA 34
HARRIS, BENJAMIN 42
HARRIS, CLARKSON 91
HARRIS, DAVID M. 27
HARRIS, ELMA 82
HARRIS, FRANKLIN 64
HARRIS, HOMER 45,114
HARRIS, JAS.A. 16
HARRIS, JESSE 14
HARRIS, L.B. 19
HARRIS, LEMUEL 52,53
HARRIS, MARY M. 95
HARRIS, MILLSTANT 19

HARRIS, PHOEBE 16
HARRIS, ROBERT 19,52,107
HARRIS, RUTH 96
HARRISON, ELIZABETH 27
HARRISON, ELLEN 31
HARRISON, GEORGE 50
HARRISON, JOSEPH 110
HARRISON, LUCINDA 51
HARRISON, M.E. 50
HARRISON, MARGARET 73
HARRISON, MARY E. 51
HARRISON, THOMAS 50,51
HARRISON, WILLIAM 7,73
HARROD, M. 1
HARROLD, ARNOLD 105
HARROLD, EPHRAIM 49
HARROLD, JOHN 77
HARROLD, REBECCA 101
HART, ALEXANDER 45
HART, ANSON B. 40
HART, D.B., DR. 53
HART, ELIZABETH 3
HART, FLORA E. 45
HART, H.B., DR. 11
HART, JENNIE 66
HART, MARGARET 45
HART, MARY E. 93
HART, SILAS 86
HARTLEY, JOSEPH S. 8
HARTMAN, ANNA 45
HARTMAN, J.H., REV. 86
HARTMAN, JAMES B. 65
HARTMAN, SUSANNAH 6
HARTSHORNE, TILLY 110
HARTSOCK, FRANK M. 18
HARTZELL, EDWARD 87
HARTZELL, SIMON 9
HARTZHORN, O.N., REV. 21
HARVEY, JOHN 56,57,60
HARVEY, MARY 107
HARVEY, REV. 5
HARWOOD, WILLIAM 85
HASKELL, O.W. 69
HASNESS, ABRAM 67
HASNESS, MARGARET 67
HASSAN, JAS.N. 36
HASSIN, ANNETTA 103
HASSIN, CHARLES F. 16
HASSIN, ELIZABETH 16,100
HASSIN, ELMER W. 100
HASSIN, J.N. 103
HASSIN, JONATHAN 16,100
HASSIN, L.N. 103
HASSLY, CHARLES 47
HASSLY, THOMAS J.H. 47
HASSON, MATILDA 116
HASTINGS, EMMA 118
HASTINGS, ISAAC 43,83,117
HASTINGS, MARY J. 35
HASTINGS, W.K. 118
HASTINGS, WILLIAM,REV. 46,117
HAUGH, MRS. 51
HAUGHTON, MARY 78
HAUGHTON, PATRICK 78
HAUGHTON, THOMAS 78
HAUN, G.W. 54
HAUPT, W., REV. 81
HAUPTMANN, CAROLINE 78
HAVIC, MARY 106
HAVIC, SAMUEL 106
HAVILAND, JOSEPH 62
HAVILAND, LYDIA 62
HAWKER, J., REV. 95
HAWKER, JOHN, REV. 83,89,96
HAWKINS, ALICE 60
HAWKINS, ANNORA 3
HAWKINS, CATHARINE 3
HAWKINS, CLARA M. 82
HAWKINS, DEBORA 100
HAWKINS, GEORGE 25,79
HAWKINS, HOWARD J. 80
HAWKINS, JAMES R. 87
HAWKINS, K.Q. 80
HAWKINS, LEE C. 116
HAWKINS, LORETTA 27
HAWKINS, MARTHA 59
HAWKINS, MARY 89,91
HAWKINS, NANCY 5
HAWKINS, ROBERT 3
HAWKINS, SUSAN 116
HAWKINS, T.G. 80

HAWKINS, THOMAS 100,101,110
HAWKINS, THOMAS, MRS. 101
HAWKINS, WM. 64
HAWLEY, BENJ. 54
HAWLEY, EMERINE 34
HAWLEY, ESQ. 34,58
HAWLEY, JESSE 56,61,69,88
HAWLEY, SAMUEL D. 42
HAYES, CHARLES 8,29,39
HAYES, GOV. 13
HAYES, LYDIA 29
HAYS, CELIA 75
HAYS, ELIZA 114
HAYS, ELLA J. 70
HAYS, HARRISON 114
HAYS, J.B. 95
HAYS, J.J., REV. 96
HAYS, LAURA 108
HAYS, MARY E. 116
HAYS, ROBT., REV. 4,5,8,11,18,
  19,23,25,30,33,35,40,43,49,
  53,54,58,63,68,70,71,73,75,
  79,81,82,85,86,87,88,93,96,
  98,101,110
HAYS, SADIE 103
HAYS, T.J., REV. 86
HAZEL, LIZZIE 70
HAZEN, MARY 21
HAZLET, MR. 23
HEACOCK, ALFRED 46
HEACOCK, EMMA 44
HEACOCK, FERDINAND 21
HEACOCK, GEO. 37
HEACOCK, JOSEPH 1
HEACOCK, MISS 110
HEACOCK, MORRIS 47
HEACOCK, R.V. 11
HEACOCK, SALLIE 28
HEADLEY, MOSES 118
HEADLY, MR. 117
HEALD, MATTHEW 87
HEASLEY, HENRY 25
HEATON, ANNA 111
HEATON, DANIEL 31
HEATON, GEORGE 65
HEATON, J.C., DR. 111
HEATON, JACOB 54,95
HEATON, JESSE 81
HEATON, LIZZIE 111
HEATON, MARY 19
HEATON, MIRIAN 96
HEATON, R.G. 12,111
HEATON, WM.WEAVER 24
HECK, CATHARINE 68
HECK, DAVID 46
HECK, HIRAM 46
HECK, MARY M. 46
HECK, OLIVER 106
HECKATHORN, MAGGIE 59
HECKENELDER, JOHANNA 75
HECKENLIVELY, MARY 35
HECKERT, GEORGE W. 28
HECKLER, GEORGE 68
HECKLER, JULIA 68
HECKLER, MARY 117
HEGGEM, CHARLES O. 69
HEILNER, ELIZABETH 6
HEINSMAN, CLEMENTINE 65
HEISTAND, WILLIAM 6
HEITSMAN, M. 19
HEITZMAN, GEORGE 61
HELDT, JOHN 109,112
HELLER, M. 46
HELMAN, CHARLES M. 2
HELMAN, EMMA B. 2
HELMAN, MAGDALENA 87
HELMAN, MARTHA J. 64
HELMAN, MARY 2,19,55
HELMAN, WILLIAM 55
HELT, KATIE 23
HELTZEL, JENNIE 105
HELTZER, MAGGIE 31
HEMPHILL, J.W., REV. 100
HENCHILLWOOD, ROBERT 10
HENDERSON, DANIEL 10
HENDERSON, ELIZABETH 3,106
HENDERSON, ELLA 53
HENDERSON, J., REV. 1,25,31
HENDERSON, JAMES 77,106,108
HENDERSON, JAMES, REV. 6,55
HENDERSON, JOHN 10

HENDERSON, L.M. 8
HENDERSON, MARY 84
HENDERSON, PETER 54
HENDERSON, RACHEL 10
HENDERSON, REV. 26,35
HENDERSON, RICHARD 49
HENDERSON, ROBERT 54
HENDERSON, SAMUEL 91,106
HENDRICK, ADALINE 42
HENDRICK, MARY E. 91
HENDRICKS, J.C. 74
HENDRICKS, LAVINA 34
HENDRICKS, LOVINA 34
HENDRICKS, MARY J. 47
HENDRICKS, MERVIN 105
HENDRICKS, NATHAN 8,20
HENDRICKS, STEPHEN 3
HENRICK, LOUISA 43
HENRY, ALLIE 110
HENRY, BARBARA 88
HENRY, HELEN 9
HENRY, JACOB 88
HENRY, JOSEPH F. 58
HENRY, MARTHA 115
HENRY, MARTIN 88
HENRY, MICHAEL, MRS. 106
HENRY, SOPHIA 78
HENRY, WILLIAM 3
HENSCHILLWOOD, T.J. 55
HENSHALL, JOHN 64
HENTHORN, C.B., REV. 97
HEPHNER, ELIZABETH 53
HEPHNER, JESSE 7
HEPHNER, MRS. 34
HEPPLEWHITE, JOHN 102
HEPPLEWHITE, MOLLIE 102
HEPPLEWHITE, ROBERT 102
HERBERT, JOSIAH 96
HERBERT, NELLIE 113
HERRICK, HATTIE A. 2
HERRON, BELLE 52
HERRON, EMMA 53
HERRON, RUFUS 81
HERRON, S.T., REV. 2,3,7,10,
  11,24,52
HERWIG, EMIL 88
HERWIG, ERNST 88
HERWIG, ROSANA 88
HERZBERGER, A.F., REV. 92
HESS, DAVID, REV. 50
HESS, WILLIAM 102
HESSIN, JOE 15
HESSIN, JOHN E. 62,69
HESSON, HENRY 59
HESTAND, ISAAC 75
HESTAND, SAMUEL 71
HESTER, GEORGE 7
HESTON, ANN 25
HESTON, JOHN 1
HETHERINGTON, JAMES 102
HETHERINGTON, JANE 102
HETHERINGTON, RICHARD 102
HETZEL, JOHN 73
HEWIT, SANSOM I. 76
HEWITT, ELIZABETH 55
HEYCOCK, SAMUEL 94
HIBBETS, DANIEL 32
HICK, MARY 1
HICKLING, THOMAS 110
HICKMAN, ISABELLA 109
HICKMAN, J.W. 69
HICKMAN, JOHN 109
HICKMAN, LEVI 110
HICKMAN, REBECCA J. 21
HICKMAN, S.M., REV. 31,54
HICKMAN, TILLIE 89
HICKOX, H.S. 118
HICKOX, MARY 118
HICKOX, S.H. 118
HICKS, JOHN 119
HIDDLESON, MAY 114
HIDDLESON, SARAH 114
HIDDLESON, TAMAR 115
HIDDLESTON, JOHN B. 87
HIESTAN, HENRIETTA 54
HIESTAN, JOHN 54
HIGBY, W.B., REV. 21
HIGGINS, CATHERINE 96
HIGGINS, OWEN, REV. 4
HIGGINS, REV. 6
HILBERT, MARTIN 113

HILBERT, MARY 113
HILBISH, H., REV. 55,56,57,69,
  76,78,79,85,87,89
HILL, AGNES M. 21
HILL, HARRY 27
HILL, J.G. 12
HILL, JACOB G. 25
HILL, JOHN 95
HILL, LILLIE 12
HILL, MARY 55,57
HILL, NANCY 1
HILL, SANFORD C. 48
HILL, SARAH 4,72
HILL, SOPHIA 12,25
HILL, SOPHIE C. 25
HILL, WILLIAM 16,104
HILLERMAN, GEORGIE 102
HILLERMAN, HANNAH J. 95
HILLERMAN, HATTIE A. 7
HILLERMAN, J.F. 8
HILLERMAN, J.H. 1,88
HILLERMAN, KATE 88
HILLERMAN, MISS 95
HILLIARD, JOHN 32,100
HILLIARD, MARGARET 27
HILLIARD, MARY 14,100
HILLIARD, REBECCA 32
HILLIARD, SARAH 100
HILLICK, JAMES,DR. 77
HILLIS, FLORA 114
HILLIS, LOUA 40
HILLIS, S.D. 40
HILLMAN, ALBERT T. 44
HILLMAN, D.H. 33
HILLMAN, J.G. 85,99
HILLMAN, ROBERT 79,99
HILLMAN, S.A. 99
HILLOCK, THOMAS, REV. 96
HILLYARD, MATILDA 60
HILTEBIDDLE, MATTIE 84
HIME, DANIEL 74
HIME, MARY 74
HINCHELIFF, C. 36
HINCHLIFFE, GEORGE 100
HINDMAN, JOHN 7
HINE, CECIL D. 17
HINE, JESSIE D. 83
HINE, JOHN 42
HINE, MARY E. 84
HINE, P.L. 83
HINE, R.R. 83
HINER, CAROLINE 88
HINER, JOHN 26
HINER, M.J. 25
HINGLEY, E.,REV.91,101,103,104
HINKLE, M.L. 33
HINSHILLWOOD, LIZZIE 76
HINSHILLWOOD, M.THOMAS 115
HISCOCK, JOHN 5
HISCOCK, SUSAN 54
HISCOX, ELIZABETH 14
HISCOX, JAMES 14
HISCOX, MARY L. 14
HISE, JACOB 80
HISER, J.A., DR. 33
HISEY, BENJAMIN 66
HISEY, BINA 95
HISEY, ELIZABETH 71
HISEY, JOSEPH 71
HISEY, SYLVANUS 64
HIVELY, AARON 44
HIVELY, C. 7
HIVELY, CHRISTIAN 109
HIVELY, ELIZABETH 44
HIVELY, GEORGE 27
HIVELY, JOHN 7,44,85
HODGEKINSON, G.W., REV. 31
HODGKINSON, JOHN, REV. 37,53
HODGSON, T.C., REV. 96
HODGSON, T.S., REV. 82
HOEY, ELIZABETH 91,97
HOEY, MAGGIE 91
HOEY, ROSE ANN 69
HOFFE, ANNIE M. 3
HOFFEE, FRANKIE 93
HOFFEE, HATTIE 97
HOFFEY, PHILLIP J. 39
HOFFMAN, A.B. 86
HOFFMAN, ADAM 85
HOFFMAN, CAROLINE 4
HOFFMAN, FERDINAND 4,5

HOFFMAN, JOHN 7
HOFFMAN, JOSEPH 95
HOFFMAN, SADIE 103
HOFFMAN, WILSON 80
HOFFSTOTT, FRANK 51
HOFFSTOTT, MARGARET 111
HOGE, FRANK B. 80
HOGE, JAMES 62,94
HOGE, LEVI 21
HOGE, RICHARD H. 35
HOGUE, HONORA 101
HOGUE, LEE 66
HOGUE, MARY ETTA 66
HOILES, EMANUEL 25
HOILES, MARTHA 25
HOKE, ISAAC E. 75
HOKE, JOHN 34
HOKE, JONAS 5,75
HOKE, PHEBE N. 5
HOKE, REBECCA 75
HOLCOMB, HIRAM 9
HOLDEMAN, MARY A. 74
HOLDERMAN, ADMIRAM 20
HOLDERMAN, ELIZA A. 20
HOLDERREED, MARY 79
HOLE, AMELIA E. 54
HOLE, ANN 72
HOLE, CAROLINE 78
HOLE, CATHARINE 38
HOLE, ELIAS 81
HOLE, I.P. 38,80
HOLE, JACOB 5,54
HOLE, JAMES L. 85
HOLE, JOHN, DR. 41
HOLE, L.C. 85
HOLE, LEONA E. 54
HOLE, MAHLON 47,80
HOLE, MARY 44,80
HOLE, NATHAN 41
HOLE, RACHEL 85
HOLE, ROBERT 78
HOLE, S.J., DR. 44
HOLE, SOPHIA 94
HOLE, THOMAS 30,44
HOLE, VESTA G. 78
HOLLABAUGH, SARAH J. 54
HOLLAND, SAMUEL 7
HOLLAND, WILLIAM 98
HOLLAR, ROSE E. 61
HOLLAR, WILLIAM B. 102
HOLLINGER, ELIZABETH 92
HOLLINGER, FRANK 110
HOLLINGSHEAD, JAMES, REV.16,
  24,55,76,84,86,91,116
HOLLINGSWORTH, THOMAS 80
HOLLISTER, J.E., REV. 117
HOLLOWAY, AARON 7
HOLLOWAY, ADA 43,63
HOLLOWAY, AMANDA 43,78
HOLLOWAY, ANNIE 93
HOLLOWAY, CALDWELL 93,101
HOLLOWAY, E.S., GEN. 115
HOLLOWAY, ELIZA 112
HOLLOWAY, ELMER 102
HOLLOWAY, EMMA 14
HOLLOWAY, EPHRAIM 7,99
HOLLOWAY, FRANK R. 63
HOLLOWAY, HARVEY 86
HOLLOWAY, J.G. 76
HOLLOWAY, JACOB 112
HOLLOWAY, JOEL 7,64,89
HOLLOWAY, JOHN W. 105
HOLLOWAY, JOSEPH 33,88,102
HOLLOWAY, JOSHUA 70
HOLLOWAY, JULIA 76
HOLLOWAY, LEONARD 43,63
HOLLOWAY, LEONORA 43
HOLLOWAY, LUCENA 34
HOLLOWAY, LYDIA 102
HOLLOWAY, MARY 89,101
HOLLOWAY, MATTIE D. 76
HOLLOWAY, MINTIE 93
HOLLOWAY, MR. 57
HOLLOWAY, ORLANDO 67
HOLLOWAY, S.M. 57
HOLLOWAY, SARAH 44
HOLLOWAY, SUSAN 70
HOLLOWAY, THOMAS 3
HOLLOWAY, VELINA 107
HOLLY, ALPHONSO 99
HOLM, LIBBIE 35

HOLMES, B.P. 87
HOLMES, S.J. 82
HOMER, ELIZA 66
HOOK, MARIA 33
HOOK, MICHAEL 33
HOOKER, BARBARA 45
HOOKER, JOHN 45
HOOKER, MARY JANE 101
HOOKER, WILLIAM 45
HOOPES, CHARITY 82
HOOPES, MARSHALL B. 23
HOOPS, ABIGAIL 27
HOOPS, ANNA 44
HOOPS, ARTHUR 106
HOOPS, DAVID S. 63
HOOPS, JAMES 45
HOOPS, JESSE 43
HOOPS, LUCINDA 106
HOOPS, MARSHAL 31
HOOPS, RACHEL 43
HOOPS, WILLIAM 106
HOOVER, EMMA E. 5
HOOVER, JOHN 7
HOOVER, KATIE 98
HOOVER, SAMUEL SR. 119
HOOVER, WILLIAM A. 5,119
HOOVER, Z.L., DR. 98
HOPKINS, H.H. 4
HOPKINS, NANCY B. 76
HOPPES, AMANDA 60
HOPPES, JANE 74
HORN, J.M. 51
HORNE, WM. 37
HORNER, CHARLES 108
HORNER, JOSEPH, REV. 108
HOSTETTER, ANNA 17
HOSTETTER, CARRIE 38
HOSTETTER, CHARLES D. 67
HOSTETTER, DAVID 55
HOSTETTER, DAVY 15
HOSTETTER, ELIZABETH 62
HOSTETTER, HIRAM 55
HOSTETTER, JACOB 18
HOSTETTER, JAMES 17,46,61
HOSTETTER, JOSEPH 62
HOSTETTER, JOSIE 112
HOSTETTER, LIDDIA 46
HOSTETTER, LYDNIA 17
HOSTETTER, MILLIE 42
HOSTETTER, SHERIFF 61
HOSTETTER, W.M. 9,112
HOSTETTER, WILLIAM 55,97
HOTRING, F.R., REV. 109
HOUK, D.A. 50
HOULETT, ENOCH 114
HOUSE, ANDREW 44
HOUSE, ELIZA 14
HOUSTON, A.Y., REV. 8
HOUSTON, REV. 4
HOUTS, MARY 97
HOUTZ, JOHN W. 23
HOWARD, CHARLES 73,81
HOWARD, GEORGE 117
HOWARD, JOHN 50
HOWARD, LETTIE 65
HOWARD, MAGGIE 52
HOWARD, RACHEL 73
HOWARD, W.D., REV. 18
HOWBETT, A.W., REV. 33
HOWE, GEORGE 19
HOWE, REV. 42
HOWEL, BENJAMIN 58
HOWEL, ELMA 59
HOWELL, BENJAMIN 113
HOWELL, ELIZABETH A. 37
HOWELL, JAMES 28,29
HOWELL, LOUIS O. 65
HOWELL, MARY 113
HOWELL, NANCY 113
HOWELL, WILLARD 104
HOWELL, YERKES 113
HOWELLS, MARGARET 36
HOWENSTINE, FREDERICK 68
HOYLES, BENJAMIN 105
HOYLES, MARIA 105
HOYTE, C. 97
HUBBARD, HENRY JR. 17
HUBBARD,BURKE & CO 17
HUCHISON, OLIVER 43
HUCKLEBOUS & ROBINSON 4
HUDD, MARY J. 116

HUDLEMYRE, LYDIA A. 33
HUDLESTON, WILLIAM 51
HUDSON, ADA 14
HUDSON, ELIZA 62
HUDSON, J.K. 14
HUDSON, JAMES 21,62
HUDSON, JOHN 41,71,100
HUDSON, KATE 88
HUDSON, LYDIA 22
HUDSON, MARGERY 62
HUDSON, MARY 14,63,100
HUDSON, MELL H. 55
HUDSON, MR. 39
HUDSON, REBECCA 41
HUDSON, REV. 91
HUDSON, TILLIE 24
HUDSON, WILLIE F. 41
HUES, SAMUEL 44
HUESTON, JAMES 103
HUEY, JOHN 24
HUEY, MARY 24
HUFF, ELSIE 99
HUFF, ISAAC 73
HUFFMAN, ANNA 113
HUFFMAN, HATTIE 50
HUFFMAN, LAURA E. 103
HUFFMAN, MOLLIE 47
HUFFMAN, REBECCA 113
HUFFMAN, SAMUEL 113
HUFFMAN, SARAH 88
HUFFMAN, WILBERT 88
HUG, MARIA 33
HUG, MICHAEL 33
HUGHES, ISAAC 107
HUGHES, JOHN 109
HUGHES, PAT 92
HUGHES, S.A., REV. 55
HUGHES, WILLIAM 101
HUKILL, HELEN V. 37
HULL, CARRIE 8
HULL, MARY A.M. 50
HULL, NANCY 6
HULME, EMMA 73
HULME, HATTIE 20
HULSE, SARAH 96
HUM, DAVID 28,112,113
HUM, ELIZABETH 51
HUM, HATTIE B. 68
HUM, JACOB 92,113
HUM, JOHN 19,112,113
HUM, MARGARET 93
HUM, MARY 68,92
HUM, R.W. 68
HUM, REUBEN 51
HUM, SUSAN ETTA 51
HUM, WILLIAM W. 79
HUMPHREY, AMANDA 101
HUMPHREY, FRANKIE 23
HUMPHREY, WILLIAM 23
HUMRICKHOUSE, JULIA 106
HUNE, CONRAD 32,40
HUNT, BENJAMIN 1
HUNT, ELISHA 78
HUNT, ELIZA 4
HUNT, FRANK 115
HUNT, JOHN 115
HUNTER, ALICE A. 45
HUNTER, AMANDA J. 31
HUNTER, ANNA 25,103
HUNTER, DAVID M. 88
HUNTER, DR. 73
HUNTER, ELIZA 8
HUNTER, ELLEN 11
HUNTER, H.A. 51
HUNTER, HARRY 33
HUNTER, JAMES H. 103
HUNTER, JAMES R. 103
HUNTER, JIMMIE 86
HUNTER, JOHN M. 105
HUNTER, N.A. 105
HUNTER, WILLIAM 24,53
HUNTER, WM., REV. 65,83,98
HUNTSMAN, WIDOW 108
HURTMAN, ISAAC 70
HUSONG, F.T. 37,105
HUSONG, HANNAH 105
HUSSEY, J.G. 21
HUSTON, ALEXANDER 77
HUSTON, ALVEN 102
HUSTON, BAXTER 116
HUSTON, CORRA E. 88

HUSTON, ELIZABETH 25
HUSTON, EMMA 73
HUSTON, EPHRAIM 50
HUSTON, GEORGE 81,88,97
HUSTON, HAMP 41
HUSTON, HATTIE J. 58
HUSTON, HOMER 11
HUSTON, J.,REV. 42,43,58
HUSTON, J.H. 35
HUSTON, JESSE 1
HUSTON, JOHN 1,21,32,119
HUSTON, JOHN, REV. 16,19
HUSTON, M.M. 77
HUSTON, MARCUS 88
HUSTON, MARY 77,93,105,119
HUSTON, MURRAY 119
HUSTON, R. 115
HUSTON, SUSAN 88
HUSTON, THOMAS G. 35,86
HUTCHINSON, SARAH 76
HUTCHISON, ELENOR 41
HUTCHISON, MAGGIE J. 41
HUTCHISON, MARY B. 41
HUTCHISON, ROBERT 41
HUTTON, ALICE L. 85
HYDE, CLARA T. 33
HYDE, D.V., REV. 3,5,10,12,14,
20,23,24,27,28,29,31,32,33,
34,43,45,49,57,58,59,63,73,
81,89,91,100,101,103,104
HYDE, ROSE 116
ICENHOUR, JOHN 7
ICKES, JOHN O. 9
ICKES, WILLIAM 3
IKERT, J.J., DR. 33
IKERT, KATE 5
IKIRT, ABRAHAM 10
IKIRT, DAVID 56
IKIRT, GEORGE 108
IKIRT, J.J. 115
IKIRT, MARY 108
ILER, B.F. 59
ILER, ELIZA J. 8
ILER, LYDIA 76
ILER, SINA E. 107
INGLEDUE, FRANK 95
INGLEDUE, FRANKLIN 91
INGLEDUE, MARGARET 21,27,91
INGLEDUE, REUBEN 10,57
INGRAM, JOHN 116
INGRAM, JOSEPH 5
INGRAM, M.J., REV. 116
INGRAM, MARY 5
INGRAM, PHEBE 5
INGRAM, W.F. 77
INMAN, EDWIN 95
INMAN, MARY E. 95
INMAN, THOMAS B. 95
IRA, LUCRETIA 23
IREY, EDEN 99
IREY, ELIZABETH 99
IRISH, CAPT. 2
IRISH, LYDIA 9
IRISH, WILLIAM 9,11
IRVIN, URIAH 12
IRWIN, CORDY 47
IRWIN, D.A. 98
IRWIN, ELLA 119
IRWIN, EMMA 3
IRWIN, GERSHOM C. 69
IRWIN, IDA 93
IRWIN, J.M. 80
IRWIN, JAMES 47
IRWIN, JAMES P., REV. 55,78
IRWIN, KATE D. 3
IRWIN, MARY 77
IRWIN, REBECCA 80
IRWIN, REV. 84
IRWIN, WILLIAM 69
ISAMINGER, G.W., REV. 51
ISEMAN, DANIEL 103,114
ISEMAN, DAVID 84
ISEMAN, SARAH 84
ISEMAN, WM. 30
JACK, FIDELAS 86
JACK, VALENTINE 103,104
JACK, WILLIAM 109
JACKMAN, EOLINE 90
JACKMAN, JAMES 5
JACKMAN, ROBERT 45
JACKMAN, STOCKDALE 102

JACKSON, ALICE 82
JACKSON, E.P. 111
JACKSON, ISABELLA 108
JACKSON, J.J., REV. 14,24,27,
38,40,44,47,72
JACKSON, JAMES 8,32
JACKSON, KATE 36
JACKSON, MARY 32
JACKSON, REV. 90
JACKSON, SAMUEL P. 82
JACKSON, WILLIAM 101
JACOBS, JOHN 101
JAGGAR, BENJAMIN 5,65
JAGGAR, ELIZABETH 65
JAGGAR, SARAH 65
JAMES, I.L. 88
JAMES, MR. 96
JAMES, RUTH B. 18
JAMES, SUSAN 29
JAMIESON, REV. 111
JAMISON, EDGAR 84
JAMISON, G.T. 87
JAMISON, W.H., REV. 5
JAMISON, WALTER 87
JEFFERSON, THOMAS 108
JEFFERY, NANNIE 110
JEFFREY, ELIZABETH 26
JEFFREY, MARETTA 116
JEFFREY, WILLIAM 26
JEHU, MURDOCK 91
JENICKSON, R.M. 14
JENKINS, A.BYRON 90
JENKINS, ELIZABETH 39
JENKINS, GEORGE W. 48
JENKINS, J.M. 52
JENKINS, JOHN 31,82
JENKINS, MATTIE 115
JENKINS, MELISSA 9
JENNINGS, ELLA 40
JENNINGS, EMMA 35
JENNINGS, SIMEON 18
JENNINGS, WILLIAM 63
JEROME, MARY A. 68
JESSOP, THOMAS 12,36
JOBE, ANN 84
JOBS, SARAH C. 5
JOHN, ELLA J. 6
JOHN, JOSIAH 113
JOHN, PHEBE 113
JOHNS, ASENITH 32
JOHNS, ELIZABETH 87
JOHNS, JNO., DR. 40
JOHNS, JOSIAH 51
JOHNSON & MILLER 15
JOHNSON, ALFRED J. 69
JOHNSON, ALICE 67
JOHNSON, C.L. 90
JOHNSON, C.S. 10
JOHNSON, CATHARINE 24
JOHNSON, CHARLES 24
JOHNSON, CHRISTOPHER 6,42
JOHNSON, D. 10
JOHNSON, D.C. 95
JOHNSON, DAVID 12,36
JOHNSON, ED 15
JOHNSON, EDWARD M. 68
JOHNSON, ELIZA 2,41
JOHNSON, ELIZABETH 58,66
JOHNSON, ELLA 101
JOHNSON, ELLIS F. 77
JOHNSON, ESTHER 78
JOHNSON, ETTIE 73
JOHNSON, FLORA E. 105
JOHNSON, G.N., REV. 101,111
JOHNSON, G.W., REV. 45,69,98
JOHNSON, GEORGE N.,REV. 60,65,
69,72,87,89,90
JOHNSON, HANNAH 58,92
JOHNSON, HELEN 81
JOHNSON, J.M. 77
JOHNSON, J.W. 65
JOHNSON, J.W., REV. 110,117
JOHNSON, JAMES 3,24,43,
47,65,67,100
JOHNSON, JANE 100
JOHNSON, JOEL 66,75,112
JOHNSON, JOHN 92,101
JOHNSON, JOHN W. 73,78,90
JOHNSON, JOSEPHINE 65
JOHNSON, LOUIS 73
JOHNSON, MARGARET 67

JOHNSON, MARTHA 76
JOHNSON, MARY E. 3,47,51,63,71
JOHNSON, MINNIE R. 67
JOHNSON, NANCY 47,65
JOHNSON, R.P., DR. 34
JOHNSON, REBECCA 76
JOHNSON, REV. 67,117
JOHNSON, ROBERT 27,93
JOHNSON, SARAH 10,90,104
JOHNSON, TACY L. 1
JOHNSON, THOMAS 12,36,58,76
JOHNSON, THOMAS P., REV. 72
JOHNSON, VILLA 67
JOHNSON, WM. 9,19,28,33,35, 67,76,104
JOHNSTON, ANDREW 53
JOHNSTON, CHARLES R. 28
JOHNSTON, G.N., REV. 92,93,95, 97,98,102,105,106,110,117,119
JOHNSTON, GEO.N.,REV. 71,73, 76,77,80,90,115
JOHNSTON, GEORGE 119
JOHNSTON, HARRY H. 75
JOHNSTON, JAMES M. 38
JOHNSTON, JANE 53
JOHNSTON, JOHN P. 50
JOHNSTON, LIZZIE 102
JOHNSTON, M.B. 114
JOHNSTON, MARGARET 93
JOHNSTON, MARY B. 50
JOHNSTON, PRISCILLA 74
JOHNSTON, REV. 56
JOHNSTON, ROBERT 53
JOHNSTON, SARAH I. 1
JOHNSTON, T.P., REV. 64
JOHNSTON, W.H. 93
JOHNSTON, WILLIAM 39,69
JOINT, JOHN 10
JOLLEY, SAMUEL 18
JOLLY, MRS. 39
JOLLY, WILLIAM 28
JONES, A.P., REV. 56
JONES, ANNA 111
JONES, CATLET 22
JONES, D., REV. 99
JONES, DALESA 29
JONES, DAVID 22
JONES, EDWARD 22
JONES, ELIZABETH T. 44
JONES, GALEN C. 42
JONES, H.C. 72
JONES, HENRY C. 62
JONES, J.F., REV. 10,11,14,35, 37,38,39,41,47
JONES, J.H. 66
JONES, J.J., REV. 40
JONES, J.O. 55
JONES, JESSIE N. 54
JONES, JOHN R. 54,59
JONES, LAURA B. 78
JONES, LIBBIE 57
JONES, LILLIE B. 56
JONES, MARY 22,62,66
JONES, ORVILLE 86
JONES, P.H., REV. 104
JONES, P.N. 90
JONES, REV. 13,22
JONES, SARAH 100
JONES, STEPHEN W. 29
JONES, THOMAS 4,44
JONES, W.B. 95
JORDAN, MARY A. 109
JORDEN, D., DR. 101
JORDEN, JOSEPHINE 101
JUDD, ISAAC 2
JUNKIN, D.C., REV. 5
JUNKIN, J.ROSS 89
JUSTICE, MORRISON 111
JUSTICE, ROBERT P. 3
KAHLER, JOSEPH 117
KAINE, LUCINDA 21
KAISER, J.H. 72
KALE, ISAAC 23
KALE, L.E.E. 23
KALE, MARY ANN 23
KANDALL, JACOB N. 62
KANNAL, EMMET 61,68,69,85
KANNAL, ERR 27
KANNAL, J. 44
KANNAL, JOHN 87
KANNAL, JOSEPH 71,101

KANNALS, IRA 104
KARNS, MICHAEL 116
KAUFFMAN, JACOB 97
KAUFFMAN, WILLIAM 97
KAUFMAN, --- 44
KAYE, SALLIE P. 71
KEATCH, THOMAS 7
KECK, CATHERINE 37
KECK, JACOB 8,26
KECK, MRS. 62
KECK, PETER 62
KECK, SOPHIA 26
KEELER, HUGH 25
KEELER, JACOB 8
KEELER, SIDNAH 43
KEELEY, HANNAH 94
KEELEY, JAMES 94
KEEN, ANNA L. 21
KEEN, ANNIE 27
KEEN, LAURA 21
KEEN, T.J. 21
KEEN, THOMAS 23,34
KEEP, SARAH 38
KEESEY, SUSAN 14,16
KEFFER, F. 36
KEGNEY, MARY 69
KEGNEY, WILLIAM 69
KEIPER, C.H. 61
KEISTER, DAVID 42
KEISTER, HENRY 93
KEISTER, ISAAC 93
KEISTER, MAGDALENA 37
KEITH, ELI 16
KEITH, HARRY S. 16
KEITH, JOSEPH 70
KEITH, JOSIAH 69
KEITH, MARY 16
KEITH, STEPHEN 9
KELLAR, ANNA 38
KELLER, LEAH 116
KELLER, MARY I. 65
KELLEY, CHALKLEY 92
KELLEY, MRS. 44
KELLEY, PATRICK 7
KELLEY, PHEBE A. 29
KELLEY, REV. 56
KELLEY, SARAH 87
KELLEY, STEPHEN 31
KELLEY, WM.A. 19
KELLINGER, KATE 2
KELLY, AMOS 42
KELLY, B.B., REV. 97
KELLY, CASS 49
KELLY, D. 115
KELLY, E. 115
KELLY, ELIZABETH 81
KELLY, JAMES 115
KELLY, LULA 115
KELLY, THOMAS 61,100
KELLY, WILLIAM 117
KELTY, ELISHA W. 83
KEMBLE, ALICE 70
KEMBLE, CYNTHIA 117
KEMBLE, JOHN 19,91
KEMBLE, K.K. 7
KEMBLE, WILLIAM 46,88
KEMP, J.W. 43
KEMP, LUCY 4
KENDALL, JAMES L. 2
KENDIG, J.M., REV. 70,83,85, 88,91,92,97,99,100,102,103, 104,118
KENDIG, W.S., REV. 16
KENMUIR, WILLIAM 44
KENNAL, JOSEPH 92
KENNAMAN, REBECCA 23
KENNAN, ANNABELLA 43
KENNAN, MARTHA 43
KENNAN, WILLIAM C. 43
KENNEDY, D.S., REV. 91
KENNEDY, ELIZABETH 110
KENNEDY, J.S., REV. 58
KENNEDY, JAMES 77
KENNEDY, LOUISE 49
KENNEDY, S.Y., REV. 62,65,66, 68,69,73,74,77,81,84,86,92, 93,94
KENNEDY, T.J., REV. 82
KENNETT, EDWARD 46
KENNETT, THOMAS 46
KENNEY, JANE 67

KENNEY, ROBERT 50
KENREICH, ELIZABETH 97
KENTNER, ELI 88
KENTNER, MARY 88
KENTNER, MR. 61
KENTY, JOSEPH B. 31
KENTY, SAMANTHA 81
KEPLINGER, MARY 14
KEPNER, BENJAMIN 2
KERNS, ANNIE 92
KERNS, ELIZABETH 103
KERNS, ESTHER 53
KERNS, JOHN 45
KERNS, RICHARD 92
KERR, ANNIE 57
KERR, ELIZABETH 100
KERR, G.R., REV. 2
KERR, HARRY D. 100
KERR, J.A. 4
KERR, J.C. 101
KERR, JOHN 50,73
KERR, L.T. 103
KERR, MARY C. 97
KERR, RACHEL 73
KERR, S.C. 19
KERR, S.J. 93
KERR, SAMUEL 97
KERR, SURVANTUS P. 11
KERR, THOMAS 47
KERR, WILLIAM 51,57,100
KESSELMIRE, C.F. 9
KETCHUM, HANNAH 47
KETCHUM, LAURA 97
KETCHUM, NANCY 98
KETCHUM, SARAH 97,98
KETCHUM, SEYMOUR 97
KETCHUM, WILLIAM 97,98
KEUGELE, HENRY 95
KEYES, M.C. 94
KEYSER, JESSE 25
KEYSER, JULIA 25
KEYSER, LOMEY 25
KEYSER, MARY 58,81
KIBLER, ADAM 3
KIBLER, DAVID 79
KIBLER, ISAAC 58
KIBLER, LAVINA 30
KIBLER, MARY E. 89
KIBLER, SOLOMON 33,34
KIDD, FLORA J. 7
KIDD, GEO.W. 32
KIDD, HARVEY 43
KIDD, WILLIAM 103
KIDDEY, CHARLES 103
KIDDEY, ELIZABETH 103
KIDDEY, MARIA 103
KIDDEY, THERESA 103
KIHN, JOHN G. 57
KILLE, JOHN 85
KILPINGER, REBECCA 45
KIMBLE, JOHN 68
KIMBLE, WM. 61
KIMES, SARAH A. 100
KINDIG, CATHARINE 19
KINDIG, MARTIN 116
KINDIG, WILLIAM 8
KINES, AARON, MRS. 113
KING, A.B. 57,69
KING, A.J. 117
KING, ALEXANDER 21
KING, ANNIE E. 70
KING, CHARLEY W. 41
KING, CORONER 64
KING, DAVID 2
KING, EDWARD 42
KING, ELIZABETH M. 74
KING, ELLA 82
KING, ELNORA 105
KING, H.E. 55
KING, HARRIET 22,25
KING, HENRY J. 12
KING, HUGH 7,47
KING, J. 72
KING, JAENETTE 25
KING, JEHU C. 25
KING, JOHN 2,7,41
KING, JONAS 91
KING, KATE 8,57
KING, L.B., REV. 109,116,119
KING, LAURA 75
KING, LEVI 29,58,63,68

KING, LIZZIE J. 18
KING, LUCY 83
KING, LYDIA A. 102
KING, MARTHA 40,41
KING, MARY E. 103
KING, MRS. 12,104
KING, NATHAN A. 5
KING, ROBERT 75
KING, THOMAS 7
KING, WILLIAM 8,94
KINGDON, REV. 24
KINGSBURY, H.G. 5
KINNAMAN, LOUISA 108
KINNEAR, G.D., REV. 1,3,8,100
KINNEAR, H., MRS. 94
KINNEAR, HAMILTON 99
KINNEAR, JAMES W. 8
KINNEAR, MARION 99
KINNEY, DAVID M., REV. 29
KINNEY, GEORGE 19
KINNEY, JOSEPH 16
KINNEY, LEWIS 7
KINNEY, MARY A. 88
KINNEY, PETER 7
KINNEY, RACHEL 62
KINSEY, AMELIA 91
KINSEY, MR. 54
KINSEY, SUSAN 31
KINSEY, ZEBULON 103
KINSEY, ZEBULUM 91
KINTY, W.D. 71
KIPP, LOUISA 8
KIRBY, HENRY 63
KIRBY, JULIA 16
KIRBY, TIMOTHY 16
KIRK, JOSEPH 87
KIRK, SARAH 35
KIRK, SUSANA 107
KIRK, W.F. 89
KIRKBRIDE, FANNIE 119
KIRKBRIDE, JOHN H. 81
KIRKBRIDE, JOSEPHINE 81
KIRKBRIDE, MARY E. 87
KIRKENDALL, JOHN 115
KIRKPATRIC, EDWARD 70
KIRKPATRIC, WM. 70
KIRTLAN, ALBERT S. 28
KIRTLAN, EVERT 118
KIRTLAN, WILLIAM 118
KIRTLAND, A.B., REV. 19,24,30, 31,32,34,38,39,41,43
KIRTLAND, ALFRED P. 17
KIRTLAND, C.B. 38
KIRTLAND, ELIZABETH 24
KIRTLAND, MORRIS O. 38
KIRTLAND, THOMAS 24
KISER, APELINE 60
KITCHEL, F.D. 91
KITCHEL, REV. 91
KLEINOGLE, JOHN 111
KLING, ADAM 96
KLING, GEORGE W. 100
KLING, J.C. 114
KLING, JOHN A. 100
KLING, SUSANNA 81
KLIPPINGER, REBECCA 45
KLYNE, LLOYD 91
KNEPPER, PETER 32
KNOBELOCK, CHAS. 73
KNOLL, GEORGE 74
KNOWELS, NANCY J. 31
KNOWKES, BELLE C. 12
KNOWLDS, FRANK 61
KNOWLES, BELLE C. 12
KNOWLES, EMMA 119
KNOWLES, ISAAC 110
KNOWLES, JNO.W. 68
KNOWLES, LIDA 119
KNOWLES, MARY 110
KNOWLES, R.B. 119
KNOWLES, W.R. 64
KNOWLS, ELIZA 36
KNOWLS, JOHN W. 36
KNULL, A.B. 12
KOCH, HENRY 97
KOCH, SOLOMON 31
KOFFEL, ISAAC 36
KOLL, CHARLES 101
KOLL, DANIEL 6,93
KOLL, MARY 93
KOLL, WILLIAM 86

Name	Page(s)
KOONTZ, JOHN	7
KOPP, ANNIE E.	40
KOPP, J.D.	40
KOPP, RACHEL	40
KOUNTZ, ANNA	87
KOUNTZ, ELIZA	90
KOUNTZ, J.G.	41,97
KOUNTZ, JACOB	90
KOUNTZ, JANE	11
KOUNTZ, MARGARET	74
KOUNTZ, MARY	97
KOUNTZ, PENINA	97
KOUNTZ, WILLIAM	80
KREIDLER, MARY M.	3
KRIDLER, EDWARD H.	7
KRIDLER, GEORGE	20
KRIDLER, LIZZIE	55
KRIDLER, MARY J.	20
KRINDLE, PETER	99
KRING, INFANT	59
KRING, JACOB	59,83
KRING, MARTHA	59
KRONK, JOHN	65
KRONK, MRS.	67
KROUCE, JACOB	8
KRUFFS, CHRISTIAN	67
KUFFEL, SARAH	113
KUHL, CATHARINE	102
KUHL, JOHN	102
KUHN, ANNA	87
KUHN, J.M., DR.	37
KUNTZ, DANIEL	49
KURTZ, ALICE	69
KURTZ, DANIEL	96
KURTZ, DAVID	77
KURTZ, ELDER	73
KURTZ, H.	79,80
KURTZ, HENRY	48,50,62,68
KURTZ, NETTIE	50
KUSK, FELIX	84
KYLE, ELIZABETH	98
KYLE, O.W.	42
KYLE, WM.	71
KYSER, ANNAMELIA	70
KYSER, B.	73
KYSER, JACOB	99
KYSER, LYDIA	99
LACEY, ELIAS	28,29
LACEY, JERRY	68
LACOCK, HENRIETTA	19
LACOCK, J.F.	93
LACOCK, J.W.	115
LACY, ELIAS	107
LACY, JOHN	31
LACY, NANCY	31
LAFFERTY, REV.MR.	99
LAFUSS, DONIE	46
LAFUSS, JOSEPH	46
LAIRD, REBECCA	23
LAMB, ELLA	83
LAMB, GEORGE	45,71
LAMBORN, JANE	102
LAMBORN, JENNIE	106
LAMBORN, LEMUEL T.	19
LAMBORN, LYMAN	89
LAMBORN, M.E.	11
LAMBORN, MARY	104
LAMBORN, SAMUEL	97
LAMBRON, JANE	102
LAMOND, ANGUS	63
LAMPSON, JAMES I.	38
LANDON, FRANKLIN	24
LANE, A.J., REV.	62,65,66,69
LANG, REV.	102
LANG, W.W., REV.	97
LANGSTAFF, JOHN SR.	23
LANNIE, JOSEPH	13
LANPHEAR, J.W.	7
LANPHEAR, MR.	23
LANPHEAR, REV.	13
LANPHEAR, S.K.	24
LANPHEAR, W.P.	11
LANT, MARY	80
LANTERMAN, WILLIAM	26
LAPSLEY, MARY	60,61
LARGE, SOPHIA	13
LARKINS, HENRY	40
LARKINS, JAMES	16
LARKINS, JOSEPH	33
LARKINS, N.	40
LARKINS, SARAH	33
LARKINS, SIMEON	116
LARVAN, LEVI	86
LARWELL, JOHN	54,103
LARWELL, JOHN, MRS.	103
LARWELL, JOSEPH H.	6
LATTA, DEURIA	83
LATTA, LOUISA	24
LATTA, SARAH ANN	30
LAU, CLAYTON F.	70
LAUBIE, JENNIE	89
LAUFFER, M.F., REV.	88,115
LAUFFER, M.J., REV.	95
LAUFFER, M.T., REV.	118
LAUGHLIN, ALVIN	31
LAUGHLIN, BETTIE	8
LAUGHLIN, HUGH	35,94
LAUGHLIN, J.F.	43
LAUGHLIN, JENNIE	23,109
LAUGHLIN, MARIA	22
LAUGHLIN, ROBERT	22
LAUGHLIN, THOMAS	48
LAUGHLIN, WILLIAM	12,36
LAVERTY, J.C., REV.	81
LAW, HENRY	67
LAWLER, J.S.V.	72
LAWRENCE, JAMES SR.	105
LAWRENCE, REBECCA	55
LAWRENCE, ROBERT	55
LAWRY, MARY	66
LAWSON, EDWARD	4
LAWSON, MARY	1
LAWSON, THOS.	70
LAWSON, VIRGINIA	35
LAWSON, WILLIAM	35
LAYING, THOMAS M.	88
LAYMAN, JACOB	51
LEA, RICHARD, REV.	93
LEA, W., REV.	102
LEACH, BENJ.	92
LEACH, ELLA	48
LEACH, JAMES W.	77
LEACH, MARY	92
LEACH, NANCY	92
LEAF, JOSHUA	110
LEAF, LYDIA	110
LEAF, SOLOMON	48
LEARY, H., REV.	6
LEASE, C.F.	74
LEASE, CHARLES F.	4,13
LEASE, E.A. & CO	56
LEASE, EDWIN	4
LEASE, FANNY E.	74
LEASE, MARY B.	4
LEASE, S.B.	13,74
LEASE, W.E.	70
LEBUS, ANTHONY N.	46
LEBUS, CATHARINE	46
LEBUS, GEORGE A.	46
LECLERE, J.M.	41
LEE, ANDREW	17
LEE, FANNY	78
LEE, GEORGE	36,47,60
LEE, HARVEY	6
LEE, JOSHUA	56
LEE, MARY F.	72
LEE, MRS.	92
LEE, SALLIE E.	64
LEE, WILLIAM	60
LEEK, JOHN	3
LEEK, RICHARD	3
LEEK, THOMAS	50
LEEPER, REV.	117
LEGGET, J.D., REV.	102
LEGGET, REV.	73
LEGGETT, ABRAHAM	62
LEGGETT, J.D., REV.	62,81
LEHMAN, SARAH	72
LEIGH, ANN	43
LEIGH, DAVID	111
LEIGH, EDWARD	109
LEIGH, HARRIET	97
LEIGH, JAMES	43,108
LEIGH, JOHN	97
LEIGHTENSTINE, JOSEPH	12,36
LEIPER, AMANDA	54
LEIPER, J.H., REV.	20,35
LEIREY, ALICE	87
LEISHMAN, MAGGIE	106
LEITH, FLORA	87
LEMMON, JESSE	111
LEMMON, MARTHA	63
LEMMON, SARAH	111
LEMON, JESSE	89
LEMON, JOHN	1
LEMON, NELLIE	89
LEMOYNE, DR.	117
LENHART, EDWIN	6
LEOCLOSH, DOMICILLA	27
LEONARD, A.B., REV.	30,56
LEONARD, ANNIE	11
LEONARD, GEORGE	68
LEONARD, HOMER	108
LEONARD, JOSEPH	101
LEPER, J.H., REV.	47,115
LEPER, JOSEPH, REV.	13
LEPPER, CHARLES W.	54
LEPPER, E.F., CAPT.	33
LEPPER, VIRGINIA	54
LEPPER, WILLIAM D.	53,115
LESHER, M.	47
LESHER, MINERVA	47
LESHER, R.	47
LESLIE, J.	64
LESLIE, J.G.	17
LEVAN, DELLA	38
LEVAN, E.P.	93
LEW, REV.	107
LEWIS, A.W.	17,105
LEWIS, ANNIE	105
LEWIS, ANTHONY	69
LEWIS, C.H.	105
LEWIS, DAVID	119
LEWIS, ETHELINDA	10
LEWIS, GEORGE	40
LEWIS, HANNAH H.	28
LEWIS, J.H.	5
LEWIS, LENA MAY	105
LEWIS, MARY	105
LEWIS, NINA L.	27
LEWIS, SAMUEL	4
LIBER, C.	78,79
LIBER, KATE	43
LIBER, LOUISA	45
LIBER, MARY	119
LICHENBERGER, H.A.	90
LIEHM, SAMUEL	76
LIGHTEAN, M.V.	77
LIGHTHILL, MRS.	111
LIGHTHILL, THOMAS	111
LILLY, CATHARINE	74
LINDERSMITH, DAVID	90
LINDERSMITH, E., FATHER	37,69,78,86,89
LINDERSMITH, FATHER	110
LINDERSMITH, HENRY B.	33
LINDERSMITH, J.	20
LINDERSMITH, MRS.	26
LINDERSMITH, T.C.	32
LINDESMITH, E.W.J.,REV.	66
LINDESMITH, SARAH S.	34
LINDSAY, ---AS	37
LINDSAY, ARABELLA	45,46
LINDSAY, ELIZABETH	67
LINDSAY, J.A.	5
LINDSAY, JOHN	78
LINDSAY, V.A.	30
LING, AGATHA	72
LING, AMELIA S.	72
LING, DENNIS	72
LING, JOSEPH	72
LING, LAWRENCE	25,72
LING, LINORA E.	72
LINGENFELTER, CLARA A.	36
LINN, NANCY J.	58
LINN, THOMAS	88
LINN, WILTON	88
LIPP, SYBILLA	64
LIPPINCOTT, JOHN	47
LIPSEY, E.L.	6
LIPSEY, EDMUND	62
LIPSEY, OLIVE	76
LIPSEY, SARAH	62
LIST, HARVEY	72
LITTLE, ANDREW	57
LITTLE, ANNIE	57
LITTLE, ARMINDA V.	31
LITTLE, IDA	114
LITTLE, JAMES	115
LITTLE, JASON	66
LITTLE, MITCHELL	67
LITTLE, MRS.	83
LIVEZEY, SIDNEY S.	47
LIVINGSTON, GEORGE	87
LIVINGSTON, IDA	102
LIVINGSTON, SUE	38
LIVINGSTON, SUSAN	87
LIVINGSTON, WILLIAM A.	87
LLOYD, ----	39
LLOYD, ABEL	104
LLOYD, CATHARINE	70
LLOYD, ELIZA J.	48
LLOYD, ELLA	39
LLOYD, HARRY	70
LLOYD, JOHN	70
LOCH, ELIZABETH	69
LOCH, ESTHER	69
LOCH, MARTHA	48
LOCH, ROBERT	69
LOCH, SARAH	69
LOCH, WILLIAM	69
LOCK, BENNETT	67
LOCK, JOHN	82
LOCK, REV.	45
LOCKARD, JAY	44
LOCKARD, JOHN	51
LOCKARD, L.B.	5,30
LOCKARD, WALTER	108
LOCKE, CLIFFORD	106
LOCKE, E.B.	106,107
LOCKE, JESSIE	107
LOCKE, LILA	107
LODEKER, WM.	32
LODGE & ZEPERNICK	26
LODGE, ABE	53
LODGE, ABEL	6,9,43,55,94,117,118
LODGE, ABNER	21
LODGE, ALLEN	28,29
LODGE, BENJAMIN	56
LODGE, BENNY	21
LODGE, ELIZABETH	46,117
LODGE, EMMA	100
LODGE, ESTHER	21
LODGE, ETTA L.	4
LODGE, EVAN	118
LODGE, HARRIET	1
LODGE, IVAN	110
LODGE, JONATHAN	94
LODGE, JOSEPH	9,27,66,68,94
LODGE, KATE E.	55
LODGE, O.L.	72,94
LODGE, REBECCA	119
LODGE, THOMAS	20,27,106
LODGE, WILLIAM	4,93
LOGAN, EDDIE	33
LOGAN, J.	115
LOGAN, J.W.	25
LOGAN, JAMES	78
LOGAN, MARY	20,33
LOGAN, PATRICK	20,33
LONG, A.J.	33
LONG, EMMA	109
LONG, EVERETHA	28,29
LONG, H., REV.	56
LONG, H.H.	28.29
LONG, J.FRANCIS	13
LONG, JOHN	73
LONG, JOHN, REV.	71,90,91,105
LONG, JUSTICE	35
LONG, LIZZIE C.	76
LONG, MAGGIE	91
LONG, MAYOR	61
LONG, R.S.	75
LONG, REV.	97
LONG, SALUTHA	58
LONG, SUSAN	13,28,29
LONG, W.W., REV.	102
LONG, WARNER, REV.	5
LONGANECKER, DANIEL	35
LONGECKER, MARIA	48
LONGENECKER, JACOB	94
LONGENECKER, LYDIA A.	82
LONGENECKER, SARAH	85
LONGHEAD, B., REV.	74
LONGSHORE, D.W.C.	63
LONGSHORE, J.D.	117
LONGSHORE, JONATHAN H.	61
LONGSHORE, MACLEAN	88
LONGSHORE, SARAH	46,63
LONGSHORE, VINCENT	46
LOOMIS, A.W.	51
LORD, REV.MR.	53
LOUDEN, ADA M.	100

LOUDEN, HIRAM	12,36	LYON, WILLIAM H.	50
LOUDEN, JANE	110	LYONS, ----	28
LOUDEN, JOHN	13,42,49	LYSETT, J.M.	93
LOUDEN, JONATHAN	100	LYTEL, MATTIE	104
LOUDEN, LAURA	100	LYTLE, J.S., REV.	14
LOUDEN, MAGGIE	33	LYTLE, JASON	66
LOUDEN, MARGARET	49	McABEE, J.W., REV.	79
LOUDEN, SARAH J.	40	McALLISTER, ALEXANDER	45
LOUDEN, THOMAS	75	McALLISTER, HECTOR	68
LOUDON, MATTHEW	39	McALLISTER, MARY	68
LOUDON, WASHINGTON	23	McANEENY, PATRICK	34
LOUNSBERRY, BELUS	54	McANULTY, JAMES	114
LOUNSBERY, MARY	19	McARDIE, MARY	87
LOUNSBURY, CHARLES E.	12	McARTER, ANNIE	36
LOUY, LEONARD	71	McARTOR, HARRY A.	77
LOVE, MATTHEW	22	McARTOR, HERMAN	75
LOVE, SARAH ANN	22	McARTOR, IRA	77
LOVE, THOMAS T.	30	McARTOR, M.P.	75
LOVE, WM.	22	McARTOR, MARGARET	75
LOW, E.E.E.KALE	23	McARTOR, MARY A.	74
LOW, ISAAC	23	McARTOR, MINNIE	74,77
LOW, JOHN	103	McARTOR, O.D.	74,77
LOW, MARY A.	23	McBAINE, MAGGIE	38
LOW, S., REV.	117	McBANE, ALEX	58
LOW, W.J.	56	McBANE, ALEXANDER	119
LOWBER, ALEXANDER	19	McBANE, ANGUS	116
LOWBER, KATE W.	19	McBANE, CATHARINE	98
LOWELL, FLETCHER	90	McBANE, D.S.	90
LOWELL, WM.	30	McBANE, JAMES	101
LOWER, CATHERINE	117	McBANE, JANETTE	98
LOWER, ELIAS	64,88	McBANE, JESSIE	32
LOWER, ELIZABETH	64	McBANE, JOHN	98
LOWER, FRANKLIN P.	95	McBANE, KATE	58,98
LOWER, GEORGE	100	McBANE, LAUGHLIN	58
LOWER, I., REV.	32	McBANE, LIZZIE	78
LOWER, JONAS, REV.	43	McBANE, MAGGIE	90
LOWER, SAMANTHA	73	McBANE, MARGERY	53
LOWERY, MARY A.	50	McBANE, NANCY	35,110
LOWERY, ROBERT	50,111	McBEAN, CATHARINE	94
LOWMAN, A.J., REV.	10	McBEAN, NANCY	89
LOWMAN, ANNA F.	6	McBETH, MAGGIE	62
LOWMAN, ANNIE	78	McBETH, MARY	75
LOWMAN, G.A.,REV.	6,61,78,99	McBETH, ROBERT	27
LOWREY, PETER	61	McBRIAR, J.T.	97
LOWREY, REBECCA	35	McBRIDE, JAMES	35,70
LOWRIE, D.W.	81	McBRIDE, JOSEPH	45
LOWRIE, JAMES	95	McBRIDE, MARGARET	61
LOWRIE, LUCINDA N.	36	McBURNEY, LT.GOV.	50
LOWRY, A.S., REV.	10	McCAFFREY, JOHN	23
LOWRY, JAMES	117	McCAIN, CHARLES C.	94
LOWRY, JOSEPH L.	100	McCAIN, MELISSA	73
LOY, ANNA	5	McCALL, MAGGIE	99
LOYD, SARAH ELLEN	47	McCALL, WM.	60,61
LOZIER, CORNETTA	66	McCALLA, DAVID	56
LUCAS, ALEXANDER	98	McCALLA, IDA M.	74
LUCAS, ENOCH	76	McCALLA, JOHN	77
LUCAS, JOHN E.	107	McCALLA, MRS.	30
LUCAS, KATE	107	McCALLISTER, ROBERT	7
LUCAS, THOMAS	56,107	McCAMMON, ROBERT	44
LUCAS, WILLIAM	70	McCAMON, JOHN A.	1
LUCKEY, JOHN B.	28	McCAN, ALICE	98
LUCKEY, KITTIE	28	McCAN, GEO.W.	21
LUCKEY, MAUD	28	McCAN, M.	9
LUCY, F.	66	McCAN, THOMAS	19
LUDLAM, RHODA	90	McCANAHEY, JAMES	107
LUDWICK, LIZZIE	33	McCANN, HENRY	8
LUDWICK, S.P.	33	McCANN, NELSON	109
LUDWICK, SAMUEL P.	1	McCARTER, A.	2
LUFFER, M.F., REV.	104	McCARTER, SAMUEL	90
LUKE, JAMES	117	McCARTNEY, CAROLINE	86
LUKE, WILLIAMSON	1	McCARTNEY, CATHARINE	61
LUNAMAKER, JANE	70	McCARTNEY, FRANK	111,119
LUPTON, DANIEL	22,30	McCARTNEY, LORENZO T.	66
LUPTON, E.	21	McCARTNEY, MR.	104
LUPTON, EMILY	22	McCARTNEY, PIERCE	12
LUPTON, MARY	22,56	McCARTY, A.C.	89
LUPTON, MAUD	22	McCARTY, BESSIE	89
LUQUIENS, JULIUS	93	McCARTY, JOHN, REV.	3,5,11,61
LUTHER, IDA V.	95	McCARTY, KATE L.	107
LUTHER, M.J.	47	McCARTY, LIZZIE	107
LUTTON, J.B.	110	McCARTY, MARY E.	89
LYNCH, MARGARET	11,66	McCARTY, T.J.	89
LYNCH, OWEN	11	McCASKEY, A.G.	8
LYNCH, REV.	101	McCASKEY, CLARA	106
LYNCH, WM., REV.	35,37,39,36,38,	McCASKEY, DUNDENA	94
40,43,44,45,48,53,61,63,64,		McCASKEY, EMPSY	94
65,69,70,71		McCASKEY, MARY	94
LYNN, HUGH	16	McCASKEY, ROBERT, REV.	12
LYNN, JAMES	81	McCASLIN, JOHN	16
LYNN, MARY	58	McCAULEY, LAURA	76
LYON, OSBORN	64	McCAUSLAND, MARTHA J.	31

McCAWLEY, ELIZABETH	27	McCOY, JAMES B.	111
McCLAIN, MARTHA	83	McCOY, JOHN	74
McCLAIN, OSCAR F.	58	McCOY, LEWIS	7
McCLEARY, ALEXANDER	21	McCOY, M.A.	80,103
McCLELLAN, JAMES	32	McCOY, NANCY	45
McCLELLAN, JOSEPH	43	McCOY, SAMUEL	9
McCLELLAN, REV.	46,54	McCOY, T.M.T., MRS.	118
McCLELLAN, SAMUEL	29	McCOY, THOMAS	85
McCLELLAN, THOMAS	34,65	McCRACKEN, ANNIE B.	81
McCLELLAND, A.C., REV.	57	McCRACKEN, ELIZABETH	32
McCLELLAND, ALBERT	89	McCRACKEN, HERBERT	35
McCLELLAND, ANNA	99	McCRACKEN, LIZZIE T.	35
McCLELLAND, ANNIE	87	McCRACKEN, M.E.	74,75
McCLELLAND, JAMES	87	McCRACKEN, NATHANIEL	32
McCLELLAND, MAGGIE	65	McCRACKEN, THORNTON	34
McCLELLAND, MARGARET	89	McCREA, ELIZABETH	42
McCLELLAND, MINNIE	89	McCREA, SAMUEL	33
McCLELLAND, R.H., REV.	72	McCREADY, A.G.	115
McCLELLAND, REBECCA	10	McCREADY, MARY	110
McCLELLAND, ROBERT S.	90	McCREADY, THOMAS	118
McCLELLAND, THOMAS	10	McCREARY, H.M.	60
McCLOSKEY, E.	42	McCREARY, MARY H.	61
McCLOSKEY, J.A.	42	McCULLOUGH, BELLE	50
McCLOSKEY, RACHEL	42	McCULLOUGH, HUGH	74,75
McCLOSKEY, W.H.	18	McCULLOUGH, JAMES	50,77
McCLOUD, DANIEL	35	McCULLOUGH, SARAH	43
McCLUE, MARTHA	115	McCUNE, FANNIE	97
McCLURE, J.T., REV.	59	McCUNE, MATTIE	18
McCLURG, F.	16	McCUNE, SAMUEL	18
McCLURG, G.A.	16	McCURDY, ALVAN	46
McCLURG, HANNAH V.	16	McCURDY, EVELYN	81
McCLUSKEY, DAVID	103	McCURDY, MARTHA D.	84
McCLUSKEY, MARY	103	McCURDY, REV.	42
McCLUSKEY, THERESA	103	McCURDY, SAMUEL	84
McCLYMONDS, LEWIS	117	McCURDY, SARAH	84
McCLYMONDS, WALTER	117	McCURDY, T.A., REV.	2,7,70,92, 116
McCLYMONDS, WILLIAM	5	McCURDY, TAMAR	81
McCLYNCHEY, JOHN	99	McDANIEL, JOHN C.	106
McCOLLY, H.	73	McDERMOTT, JAMES	77,99
McCONAUGHEY, SARAH	86	McDERMOTT, MARY E.	99
McCONNAUGHY, GEORGE	77	McDERMOTT, NANNIE	99
McCONNEL, JOSEPH	7	McDEVIT, ACLIMISIA	41
McCONNELL, JOHN	8	McDEVIT, AUSTIN	39
McCONNELL, SARAH A.	27	McDEVIT, DAVID	41
McCONNELL, W.A., REV.	36	McDEVIT, MATILDA	41
McCONNER, ALONZO	89	McDEVITT, CHAS.	28
McCONNER, ENOCH	35	McDEVITT, ELIZABETH	98
McCONNER, MRS.	35	McDEVITT, JOHN	62,118
McCONNER, NANCY	56	McDEVITT, SALLIE	88
McCOOK, DANIEL	27	McDEVITT, SARAH J.	89
McCOOK, DR.	49	McDIVITT, DAVID	58
McCOOK FAMILY	51	McDIVITT, NANNIE	79
McCOOK, GEORGE , DR.	24,26,27, 39,50,77,82	McDONALD, A.J.	46
McCOOK, H.C., DR.	24	McDONALD, ALLAN	70
McCOOK, KATE FISHER	39	McDONALD, ANGUS	27
McCOOK, LATIMORE, DR.	27	McDONALD, D.	46
McCOOK, MARTHA	24	McDONALD, DAVID	34
McCOOK, POLLY	26	McDONALD, DUNCAN	5
McCOOK, W.P.	73	McDONALD, ELIZA ANN	53
McCORD, ALEXANDER	73,89	McDONALD, F.C.	78
McCORD, ARTHUR	86,98	McDONALD, GEORGE	9,42
McCORD, ELIZABETH	98	McDONALD, ISABELLA	13
McCORD, GEORGE	72	McDONALD, JAMES	3
McCORD, H.	21	McDONALD, JOHN	12,36
McCORD, HIRAM	30	McDONALD, LIZZIE	3
McCORD, JAMES	107	McDONALD, MAGGIE	97
McCORD, JESSE	73	McDONALD, MARY	113
McCORD, MAGGIE	1,93	McDONALD, MATTIE C.	16
McCORD, MARY	107	McDONALD, NANCY	96
McCORD, MELISSA J.	73	McDONALD, PATTERSON H.	104
McCORD, MERVIN	107	McDONALD, SARAH	57
McCORD, SARAH	19,73,98	McDONALD, TENIE	20
McCORD, THOMAS	19	McDONALD, WILLIE	46
McCORD, W.B.	70,115	McELHENNY, G., REV.	4
McCORD, WILLIAM B.	70	McELROY, AUGUSTA	80
McCORMICK, ALEXANDER	109	McELROY, JOHN	11
McCORMICK, GEORGE	83	McELWEE, THOMAS	21,37
McCORMICK, ISAIAH G.	43	McENTEE, GEORGE W.	34
McCORMICK, JAMES	48,55	McENTEE, SOPHIA	64
McCORMICK, JOHN	19,86	McENULTZ, ELIZABETH	84
McCORMICK, MARTHA J.	24,25	McFALL, J.	83
McCORMICK, PATRICK	18	McFALL, JOHN	47,48,73,108
McCORMICK, THOMAS	24,25	McFALL, SQUIRE	85,111
McCOWEN, S.S., REV.	32	McFATE, WILLIAM	30
McCOWN, HARVEY	66	McFERRAN, ALBERT	48
McCOY, A.A.	94	McFERRAN, NANCY	48
McCOY, ELIZA	116	McFERRAN, PHEBE J.	48
McCOY, ELIZABETH	112	McGAFFIC, JOSEPHINE	64
McCOY FARM	39	McGAFFICK, ANDREW	57
McCOY, GEORGE	110	McGAFFICK, CAROLINA	25

Name	Page(s)
McGAFFICK, JANET	84
McGAFFICK, JOHN	84
McGAFFICK, JOSEPH	84
McGAFFICK, MARGARET	10
McGAFFICK, MARY	57
McGAFFREY, J.	10
McGAFFY, JOHN	28,29
McGARVEY, ELIZABETH	22
McGARVEY, JANE	48
McGARVEY, JOSEPH	48,53
McGARVEY, MARY	48
McGARVEY, ROSAAN	53
McGARVEY, SARAH	79
McGARY, DANIEL	94
McGARY, ELLEN	23
McGARY, JOHN	23,80
McGARY, MARY JANE	94
McGAVERN, JOHN	72
McGAVERN, MAGGIE J.	27
McGAVRAN, SARAH E.	69
McGAVRAN, W.E.	98
McGAW, CATHARINE	37
McGAW, HUGH	37
McGEE, PATRICK	45
McGEEHEN, MARGARET	32
McGEHAN, THOMAS	50
McGHAR, J.H.	35
McGHIE, MAGGIE	12
McGILL, R.A.	61
McGILL, W.W.	69
McGILLIVARY, ELIZABETH	118
McGILLIVRAY, JOHN	65
McGILLIVRAY, NICHOLSON	68
McGILLIVRAY, PETER	75
McGILLVARY, ALEX	12
McGILLVARY, MAGGIE	62
McGILLVARY, PERCILLA	12
McGILVARY, MARY	53
McGILVERY, MARGARET	78
McGILVERY, NANCY	5
McGILVRAY, CATHARINE	38
McGINNERY, LIZZIE	83
McGINNIS, GEORGE W.	103
McGINNIS, JAMES	79
McGINNIS, JENNIE	103
McGINNIS, L.E.	117
McGLENEN, ROSE	16
McGLENNEN, JOHN	90
McGLYNN, MARIA	37
McGONAGLE, ROBERT	27
McGOUGH, MARY	95
McGOWAN, MISS	58
McGOWAN, SAMUEL	109
McGOWN, REV.	34
McGRAHAM, FRANCIS	104
McGREE, MOLLIE	104
McGREGGOR, ALEX	54
McGREGGOR, CHARLES	104
McGREGGOR, CHARLOTTE	104
McGREGGOR, CLYDE	104
McGREGGOR, WILLIAM	6
McGREGOR, ANNIE	78
McGREGOR, DANIEL	87
McGREGOR, DONALD	80
McGREGOR, EMMA	38,72
McGREGOR, WM.	78
McGREW, FINDLEY	52
McGREW, MOLLIE	105
McGUAGHEY, A., REV.	116
McGUERN, JAMES	46
McGUINTY, NANCY	33
McGUIRE, FATHER	20,46,56
McGUIRE, GEORGE	79
McGUIRE, J.P., REV.	60
McGUIRE, JOHN	109
McGUIRE, P.J., FATHER	119
McGUIRE, P.J., REV.	1,19,55,69
McGURTY, MARY	82
McHENRY, MAGGIE	81
McHENRY, RACHEL	82
McILLVAINE, DOC	109
McILVAIN, HERMAN C.	116
McILVANE, DOC	112
McINTIRE, E.A.	21
McINTOSH, ALEVENIA	114
McINTOSH, ALEXANDER	33,49,90
McINTOSH, ANDREW	90
McINTOSH, ANN	68
McINTOSH, ANNA	93
McINTOSH, BELLE	79
McINTOSH, D.A.	90
McINTOSH, DANIEL G.	93
McINTOSH, ELIZABETH	42
McINTOSH, EVAN	20
McINTOSH, FRANCIS	42
McINTOSH, JAMES	91,108
McINTOSH, JANE	65
McINTOSH, JOHN	41,109
McINTOSH, JOHNSON	93
McINTOSH, MAGGIE	101,119
McINTOSH, MARGARET	109
McINTOSH, MARY	56
McINTOSH, MR.	27
McINTOSH, NANCY	33
McINTOSH, PHILIP	90
McINTOSH, W.G.	9
McINTOSH, W.S.	90
McINTOSH, WILLIAM	50,68,70
McKAGE, ROBT.	60
McKAIG, PETER	7
McKAIG, W.W.	49
McKANE, MARY C.	5
McKARNES, JOHN	117
McKARNS, THOS.F.	20
McKAY, DANIEL	26
McKEAG, SQUIRE	21
McKEAGE, ROBERT	51
McKEE, ANNIE	116
McKEE, DANIEL T.	19
McKEE, E.H.	79
McKEE, ELLA	83
McKEE, JOSEPH T.	102
McKEE, LUCINDA	101
McKEE, MARGARET	21,103
McKEE, MARY E.	40
McKEE, S.G.	105
McKEE, SARAH	108
McKEE, STUART G.	104
McKEE, TOOLEY	103
McKEE, WILLIAM	24,30,79
McKELVEY, SADIE	91
McKENNA, JOHN E.	19
McKENNA, PATRICK	44
McKENNA, PETER	22
McKENZIE, JAMES	35,48,94
McKENZIE, KATE	12
McKENZIE, LAUGHLIN	9
McKENZIE, LAURA	117
McKENZIE, N.K., MRS.	79
McKENZIE, RETTIE A.	45
McKERE, JENNIE	2
McKIBBEN, E.E.	56
McKIBBON, MICHAEL SR.	86
McKINLEY, ABNER O.	17
McKINNEL, JAMES H.	60
McKINNELL, AGNES	106
McKINNEY, W.J.	116
McKINNON, GEORGE	31
McKINNON, JOHNNY	118
McKINNON, JOSEPH	45
McKINNON, MARY	117
McKINNON, MICHAEL	45
McKINSEY, JOHN	111
McKINSTRY, MRS.	63
McKOWN, JAMES	91
McKOWN, MAGGIE	91
McKOWN, S.S., REV.	4,18,27,62, 84,93,114
McLAIN, D.B.	39
McLAIN, D.W.	67
McLAIN, DAVID	2
McLAIN, EDITH E.	14
McLAIN, F.T.	82
McLAIN, HANNAH	14,18
McLAIN, JOHN	38
McLAIN, LEONARD	14,18
McLAIN, VIRGINIA B.	18
McLANE, DANIEL	4,8
McLANE, EUPHEMA	93
McLANE, JAMES	93
McLANE, MARGARET	79
McLANE, MARTHA J.	11
McLANE, MATHEW	79
McLANE, ROSE	96
McLANE, SAMUEL	92
McLANE, WARREN	93
McLANE, WM.	32
McLARAN, THOMAS	49
McLAUGHLIN, ----	13
McLAUGHLIN, A.J.	49,100
McLAUGHLIN, ANNIE	116
McLAUGHLIN, CAPT.	7
McLAUGHLIN, CATHARINE	110
McLAUGHLIN, ELIZABETH	73
McLAUGHLIN, HOMER	86
McLAUGHLIN, JACOB	73
McLAUGHLIN, JAMES	8
McLAUGHLIN, JEREMIAH	7
McLAUGHLIN, JOHN	7,103,110,116
McLAUGHLIN, JOSEPH	4,86
McLAUGHLIN, LEONARD	106
McLAUGHLIN, MARIA	116
McLAUGHLIN, MARTHA	46,100
McLAUGHLIN, MARY L.	1
McLAUGHLIN, MOSES	107
McLAUGHLIN, NEWTON	4
McLAUGHLIN, REBECCA	100
McLAUGHLIN, W.	107
McLEAN, ABIJAH	86
McLEAN, CHARLES	100
McLEAN, DANIEL S.	5
McLEAN, DAVID B.	15
McLEAN, EMMA	69
McLEAN, JOHN A.	100
McLEAN, LAUGHLIN	67
McLEAN, MAGGIE	51
McLEAN, NANCY	77
McLEAN, REBECCA	25
McLEAN, S.	47
McLEARN, JENNIE	44
McLEARN, JOHN	44
McLEARN, MARY	21
McLENEN, MRS.	72
McLERAN, E.	55
McLERAN, JOHN	11
McLONEY, SARAH	55
McMAHON, ROBERT, REV.	110
McMANIMON, HANNAH	110
McMANNUS, MARGARET	97
McMASTER, JAMES	28
McMASTERS, ALDERMAN	61,70
McMASTERS, LYDIA	32
McMICHAEL, MARY	100
McMICHAEL, R.H.	100
McMILLAN, ELEANOR	76
McMILLAN, ELIZABETH	33
McMILLAN, HENRY	93
McMILLAN, JOEL	33
McMILLAN, JOHN	95
McMILLAN, LIZZIE	95
McMILLAN, MAGGIE	95
McMILLAN, MARY E.	95
McMILLAN, SELL	87
McMILLAN, SMITH	95
McMILLEN, ANNA B.	111
McMILLEN, ELIZA A.	32
McMILLEN, GEORGE W.	45
McMILLEN, J.S.	40
McMILLEN, JAMES	89,103
McMILLEN, JOHN	111
McMILLEN, MARY J.	111
McMILLEN, MILTON, REV.	56
McMULLEN, JAMES	6
McMULLEN, LOUISA	21
McMULLEN, THERESA	88
McMURPHY, A.T.,REV.	3,4,5,13
McNAMARA, MARY	97
McNAMARA, MICHAEL	97
McNAMARA, PATRICK	97
McNAMARAH, EDWARD	89
McNANNY, JAMES	32
McNICHOL, MAGGIE	20
McPHEE, JANE	88
McPHEE, MAGGIE	93
McPHERSON, ANDREW	107
McPHERSON, ANDREW SR.	107
McPHERSON, ELIZA	32
McPHERSON, EVA	116
McPHERSON, JAMES	98
McPHERSON, JOHN	75
McPHERSON, MARY	70
McPHERSON, NAN	67
McPHERSON, NANCY J.	39
McQUADE, PATRICK	47
McQUEEN, JAMES	117
McQUILKEN, D.L.	10
McQUILKEN, DAVID	12
McQUILKEN, ELIZABETH	74
McQUILKIN, ANNIE S.	27
McQUILKIN, CATHARINE	32
McQUILKIN, ELIZABETH	16
McQUOID, ELIZABETH	48
McSHADDEN, JOHN	81
McSHANE, MAGGIE	119
McSKIMEN, HATTIE	60
McSPADDEN, WILLIAM	1
McSTEPHENSON, MARY	13
McVANE, BELL	58
McVICKER & CLARKE	30
McVICKER, JOHN	2,5,8,14,15, 16,19,25,30,37,38,49,65
McVICKER, R.	65
McVICKER, SQUIRE	11
MACHAN, MICHAEL	78
MACK, GEORGE	69
MACKALL, GEORGE H.	105
MACKALL, JACKSON E.	31
MACKALL, MONTERVILLE	88
MACKALL, SAMUEL	8
MACKENTIRE, JAMES	47
MacKENZIE, ALEXANDER	90
MADIGAN, PATRICK	92
MADISON, ALFRED	73
MADISON, HANNAH	73
MADISON, HUGH J.	65
MADISON, JOHN	73
MADISON, SAMUEL	66
MADISON, SARAH	42
MADSON, ELIZA	21
MAERKT, WILLIAM	2
MAGEHAN, HUGH	111
MAGUIRE, FATHER	53
MAHAN, ED M.	30
MALEY, BRIDGET	34
MALEY, JOHN	93
MALL, MRS.	20
MALONE, WILLIAM S.	93
MALONEY, CORA	115
MALONEY, J.M., DR.	115
MALONEY, LAURA	115
MALONY, JAMES	19
MALONY, RACHEL	19
MALOY, J.C., REV.	57
MANLEY, JETHRO	55,60,72,75,78, 81
MANNING, J.M.	109
MANNING, J.W.	109
MANNING, WILLIE	109
MANNIST, D.	81
MANNIST, DAVID	57
MANSBRIDGE, JAS.	80
MANSFIELD, FRANK	17
MANSFIELD, I.F.	76,83
MANSFIELD, JUSTICE	116
MANSFIELD, P.	99
MANTI, JACOB	40
MAPLE, JAMES	58
MAPLE, KEZIAH	10
MARBLOW, LINNIE	89
MARBLOW, SAMUEL	89
MARCH, ISADORE	85
MARCH, JOHN	18,51
MARCH, MARTHA J.	20
MARCH, MARY	53
MARCH, MELISSA E.	12
MARCH, SARAH A.	40
MARCHAND, J.I., DR.	11
MARCHAND, JOHN F.	116
MARIETTA, ADRIAN	30
MARIS, BARCKLEY	86
MARKER, MARY	102
MARKHAM, MATILDA	28
MARKS, GEORGE W.	55
MARKS, LAFAYETTE, REV.	99
MARKS, R.ISABELLA	99
MARLANEE, JANE	102
MARLATT, WM.	58
MARLNEE, REBECCA E.	2
MARLNEE, WILLIAM	102
MARLOW, ROBERT	21
MARQUIS, JOHN	64
MARQUIS, SAMUEL	99
MARSDEN, CATHARINE	56
MARSDEN, HANNAH	110
MARSDEN, JOB	110
MARSDEN, JOHN	58
MARSDEN, SARAH	110
MARSH, A.	104
MARSH, ELIZABETH	46
MARSH, MARY A.	35
MARSH, W.G., REV.	45
MARSHAL, E.	9
MARSHALL, E.J.	19
MARSHALL, EMMA	97,98

MARSHALL, ISABELLA	22
MARSHALL, JAMES M.	66
MARSHALL, JOHN	97,98
MARSHALL, LUEMMA	104
MARSHALL, MATILDA	33
MARSHALL, WM.E.	95
MARSHE, DAVID M.	58
MARTIN, A.R.	1
MARTIN, ABIGAIL	11
MARTIN, ALBERT	109
MARTIN, ALFRED	82
MARTIN, ARA	28
MARTIN, CHARLEY	97
MARTIN, CYNTHIA M.	4
MARTIN, D.B.	115
MARTIN, DAVID B.	41
MARTIN, EDWIN L.	106
MARTIN, EMILY	14,108
MARTIN, EMMA	80
MARTIN, GEORGE H.	93
MARTIN, H.	78
MARTIN, HANNA	71
MARTIN, HUGH	32
MARTIN, J.R.	14
MARTIN, J.W., REV.	6
MARTIN, JAMES	27,109
MARTIN, JANE	97,108
MARTIN, JOHN	8,11,24,29,32
MARTIN, JONATHAN	86
MARTIN, JULIA	90
MARTIN, MAGGIE	55,114
MARTIN, MR.	57
MARTIN, RUFUS	43
MARTIN, SALOME	10
MARTIN, SAMUEL	81,97,108
MARTIN, W.T.	1
MARTIN, WARRICK	55
MARTINVALE, C.P., REV.	54
MARTTA, ANNA	64
MARTTA, SAMUEL	64
MASKREY, HANNAH	88
MASKREY, J.E.	10
MASON, CHARLES	11
MASON, HATTIE	108
MASON, JOHN	6,108,112
MASON, LINNIE	6
MASON, MARTIN	7
MASSEY, WILLIAM	55
MASTERSON, ELIZABETH	101
MASTERSON, MARGARET	101
MASTERSON, OWEN	101
MATHER, ALBERT	79
MATHER, J.T.	111
MATHER, WILLIAM H.	60
MATHERS, B.R., REV.	20
MATHERS, KATE	101
MATHERS, SARAH	107
MATHERS, THOMAS	107
MATHERS, WM.	33
MATHEWS, CHARLES	20
MATHEWS, EDDIE	1
MATHEWS, JOHN	17,63
MATHEWS, MARY ANN	1
MATHEWS, PHILIP	1
MATTHEWS, ELLA	43
MATTHEWS, MONROE	46
MAUCK, E.W., REV.	27
MAUNTY, S.B.	9
MAUS, FRED	11
MAUS, JOSEPH	65
MAUTZENBAUGH, MRS.	116
MAXWELL, A.B., REV.	1,2,3,4,11, 14,16,18,29,31,32,33,37,42, 49,51,57,61,64,70,72,87,93, 99,106,111,115,116,118
MAXWELL, O.C.	50
MAXWELL, WILLIAM	99
MAY, MRS.	91
MAYER, ADA F.	33
MAYER, DR.	57
MAYER, HANNAH	33
MAYER, WM.	33
MAYERHOEFER, HERMANN	105
MAYLONE, J.M.	64
MAYLONE, OMA	54
MAYLONE, WILLIAM C.	102
MAYRES, WILLIAM	110
MEACE, PHILIP	8
MEACHAM, MARTIN	72
MEAD, ABEL	90
MEAD, JOHN	72
MEAD, MARY	72
MEAD, SAMUEL	97,102
MEEK, FRANK	109
MEEK, JAMES H., REV.	91
MEEK, SETH	8
MEEK, SOLOMON	68
MEEKER, CYNTHIA D.	74
MEEKER, ORIE	61
MEEKS, ELCEY M.	3
MEEKS, JOSEPH	43,74
MEESE, EDWIN	108
MEGARGE, AMANDA	95
MEGARGE, WILLIAM	104
MEGAVENRY, ANDREW	63
MEHAN, JOHN	70
MEHEN, LYDIA	96
MEIGH, FRED	116
MEIGH, MARY	116
MEIGHER, SALON J.	68
MEISTER, ANASTACIA	108
MEISTER, JOHN	108
MELANY, F.I.	74
MELGRIM, CHARLES	97
MELLINGER, MOLLIE A.	79
MELLINGER, NOAH	65
MELLON, BRIDGET	40
MELLON, THOMAS	41
MELLOR, ANNA	28,29
MELLOR, CHARLES M.	10
MELLVANE, JAMES	52
MELON, PATRICK	106
MELOY, J.C., REV.	59,64,68,70, 82,90,110
MELVIN, W.H.	2
MENDANHALL, REV.	98
MENDELL, WM.S.	71
MENDENHALL, ELIZA A.	7
MENDENHALL, GEORGE, DR.	87
MENDENHALL, ISAAC	7
MENDENHALL, REBECCA	3
MENDENHALL, REV.	74
MENOUGH, FRANK H.	10
MENTZER, JOHN W.	85
MENTZER, LYDIA L.	6
MENTZER, WILLIAM	14
MERCER, DANIEL	10,22
MERCER, LIZA ANN	22
MERCER, MR.	110
MERCER, SAMUEL C.	22
MERCER, WILLIAM H.	88
MEREDITH, ANN	27
MEREDITH, EDDIE	46
MEREDITH, JOHN	83
MEREDITH, NANNIE	46
MEREDITH, WILLIAM	8,46
MERRICK, MINER	72
MERRILL, ARAMINTA	71
MERRILL, LAURETTA	71
MERRIMAN, MISS	49
MERRITT, REV.	99
MERTON, JAMES H	60
MERTZ, PHILIP	118
MESSER, DAVID	31
MESSIMORE, CATHARINE	78
MESSIMORE, WASHINGTON	11
METCHUM, GEORGE	4
METZ, ADELIA	79
METZ, ANN	51
METZ, BEN F.	102
METZ, ISAIAH	55
METZ, JONAH	10
METZ, SAMANTHA	80
METZGAR, ANNA E.	14
METZGAR, JOHN	52
METZGAR, M.E.	52
METZGAR, MARY A.	93
METZGAR, PAUL	81
METZGAR, SALOME	52
METZLER, EPHRAIM	85
METZLER, JOHN B.	62
MEYERS, THOMAS J.	86
MICHAELS, ARENA	51
MICHAELS, HARMON	51
MICHAELS, MARY	51
MICHELL, JOHN	46
MICHELL, MARY	46
MICHINER, PARK P.	77
MICHNER, HENRY	9
MICK, JOHN W.	85
MICK, TWIN GIRLS	85
MILBOURN, WILLIAM	83
MILBURN, ANN MARIA	44
MILBURN, JEFFERSON	61
MILBURN, JOHN L.	44
MILBURN, LOT R.	44
MILBURN, NANCY	67
MILBURN, THOMAS F.	44
MILINGER, JACOB	8
MILLARD, EDWIN	101
MILLARD, ELIZABETH	79
MILLARD, JOHN B.	79
MILLER & JOHNSON	15
MILLER, A.	104
MILLER, ABBADENIA	37
MILLER, ADAM	109
MILLER, ALEXANDER	87
MILLER, ANDREW	26,28,78
MILLER, ANNA M.	78
MILLER, ARCH	57
MILLER, B., REV.	43
MILLER, CATHARINE	94
MILLER, CLARA	106
MILLER, DANIEL	96
MILLER, DAVID	67
MILLER, E.A.	96
MILLER, ELIZABETH	1,78
MILLER, EMMA S.	90
MILLER, F.M.	74
MILLER, FRANCIS	86
MILLER, FRANK	60,106
MILLER, GEORGE	1,14,21,67
MILLER, GILENA	36
MILLER, HARRY	20,37
MILLER, HATTIE S.	39
MILLER, IDELLA	96
MILLER, J.A., REV.	88
MILLER, J.B., REV.	1,29,31,35
MILLER, JACOB	94
MILLER, JESSE	11
MILLER, JOHN	12,34,36,40,84
MILLER, JOHN B., REV.	14,21, 23,25,62,84
MILLER, JOHN C.	38,81
MILLER, JOHN H.	89
MILLER, JOHN W.	70
MILLER, KATE E.	99
MILLER, LAURA	22
MILLER, LEANDER	76
MILLER, LEVI	17
MILLER, LIZZIE	106
MILLER, LIZZIE	76
MILLER, M.	115
MILLER, M.A., REV.	50
MILLER, MARIA	11
MILLER, MARSHALL	12
MILLER, MART R.	82
MILLER, MARY	37,50
MILLER, MORRIS	54
MILLER, NANCY	44,91
MILLER, NANNIE	86
MILLER, O.B.	87
MILLER, PETER	8
MILLER, REUBEN	8
MILLER, REV.	31,85
MILLER, SAMANTHA	82
MILLER, SIMON	82
MILLER, SOLOMON	1
MILLER, SUE	106
MILLER, W.C.	83
MILLER, W.S., DR.	110
MILLER, W.W.	29
MILLER, WILLIAM	18,63,99
MILLIGAN, ANNA G.	25
MILLIGAN, JAMES	66
MILLIGAN, LUCINDA	74
MILLINAUX, MARTHA M.	8
MILLS, BELLA	67
MILLS, J.	19
MILLS, J.B.	13,18,23,28, 29,30,39
MILLS, JAMES H.	111
MILLS, JOHN B.	30
MILLS, JUSTICE	13,14
MILLS, LIZZIE	66
MILLS, REV.	11
MILLWARD, JOHN	65
MILLWOOD, LAVINIA	8
MILNER, AGGIE	77
MILNER, GEORGE	84
MILNOR, RODNEY	85
MINARD, LEAH	63
MINER, ISADORE	21
MINER, JOHN	57
MINER, VIOLA	82
MITCHEL, JOHN	93
MITCHEL, MARY	109
MITCHELL, CATHARINE	89
MITCHELL, JACOB	12,36
MITCHELL, JAMES R.	58
MITCHELL, JOHN	12,36
MITCHELL, JOSEPH R.	64
MITCHELL, MARTHA E.	84
MITCHELL, REV.	5
MITCHENOR, HENRY	11
MITCHENOR, SARAH	11
MITE, ALFRED	2
MITE, JAMES C.	2
MOFF, DORATHA	3
MOFF, JOHN	3,32,39
MOFF, MARGARET	39
MOFFET, ISABELLA	100
MOFFET, JOSEPH	100
MOFFET, SUSAN	100
MOFFETT, JOHN, REV.	45
MOFFETT, WM.S.	19
MOFFIT, ANDREW	81
MOFFIT, J.J., REV.	11,12,19, 20,21
MOFFIT, JOHN J., REV.	11
MOFFIT, JOS.	49
MOFFIT, MARY J.	23
MOMFORD, MARY	37
MONAGAN, JOHN	27
MONAGAN, WILLIAM	27
MONAGHAN, ALICE E.	52
MONAGHAN, MAGGIE	52
MONAGHAN, WILLIAM	52
MONCRIEF, DAVID	21
MONDAY, CHARLES	102
MONTGOMERY, ALBERT	19,48
MONTGOMERY, ANNA	22
MONTGOMERY, CHAS	85
MONTGOMERY, ELLEN	115
MONTGOMERY, HANNAH	109
MONTGOMERY, ISADORE	31
MONTGOMERY, JANE	70
MONTGOMERY, JOHN	97
MONTGOMERY, JOSEPH	115
MONTGOMERY, LAURA E.	69
MONTGOMERY, MARCUS	79
MONTGOMERY, MARTHA	56
MONTGOMERY, MR.	40
MONTGOMERY, SADIE	88
MONTGOMERY, SAMUEL	91
MONTGOMERY, WILLIAM	6,25,79 97,98
MOODY, BENJAMIN	97,98
MOODY, EMMA	97,98
MOODY, GRANVILLE, REV.	42
MOON, WINNIE A.	107
MOOR, GEORGE	93
MOORE, ABBIE	16
MOORE, ABRAM	43
MOORE, ALMIRA	30
MOORE, BILLY	34
MOORE, CAROLINE M.	68
MOORE, CATHARINE	101
MOORE, DANIEL W.	101
MOORE, DAVID C.	30
MOORE, ED F.	115
MOORE, ELIAS	80
MOORE, ELISA J.	40
MOORE, ELIZABETH E.	30
MOORE, EMMA	30
MOORE, EZEKIEL J.	40
MOORE, FRANK	15
MOORE, G.S.	46
MOORE GALLERY	23
MOORE, J.Z., REV.	96,97,100, 101,105,107
MOORE, JACOB SR.	90
MOORE, JAMES	30,106,115
MOORE, JOHN	35,58
MOORE, JOSEPH F.	119
MOORE, LINNA	46
MOORE, LIZZIE M.	35
MOORE, M.	7
MOORE, M.S.	112
MOORE, MAGGIE	30
MOORE, MARY	104,106
MOORE, MARY	36
MOORE, MILLIE	40
MOORE, MISS	15,33

MOORE, MR.	7
MOORE, ROBERT	101
MOORE, ROSA BELL	40
MOORE, ROSS	94
MOORE, SALLIE	9
MOORE, SETH	111
MOORE, SUSAN	22
MOORE, THERESA	89
MOORE, WILL	115
MOORE, WILLIAM	4,30,34,46,49,66,91
MOORE, WILLIAM,DR.	36
MORELAN, ISABEL	81
MORELAND, ALBERT M.	77
MORELAND, H.	115
MORELAND, JOEL	4
MORGAN, CATHARINE	20
MORGAN, EMMA	68
MORGAN, JAMES	31,109
MORGAN, JASON	20
MORGAN, JOHN	11,15,19,20
MORGAN, JOSEPH B.	9
MORGAN, JOSIAH	9,12
MORGAN, MARY	108,110
MORGAN, NANCY	31,33
MORGAN, WILLIAM	7,20,33,92
MORGANS, EDWARD	61
MORGANS, MARY ANN	95
MORLAN, AMELIA E.	5
MORLAN, CATHARINE	2,44
MORLAN, HENRY	2
MORLAN, JULIA	2
MORLAN, LOVINA	43
MORLAN, MARCUS B.	42
MORLAN, MARY	117
MORLAN, SARAH	84
MORLEY, MARY J.	66
MORLEY, SAMUEL	87,96
MORNINGSTAR, HENRY	101
MORRIS, ALBERT	54
MORRIS, CORNELIA	102
MORRIS, GEORGE	102
MORRIS, HANNAH	64
MORRIS, HENRY E.	102
MORRIS, JONATHAN	93
MORRIS, LINDLAY	48
MORRIS, LOT	82
MORRIS, LOUISA C.	68
MORRIS, LYDIA	75
MORRIS, MARY	85,102
MORRIS, MORRIS E.	64
MORRIS, S.	4
MORRIS, SARAH	93
MORRIS, SHERIFF	60
MORRIS, ZACHARIAH	118,119
MORRISON, EMMA	28
MORRISON, FREEMAN	3,12,14
MORRISON, GUSSIE	70
MORRISON, HARVEY	46,65
MORRISON, J.N.	14
MORRISON, J.W.	4,5
MORRISON, JAMES B.	84
MORRISON, JENNIE	55
MORRISON, JOHN	6,7,15,46
MORRISON, JUSTICE	5
MORRISON, LOU	65
MORRISON, MARY	3,14,84
MORRISON, SAMUEL P.	3
MORRISON, SUSANNA	19
MORRON, AMANDA	89
MORRON, JOHN A.	89
MORROW, HUGH	19,36
MORROW, JONAH	90
MORROW, LULU DELL	48
MORROW, P.A.	48
MORROW, ROBERT	112
MORROW, W.	115
MORROW, W.C.	48
MORSE, HENRY G.	17
MORSE, SIDNEY	84
MOSELY, SIDNEY	84
MOSSMAN, WASHINGTON	55
MOTE, WILLIAM	106
MOTTINGER, GEORGE	7
MOUGH, JOHN A.	82
MOUNTFORD, MRS.	81
MOUNTFORD, WILLIAM	101
MOUNTS, LIZZIE	87
MOWER, SAMUEL, REV.	94
MOWERY, EUNICE	67
MOWREY, J.M.	9
MOWREY, JACOB M.	38
MOWREY, JESSE	38
MOWREY, SALINDA	38
MOWRY, JACOB M.	119
MUIR, THOMAS	76
MULFORD, CHARLES C.	7
MULHERIN, CHARLES SR.	74
MULHERRIN, CHARLEY	109
MULHOLLEN, JOHN	6
MULHURN, MARY	11
MULLEN, CLARA	18
MULLEN, MR.	111
MULLEN, SALLIE	43
MULLER, EMMA	86
MULROY, STEPHEN	21
MUMFORD, MARY	25
MUNK, MARY	89
MUNTZ, JOHN	102
MURDOCH, J.M., DR.	115
MURPHY, AMY	12
MURPHY, E.W.	12
MURPHY, EPHRAM	70
MURPHY, J.F.	26
MURPHY, MARY	62
MURPHY, MILLIE H.	3
MURPHY, MOLLIE	48
MURPHY, MR.	62,115
MURPHY, REV.	109
MURPHY, SALLIE	26
MURPHY, SETTA	60
MURPHY, WILLIE C.	26
MURRAY, HARVEY D.	67
MURRAY, JOHN	67,107
MURRAY, LYDIA	92
MURRAY, MARY D.	67
MURRAY, MICHAEL	119
MURRAY, MRS.	107
MURRAY, THOMAS	52,116
MURRY, HANNAH A.	9
MURRY, JOHN	9
MUSGRAVE, MYRA	33
MUSSELMAN, MARY V.	74
MYERS, ---	50
MYERS, ALICE S.	51
MYERS, ANDREW	88
MYERS, CAPT.	31
MYERS, EMMA	107
MYERS, GEORGE	118
MYERS, HIRAM	12,36,38
MYERS, ISAAC	112
MYERS, J.A.	72
MYERS, J.M.	55
MYERS, JANE ANN	38
MYERS, JEREMIAH E.	75
MYERS, JOHN	72,110,114
MYERS, LYDIA	20,22
MYERS, MARY	29,30,62,104
MYERS, MR.	22
MYERS, NANCY	51
MYERS, WILLIAM	44,51,92
MYGATT, HANNAH	116
MYRES, ALFRED	83
NAASER, LIZZIE	58
NACE, CHRISTIANA	16
NACE, GEORGE S.	53
NACE, MATTHIAS	16,31,54,97
NACE, WILLIE G.	53
NAEBART, MARY	69
NALL, JEROME	43
NANGLE, GEORGE	109,112
NAUGHTON, JAMES	12
NAUGHTON, MAGGIE	101
NAUGHTON, MARY	101
NAUGHTON, THOMAS	101
NAUGLE, D.A.	80
NAYLOR, JAMES JR.	23
NEASE, BARNEY, MRS.	2
NEEDHAM, JOHN	48
NEEDHAM, REBECCA	48
NEEDHAM, REV.	6
NEEMES, GEORGE	84
NEGUS, MARY	32
NEGUS, WEST	19,32
NEIGH, EMMA	82
NEIL, ELIZABETH	64
NEIL, JOHN E.	64
NEILL, ANN	88
NEILL, EDITH C.	11
NELSON, ANN	85
NELSON, J.B.	43
NELSON, JANE	1
NELSON, JEROME	85
NELSON, LIZZIE	38
NELSON, LOUIS B.	11
NELSON, MIROM	85
NELSON, NANCY	34
NELSON, SUSAN	62
NELSON TANNERY	68
NELSON, THOMAS	62,82,85
NELSON, W.D.,REV.	117
NELSON, W.L.,REV.	33,61,75,93
NESBIT, REV.DR.	98
NEUSBAUM, FREDERICK	85,99
NEVILL, E.T.	23
NEVILLE, EDDIE	97
NEVILLE, ELLA	97
NEVILLE, JOSIAH	84
NEVILLE, SANFORD	59,97
NEVIN, EMMA	98
NEVIN, JAMES	44,86
NEVIN, R.E.	96
NEVIN, SADE J.	4
NEVIN, W.G., REV.	92,95,97,98,111
NEWBERRY, AGNES	6
NEWBERRY, JOHN H.	6
NEWELL, MAGGIE J.	1
NEWHOUSE, ELIZABETH	27
NEWHOUSE, FAMILY	112
NEWHOUSE, GIDEON	112
NEWHOUSE, ISAIAH	27
NEWHOUSE, MARY	23
NEWHOUSE, REBECCA	103
NEWHOUSE, REZIN	66
NEWHOUSE, S.S.	35
NEWHOUSE, THOMAS	23,44
NEWMAN, FERDINAND	102
NEY, CHARLOTTE	38
NEY, MARGARET	48
NEYE, W.B.	73
NIBLO, ELLEN	75
NICHOLS, E.W.	79
NICHOLS, HARRIET	19
NICHOLS, JESSIE A.	19
NICHOLS, M.J.	51
NICHOLS, MAHLON J.	92
NICHOLS, MARY	95
NICHOLS, NATHAN	66
NICHOLS, SALLIE	114
NICHOLS, W.A.	9
NICHOLS, W.M.	9
NICHOLS, WILLIAM	19,116
NICHOLSON, GEORGE W.	4
NICKUM, ANN	103
NICKUM, JOHN	52
NICKUM, S.A.	85
NIGHT, W.H.	112
NILES, MARY C.	35
NITREWER, JOHN J.	76
NIXON, HENRY	104
NIXON, J.B.	12
NIXON, LIBBIE	12
NIXON, WILLIAM M.	73
NOBLE, ALEXANDER	37
NOBLE, D.S.	100
NOBLE, DONALD	84
NOBLE, ELIZABETH	37
NOBLE, F.A., REV.	32,40
NOBLE, GEORGE	79
NOBLE, JOHN A.	4
NOBLE, LAUGHLIN	33
NOBLE, MARY A.	79
NOBLE, ROSE M.	89
NOBLE, WILLIAM	76
NOGAL, A.	63
NOGAL, LOUISA	53
NOLD, EMMA	89
NOLD, ENOS	67
NOLD, MR.	57
NOLD, NOAH E.	55
NOLD, SAMUEL	67
NOLD, SOL	112
NOLD, VELINA	67
NOLF, MATHIAS	12
NORRIS, ANNA	2
NORRIS, DELILAH	20
NORRIS, JAMES	20
NORRIS, JASPER N.	27
NORRIS, JOHN	16
NOSS, MAGGIE	77
NOSS, RAYMOND	77
NOSS, W.J.	77
NUZEM, THOMAS	90
NUZUM, FRANK	92
O'BRIEN, CHARLES	10
O'BRINE, JULIA	93
O'CONNEL, JOHN	33
O'CONNER, MARY	100
O'DONNEL, MARGARET	62
O'DONNEL, PETER	16,62
O'DONNELL, BERNARD	106
O'DONNELL, LIZZIE	60
O'HARE, PATRICK	79
O'HEGGEM, CHARLES	69
O'HERIN, RICHARD	21
O'KANE, JOHN	92
O'NEAL, JOHN	93
O'ROURKE, EDWARD	57
OBENAUF, HULDA	3
OBERHOLTZER, JOEL	12
OBRINE, NETTIE	62
ODENBAUGH, MARY E.	16
OEHRIE, JOHN J.	73
OGDEN, B.B., DR.	60,115
OGDEN, J. & CO	15
OGDEN, JOHN	5
OGLE, BARBARA	86
OGLE, HENRY	12,36
OGLE, LIZZIE	88
OGLE, WM.	8
OGLINE, WILLIAM	84,90
OHL, DAVID	92
OLDHAM, WILLIAM	54
OLDRIDGE, LEWIS	82
OLIVER, ELNORA	106
ORMES, ANN	54
ORMES, BROTHERS	20
ORMES, JOHN	54
ORMES, LAVINA	11
ORMES, WILLIAM JR.	11
ORMS, B.F.	117
ORMS, LORENZE	117
ORMS, S.	117
ORNER, ALLIE	33
ORR, A.B.	57
ORR, BENJAMIN F.	12,36
ORR, CHARLES	118
ORR, DAVID	109
ORR, HELEN W.	11
ORR, JAMES S.	11
ORR, JOSEPH F.	12,36
ORR, KITTIE	28
ORR, LIZZIE H.	11
ORR, MARY	52,53
ORR, MATHEW	31
ORR, S.W.	52,53,57,71
ORR, SAMUEL	28
ORR, THOMAS Y., REV.	3
ORR, WILL	118
ORR, WILLIAM	7
ORT, E.B., REV.	73
OSBORN, EMMA	48
OSBORN, HETTIE	31
OSBORN, JOSEPH	48
OSBORN, MARCUS L.	40
OSBORNE, D.C., REV.	16,28
OSWALD, CORA	112
OTT, BARBARA	42
OTT, JOHN MARTIN	42
OTT, JOSEPH	61,85
OTT, MAGGIE	85
OTT, MARY ANN	61,85
OTT, VIOLA C.	61
OVERHOLT, AARON	38
OVERLANDER, FERDINAND	102
OVINGTON, MARY M.	3
OWENS, HARRISON	14
OWREY, HETTIE	30
OYSTER, AMOS	22
OYSTER, M.A.	22
OZENGER, A.	106
OZENGER, NANCY	106
PACKSTON, CHARLES	21
PAGE, D.C., REV.	85
PAIK, SYLVESTER	32
PAINE, JUDGE	77
PAINE, L., REV.	21
PAINTER, ANN	1
PAINTER, EMMA F.	5
PAINTER, ISABELL F.	75
PAINTER, ISABELLE	74
PAINTER, JACOB	74
PAINTER, MARY	1,86

Name	Page	Name	Page	Name	Page	Name	Page
PAINTER, REUBEN	74,75	PEARSON, D., MRS.	43	PHILLIPS, JOHN	44	PORTER, MINNIE	71
PAISELY, RACHEL	102	PEARSON, MARTHA L.	31	PHILLIPS, JOSEPH	112	PORTER, MR.	57
PAISLEY, DAVID	118	PECK, ELEANOR	13	PHILLIPS, MARTHA M.	87	PORTER, MRS.	71
PAISLEY, ELIHU	40	PEDEN, JAMES, MRS.	90	PHILLIPS, NATHAN	93	PORTER, S.H.	110
PAISLEY, GEORGE	89	PEEK, D.W.	92	PHILLIPS, OLIVER	34	POST, SARAH	19
PAISLEY, ROSALI J.	40	PEEK, THEODORE M	92	PHILLIPS, WM.	19	POST, THOMAS	118
PALMER, BARBARA	72	PEEPLES, HANNAH	102	PHILMAN, JONATHAN	12	POSTLETHWAITE, CORDELIA	69
PALMER, C.G., REV.	95	PEEPLES, JOSIE	42	PHILPOT, ARABELLA	39	POTTER, ANDREW	91
PALMER, ELIZABETH	35	PEEPLES, LAURA F.	50	PHILPOT, CHRISTINA	58	POTTER, BROWN & ARTER	72
PALMER, H., REV.	117	PEEPLES, LIDIE	42	PHILPOT, S.M.	107	POTTER, ELDERKIN	7
PALMER, MARY	31	PEEPLES, MAGGIE	104	PHILPOT, SARAH	78	POTTER, ELLA	25
PANCAKE, MR.	34	PEEPLES, SQUIRE	114	PIATT, DONN, MRS.	16	POTTER, H.N., REV.	67
PARISH, JULIA A.	68	PEEPLES, WILLIAM A.	42	PICKENNY, THOMAS	76	POTTER, HORACE, DR.	25
PARISH, LIZZIE S.	67	PEIFFER, MARY	72	PICKET, ALLIE	33	POTTER, K.G.	21
PARISH, MAGGIE	67	PEIFFER, PERCILA	72	PICKET, J.P.	33	POTTER, KATE E.	21
PARISH, WM.	67	PENDERGRAST, L.M.	14	PICKET, OTTIE	33	POTTER, SOPHRONIA	14
PARK, JOHN B.	72	PENGILL, S.J.	113	PICKETT, DAVID	101	POTTER, WILLIAM	74,90
PARK, JOSEPH	110	PENGILL, T.W.	113	PICKETT, J.K.	65	POTTS, GEORGE	65
PARK, SARAH	32	PENGILL, WILLIAM H.	113	PICKETT, MARY ANN	19	POTTS, HENRY C.	118
PARKER, ELIZA	28,29	PENNOCK, MARTHA J.	70	PICKFORD, WM.W.	79	POTTS, ISAAC W.	65
PARKER, ELLA	104	PENNOCK, MATILDA	83	PIDGEON, AQUILLA	30	POTTS, MARIA	42
PARKER, J.M.	63	PENROSE, R.A.	77	PIDGEON, CATHARINE	77	POTTS, MARY A.	32
PARKER, JUDGE	103	PENTZ, ELIZA	115	PIERCE, CHARLES H.	50	POTTS, MR.	115
PARKER, MARY	103	PEPIN, CAROLINE	31	PIERCE, ELDRIDGE	92	POTTS, SALLIE	65
PARKER, SHELDON	104	PEPIN, G., MRS.	105	PIERCE, FRANK, REV.	33	POTTS, W.S.	77
PARKINS, MARTHA	64	PEPPARD, STANDISH	82	PIERCE, JOHN F.	6	POULSON, SAMUEL	75
PARKINSON, A.M.,REV.	118	PEPPEL, DANIEL	99	PIERO, GEORGE J.	89	POW, GEORGE	47,90
PARKINSON, M.A.,REV.	73,101,102	PEPPEL, E.A.	103	PIERSOL, JAMES K.	2	POW, RICHARD	64
PARKS & WENTZ	10	PEPPEL, EVA M.	99	PIFER, THOMAS	93	POWELL, ANGELINE	104
PARKS, JOHN	105	PEPPEL, HENRY S.	30	PIGEON, WILLIAM	8	POWELL, CORA	104
PARLINGTON, FRANK	58	PEPPEL, LUCINDA	61	PIKE, CYNTHIA ANN	81	POWELL, JAMES	104
PARMALEE, H.C.	8	PEPPEL, MARY	99	PIKE, HANNAH I.	28	POWELL, JOHN	60
PARMLEY, AGNES S.	42	PEPPER, REV.MR.	61	PIKE, J.C.	110	POWELL, LIZZIE	75
PARSON, AMELIA	92	PEPPLE, DAVID S.	68	PIKE, JENNIE	32	POWELL, REV.	8
PARSONS, AGNES	115	PEPPLE, SYLVANUS	30,41	PIKE, JOHN C.	114	POWELL, THOMAS	7
PARSONS, ELIZABETH	102	PERDUE, HENRY	78	PIKE, LEAH	81	POWERS, CHARLES	9
PARSONS, JENNIE	109	PERDUE, MARY	21	PIKE, MARIA	114	POWERS, CLINTON J.	63
PARSONS, WM.	12,36	PERINE, GEO.W.	37	PIKE, SIMON	117	POWERS, E.	119
PARTHE, L.	85	PERINE, LYDIE D.	37	PIKE, THOMAS	81	POWERS, F.	119
PATRICK, MARY	37	PERINE, WILFRED C.	37	PIKE, WILLIAM	84,92	POWERS, JAMES H.	18
PATRICK, WM.A.	37	PERKINS, ANNIE	103	PILLMAN, ROBT	22	POWERS, R.J.	9
PATTEN, JOSEPH	119	PERKINS, ELI	103	PIM, ANNA	86	POWERS, WILLIAM A.	119
PATTEN, SARAH	119	PERKINS, L.B., REV.	2,85	PIM, SADA	4	PRENTISS, MATTIE	48
PATTERSON, A.O., REV.	20	PERKINS, MARY	85,103	PINEER, FREDERICK	12,36	PRESLEY, ALICE	88
PATTERSON, AGNES	96	PERKINS, MR.	45	PINKHAM, EMMA C.	26	PRESSEY, CLARA	98
PATTERSON, ALEXANDER	84,104	PERKINS, SARAH	103	PINKHAM, HOWARD	26	PRESTON, ELIZABETH M.	77
PATTERSON, ARABELLA	44	PERRIN, MR.	43	PINKHAM, WM.	26	PRICE, JAMES	7
PATTERSON, CATHARINE	50	PERRY, N.J.	118	PINKHURST, SARAH	39	PRICE, JENNETT	47
PATTERSON, DAVID	11,98	PERSHING, I.C., REV.	39,104	PIPER, APPA	57	PRICE, JOHN	47
PATTERSON, DELLA	81	PETERS, S.A.	76	PITCAIRN, ALEXANDER	92	PRICHETT, REUBEN E.	73
PATTERSON, DR.	16	PETERS, WARNER SR.	86	PITCAIRN, ANNIE	92	PRIDE, CHARLES	116
PATTERSON, ELLA	44,113	PETERSON, JACOB D.	25	PITCAIRN, CATHARINE	96	PRINCE, H.	14
PATTERSON, EMMA	98	PETERSON, M.C.	105	PITCAIRN, FLORENCE M.	19	PRISBY, MARIA	14
PATTERSON, HARRIET	67	PETERSON, SAMUEL F.	76	PITCAIRN, JOHN	92,96	PRITCHARD, B.W.,MRS.	2
PATTERSON, JAMES	32,33,78	PETERSON, WILLIAM	67,84	PITCAIRN, LAURA	96	PRITCHARD, BENJAMIN	14
PATTERSON, JEANNETTE	101	PETERSON, WOSHER	61	PITTINGER, ABRAM	81	PRITCHARD, CARRIE	66
PATTERSON, JENNIE J.	44	PETTIT, A.J., REV.	83,87,91	PITTINGER, N.	40	PRITCHARD, CELIA D.	42
PATTERSON, JESSIE	113	PETTIT, CELESTIA C.	10	PITTS, THOMAS, REV.	88	PRITCHARD, CYRUS B.	15,36
PATTERSON, JOHN	54,67,74	PETTIT, DANIEL R.	111	PITZER, CLARA V.	26	PRITCHARD, D.A.	61
PATTERSON, JOHN, REV.	47	PETTIT, EDWARD	13,19,25,42,	PITZER, SADIE E.	5	PRITCHARD, DAVID	80,101
PATTERSON, JOSHUA	8,63		48,68,84,89,92,106	PLATT, LAURA	5	PRITCHARD, JOANNA	66
PATTERSON, LEAH	101	PETTIT, EDWARD, REV.	6	PLATT, NATHAN	76	PRITCHARD, R.B.	15,66
PATTERSON, MAGGIE	32	PETTIT, EDWIN	90,93	PLUNKET, ARTHUR	104	PRITCHARD, THERESA	61
PATTERSON, MARIA	3	PETTIT, ELIZA J.	82	POE, ADAM	103,113	PROBERT, CHAS.R.	49
PATTERSON, MARY	2,44,63	PETTIT, ELLA	91	POE, ANDREW	7,103	PROBERT, ELIZA	105
PATTERSON, MATILDA	107	PETTIT, JOHN	78	POE, ESTHER	32	PROBERT, MARIA	4
PATTERSON, NANCY	32,84	PETTIT, MATTIE	84	POE, GEO.	115	PROBERT, MR.	31
PATTERSON, ROBERT	86	PETTIT, SAMUEL	53,55	POE, JAMES	48	PROBERT, REUBEN	13
PATTERSON, THOMAS	3	PETTIT, SQUIRE	69,99,109	POLAN, J.M.	93	PROCTOR, DAVID	79
PATTERSON, W.E., DR.	44	PETTIT, WILLIAM B.	21	POLAND, CYNTHIA B.	89	PROCTOR, ELIZABETH	79
PATTERSON, WILLIAM	59,113	PFOFFENBAUGH, ANNIE	44	POLAND, MARIETTA	101	PROSSER, LAURA	82
PATTON, JAMES	51	PFOFFENBAUGH, JOHN	44	POLAND, MARTIN	89	PROSSER, MARY A.	91
PATTON, JAMES, MRS.	51	PFOFFENBAUGH, ROSA	44	POLLOCK, JOHN	94	PROUSE, ELIZABETH	51
PAUL, JAMES	94	PHELEN, R., REV.	110	POLLOCK, MARY	94	PROUSE, FRANK	12
PAUL, JOHN	35	PHILIPS, CURTIS R.	36	POLLOCK, SAMUEL	24,27,48	PROUSE, MICHAEL	51
PAUL, P.W.	96	PHILIPS, DAVID	91	POLLOCK, WILLIE	94	PROUSE, WILLIAM	51
PAULY, DANIEL	24	PHILIPS, HENRY	44	POMEROY, S.W., REV.	69	PROUTY, MILLIE E.	24
PAXON, ALFRED	24	PHILIPS, JESSE	116	POORMAN, PHILIP	52	PROVINES, ALLIE	60
PAXON, ELIZABETH	24	PHILIPS, MARY	22	PORTER, AELINE	71	PROVINES, JOHN	60
PAXON, JOSEPH, REV.	16	PHILIPS, NANCY	116	PORTER, ANNA FRANK	22	PROVINES, MARY	60
PAXON, MARY A.	24	PHILLIPS, ABIGAL	6	PORTER, ANNIE E.	74	PROVINES, ROSELLA	60
PAXON, NANCY ANN	24	PHILLIPS, ALBERT G.	63	PORTER, BIRDIE	110	PUGH, GEO.E.	50
PAXON, OLIVER	94	PHILLIPS, ANNA S.	83	PORTER, D.G.	33	PUGH, R.P.	4
PAXON, PHEBE B.	56	PHILLIPS, ANNIE	104	PORTER, DAVID	74,111	PUMPHREY FARM	23
PAXSON, ELIZABETH	7	PHILLIPS, DAVID	6	PORTER, ELLA	110	PUMPHREY, MARY	65
PAYNE, A.F.	50	PHILLIPS, DELLA	90	PORTER, ERBEN	71	PUMPHREY, W.W.	35
PAYNE, ROBERT	99	PHILLIPS, F.	3	PORTER, FLORA	91	PURDY, ADA	98
PEARCE, AARON	7	PHILLIPS, FRANCIS	19	PORTER, FRANCES	22	PURNELL, CARRIE L.	59
PEARCE, R.A.	93	PHILLIPS, ISAAC	44	PORTER, HENRY H.	22	PURVIANCE, W.C.	57
PEARCE, REV.	73	PHILLIPS, JAMES	19	PORTER, IRWIN G.	71,82,103	PYBURN, MARY	50
PEARIES, S.E., REV.	42	PHILLIPS, JENNIE	119	PORTER, JENNIE	110	PYLE, CALLIE	109

Name	Page(s)
PYLE, GEORGE W.	13
PYLE, HENRY	2
QUAIL, ELIZA J.	3
QUAIL, ELLEN	54
QUAIL, MAGGIE	19
QUAIL, MARY	25
QUAILY, ANTHONY	6
QUEST, MELISSA E.	2
QUIGLEY, SAMUEL, DR.	99
QUINLAND, MARY	72
QUINN, DENNIS	107
QUINN, EMMA	72
QUINN, JOHN	89
QUINN, MARTHA	68
QUINN, NELLIE	72
QUINN, THOMAS	72
RABISKA, MARIBAH	73
RAETHER, P., REV.	102
RAFFERTY, THOMAS	111
RAFFLE, LIZZIE	42
RAGAN, ZACHARIAH, REV.	104
RAHMANN, JOHN	60
RAILEY, MILTON	77
RAKESTRAW, JOHN	85
RAKESTRAW, MARY	95
RALEY, JAMES	70
RALEY, JEHU	112
RALEY, ROBERT	6
RALEY, THOMAS	112
RALPH, NATHANIEL	106
RALSTON, H.B.	114
RALSTON, LOUISA	97
RALSTON, M.BELLE	99
RAMAGE, LIZZIE	62
RAMSDEN, ANN	114
RAMSDEN, RICHARD	114
RAMSEY, ANDREW C.	54
RAMSEY, ELIZABETH	46,47
RAMSEY, ELLA F.	35
RAMSEY, HANNAH	23
RAMSEY, HENRY	16
RAMSEY, HOMER	101
RAMSEY, JAMES	38
RAMSEY, JOHN	35,54
RAMSEY, KEZIAH	35
RAMSEY, KEZIE	115
RAMSEY, ROBERT W.	1
RAMSEY, SUSAN	101
RAMSEY, W.K.	99
RAMSEY, WILLIAM	46,47,56,99
RAMSEY, WILSON	63,101
RANDALL, D.A., REV.	19
RANDALL, VIRGINIA	99
RANDEL, ANN	108
RANDELS, JOHN	98
RANDELS, LUCINDA	98
RANDLES, JOHN	33
RANDOLPH, BAILEY F.	64
RANDOLPH, CAL	102
RANDOLPH, CAROLINE	44
RANDOLPH, E.L.	98
RANDOLPH, ISAAC	7
RANDOLPH, JAMES	38
RANDOLPH, JOSEPH F.	77
RANDOLPH, KERSEY	15
RANDOLPH, NICHOLAS J.	44
RANDOLPH, RESIN	44
RANDOLPH, REUBEN F.	6
RANDOLPH, RICHARD	40
RANDOLPH, WILLIAM H.	8
RANK, A.	40
RANK, AMOS	30,62
RANK, HOWE	62
RANK, REBECCA	62
RANKIN, F.B.	102
RANKIN FAMILY	65
RANKIN, LAURA	102
RANKIN, PETER	65
RANKIN, R.J.	102
RANKIN, ROBERT	65
RANSOM, JENNIE	98
RANSOM, MARY	83
RAPPLES, ANN	11
RASH, ELIZABETH	22
RATHGEB, SOPHIA	96
RATTERY, ANDREW	90
RAUCH, G.F.	54
RAUCH, JONATHAN	8
RAVER, SARAH	79
RAY, ANNA C.	17
RAY, CELESTIA	24
RAY, HENRY W.	17
RAY, JAMES H.	101
RAY, JOSEPH	3,101
RAY, MARY	17,101
RAYL, S.AMANDA	106
READ, ALLEN B.	28,29
READ, MARY B.	28,29
READ, THOMAS	28,29
READ, WILLIS B.	4
REASNER, CHARLOTTE	107
RECK, WILLIAM H.	43
REDDICK, CUMMONS C.	20
REDDICK, CYNTHIA	95
REDDICK, JOHNIE	20
REDDICK, SAMUEL	95
REDDICK, SARAH E.	20
REDFOOT, DAVID	79
REDMAN, DANIEL	86
REED, A.C.	108
REED, ALLEN G.	32
REED, ELIZA A.	88
REED, ELIZABETH	102
REED, FISHER	3
REED, FLORENCE	92
REED, GEO.	20
REED, HANNAH	3,21
REED, HATTIE	110,111
REED, J.H.	85
REED, J.S., REV.	8
REED, JAMES	92
REED, JANE	28,29
REED, LEVADA	108
REED, LEWIS	7
REED, MRS.	119
REED, S.F.	88
REED, S.V.	108
REED, TAYLOR B.	58
REEDER, A.J.	13
REEDER, D.W.	88
REEDER, DAVID B.	26
REEDER, EDEN	66
REEDER, IVANNA	19
REEDER, JACOB F.	30
REEDER, JESSE W.	91
REEDER, LYDIA	19
REEDER, MAHALA	13
REEDER, THOMAS L.	36
REEDER, WEALTHY	111
REEP, ANNA	115
REEP, M.M.	33
REES, DAVID	103
REESE, ANNA M.	33
REESE, CAROLINE	84
REESE, JOHN	113
REESE, JULIA E.	10
REESE, LYDIA	10
REESE, MARY	113
REESE, MR.	57
REEVE, ELIZABETH	112
REEVE, JOSHUA	112
REEVES, HARMON	100,102,104
REEVES, HARMON,REV.	96,98,105
REEVES, REV.	82
REGAL, LETTIE	39
REGAL, SUSAN	23
REID, ELLEN B.	50
REILLY, I.B.	4
REINHART, ELIZABETH	56
REINHART, J., REV.	24,35
REITER, ISAAH, REV.	100
REITZELL, JOSEPH	69
RENEKER, OLIVER	73
RENKENBERGER, B.	55
RENO, CAPT.	12
RENS, ARBANA	67
RENS, DALLAS	8,67
RENS, HARRY	67
REVES, JOSHUA	22
REYNOLDS, JAMES	18
RHINEHART, ALICE	40
RHINEHART, ELIZABETH	40
RHINEHART, MARY	77
RHINEHART, SOLOMON	40
RHODES, DR.	58
RHODES, ISAAC	74,116
RHODES, LOUISA	82
RHODES, MARY	95
RHODES, WILLIAM	18
RHORBAUGH, JOSIAH	95
RICE, ANTHONY	40,41
RICE, BAKER	4
RICE, HENRY A.	38
RICE, MARGARET	40,41
RICE, REV.	4
RICE, SARAH	24,40
RICH, AUSTIE A.	57
RICH, DANIEL	8
RICHARD, HARRIET	97
RICHARD, WILLIAM H.	97
RICHARDS, ADAM	58
RICHARDS, CHARLES	19
RICHARDS, CLARA	46
RICHARDS, EDWARD	32
RICHARDS, FRANK,REV.	12,21,74
RICHARDS, GEORGE	92
RICHARDS, HANNAH	96
RICHARDS, HARRIET	46
RICHARDS, JANE	32
RICHARDS, MARTHA	77
RICHARDS, STEPHEN B.	87
RICHARDS, THOMAS	96
RICHARDS, W.K.	46
RICHARDS, WILLIE S.	74
RICHARDSON, A.	36
RICHARDSON, ALCINUS	3,4,12
RICHARDSON, ETTIE	102
RICHARDSON, JOSEPH	7
RICHARDSON, LYDIA	116
RICHARDSON, SAMUEL, REV.	51
RICHER, SAMUEL	13
RICHEY, ELIZA	3
RICHEY, GEORGE	56
RICHEY, JOSEPH	94
RICHEY, LEVI	94
RICHEY, MATILDA	56
RICHEY, SARAH	58
RICHEY, THOMAS	116
RICHEY, WILLIAM	3
RICKERT, ALLEN F.	72
RIDDLE, GEORGE T.	108,118
RIDDLE, GERTRUDE	118
RIDDLE, HENRIETTA	48
RIDDLE, J.A., MRS.	57
RIDDLE, JUDGE	71
RIDINGER, MATTIE	104
RIDOUT, WILLIAM	70
RIEL, MARY	78
RIGBY & FOSTER	11
RIGBY, CARRIE	85
RIGBY, ELIZA E.	72
RIGBY, MARY	85
RIGBY, TIMOTHY	81
RIGBY, WM.	85
RIGGLE, GEO.W., REV.	6,19,21,23,31,40,57,58,67,77,80,88,93,96
RIGGS, EMMA	118
RIGGS, THOMAS W.	26
RIGHT, AMANDA V.	1
RIGHTER, J.W., REV.	114
RIGHTER, LEWIS	100
RIGHTER, LEWIS, MRS.	100
RILEY, MATTIE E.	66
RILEY, MR.	3
RILEY, SOPHIA	102
RINEHART, CELESTA C.	6
RINEHART, ELIZABETH	68
RINEHART, JAMES, REV.	40
RINEHART, LYDIA	1
RINEHART, SOLOMON	68
RIPLEY, SARAH	118
RIPPLE, JERRY P.	103
RIPPLEY, JOHN	109
RISDEN, ELIAS D.	46
RISDEN, ISABELLA	46
RISDEN, JOHN W.	46
RISH, ANDREW	19
RISH, ANTHONY	35
RISH, JACOB	35
RISH, MARY	35
RITCHEY, ARBANA	8
RITCHEY, ELLA	81
RITCHEY, ISAIAH	7
RITCHEY, J.B.	102
RITCHEY, REBECCA J.	56
RITCHIE, MAGGIE	20
RITCHIE, MARION	90
RITCHLY, GEORGE	24
RITTENHOUSE, BARTLEY B.	7
RITTENHOUSE, ISAAC	91
RITTENHOUSE, ROSANNA	91
RITTER, ELIZABETH	101
RITTER, JACOB	70
RITTER, SAMUEL G.	99
RITZ, CATHARINE	98
RITZ, DENT L.	98
RITZ, JAMES	98
RIVERS, BOB	64
RIVERS, THOMAS	64
ROACH, ANDREW	20,54
ROACH, J.B.	61
ROANERT, AMELIA	67
ROBB, ANNA M.	42
ROBBIN, JAS.	37
ROBBINS, CATHARINE	80
ROBBINS, H.C.	23,44
ROBBINS, JAMES	37
ROBBINS, SALLIE	55
ROBBINS, WILL, REV.	85
ROBERTS, BENJAMIN	98
ROBERTS, EASY	54
ROBERTS, GEORGE M.	3
ROBERTSON, ANNA E.	105
ROBERTSON, BERT	22
ROBERTSON, CLEMENT S.	95
ROBERTSON, D.	105,109
ROBERTSON, J.L.	65
ROBERTSON, J.S., DR.	65
ROBERTSON, JAMES, DR.	19
ROBERTSON, JAMES L.	11,82
ROBERTSON, JOHN	9,30,53,82
ROBERTSON, JOHN S.,DR.	23,95
ROBERTSON, KATE R.	3
ROBERTSON, LIZZIE	38,95
ROBERTSON, M.	82
ROBERTSON, MARGARET E.	53
ROBERTSON, MARTHA	105
ROBINS, HENRY C.	13
ROBINSON, ALBERT H.	62
ROBINSON, ALEXANDER S.	81
ROBINSON, CHARLOTTE B.	20
ROBINSON, ELLA	63
ROBINSON, FLORA	93
ROBINSON, GEORGE	116
ROBINSON, HARVEY	118
ROBINSON, JACOB	116
ROBINSON, JOANNA	116
ROBINSON, JOHN	5,8,12,15,22,64,90,104
ROBINSON, JONAH	116
ROBINSON, KINSEY	116
ROBINSON, LOUISA	105
ROBINSON, MARY	85
ROBINSON, MILTON C.D.	42
ROBINSON, MR.	39
ROBINSON, MRS.DR.	37
ROBINSON, PRESLEY	24
ROBINSON, WALTER	42
ROBSON, ROBERT	43
RODEBAUGH, WILLIAM	101
RODGERS, ABIE A.	22
RODGERS, AMANDA M.	16
RODGERS, ANNA B.	13
RODGERS, J.M.	93
RODGERS, JOSEPH G.	93
RODGERS, M.C.	93
RODGERS, MARY C.	102
RODGERS, Z.R.	22
ROGAN, ELLEN	48
ROGEN, DANIEL	88
ROGER, GEORGE	63
ROGERS, DIOGENES	81
ROGERS, EDIE G.	1
ROGERS, ELI H.	62
ROGERS, G.FRANK	6
ROGERS, JOHN A.	78
ROGERS, JONATHAN S.	62
ROGERS, LINDLEY	62
ROGERS, MARY L.	58
ROGERS, MATTIE	9
ROGERS, PHOEBA	45
ROGERS, RAGAN	16
ROGERS, REV.	69,70
ROGERS, SUSAN	2
ROGERS, SUSANNAH	58
ROHER, EMMA	57
ROHER, JAMES	57
ROHER, LYDIA	39
ROHER, REBECCA	57
ROHOR, JAMES	71
ROHRBAUGH, EST.	67
ROHRBAUGH, FRANK	79

ROHRBAUGH, JOSIAH 35,36,48, 67,68,70,76,78,89
ROHRBAUGH, MARGARET 79
ROHRBURGH, JOSHUA 34
ROHRE, ELLEN 51
ROLLER, CAROLINE H. 1
ROLLER, EMMA 73
ROLLER, GENERAL 46
ROLLER, HENRY 8
ROLLER, J.R., REV. 1,27
ROLLER, JACOB 7,8,44,54,82
ROLLER, JAMES 26
ROLLER, JESSE IRA 1
ROLLER, JONES W. 28
ROLLER, JOS. 73
ROLLER, JOSHUA 20
ROLLER, LAVINA 40
ROLLER, LYDIA 20
ROLLER, M.L. 102
ROLLER, M.S. 16
ROLLER, MARSHALL 71
ROLLER, MARY 49,82,102
ROLLER, MAUDA L. 28
ROLLER, REV. 8,40
ROLLER, SAMANTHA A. 28
ROLLER, SAMUEL 1,81
ROLLER, W.B., REV. 82
ROLLER, WILLIE 20
ROLLER'S DAM 6
ROLLIE, JESSIE 100
RONEY, JAMES B. 23
ROOK, MARTHA M. 14
ROOSE, ELLA C. 24
ROOSE, MICHAEL 27
ROOSE, OELA 78
ROOSE, WILSON A. 24
ROOT, MONTERVILLE 78
ROOT, MR. 44
RORHL, SAMUEL 60
ROSE, DAVID 7
ROSE, MARJORY 86
ROSE, MARY 54,86
ROSE, WILLIAM 68,86,110
ROSEBERG, MRS. 9
ROSEBURGH, JOHN 31
ROSENBERRY, MARY 45
ROSETTE, JOHN 77
ROSH, MELISSA 30
ROSS, JOHN 74
ROSS, MAGGIE 23
ROSS, R.S., REV. 98
ROSS, W.D. 70
ROSS, WM., REV. 115
ROSSTON CIRCUS 64,66
ROTHGEIB, TOBIAS 79
ROTHWELL, MR. 113
ROUDEBUSH, LYDIA 24
ROUGH, BAZIL 63
ROW, CAROLINE 88
ROW, ELIZABETH 78
ROW, EMMA C. 31
ROWE, DORA 97
ROWE, LIZZIE 65
ROWELL, CHARLES 48
ROWLAND, ANNA 89
ROYER, ABRAHAM F. 10
ROYER, EMMA A. 64
ROYER, JOHN 70
ROYER, SARAH 18
RUBLE, DAVID L. 18
RUDER, EARNEST 65
RUDER, LENA 65
RUDESIL, WM.H. 28
RUFF, JOHN 6
RUFF, SAMANTHA 88
RUFFINGTON, A.J. 102
RUGGY, GEORGE A. 63
RUKENBROD, ED F. 25,30,115
RUKENBROD, EMMA F. 14
RUKENBROD, J.K. 44,115
RUMMEL, CELESTIA 91
RUMMELL, EDWIN 32
RUNDLE, WM.B. 77
RUNYAN, EMMA 31
RUPERT, REBECCA 110
RUPP, ANN 84
RUPP, CHARLEY 84
RUPP, EMMA 93
RUPP, HENRY 84
RURDAL, WM. 73
RUSELL, MAGGIE 81

RUSH, HELEN 84
RUSH, R.B., DR. 84,105
RUSLER, CATHARINE 40
RUSSEL, ANNIE S. 68
RUSSEL, MARY A. 79
RUSSEL, STEWART 68
RUSSEL, W.W. 79
RUSSELL, ALICE 78
RUSSELL, ANNIE 36
RUSSELL, ARIEL 108
RUSSELL, CHARLES A. 1,68
RUSSELL, DR. 113
RUSSELL, ELIZABETH 87
RUSSELL, GEORGE 4,102
RUSSELL, HARPER 61
RUSSELL, JAMES 98
RUSSELL, JANNETTA 76
RUSSELL, JNO.W. 107
RUSSELL, M.A. 76
RUSSELL, M.N. 26,33
RUSSELL, MYRON 36
RUSSELL, W.W. 76
RUSSI, FRIEDMAN 42
RUTH, DAVIS T. 63
RUTH, WM. 82
RUTHRAUFT, J., REV. 118
RUTLEDGE, EDWARD 46
RYAN, CATHARINE 100
RYAN, ELLEN 46
RYAN, J.C. 64
RYAN, KATIE 51
RYAN, MARY 107
RYAN, TIM 109
"SAINT GEORGE" 31
SACKETT, SIMMONS 25
SAINT, JOSEPH F. 81
SAINTCLAIR, MARION 9
SALTER, HENRY 65
SALTER, JOHN H. 90
SALTERWAIT, HUTCHEON 8
SALTSMAN, ALSIGNA 89
SALTSMAN, JAMES 89
SALTSMAN, MELINDA 78
SALTSMAN, WILLIAM A. 78
SALTSMAN, WOOSTER 78
SALYARDS, REUBEN 104
SAMPSELL, JOSEPH 36,42,44
SAMPSELL, REBECCA 99
SAMPSON, SADIE 99
SANDERS, HARRIET 68
SANDERS, THEODORE 107
SANDERS, WILLIAM P. 81
SANKERS, HARRIET 70
SANOR, CATHARINE 61
SANOR, FANNY 56
SANOR, G.W., DR. 34
SANOR, GEORGE 48
SANOR, JACOB 24
SANOR, JOHN 29,56
SANOR, PERRY 94
SAPP, MATILDA 96
SARAN, LIZZIE 57
SATTERTHWAIT, JOHN 74
SAUNDERS, ELLA 51
SAVACOOL, JOHN 31
SAVACOOL, MARY 77
SAXON, JOSEPH 74
SAXTON, JOHN 48
SAYLER, DANIEL 38
SCADDEN, SARAH 89
SCAIFFE, LILL 104
SCANDRETT, ALF K. 89
SCANNEL, ROBERT O. 18
SCATTERGOOD, A.L. 33
SCATTERGOOD, BENJAMIN 8
SCATTERGOOD, DAVID 9
SCATTERGOOD, SARAH E. 77
SCHAEFER, DAVID 43
SCHAFER, HELEN 67
SCHAFER, HENRY 67
SCHAFFER, AVINA 76
SCHAFFER, CHARLES B. 99
SCHAFFER, EMMA 89
SCHAFFER, HENRY 99
SCHAFFER, MATTHEW 1
SCHAFFER, SARAH E. 99
SCHAUWEKER, FRANKLIN 70
SCHAWECKER, ELVINA 115
SCHAWECKER, FREDDIE 115
SCHAWECKER, ROBERT 76,115
SCHERER, MARTIN 79

SCHILLING, CAROLINE 14
SCHILLING, JACOB F. 52
SCHISSLER, IRA P. 81
SCHLEY, CHARLOTTE 108
SCHMICK, C.N. 2
SCHNARENBERGER, SARAH 40
SCHOFIELD, REBECCA 33
SCHOLFIELD, DAVID 8
SCHOOLEY, ELIZA H. 66
SCHOOLEY, EMMA 5
SCHOOLEY, RACHEL 73
SCHOOLEY, RICHARD 73,95
SCHOOLY, LYDIA A. 20
SCHOOLY, WILLIAM 20
SCHOTT, MATHIAS 6
SCHROEDER, MARY 118
SCHUKERT, WILLIAM 112
SCHWITZER, MAYOR 103
SCINTHIEL, MRS. 94
SCIPLE, SARAH 63
SCOTT, A.T., REV. 47
SCOTT, ALEX, REV. 28,29,31,36
SCOTT, COE 86
SCOTT, ELDORADO 99
SCOTT, JAMES 115
SCOTT, JENNIE 120
SCOTT, JOHN 9,117
SCOTT, JOSEPH 73
SCOTT, JOSIAH 68
SCOTT, MARY J. 38,76
SCOTT, POLLY 27
SCOTT, REV. 78
SCOTT, ROBERT 12,36
SCOTT, T.A., REV. 30,34,35, 38,39,46,48,55,58,61,64,67, 69,70
SCOVIL, IDA 118,119
SCOVIL, LEMUEL 119
SCRAGG, RALPH 102
SCROGGS, ANNIE E. 100
SCROGGS, ELIZABETH 47
SCROGGS, J.J. 11,100
SCROGGS, JOSEPH J. 109
SCROGGS, M.Y. 100
SCROGGS, MARGARET 43
SCROGGS, REV. 109
SCULLY, PETER 74
SEACHRIST, ENOS 2
SEACHRIST, ISAAC 10
SEACHRIST, MR. 62
SEACHRIST, SUSAN 94
SEACRIST, WILLIAM 37
SEARS, MARSHAL 64
SEATON, JAMES 14
SEATON, KATE M. 58
SELL, FELIX 117,118
SELL, WM. 57
SEVIHART, JEREMIAH 56
SEVIHART, NANCY 56
SEYFORT, E.A. 62
SEYMOUR & BLAIR 18
SHACKLETON, FRED 108
SHAEFFER, A. 46
SHAFER, HOWARD 33
SHAFFER, ANNA C. 51
SHAFFER, ANTOINETTE 95
SHAFFER, ARHART 78
SHAFFER, AUGUST 115
SHAFFER, CLARA 115
SHAFFER, DAVID 14
SHAFFER, ELLEN 75
SHAFFER, FRED 115
SHAFFER, FREDDY W. 101
SHAFFER, GEORGE 41
SHAFFER, HENRY 64
SHAFFER, JANE 101
SHAFFER, JOHN 47
SHAFFER, LETITIA 79
SHAFFER, MARY 95
SHAFFER, MATTIE 99
SHAFFER, SAMUEL M. 40
SHAFFER, THOMAS 2,5,101
SHAFFER, WILLIAM 95
SHANE, ABRAM M. 72
SHANKS, J.D, REV. 58
SHANNON, JOHN P. 59
SHANNON, MRS. 59
SHANNON, WM.B. 63
SHARLEY, MARY E. 69
SHARP, ANNA 18
SHARP, B.F., REV. 42

SHARP, FRANK 67
SHARP, GEORGE S. 89,113
SHARP, JESTEEN 85
SHARP, LUCY 104
SHARP, MARY 91
SHARP, MR. 111
SHARP, REBECCA 113
SHARP, RENA 113
SHARP, THOMAS 91
SHARPE, W.J., REV. 22
SHARPNACK, ALVIRA 99
SHARPNACK, AMANDA 65
SHARPNACK, CHARLES 28
SHARPNACK, D.H. 88
SHARPNACK, DANIEL 2,47,99
SHARPNACK, FRANK, MRS. 2
SHARPNACK, HETTY 16
SHARPNACK, JOHN H. 65
SHARPNACK, PERCY 88
SHARPNACK, TINE 19
SHATER, JOSEPH 87
SHAUB, HENRY 70
SHAUB, JACOB 8
SHAW, ALEXANDER 72
SHAW, CATHARINE 23
SHAW, E.P. 92
SHAW, ELIZABETH 56
SHAW, GEORGE 40
SHAW, ISAAC 25,34
SHAW, ISABEL 23
SHAW, JAMES 23,56
SHAW, JOHN 23,104
SHAW, JONATHAN 10
SHAW, LOUISA 65
SHAW, MARIAH E. 30
SHAW, MARY E. 6
SHAW, ROBERT 105
SHAW, SARAH 76
SHAW, SUSANNA 43
SHAWBER, PHILIP 20
SHAWBER, SUSAN 20
SHAWECKER, MALINDA 76
SHAWK, E.M. 67
SHAWK, G.W. 67
SHAWK, GEORGIE 67
SHAWK, JOHN 60
SHAWK, MRS. 67
SHAWKE, ELIZABETH 99
SHAWKE, JACOB 54,99
SHEAN, MARTHA 98
SHEARER, ROBERT 91,93
SHEARMAN, ANNIE M. 1
SHEARMAN, ELLEN F. 5
SHEARS, M.B. 17
SHEARS, MARY J. 17
SHEASLEY, F.M. 75
SHEATZLEY, WINFIELD 100
SHECKLER, ELIZABETH 5
SHECKLER, GEO. 66
SHECKLER, JOHN 85
SHECKLER, SIMEON 119
SHECKLOR, MARY E. 117
SHEEHAN, --- 13
SHEEHAN, SARAH E. 56
SHEELY, JOHN 46
SHEEN, CHARLES 53
SHEEN, EMMA 101
SHEEN, JAMES 28,101
SHEETS, ALICE E. 117
SHEETS, B.E. 51
SHEETS, ELLA M. 63
SHEETS, GEORGE 74
SHEETS, HARRIET E. 2
SHEETS, HATTIE 47
SHEETS, HENRY 63
SHEETS, IRA 63
SHEETS, ISABELLA 86
SHEETS, JENNIE C. 100
SHEETS, JOHN 8,22
SHEETS, SAMUEL 47
SHEETS, SUE E. 8
SHEETS, W.H. 63
SHEETS, WARREN 16
SHELENBERGER, ANNA 77
SHELLENBARGER, MINERVA 19
SHELTON, ALICE A. 1
SHELTON, CATHARINE 4
SHELTON, DAVIS 24
SHELTON, H.B. 118
SHELTON, LETHA 77
SHELTON, MARY E. 40

SHENKEL, JANE BELL	43		
SHENKLE, ALBERT	21		
SHENKLE, JACOB	8		
SHENKLE, JOHN N.	4		
SHEPHARD, A.S.	48		
SHEPHARD, DR.	54		
SHEPHERD, CAPT.	88		
SHEPHERD, CARLISLE	88		
SHEPHERD, JOHN	108		
SHEPPARD, FORGE	118		
SHERBINE, W.C.	10,110		
SHERKS, GEORGE	47		
SHERMAN, ANNA J.	1		
SHERMAN, CHARLES W.	34		
SHERMAN, GEN.	74		
SHEROW, ELIZABETH	94		
SHEROW, MARY F.	8		
SHEROW, WILLIAM	94		
SHERRARD, ROBERT A.	82		
SHERROW, MR.	51		
SHERROW, SARAH ANN	9		
SHIDLER, J.H.	42		
SHIELDS, GEO.	63,95		
SHIELDS, JAMES	100		
SHIELDS, LAURA	95		
SHIMP, MARTHA E.	46		
SHIMP, PETER	46		
SHINGLER, JOHN	76		
SHINN, EDWARD L.	89		
SHINN, ELIJAH	119		
SHINN, HARRIET	52		
SHINN, JOS.A.	39		
SHINN, LOUISA	81		
SHINN, MARGARET	27		
SHINN, MARY A.	89		
SHINN, SAMUEL	77,78		
SHINN, THOMAS	8		
SHINN, WILLIAM	52,68,85		
SHIPMAN, G.	6		
SHISLER, NETTIE	111		
SHIVE, DAVID	26,65,83		
SHIVE, JOHN	54		
SHIVE, LUCINDA	65		
SHIVE, MAGGIE	70		
SHIVE, SIMON	104		
SHIVELY, A.	38		
SHIVELY, JOHN H.	23		
SHIVELY, LUSETTA	101		
SHIVELY, REV.	106		
SHIVELY, SOLOMON	28		
SHIVELY, THOS.J.	35		
SHIVERS, SARAH	96		
SHIVES, MARY A.	36		
SHIVES, TIMOTHY	36		
SHOEMAKER, ALICE	48		
SHOEMAKER, F.A.	46		
SHOEMAKER, JOSEPH	20		
SHOEMAKER, MARGARETANN	21		
SHOEMAKER, MARTHA	6		
SHOEMAKER, MICHAEL	9		
SHOEMAKER, SUSAN	72		
SHOEMAKER, SUSANNA	20		
SHOEMAKER, WILLIAM	21,59		
SHOFFT, MR.	114		
SHONS, SARAH J.	7		
SHONTZ, J.W.	89		
SHORTEN, JAMES	42		
SHORTEN, LIBBIE P.	42		
SHOUVER, PHILIP	73		
SHREVE, OSBORN	105		
SHRIVER, LEANDER	10		
SHRIVER, LIZZIE	105		
SHRIVER, P.	36		
SHRODER, ELIZABETH	30		
SHRODER, PHILIP	30		
SHUGART, JENNIE	81		
SHULL, GEORGE C.	5		
SHULTZ & BRO.	15		
SHULTZ, D.C.	35		
SHULTZ, DAVID	43		
SHULTZ, LADY	95		
SHULTZ, LYMAN H.	15		
SHULTZ, M.H.	35		
SHULTZ, MARTIN	43		
SHULTZ, MARY M.	35		
SHURTZ, ANNIE E.	3		
SHURTZ, JAMES	89		
SHUTS, MRS.	13		
SHUTT, DANIEL	13,14,15		
SHUTTER, MATTIE	83		
SIDDALLS, WILLIAM	89		
SIDLER, SOLOMON	8		
SIDWELL, ISAAC	22		
SIGLE, JULIUS T.	3		
SILLIMAN, WILLIAM S.	31		
SILVER, ABEL	4		
SILVER, DAVID	2		
SILVER, E.W.	38		
SILVER, WILLIAM	14,16		
SILVERS, MELIZZA	35		
SILVERTHORN, MAGGIE	28		
SIMKINS, JENNIE	94		
SIMMONITE, ELIZABETH	90		
SIMMS, J.H.	101		
SIMMS, MART B.	31		
SIMMS, MR.	84,115		
SIMON, ADAM	28		
SIMON, ANDREW	53		
SIMON, MISS	53		
SIMON, MR.	38		
SIMON, SUSANNA	28,80		
SIMPSON, DAVID	83,95		
SIMPSON, GEORGE A.	48		
SIMPSON, J.A., REV.	57,78		
SIMPSON, JOHN	93		
SIMPSON, L.	52		
SIMPSON, MAGDALENE	70		
SIMPSON, REV	42		
SIMPSON, T.C.	16		
SIMPSON, V.	52		
SIMSELL, H.E.	75		
SINCALIR, BENJAMIN	81		
SINCLAIR, A.F.	75		
SINCLAIR, CHARLES F.	75		
SINCLAIR, ELIZA	119		
SINCLAIR, EMMA	13		
SINCLAIR, LUCINDA	76		
SINCLAIR, M.A.	75		
SINCLAIR, O.C.	119		
SINCLAIR, W.	99		
SINCLAIR, WILLIE	75		
SINGER, JNO.	71		
SINNING, C.C.	68		
SINNING, ELIZABETH	68		
SINNING, LIZZIE	68		
SINSELL, EMMA	100		
SINSELL, HENRY	66		
SIPLE, FRANK	119		
SIPLE, LIZZIE	86		
SIPLE, MARY ANN	22		
SITLER, ALICE	98		
SITLER, ELIZABETH	98		
SITLER, EMARR T.	61		
SITLER, J.M.	25		
SITLER, S.H.	98		
SITLER, SOLOMON SR.	47		
SITTLE, MITCHELL	67		
SITTLER, HENRY O.	102		
SKEETER, AMOS	25		
SKELLEY, GEORGE	9		
SKILLMAN, J.B.	2		
SKINNER, GEORGE	91		
SKINNER, MARY JANE	66		
SKINNER, W.A.	66		
SKYLES, ROBERT	86		
SLACK, EDWARD C.	59		
SLACK, JACOB R.	52		
SLACK, JAS.H.	59		
SLAGLE, JONAS	102		
SLAGLE, KATIE	102		
SLAGLE, S.	82		
SLAVEN, ANDREW	18		
SLOAN, GEORGE	6,43		
SLOAN, J.W., REV.	25		
SLOAN, M.B., REV.	23		
SLOAN, MARGARETTA M.	6		
SLUSSER, MELISSA	74		
SLUTTS, J.J., REV.	77		
SLUTZ, M.J., REV.	92		
SMALL & SONS	15		
SMALL, C.F.	63,92		
SMALL, CLARENCE F.	55		
SMALL, FRANK	15		
SMALL, HELEN	68		
SMALL, PHIL	15		
SMALL, S. & SONS	5		
SMALL, STEPHEN	72		
SMALLEY, ANN	98		
SMALLEY, ISAAC	7		
SMART, ESQ.	88		
SMELTZ, DENNIS	39		
SMELTZ, FRANK	36		
SMELTZ, JOSEPH	62		
SMELTZ, SARAH	112		
SMILEY, DR.	98		
SMILEY, E.B.	92		
SMILEY, ELIZABETH	57		
SMILEY, EMMA	98		
SMILEY, S.	73		
SMILEY, WILLIAM R.	30,61,63		
SMITH, A.R., REV.	21		
SMITH, AGNES	81		
SMITH, ALCINDA	91		
SMITH, ALEXANDER	68,73,80		
SMITH, ALLIE	79		
SMITH, ANDREW	5		
SMITH, ANN	75		
SMITH, ANNA	78		
SMITH, BENJAMIN	8		
SMITH, BILLY	15,26		
SMITH, C., REV.	61		
SMITH, CALVIN	119		
SMITH, CHARLES	28,55,67		
SMITH, CHRISTINA	48		
SMITH, CLEMENTINE	114		
SMITH, D.J.	70		
SMITH, DANIEL	48,51,56,64,70, 72,85,92,120		
SMITH, DAVID	81		
SMITH, E.	78		
SMITH, E.A.	9		
SMITH, EDGAR	88		
SMITH, EDWARD	105		
SMITH, ELIZABETH	20,34		
SMITH, ELLEN	116		
SMITH, F.	109		
SMITH, FREDERICK	28		
SMITH, G.G., REV.	94		
SMITH, GEORGE	34,39,58,82, 87,91,97		
SMITH, HARVEY J.	45		
SMITH, HENRY	107		
SMITH, HERBERT	68		
SMITH, ISABELLA	120		
SMITH, J.B.	61		
SMITH, J.L.	1,31,120		
SMITH, J.L., REV.	95		
SMITH, JACOB	20,45		
SMITH, JAMES	75,78,89,103		
SMITH, JANE	68,75,103		
SMITH, JERRY	40		
SMITH, JESSE	106		
SMITH, JOHN	8,12,37,68,76,89		
SMITH, JOSEPH T.	109		
SMITH, JOSEPHINE	64		
SMITH, KATE E.	48		
SMITH, KATHRINE	79		
SMITH, L.W.	85		
SMITH, LIZZIE A.	109		
SMITH, LOU	99		
SMITH, M.S.	79		
SMITH, MAGGIE	22,82		
SMITH, MARGERY	53		
SMITH, MARTHA	55		
SMITH, MARY	27,31,80		
SMITH, MATILDA	19		
SMITH, MISS	72		
SMITH, MR.	27,66		
SMITH, MRS.	16,77		
SMITH, NANCY	111		
SMITH, NORA	119		
SMITH, ORSINA	55		
SMITH, P.W.	26,102		
SMITH, PHEBE	85		
SMITH, PRESTON	105		
SMITH, REV.	89		
SMITH, SADE	33		
SMITH, SARAH A.	107		
SMITH, SIMON	12,36		
SMITH, SUSAN	75,119		
SMITH, SUSIE	77		
SMITH, W.J.	69		
SMITH, WESLEY, REV.	20		
SMITH, WILL A.	106		
SMITH, WILLIAM	2,75,112		
SMITH, WILLIAM C., REV.	35,60		
SMYERS, PHILIP L.	18		
SNIDER, A.	54		
SNIDER, ALICE	101		
SNIDER, ANNA	25		
SNIDER, CHAS.C.	59		
SNIDER, ETTIE T.	11		
SNIDER, FLORENCE	58		
SNIDER, HATTIE	87		
SNIDER, JOHN	8		
SNODGRASS, ALEX	7,119		
SNODGRASS, MATTIE	23		
SNODGRASS, REV.	118		
SNODGRASS, S.W.	115		
SNOOK, JOHN	70,99		
SNOOK, MARY	99		
SNOWDEN, MARY J.	9		
SNYDER & STEELE	62		
SNYDER, ANNA	70,78		
SNYDER, CHARLES C.	78		
SNYDER, CLARK	85		
SNYDER, EDWARD	64		
SNYDER, ESTHER	80		
SNYDER, FRANK	88,89		
SNYDER, G.S.	54		
SNYDER, GRACE	84		
SNYDER, IRENE	95		
SNYDER, JACOB	74,86		
SNYDER, JOHN	80		
SNYDER, JOSEPHINE	19		
SNYDER, MAGGIE	118		
SNYDER, NANNIE	74		
SNYDER, SOLOMON	84		
SNYDER, SUSAN	12,84		
SNYDER, WILSON	80,103		
SOLCOTT, MARTHA	16		
SOMERS, LABAN	111		
SOMERS, LYMAN	24		
SOMERS, SARAH M.	9		
SOMMER, MARY ANN	61		
SOUDER, JOHN	9,79		
SOUDERS, MISS	13		
SOURBECK HOUSE	30		
SOUTHWORTH, DALLAS	66		
SOWDER, JOHN	27		
SOWERS, GEORGE	110		
SPAETH, JACOB	79		
SPAULDING, JUDGE	51		
SPAULDING, W.J., REV.	74		
SPENCE, EMMA	107		
SPENCER, ADALINE	77		
SPENCER, E.L.	80		
SPENCER, ELIZABETH	45,101		
SPENCER, JAMES	114		
SPENCER, JULIAN N.	36		
SPENCER, THOMAS	45,91		
SPIKER BLDG.	30		
SPIKER, QUINCY	53		
SPIKER, SIMON	53,54		
SPINDLER, W.R., REV.	69,70,72, 73,77,81,90,91,104,105,108, 109		
SPIRES, SUSAN	21		
SPITLER, MILLER M.	39		
SPONSELLER, CONRAD	42		
SPRINGER, AMELIA	3		
SPRINGER, ANNA	118		
SPRINGER, ARVILLA	59		
SPRINGER, DAVID	12,36		
SPRINGER, DR.	57		
SPRINGER, ELIZA	118		
SPRINGER, ELIZABETH	116		
SPRINGER, EMMA	59,120		
SPRINGER, GEORGE	6,120		
SPRINGER, IDA	96		
SPRINGER, JACOB	105		
SPRINGER, JAMES	12,36,82		
SPRINGER, JOHN	80,92		
SPRINGER, JOSEPH	59,67		
SPRINGER, LEONARD	12,36		
SPRINGER, M.E.	4		
SPRINGER, M.O.	16,23		
SPRINGER, MARCUS O.	57,58		
SPRINGER, MARY K.	27		
SPRINGER, NANCY	96		
SPRINGER, O.M.	57		
SPRINGER, PETER	39,86,118		
SPRINGER, REBECCA	105		
SPRINGER, REUBEN	96		
SPRINGER'S GRAVEYARD	78		
SPROWEL, EMMA	88		
SPROWL, B.	63		
SPROWL, C.	63		
SPROWL, LOUISA	37		
SQUIRE, E.R., REV.	59		
STABLEY, JOHN E.	72		
STACKHOUSE, ANNA	14		
STACKHOUSE, CHARLES	111		
STACKHOUSE, GEO.	33		

STACKHOUSE, MR. 110	STEVENS, GEORGE 115	STOKESBERY, ISAAC 73	SULIOT, EUGENE 110
STACKHOUSE, SADIE E. 69	STEVENS, JAMES W. 64	STOKESBERY, MYRA 73	SULLIVAN, BRIDGETTA 52,70
STAFFORD, DANIEL, REV. 110	STEVENS, JOHN 12,19	STOKLEY, MAYOR 98	SULLIVAN, WILLIAM 52,70
STAFFORD, JOHN 55	STEVENS, M.C. 46	STOLL, WILLIAM F. 51	SULTNER, GEORGE 4,43
STAHL, ROTCHET 67	STEVENS, MAGGIE 19	STONE, BENJAMIN 114	SULTNER, HENRY 62
STAHL, TOCHET 67	STEVENS, SARAH 23	STONE, STEPHEN 26	SUMMER, EMMIT 61
STALCUP, MINERVA 105	STEVENSON, ELLA 59	STONEBRAKER, IRWIN 31	SUMMER, GEORGE D. 110
STALCUP, WILLIAM 1	STEVENSON, HANNAH 103	STORY, GEORGE 72	SUMMER, MARY ANN 61
STALLCUP, ANNA 96	STEVENSON, MARY 15,104	STORY, MARY 72	SUMMER, SOLOMON 61
STALLCUP, FRANKLIN 91	STEVENSON, MR. 64	STOTHARD, J., REV. 74	SUMMERS, AMOS 11
STAMP, J.H. 14	STEVENSON, R.R., DR. 117	STOUFFER, DANIEL A. 110	SUMMERS, ANNA 11
STAMP, MARSHALL 89	STEVENSON, ROBERT B. 99	STOUFFER, JOHN 47	SUMMERS, CLEMENTINE 71
STANGEE, HENRY 92	STEVENSON, S.B., REV. 95,96,104	STOUFFER, LAURTES 93	SUMMERS, GALEN W. 71
STANLEY, AMELIA F. 45	STEVENSON, SAMUEL 64	STOUGH, CLARK 18	SUMMERS, HENRY D. 11
STANLEY, ANDREW 46	STEWART, ARCHY 101	STOUGH, J.HOWARD, REV. 80,81	SUMMERS, JOHN A. 61
STANLEY, BENJAMIN 18,64	STEWART, CATHARINE 19,21	STOUGH, SAMUEL 18	SUMMERS, LEVI 11,45
STANLEY, ELIZABETH 32	STEWART, DANIEL 46,60	STOUT, ANN 45	SUMMERS, MARY 11
STANLEY, ELLA 111	STEWART, DAVID 60	STOUT, DANIEL 45	SUMMERS, MELINDA 95
STANLEY, EZRA 89	STEWART, EDWARD 24	STOW, BARON, REV. 25	SUMMERS, ROSANNA 55
STANLEY, JOHN 11,54,96,100, 112,113	STEWART, ELIZABETH 46	STOWELL & WHITNEY 22	SUMMERS, SIMEON 53
STANLEY, JONATHAN 45,75	STEWART, EMANUEL 35,49,60, 61,64	STRABLEY, TILLIE 104	SUMMERVILLE, ADAM 93,109
STANLEY, JOSIAH B. 59	STEWART, EUPHEMA 92	STRAGER, AMANDA 7	SUMMERVILLE, ESAU 74,80
STANLEY, MARGARET 60	STEWART, GEORGE 115	STRAIN, MICHAEL, MRS. 43	SUMMERVILLE, EVALINE 80
STANLEY, MARTHA 96	STEWART, HOMER 14	STRAIT, CORNELIUS Y. 12	SUMMERVILLE, LOU 93
STANLEY, MARY 64	STEWART, HUGH 80	STRATTON, DELINA 23	SUMMERVILLE, MISSOURI 80
STANLEY, MATTIE C. 30	STEWART, JACOB 8,108	STRATTON, ELI 14	SUMMERVILLE, WILLIAM J. 74
STANLEY, MR 114	STEWART, JAMES 36,59,88,92	STRATTON, ELLA J. 23	SUPER, CAL 21
STANLEY, OVERTON 60	STEWART, JEHU W. 64	STRATTON, ESTHER 51	SURTZER, SOLOMON 2
STANLEY, REBECCA 59	STEWART, JENNIE M. 2	STRATTON, H.W., REV. 75	SUTTON, WILLIAM 27
STANLEY, SAMUEL 8	STEWART, JOHN 2,37	STRATTON, LAURA 112	SWAIN, REV. 78
STANLEY, THOS.L. 75	STEWART, JOSEPH 3,19,69	STRATTON, LIZZIE 112	SWALLOW, ANNA 111
STANSBURY, EVALINE 101	STEWART, JOSIAH 14,17	STRATTON, MARY 1	SWAN, J.N., REV. 2,4,8,10,11, 12,20,23,33,35,36,39,41,43, 47,48,49,50,51,52,53,58,67, 70,72,79,80,83,90,95
STANSBURY, JOSEPH 101	STEWART, JUSTICE 113	STRATTON, OLIVE 50	
STANTON, E.M. 51	STEWART, LOUISA 24	STRATTON, SALLIE 98	
STAPLETON, HARRY 80	STEWART, MAGGIE 119	STRATTON, SIMON 23	
STAPLETON, M.E. 54	STEWART, MARTHA 19,119	STRATTON, WILLIAM 7,50,72,98	SWAN, REV. 3,5
STAPLETON, OLIVE J. 54	STEWART, MARY 88	STRAUGHN, HARRY 120	SWANDER, J.I., REV. 103
STAPLETON, SUSANNA 19	STEWART, MATTIE 35	STRAUGHN, J.L. 64	SWANEY, ALSINUS 16
STAPLETON, WILLIAM 54,80	STEWART, R.MARION 46	STRAUGHN, JOHN 85,100,120	SWANK, CHARLES 14
STARKE, ANNIE 105	STEWART, ROBERT 109,119	STRAUGHN, JOSEPH 3,103	SWANK, ELIZABETH 102
STARKEY, HANNAH 89	STEWART, ROSANNA 35,49	STRAUGHN, LOIS L. 100	SWARTHY, EMMA 105
STARKEY, LEVI G. 65	STEWART, ROSENA 24	STRAUGHN, MARY 100,120	SWEANNY, HARRIET 66
STARKEY, MATILDA 65	STEWART, SAMUEL 13,60	STRAUGHN, MORRIS 1	SWEARENGER, ELIMELECH 25
STARKEY, NANCY 65	STEWART, SARAH 14,17	STRAUGHN, MRS. 103	SWEARINGEN, ALETHA 14
STARR, CALVIN 12	STEWART, SOPHIA 34	STRAWN, A.J. 61	SWEARINGEN, ELIMELECH 75,97,108
STARR, CLINTON 12	STEWART, WILLIAM 16,76	STRAWN, CHARLES 26	
STARR, ELLA E. 3	STIFFEY, REV. 97	STRAWN, DORA 94	SWEARINGEN, FANNY 94
STARR, HATTIE K. 120	STIGLEMAN, JENNIE 99	STRAWN, ESTHER M. 83	SWEARINGEN, G.T. 5
STARR, JAMES 2,16,59	STILSON, ALICE B. 4	STRAWN, JENNIE 61	SWEARINGEN, HARRY 94
STARR, JOHN 16	STILSON, FREDERICK W. 68	STRAWN, LOU 13	SWEARINGEN, JENNIE 94
STARR, SOPHIA 2	STITT, ALEXANDER 66	STRAWN, SAMANTHA 21	SWEARINGEN, JOHN T. 73
STARR, THOMAS 3,20,49	STITT, ELLAS 101	STRAWN, WILLIAM 6	SWEARINGEN, LISSA 32
STARR, WILLIAM 14	STITT, J.M. 66	STREET, ALTON 52	SWEARINGEN, LUCY 107
STATELER, LAURA 100	STITT, J.W. 107	STREET, ANNA 85	SWEARINGEN, MARGARET 4
STAUFFER, CELESTIA 45	STITT, JAMES 4,107	STREET, DAVID, REV. 119	SWEARINGEN, MARIA 75
STAUFFER, HENRY 8,22	STITT, JANE 81	STREET, JOHN 119	SWEARINGEN, RUTH 97
STEEL, ELIZA J. 71	STITT, JOSEPH 100	STREET, MARY J. 119	SWEARINGEN, SARAH 5,75,97,108
STEELE & SNIDER 59,62	STITT, LAURA 81	STREET, NANNIE 52	SWEARINGEN, THOMAS E. 99
STEELE, AMOS 119	STITT, MAGGIE 51	STREET, S.T. 69	SWEARINGEN, TOM 52,113
STEELE, HELLEN 90	STITT, MARGARET 101	STREET, SARAH E. 69	SWEENEY, A., REV. 81
STEELE, JOHN 13,87	STITT, THOMAS J.W. 32	STREET, WEBSTER 25,75	SWEET, THOMAS 108
STEELE, LOUIS 28	STITT, WILLIAM 101	STREET, WILLIAM J. 49	SWEITZER, DANIEL 67
STEELE, NELSON 62	STIVER, WILLIAM 111	STREET, ZADOK 30,37,52,54	SWICK, J.W. 105
STEELE, SARAH 62,69	STOCK, CLARA 52	STRICKLER, BARBARA 26	SWICK, J.W., REV. 103,104,112
STEELE, WALTER 13	STOCK, ELIZABETH 52,105,107	STRICKLER, DANIEL 71,78	SWICK, S.W., REV. 96,103
STEELS, WM. 87	STOCK, HENRY 105	STRICKLER, ELIZABETH 71	SWIFT, REV. 30
STEEN, ANNIE C. 7	STOCK, JASON 105	STRINGER, E.T. 94	SWIHART, JEREMIAH 56
STEEN, D.G. 16,55	STOCK, MARIA 105	STRINGER, THOMAS 94	SWIHART, NANCY 56
STEER, ELISHA 86	STOCK, MARY E. 72,89	STRINGFELLOW, MARY 113	SWITZER, --- 74
STEIN, MARY E. 73	STOCK, MINERVA 105	STRINGFELLOW, WILLIAM 113	SWITZER, AMELIA M. 32
STEINBECK, GEORGE 63	STOCK, REBECCA 105	STRINGFELLOW, WILLIE 113	SWITZER, CATHARINE 109
STELLER, JOSEPH 96	STOCK, SAMUEL 52,105,107	STROBLE, MARY 40	SWITZER, ELIZA 109
STEMLEY, KATE 19	STOCK, WILLIAM 105	STROHN, EDWARD L. 34	SWITZER, ELLEN J. 32
STEPHENS, JAMES 64	STOCKMAN, HESTER 98	STROUSE, BARTLETT 66	SWITZER, FLORIAN 74
STEPHENSON, M. 14	STOCKMAN, MARTHA J. 62	STUART, ARCHIBALD 77	SWITZER, JAMES 109
STEPHENSON, MARY 13	STOCKMAN, MARY 62	STUART, HUGH 8	SWITZER, JOHN 5
STEPHENSON, PETER 8	STOCKMAN, W.A. 62	STUART, JIMMY 59	SWITZER, LEATHY 21
STEPHENSON, SAMUEL 3	STOCKWELL, M.J. 74	STUART, JOHN 26	SWITZER, MARIA 7,92
STEPHENSON, THOMAS 3	STODDARD, HENRY 18	STUART, MARIA 77	SWITZER, MARTIN 44
STERLING, D. 118	STOFFEL, FRED S. 61	STUART, MOLLIE 81	SWITZER, MARY 44,55
STERLING, DAVID 93	STOFFEL, JOSEPH 72	STUCKMAN, LOMIE 67	SWITZER, SAMANTHA A. 43
STERLING, JAMES 21,97	STOFFER, DAVID 31	STUCKMAN, MARY E. 84	SWITZER, SAMUEL 8
STERLING, JOHN 60	STOFFER, ELIZA A. 84	STUCKRATH, JACOB JR. 75	SWITZER, SARAH ANN 43
STERLING, MARY 21	STOFFER, GEORGE 9	STULL, CARRIE 113	SWITZER, SOLOMON-SURTZER 2
STERLING, ROBERT 20	STOFFER, JACOB 7	STULL, JOHN M. 113	SYFORT, DORA 117
STERLING, VIRGINIA 75	STOFFER, LEWIS I. 9	STUNMAN, JOSIAH 35	SYKES, LORETTA 78
STERNE, CHARLES 68	STOKESBERRY, HENRY 89	STURGEON, A., MRS. 101	SYLVA, WILLIAM 104
STEVENS, ABIGAIL 64	STOKESBERRY, WARREN 87	STURGEON, H., REV. 110	SYNE, THOMAS G. 115
STEVENS, ALICE 103	STOKESBERRY, WILLIAM 3,91	STURGEON, LIZZIE 85,104	TAGGART, BROWN 87
STEVENS, CORA MAUD 19	STOKESBERY, ANNA 73	STURGEON, MARY ELLEN 24	TAGGART, C., REV. 58
		STURGEON, OTHELLO 116	

TAGGART, J.C., REV.31,41,69,97, 98,99,110,114,115,117
TAGGART, JOHN 7,115
TAGGART, M.E. 7,112,115
TAGGART, MARGARET 88
TAGGART, MARY 112
TAGGART, R.C. 98
TAGGART, R.F. 72
TALBOT, REUEL 85
TALCOTT, MARTHA 14
TALER, EVA 94
TALMAGE, EMMA 114
TALMAGE, MARY 100
TANNAHILL, CORA 77
TANNAHILL, JAMES 77
TANNAHILL, MARGARET 77
TANNER, HADLEY 68
TANNER, JAMES 2
TANNER, M.A. 98
TARR, WILLIAM 100
TATEM, JESSIE N. 3
TATUM, MATTIE 8
TAYLER, JOHN W. 12
TAYLOR, A.B. 31
TAYLOR, AMANDA 35
TAYLOR, ANNIE 35
TAYLOR, BELLE C. 26
TAYLOR, BUCYRUS 56
TAYLOR, C.H., REV. 81
TAYLOR, CALEB M. 4
TAYLOR, CHARLES 22
TAYLOR, CLEM 48
TAYLOR, COLBERTSON 35
TAYLOR, ELIZA 98
TAYLOR, ELMER 21
TAYLOR, EZRA 83
TAYLOR, HOWARD 31
TAYLOR, J.L. 107
TAYLOR, JACOB 30
TAYLOR, JAMES M. 59
TAYLOR, JESSE 32,91
TAYLOR, JOHN 26,103
TAYLOR, JOSEPH 60,92
TAYLOR, JULIA A. 30
TAYLOR, LEOTA 41
TAYLOR, LIZZIE 69
TAYLOR, MARY 24,56,90
TAYLOR, PLUMER 22,23
TAYLOR, R.W. 109
TAYLOR, RACHEL A. 22,23
TAYLOR, REBECCA J. 4
TAYLOR, REV.DR. 65
TAYLOR, ROBERT 19
TAYLOR, SADIE J. 49
TAYLOR, SUSAN 14,91
TAYLOR, SUSANNA 35
TAYLOR, THOMAS 4
TAYLOR, WILLIAM 4,104
TAYLOR, WM.M., REV. 95
TAYLOR, ZILLA B. 68
TEAGARDEN, S.B.,REV. 5,6,21,33
TEDROWE, V.A. 54
TEEGARDEN, ELDER 116
TEEGARDEN, FAMILY 110
TEEGARDEN, GEORGE 91
TEEGARDEN, MARY 91
TEEGARDEN, MATILDA 50
TEEGARDEN, REV. 86
TEEGARDEN, S.B. 74,75
TEEGARDEN, S.B., REV. 95,102
TEEGARDEN, S.T. 108
TEEGARDEN, URIAH 44,50
TEEGARDEN, URIAL 110
TEEGARDEN, WILLIAM 7,49
TEEGARDEN, WILLIAM, REV. 110
TEES, WM. 70
TEETERS, JOHN 8
TEETERS, R.W. 59
TEGARDEN, ELIZABETH 60
TEIL, SARAH 10
TELLIS, LOUIS 23
TEMPLE, EDWIN 59
TEMPLE, ELLA 59
TEMPLE, MENEMA 59
TEMPLIN, ELIZABETH 51
TEMPLIN, JOHN 85
TESCHER, ANNA 42
TEST, ALBERT B. 18
TEST, BENJAMIN 102,104
TEST, DRUCILLA 74
TEST, ISAAC 8

TEST, J.S. 94
TEST, JOHN B. 100
TEST, MARY L. 100
TEST, ROLAND 100
TEST, ZACHEUS 8,74
TETERS, JOHN 90
TETERS, MARY 90
TETLOW, MARTHA 111
THACKERAY, SARAH 108
THACKERY, ANN 27
THACKERY, CHARLES E. 27
THACKERY, THOMAS 27
THACKSTON, LILY 103
THACKSTON, VIRGINIA 103
THACKSTON, WILLIAM 103
THARP, BARBARA 75
THAYER, THOMAS 90
THEAKSTAN, JOHN C. 55
THEANA, OSCAR 38
THEISSE, MARGARET 63
THIEME, WALDEMAR 6
THOMAN, DANIEL 24
THOMAS, A.A. 2,4,5,8,56
THOMAS, A.H. 107
THOMAS, A.H., REV. 38
THOMAS, ANNIE E. 58
THOMAS, CATHARINE L. 46
THOMAS, CHARLES 118
THOMAS, EDWARD 21
THOMAS, ELIZABETH 87
THOMAS, EMMA 115
THOMAS, ENOS 45
THOMAS, EVA 115
THOMAS, EVAN 92
THOMAS, GEORGE W. 81
THOMAS, H.G. 58
THOMAS, HARRY G. 58
THOMAS, HENRY 38
THOMAS, J.M., REV. 100
THOMAS, JEFF 99
THOMAS, JEFFERSON 38
THOMAS, JENNIE 86
THOMAS, JOHN 12,36,95,102,119
THOMAS, LIZZIE 102
THOMAS, LYDIA J. 61
THOMAS, MARTIN 9,90
THOMAS, MARY 55,74,99
THOMAS, MOLLIE 120
THOMAS, OLIVER A. 85
THOMAS, RENNIE 99
THOMAS, ROBERT 38
THOMAS, SARAH 54,76
THOMAS, SQUIRE 114
THOMAS, STANTON 110,117
THOMAS, T.B., REV. 120
THOMAS, URIAH 13,45
THOMAS, VIRGINIA 32
THOMAS, WILLIAM 11,31
THOMPSON, ALICE B. 73
THOMPSON, B.F. 78
THOMPSON, BENEZETTE 66
THOMPSON, BESSIE 43
THOMPSON, CASSIUS C. 28
THOMPSON, CURT 9
THOMPSON, EDDY 57
THOMPSON, ELIHU 50
THOMPSON, ELIZA 109
THOMPSON, ELIZABETH 79,116
THOMPSON, ELLEN 19
THOMPSON, ELMIRA 78
THOMPSON, EMMA G. 89
THOMPSON, GEORGE L. 97
THOMPSON, HANNAH A. 32
THOMPSON, HARRIET L. 70
THOMPSON, ISABELLA 110
THOMPSON, ISABELLE J. 4
THOMPSON, J.R., REV. 73
THOMPSON, JENNIE 117
THOMPSON, JOHN 112
THOMPSON, JOSEPH 32,79,109
THOMPSON, JOSIAH 92
THOMPSON, KATE 33,101
THOMPSON, LEWIS 31
THOMPSON, LILLY F. 74
THOMPSON, LIZZIE 4,33
THOMPSON, LOUISA 98
THOMPSON, M. 29
THOMPSON, MAGGIE 95
THOMPSON, MAMIE 113
THOMPSON, MARY 4,32,81
THOMPSON, MINERVA 113

THOMPSON, MRS. 11
THOMPSON, R.G., REV. 75
THOMPSON, RALPH JR. 33
THOMPSON, REV. 117
THOMPSON, ROBERT 113
THOMPSON, S.I. 77
THOMPSON, SAMMY 16
THOMPSON, SAMUEL C. 30
THOMPSON, THOMAS 64,89
THOMPSON, TOMMY 16
THOMPSON, WILLIAM 110,112
THOMSON, AMY 20
THOMSON, JOHN, DR. 78
THOMSON, LAWRENCE 11
THOMSON, MARTHA 78
THORN, CHARLES, REV. 2
THORNTON, --- 25
THURMAN, A.G. 50
THURSTON, THOMAS R. 57
TIBBETTS, CHARLOTTE M. 42
TIFFANY, C.B., DR. 52
TILBROOK, WILLIAM J. 57
TILL, LIZZIE 67
TILTON, H.C., REV. 62
TOBEY, JACOB 73
TODD, ALBINA 104
TODD, ALEXANDER 107
TODD, BETHUNA 104
TODD, ELIZABETH 77,118
TODD, EMMA 107
TODD, G.E. 104
TODD, GEORGE 73,78
TODD, ISABEL 8
TODD, J.P. 12,34
TODD, JACOB B. 100
TODD, JOHN 13,77,87
TODD, JOSEPHINE 13
TODD, JOSHUA 9
TODD, L.E. 72
TODD, LAURA V. 43
TODD, LELAND 34
TODD, MAGGIE J. 34
TODD, NANCY C. 86
TODD, O.M., REV. 1,2,6
TODD, SHIVERS 99
TODD, THOMAS T. 100
TODD, WILLIAM 26,79
TOEFFINGER, HENRIETTA 41
TOLERTON, FANNIE M. 21
TOLERTON, H.A. 105
TOLERTON, HILL 90
TOLERTON, JAMES D. 4
TOLLERTON, JAMES SR. 43
TOLLERTON, ROBERT 74
TOLSON, DANIEL 50
TOLSON, DELILAH 13
TOLSON, GEORGE 42
TOLSON, JOSEPH 40
TOLSON, RACHEL 91
TOLSON, THOMAS C. 100
TOMAN, LEMUEL 102
TOMBAUGH, ELIZABETH A. 77
TOMLINSON, ALLEN J.R. 41
TOMPKINS, HENRIETTA 2
TOMPKINS, JAMES 107
TOMS, SARAH E. 79
TOOLE, JOHN 109
TOOT, J.M. 65
TORRENCE, H.M. 86
TORRENCE, J.W., REV. 6
TORRENCE, JOSEPH E. 22
TORRENCE, MILO 53
TORRENCE, OLIVER 53
TORRENCE, REBECCA 86
TOWNER, S.ELIZA 120
TOWNSEND, D.W., REV. 3,4,12
TOWNSEND, HARRIET M. 67
TOWNSEND, JAMES R. 98
TRAGO, SARAH E. 64
TRAIL, CHARLES 95
TRAIL, CONSTABLE 84
TRAIN, CELESTIA 25
TRAIN, EDMUND 25
TRAINER, LAURA 16
TRAIT, ALFRED 67
TRAIT, FRANCIS 67
TRANSUE, ELIZABETH 4
TRAVIS, ANNA 18
TRAVIS, JOHN 35,104
TRAVIS, MILTON 11
TREFFINGER, HENRIETTA 41

TREFFINGER, WILLIAM 33,57
TRENT, MOTTIE 72
TRESCOTT, ALLA 16
TRESCOTT, IDA 79
TRESCOTT, PHEBE 4
TRESH, LIBBY 93
TRIEP, ALICE 66
TRIFFINGER, HUBER 110
TRIMBLE & WRIGHT 50
TRIMBLE, BIANCA 7
TRIMBLE, R.P. 50
TRIMMEN, MARY A. 83
TRITT, CASPER 71
TRITT, H. 13
TRITT, HENRY 13
TROESCHER, CHARLES 64
TROTTER, ELIZABETH 105
TROTTER, HENRY 95
TROTTER, JAMES 105
TROTTER, JOHN 35,91
TROTTER, MARY 116
TROTTER, SARAH 91
TROXEL, REBECCA 50
TRUNIC, EDGAR 19
TRUNICK, BEULAH A. 28
TRUNICK, EDGAR 81,82
TRUNICK, ELIZABETH 38
TRUNICK, HENRY 54,82
TRUNICK, JOHN 65
TRUNICK, JOSEPH 38
TRUNICK, KITTY 81
TRUNICK, MARIA 38
TRUNICK, MARY 81
TRUNICK, NANCY 65
TRUNICK, RACHEL 2
TRUNICK, SENETH 112
TRUNICK, SOPHIA 65
TUCKER, FLORIEN 100
TUCKER, HANNAH C. 100
TUCKER, W.A. 100
TUCKER, W.ALLAN 27
TULLIS, ELLEN 76
TULLIS, IRA T. 68
TULLIS, IRENE 79
TULLIS, LOUIS 23
TULLIS, MANT M. 72
TULLIS, W.A. 21
TUNNISON, T.G., REV. 69
TURNER, GEORGE, MRS. 1
TURNER, MARTHA 97
TURNER, REV. 57,84
TURNER, ROBERT 20
TURNER, SARAH 63
TURNER, SUSANNA 13
TURNER, THOMAS 37
TURNER, WM.P., REV. 67,69,73, 90,107
TURRINGTON, PHEBE 57
TUTTLE, HENRIETTA 10
TWADDLE, JOHN 9,88
TWITCHEL, REV. 80
TYLER, HENRY 38
TYSON, ELIZABETH 73
ULERY, EMELINE 88
ULERY, JOHN 88
ULERY, MUZELLA 88
ULRICK, CARRIE 88
UMSTEAD, WM.H. 21
UNDERWOOD, EMANUEL 87
UNDERWOOD, JESSIE 62
UNDERWOOD, KATE 8
UNDERWOOD, LIZZIE 44
UNDERWOOD, MAHLON 98
UNDERWOOD, MARY 63
UNDERWOOD, MATTIE M. 7
UNDERWOOD, MILES 25
UNDERWOOD, RATIE 61
UNDERWOOD, WILLIAM 49,98
UNDERWOOD, ZULICA M. 47
UNGER, MRS. 9
UNKEFER, ELIZABETH 114
UPDEGRAFF, ELIZABETH 91
UPDEGRAFF, JACOB 91
UPDEGRAFF, WILLIE 91
URIE, MARTHA A. 8
URIE, WM.G. 22
URQUHART, WILLIAM 46
VALE, E.O. 37
VALE, JOHN T. 106
VALE, JOSEPH 106

VALLANDIGHAM, C.L. 3,34,38,53
VALLANDIGHAM, CLEMENT H. 37
VALLANDIGHAM, CLEMENT L. 50,51,56
VALLANDIGHAM, GEO.S., REV. 43,52, 69,73
VALLANDIGHAM, GEO.S.,DR. 37,49
VALLANDIGHAM, IRVING S. 19
VALLANDIGHAM, J.L. 65
VALLANDIGHAM, J.L., REV. 19,56
VALLANDIGHAM, JAMES, REV 51
VALLANDIGHAM, JOSEPH 62,87
VALLANDIGHAM, MARGARET 53
VALLANDIGHAM, MARMIAN 49
VALLANDIGHAM, MRS. 53
VAMMETER, MARTHA J. 29
VAN FOSSEN, NANNIE 106
VAN HORN, J.M. 76,80,89,90
VAN HORN, J.N., REV. 86
VAN HORN, REV. 104,106
VAN VOORHEES, C.E. 49
VANCE, CHARLES D. 59
VANCE, FRANK 108
VANCE, HELEN 25,109
VANCE, JOSEPH E. 52
VANCE, LYDIA 108
VANCE, ROBERT 95
VANCLEVE, WM., REV. 77
VANCYOC, EMMA 108
VANDEGRIFFT, ANN J. 36
VANFOSSAN, DANIEL D. 75
VANFOSSAN, MARY A. 18
VANFOSSAN, MILO 26
VANFOSSEN, ADELINE 47
VANFOSSEN, CARRIE 92
VANFOSSEN, GEORGIANNA 76
VANFOSSEN, ICAPHENIA 31
VANFOSSEN, JAMES 31,64,76
VANFOSSEN, LINNIE 55
VANFOSSEN, MARTHA 33,76
VANFOSSEN, WILSON H. 87
VANHORN, J.M., REV. 66,81
VANHORN, LARENA 77
VANHORN, WILLIAM 110
VANKIRK, B.H. 33
VANKIRK, ELIZABETH 26
VANPELT, MR. 39
VANSICK, SAMUEL 69
VANSKIVER, EMMA 88
VANSKIVER, F. 58
VANSYCKLE, SAMUEL 69
VANSYCLE, JOHN L. 78
VANSYOC, E.P. 6,8,9,11,19
VANVOORHES, C.E. 75
VATMAN, EDWARD, FATHER 49
VATTLES, LAURA 54
VATTMAN, E., FATHER 40
VATTMAN, REV. 69,89
VAUGHAN, J.C. 73
VAUGHAN, LUA 73
VAUGHN, ANNA M. 76
VAUGHN, ELIZA 96
VAUGHN, HOMER W. 106
VAUGHN, J.C. 79
VAUGHN, JANE 38,94
VAUGHN, JONATHAN 76
VAUGHN, JOSEPH 59
VAUGHN, LYDIA 106
VAUGHN, LYMAN H. 38
VAUGHN, MILLIE 10
VAUGHN, MISS 52
VAUGHN, REBECCA 85
VAUGHN, ROBERT 59
VAUGHN, W.G. 96
VAUGHN, W.H. 85
VAUGHN, WILLIAM 22,106
VEERS, JAMES 65
VEIGLE, ALICE 102
VENABLE, GEORGE 16
VENABLE, SARAH 16
VERNER, EDDIE 25
VERNER, ELIZABETH 109
VERNER, GIBSON 25
VERNON, S.M., REV. 105
VICKERS, E.L. 12
VICKERS, JAMES 4
VICTOR, MRS. 13
VIEGLE, JACOB A. 68
VIEGLE, JOHN 68
VIEGLE, LOUISA 68
VIERS, MADISON 106

VIVIAN, JAMES E. 84
VIVIAN, JOHN 84
VIVIAN, LOUISA 84
VOETTER, FREDERICK 10
VOETTER, JULIUS 10
VOETTER, MARGARET 10
VOGAN, C.B. 27
VOGAN, EDDIE W. 49
VOGAN, G.W. 49
VOGAN, J.W. 70
VOGAN, JOHN V. 26,36
VOGAN, M.J. 49
VOGAN, SARAH A. 70
VOGAN, SOPHRONIA 87
VOGAN, WILSON 3
VOGLESONG, CATHARINE 92
VOGLESONG, EMMA H. 88
VOGLESONG, GEO., REV. 22,24, 30,45,70,88,97
VOGLESONG, GEORGE A. 14
VOGLESONG, GEORGIA 97
VOGLESONG, J.E. 5
VOGLESONG, JOHN 5
VOGLESONG, SANFORD W. 92
VOGLESONG, SUSAN M. 24
VOGLESONG, WESSIE 45
VOLKERS, A.J. 76
VOLKERS, CHARLOTTE 104
VOLKERS, ELIZA 88
VON GOHREN, CLARA 75
VOTAW, AARON 116
VOTAW, CURTIS 81
VOTAW, FREMONT 116
VOTAW, JOHN 7
VOTAW, MATTIE 27
VOTAW, MOSES 8
VOTAW, RUTH 116
VOTE, J., REV. 91
WADDLE, J.L. 64
WADINGTON, JOHN 76
WADINGTON, MARY ANN 76
WADSWORTH, ADELINE 3
WADSWORTH, HATTIE L. 3
WAGELY, SOPHIA 3
WAGELY, WILLIAM 88
WAGNER, G., REV. 114
WAGNER, GOTTFRED 99
WAGNER, L., REV. 103
WAGNER, S., REV. 2,33,79,81, 82,95,96,119
WAGNER, T., REV. 7
WAGONHOUSER, ELIZABETH 79
WAGSTAFF, MAGGIE 104
WALKER, ANDREW 65
WALKER, ELLA 97,114
WALKER, EMMA G. 26
WALKER, FAMILY 45
WALKER, J.C. 36
WALKER, JACOB 83,87
WALKER, JANE 55
WALKER, JOHN M. 76
WALKER, KATE 63
WALKER, LEWIS 55,62,87
WALKER, MARTHA 95
WALKER, MARY ANN 99
WALKER, NANCY 46
WALKER, ROSA 91
WALKER, S.A. 68
WALKER, SAMSON 62
WALKER, WILLIAM 56,111
WALL, ELIZABETH 28,29
WALL, JOHN 28,29
WALL, PETER 28,29
WALL, THOS.M. 37
WALLACE, ANN 44,74
WALLACE, EDWARD 107
WALLACE, GEORGE 104
WALLACE, HANNAH 90
WALLACE, HARRY H. 69
WALLACE, J.B., REV. 66,68,69
WALLACE, J.H. 109
WALLACE, J.M., REV. 98
WALLACE, JOHN 26,73
WALLACE, M., REV. 81
WALLACE, MARTHA 44
WALLACE, MARY 69,109
WALLACE, NELSON 98
WALLACE, R.J. 73
WALLACE, REBECCA 104
WALLACE, REV. 65

WALLACE, SARAH 21
WALLACE, STACY 98,107
WALLACE, VIRGINIA 107
WALLACE, W.H. 104
WALLACE, WILLIAM 21
WALSER, HENRY 116
WALTER, DAVID 110
WALTER, HARRISON 110
WALTER, HENRY 80
WALTER, J.M. 100
WALTER, THOMAS 55,110
WALTERS, ANNA W. 11
WALTERS, ELLA 25
WALTERS, GEORGE, MRS. 114
WALTERS, LYDIA 110
WALTON, DANIEL 70
WALTON, FLORA 70
WALTON, JOSIAH 8
WANEY, CHARLES 44
WANEY, SARAH 44
WANEY, WM.S. 74
WANSETLER, ANNIE 76
WANSETLER, CATHARINE 98
WARD, A.E., REV. 18,19,109, 114,118
WARD, A.S. 69
WARD, ALBION M. 10
WARD, ALEXANDER 75
WARD, ALICE 90
WARD, AMELIA 95
WARD, AMFIELD C. 88
WARD, DAVID 19,95
WARD, DENNIS 95
WARD, E.D. 37
WARD, ELIZA N. 90
WARD, ELIZABETH J. 82
WARD, ENGELINE 41
WARD, ETTA 37
WARD, EUGENE J. 38
WARD, F.J. 82
WARD, FRANK D. 86
WARD, HARRY 41,95
WARD, J. 82
WARD, JACOB A. 68,80
WARD, JAMES 53,110
WARD, JOSHUA 75
WARD, LEVI 41
WARD, LYDIA A. 68
WARD, M. 116
WARD, MARGARET 39,82
WARD, MARY A. 40
WARD, MAXIN 68
WARD, MICHAEL 99
WARD, MORRIS 95
WARD, NANCY 61
WARD, P.J., REV. 111,113
WARD, PHEBE 95
WARD, REBECCA 57
WARD, S.J. 37
WARD, WILDLY 30
WARD, WILLIAM E. 68
WARE, SARAH E. 20
WARICK, W. 78
WARNER, A.H., REV. 115
WARNER, E.O. 17
WARNER, ISRAEL 7
WARNER, JACOB 23
WARNER, PHOEBE 94
WARNER, SAMUEL 85,89
WARNER, THOMAS 94
WARNER, W.F., REV. 65
WARR, WILLIAM 79
WARREN, JOB 114
WARREN, REBECCA 114
WARREN, SAMUEL 53
WARRICK, ELLA 42
WARRICK, CATHARINE 45
WARRICK, HARROLD M. 103
WARRICK, J.F. 103
WARRICK, JONATHAN 45
WARRICK, JOSEPH 11
WARRICK, LAWRENCE J. 45
WARRICK, M.J. 103
WARRING, DEBORAH 101
WARRINGTON, CHARLES 87
WASHBURN, REV. 82
WASHBURN, SILAS W. 69
WATERS, EMILY 80
WATERS, GEORGE 79
WATERS, LIZZIE 12

WATERS, MELISSA 83
WATERS, MRS. 79
WATSON, ALLEN 89
WATSON, ALVA T. 67
WATSON, CHARLES M. 108
WATSON, DAVID 50
WATSON, ELIZABETH 67
WATSON, ELVIN 67
WATSON, HANNAH 50
WATSON, HARRY 113
WATSON, JAMES H. 45
WATSON, JOHN 87
WATSON, JOSEPH 7,29
WATSON, MR. 39
WATSON, NATHAN B. 67
WATSON, ROBERT 28
WATSON, THOMAS 5
WATSON, W.H. 55,115,116
WATSON, WILLIAM 96
WATT, DANIEL 12,36
WATT, ESQ. 55
WATT, JOHN 12
WATT, REUBEN 5,44
WATT, WM. 57
WAY, A.B., REV. 50,57,59
WAY, ANNA M. 78
WAY, B.F. 60
WAY, CALEB 66
WAY, FORTUNE 66
WAY, JESSE W. 53
WAY, JOHN 105
WAY, THOMAS 32
WEAVER, ADA 111
WEAVER, ANDREW 7,73
WEAVER, ANNA 100
WEAVER, ANNIE 114
WEAVER, CORNELIA F. 30
WEAVER, ELIZABETH 13
WEAVER, ELLA 91
WEAVER, EMMOR T. 6
WEAVER, GEORGE E. 107
WEAVER, GULIELMA 89
WEAVER, HENRY B. 34,107
WEAVER, ISAAC 2,3,5,6,8,9,63, 75
WEAVER, JENNIE 77,78
WEAVER, JOHN 25,91,95,98, 106,114
WEAVER, LOMINA 46
WEAVER, LUCENA 107
WEAVER, MARY 6,31,46
WEAVER, N.H., REV. 14,23,25, 30,64,70,80,82,86
WEAVER, ROSE 25,72
WEAVER, S., REV. 30
WEAVER, WILLIAM 111,115
WEAVER, WILLIS 87
WEBB, ANGELINE 36
WEBB, ANN 77,78
WEBB, ANNA 59
WEBB, ELLA 64
WEBB, H., REV. 98
WEBB, ISAAC 21,78,87
WEBB, J.MORRIS 97
WEBB, JOHN D. 96
WEBB, JOSEPH 23
WEBB, JOSHUA 13
WEBB, LAURA A. 7
WEBB, MARY 14
WEBB, REBECCA 76
WEBB, RICHARD 1
WEBB, THOMAS 8
WEBB, URBAN F. 100
WEBBER, ALBERT 93
WEBBER, ELLA 119
WEBER, AUGUSTA 85
WEBER, ELIZABETH 21
WEBER, J.A. 85
WEBER, WILLY A. 85
WEBSTER, DOLLY 82
WEBSTER, GEORGE 111
WEBSTER, JOHN 30
WEBSTER, LARY 89
WEBSTER, M.A. 89
WEBSTER, SARAH 23
WEDDLE, P.W., REV 10
WEDEN, WILLIAM W. 2
WEDLOCK, MARTHA 84
WEEDON, W.W. 92
WEEKS, CHARLES H. 16

WEIGAND, ANDREW 99
WEIGAND, CAROLINE 99
WEIGHTENHOUSER, ELIZ'TH 79
WEIKART, DAVID 86
WEIKART, JAMES C. 115
WEIKERT, HIRAM 57
WEIKERT, JAMES 51
WEIKERT, MARY A. 57
WEIKERT, W.D. 82
WEISS, DENNIS 39
WEKER, EMMA 114
WELBORNE, SUSAN 66
WELCH, ALBERT 51
WELCH, ED. 14
WELCH, FRANK E. 24
WELCH, GEORGE 90
WELCH, JACOB 97
WELCH, JOSEPH 111
WELCH, JOSIE 111
WELCH, KATE 24
WELCH, LOUISA J. 54
WELCH, MARCELLA 97
WELCH, MARY 2
WELCH, REASON 96
WELCH, ROBERT 24
WELCH, THOMAS 93
WELDMAN, JOSHUA 22
WELDON, LOUISA 96
WELHELMENA, MRS. 30
WELK, ANNA M. 46
WELKER, CHARLES E. 27
WELKER, CHRISTIANA 63
WELKER, JACOB 27
WELKER, JAMES 52
WELKER, JENNIE 2
WELKER, KATE 115
WELKER, MR. 27
WELKER, PERRY 95
WELKER, PHOEBE ANN 52
WELKER, RACHEL 27
WELKER, VIOLET 92
WELKER, WALLACE W. 106
WELKER, WILLIAM 94
WELLER, J.Q.A., REV. 35
WELLINGTON, CATHARINE 39
WELLINGTON, J.L. 70
WELLINGTON, JASON 48
WELLINGTON, LENA D. 48
WELLINGTON, MARTHA 48
WELLMAN, CARRIE D. 29
WELLMAN, JULIA 63
WELLS, EMMA 91
WELLS, ESTHER 103
WELLS, GEO. JR. 33
WELLS, HOMER C. 51
WELLS, JOSEPH 116
WELLS, PETER 7
WELLS, W.G. 103
WELLS, W.P. 51
WELLS, WILLIE 103
WELSH, EDWARD 63
WELSH, MISS 113
WELSH, PETER 37
WELTON, JAMES W. 30
WENTZ & PARKS 10
WERE, DORLISHA 50
WERNET, MAGGIE 67
WERTZ, ALONZO 9
WEST, ANNIE M. 106
WEST, CONSTABLE 108
WEST, EMMA 109,115
WEST, GEORGE 22,45
WEST, ISABEL 32
WEST, MAGGIE 35
WEST, NANCY McCOY 45
WEST, PHOEBE 64,65
WESTFALL, ADDIE 88
WESTFALL, ELI 10,94
WESTFALL, NANNIE 94
WESTON, BYRON 66
WESTON, JESSIE 66
WESTON, UNDINE 66
WETHERSPOON, TRESSA 75
WEYL, CALVIN 58
WHAN, JAMES 119
WHAN, JENNIE 105
WHAN, MARY 95
WHAN, WILLIAM 58,103
WHANG, MR. & MRS. 24
WHARTON, DANIEL 4
WHARTON, J.T. 97

WHARTON, MARTHA 4
WHEATLEY, JOHN 66
WHEATLEY, MICHAEL 45
WHEATLEY, ROBERT W. 45
WHEDON, FRANC 104
WHEELER, OGDEN 36
WHEELER, REBECCA 90
WHERRY, HIRAM 64
WHIMPEY, ELIZA 41
WHIMPEY, ISAAC 41
WHINERY, ABIE 28,29
WHINERY, AMY 94
WHINERY, CHARLES L. 76
WHINERY, DAVID 94
WHINERY, FOSTER 48
WHINERY, GERTRUDE 87
WHINERY, JEREMIAH 40
WHINERY, JOSEPH B. 28,29
WHINERY, JOSEPHINE 85
WHINERY, MAHLON 38
WHINERY, MATTIE 94
WHINERY, REBECCA 19
WHINERY, SAMUEL 112
WHINERY, THOMAS 33
WHINERY, ZIMRI 10
WHITACRE, AGLINE 117
WHITACRE, ALCY 110
WHITACRE, ANNIE 75
WHITACRE, CATHARINE 28,29,49
WHITACRE, CORNELIUS 42
WHITACRE, DAVID 49,66
WHITACRE, E. 2
WHITACRE, EDWARD 92
WHITACRE, ELBRIDGE 119
WHITACRE, FRANK P. 81
WHITACRE, GEORGE 74
WHITACRE, HANNAH 94
WHITACRE, IDA M. 93
WHITACRE, JANE 64
WHITACRE, JOHN 25,64,94,104
WHITACRE, JOHN JR. 12,36
WHITACRE, JONATHAN 23,94
WHITACRE, JOSEPH Y. 101
WHITACRE, JOSHUA 3
WHITACRE, MAGGIE 103
WHITACRE, MARION 66
WHITACRE, MARY 66,116
WHITACRE, ROBERT 54,117
WHITACRE, SAMANTHA 3
WHITACRE, SEYRENE 59
WHITACRE, URIAH 8
WHITACRE, WILLIAM 83,103,117
WHITAKER, MARY 66
WHITE, AMELIA 24
WHITE, AUZY 11
WHITE, D.J. 4,8,10,18
WHITE, ELIZABETH A. 10
WHITE, GEORGE 95
WHITE, H.J., REV. 48
WHITE, HANNAH 25
WHITE, I.N., REV. 4,6,18,21,-
28,29,30,31,34,58,82,96,97
WHITE, ISAAC 25
WHITE, J.D. 7
WHITE, JOHN 24,34,37
WHITE, LOU C. 88
WHITE, MARY 34,71
WHITE, MOSES S. 23
WHITE, REV. 20,98
WHITE, SAMUEL 54,104
WHITE, T.H. 92
WHITE, THOMAS H. 16
WHITEFOOT, JOHN 72
WHITEFOOT, SARAH 72
WHITELEATHER, CLARISSA 26
WHITELEATHER, FRANKLIN 115
WHITELEATHER, J.M. 96
WHITELEATHER, O.H. 108
WHITELEATHER, SIMON 26
WHITELY, KATE 19
WHITESTONE, CATHARINE 44
WHITESTONE, CHARLIE 44
WHITESTONE, RICHARD 44
WHITLA, JOSEPH L. 85
WHITNEY & STOWELL 22
WHITNEY, LEE 98
WHITNEY, LENA J. 92
WHITNEY, MATTIE 92,98
WHITNEY, W.C. 92
WHITNEY, WATSON 9,98
WHITTON, EDMUND J. 9

WICKART, JOHN 8
WICKERSHAM, ALLEN 33
WICKERSHAM, AMY 26,27
WICKERSHAM, LYDIA C. 75
WICKERSHAM, PHILIP 26,27
WICKERSHAM, WILLIAM 8
WICKES, THOS., DR. 18
WICKLINE, BELLE J. 27
WIGNET, C.L., REV. 72
WILAMAN, NANCY 5
WILCOX, JEREMIAH 54
WILCOXEN, JOHN L. 14
WILCOXEN, NATHAN 116
WILCOXIN, CLARENCE V. 70
WILCOXON, JENNIE 90
WILDERSON, ELIZABETH 77
WILDMAN, JOSHUA 22
WILDWOOD, JAMES 8
WILES, FRANK 106
WILES, POLLY 20
WILEY, ELLEN E. 31
WILEY, JAMES 62,63
WILEY, JOHN 60
WILEY, LOU A. 35
WILEY, MARY E. 60
WILHELM, HENRY 93
WILHELM, JACOB 88
WILHELM, VALENTINE 43
WILKENS, JOSEPH 22
WILKENS, WARREN H. 22
WILKIN, J.B., REV. 69,91,104
WILKIN, MAGGIE 104
WILKINS, JOSEPH 83
WILKINS, WM. 90
WILKINSON, MARY 82
WILL, ALONZO 90
WILL, CHRISTIAN 90
WILLARD & CHILD 2
WILLETS, GEO 7
WILLETS, JOHN 103
WILLETS, MARY ANN 25
WILLETTS, MARY 103
WILLHELM, MR. 64
WILLI, GEO. 53
WILLIAMS, ANN 25
WILLIAMS, BAZIL 98
WILLIAMS, BELLE 118
WILLIAMS, BEN 82
WILLIAMS, CAROLINE 96
WILLIAMS, CASPER 90
WILLIAMS, CHAS. 81
WILLIAMS, DANIEL 96
WILLIAMS, DAVID 8,25,72
WILLIAMS, DORA 93
WILLIAMS, ELIZABETH 8
WILLIAMS, ELLA 98
WILLIAMS, EUPHEMIA 11
WILLIAMS, FRANCES 35
WILLIAMS, FRANK 118
WILLIAMS, GEORGE 80
WILLIAMS, HARRIET 93
WILLIAMS, HENRY 63
WILLIAMS, J.A. 91
WILLIAMS, JOHN 6,73,74,96
WILLIAMS, JOHN, REV. 1
WILLIAMS, JOSEPH B. 106
WILLIAMS, LIZZIE 1
WILLIAMS, LYDIA 22
WILLIAMS, MAGGIE J. 6
WILLIAMS, MARY 18,106
WILLIAMS, MATTIE 40
WILLIAMS, MINUS A. 19
WILLIAMS, MOLLIE 114
WILLIAMS, N.P. 73
WILLIAMS, REBECCA 73,85
WILLIAMS, RICHARD 88
WILLIAMS, ROBERT 44
WILLIAMS, ROSANNA 97
WILLIAMS, SAMUEL 45,54,81
WILLIAMS, SUSAN 43
WILLIAMS, TAMER 40
WILLIAMS, TRACY 72
WILLIAMS, WESLEY 118
WILLIAMS, WEST 93
WILLIAMS, WM.C. 26
WILLIAMSON, CLARISSA 1
WILLIAMSON, ISAAC 95
WILLIAMSON, LAVINA 1
WILLIAMSON, LIZZIE 93
WILLIAMSON, LUCINDA 85
WILLIAMSON, THOMAS 85

WILLIARD, ADAM 5
WILLIARD, DEWALT 98
WILLIARD, ELIZABETH 23,77
WILLIARD, G.W., REV. 117
WILLIARD, GASPER 8
WILLIARD, JOHN 23,26,63
WILLIARD, M.T. 9
WILLIARD, ROSA 11
WILLIARD, RUSSELL 3
WILLINGTON, CHARLES 22
WILLINGTON, JASON 22
WILLISTON, JOHN 45
WILLITS, S.R. 8
WILLS, GEORGE 75
WILLYARD, MAGDELENA 50
WILSON, A., REV. 105
WILSON, AARON 26
WILSON, AARON, MRS. 100
WILSON, ADDIE 94,103
WILSON, ALVIRA 47
WILSON, AMASETT C. 45
WILSON, ANDREW, REV. 9
WILSON, ANNA 80
WILSON, B.F. 21
WILSON, BYRON F. 42
WILSON, CATHARINE 42
WILSON, DAVID 7
WILSON, DELLA 24
WILSON, DR. 78
WILSON, E.W. 106
WILSON, EDWARD C. 84
WILSON, EMMOR R. 29
WILSON, FLORA 104
WILSON, GERTIE 41
WILSON, HARRIET 80,106
WILSON, HARRY 75
WILSON, HOMER H. 110
WILSON, IDELIA 24
WILSON, ISAAC 50
WILSON, ISADORE 42
WILSON, J. 54
WILSON, J.B. 106
WILSON, J.R. 41
WILSON, JAMES 8,14,18,65,94
WILSON, JENNIE 116
WILSON, JESSE 21,54
WILSON, JOHN 24,35,39,40,42,
102
WILSON, JOHN N., REV. 31
WILSON, JOSEPH 32
WILSON, K.AUGUSTA 65
WILSON, LIZZIE 25,90
WILSON, M.A. 24
WILSON, M.J. 41
WILSON, MAGGIE 66,99
WILSON, MARY 24,50,94,99
WILSON, R.C. 84,93
WILSON, REV.MR. 83
WILSON, RHODERICK 66
WILSON, RODRICK 99
WILSON, SADIE A. 24
WILSON, SAMUEL 3,35,110
WILSON, SARAH 61
WILSON, SUSAN W. 21
WILSON, TACY 46
WILSON, THOMAS B. 1,50
WILSON, URIAH 24
WILSON, W., REV. 75
WILSON, W.T. 46
WILSON, WILLIAM 110,118
WILT, SYLVESTER 117
WIMER, CHRISTIANA 92
WIMER, WILLIAM 92
WINDELL, ALPHARETTA 45
WINDELL, BENJAMIN 38
WINDER, A.A. 9
WINDER, AARON 73
WINDER, E.J. 69
WINDER, L.H. 69
WINDER, MARTHA J. 69
WINDLE, EDWIN 94
WINDLE, FRANK 104
WINDLE, IDA 88
WINDLE, JOSEPH J. 107
WINDLE, MARY J. 63
WINDLE, SUSAN 69
WINES, ABNER 63,81
WINES, FRANK 6
WINES, HEDGEMAN 1
WINES, HELEN 52
WINES, MRS. 1

147

WINGET, C.L., REV. 63,64,73,75, 85,91,93,95,97,102,104,105, 108,116,117
WIREBAUGH, G.W. 13
WIRT, ELMIRA 62
WIRTS, MELISSA 105
WISDEN, LIZZIE 77
WISDEN, SIMON 37
WISE, JOHN 27
WISE, MARY ANN 27
WISEMAN, S.P. 73
WISLER, ANTHONY 58
WISLER, MAGDELENA 58
WISMAN, JANE 28,29
WISMAN, LEVI 20
WISMAN, MARTHA 20
WISMAN, MARY ANN 20
WISNER, ELIZA J. 54
WISNER, ELLEN S. 34
WISNER, SAMUEL 79
WITNEY, ETTIE 62
WITNEY, JAMES R. 62
WITNEY, STEPHEN 62
WITT, F.A. 115
WITTER, DAVID 65
WOLF, ANGELINE 20
WOLF, ANNIE 93
WOLF, CHARLEY 63
WOLF, DANIEL 5
WOLF, EMMA 91
WOLF, FREDERICK 40
WOLF, HARRY 63
WOLF, HENRY 98
WOLF, RACHEL 61
WOLF, RADY 63
WOLFE, JOS. 74
WOLLAM, MAGGIE 117
WOLLAM, MARGARET 77
WOLLAM, MARY 48,116,117
WOLLAM, URIAH 117
WOLLOM, DANIEL 41
WOOD, E.M., REV. 37
WOOD, JOHN F. 102
WOOD, JOSHUA G. 23
WOOD, ROBERT B. 66
WOOD, SIDNEY J. 89
WOOD, WILLIAM M. 104
WOODARD, SUSAN 1
WOODARD, WILLIAM 1
WOODBRIDGE, HELEN 11
WOODBRIDGE, SARAH 103
WOODBRIDGE, T., DR. 40
WOODBURN, B.F., REV. 89
WOODRICH, JAMES 78
WOODRUFF, DAVID 6
WOODRUFF, HARRIET 10
WOODRUFF, JAMES 10,39,71
WOODRUFF, JOHN 109
WOODRUFF, LOU 73
WOODRUFF, MARY E. 39
WOODRUFF, MARY E. 116
WOODS, A. 38
WOODS, CARL 98
WOODS, F.T. 98
WOODS, HANNAH E. 99
WOODS, J.F. 99
WOODS, JAMES 45,108
WOODS, JANE 99
WOODS, JOHN L. 98
WOODS, JOSEPH 9,60,82
WOODS, KATE G. 105
WOODS, MARY 78
WOODS, MOLLIE E. 14
WOODS, O.SCOTT 36
WOODS, R.G. 38
WOODS, ROBERT G. 80
WOODS, SAMUEL 74
WOODS, T.S. 16,21,22
WOODS, THOMAS S. 38
WOODWARD, ELIZABETH 69
WOODWARD, ELMER 69
WOODWARD, JOSHUA 10
WOODWARD, PETER 69
WOODWORTH, E. 22
WOODWORTH, GEORGANNA 108
WOODWORTH, HARRY 111
WOODWORTH, MARIA 111
WOODWORTH, NELLIE 111
WOODWORTH, P.H. 108
WOOLAM, LAVINA E. 23
WOOLF, ANNA 96,108

WOOLF, GEORGE S. 88
WOOLF, HOMER H. 98
WOOLF, MAGGIE 83
WOOLF, S.A. 101
WOOLF, S.P., REV. 111
WOOSTER, H.C. 61
WORCHESTER, SAMUEL, REV 20
WORKMAN, MATTIE 42
WORMAN, ALICE R. 48
WORMAN, AMELIA 80
WORMAN, ANNA 25
WORMAN, ELIZABETH 3
WORMAN, JACOB 42
WORMAN, JOHN 31,43,48
WORMAN, JOSEPH 21,25
WORMAN, LIZZIE 92
WORMAN, MAGDALENA 48
WORMAN, NOAH 99
WORMINGTON, ELLEN 76
WORMINGTON, FRANCIS 76
WORMINGTON, JAMES 39,70,73,76
WORMLEY, SARAH C. 13
WORTMAN, M.L., REV. 66,85
WRIGHT & TRIMBLE 50
WRIGHT, A.B. 16
WRIGHT, ANNIE 112
WRIGHT, DANIEL 4,95
WRIGHT, E.A. 3
WRIGHT, HENRIETTA 95
WRIGHT, I.N. 27
WRIGHT, JOHN 62
WRIGHT, JOHN, REV. 62
WRIGHT, JOSEPH 8
WRIGHT, MARIA 58
WRIGHT, MARY J. 62
WRIGHT, MELISSA E.M. 24
WRIGHT, N.E., DR. 109
WRIGHT, RACHEL E. 79
WRIGHT, REV. 53
WRIGHT, RUEL 16
WRIGHT, SARAH 95
WRIGHT, WILLIAM S. 95
WYANT, SAMUEL 4
WYCKOFF, REV. 26,33
WYCOFF, J.L.R., REV. 39
WYCOFF, JAMES P. 75
WYLIE, LEWIS C. 86
WYLIE, SABINA 86
WYLLEY, ELLEN 96
YANT, GEORGE W. 88
YANT, JOHN 36
YARIAN, MARY A. 49
YARIAN, SOLOMON 114
YARWOOD, THOMAS 67
YATES, JAS. 34
YATES, JOEL 105
YATES, MARGARET 19
YATES, MINERVA 20
YEALY, MARY 18
YENGLING, A.C. 45
YENGLING, D.F. 1
YENGLING, JOHN 67,86
YENGLING, LEWELLA 67
YENGLING, MARY 67
YENGLING, NANCY 83
YEOMANS, JOHN 119
YERGER, G.W. 3
YODER, DAVID 27
YODER, LEAH 87
YOST, CAROLINE 4
YOST, MISS 5
YOUNG, A.I., REV. 54
YOUNG, A.J., REV. 46
YOUNG, A.T., REV. 57
YOUNG, ALCINOUS, REV. 108
YOUNG, ANDREW 14
YOUNG, ANN E. WEBB 77
YOUNG, B.A. 89
YOUNG, BRIGHAM 14,77
YOUNG, CYRUS 74
YOUNG, DAVID 87
YOUNG, DAVID B., DR. 82
YOUNG, EDWARD F. JR. 53
YOUNG, EDWARD P. 56
YOUNG, FLORENCE L. 79
YOUNG, FRANCES 99
YOUNG, G.I. 45
YOUNG, GEORGE F. 28,29
YOUNG, HATTIE 74
YOUNG, I.C. 11
YOUNG, ISA C. 9

YOUNG, ISABELLA 69
YOUNG, J.M. 99
YOUNG, JAMES 60
YOUNG, JOHN 27,63
YOUNG, JOSEPH 118
YOUNG, LYDIA 80
YOUNG, M.L. 29
YOUNG, MISS 71
YOUNG, MRS. 98
YOUNG, NAPOLEAN 13
YOUNG, P.C. 57
YOUNG, PETER 5,6,43,64,69
YOUNG, REBECCA 2
YOUNG, SAMUEL 98
YOUNG, SARAH J. 71
YOUNG, W.H. 98
YOUNG, W.L. 109
YOUNG, WILLIAM 96
ZANG, JULIUS 98
ZEHERNICK, FRANKLIN 61
ZEHRING, ANGIE 78
ZEIGER, FRANCIS 66
ZEIGER, G., REV. 45
ZEIGLER, CHRISTENA 82
ZEIGLER, HANNAH 55
ZEIGLER, JENNIE 114
ZEIGLER, MICHAEL 82
ZELLARS, ENGLEBRECHT 27
ZELLEY, REBECCA 10
ZENGER, MARY 40
ZEPERNICK & LODGE 26,55
ZEPERNICK, AMELIA 95
ZEPERNICK, CARRY 61
ZEPERNICK, ELLIOT 117
ZEPERNICK, FRANKLIN 61
ZEPERNICK, LOVINA 61
ZEPERNICK, SUSAN 90
ZEPPERNICK, F. 2
ZEPPERNICK, SUSAN 2
ZIEGER, WILHELMINA 51
ZIMMER, ADOLPH 35
ZIMMERMAN, ALBERT 43,73
ZIMMERMAN, ALPHONSO 115
ZIMMERMAN, CONRAD 8
ZIMMERMAN, EMMA 68
ZIMMERMAN, FRANK 81,88
ZIMMERMAN, HENRY 8,104
ZIMMERMAN, J.C. 3
ZIMMERMAN, JEREMIAH 96
ZIMMERMAN, JOHN 8,11,29,91
ZIMMERMAN, JOHN, MRS. 30
ZIMMERMAN, JOSEPH 8
ZIMMERMAN, LAVINA 73
ZIMMERMAN, LIZZIE 80
ZIMMERMAN, MARGARET 28
ZIMMERMAN, MARTHA 43
ZIMMERMAN, MARY 9,11,79,98
ZIMMERMAN, SARAH 38,105
ZIMMERMAN, WILLIAM R. 40
ZOOK, LIZZIE 81
ZUMPE, J.B., REV. 86
ZURBRUGG, S.E. 116